NEW DIRECTIONS IN MUSIC

NEW DIRECTIONS IN MUSIC
FIFTH EDITION

DAVID H. COPE
UNIVERSITY OF CALIFORNIA,
SANTA CRUZ

wcb

WM. C. BROWN PUBLISHERS
DUBUQUE, IOWA

Consulting Editor
Frederick W. Westphal
Sacramento State College

Cover illustration by Ben Neff.

Library of Congress Catalog Card Number: 88-71225

ISBN 0-697-03342-2

Printed in the United States of America by Wm. C. Brown Publishers
2460 Kerper Boulevard, Dubuque, IA 52001

10 9 8 7 6 5 4 3 2 1

Dedicated to my wife,
without whom this book
would not have been written;
and to my parents, whose
faith started it all.

CONTENTS

PREFACE

This fifth edition of *New Directions in Music* contains a number of major changes. A new chapter, "Automated and Cybernetic Music," attempts to cover very recent advances in computer-centered artificial intelligence and music. Another new chapter, "The New Conservatism," recounts attempts at returning to tonality and suggests a cyclic nature to the past thirty to fifty years in contemporary music. The book has also been reorganized into what the author feels represents a more logical succession of ideas and developments. "Indeterminacy" and "Experimentalism" come earlier in the text, for example. "Improvisation" is now included as part of Chapter 5. Each vectoral analysis now includes a comparison with those in other chapters pointing out the similarities between works as well as their diversity. New information will be found on the CD revolution, MIDI interfaces, and sampling techniques, each with attendant charts of relevant equipment and software (as well as developer addresses in Appendix 4). Over one hundred new examples have been included and bibliographic citings for reference and further study have been increased and updated. In this latter area, CDs and videos have been included. "Quotation" has been moved from "Extended Media Resources" to the "Post Avant-garde" (Chapter 11) where it is more relevant.

The annotated chapter bibliographies include not only materials discussed in the chapters but supplemental materials which would be of use to the reader seeking greater detail. Each chapter bibliography is divided into two categories:

1. Readings: books and articles relevant to the subject matter of the chapter (listed alphabetically by author, or subject). Also included are reference materials for in-depth biographical study of the composers mentioned in the chapter.

2. Recordings and Publishers: these include record/CD/video numbers and publishers (when available) of works referred to in the chapter as well as other works the author feels demonstrate chapter content (listed alphabetically by composer).

Though by no means all-inclusive, these bibliographies are sufficiently comprehensive to serve the reader. They are intended to be used as lists of information selected as examples of chapter material, and as *sources* in themselves for bibliographical information to support more intensive research. The bibliographies have been extensively updated and their scope broadened since the fourth edition. This, combined with the updating of the composer biographies (Appendix 2), the expansions of terms and their definitions (Appendix 1), and the source addresses of Appendix 4, should make the materials discussed more easily understood by and accessible to the reader. Composition or publication dates are included if available. They are mentioned with the first appearance of the name of the work and not thereafter (i.e., if the work is discussed and date listed in the body of the chapter, the date will not be included in the chapter bibliography under *Recordings and Publishers*).

One is often confronted by readers holding a variety of misconceptions, two of which this composer-author would like to dispel with brevity and singular decisiveness. First of all, just as writing about Greek mythology does not make one either a Greek or a believer in myths, so writing about various types of *avant-garde* musics does not *necessarily* make one an admirer of those selfsame musics. Second, due to the volatile nature of much of the subject matter under discussion, one must weigh carefully a most important statement in the *Preface* to the first edition:

> The lack of material herein related to more traditional (mainstream) techniques is not intended to reflect or suggest their unimportance (they are *most* important), but is rather due both to the fact that there is a wealth of material already available on these subjects, and to the necessarily limited scope of this text.

Whether one agrees or disagrees with the concepts, philosophies, and resultant sound activities and/or silences discussed herein is simply beside the point. These musics *do* exist and to avoid either their manifestations or significance is simply playing ostrich.

It is quite possible that more compositions have been brought into the world during the past 50 years than during the entire previous 120-year period. Many of these works are experimental, destined to become, like P.D.Q. Bach, "hopelessly lost," or to help found a broad and more creative base for artistic endeavor. In any event, they can no longer be considered external to the history of this era, or to its future existence.

Directions seem as numerous or as diverse as composers or works. And yet there exists behind these directions historical motives and constant aesthetic values, traceable and uniquely observable due to their singularly radical nature. Electronic instruments and techniques, aleatoric methods, adoption of scientific procedures and theatrical participation, once held as highly controversial and innovative, have entered a large number of current mainstream compositions, due in part to the recent sophistication of international communications media. It was not always so. Berlioz's innovations in orchestration waited half a century for recognition and acceptance. Charles Ives's experiments took many years to be discovered—many more to be considered even rational.

The purpose of this book, then, is to explore the history, philosophies, materials, composers, and works pertaining to those directions in music since the late 1940s which express a radical departure from tradition in concept and/or production, with special emphasis on the relationship of these to significant and realistic directions of style and thought.

New Directions in Music is intended as an introduction and general survey of *avant-garde* and post *avant-garde* music in the twentieth century to the present, in the hope that it will stimulate the reader to further listening and research. Designed for music students at the college and graduate level, it may be suitably integrated into any course incorporating the study of various aspects of twentieth-century composition: forms, techniques, philosophy. It can be a valuable supplement to the well-rounded education of any serious musician. By the very fact that most of the years discussed have not yet become "history" in the academic sense, the author has intentionally avoided the standard historical approach and rhetoric in order to develop *concepts* and *interest* in the *New Directions in Music*.

I would like to thank the following reviewers who worked with me on this edition: Roy J. Guenther, George Washington University; Judith Lochhead, SUNY at Stony Brook; Dean Madsen, Utah State University; Charles N. Mason, Birmingham Southern College; Neil Tilkins, George Washington University; Michael Schelle, Butler University.

David Cope

INTRODUCTION

As work neared completion on the fourth edition of *New Directions in Music,* I was struck with the notion of including an original Cage mesostic (text arranged to create names and ideas in vertical simultaneity). I wrote to John in New York half suspecting he wouldn't even receive my letter before the deadline passed. He responded in less than ten days (he is amazing in keeping up on correspondence) and promised something as soon as he could get to it. He had just returned from Europe and now must fly to Oakland. Since I had thought to send a copy of the third edition with my request, I was overjoyed to think that he would now be able to contribute a mesostic on the text.

After a few days had passed, John phoned from Oakland. He was quite apologetic. It seems that he had placed *New Directions in Music* in a drawer in New York City. When he went to retrieve it for creating the mesostic, the drawer would not open; something was stuck between the upper shelf and the contents (probably *New Directions in Music*) and no subsequent pulling and tugging would pry it open. John called a carpenter. Time passed, however; and since he had to get to the airport to fly to Oakland, he left the book "locked" in the drawer.

I, of course, was aghast at this trick of fate but more than understanding of John's plight. In fact, I guess I was so delighted that he would *think* of doing a mesostic, I momentarily forgot that I was not going to receive same.

I quickly mailed John a new copy of the third edition (actually not "new" since the only copy I had was the one in which I had made editorial changes for edition four). But time was getting short and my optimism was fast retreating. I did have hope, however, since it could have been worse: John could have read the will of fate into my book's active reluctance to allow his drawer to act normally.

Finally, John wrote a lovely note and attached the following correspondence. While nothing could truly surpass a personal Cage mesostic, as far as I was concerned, this serial came close. The articulate and perceptive dialogue present speaks for itself. It does, I hope, give the reader a spirit of inquiry which accompanies the soul bent on these kinds of exploratory journeys. Mr. Berry's kind permission to use his letters is gratefully appreciated.

1 November, 1982

Dear Mr. Cage,

What follows is the angry cry of a young composer demanding explanation and justification for what he perceives as folly in an older colleague. It is offered as a tossed gauntlet. I challenge you to defend yourself so I may understand you better. And be assured I sincerely prefer understanding over anger.

Mr. Cage: I accuse you for items #1 and #2, and hold you directly responsible for the situation described in item #3.

ITEM #1: You have systematically bastardized the art of music composition through the abuse of language. By redefinition of the word 'music', in a way which says, 'anything and everything is music' you have made the word 'music' meaningless. If everything is music, then *nothing* is music. And therefore, composers can no longer exist . . . there is simply nothing left for them to do.

ITEM #2: You have declared, 'My purpose is to eliminate purpose.' You would have all composers eliminate beauty, sincerity, joy, compassion, expression, and love from their music. You would have all composers ignore these basic qualities in music which humanity has enjoyed for several thousand years.

ITEM #3: As a result of your nihilistic philosophy of music, and your pointless musical-sociological experiments, most young composers have been completely alienated from other musicians and from concert audiences. Concert audiences (in the U.S.) are for the most part completely disinterested in New Music, having been convinced there is no purpose or sincerity in the work of most 20th century composers. You have caused a near-total collapse of musical culture in this country, and left nothing for us (the young composers) to work with. We have no patrons, and our motives for composing music are constantly suspect.

I believe the Great John Cage, 'grandfather of modern music', is a nihilistic comedian playing to an audience of indoctrinated sheep. His art is not art at all: it is blasphemy.

Sincerely,

Charles Berry

8 Dec 1982

JOHN CAGE
101 West 18 Street (5B) • New York,
New York 10011

MESSAGE	REPLY
TO Mr. Charles Berry 3571 Ruffin Rd. #238 San Diego, Calif. 92123 DATE Nov. 21, 1982 It seems that what angers you are my writings, my ideas. I suggest you drop interest in them and focus on your own. Turn your attention to what you believe in. That is what I did. Thus I found alternative compositional means that would permit the introduction of noises and sounds available through new technology into musical works. I rediscovered the traditional purposes for making music	a) to imitate nature in her manner of operation, and b) to sober and quiet the mind thus making it susceptible to divine influences. Thus I was freed from self expression. Music became a discipline, a way of life. I have always noticed that very few people are interested in New Music. I was 50 years old before there was any supportive acceptance of my work. I am now much older but my work remains controversial as your feelings testify. Sincerely, *John Cage*

Detach and File for Follow-up

8 Dec 1982

Dear Mr. Cage,

Thank you for your letter. It has given me a much better understanding of the intent and substance of your ideas and your music. For the present I will take your advice and concentrate on my own creative instincts. However, I do feel compelled to study your work further.

At some future date I may, quite possibly, approach your work from a different perspective and find it refreshing and enjoyable.

Sincerely

Charles Berry

Charles Berry

THE CHALLENGE
TO TONALITY

1

Nineteenth century humankind, reasonably cloaked in the gifts of the industrial revolution, entered the final one hundred years of the millennium with optimistic and exploratory vision. H. G. Wells' prophetic "War of the Worlds" (1898) introduced millions to the planet earth, viewed finally as a sum of its parts, and to an electrical and even atomic future. It was an era of incredible change and challenge to established traditions. The very essence of its spirit rode tether with Orville and Wilbur Wright on a North Carolina beach in 1903.

    The arts rarely detach themselves from social dynamics. The visual arts began (as early as the 1860s) to question the photographic realism of classicism with impressionistic and pointillistic explorations. Georges Seurat's 1886 oil painting *A Sunday Afternoon on the Grande Jatte,* for example, is composed of small dots of intense color systematically covering an enormous 6′ 9″ by 10′ canvas. The docile and immobile figures are relaxed in a timelessness almost antithetical to the passionate points that bring it forth. Poets Paul Verlaine (1844–1896) and Stéphane Mallarmé (1842–1898, whose poem *L'Après-midi d'un faune* was the source for Debussy's seminal Prélude) mirrored the sensuous and coloristic impressionist painters.

    The Expressionists contrasted this exotic lyricism with intensely personal and emotive concepts. Vincent Van Gogh's (1853–1890) visionary early work produced violent and often tormented canvases. Georges Rouault's *Head of Christ* (see Figure 1.2) gives example of the Gothic brutality in Expressionism. T. S. Eliot (1888–1965) and James Joyce (1882–1941) exemplified these qualities in their "stream of consciousness" novels and poetry.

    Both Expressionism and Impressionism, while in their own right significant schools of art, served as precursors for the abstractionists of the 20th century. Kandinsky's (1866–1944) *Sketch I for "Composition VII"* is a subtle Impressionist "shaping" *and* an Expressionist "personal insight" while avoiding any covert realism or objectivism. Ambiguity of representation thereby creates another level of viewing color and balance.

    Concomitant to (possibly even subscribed within) abstractive art is Cubism with its principal exponent Pablo Picasso (1881–1973). If abstract art "removes" image, then Cubism "abstracts" the removal. While *Three Musicians* is clearly that, the

Prelude

Figure 1.1. Georges Seurat (1859–1891): *A Sunday Afternoon on the Grande Jatte* (1886). Helen Birch Bartlett Memorial Collection. An example of Impressionism.

Figure 1.2. Georges Rouault (1871–1958): *Head of Christ* (1905). Walter Chrysler Museum, Provincetown. An example of Expressionism.

The Challenge to Tonality

Figure 1.3. Wassily Kandinsky: Sketch I for "*Composition VII*" (1913). Collection Felix Klee, Bern. An example of abstract art.

angular and often perspective-lacking juxtaposition of "cut-out"-like figures distorts the view, creating an amorphous catalog of queries into the underlying rationale. Picasso, like so many of the century's artists and authors, pursued active relationships with composers, playwrights and dancers.

By 1919 two endemically 20th century schools of art were born. The first, the Bauhaus, was a group of visual artists (both two- and three-dimensional) headed by Walter Gropius (a German-born architect) whose visionary work created a model for today's steel and glass skyscrapers. The second, the "Dadaists," was formed by poets André Breton and Tristan Tzara and spawned the talents of (among others) Marcel Duchamp (1887–1968), Man Ray (1890–1976) and Salvadore Dali (1904–1989). Dali also forged a third school called *surrealism*. His canvases often depicted plastic figures melted into impossible shapes similar to Picasso's Cubism but lacking its formal line, and creating power through supernatural images.

During this time the film medium was born, raised through its puberty and matured to an art form all in a microcosm of dynamic energy unmatched at any other time (with the possible exception of current digital technologies). Beginning with simple narratives, the silent film proceeded to create illusions the extent of which we still have not explored completely.

Each development and contrary turn in the road, whether it be in the style or content of art or literature, reflects the tenacity of the individual in times of great

Figure 1.4. Pablo Picasso: *Three Musicians* (1921). The Museum of Modern Art, New York; Mrs. Simon Guggenheim Fund. An example of Cubism.

Figure 1.5. Left to right: Jean Cocteau, French surrealist author and filmmaker; Pablo Picasso; Igor Stravinsky, Russian composer; Olga Picasso; 1925.

uncertainty. It is no accident that art parallels the tempo of world events. Contextualized by the "winds of change" in the visual and narrative arts, composers began similarly to divest themselves of the often unspoken presumptions of tradition and strike out for the edges of discovery.

The Challenge to Tonality

Figure 1.6. Salvadore Dali: *The Persistence of Memory* (1931). Collection, The Museum of Modern Art, New York. An example of *surrealism*.

The "common-practice" period of music history (roughly 1600–1900) witnessed a flowering of musical resources into an enormously rich and complex language. Its basic force (tonality) still pervades much of today's popular and world musics. While a just summary of tonal vocabulary and techniques could take hundreds of pages, there are three primal forces that are important to note. The inexorable challenges to these central concepts spawned "new directions in music."

First, concepts of "key" define the basic pitch material (the vocabulary) of tonality. Melodies reduced to source material become scales of ordered intervals. Figure 1.7 shows a melodic line and the projection of a scale. Tonality defines these pitches as *diatonic* and those foreign to the "key" as *chromatic*.

An Overview of Tonality

- or -

Figure 1.7. Wolfgang Amadeus Mozart (1756–1791): *Theme and Variations: "Ah! Vous Dirai-je, Maman"* and a derived C major scale.

Secondly, concepts of consonance (relaxation) versus dissonance (tension) permeate the relationships of tonal materials. The overtone series (pitches present in acoustic sound) is often argued as the rationale for vertical consonance. This series (infinite; shown here through 8 pitches) gives prominence in its lower (more audible) spectrum to three primary intervals: octaves, fifths and thirds—see Figure 1.8. When projected as a simultaneity these create a triad (three-note chord built in thirds). Pitches outside these basic sonorities are called "non-harmonic" and typically resolve (move towards) a chord member. Most tonal music consists of these harmonic triads contextualized by key (e.g. *diatonic* or *chromatic*).

Figure 1.8. The overtone series on C with primary lower intervals marked and a derived C major triad.

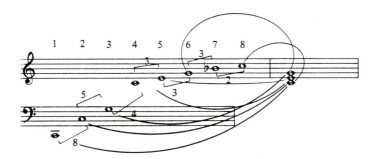

Finally, subtle concepts of hierarchical relationships pervade most tonal music. Two primary pitches provide fulcrum and weight. The *dominant* note (or triad) is the fifth of the key. It acts principally as a penultimate (second to last) pitch to each gesture of tonal music (be it a single phrase or an entire piece). It begs resolution to the *tonic* note (or triad) which answers the dominant "question." The tonic is the first note of each key scale. Figure 1.9 shows the primary chords of tonic and dominant in tonal hierarchy with examples of other "secondary" chords. As well, the figure shows a fragment of a piece with the three tonal principles at work: key, consonance and hierarchy.

The interplay of these and other tonal principles has provided a common language for thousands of composers. Their music, steeped in rich tonal traditions, parallels that of classic realism in the visual arts. So complex is the syntax of this language that relationships are often implied but not present.

As the century turned, tonal composers faced critical challenges with sophistication of syntax developing "slang" counterparts. The *chromatic* outweighed the *diatonic,* the non-harmonic overshadowed the harmonic, the hierarchy had become so implied as to become unreal.

Figure 1.10 demonstrates the complex tonal ambivalences of late 19th century (Romantic period) music.

Each of the three principal elements of tonality are barely perceivable. The very fabric of *diatonic* and *consonant* hierarchy is in crisis here. While many composers clung to tonal traditions (neo- Romanticists such as Elgar, Rachmaninoff, etc.), many felt the need to strike out for new soil (though as with all historical models, based on older techniques).

x = non-harmonic tones

Figure 1.9. (a) chords listed in tonal hierarchy; (b) Ludwig van Beethoven (1770–1827): *Sonata* Op. 2, No. 3.

Figure 1.10. Richard Wagner (1813–1883): *Tristan und Isolde* (Prelude)—1859.

Expanded Scale Resources

Exploration of alternative scales was one of the initial ways composers sought for new order. Traditional and quasi-traditional modes, direct (16th century) antecedents of tonality, returned in new guises. Impressionism in music (*circa* 1894–1915), as in the visual arts, chose methods of alluding to yet blurring classic realism (in this case tonality).

Figure 1.11 shows six somewhat standard modes often used in impressionistic works, with their Renaissance (16th century) nomenclature.

Note that in each of the modes, the half-step patterns apply to different members of the series, giving a significantly different sounding scale even though the pitch content of each is the same (piano white keys). Figure 1.12 shows Debussy's use of Aeolian mode on D as the basis for pitch materials.

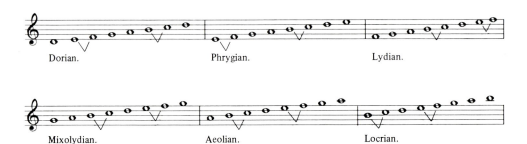

Dorian.   Phrygian.   Lydian.

Mixolydian.   Aeolian.   Locrian.

Figure 1.11. The standard modes.

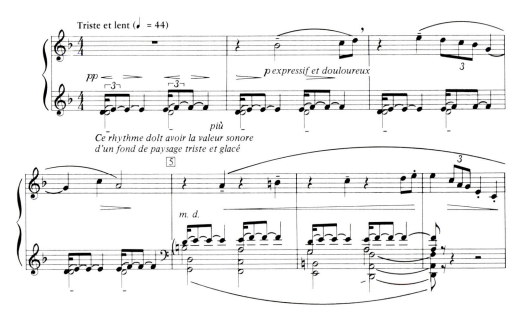

Figure 1.12. Claude Debussy (1862–1918): *Prélude, Des pas sur la neige* (Footsteps in the Snow) (1910). A. Durand, Paris. An example of modal composition.

The Challenge to Tonality

Figure 1.13. Claude Debussy. Dover Publications, Inc. Permission granted.

The first four measures state the mode through repeated tonic (D in the lowest voice) and a scale-like melodic line. The B♭ creates a transposed mode with Aeolian half-steps between 2–3 and 5–6 (see figure 1.11). The C♯, which was often common as leading tone in the late Renaissance, is conspicuously missing here. Debussy is obviously concerned about establishing modal integrity so that the variances with D minor can be emphasized. The B♮ beginning in measure 5 might briefly suggest D melodic minor, but the constant use of C♮ clearly identifies a modulation to D-Dorian (half-steps between 2–3 and 6–7; see Figure 1.11). "Tonal" ears can often bend modal materials into tonal leanings. Debussy fights this tendency, avoiding leading tone implications wherever possible.

Another popular resource in early music of this century was the whole-tone scale. This scale divides the octave into six equal whole steps, creating an interesting and definitely non-tonal mode. Figure 1.14 shows the basic whole-tone scale beginning on C, and a second whole-tone scale beginning on D♭. In actuality these are the only two different possibilities, since beginning on D duplicates both the tones and intervals present in the C scale.

Figure 1.14. Two whole-tone scales.

Composers discovered that this limitation (lack of the real potential of modulating to different whole-tone "keys") is a severe drawback. As well, the characteristic sound of the scale soon wears thin. Figure 1.15 presents an example of the C whole-tone scale in use.

Composers of the early 20th century adopted folk modes and materials as well as traditional modes and whole-tone scales. In Figure 1.17, Debussy employs a Spanish mode in *Habañera* style.

Figure 1.15. Béla Bartók: (1881–1945): *Mikrokosmos* (1926–37) Volume 5, No. 136: "Whole-tone Scale." Boosey and Hawkes, New York City.

Figure 1.16. Béla Bartók. Dover Publications, Inc. Permission granted.

Figure 1.17. Claude Debussy: *Soirée dans Grenade,* from *Estampes* (1903). A. Durand, Paris. Use of folk modes in classical music.

Figure 1.18. Mode derived from Figure 1.17.

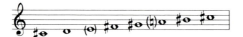

The Challenge to Tonality

The melodic line (here at the bottom) convincingly states a D-based mode different from any yet mentioned.

The scale is clarified and established by repetition of the important intervals of difference between it and traditional tonality and modality. The augmented second suggests the harmonic minor on C♯, but the use of the D♮ (which would be a half-step above the tonic) negates that possibility.

Pentatonic (five-note) scales derive in part from simplified versions of *oriental* and *Indonesian* folk music. These latter folk traditions encompass complicated and exotic tunings as well as subtle cultural connotations. Western tradition, however, extracted the simplified scale elements of five notes as shown in Figure 1.19.

Figure 1.19. (a) Two pentatonic scales; (b) Claude Debussy: *Pagodes* from *Estampes* (1903). A. Durand, Paris.

The melody here is completely constructed of piano keyboard black-notes (as opposed to the white-key modal constructions of Figure 1.11). As with whole-tone scales, the lack of half-steps creates tonal ambiguity. As well, notice the reference to oriental temples in the title.

Synthetic scales involve the creation, usually by the composer, of unique scales for the purpose of composition. Figure 1.20 shows an example of a work (by an American impressionist, Charles Griffes, 1884–1920) based on a synthetic mode.

Figure 1.20. Charles Tomlinson Griffes: *Sonata* (1918). G. Schirmer, New York. Use of synthetic modes in 20th century music.

Figure 1.21. Synthetic modes derived from Figure 1.20.

Here the scale used does not conform to traditional tonal-modal shapes. In Figure 1.21a, the scale based on F is clearly derived from these opening notes. In Figure 1.21b, the scale of the entire movement is shown (space does not permit reproduction of the entire work). With synthetic scales, composers are able to freely determine their own functional relationships. This is accomplished through the same resources available to the common-practice composer: repetition and cadence. Unfortunately, real definition of expectancy and fulfillment, so characteristic of tonal music, can only be suggested here since often only one piece (or at best a few) exists in any particularly synthetic scale. Moreover, the composer using such scales must constantly be aware of the tonally-based experience of the listener. Synthetically derived materials can often be mistaken as tonal or modal in origin when this is not the case.

Any one of the scales mentioned herein, or an assemblage of two or more, might act as tonal substitute were it not for the lack of a consistent body of work utilizing the materials and techniques. More often than not, these new scales were exploited and then abandoned, victims of the lust for yet newer devices in hopes that a stable system might surface to replace tonality. At the same time, the engaging qualities of works whose materials are unique cannot be overlooked.

Extensions of Tertian Harmony

As melodic materials developed into more complex and subtle variants, so too did their harmonic counterparts. In early Western tonal traditions, one finds triads used without a great deal of non-triadic dissonances. As the common practice developed, non-harmonic tones increased in number and, while still embellishing their harmonic function, began to pull gently at the triadic structure. As explorations continued, a hierarchy of dissonances surfaced. Some tones outside the triad itself seemed more consonant than others. Often these latter tones are extensions of building thirds upon thirds (the source of the triad itself). Figure 1.22 shows a series of triads with added thirds creating continuous 7th chords.

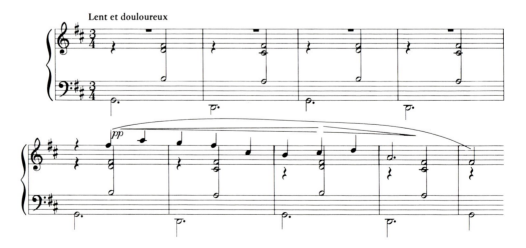

Figure 1.22. Eric Satie (1886–1925): *3 Gymnopédies* (No. 1)—1888. G. Schirmer, New York. An example of 7th chords.

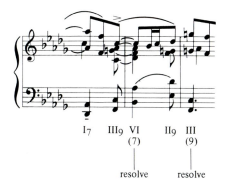

Figure 1.23. Maurice Ravel (1875–1937): *Sonatine* (1903). An example of 7th and 9th chords.

Note that where the non-harmonic tone "resolves" into the triadic structure, the 7th chord projections indicate no "resolution." Figure 1.23 shows a series of expanded harmonic structures (7th and 9th chords) with some tones resolving to chord tones and others not. This ambiguity is a trademark of turn of the century impressionistic composers.

Further expansion of triads by thirds creates further complexity and depth of texture. Figure 1.24 shows a dominant 13th chord. Note how chord members remain fixed (do not resolve into a triadic structure).

Figure 1.24. Claude Debussy: *Prélude à "L'Après-midi d'un Faune"* (1894). An example of a dominant 13th chord.

Spacing is also a critical component. If the 13th chord of Figure 1.24 is collapsed within a single octave, a dissonant chord occurs where seconds rather than thirds seem to be the basic substructure. These tend to resemble "clusters" of sound (discussed in Chapter 3).

Figure 1.25. Collapsed 13th chord and resultant dissonance.

Because 9th, 11th and 13th chords are often vertically oriented (since non-harmonic movement is reduced with so many tones already present in the chord), constant contrary motion with chords of so many members can create contrapuntal chaos, with few of the voices distinguishable and often colliding with one another. Thus they are often used in parallel voice motion. This is called *planing* (creating "planes" or "levels" of register).

Planing basically involves "freezing" a chord structure and then moving it as if it were a single melodic line. Harmonies become a by-product of melodic movement and are heard as moving groups of notes rather than separate entities. Figure 1.26 is an example of diatonic planing.

Figure 1.26. Claude Debussy: *Feuilles mortes* ("Dead Leaves," from the Préludes, Book II). (1913). A. Durand, Paris. An example of diatonic planing.

While the intervals change (e.g. major to minor) and the functions could be said to change on each chord, it is the horizontal movement that carries the vertical structure along. To evaluate "tonics," "dominants," and other functions within this is to simply ignore the real meaning of the music.

Figure 1.27 shows a more substantial use of planing from the same composer. Here the *freezing* of the basic pattern remains so fixed that the passage obtains a great variety of chromaticism. Again, it would be possible to carefully go through each and every harmonic structure and detail function. The vertical sonorities are, however, simply a by-product of the melodic line and the resulting chords and chromaticism formed by this planing. The triads of Figure 1.28 create a full chromatic complement (all 12 tones) to the resolute "pedal point" G in the bass.

Composers also sought to create complex vertical structures (while hoping to retain some tonal identity) by combining two or more keys simultaneously. This "polytonality" produces a rich fabric of chromatic textures, especially when the keys have few common tones. Figure 1.30 (reduced from orchestral score) shows an example of polytonality using the keys of C major and F♯ major simultaneously (note how the scales shown have only 2 notes in common: B and F [E♯]).

The dissonance of the passage is greatly reduced by the simple use of triads in each key. The listener, though certainly pummeled with dissonance, can grasp the basic duality of the elements in this context. To create this counterpoint of keys,

Figure 1.27. Claude Debussy: *La Soirée dans Grenade* from *Estampes* (1903). A. Durand, Paris.

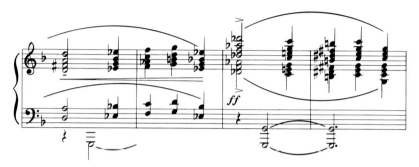

Figure 1.28. Maurice Ravel: *Le Tombeau de Couperin,* "Minuet" (1917). A. Durand, Paris. An example of triadic *planing.*

Figure 1.29. Maurice Ravel. Dover Publications, Inc. Permission granted.

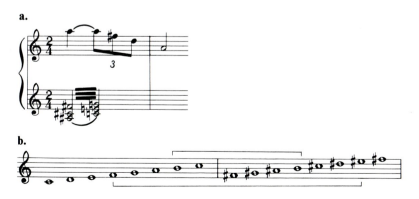

Figure 1.30. (a) Igor Stravinsky (1882–1971): *Petrushka* (1911). (b) Scales of C and F♯ major.

Figure 1.31. Igor Stravinsky. Dover Publications, Inc. Permission granted. Stravinsky (seen here fourth from left) appears with the Hindemith Quartet (composer Paul Hindemith is standing).

composers often establish strong key centers rather than allowing the variants to intermingle and reduce the bi-tonal recognizeability. In Figure 1.32, Bartók uses different key signatures, different staves, and particularly different material for each key (B major melodic figuration versus C major harmonic planing).

Figure 1.32. Béla Bartók: *Out of Doors Suite* (1926). Universal Edition.

Some composers add the element of "collage" to polytonal techniques. This effect combines polytonality with quotation (usually popular or folk in origin). The result often creates polyrhythms, polymeters, polytextures and polyconcepts from the overlapping of widely diverse musical types. Figure 1.33 shows this process in use.

Here one idea is in B♭ major (flutes, clarinets, trumpets, bass and lower violas), another in D minor (piano, violins, and horns), with a third suggesting F major (trombones). One line wavers slowly (top 'celli) around chromatic pitches B♭, A and C♭. The result might be chaos, but because each idea is uniquely orchestrated and identifiable as quotation, the "poly" concept works effectively. Collage techniques are therefore viable procedures to clarify and establish polytonality.

Figure 1.33. Charles Ives (1874–1954): "Putnam's Camp," from *Three Places in New England* (1914).

Composers also sought ways of constructing chords from intervals other than thirds. In Figure 1.35, the basic harmonic fabric is clearly 4th chords (four 4ths creating five notes). Only the first chord of the second measure (with the word "wonder") defies this analysis.

Note how the melodic line contrasts with the harmonic structure by moving almost exclusively in seconds. The "stacked" nature of the chords makes planing almost unavoidable. There is no doubt of the non-tertian nature of these chords since no tones resolve or even hint of a triadic base.

Figure 1.34. Charles Ives. Dover Publications, Inc. Permission granted.

A boy who had been there three hours be-gan to won-der, "Is life an-y-thing like that?"

Figure 1.35. Charles Ives: *The Cage* (from *114 Songs:* 1884–1921). Published by the composer and later by New Music Edition. An example of chords built with fourths.

Figure 1.36 is a more complex interplay of non-tertian harmonies and develops a more contrapuntal basis of voice motion. The first chord is a "stacked" 4th chord (B—E—A) with a doubled B in the top voice. The third, fourth and sixth chords are similarly stacked in fourths. Chords five and seven are inversions of 4th chords and need only an octave displacement of one pitch (B below E for chord five, and F♯ between C♯ and B for chord seven) to be seen as similar projections of fourths. Chords two, eight and nine are ambiguous with either a note missing (e.g. chord two could be seen as stacked fourths if the B were in the bass and an E added just above it) or a triad with an added pitch.

The final chord is a triad which by its simplicity seems almost dissonant (i.e. in its "contrary to context" meaning). Chromatic pitches here are not derived from tonal inflections but are the result of projections of "perfect" fourths.

Expanding triads into dense sonorities (9th, 11th and 13th chords), using more than one key simultaneously (polytonality) and exploring new interval foundations for harmonies all expand the composer's menu of available materials for vertical

Figure 1.36. Paul Hindemith (1895–1963): *Le Cygne* (from *Six Chansons*)—1939. *B. Schott's Soehne, Mainz.* Contrapuntal techniques in non-tertian harmony.

simultaneities. Each of these avenues, while initially focused on as elaborations of tonality, helps to defuse its very center—the triad—and in so doing provides exit routes into less widely interpretable vocabularies.

Layer Hierarchies

As harmonic cohesiveness seeps from tonality, hierarchical structure slips away. Subtle chromatic embellishing chords with complex but expected resolutions grow so distant from basic key concepts that recognition of tonic and dominant becomes obscured. Simply rhyming phrases of tonality appears too obvious and phrases blur into a continuity which lacks clear hierarchical structure (i.e. primary structure: I, V; secondary: II, III, etc.; tertiary: chromatic chords, etc.). Busoni possibly says it more eloquently: "Let me take thought, how music may be restored to its primitive, natural essence; let us free it from architectonic, acoustic and esthetic dogmas; let it be pure invention and sentiment, in harmonies, in forms, in tone-colors (for invention and sentiment are not the prerogative of melody alone); let it follow the line of the rainbow and vie with the clouds in breaking sunbeams."[1]

With tonal superstructure gone, composers evolved uniquely "personal" languages that often did not last for more than a few works. As well, tonal emphasis on phrase structure and cadence imploded into a preoccupation with single events. Scriabin's *mystic chord,* for example, is a kind of 4th chord (inclusive of both augmented and diminished forms).

Figure 1.37. Alexander Scriabin's *mystic chord.*

This became the organic source for melodic and harmonic development. Figure 1.38 shows a brief sample of how this structure permeates the fabric of Scriabin's work. The "event" concept, taken to the extreme, implies a momentary collapse of the lyric in music. The emphasis turns to the vertical subtleties of the event—its texture, timbre and duration—with a focus separate from cadence-directed motion.

1. Ferruccio Busoni, *Sketch of a New Esthetic of Music* (New York City: G. Schirmer, Inc., 1911). Translated from German by T. Baker.

Figure 1.38. Alexander
Scriabin (1872–1915): *Poème*
Op. 69, no. 1 (1913).

Figure 1.39 shows how groups of events can be organized into linear direction. The texture here is fluid, yet shaped by a set of events or points of sound (see Figure 1.1 and note the differences between pointillism in art and music. In the former, the "points" group to form images; in the latter, the focus is on points of color).

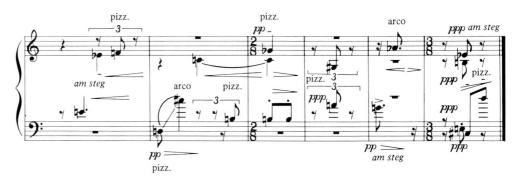

Figure 1.39. Anton Webern (1883–1945): *Six Bagatelles* for string quartet (1913). An example of musical pointillism.

With music freed, as it were, from "architectonic" expectation, areas other than pitch also became available for experimentation. The rigor of the barline relaxed into what some have called "time-suspension." Figure 1.40 shows two of the many

Figure 1.40. Arnold Schoenberg (1874–1951): *Sechs Kleine Klavierstücke* Opus 19 (1911). Universal Edition.

ways composers used to free music from the "tyranny" of the beat. First, on-beats are avoided (especially downbeats) to diminish their import. Secondly, irregular small subdivisions of the beat are created to blur suggested beat accent.

The *atonal* (derogatory word often used to describe early works of this century) qualities of the pitch material are similar to that of Scriabin's *Poème* (Figure 1.38) and triadic references are rare. Public acceptance of these *atonal* works was quite mixed as the following (a review in the *Paris-Midi,* of May 29, 1913) indicates:

> . . . musical cubism has made its appearance in the fair city of Paris. By singular irony of fate, it was in the venerable hall of the Conservatoire, the temple of all tradition, that this revelation took place . . . offering to its habitués the first performance of three piano pieces by Arnold Schoenberg. This composer hails from Vienna, preceded by an intriguing reputation. Every performance of one of his works in Austria and Germany has provoked disorders, police intervention, transportation of the wounded to the hospital and of dead bodies to the morgue. At the sound of the last chord the listeners would come to blows, and music lovers strewn on the floor would be picked up in bunches. So we waited with impatience the first contact of this explosive art with French sensibilities . . . But all expectations were deceived. True, there were some uncomfortable smiles, some anguished sighs, some stifled groans, but no scandal erupted. Arnold Schoenberg would not believe it.[2]

Timbral explorations were likewise important and composers continued to expand the repertoire of acceptable musical sounds. Percussion sections of orchestras often "wagged the dog," as in works by Edgard Varèse. *Amériques* (1922) for orchestra, for example, requires ten percussionists utilizing 21 different instruments. This work also expands the resources of the traditional orchestra with normal complements of winds often doubled in size (e.g. six trumpets, five trombones, etc.). He also employs the Hecklephone, contrabass tuba and contrabass trombone. *Amériques* is a culmination of the post-Romantic tradition of gargantuan orchestras exemplified by Schoenberg's *Gurrelieder* (1911 for 5 soloists, choir and large orchestra).

While some composers clung to tonal inheritance, content to articulate their musical thoughts through revisions of Western tradition, others saw this as a turning point for their musical style. The common language was gone for them and each was free to pursue an experimental direction. For some this meant the construction of new vocabularies and/or a complete reexamination of the very nature of sound and the complicated way in which the human animal acts and interacts in its presence.

2. Nicolas Slonimsky, *Lexicon of Musical Invective: Critical Assaults on Composers since Beethoven's Time* (second ed.) Seattle, Washington: University of Washington Press, 1969, pp. 310–11.

Figure 1.41. *Arnold Schoenberg.* A caricature by Vera Jackovich (1948). Trumbell Collection, New York City.

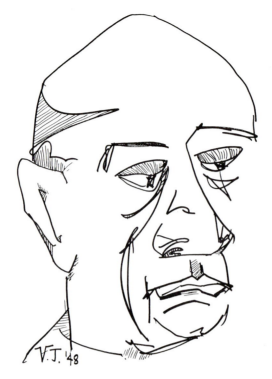

Vectoral Analysis: Edgard Varèse: *Density 21.5*

Vectoral[3] analysis will be used for all larger in-depth analysis throughout the text. Its seven-pronged view of each piece provides the perspective and thorough analysis necessary to understand contemporary music more fully, especially that of recent experimental vintage.

The following is a basic synopsis of the analytical process to be used.

1. Historical Background: This includes information of relevance to the piece under discussion relating to period of composition, school of composition (if any), inclusive dates of composition, country of origin, historical influences, and the composer's important teachers.

2. Overview, Structure and Texture: This includes general formal analysis and a careful look at composite structures (e.g., homophonic, monophonic, contrapuntal), general notational principles used, rhythmic ideas generated, compositional techniques influencing structure (e.g., mobile forms, graphic notation), and texts employed.

3. Orchestration Techniques: Basic timbre analysis, general instrumentation, unusual techniques (e.g., multiphonics, preparations), extreme ranges, unusual balance and/or inverted structures, relevant relation of timbre to form, and structure.

3. From *vector,* a quantity with both force and direction, here defined as a three-dimensional analytical technique rather than two-dimensional form analysis or one-dimensional harmonic analysis.

The Challenge to Tonality

Figure 1.42. Edgard Varèse. BMI Archives. Used by permission.

4. Basic Techniques: Includes pitch organization (e.g., tonal), motivic structures, and rhythmic detail.

5. Vertical Models: Presentation of significant samplings of vertical structures from the piece, including chord roots, centers, and voice leading between chord structures.

6. Horizontal Models: Presentation of significant samplings of horizontal melodic structures including cadence, balance, and motion.

7. Style: An integration of 1 through 6; a summary of the stylistic parameters employed by the composer; any relevant material not discussed above; general summation of harmonic, melodic, rhythmic, and formal techniques used; and their correlation.

Limitations of space do not allow for extensive dissertations for each of these categories (which indeed becomes a possibility when one begins to delve deeply into the bowels of most contemporary works), but rather a synoptical summary of the techniques and applications found under each reference.

1. Historical Background. Edgard Varèse (1883–1965) was born in Paris of Italian-French parents and studied principally mathematics and science at school until he was 18. He then entered the Schola Cantorum where he studied composition with Vincent d'Indy, Albert Roussel, and Charles Widor,

becoming as well a very close friend and confidant of Ferruccio Busoni. He came to the United States in 1915, organizing both orchestras and concert societies for new music in New York City. Many of his early works were destroyed by fire. The greater part of the music we are now aware of was written during the twenties and thirties; for example, *Octandre* (1924), *Intégrales* (1925), and *Ionisation* (1931). From that time until the early fifties Varèse did not compose. The fifties brought *Déserts* (1954) and *Poème électronique* (1958) into existence, both works involving electronic forces. Varèse was clearly influenced by the iconoclastic Busoni and Carlos Salzedo (with whom he founded the International Composers' Guild in 1921). As well, his work shows marked influence of Stravinsky (particularly Stravinsky's early "primitive" period).

2. Overview: *Density 21.5* was completed in 1936 and written for Georges Barrere for the inauguration of his platinum flute (21.5 is the density of platinum). The work was revised in April of 1946 for a *New Music Quarterly* release in July of that year, and subsequent performances follow this latter form. The work is in three main continuous sections with the first and last having similar lyric qualities. The middle section is event-oriented.

   It is interesting that the first note of each of these sections, when taken out of context but grouped together, become the first three notes of the piece (F—E—F♯). This kind of "organic" writing (all materials flowing naturally from a single seed) replaces some of the tonal expectations of key, triad and hierarchy and provides a kind of consistency that gives a natural sense of flow to the work.

3. Orchestration: Most timbral features available on the flute are explored in this piece: range differences, dynamics within the various registers, articulations, etc. Figure 1.43 shows an excerpt employing "slapped" keys, a percussive effect produced by playing softly and hitting the key simultaneously (+).

4. The motive of the piece is clearly stated and separated from the body of the first phrase: F—E—F♯ (see Figure 1.44). Note that this motive also implies a concept of statement (F), new statement (E) and return to the first statement with variation (F♯) which characterizes the work's form. Within the first section, one finds constant references to the opening motive. Measure 2 continues the first phrase with basic expansion of intervals and extension (four notes instead of three). The second phrase begins exactly as the first, but continues with variations based on inversion (F♯—G—F♯) and repetition. The third phrase retrogrades the extension of the first phrase and intervallically expands the motive to G—B♭—G. Every note of the first section can realistically be evolved from the opening three-note motive. Some are extensive variations, while others are simple inversions. However, all reflect in some way the concept of statement—new statement—return, with variation implicit in the motive of the piece. One can also note the synthetic

Figure 1.43. Opening materials of each section for *Density 21.5.* © 1946 by Colfranc Music Publishing Corp.

Figure 1.44. The opening 8 bars of *Density 21.5* © 1946 by Colfranc Music Publishing Corp.

scale use at the beginning and throughout the work (based on the 8-pitch base of the opening 8 bars).

Also noteworthy is the way in which Varèse "saves" important notes—notably D (which does not occur until bar 11) and B (which does not occur until bar 18).

The second section establishes a contrasting pointillistic theme (see Figure 1.43). However, note the "real" material here: E—C♯—E is clearly a variant of the opening motive. Even the highly contrasting and repetitive climax of the work is an extended inversion of the opening motive. The third section returns to the opening lyric style, but pitch content is varied (based on opening materials).

Varèse may have even attempted numerical relationships with the title of the piece. Interestingly, 70 out of the first 83 intervals of the piece are seconds (2) primes (1) or fifths (5). Whether Varèse intended such relationships is really beside the point; such extreme consistency of intervallic structure contributes to the overall tightly integrated structure of the piece.

Figure 1.45. Repetition in *Density 21.5.* © 1946 by Colfranc Publishing Corp.

5. Vertical model: One does not expect to find vertical possibilities in a work for solo flute. However, it is interesting to note how figure repetition, after a period of time, blends and begins to suggest vertical simultaneities. In Figure 1.45 two of the prominent intervals (seconds and fourths) are underscored by notable repetition. The passage emphasizes tonal ambiguities (non-resolution of tritones) and contrasts these with highly directed dynamics. Note as well how the D♮ is "saved" and finally reached in an explosive triple *forte*.

6. Horizontal models: The expansion of the original motive is prevalent. Figure 1.46 shows how the second expands to the augmented 4th (as mentioned in vertical models). Note how the passage is a kind of "suspension" of musical time. Only the opening note is a downbeat with the remainder of the phrase freely sculpted from available duration rather than splintered from beats and sub-beats.

Figure 1.46. Expansion techniques in *Density 21.5.* © 1946 by Colfranc Publishing Corp.

7. Style: Varèse's *Density 21.5* is a three-part work consistently hewn from an initial three-note motive of major and minor seconds. The instrument's range and available effects are explored as are the concepts of expansion and diminution of intervals, saving pitches for intense climaxes. A "free" phrase structure dominates but without marked tonal references or resolutions. Lines are freely spun through time in a musical and balanced manner. The musical language used, however separate from a tonal sphere, is articulate and consistent. Varèse belongs to that group of composers intent on creating a new syntax from rich vocabularies of sound.

Readers should compare this vectoral analysis with those of the next two chapters (for the extraordinary differences) and then the last two chapters of the book (for the similarities). The chromaticism of the Webern example in the next chapter compares favorably except in its serial approach. The line of the Varèse contrasts significantly with the pointillism of the Webern. The Glass example in the final chapter, however, is comparable in the latter case and not in the former.

Austin, William. *Music in the Twentieth Century*. New York: W. W. Norton, 1966. Good general coverage of mainstream developments of the post-Romantic tradition.

Backus, John. *The Acoustical Foundations of Music*. New York: W. W. Norton, 1969. This is the standard reference for acoustical information relating to music.

"The Composer Between Man and Music (Contemporary Music in the 1970s)" *Interface* Vol. 9, no. 3–4, 1980. Results of a widely broadcast questionnaire on contemporary music.

Forte, Allen. *Contemporary Tone Structures*. New York: Columbia University Press, 1955.

Gagne, Cole and Tracy Caras. *Soundpieces: Interviews with American Composers*. Metuchen, N.J.: The Scarecrow Press, Inc., 1982. Insightful interviews with a wide range of contemporary composers (alive in 1980). Notable are those with Glass, Shapey and Druckman.

Griffiths, Paul. *A Concise History of Avant-Garde Music*. New York: Oxford University Press, 1978. An excellent overview of the origins of the *avant-garde,* though very biased toward European composers and works.

Machlis, Joseph. *Introduction to Contemporary Music* (2nd edition). New York: W. W. Norton and Company, 1979. The most complete work covering all aspects of 20th century music. Though the *avant-garde* is not its main thrust, it does give it more than "nodding" mention. The addition of short biographies of a wide diversity of younger composers is most useful.

Martin, W. R. and Drossin, J. *Music of the Twentieth Century*. Englewood Cliffs: Prentice-Hall, 1980. This book provides good coverage of 20th century music of all types.

Mellers, Wilfred. *Romanticism and the Twentieth Century*. New York: Schocken, 1969. Continues tonal idioms where this chapter leaves off.

Myers, Rollo W. *Modern French Music from Fauré to Boulez*. New York: Praeger Books, 1971. A very good study of French music from the impressionists to IRCAM (inclusive of the *avant-garde*).

Persichetti, Vincent. *20th Century Harmony*. New York: W. W. Norton, 1961. This is a good source book for those interested in continuing study of non-tertian chord structures and polytonality.

Rochberg, George. *The Aesthetics of Survival. A Composer's View of Twentieth-Century Music*. Ann Arbor: The University of Michigan Press, 1984. A collection of articles and pieces which have appeared elsewhere. "No Center," first published in 1969 by *Composer Magazine,* is a classic as is "Indeterminacy in the New Music." While it is helpful to have all of these in one place, the book does not particularly hold together due to the time period covered. The choice of title is an odd one given most of the material in the book.

Salzman, Eric. *Twentieth-Century Music: An Introduction*. Englewood Cliffs: Prentice-Hall. Second Edition, 1974. A good general introduction to mainstream composers and works.

Satie, Erik. *écrits (réunis, établis et annotés par Ornella Volta)*. Paris: Editions Champ Libre, 1977. Although this only exists in French, the voluminous drawings and graffiti provided give wonderful insight into this composer of many talents.

---

*Addresses for record companies, periodicals, and music publishers mentioned in this Bibliography can be found in Appendix 4.

Simms, Bryan R. *Music of the Twentieth Century, Style and Structure*. New York: Schirmer Books, 1986. An excellent general purpose text in 20th century music. There is little or no coverage, however, of computer music or music in the "new age." The author tends to focus on a few well-known composers rather than seeking diversity.

Slonimsky, Nicolas. *Music Since 1900*. New York: Charles Scribner's Sons. 4th Edition, 1971. A master work of research and a most valuable tool for those interested in the details of a great number of events of this century.

Sternfeld, F. W., ed. *Music in the Modern Age*. Praeger History of Music, Vol. V. New York: Praeger Books, 1973. Interesting anthology of thoughts on twentieth-century music (what it lacks in continuity, it makes up for in insight).

Stuckenschmidt, H. H. *Twentieth-Century Music*. New York: McGraw-Hill, 1969. An excellent general introduction but overly geared to the European scene.

Thompson, Oscar. *A Dictionary of Twentieth-Century Composers (1911–1971)*. London: Faber and Faber, 1973. Good source for information on mainstream composers.

Yates, Peter. *Twentieth-Century Music*. New York: Pantheon, 1967. While in some ways outdated, this is a very important book dealing with issues as well as chronicling the "new music" scene at mid-century.

Recordings and Publishers

Bartók, Béla. *Mikrokosmos,* Volume V (1935). Boosey and Hawkes. Recorded on DG 2740239.

———. *Out of Doors Suite* (1926). Universal Edition. Recorded on Nonesuch 71175.

Beethoven, Ludwig van. *Sonata* Op. 2, No. 3. C. F. Peters. Recorded on London 7028.

Busoni, Ferruccio. *Indianisches Tagebuch, for Piano* (1915). Recorded on Orion 74154.

Debussy, Claude. *Pelleas and Melisande* (1907). A. Durand. Angel Records SZX-3885.

———. *Préludes* Books I and II (1910–13). A. Durand. Recorded on Phillips 9500676 and 9500747.

———. *Prélude à "L'Après-midi d'un faune."* (1894). A. Durand. Recorded on Columbia Records MS-7361. CD: Decca; 414 040-2DM. This seminal work made significant challenges to the common-practice and is *the* major example of musical impressionism.

———. *La Soirée dans Grenade* (1903). International Music Corporation. Phillips 9500965.

Griffes, Charles Tomlinson. *Sonata*. G. Schirmer. Recorded on Orion 77270. CD: GASP; GSCD233.

Hindemith, Paul. *Chansons* (6) 1939. B. Schott's Soehne, Mainz. Recorded on Nonesuch 71115.

Ives, Charles. *Concord Sonata* (1915). Associated Music Publishers. Columbia MS-7192. A masterwork of polytonality and collage.

———. *114 Songs* (1884–1921). Published by the composer and subsequently by New Music Edition. See the Schwann Record Catalog for currently available recordings of various songs. CD: ETCE; KTC1020.

———. *Three Places in New England* (1914). Mercury Music Corporation. Recorded on DG 2530048.

Mozart, Wolfgang Amadeus. *Theme and Variations: Ah! Vous Dirai-je, Maman.* (K. 265) Kalmus Edition. Recorded on DG 2535115.

Ravel, Maurice. *Daphnis et Chloe Suite #2* (1913). A. Durand. Columbia M-31847. CD: London, 400055-2 LH.

———. *Le Tombeau de Couperin* (1977). A. Durand. Recorded on Quintessence 2712. CD: Decca; 400 051-2DH.

———. *Sonatine* (for piano). International Music Publishers. Recorded on DG 2530540. CD: Denon; CD-7805.

Satie, Erik. *Trois Gymnopédies*. Kalmus Edition. Recorded on CBS M-36694. CD: Decca; 410 220–2DH.

Schoenberg, Arnold. *Pierrot Lunaire* (1912). Universal Edition. Recorded on Turnabout 34315.

———. *Sechs Kleine Klavier stucke* Op. 19 (1911). International Editions. Nonesuch 71309. CD: Denon; CO-1060/1.

Scriabin, Alexander. *Poème* Op. 69, No. 1 (1913). C. F. Peters. Recorded on VOX SVBX-5474.

Stravinsky, Igor. *Petrushka* (1911). Edition Russe de Musique. Recorded on Columbia D3S-705. CD: DG; 419 202-2GH.

Varèse, Edgard. *Amériques*. Colfranc Corporation. Recorded on Vanguard S-308.

———. *Density 21.5* (1936). Colfranc Corporation. Recorded on Nonesuch 73028.

Wagner, Richard. *Tristan und Isolde* (1859). Eulenberg Scores. Recorded on Angel S-3777. CD: CBS; MK-37294.

Webern, Anton. *Six Bagatelles* (for string quartet)—1913. Universal Edition. Recorded on DG 2720029.

2 · ROOTS OF THE EXPERIMENTAL TRADITION

12-Tone Techniques

As artists stretched ever outward to explore new visions, musical traditions continued to collapse. Audiences groped for tangible indications of commonality of style. Stravinsky remarks: "Is it any wonder, then, that the hypercritics of today should be dumbfounded by a language in which all of the characteristics of their aesthetic seem to be violated?"[1] Natural too is the composer's desire for new order to be able to spend more time "composing" and less "experimenting" with new materials and techniques.

During the first two decades of the 20th century, a number of mainstreams derived from Romantic traditions of the nineteenth century developed. The Germanic style (often presented as a Beethoven-Wagner-Mahler-Schoenberg lineage) was steeped in motivic microdevelopment and metatonal (chromatic) concepts. The Franco-Russian composers (particularly Debussy, Ravel, and Stravinsky), the Primitivists (especially Béla Bartók), and the Iconoclastic composers (particularly Charles Ives in America) developed more fluid, less systematic techniques, often effecting fewer works in freer application.

One of the more important developments during this time was twelve-tone composition (often called *serialism*). It was clearly derived from a base of Germanic tradition, and presented composers with the prospect of a common language and context. The twelve-tone approach was developed primarily by Arnold Schoenberg during the years 1917–1923, during which time he wrote little music, devoting his energies to performance and development of the new techniques and applications he had discovered. Serialism seemed to him to be the natural conclusion of the extended complex chromaticism that had been developing in Western European music during the previous 120 years (since mid-Mozart).

One of the basic properties of twelve-tone writing is the creation of a row. The only basic requirement of this line of twelve notes is that they all be different (i.e., the row must contain all twelve notes of the chromatic scale). Figure 2.1 shows how three different serial composers applied this principle. Note how Schoenberg's row (a) tends to void suggestions of tonal centers (i.e., successive notes tending not to

---

1. Igor Stravinsky, *An Autobiography* (New York: W. W. Norton, 1936), p. 176.

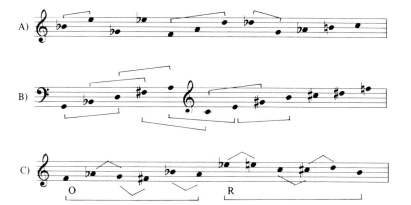

A)

B)

C)

O   R

Figure 2.1. Schoenberg *Variations for Orchestra,* op. 31; (b) Berg, *Violin Concerto;* (c) Webern, *Symphonie,* op. 21.

Figure 2.2. Arnold Schoenberg. Dover Publications, Inc. Permission granted.

Figure 2.3. Alban Berg. Dover Publications, Inc. Permission granted.

exist in the previous note's key signature). On the other hand, Berg's row (b) holds strong tonal ties with continuous triadic reference (the first seven notes, moreover, existing in the G melodic minor scale). Webern (c) tends to develop certain integrated cross-referencing within the row itself (e.g., the second half of the row is a reverse of the first half).

Once a composer has created a row (called "prime"), certain variants are created: *retrograde* (the row played backwards), *inversion* (the row played upside down), and *inversion-retrograde* (the row played both upside down and backwards). Each of these is shown in Figure 2.4 based on the Schoenberg row of Figure 2.1. It is important to note from the outset that interval integrity must be maintained throughout (i.e., each interval is reproduced exactly with each variant). However, it is not necessary for the new pitch to remain in the octave shown. Once determined, the pitch belongs to a "class" of pitches with the same name. Therefore, all C's belong to the same "pitch class."

The numbers above each note of the prime version (Figure 2.4) indicate the number of half steps separating each row member from the first note. In chromatic scale order, the initial pitch is labeled "O" and the last "11," accounting for the eleven half steps between the twelve different notes present. Composers find this approach more laden with information about rows than one which simply indicates row order (i.e. 1, 2, 3, etc., pitches of the series).

Figure 2.4. Prime, retrograde, inversion, and inversion-retrograde of row for Schoenberg's *Variations for Orchestra*, op. 31.

Each of these variants can now exist in twelve transpositions (each beginning on twelve different notes, again keeping their respective interval integrity intact). Figure 2.5 shows the original row beginning on B♭, then A, then A♭, etc., clearly demonstrating the different levels. Notice that the variations Schoenberg chose to develop his row properties are an extension of motivic development that German composers (particularly since Beethoven) used with extreme vitality. The arabic numeral next to the "prime" indicates a new beginning pitch referenced to the ordinal numbering of the initial series.

Figure 2.5. Transpositions (beginning on successively lower notes) of row for Schoenberg's *Variations for Orchestra*, op. 31.

One way composers chose to show all the versions of a row at once is called a *matrix*. This "box" of 144 squares is created by cross-thatching twelve vertical lines with twelve horizontal lines (actually thirteen in each case to provide the outer layers of the box itself). If the original row is placed across the top of the box (left to right) and the inversion placed down the left of the matrix (top to bottom), a frame can be created to define the interior rows. To complete the matrix, the composer fills in (left to right) the transpositions of the original, allowing the notes of the inversion to dictate the beginning notes. Figure 2.6 shows a completed matrix (again based on the Schoenberg row of figure 2.1). Note that one can now quickly read any version of the row from the completed matrix (originals, left to right; inversions, top to bottom; retrogrades, right to left; retrograde-inversions, bottom to top). The matrix can become an extremely important tool for use in analysis or composition of twelve-tone music.

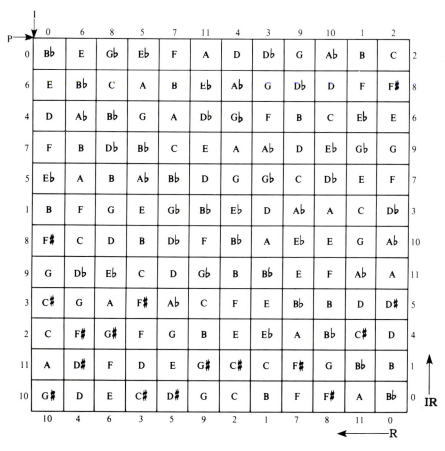

Figure 2.6. Matrix of row from Schoenberg's *Variations for Orchestra*, op. 31.

A row seen in a matrix is void of absolute register. The B♭ (upper left corner) could appear in any octave. Each pitch becomes part of a distinct and related (by octave) "set" of pitches (all B♭'s in this instance). As mentioned earlier, they belong to the same "pitch class." Composers are able to choose freely from any member of a certain pitch class and not be restricted to a given octave. Also noteworthy is the observation that the ordinal numbers of the inversion can be derived by subtracting the appropriately paired prime number from 12. For example, moving left to right and top to bottom, $12 - 0 = 12$ (or 0); $12 - 6 = 6$; $12 - 8 = 4$; etc.

Composers typically utilize rows in two ways in serial composition. The first (here called category A) derives all successive notes from one version of the row at a time. Figure 2.7A shows a category A type of composition using the Schoenberg row. Notice that all notes of both melody and harmony are extracts from the single version of the original form of the row. In order to show this, numbers here refer to row ordering and not interval relationship to the initial pitch. The work could continue from this point with a repeat of this version or any other version used in a similar manner.

A second type of twelve-tone composition employs more than one version of the row at a time and is called category B. Figure 2.7B shows three versions of the Schoenberg row used simultaneously. Unlike the category A composition, it is difficult here to maintain a twelve-tone integrity (e.g., notes are frequently repeated immediately or simultaneously, often creating non-row-centered sonorities).

Early in the development of twelve-tone theory, Schoenberg and others adopted a variety of techniques which aid the composer in expanding the potential of the approach. These create interesting anomalies which can eventually lead to unique

Figure 2.7. Category A (a) and category B (b) types of twelve-tone composition using Schoenberg row from *Variations for Orchestra*, op. 31.

styles and works. The most simple of these variations is *repetition*. Since most music includes repetition of individual notes as inherent to an important motive or line, this same attribute can be utilized in twelve-tone composition. Therefore, repeated notes and chords are acceptable, and not considered deviations from the basic structure of twelve-tone concepts. Patterns of notes (e.g., two-, three-, and four-note groupings) may also be repeated immediately after they have sounded, making it possible for the composer to initiate individual stylistic motives.

Overlapping one version of the row with another is also fairly common in twelve-tone compositions. In this variant, the last note (usually) of one version becomes the first note of the next. Composers also use *anticipations* of coming material, creating interesting implosions of row contents. Figure 2.8 has the first eight notes of the row in the voice part. The ninth through twelfth notes of the row are stated in the piano part even before the voice part begins (anticipation). These then are repeated with variation as accompaniment until they fall in their right place numerically.

Figure 2.8. Arnold Schoenberg: *Sommermud.* Example of note repetition and anticipation in twelve-tone composition.

Combinatoriality

Category B twelve-tone composition poses unresolved problems of harmonic continuity and homogeneity. While these problems do not exist in category A composition, composers seem more interested in the complexities available in the contrapuntal use of many variants of the row used simultaneously. Combinatoriality mechanics tend to absorb the discontinuities resulting from category B usage.

One of the first steps in understanding combinatoriality involves applying principles of subsetting. A *subset* is a group of notes, smaller than twelve, which is an evenly divisible integer of the whole (e.g., 2, 3, 4, and 6 are each evenly divisible into 12). Terminology includes: *hexachord,* a group of six notes (two in a twelve-tone row); *tetrachord,* a group of four notes (three in a twelve-tone row); *trichord,* a group of three notes (four in a twelve-tone row); and *dichord,* a group of two notes (six in a twelve-tone row).

Combinatoriality, the combining of versions of mutually exclusive note contents, is best understood when carefully observing the matrix. Looking back at Figure 2.6, one notices that the second hexachord of the original row (i.e., D, Db, G, Ab, B, C of P° in that order) equals the pitch content of the first hexachord of the inversion of the row beginning on G (I⁹ top to bottom beginning in the ninth square left to right). Important however, is that the order of the notes involved has changed remarkably (i.e., they now read G, Db, B, D, C, and Ab; 9, 3, 1, 4, 2, 10 instead of 4, 3, 9, 10, 1, 2). As would be expected, the second hexachord of this inversion has the same note content as the first hexachord of the original nontransposed version. This feature becomes important when one realizes that combining these two versions in a category B type composition provides a continuous twelve-tone (category A type) continuity and homogeneity, while at the same time providing the explorations possible in the contrapuntal environment of category B frameworks.

In Figure 2.9 the top voice uses the twelve notes of the original form of the row, with the twelve notes of the inversion from G used in the bass voice. Note, however, that unlike Figure 2.7B where the vertical chromaticism often produces irregularities such as octaves and repeated notes, this example does not. Clearly the first bar contains twelve different notes as does the second bar. This kind of hexachordal subsetting in the right combinations provides the basis for combinatorial composition.

Figure 2.9. Combinatoriality using the original (top voice) and the inversion (bottom voice) of the row from Schoenberg's *Variations for Orchestra*, op. 31.

Set Theory

A number of composers have employed theories of unordered pitch sets in their compositions. This theory suggests that contiguous pitch groupings (whether melodic or harmonic) can be recognized regardless of their order or transposition. Only 220 unique pitch class (pc) sets exist mathematically (shown here in Figure 2.10).

Pitch class sets									
		5-7	0,1,2,6,7	6-18	0,1,2,5,7,8	7-Z17	0,1,2,4,5,6,9	8-27	0,1,2,4,5,7,8,10
		5-8(12)	0,2,3,4,6	6-Z19	0,1,3,4,7,8	7-Z18	0,1,2,3,5,8,9	8-28	0,1,3,4,6,7,9,10
3-1(12)	0,1,2	5-9	0,1,2,4,6	6-20(4)	0,1,4,5,8,9	7-19	0,1,2,3,6,7,9	8-Z29	0,1,2,3,5,6,7,9
3-2	0,1,3	5-10	0,1,3,4,6	6-21	0,2,3,4,6,8	7-20	0,1,2,4,7,8,9	9-1	0,1,2,3,4,5,6,7,8
3-3	0,1,4	5-11	0,2,3,4,7	6-22	0,1,2,4,6,8	7-21	0,1,2,4,5,8,9	9-2	0,1,2,3,4,5,6,7,9
3-4	0,1,5	5-Z12(12)	0,1,3,5,6	6-Z23(12)	0,2,3,5,6,8	7-22	0,1,2,5,6,8,9	9-3	0,1,2,3,4,5,6,8,9
3-5	0,1,6	5-13	0,1,2,4,8	6-Z24	0,1,3,4,6,8	7-22	0,1,2,5,6,8,9	9-4	0,1,2,3,4,5,7,8,9
3-6(12)	0,2,4	5-14	0,1,2,5,7	6-Z25	0,1,3,5,6,8	7-23	0,2,3,4,5,7,9	9-5	0,1,2,3,4,6,7,8,9
3-7	0,2,5	5-15(12)	0,1,2,6,8	6-Z26(12)	0,1,3,5,7,8	7-24	0,1,2,3,5,7,9	9-6	0,1,2,3,4,5,6,8,10
3-8	0,2,6	5-16	0,1,3,4,7	6-27	0,1,3,4,6,9	7-25	0,2,3,4,6,7,9	9-7	0,1,2,3,4,5,7,8,10
3-9(12)	0,2,7	5-17(12)	0,1,3,4,8	6-Z28(12)	0,1,3,5,6,9	7-26	0,1,3,4,5,7,9	9-8	0,1,2,3,4,6,7,8,10
3-10(12)	0,3,6	5-Z18	0,1,4,5,7	6-Z29(12)	0,1,3,6,8,9	7-27	0,1,2,4,5,7,9	9-9	0,1,2,3,5,6,7,8,10
3-11	0,3,7	5-19	0,1,3,6,7	6-30(12)	0,1,3,6,7,9	7-28	0,1,3,5,6,7,9	9-10	0,1,2,3,4,6,7,9,10
3-12(4)	0,4,8	5-20	0,1,3,7,8	6-31	0,1,3,5,8,9	7-29	0,1,2,4,6,7,9	9-11	0,1,2,3,5,6,7,9,10
4-1(12)	0,1,2,3	5-21	0,1,4,5,8	6-32(12)	0,2,4,5,7,9	7-30	0,1,2,4,6,8,9	9-12	0,1,2,4,5,6,8,9,10
4-2	0,1,2,4	5-22(12)	0,1,4,7,8	6-33	0,2,3,5,7,9	7-31	0,1,3,4,6,7,9		
4-3(12)	0,1,3,4	5-23	0,2,3,5,7	6-34	0,1,3,5,7,9	7-32	0,1,3,4,6,8,9		
4-4	0,1,2,5	5-24	0,1,3,5,7	6-35(2)	0,2,4,6,8,10	7-33	0,1,2,4,6,8,10		
4-5	0,1,2,6	5-25	0,2,3,5,8	6-36	0,1,2,3,4,7	7-34	0,1,3,4,6,8,10		
4-6(12)	0,1,2,7	5-26	0,2,4,5,8	6-Z37(12)	0,1,2,3,4,8	7-35	0,1,3,5,6,8,10		
4-7(12)	0,1,4,5	5-27	0,1,3,5,8	6-Z38(12)	0,1,2,3,7,8	7-Z36	0,1,2,3,5,6,8		
4-8(12)	0,1,5,6	5-28	0,2,3,6,8	6-39	0,2,3,4,5,8	7-Z37	0,1,3,4,5,7,8		
4-9(6)	0,1,6,7	5-29	0,1,3,6,8	6-Z40	0,1,2,3,5,8	7-Z38	0,1,2,4,5,7,8		
4-10(12)	0,2,3,5	5-30	0,1,4,6,8	6-Z41	0,1,2,3,6,8	8-1	0,1,2,3,4,5,6,7		
4-11	0,1,3,5	5-31	0,1,3,6,9	6-Z42(12)	0,1,2,3,6,9	8-2	0,1,2,3,4,5,6,8		
4-12	0,2,3,6	5-32	0,1,4,6,9	6-Z43	0,1,2,5,6,8	8-3	0,1,2,3,4,5,6,9		
4-13	0,1,3,6	5-33(12)	0,2,4,6,8	6-Z44	0,1,2,5,6,9	8-4	0,1,2,3,4,5,7,8		
4-14	0,2,3,7	5-34(12)	0,2,4,6,9	6-Z45(12)	0,2,3,4,6,9	8-5	0,1,2,3,4,6,7,8		
4-Z15	0,1,4,6	5-35(12)	0,2,4,7,9	6-Z46	0,1,2,4,6,9	8-6	0,1,2,3,5,6,7,8		
4-16	0,1,5,7	5-Z36	0,1,2,4,7	6-Z47	0,1,2,4,7,9	8-7	0,1,2,3,4,5,8,9		
4-17(12)	0,3,4,7	5-Z37(12)	0,3,4,5,8	6-Z48(12)	0,1,2,5,7,9	8-8	0,1,2,3,4,7,8,9		
4-18	0,1,4,7	5-Z38	0,1,2,5,8	6-Z49(12)	0,1,3,4,7,9	8-9	0,1,2,3,6,7,8,9		
4-19	0,1,4,8	6-1(12)	0,1,2,3,4,5	6-Z50(12)	0,1,4,6,7,9	8-10	0,2,3,4,5,6,7,9		
4-20(12)	0,1,5,8	6-2	0,1,2,3,4,6	7-1	0,1,2,3,4,5,6	8-11	0,1,2,3,4,5,7,9		
4-21(12)	0,2,4,6	6Z3	0,1,2,3,5,6	7-2	0,1,2,3,4,5,7	8-12	0,1,3,4,5,6,7,9		
4-22	0,2,4,7	6-Z4(12)	0,1,2,4,5,6	7-3	0,1,2,3,4,5,8	8-13	0,1,2,3,4,6,7,9		
4-23(12)	0,2,5,7	6-5	0,1,2,3,6,7	7-4	0,1,2,3,4,6,7	8-14	0,1,2,4,5,6,7,9		
4-24(12)	0,2,4,8	6-Z6(12)	0,1,2,5,6,7	7-5	0,1,2,3,5,6,7	8-Z15	0,1,2,3,4,6,8,9		
4-25(6)	0,2,6,8	6-7(6)	0,1,2,6,7,8	7-6	0,1,2,3,4,7,8	8-16	0,1,2,3,5,7,8,9		
4-26(12)	0,3,5,8	6-8(12)	0,2,3,4,5,7	7-7	0,1,2,3,6,7,8	8-17	0,1,3,4,5,6,8,9		
4-27	0,2,5,8	6-9	0,1,2,3,5,7	7-8	0,2,3,4,5,6,8	8-18	0,1,2,3,5,6,8,9		
4-28(3)	0,3,6,9	6-Z10	0,1,3,4,5,7	7-9	0,1,2,3,4,6,8	8-19	0,1,2,4,5,6,8,9		
4-Z29	0,1,3,7	6-Z11	0,1,2,4,5,7	7-10	0,1,2,3,4,6,9	8-20	0,1,2,4,5,7,8,9		
5-1(12)	0,1,2,3,4	6-Z12	0,1,2,4,6,7	7-11	0,1,3,4,5,6,8	8-21	0,1,2,3,4,6,8,10		
5-2	0,1,2,3,5	6-Z13(12)	0,1,3,4,6,7	7-Z12	0,1,2,3,4,7,9	8-22	0,1,2,3,5,6,8,10		
5-3	0,1,2,4,5	6-14	0,1,3,4,5,8	7-13	0,1,2,4,5,6,8	8-23	0,1,2,3,5,7,8,10		
5-4	0,1,2,3,6	6-15	0,1,2,4,5,8	7-14	0,1,2,3,5,7,8	8-24	0,1,2,4,5,6,8,10		
5-5	0,1,2,3,7	6-16	0,1,4,5,6,8	7-15	0,1,2,4,6,7,8	8-25	0,1,2,4,6,7,8,10		
5-6	0,1,2,5,6	6-Z17	0,1,2,4,7,8	7-16	0,1,2,3,5,6,9	8-26	0,1,2,4,5,7,9,10		

Figure 2.10. A chart of unordered pitch class sets.

The names derive from (a) the number of pitches in the set, (b) a dash and (c) the number in the series. The numbers in the set that follow equate to O = C, 1 = Db, 2 = D, etc. in ascending numerical order with intervals reduced within the octave (12 = pitch class equivalency). Two pitch-class sets are equivalent if they are reducible to the same prime form by transposition or by inversion followed by transposition. Figure 2.11 shows how such reductions demonstrate similarities

Figure 2.11. Chords from (respectively) works by Berg and Stravinsky.

between otherwise (apparently) dissimilar constructs. Here the two sets would seem to be different. Using the above model, however, they reduce to the same pc set. The process follows:

1. Placing the numbers in "normal [ascending] order" ([3,5,6,9,0(12)] and [5,7,8,11,2(14)]) with the least possible differences between first and last numbers (adding 12 to each number moved beyond the highest below 11; if 2 or more orderings are the same, then the next inner values are compared);
2. Transposing the set to 0 level (i.e., subtracting the first number from all others)—[0,2,3,6,9] and [0,2,3,6,9] respectively;
3. Finding and naming the set from the list in Figure 2.10.

In the above case, however, no such set is found in the list. In this case, theory argues that the set is not yet in its *best* possible order. To accomplish this, one must

1. invert the set by subtracting each number from 12 with 0 = 12[0,10,9,6,3];
2. place numbers in ascending order [0,3,6,9,10];
3. find the new normal order (as in 1 above) [9,10,0,3,6];
4. transpose the set to 0 level [0,1,3,6,9].

This set does appear in the list as 5–31 thus demonstrating set theory equivalency. Figure 2.12 shows another more contextual example. The pc-set analysis below

Figure 2.12. Opening of Schoenberg's Opus 11, No. 2 with analysis using set theory.

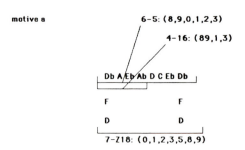

Figure 2.12. *(Continued)*

motive b:

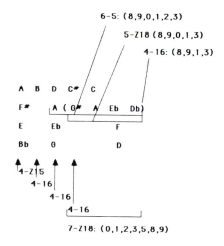

6-5: (8,9,0,1,2,3)

5-Z18 (8,9,0,1,3)

4-16: (8,9,1,3)

A	B	D	C#	C
F#		A (G#	A	Eb	Db)
E		Eb			F
Bb		0			D

4-Z15
4-16
4-16
4-16

7-Z18: (0,1,2,3,5,8,9)

the example demonstrates the interrelationships between unordered sets of pitches (repeated pitches count only once). Note the number of comparable pitch set names. The 6–5 set located in the top voices of both phrases is not readily apparent without using the pc-set manipulations. The music hints at it, however, in the Eb–Db dyad (2-note set) at the end of each phrase. The harmonic repeat of 7–Z18 (the Z stands for pitch-class sets which have the same total interval content, but are unrelated by transposition or inversion) and the very consistent 4–16 harmonic vocabulary related to the first tetrachord (4-note set) of the melody suggest serious motivic interweavings.

Pitch set theory is not without its critics, however. Many argue against composer intention while others claim that these relationships, for the most part, are unheard and hence useless. In Berg's *Wozzeck,* for example, pc-set analysis of the themes of each character is serious evidence of composer-intended relationships (only understood by a thorough set analysis). Pioneering work on Stravinsky's *Rite of Spring* by Allen Forte suggests serious intent by the composer to draw links between various pitch sets (principally harmonic) in the work.

Regardless of past intention or future use, set theory has caused a number of mathematically inclined composers to define their work by the use of unordered pitch sets. The more works under set theory scrutiny, the more that seem to be thus composed. Certainly the bulk of current interest in this approach as a compositional process resides on the East Coast of the United States.

Total Control

Pantonality (this, not *atonality,* was the term used by Schoenberg), or "inclusive of all tonalities," is not important because of chromaticism, but in its extreme control over compositional elements, a control that is predominantly inaudible and recognizable in general stylistic terms only. Total control or serialization of the other parameters of musical composition begins as it does in pitch organization, with the creation of a row and extended by the basic variant sets.

Anton Webern's *Variations for Piano,* opus 27 (second movement) employs a dynamic row of nine values as shown in Figure 2.13

Figure 2.13. Anton Webern: *Variations for Piano,* opus 27, second movement. Dynamic row.

$f \ p \ f$ $p \ f \ p$ $f \ p \ ff$

Webern follows this prime order with a variation of the retrograde (the third trichord—now the first—left in original order):

Figure 2.14. Retrograde (variation) of the dynamic row of Figure 2.14.

$f \ p \ ff$ $p \ f \ p$ $f \ p \ f$

Articulations are directly related to individual pitches of the row. Figure 2.15 shows how this is accomplished.

Figure 2.15. Articulation row of Webern's *Variations for Piano,* opus 27.

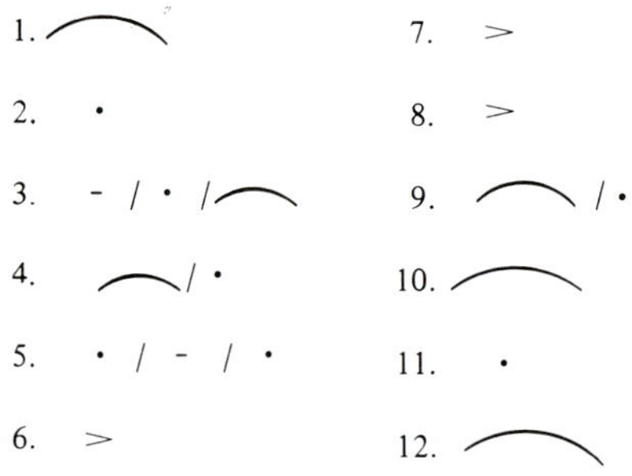

For example, the second note of every version of the row used in the second variation is staccato, etc. Careful analysis of rhythm and form (a cyclic mirror canon) shows that these are also related serially to the basic structure of this piece. Whether any of these elements are audible is beside the point. Most tonal composers worked constantly with intricate motivic and chromatic techniques which become evident to the ear only after repeated listening and score study. Some critics of these techniques claim that their basic use is inherently "non-musical." Here again, the point relates to the particular composer using them; if used musically, they aid in the creation of good music. If used as a crutch to simply produce notations of mathematical import and interest without real aural meaning, then certainly they are "nonmusical."

The piano composition by Milton Babbitt shown in Figure 2.16 demonstrates serialized control of dynamics, rhythm, and pitch. The pitch content of this piece is based on combinatorial principles. The basic row is shown in Figure 2.17.

Figure 2.16. Milton Babbitt: *Three Compositions for Piano*, 1947 (measures 1–8, Piece No. 1). Published by Boelke-Bonart, Inc., Hillsdale, N.Y. Key: P = prime; R = retrograde (backwards); I = inversion; IR = inverted retrograde.

Figure 2.17. Row for Milton Babbitt's *Three Compositions for Piano.*

Note that this form of the row appears in the lower voice of the first two bars. Babbitt carefully observed that the first hexachord of the original form of the row beginning on E contained notes that were mutually exclusive of those in the first hexachord of the original beginning on B♭. Therefore, by combining this version (as the upper voice) with the original nontransposed version, he was able to create combinatoriality. Note that the first bar contains twelve different notes as does the second bar, thus avoiding inconsistent repetitions or octave-unison doublings.

The rhythm of the piece also involves serial principles. If one looks carefully at the hexachordal subgroupings within each bar of the composition, it becomes clear that a held note balances the other notes of equal duration. In the bass voice, for example, the held tone (fifth in the six-note sequence), suggests a five grouping followed by a single note. The same is true of the first hexachord of the row in the upper voice (i.e., 5/1). In the second bar, the grouping is distinctly different. Here the held note (fourth of the sequence), divides the hexachord into groups of four and two notes each (the same being true in the upper voice). The rhythm clearly follows a pattern based on the principle of 5/1/4/2; each voice holds that row intact. In the upper voice in bar 3 one encounters the order 2/4, with the next bar developing 1/5 (again, in the upper voice). This ordering (2/4/1/5) is the retrograde of the original rhythmic row.

To create an inversion of such rows becomes obviously different from similar groupings in tone rows. Babbitt creates such "inversions" here by inverting dichordal subsets (that is, reversing the order of the outer groups of two numbers each). Therefore, the inversion of 5/1/4/2 becomes 1/5/2/4 (and the inversion retrograde, 4/2/5/1).

Examining Figure 2.16, bars 3 and 4 (bass voice), one can immediately recognize that the rhythm here is an inversion retrograde of the original row. Serialization of rhythmic principles continues in this manner for the remainder of the piece.

Dynamic serialization, while simpler in this piece, is still important to its basic structure. Here, each version of the row links with a dynamic (i.e., original, *mp;* retrograde, *mf;* inversion, *f;* and inversion retrograde, *p*).

Figure 2.18. Rhythm rows for Babbitt's *Three Compositions for Piano.*

P: 5 - 1 - 4 - 2
I: 1 - 5 - 2 - 4
R: 2 - 4 - 1 - 5
IR: 4 - 2 - 5 - 1

In his now-famous article "Who Cares if You Listen," Milton Babbitt speaks of this "high degree of determinacy":

In the simplest terms, each such "atomic" event is located in a five-dimensional musical space determined by pitch-class, register, dynamic, duration, and timbre. These five components not only together define the single event, but, in the course of a work, the successive values of each component create an individually coherent structure, frequently in parallel with the corresponding structures created by each of the other components. Inability to perceive and remember precisely the values of any of these components results in a dislocation of the event in the work's musical space, an alteration of its relation to all other events in the work, and—thus—a falsification of the composition's total structure. For example, an incorrectly performed or perceived dynamic value results in destruction of the work's dynamic pattern, but also in false identification of other components of the event (of which this dynamic value is a part) with corresponding components of other events, so creating incorrect pitch, registral, timbral and durational associations.[2]

Babbitt speaks of the confusion surrounding his article in an interview:

I gave a lecture at Tanglewood in 1957 about the state of the contemporary composer. The then-editor of *High Fidelity* heard it and asked me to write it down. I had been improvising it and didn't want to write it down, but they had a copy of the tape and asked me if I would take it and put it in some kind of publishable shape. The title of the article as submitted to *High Fidelity* was "The Composer as Specialist." There was no imputation whatsoever of "who cares if you listen," which as far as I am concerned conveys very little of the letter of the article, and nothing of the spirit. Obviously the point was that I cared a great deal who listened, but above all how they listened. I was concerned about the fact that people were not listening. But theirs of course, was a much more provocative title, and journalists are concerned to provoke, and do. It wasn't "who cares if you listen." It was this: If you're not going to take our activities in as serious and dignified a manner as we take them, then of course we don't want you to listen.[3]

Oliver Messiaen (b. 1909 in France) was one of the first to use rigid rhythmic control (augmentation, diminution by one half, one third, one fourth, etc., of the original) over his materials. His *Quatre études de rhythme* (especially number 2, *Mode de valeur et d'intensités*), published in 1949, was one of the first works to include integral organization of the "whole." Though based more on modal than twelve-tone principles, it did in fact serialize the basic musical components (36 sounds; 24 durations; 7 dynamics; 12 articulations).

Messiaen's influence over the younger composers of France, combined with twelve-tone theory, enabled Pierre Boulez to arrange twelve different durations, twelve articulations, and twelve dynamics in row forms, thus creating serialization possibilities over more compositional elements. This is particularly effective and noticeable in Boulez's *Structures* (1952) and *Second Piano Sonata* (1948). Figure 2.19 shows each of these series.

---

2. Milton Babbitt, "Who Cares if You Listen," *High Fidelity* 8, no. 2 (February 1958):38–40, 126–27.
3. Cole Cagne and Tracy Caras, *Soundpieces: Interviews with American Composers* (London: The Scarecrow Press, Inc., 1982), p. 37.

Figure 2.19. Boulez: *Structures* Serialization of parameters.

Figure 2.20. Pierre Boulez.

Bernd Alois Zimmermann's *Perspectives* for two pianos (1956) is row controlled from an aggregate of procedures pertaining to pitch, density, rhythm, dynamics, attacks and pedaling representing somewhat of a landmark in its degree of systematic composer control (see the article on the work in *die Reihe* #4 for complete analysis). Ruth Crawford's (1901–53) innovative String Quartet (1931) employs procedures of total organization. The third movement of this work includes an obvious systematic procedure of control in which the compositional elements (pitch, duration, dynamics, and rhythm) are related and serialized. The foundation of the movement is a double canon in dynamics only (first canon in the viola and 'cello and the second in the two violins). The resulting dovetailing of dynamics (one voice in crescendo and the other in simultaneous diminuendo) foreshadows yet another technique of experimentation: timbre modulation (the opening intervals are major and minor seconds with the undulating dynamics creating timbre movements from one instrument to another).

These mathematical approaches are new only in their applications, for since Pythagoras and his followers, music theory has evolved through a process of scientific formulas applied during, though more often after, the compositional process. The increased requirements on both performer and audience must certainly have been in part responsible for the replacement of one by tape, and the diminishing size of the other (leaving even fellow professionals interested, but often confused, bystanders). Even without serialism, performance conflicts appeared to Charles Ives who, in the Postface to his *114 Songs* (1922) explained: "Some of the songs in this book, particularly among the later ones, cannot be sung, and if they could, perhaps might prefer, if they had to say, to remain as they are; that is, 'in the leaf'—and that they will remain in this peaceful state is more than presumable."[4]

In America the colleges and universities have replaced the courts, the church, and patrons of earlier times, offering the composer the only realistic terms for physical survival. The need in this academic environment to present composition as an ordered and intellectual pursuit, and the close physical proximity of so-called "disciplines" of scientific teachings, have contributed no small part to the large volume of systems and aesthetics in the past forty years. Pierre Boulez, in an interview with the author, referred to this environment:

> Yes, academic, and in the strong sense of the word. It does not matter whether the academic is after Schumann, after Bach, after Wagner, or after a new serial type; the academic is something which I cannot accept at any time. The main problem, to my mind, is to find a purely musical way of thinking and not something which is parascientific.[5]

Clearly, then, composers began to define their actions and reactions in terms of highly intellectual processes. By the late forties, the lines between "more" control and "less" control had been clearly drawn and defined. The roots of this disagreement seem to lie, both nationalistically (Europe vs. America) and compositionally, in the concept that extremely highly organized music sounds very often like extremely unorganized music, with the row and total serialization representing the parting of the ways (see Figure 2.21).

This mobile shows the turn-of-the-century experimental tradition to the left of the *mainstream* composers (those bent on continuing tonal or quasi-tonal models of the nineteenth century). In the mid-thirties the experimental tradition branched and accelerated into a flurry of activity at the forefront of discovery and ever-reaching into the unknown: the *avant-garde*.

---

4. Charles Ives, "Postface to 114 Songs," in *Essays before a Sonata, and Other Writings,* ed. Howard Boatwright (New York: W. W. Norton & Co., 1961), p. 131.
5. Galen Wilson and David Cope, "An Interview with Pierre Boulez," *Composer* 1, no. 2 (September 1969):79–80.

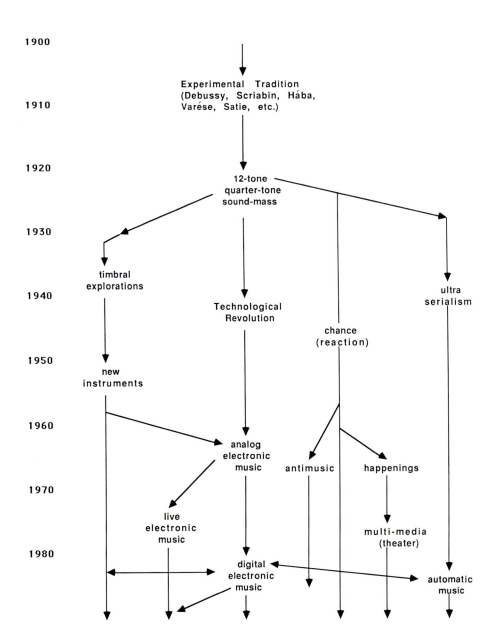

Figure 2.21. An *avant-garde* mobile.

1900

Experimental Tradition
(Debussy, Scriabin, Hába,
1910   Varése, Satie, etc.)

1920

12-tone
quarter-tone
sound-mass

1930

timbral
explorations

1940

Technological
Revolution   ultra
serialism

chance
(reaction)

1950

new
instruments

1960

analog
electronic
music   antimusic   happenings

1970

live
electronic
music

multi-media
(theater)

1980

digital
electronic
music   automatic
music

**Vectoral Analysis:
Anton von Webern:
Symphonie, op. 21**

(For information on vectoral analysis and procedures see Chapter 1).

1. Historical background: Webern was born in Vienna in 1883 and died in
   Mittersill (near Salzburg), where he had moved to avoid the Allied
   bombings. He studied with Guido Adler at the University of Vienna and
   received a doctorate in musicology in 1906. He conducted in the provincial

theaters and the Vienna Workers Symphony Concerts (organized by the then socialist city). He stayed in Germany during the Second World War, even though performances of his music were banned by the Third Reich (he worked as a proofreader for a Viennese publisher). He died in 1945 of gunshot wounds delivered accidentally by an American occupation troop stationed in Mittersill.

2. Overview: This work is in two short movements (I, ♩ = 50; II, ♩ = 54). The first movement is a kind of two-part (each is repeated) 'binary' form with the second a large canonic development of the first. The second movement is a theme and seven variations.

3. Orchestration Techniques: The *Symphonie* is scored for nine solo instruments: clarinet, bass clarinet, two horns, harp, two violins, viola, and 'cello. The major difference between this and Webern's previous work (op. 20) is *klangfarbenmelodien* (defined as a kind of *pointillism*—see Chapter 1's discussion of origins in the visual arts—that involves timbre). Note that in the opening of the work, Webern casts few notes without range, rest or timbre separations (e.g., horn vs. harp vs. pizzicati cello, etc.).

4. Basic Techniques: The row of the piece is as follows.

This palindrome row (one which reads with the same intervals in both directions) makes the initial series identical with its retrograde (transposed) and the inversion identical with the retrograde-inversion (transposed). Therefore only 24 forms of the row are actually possible (not the usual 48).

    The work begins with a double canon in contrary (inverted) motion in four parts. Horn 2 begins the original on A with imitation beginning in

Figure 2.24. First 14 bars of Anton Webern's *Symphonie,* opus 21, first movement. Beginning of double canon shown in first 7 bars.

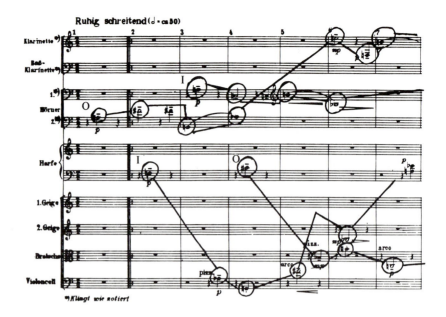

Roots of the Experimental Tradition

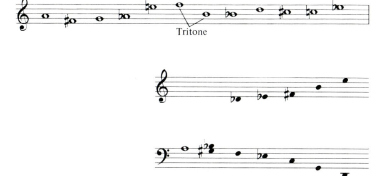

Tritone

Figure 2.24. Row for Webern's *Symphonie,* opus 21 showing palindrome characteristic.

Figure 2.25. Frozen notes and rotation around "A" in opening section of Webern, *Symphonie,* opus 21.

measure 4 (the original a major third higher) in the harp. The harp begins (in measure 2) the inversion on F, which is imitated by the first horn (in inversion beginning on A, measure 3).

Note as well how the opening section "rotates" around A. These thirteen notes (E♭ is doubled) are all that are sounded (register frozen). This is category B composition. All twelve notes do not appear until the twenty-third pitch (E♭) is sounded in the harp.

5. Vertical Models: Harmonic identities do not play a major role in this work. When more than one note sounds at a time, a consistent vocabulary appears which is based on the minor second (and concomitant projections, e.g., the ninth and seventh), augmented fourth, and the major sixth. These are the intervals most commonly found and provide a perceptible model for the category B compositional techniques.

6. Horizontal Models: The horizontal or melodic techniques are framed in the row itself reflected in the complex canonic treatment and the variants based on *klangfarbenmelodien.* The constant leaping of lines often voids a real linear function as do the rests that abound. Certainly the opening four bars in the second horn provide the frame or model for the entire work in terms of horizontal vocabulary.

7. Style: Webern's *Symphonie* (op. 21) is an enormously complex pantonal (twelve-tone) work whose pointillism, *klangfarbenmelodien,* and canonic interweaving of lines project a highly intellectual approach to the compositional process. The miniature ensemble (in contrast to the late Romantic orchestras of one hundred or more performers) as well as short duration create a crystalline edge to each note contributing critical material to the larger structure. The lack of doubling, the serial feel to articulations and dynamics, and the imitations of rhythmic developments all contribute to its synthesis of clarity and complexity.

Compare this work with the analysis of the Penderecki of Chapter 3. Note that while the chromaticism remains (in the 12-tone clusters), the latter expounds dramatic gestures and thick textures while the former centers explicitly on single note pointillism. The Webern resembles the Xenakis example at the end of Chapter 10 in that both pay serious attention to rigorous forms of serialism; the first by virtue of the twelve-tone base and permutations of other elements and the latter because it has automated features based on stochastic principles. This points out the fact that the two seemingly opposed concepts of *serialism* and *indeterminacy* are not mutually exclusive.

Bibliography

*Further Readings**

American Society of University Composers. *Proceedings* I–VIII. A clear cross section of contemporary thought concerning the issues encountered in chapter 2.

Anderson, E. Ruth. *Contemporary American Composers: A Biographical Dictionary.* Boston: G. K. Hall, 1976.

Babbitt, Milton. "Set Structure as a Compositional Determinant." *Journal of Music Theory* 5 (April 1961):72–94. A good study in the thoughts and directions of the materials derived from this "determinate" composer.

Basart, Ann Phillips. *Serial Music: A Classified Bibliography of Writings on Twelve Tone and Electronic Music* (Berkeley: University of California Press, 1961). An excellent reference tool.

Beckwith, John, and Udo Kasemets. *The Modern Composer and His World.* Toronto: University of Toronto Press, 1961. A series of reports and discussions from the International Conference of Composers (1960) on the various aspects covered in this chapter.

Berg, Alban. "Why is Schoenberg's Music So Hard to Understand?" *The Music Review* (May 1952), pp. 187–96. The first printed translation—a fascinating early source for such information.

Boretz, Benjamin, and Edward T. Cone, eds. *Perspectives on American Composers.* New York: W. W. Norton and Co., 1971.

————. *Perspectives on Contemporary Music Theory.* New York: W. W. Norton and Co., 1972. Both of the above are useful books dealing with issues facing the contemporary composer in articles by contemporary composers.

Boulez, Pierre. *Orientations.* London: Faber and Faber, 1986. A tome of Boulez articles, reviews and program notes to concerts and recordings. His "Schoenberg the Unloved?" and "Constructing an Improvisation" are excellent. Also, Boulez's "The System Exposed" presents an excellent analysis of *Polyphonie X* and its serial sources.

Brindle, Reginald Smith. *The New Music: The Avant-Garde since 1945.* New York: Oxford University Press, 1975. A good source of information, particularly on European composers.

Chase, Gilbert. *The American Composer Speaks.* Baton Rouge: Louisiana State University Press, 1966. Very valuable, especially pp. 184–305. Consists of articles and statements by the composers themselves.

Composer Magazine, 1–20. A good source for a wide cross section of articles and interviews concerning subject matter in chapter 2.

*Addresses for record companies, periodicals, and music publishers mentioned in this Bibliography can be found in Appendix 4.

Contemporary Music in Europe. Reprinted from *Musical Quarterly,* January 1965. Valuable but somewhat outdated view of the *avant-garde* on the continent.

Dallin, Leon. *Techniques of Twentieth Century Composition.* 3rd ed. Dubuque, Iowa: Wm. C. Brown Company Publishers, 1974. Includes a wide variety of new music in addition to excellent discussion of mainstream music, presenting a very sensible balance of musical styles.

Forte, Allen. *The Structure of Atonal Music.* New Haven: Yale University Press, 1973. The standard reference tool for set-theory. Contains a charting of the 220 distinct pitch-class sets. The theory remains somewhat controversial at this time. However, one should refrain from judgment until fully understanding all of the ramifications of the process of analysis with unordered pitch sets.

———. "Pitch-Class Set Analysis Today." *Music Analysis* 4:1/2 (1985): 29–58. A followup article to *The Structure of Atonal Music* 20+ years previous. Forte takes on the critics of his theory with excellent results. Z-related hexachords are more thoroughly explained here than in his earlier book.

———. *The Harmonic Organization of The Rite of Spring.* New Haven: Yale University Press, 1978. Set theory applied to the non-atonal domain (in fact, Forte probably deliberately chose this work to prove that set-theory was not expressly for serial music). Many of the insights here are valuable in understanding some of the seeming inconsistencies in other analyses of the work.

Griffiths, Paul. *Modern Music.* New York: George Braziller, 1981. Post-Second World War music covered in a socio-analytical and methodological manner. The book is quite rich in good musical examples.

Hansen, Peter. *An Introduction to Twentieth Century Music.* Boston: Allyn & Bacon, 1967. Includes material to the point of this chapter, especially pp. 359–96.

Hitchcock, H. Wiley. *Music in the United States: An Historical Introduction.* Englewood Cliffs, N.J.: Prentice-Hall, 1969. Quite good as an introduction to new music in America, especially pp. 221–61.

"Hommage to Messiaen." *Melos,* 25: December 1958, entire issue. A good study of this man and his musical contributions.

Journal of Music Theory. Often contains articles pertaining to this subject matter.

Kolneder, Walter. *Anton Webern: An Introduction to His Works.* Berkeley: University of California Press, 1968.

Lang, Paul Henry, ed. *Problems of Modern Music.* New York: W. W. Norton and Co., 1960. A collection of chapters by various individuals deeply involved in the *avant-garde,* inclusive of Babbitt, Carter, Ussachevsky, and Krěnek, among others.

Lewin, David. *Generalized Musical Intervals and Transformations.* New Haven: Yale University Press, 1987. A highly complex Forte-based set-theory expansion analysis theory. An important resource for those already versed in set-theory; definitely *not* for the layman.

Machlis, Joseph. *Introduction to Contemporary Music,* 2nd ed. New York: W. W. Norton and Co., 1979. An extraordinary book covering a wide scope of new music since 1900.

Messiaen, Oliver. *The Technique of My Musical Language.* Paris: Alphonse Leduc & Cie., 1950. A complex theoretical and philosophical treatise of his highly specialized rhythmic control procedures.

Neighbour, Oliver, Paul Griffiths and George Perle. *The New Grove Second Viennese School.* London: Macmillan, 1980. An in-depth look at Schoenberg, Webern and Berg (biographies and analysis of works). The three authors' expertise works effectively here and provides readers with a succinct and invaluable reference tool on the interrelations of these composers. Excellent worklists and bibliographies.

The New Oxford History of Music (*The Modern Age 1890–1960*). London: Oxford University Press, 1974. Good introductory material on new music by country.

Numus West, 1–5. An excellent periodical devoted to the various aspects of *avant-garde* music.

Perle, George. *Serial Composition and Atonality.* Berkeley: University of California Press, 1962. Contains numerous analyses, especially of completely serialized compositions, and lists a large number of them as well for further study.

Perle, George. *Twelve-Tonality.* Berkeley: University of California Press, 1977. An excellent resource that truly dispels the concept that these two resources are not necessarily mutually exclusive. Not surprisingly, the definition of "tonality" has been used somewhat loosely and a good portion of the musical examples are Berg and Perle.

Perspectives of New Music. A periodical dedicated to new music idioms.

Rossi, Nick. *Music of Our Time.* Boston: Crescendo Publishing Co., 1969. Excellent source of examples, composers, and photos of new music (unfortunately segregated by country as in so many other books of this type).

Salzman, Eric. *Twentieth-Century Music: An Introduction.* Englewood Cliffs, N.J.: Prentice-Hall, 1988. Extremely good book on new music, its only drawback being brevity. Pages 155–86 especially good in treatment of "ultrarationality" vs. "antirationality."

Schaefer, John. *New Sounds, A Listener's Guide to New Music.* New York: Harper and Row, Publishers, 1987. Written in a glib and popular style, this book gives perspective to the layman. A somewhat eclectic view of music since about 1950. Excellent resource for recordings. Most interesting chapters include "World Music" and "A Tale of Two Labels" (ECM and Windham Hill).

Schwartz, Elliott, and Barney Childs, eds. *Contemporary Composers on Contemporary Music* (New York: Holt, Rinehart and Winston, 1967). Superb book and a continuation in spirit of Cowell's *American Composers on American Music.* It is a collection of articles by the composers themselves inclusive of a full range of topics relating to *avant-garde* musics (see especially Stefan Wolpe's "Thinking Twice," pp. 274–307, on complex serial and philosophical ideas; and "The Liberation of Sound" by Edgard Varèse, pp. 195–208, as well as a host of other very important articles which will be cited many times later in this book).

Sonorum Speculum. A valuable reference source for information on new music in the Netherlands.

Soundings 1–10. A very important periodical on new music. *Soundings* has likewise printed several extremely important books: *Soundings: Ives, Ruggles and Varèse, Music is Dangerous,* and a new series of books on Conlon Nancarrow. 948 Canyon Rd. Santa Fe, New Mexico 87501.

Spinner, Leopold. *A Short Introduction to the Technique of Twelve-Tone Composition.* (London: Boosey and Hawkes, 1960). Useful to the uninitiated.

Tremblay, George. *The Definitive Cycle of the Twelve-Tone Row.* New York: Criterion Music Corp., 1974. An extremely complex text dealing in part with the 288 rows of any "cycle" from the 479,001,600 discrete twelve-tone rows possible: an eyeful of complex note control.

Vinton, John, ed. *Dictionary of Contemporary Music*. New York: E. P. Dutton & Co., 1974. An excellent source for subject headings listed in this chapter as well as biographical material on all the composers listed.

Yates, Peter. *Twentieth Century Music*. New York: Pantheon Books, 1967. A superb book dealing with the philosophies and backgrounds of the current *avant-garde*.

Babbitt, Milton. *Quartet No 2* (1954). Recorded on Nonesuch 71280.

————. *Quartet No. 3* (1969–70). Recorded on Turnabout 34515.

————. *Three Compositions for Piano* (1947). Boelke-Bonart. Recorded on CRI S-461. CD: HARM; HMC90.5160.

————. *Vision and Prayer* (1961). AMP Publishers. Recorded on CRI-268.

————. *Composition for Four Instruments.* [flute, clarinet, violin and 'cello] (1948). New Music. Recorded on CRI-138.

————. *Composition for Twelve Instruments* (1948). Associated. Recorded on Son Nova 1.

Bartók, Béla. (Recordings too numerous to mention here may be found by consulting the Schwann Record Catalog.)

Berg, Alban. *Concerto for Violin and Orchestra.* Universal Edition. Recorded on Columbia MS 6373.

Boulez, Pierre, *Le Marteau Sans Maître* (1955). Universal Edition. Recorded on Columbia MQ 32160. CD: Adès; ACD-14073-2.

————. *Second Piano Sonata* (1948). Heugel Publishers. Recorded on FIN 9004.

————. *Structures* (1952). Universal Edition. Recorded on Vox 678.028. CD: DG; 419 202-2GH.

————. *Structures: premier livre* for two pianos (1951–2). Universal edition. Recorded on Wergo 60011.

Crawford, Ruth. *Quartet* (New Music Edition). Recorded on Nonesuch 71280 (along with quartets by Perle and Babbitt).

Dallapiccola, Luigi. *Sei cori di Michelangelo Buonarroti it Giovane* (for chorus and orchestra, 1933–36). Carisch Publishers. Recorded on Telefunken S-43095.

Krěnek, Ernst. *Sestina* for voice and instrumental ensemble. Recorded on Orion 78295. An early example of total serialization.

Messiaen, Oliver. *Chronochromie* (1960). Leduc Publishers. Recorded on Angel S-36295.

Rudhyar, Dane. *Granites* (for piano, 1929). Published by Lengnick. Recorded on CRI S-247. Released in the July 1935 *New Music Quarterly*.

Satie, Erik. *La belle eccentrique* (1920). Sirene. Recorded (with a large group of Satie works) on Vanguard C-10037/8. CD: Denon; C37-7487.

Schäffer, Boguslaw. *Introduction to Composition*. PWM, 1976. An excellent source for score excerpts and general overview of European developments to the mid-seventies.

Schoenberg, Arnold. *Variations for Orchestra,* op. 31 (1928). Universal Edition. Recorded on DG 2530627. CD: DG; 415 326-2GM.

Webern, Anton. *Symphonie,* op. 21. Universal Edition. Recorded on DG 2711014.

————. *Variations,* op. 27. Universal Edition. Recorded on DG 2530803. N.B. The complete works of Webern (published primarily by Universal Edition), including his pointillistic orchestration of Bach's *Fuga* from *The Musical Offering*, are recorded on Columbia's four-record set, M4-35193 (supervised by Pierre Boulez). CD: DG; 419 202-2GM.

Recordings and Publishers

For further works, one should consult the separate chapter bibliographies along with the following important sources: *Internationales Musikinstitut Darmstädt Informationszentrum für zeitgenössische Music: Katalog der Abteilung Noten* (Druckerei and Verlag Jacob Helene KG., Pfungstadt, Ostendstrasse 10), a very fine listing of works of new music by *avant-garde* composers, published yearly; *New Music Quarterly* (a publication of modern compositions which Henry Cowell edited from 1927–1945, followed by Lou Harrison and others; now out of print, it is still a fascinating source of music of twentieth-century American *avant-garde* composers); *Source Magazine* which, like *New Music,* published music, not articles, is an excellent source for new music.

SOUND-MASS AND MICROTONES

3

Sound-mass, in constrast to serialism, minimizes the importance of individual notes (and their order) while maximizing the importance of texture, rhythm, dynamics, and/or timbre of broad gestures. This refocusing is of great significance in the development of the *avant-garde* movement. Sound-mass confronts one of the most profound technicalities of the music world—the fine differentiation between sound and noise (a derogatory term applied to sounds antithetical to music).

Mainstream composers utilized sound-mass (often called clusters) in a variety of ways. Gustav Mahler, for example, used two large panchromatic chords (inclusive of all twelve tones) in the first movement of his *Tenth Symphony* (1910). Béla Bartók employed cluster motions in his 1926 *Piano Sonata*. It is possibly most challengingly utilized, however, in Igor Stravinsky's *Le Sacre du Printemps* (1912), where a driving and repetitive string mass of sound is "charged" with unpredictably harsh accents. The rhythm of the accents becomes the thrust of the work at this point ("Danse des Adolescentes"), reducing the importance of pitch. Figure 3.1 shows

Sound-Mass Evolution

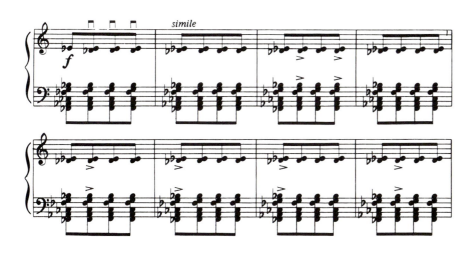

Figure 3.1. Igor Stravinsky: *Le Sacre Du Printemps:* "Danse des Adolescentes." Piano reduction of the string parts.

Figure 3.2. Henry Cowell: *The Hero Sun* (1922). Page 3. © Copyright Breitkopf and Härtel, Inc. Permission granted by the publisher. Associated Music Publishers, Agents in U.S.

the "dance" and the resultant increased importance of rhythm (accents) and decreased importance of pitch as integral linear (melodic) or vertical (harmonic) contributors to the work. Clearly this chord is an F♭ (enharmonically E) ninth chord. However, the status use of this vertical sonority offers little pitch importance in the string orchestration of harshly placed down-bows (frog: extremely close to the nut of the bow).

Henry Cowell's *The Tides of Manaunaun* (1911) and Charles Ives's *Majority* (piano and voice, 1921), present some of the first uses of traditional "noise" as an acceptable musical element. Cowell's *The Hero Sun* (1922) includes a right forearm cluster on the black keys (see Figure 3.2; note that the ♯ above indicates black keys while a ♮ indicates white keys), a striking use of sound-mass as both a melodic and percussive device against the open consonances of the left-hand harmonies. Cowell's notations for clusters differ occasionally from piece to piece, but the basics are shown and explained in Figure 3.3 taken from *What's This* (also 1922). These works, along with Cowell's innovative pieces (such as *The Banshee* discussed under *Instrument Exploration*) impressed a large number of composers (Béla Bartók in particular) and culminated in authorship of *New Musical Resources* (1930). Figure 3.4 reveals

Sound-Mass and Microtones

The Symbol (♦, ♦, ♦, etc.) represents a silent pressing down and holding of the key in order that the open string may be subjected to sympathetic vibration.

The Symbol  should be played as

It will be noticed that half and whole notes are written open, or white; while notes of other time values are written closed, or black.

When such tone clusters are small, the fist or open hand is to be used (The symbol **x** indicates the use of the fist).

In the larger tone clusters the forearm is to be employed. Care should be taken to play all the tones exactly together, and in legato passages to press the keys rather than strike them, thus obtaining a smoother tone quality.

Tone clusters to be played in the manner indicated by the symbol (♦) will be written as:

An arrowhead is used in connection with arpeggiation marks to indicate whether the arpeggiation is to be from the lowest tone upwards, as is customary, (↑) or from the highest tone downwards (↓)

R. F. Stands for right fist; L.F. for left fist.

R. A. Stands for right arm; L. A. for left arm.

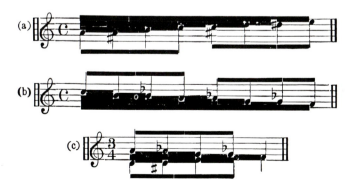

Figure 3.5. Henry Cowell. BMI Archives. Used by permission.

the depth to which Cowell studied both the musical properties and notation of sound-mass. About this example he has written: "Clusters that do in a certain sense move are, however, quite possible, and it is interesting to consider the various ways in which such movement can be introduced."[1] He notes both additive and subtractive clusters (subtractive in Figure 3.4), and thus predates a great deal of music (especially that of Penderecki) and articles (especially Kagel's "Tone-clusters, Attacks, Transitions" in *Die Reihe* #5).

John Becker (1886–1961), regrettably a relatively unnoticed innovator of the twenties and thirties, included large clusters in most of his works. His *Symphonia Brevis* (Symphony No. 3, which first appeared in Cowell's *New Music* in January of 1930) derives large sound-mass structures from long sustained chords built of seconds with instruments of similar color. In other sections the clusters twist sections of the orchestra into single percussion instrumental sounds by means of articulation (short, very loud, heavy accents).

Figure 3.6 shows the final five bars of the opening section from this work. As lines are overlaid in the rich contrapuntal fabric, the pitch becomes pantonal (all twelve tones of the chromatic scale are presented) with the F♯ rooted chord spread over five octaves.

Edgard Varèse used brass, organ, and Ondes Martenot in his *Equatorial* (1934) to achieve sound-mass. In reference to the work of Varèse, Robert Erickson writes: "These highly individual sound-blocks are images, ikons, in their own right. They exist as entities in the same way as a melody can be felt to be an entity."[2] Many

1. Henry Cowell, *New Musical Resources* (New York: Alfred A. Knopf, 1930), p. 126.
2. Robert Erickson, "Varèse: 1924–1937: Sound-Ikon," *Composer* 1, no. 3 (December 1969): 144.

Figure 3.6. John Becker: *Symphonia Brevis* (Symphony No. 3), page 3. Copyright © 1972 by C. F. Peters Corporation. By permission.

consider Varèse's music the extension of Stravinsky's "primitive" period (e.g., *Le Sacre du Printemps;* period extending to the mid-twenties of this century when Stravinsky's so-called *neoclassic* period began). The massive dissonances of his *Hyperprism* (1923) and *Octandre* (1924) are strikingly percussive.

In *Octandre*, Varèse created mirror-type sound-mass as shown in Figure 3.7*A* and *B*. In *A*, Varèse balances the "stacked" chromatic pitches with a central B♮ (a minor third from each end of the cluster). In *B*, he separates two small groupings of chromatic half-steps by equal intervals (this time the major third). Each of these structures (bars 15 and 20 respectively) includes octave transpositions and interesting orchestration (inverted, with flute over an octave below the clarinet, for example) to create harsh dynamic thrusts of sound. The work abounds with similar vertical sonorities.

Figure 3.6 *Continued*

Wallingford Riegger's *Music for Brass Choir* (1949) is one of the first large ensemble works to use large "closed" clusters. The work opens with ten trombones, each with a different chromatic note, encompassing the range of a diminished seventh. The panchromatic final chord (ten trumpets, eight horns, ten trombones, two tubas, and percussion) expresses subtle dynamic shadings with the final four bars *lento e pianissimo.*

Twelve-note or panchromatic chords are logically derived from twelve-tone music. While wide spacing avoids "cluster chord" terminology, the effect is the same. *Sonate Harmonique* by Galen Wilson contains a near-panchromatic (nine-note) cluster effect (see Figure 3.8).

Figure 3.7. From Edgard Varèse, *Octandre.*

Figure 3.8. Galen Wilson: *Sonate Harmonique.*

Luigi Nono's three choral works *Il canto sospeso* (1956), *La terra e la campagna* (1957), and *Cori di Didone* (1958) are based almost entirely on twelve-tone aggregate choral clusters creating masses of white sound within which the voices move as "fish through water."

Apart from the aforementioned Becker work, clusters (or sound-mass) occurred in orchestra works like *Metastasis* (1955) by Iannis Xenakis, and *Threnody for the Victims of Hiroshima* (1960) by Krzysztof Penderecki. Probably one of the best-known orchestral works of the past forty years, *Threnody* employs a wide variety

Cluster Techniques

of string techniques (fifty-two string parts), surprisingly few of which are actually new. More immediately recognizable are the solid bands of sound which widen and contract by means of glissando. These clusters, involving quarter tones, create a "white sound" effect resolved by movement to a single pitch, and contain such heavy overtone influence that, even though only the area of a fifth may actually be covered, the aural impression is one of all audible sounds occurring simultaneously.

Figure 3.9 is the final 54 seconds of *Threnody*. Even though the notation is proportional (see Appendix 3), the visual cluster bands are similar to those that were suggested by Cowell in his *New Musical Resources* thirty years earlier (refer to Figure 3.3).

Iannis Xenakis utilizes sound-mass as a result of his stochastic procedures (see Chapter 9 for more detailed discussion). Most of his works employ large "sonic-clouds" which sound incredibly dense as a result of large numbers of individual voices usually of like timbre (pizzicato or glissando clusters, for example). Indeed it is difficult to pick out a single one of his works which does not employ an elegant use of sound-mass (both in terms of rhythm and pitch). Xenakis has had considerable impact in Europe and many have attributed Penderecki's and the Polish School's use of sound-mass to his influence. In a 1955 article "The Crisis of Serial Music," Xenakis remarks:

> Linear polyphony destroys itself by its very complexity; what one hears is in reality nothing but a mass of notes in various registers. The enormous complexity prevents the audience from following the intertwining of the lines and has as its macrocosmic effect an irrational and fortuitous dispersion of sounds over the whole extent of the sonic spectrum. There is consequently a contradiction between the polyphonic linear system and the heard result, which is surface or mass.[3]

Henryk Górecki's (b. 1933 in Poland) *Scontri* for orchestra (1960), includes graphically notated blocks and bands of tones (large black boxes overlapping entire sections of the score).

In *Sonant* (1960), Mauricio Kagel calls for speaking and whispering from the ensemble at various pitch levels *ad libitum,* the result being a huge block or "cluster" sound-mass. The consequence of such experimentations is not only new notations, but direct applications of partially indeterminate procedures: though clusters are inevitable, exact duplication of numerous highly variable factors creates unpredictable results.

In the last few years, it has become increasingly difficult to ascertain whether cluster effects have created improvisational (partially aleatoric) procedures or vice versa. *Improvisation ajoutée* (1962) by Mauricio Kagel, for four-manual organ and two or three adjunct performers, includes huge block clusters of sound, performed with hands, forearms, and feet, and rapid multichanges in registration with, as the composer states, "the improvisation arising through the statistical nature of timbre transformations."

3. Iannis Xenakis, "The Crisis of Serial Music," *Gravesaner Blatter*, no. 1 (1955).

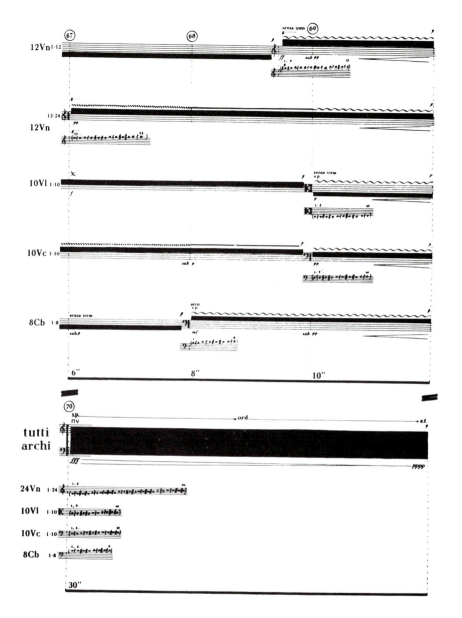

Figure 3.9. Krzysztof Penderecki: *Threnody for the Victims of Hiroshima* (final page of score). The notes for each cluster band are written out in traditional form beneath them in this proportional notation. Copyright © 1961 Deshon Music, Inc., & PWM Editions. Used with permission. All rights reserved. The two systems here are 24″ and 30″ in duration respectively.

The *Trois Poèmes d'Henri Michaux* for mixed chorus and orchestra (1963) by Witold Lutoslawski includes cluster chords derived of approximate pitch notation. The rhythmic clusters in the second part ("Le grand combat") are created by extremely complex composite rhythms.

Stockhausen's *Mixtur* (1964) demonstrates huge cluster effects (spatially, as the five groups are placed around the audience) as a result of traditional notation (only approximated by lack of staves or other exact pitch identification). Obvious motivic structures occur, yet each performer's independent decision regarding pitch and rhythmic variety results in extremely complex sound-mass structures.

Penderecki's *Passion According to St. Luke* (1965) compounds simple structures into dense bands of twelve-tone or panchromatic clusters. A continuous thread of contrapuntal material, even during these cluster effects, represents a unique approach to sound-mass construction. Half-sung, half-spoken backgrounds to crowd scenes create equally massive constructs of sound which owe their intensity to drama as well as to dissonance.

Pauline Oliveros's *Sound Patterns* (1961) creates cluster sound-mass effects with voices, employing whispers, tongue clicks, lip pops, and improvised pitches within areas of high, middle, and low registers. The results are often similar to the choral effects in Penderecki's *Passion,* yet exist more as timbre clusters than as pitch clusters.

György Ligeti's *Atmosphéres* (1961) involves the full complement of winds, strings, and percussion, orchestrated in such a manner as to create unique "clusters" of sound by overtones and resultant tones. In *Lux Aeterna (1966)* and *Requiem* (1965) (for soprano, mezzo-soprano, two mixed choirs, and orchestra), Ligeti approaches effects in which instruments and individual voices are unrecognizable.

Ligeti's *Lontano* (1967) for orchestra often employs over fifty separate instrumental voices (Ligeti's music, unlike Penderecki's, is traditionally notated) creating an ever-evolving and developing sonic texture. While seeming to lack recognizable melodic direction, this piece maintains an enormous musical impact in terms of the other available parameters (dynamics and timbre in particular).

"The important tones, the ones that are most plainly heard, are those of the outer edges of a given cluster."[4] Thus both composer and performer realized that order and exact notation of clusters could be described verbally or graphically. Theodore Lucas, in *Aberrations No. VII* for piano (Figure 3.10), evolves a system of cluster notation (white and black keys) denoting duration by horizontal length. Graphic structures show only approximate pitch and relative motion (notice here that the two sets of clusters remain static). Various cluster effects are dramatically notated by Stanley Lunetta in his *Piano Music.* Notice (especially with the indication "wiggle all fingers" in Figure 3.11) the interpretative possibilities for the performer.

for concert band, demonstrates another means of achieving sound-mass: rhythmic densities so thick as to produce vibrating columns of sound. This approach allows for continuous development of motivic and melodic fragments.

North/White by R. Murray Schafer was, in the words of the composer, "inspired by the rape of the Canadian North . . . carried out by the nation's government in conspiracy with business and industry." The title derives from "white light" which contains all visual frequencies (the piece then contains all audible frequencies producible by a symphony orchestra). The work begins and ends on single notes

4. Henry Cowell, *New Musical Resources* (New York: Alfred A. Knopf, 1930), p. 122.

Figure 3.10. Theodore Lucas: *Aberrations No. VII* for piano. Copyright 1969 by the composer.

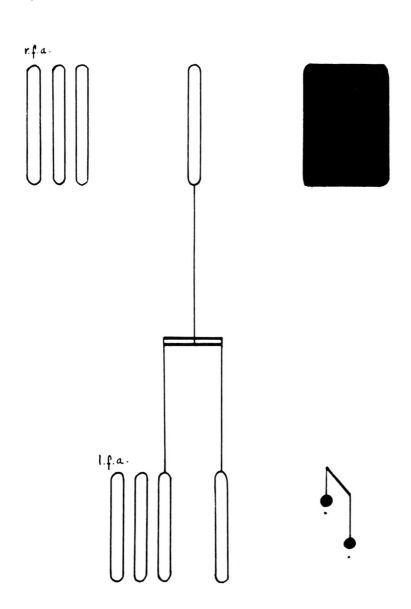

enclosing tapering clusters of sound. The form is a kind of "crab" structure with the first three main sections (slow cluster buildup; repeated notes; chromatic scales) presented in retrograde order in the second half of the piece. Schafer has created a dynamic and sometimes hostile work.

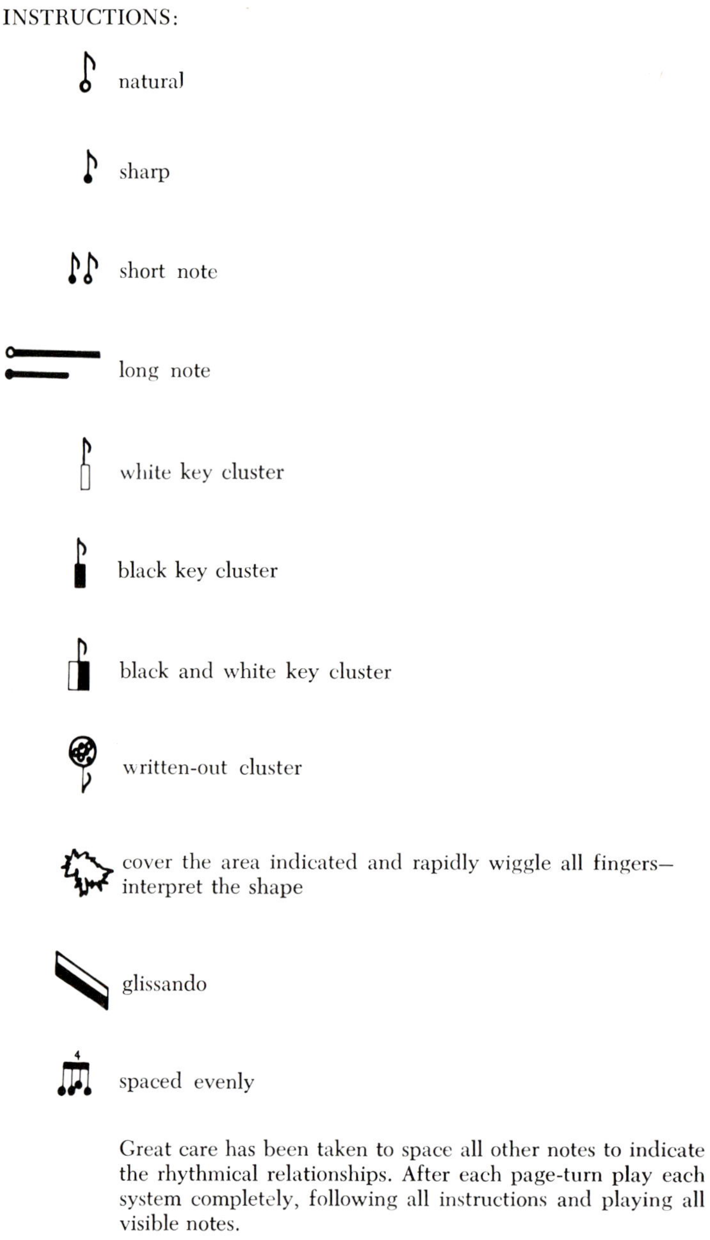

Figure 3.11. Stanley Lunetta: *Piano Music.* Performance instructions. Permission granted by *Source: Music of the Avant-Garde* Composer/Performer Edition, Davis, California.

INSTRUCTIONS:

♪   natural

♪   sharp

♪♪   short note

○━━━━   long note

♪   white key cluster

♪   black key cluster

♪   black and white key cluster

♪   written-out cluster

    cover the area indicated and rapidly wiggle all fingers— interpret the shape

    glissando

     spaced evenly

Great care has been taken to space all other notes to indicate the rhythmical relationships. After each page-turn play each system completely, following all instructions and playing all visible notes.

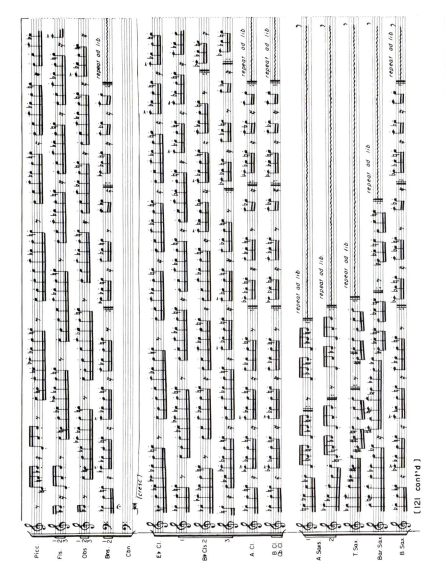

Figure 3.12. Karel Husa: *The Apotheosis of This Earth.* © Copyright 1971 by Associated Music Publishers, Inc. Used by permission.

Figure 3.12 *Continued*

While notation and performance continue to confound composers bent on freeing their music from the rigidity of the bar line, they also block microtonal possibilities (see Appendix 3). While twelve-note scales and the search for a single *stable* tuning system have existed for many centuries,[5] it seems to many contemporary composers that this search is a fruitless one, which results in a hybrid intonation (equal temperament) lacking the multifold potentials of flexible tunings. It is important to note here that while the piano may remain "fixed" in equal-tempered tuning, other instruments do not. Orchestral performers create a wide range and variety of tunings, usually a combination of *just* (based on the overtone series) and *equal* (each semitone equidistant from the next) temperaments applied at the discretion of their "musical ears." Similarly, tonal key regions with "leading tones," sevenths of dominant seventh chords and the like call for *adjusted* intonations. Mozart, for example, worked and *taught* with a 17-note scale, clearly identifying microtones through spelling (e.g., C♯ and D♭ were quite differently tuned, the first being higher).

Julian Carrillo in "The Thirteenth Sound" divides the octave into ninety-five different pitches, numbering each pitch at the end of the stem where one would ordinarily find the note head.[6] Harry Partch's forty-three-note approach (discussed as well under *Instrument Exploration*) is much freer. Through his creation of an entirely new set of instruments he has created a virtually "infinite" variety of both timbres and tunings. Most of these approaches, however, seemed doomed to either extremely limited usage or complete neglect. The main problem is that most theorists and composers continue to search for new *systems* not realizing that the devising of any such system is little better than the *system* in present use (a restricted set of pitches). It is indeed the flexibility or "nonsystematic" use of intonations which is most valuable. Composers such as Ben Johnston, Lou Harrison, James Tenney, Kenneth Gaburo, and many others have composed sections, movements, or works to multiple sets of intonations. Ben Johnston's *Fourth String Quartet* uses a varying number of proportional octave divisions from five to twenty-two, thus creating a flexible set of intonations based on the composer's ear and musical intuitions.

Johnston has written extensively on microtonal music and in writing about his *Fourth String Quartet* he sums up a great complexity in a few concise words:

> Over the whole of the historical period of instrumental music, Western music has based itself upon an acoustical lie. In our time this lie—that the normal musical ear hears twelve equal intervals within the span of an octave—has led to the

Microtones

5. Cf. Zarlino (1558), Salinas (1577), Mattheson (1725), Jackson (1726), Liston (1812), Delezenne (1827), Poole (1850), Drobesch (1855), Bosanquet (1875) and Keonig (1876), to name but a few. See Fred Fisher, "The Yellow Bell of China and the Endless Search," *Music Educators Journal* (April 1973): p. 30.
6. Julian Carrillo, "The Thirteenth Sound," trans. Patricia Ann Smith, *Soundings* 5, p. 64. This volume also contains a number of works by Carrillo using his number notations.

Figure 3.13. Ben Johnston.

impoverishment of pitch usage in our music. In our frustration at the complex means it takes to wrest yet a few more permutations from a closed system, we have attempted the abandonment of all systems, forgetting that we need never have closed our system.[7]

Johnston further describes the situation quite accurately in his "How to Cook an Albatross": "In our laziness, when we changed over to the twelve-tone system, we just took the pitches of the previous music as though we were moving into a furnished apartment and had no time to even take the pictures off the wall. What excuse?"[8]

Continued interest in intonation, microtones, and tuning systems abounds with notable recent activity, particularly on the American west coast. Periodicals such as *Interval* and *Xenharmonikon* (see in the chapter bibliography) are indicators of increased interest. The potential of microtones is bounded only by the ability of the composer to hear ideas, the notation to express these ideas (see Appendix 3), and the performer to accurately perform the results.

7. From the April 28, 1974 program notes of a concert at the University of Wisconsin-Milwaukee by the Fine Arts Quartet.
8. Ben Johnston, "How to Cook an Albatross," *Source* 7:65.

Microtones do not correspond to pitches in equal temperament. Microtonal "systems" usually involve more than twelve tones per octave, thereby forcing one or more intervals to be less than an equal-tempered semitone apart. Quarter-tones (24 tones per octave) present a type of microtonal system with twelve pitches in equal temperament and twelve in the equidistant "cracks."

Many composers felt that the creation of equal temperament, and the resolution of the octave into twelve parts, created arbitrary musical systems. Alois Hába (1893–1972) constructed a quarter-tone piano in the early twenties[9] and employed a sixth-tone system in the late thirties. Charles Ives (1874–1954) experimented with microtones in his *Three Quarter Tone Pieces* (1918?) for two pianos tuned a quarter tone apart. Harry Partch (1901–74),[10] in the process of working with microtones (an acoustical division of the octave into 43 tones), developed new instruments necessary for the realization of his experiments. He worked more in isolation than Hába, but has received much attention in the past few years.[11] Composers such as Teo Macero, Calvin Hamilton and Donald Lybbert have recently continued similar experimentation.

Though quarter tones were used sparsely by Bartók (especially in his *Violin Concerto,* 1938) and Milhaud in the late thirties and forties, their true import had not fully been discovered. The use of twenty-four or more divisions of the octave requires abandonment or total revision of techniques of traditional instruments, creation of new or revised systems of notation, and increasingly complex harmonic and melodic vocabularies. New instruments (e.g., the tape recorder), notations (graphs, punch cards), and scientific vocabularies developed in the early fifties, often as a direct result of experiments with tuning systems.

While microtones are used to embellish music and to provide variety in an otherwise strictly 12-note vocabulary, tuning systems afford whole new territories for experimentation. The definition of a tuning system is that it rigorously applies its approach to *all* of the notes available. Such systems typically utilize fixed-tuned instruments (usually percussion). These divide into three basic types: "just" tuning systems, "equal" tuning systems, and "varied" tuning systems. In the first case, all of the information about the scale is derived specifically from the overtone series (see Chapter 1). This series (infinite) possesses much information about tuning with the true resonance in its nature being the source of much of our music. (Tonality, as shown in Chapter 1, could be said to come from projections of the series; trombones and other wind instruments overblow into the series in order to complete a full range of notes, etc.) The second or "equal" tuning system simply divides the octave into equal intervals (or "cents"). Since the series is exponential in nature, the actual frequency divisions are small in the lower registers and large in the upper. Finally, combinations of these two approaches, or wholly new approaches not using

9. See Alois Hába, *The Theory of Quartertones* (out of print).
10. See Harry Partch, *Genesis of a Music* (Madison: University of Wisconsin Press, 1949).
11. See also Elliott Friedman, "Tonality in the Music of Harry Partch," *Composer* 2, no. 1 (June 1970):16–24.

either of these two, exist in the "varied" tuning systems characteristic of many used by world cultures. Western music, though couched in its secure twelve divisions of the octave, has (but to a much lesser extent) had its proposals, experiments, and protagonists for new intonations. Gerhardus Mercator's (16th century) fifty-three tones per octave scale is a particularly notable example.

In Javanese music the gamelan uses many instruments involved with "varied" tuning systems. The *gambang* (xylophone), *gender, saron* and *demoeng* (all bronze slabs), and *bonang* (set of gongs) use either the *slendro* or the *pelog*. The *slendro* consists of wide intervals and the *pelog* of narrower steps. The *slendro* is constructed of a pentatonic scale consisting of five nearly equal intervals of 240 cents (something close to a whole-tone and quarter-tone scales) as shown in Figure 3.14. The *pelog*, in contrast, consists of two conjunct tetrachords each of which is divided (approximately) into a half-step and a major third, similar to a good deal of ancient Greek music. The two thirds are filled in by two additional tones creating a septatonic scale shown in Figure 3.15. The + and − signs here indicate the lowering or raising necessary to achieve the correct pitch in the series.

Figure 3.14. The *slendro* pentatonic scale consisting of five nearly equal intervals of 240 cents.

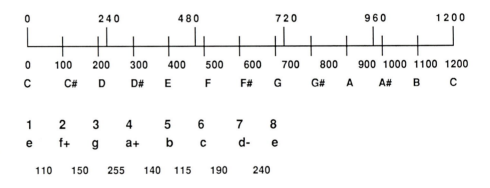

Figure 3.15. The *pelog* scale of two conjunct tetrachords each of which is divided (approximately) into a half-step and a major third filled in by two additional tones creating a septatonic scale.

Composers on the Pacific Rim have imitated such tuning systems and approaches to music. Lou Harrison, for example, has created what has been termed the American Gamelan, where his own versions of instruments in Southeastern Asian music are substituted in gamelans for which he composes. Such gamelans have produced a number of serious protagonists and composers including Jody Diamond, Vincent McDermott, Daniel Schmidt, Jarrad Powell, Jim Madara, Daniel Goode, David Demnitz, Jeff Morris, Shin Nakamura and Laura Liben.

Rhythmic Developments

Rhythm, viewed without the melodic or harmonic drive of most works prior to this century, is a rather simply used parameter of musical structure. It often seems strangled by the bar line or tied down to basic repetitions related to dance forms. Ligeti

Figure 3.16. György Ligeti: *Lontano.* Typical rhythmic entrances.

comments about freeing this in notes for *Lontano* (1967): "The bar lines serve only as a means of synchronization; bar lines and beats never mean an accentuation, the music must flow smoothly. . . ."[12] The score is filled with double- and triple-dotted notes, entrances on inner positions of triplets, quintuplets, septuplets, etc., as shown in Figure 3.16 ever diffusing the bar line and beat and giving the rhythm a development and tangible diversity.

Boulez speaks to this point in *Boulez on Music Today:*

> The rational use of the opposition between multiplication and division of the [beat] unit will, moreover, give rise to striking contrasts due to the broader span of values brought into play . . . interaction of these various methods of organization can be extremely fertile, and will create an inexhaustible variety of objects—in the same way as in the field of pitch.[13]

Some composers turn to proportional notation to avoid the accent implications of bar lines and simplicity of beat structures. Thus a section is marked 30 seconds and the notations within performed as they reach the eye (as if the visual action of reading would take 30 seconds). No accents, other than those specifically marked, are implied by such notation, creating a great deal of rhythmic variety. By the same token, this inexactness of notation disturbs some composers in that results often differ markedly from one performance to another.

Elliott Carter attempts the same goal, but from quite a different perspective. In *Flawed Words and Stubborn Sounds* Carter speaks of his directions: "The result in my own music was, first of all, the way of evolving rhythms and continuities now called 'metric modulation,' which I worked out in the composition of my *Cello Sonata* of 1948." Later in the same book he speaks of new music in general: ". . . what is needed is never just a string of interesting passages, but works whose central interest is constituted by the way everything that happens in them happens *as* and *when* it does in relation to everything else."[14]

Metric modulation, though not an entirely new concept to Eastern music or music in the Western World prior to the advent of the so-called "common-practice period," is a highly complex procedure. In Carter's *Double Concerto* (1961) for

---

12. György Ligeti, *Lontano* (New York: Schott Music Corp., 1969), from the performance notes in the score.
13. Pierre Boulez, *Boulez on Music Today* (Cambridge, Mass.: Harvard University Press, 1971), p. 58.
14. Allen Edwards, *Flawed Words and Stubborn Sounds* (New York: W. W. Norton and Co., 1971), pp. 91–92.

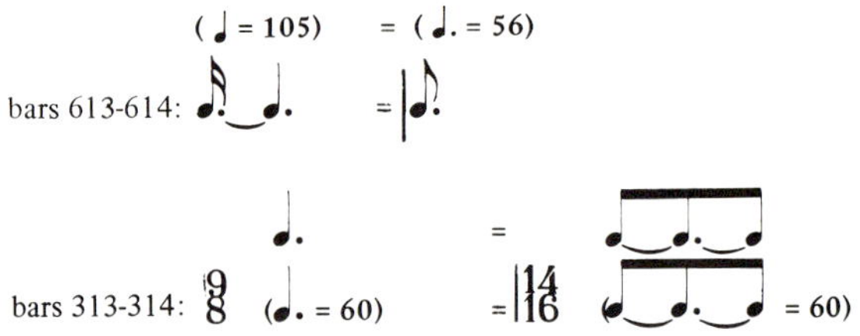

Figure 3.17. Metric Modulations from Elliott Carter's *Double Concerto*.

(♩ = 105)   = (♩. = 56)

bars 613-614: ♪ ♩. = ♩♪

bars 313-314: 9/8 (♩. = 60) = 14/16 (= 60)

harpsichord and piano with two chamber orchestras, there are many such modulations. As seen in Figure 3.17, the meter and the tempo often change at bar lines. This, combined with a rich variety of complex rhythmic development within the bar, achieves a highly structured yet "bar-line" free momentum of sounds (though many of Carter's critics expess grave doubt as to whether such "metric modulations" can actually be accurately performed). Carter's earlier *Cello Sonata* has surprisingly few metric modulations compared with the highly technical complexities of the renowned *Double Concerto*.

Most composers take a middle road between the proportional and "modulation" principles examined here, utlizing both within a single work as does Ligeti in his *Aventures* (see Figure 4.14 under Instrument Exploration).

Figure 3.18. Elliott Carter. BMI Archives. Used by permission.

Electronic and computer music present an ever-growing potential source for complex rhythmic structures and rhythm freed from bar lines. The author discusses this in his own contribution to *Electronic Music: A Listener's Guide* by Elliott Schwartz:

> The major advantage to working with electronic equipment and sounds which seem undiminished by overdone "exploration" is rhythmic freedom. No other ensemble of instruments is equally capable of fractioning time into controllable particles as the components of a well-equipped electronic music studio. While some listeners feel that the opportunity to free rhythm from any immediately recognizable meters removes some inalienable musical basic, it must be pointed out that to a large degree meter was introduced only to keep performers together in ensembles; while necessary, it was certainly not particularly musical in itself. The disposition of time is much more controllable in the electronic studio.[15]

(For information on vectoral analysis and procedures, see Chapter 1)

1. Historical Background: Krzysztof Penderecki (*c* is pronounced as if it were an *s*) was born in Debica, Poland, in 1933. He studied at the Music Academy in Cracow, where he eventually taught. Influences on his style include Iannis

Vectoral Analysis: Krzysztof Penderecki: *Capriccio for Violin and Orchestra*

Figure 3.19. Krzysztof Penderecki.

15. Elliott Schwartz, *Electronic Music: A Listener's Guide* (New York: Praeger Publishers, 1972); from "Observations by Composers," p. 214.

Xenakis (for sound-mass structures of thick multi-timbred densities) and Luigi Nono:

> In 1957, Luigi Nono came to Poland, to visit. He brought some scores with him, and he gave me some. I remember the *Five Pieces* of Webern. I was already writing my own music at that time (1957 or 1958). He gave me some of his music also. I think it was *Il Canto di Spezzo, Varianti* for violin and orchestra, *Cori di de Doni*, the piece for chorus, then *Improvisation sur Mallarmé*, by Boulez. All this was very new for me, and I tried to incorporate these techniques in a very short time. This was in 1958, till the middle of 1959. And then I decided to go my way.[16]

Most of his early works require large forces for performance, and range from short experiments in sound (especially *Threnody*, 1960; *Polymorphia*, 1961; and *De Natura Sonoris*, 1967 for string orchestras) to large dramatic opera/oratorios (notably *The Passion According to St. Luke*, 1965, and *The Devils of Loudon*, 1969). The thread of intense drama linked with subtle mystical religious overtones weaves through his musical style (until his recent turn to neo-romanticism).

2. Overview: The *Capriccio for Violin and Orchestra* (completed in 1967) is a concise concerto-type work in an abbreviated rondo-variations form (i.e., a set of variations with alternate variants referring noticeably to the opening material). After the brief opening timpani roll, a sound-mass occurs softly in the winds. Out of this texture grow individual crescendi contrapuntally increasing in number. This serves as a conceptual model for the remainder of the work, with variations deriving momentum from a variety of parameters, such as timbre, dynamics, rhythm, and texture, rather than the more typical variants of pitch that one usually associates with this form.

3. Orchestration Techniques: The orchestra splits into sections (i.e., generally instruments of like timbre). Penderecki utilizes his large percussion battery (five players needed for performance) to create large slashes of sound (e.g., vibraphone, bells, triangles, chimes, harp, and piano used simultaneously on page 5 of the score for a bright attack of cluster material). Effects include playing on the other side of the bridge (strings) and bowing for noise (extra hard pressure on the string) with pizzicato (plucking) used on the piano. Double- and triple-tongued repeated notes in the winds give rhythmic drive to stacked clusters.

4. Basic Techniques: *Capriccio* is a free twelve-tone work. This means free use of the serial concept (i.e., eleven-note rows), as well as continual development of new rows rather than clinging to a single series. Interval content evolves from the minor second (chromatic clusters from the outset) and resulting octave displacements (major seventh, minor ninth). The major second and

---

16. David Felder and Mark Schneider, ''An Interview with Krzysztof Penderecki,'' *Composer* 8, no. 1 (1977):12.

various thirds become important as the work progresses. Throughout the piece there is the feeling of expansion, the result of intervals opening up, as well as general ideas becoming longer and more developed.

5. Vertical Models: Figure 3.20 demonstrates the kind of vertical clustering that is a mainstay of this work. Notation defines pitch content followed by duration in terms of thick black proportional lines.

> I had to write in shorthand—something for me to remember, because my style of composing at that time was just to draw a piece first and then look for pitch. . . . I just wanted to write music that would have an impact, a density, powerful expression, a different expression. . . . I think this notation was for me, in the beginning, like shorthand, really, coming from drawing the piece. I used to see the whole piece in front of me—*Threnody* is very easy to draw. First you have just the high note, then you have this repeating section, then you have this cluster going, coming—different directions from the one note, twelve, and back—using different shapes. Then there is a louder section; then there's another section, then there is the section which is strictly written in 12-tone technique. Then it goes back to the same cluster technique again, and the end of the piece is a big cluster, which you can draw like a square and write behind it *fortissimo*. . . . I didn't want to write in bars, because this music doesn't work if you put it in bars.[17]

In this example, the *arm* (*armonium* or "harmonium," a reed-type organ) and piano (using wire brushes on the inside) cover their approximate visual areas in the time allowed (2/4, with the quarter note approximately equal to M.M. 76, though no tempo is given in the score; the author determined such by carefully dividing the number of bars into the duration [ten minutes], including combinations of *ritardandi*, etc.). The resultant vertical textures vary, but nonetheless continue the chromatic clusters. A third type of vertical structure is shown in the upper right-hand corner of this score page. A spread sound-mass moves by the use of microtonal (here, quarter tones) inflections in contrapuntal alternation.

Penderecki continually concentrates on the ever-widening possibilities of cluster techniques. In the opening sections, the work centers on minor second stacked clusters. Within the first minute he expands this to major second clusters (whole-tone). These eventually widen to octave-displaced minor second clusters.

6. Horizontal Models: As with the vertical concepts explored in this work, Penderecki concentrates on the use of seconds. Over 80 percent of the intervals in the opening solo violin line are half or whole steps. Often even thirds are augmentations of seconds. These lines become more angular by

17. Ibid., p. 13.

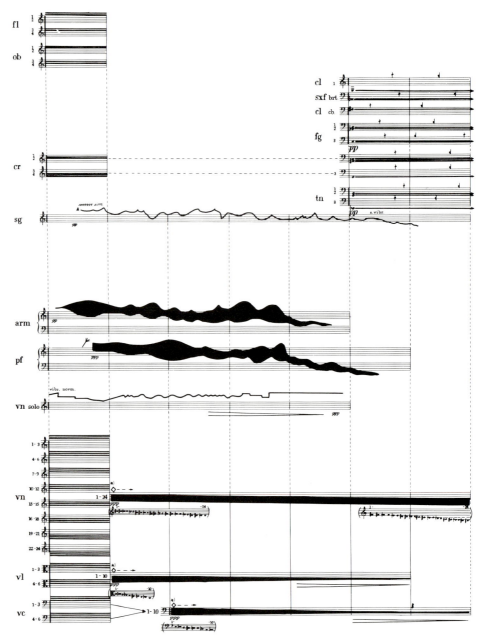

Figure 3.20. Krzysztof Penderecki: *Capriccio for Violin and Orchestra* (p. 29). Copyright © 1968 by Moeck Verlag. Used with permission. All rights reserved. See Figure 3.9 for explanation of these symbols.

octave displacement creating sevenths and ninths. The improvisatory solo violin line of Figure 3.20 gives a strong impression of the "seconds" concept. Penderecki joins the vertical and horizontal developments so that one feels each proceeding at a similar rate of speed.

It is interesting to note Penderecki's own remarks concerning his linear writing for the violin in this piece.

Sometimes when writing a group of notes in a very fast tempo, like in *Capriccio* for example, I know it is impossible to play all of them. But I did it because then I had achieved a tension in the sound. If I would have written only four or five notes, he would just do it, you know, so you would lose all the tension I have in the piece. I know this exactly. Performers ask me all the time: "Please, this is impossible." I reply that it is absolutely possible—"You will do it." Maybe the player will miss two or three of them, but there is a tension there.[18]

7. Style: Penderecki's *Capriccio for Violin and Orchestra* is a tightly woven, freely chromatic work based on the exploration of the interval of a second (both melodically and harmonically). These explorations slowly expand through a variation form, over a rondo template.

The dramatic context within which the work proceeds depends on large orchestral forces (especially large percussion), contrapuntal interweaving of nonpitch parameters (especially dynamics and rhythm), and various effects (including microtones). In contrast to the *Symphonie* of Webern (analyzed in Chapter 2), Penderecki has produced dramatic style packed with sound-mass, rhythmic development, and microtonal inflections. This example should also be compared to the Vectoral Analysis of Chapter 4 and Chapter 11 for similarity in terms of reliance on dramatic elements and explorations in orchestration. Its lack of lyricism also contrasts with the typical outcome of the Cage (Chapter 5). The clusters hold similarities to the performances of the Oliveros work in Chapter 6 and the score and tape of Erb's *Souvenir* in Chapter 8. Some of the textures, especially the thick sonorities where individual pitches lose distinction, resemble those used by Varèse in the Vectoral Analysis of Chapter 7.

Ashley, Robert. His interesting accounts of the ONCE group may be found in both *Arts in Society* (Spring 1968):86, and *Tulane Drama Review* 10:187.
Babbitt, Milton. "Twelve-Tone Rhythmic Structure and the Electronic Medium." *Perspectives of New Music* 1, no. 1 (1962):49–79.
Boatwright, Howard, ed. *Essays before a Sonata, The Majority, and Other Writings by Charles Ives.* New York: W. W. Norton & Co., 1962. A superb and fascinating study of the writings and thoughts of this man, many of which relate to sound-mass and rhythm.

Bibliography

*Further Readings**

18. Ibid., p. 14.
*Addresses for record companies, periodicals, and music publishers mentioned in this Bibliography can be found in Appendix 4.

Boatwright, Howard. "Ives' Quarter-Tone Impressions." *Perspectives of New Music* 3, no. 2 (1965):22–31. A good study of Ives's thoughts on the subject.

Boulez, Pierre. *Boulez on Music Today.* Cambridge, Mass.: Harvard University Press, 1971. Sheds a good deal of light on his own personal "controlled" approach to rhythmic structures.

Boulez, Pierre. "Aléa." *Nouvette Revue Française* 59 (November 1, 1957). The tight comparisons between European concepts of improvisation and so-called "aleatoric" music are drawn herein by the author in regard to his own work *Improvisations sur Mallarmé.*

Brinkman, R., ed. *Improvisation Und Neue Musik.* Mainz: B. Schott, 1979.

Burkholder, J. Peter. *Charles Ives: The Ideas Behind the Music.* New Haven: Yale University Press, 1985. A lively recount (actually a dissertation) of the composer's life, though without a chronology.

Carter, Elliott. "The Rhythmic Basis of American Music." *Score* 12, no. 27, June, 1955.

Christiansen, Louis. "Introduction to the Music of György Ligeti," *Numus West* 2, Feb. 1972. Excellent overview of the works of this man and his contributions both in terms of sound-mass and rhythm.

Cowell, Henry, ed. *American Composers on American Music.* New York: Frederick Ungar Publishing Co., 1933. Gives excellent insight into two composers using sound-mass: John Becker on p. 82, and Wallingford Riegger on p. 70.

Cowell, Henry. *New Musical Resources.* New York: Alfred A. Knopf, 1930. Contains an entire chapter devoted to the structuring and techniques of clusters and sound-mass.

Creston, Paul. *Principles of Rhythm.* New York: Franco Columbo, 1964.

Dallin, Leon. *Techniques of Twentieth Century Composition.* 3rd ed. Dubuque, Iowa: Wm. C. Brown Company Publishers, 1974. Part of a chapter is devoted to "New Rhythmic Concepts" (p. 66).

Edwards, Allen. *Flawed Words and Stubborn Sounds.* New York: W. W. Norton & Co., 1971. Subtitled: *A Conversation With Elliott Carter,* this is an excellent source for thoughts on rhythmic complexities and development by this American composer.

Erickson, Robert. "Time Relations." *Journal of Music Theory* 7 (Spring, 1963): 174–92.

Felder, David, and Mark Schneider. "An Interview with Krzysztof Penderecki," *The Composer* 8, no. 1 (1977):8–20.

Forte, Allen. *Contemporary Tone-Structures.* New York: Columbia University Press, 1955. Has brief discussions of sound-mass.

Foss, Lukas. "The Changing Composer-Performer Relationship: a Monologue and a Dialogue." *Perspectives of New Music* 1, no. 2 (Spring 1963).

———. "Work-Notes for *Echoi.*" *Perspectives of New Music* 3, no. 1, (1964).

Garland, Peter. "Dane Rudhyar." *Soundings.* 14/15 (1986):4–5. An excellent account of this often-misunderstood composer who attempted a marriage between astrology and music (as well as poetry).

Glasier, Jonathan, ed. *Interval (Exploring the Sonic Spectrum).* Published at Box 8027, San Diego, California 92102. Dedicated to microtonal exploration.

Hibbard, William. "Some Aspects of Serial Improvisation." *American Guild of Organists Quarterly.* (October 1966), and (January 1967). A fascinating study into this rarely explored area of improvisation.

Hitchcock, H. Wiley. *Music in the United States: A Historical Introduction.* Englewood Cliffs, N.J.: Prentice-Hall, 1969. Contains a number of interesting comments on improvisation (see the index), some relating to its early roots in nineteenth-century America.

Johnson, Tom. "Exotic Music: borrowing is not so bad." *Village Voice* 25:68 (April 14, 1980). This is an excellent article on world musics in the *avant-garde*.

Johnston, Ben. "Proportionality and Expanded Pitch Relations." *Perspectives of New Music* 5, no. 1:112–20.

Johnston, Ben and Edward Kobrin. "Phase 1-a." *Source* 7. As is his article in Vinton's *Dictionary of Contemporary Music* on microtones, this is an excellent exposition of Johnston's learned ideas on microtonality.

Kagel, Mauricio. "Tone Clusters, Attacks, Transitions." *Die Reihe* 5 (1959); 40–55. Interesting as a source of notations for opening and closing keyboard clusters and concepts.

Kirkpatrick, John. "The Evolution of Carl Ruggles: A Chronicle Largely in His Own Words." *Perspectives of New Music* 6, no. 2:146–66. An excellent study of this man of few works employing highly chromatic polyphonic sound-mass.

Makeig, Scott. "Expressive Tuning: The Theory of Interval Effect." Published in *Interval* (see above). A fascinating account of how tuning can affect emotions.

Marquis, G. Welton. *Twentieth Century Music Idioms.* New York: Prentice-Hall, 1964. Contains brief discussions of sound-mass.

Messiaen, Oliver. *The Technique of My Musical Language.* Paris: Alphonse Leduc & Cie., 1950. Excellent source for information on the extremely intricate and involved combination of proportional and metrical rhythmic language. Also a necessity for the understanding of much of Messiaen's rhythmically technical music.

"Microtonal Music in America." *Proceedings* 2, American Society of University Composers. Very good general discussion of the subject.

Mumma, Gordon. "Creative Aspects of Live Electronic Music Technology." Audio Engineering Society Reprint No. 550. A brief but credible account of how improvisation has been introduced into electronic music.

———. "The ONCE Festival and How it Happened." *Arts in Society* 4, no. 2:381.

Nono, Luigi. "Geschichte und Gegenwart in der Musik von Huete." *Darmstädter Beiträge zur Neuen Musik* 3 (1960) pp. 41–47. Most interesting study of all the materials of this chapter as well as the remainder of the book.

Orga, Ates. "Alois Hába and Microtonality." *Musical Opinion,* July 1968. Reflects a distinctly Hába viewpoint but is excellent bibliographical material.

Partch, Harry. *Genesis of a Music.* New York: Da Capo Press, 1973. Second Edition.

Persichetti, Vincent. *Twentieth Century Harmony.* New York: W. W. Norton Co., 1961. Has brief discussions of sound-mass.

Pound, Ezra. *Antheil.* New York: Da Capo Press, 1968. Contains Antheil's "Treatise on Harmony" which might better be titled "Treatise on Rhythm," as the author-composer spends the majority of the article reflecting on the importance of *when* things happen rather than *what* happens in terms of harmony.

Riegger, Wallingford. "John J. Becker." *Bulletin of the ACA* 9, no. 1 (1959):2–7. Good study of this iconoclast and his rugged music.

Rudhyar, Dane. "When does Sound Become Music." *Soundings.* 14/15 (1986):82–84. Skepticism about central European development of new music during the early part of the 20th century. Also, some interesting correlations between political events and music style changes.

Schuller, Gunther. *Early Jazz: Its Roots and Development.* New York: Oxford University Press, 1968. Good source for this stylistic type of improvisation and its inherent roots in today's improvisational concept.

————. See his contribution to *The Modern Composer and His World* (edited by John Beckwith and Udo Kasemets. Toronto: University of Toronto Press, 1961) for an excellent and forthright argument favoring the use of improvisation, and his comments about Boulez (especially pp. 38 and 39).

Source 2, no. 1 (January 1968). Contains interviews, remarks, and thoughts of the New Music Ensemble, ONCE Group, Sonic Arts Group, and the *Musica Elettronica Viva* which provide an excellent study of the conflict and interrelation between improvisation and indeterminacy.

Stockhausen, Karlheinz. ". . . How Time Passes. . . ." *Die Reihe* 3:10–40.

Varèse, Edgard. "New Instruments and New Music." In *Contemporary Composers on Contemporary Music*. Edited by Elliott Schwartz and Barney Childs, pp. 196–98. New York: Holt, Rinehart, and Winston, 1967.

Vinton, John, ed. *Dictionary of Contemporary Music*. New York: E. P. Dutton & Co., 1974. Includes a well-written analysis by Frederic Rzewski of contemporary ideas, pp. 618–25, along with an excellent bibliography.

Weisgall, Hugo. "The Music of Henry Cowell." *Musical Quarterly* 45 (1959). A good source of information on the works of this man contrasting the innovative with the conservative.

"Iannis Xenakis: The Man and his Music." Boosey & Hawkes, 1967. A good if brief look into the music of this composer who works almost exclusively with sound-mass.

Xenharmonikon. Published by Ivor Darreg, 349½ W. California Avenue., Glendale, California 91203. Annual periodical devoted to microtones.

Yannay, Yehuda. "Toward an Open-ended Method of Analysis of Contemporary Music." Doctoral Dissertation, University Microfilms, Ann Arbor, Michigan. Includes a strong analysis of *Octandre* by Varèse.

Yasser, Joseph. *A Theory of Evolving Tonality*. American Library of Musicology, 1932. Quite extensive in its tracing of the history of microtones, but gets bogged down in the author's own equally "bogged" 19-note scale.

Recordings and Publishers

Andriessen, Louis. *Hoe het* (1969). For electronic improvisation group and 52 solo strings.

Ashley, Robert. *In Memoriam Esteban Gomez* (1963). CPE-*Source*.

Austin, Larry. *Improvisations for Orchestra and Jazz Soloists* (1961). Recorded on Columbia MS-6733.

Ayler, Albert. *Music is the Healing Force*. Recorded on Impulse 9191. Excellent *avant-garde* jazz improvisation.

Bartók, Béla. *Sonata* (1921). Universal Edition. Recorded on Capitol P8376.

————. *String Quartet No. 5* (1934). Boosey & Hawkes. Recorded on Columbia ML 4280. CD: Hungaroton HCD-12502/04

Becker, John. *Symphony No. 3*. C. F. Peters. Recorded on Louisville S-721.

Berio, Luciano. *Circles* (1962). Universal Edition. Recorded on Candide 31027.

Bernstein, Leonard. *The Age of Anxiety*. G. Schirmer. See p. 59. Recorded on Columbia MS 6885.

Blackwood, Easley. *Symphony No. 1* (1958). Recorded on RCA LM-2352.

Blomdahl, Karl-Birger. *Aniara* (1959). Schott. See pp.1–3.

Boucourechliev, Andre. *Archipel I*. Recorded on Angel S-36655. Two versions of this improvised work for two pianos and percussion.

————. *Archipel IV* (for solo piano). Recorded on Finnadar 9021.

Boulez, Pierre. *Improvisations sur Mallarmé* (see Further Readings). Universal Edition.

Boulez, Pierre. *Le Marteau sans Maître* (1959). Universal Edition. Recorded on Odyssey 32–160154.

Britten, Benjamin. *The Turn of the Screw* (1954). Boosey & Hawkes. See p. 5.

Carrillo, Julian. *Mass for Pope John XXIII in Quarter-Tones* (1962). Recorded on CRI 246-SD.

Carter, Elliott. *Double Concerto*. Associated Music Publishers. Recorded on Columbia 7191.

———. *Cello Sonata*. G. Schirmer. Recorded on Nonesuch 71234.

———. *String Quartets* No. 1 (1951) and 2 (1959) AMP. Recorded on Nonesuch 71249.

Chiari, Giuseppe. *Quel Che Volete* (1965). CPE-*Source*. Along with the Ashley work cited above, represents borderline improvisation with indeterminacy, depending upon performance circumstances.

Coltrane, John. *The Mastery of John Coltrane*. A four-volume recording set (Impulse IZ-9 345–46–60–61) showing the improvisatory techniques of this jazz master.

Constant, Marius. *24 Preludes for Orchestra* (1958). Ricordi. Recorded on Heliodor HS-25058.

Cope, David. *Iceberg Meadow* (1969). Carl Fischer. Recorded on Capra 1201.

Cowell, Henry. *The Hero Sun*. Breitkopf & Härtel.

———. *The Tides of Manaunaun*. Breitkopf & Härtel, recorded on CRI 109.

———. *What's This*. Breitkopf & Härtel. (A number of Cowell's piano works are recorded on CRI S-281).

Crumb, George. *Black Angels* (1970). C. F. Peters. Recorded on CRI S-283.

Curran, Alvin. *Home-Made*. CPE-Source.

Davis, Miles. *Bitch's Brew*. Columbia PG-26. Incredible demonstration of improvisatory techniques.

Dempster, Stuart. *Standing Waves* (1976). Recorded on 1750 Arch Records S-1775. Improvisations in the great Abbey of Clement VI.

Douglas, Bill. *Improvisations III* (1969). Recorded on Orion 73125.

Duckworth, William. *Pitch City*. CAP.

Erb, Donald. *Concerto for Percussion and Orchestra*. Merion Music. Recorded on Turnabout TV-S 34433.

Erickson, Robert. *Ricercar á 5* (1966). Okra Music. Recorded on DG-0654084.

Foss, Lukas. *Echoi*. Recorded on Helidon 2549001.

———. *Etudes for Organ*. CPE-Source.

———. *Fragments of Archilocos*. Recorded on Helidon 2549001.

———. *Music for Clarinet, Percussion and Piano*, 1961 (out of print). Recorded on RCA LSC-2558.

———. *Time Cycle*. Recorded on Columbia MS-6280.

Globokar, Yinko. *Ausstrahlungen* (1969) for soloist and 20 players. Peters. Harmonia Mundi HMU 933.

Helm, Everett. *Concerto for Five Solo Instruments, Percussion and Strings* (1954). Schott. See p. 15.

Husa, Karel. *Apotheosis of this Earth* (1971). AMP. Recorded on Golden Crest 4134.

———. *Music for Prague* (1968). AMP. Recorded on Louisville S-722. Represents excellent use of sound-mass created both rhythmically in layers and by clusters.

Ives, Charles. *Majority*. AMP.

———. *Sonata #2* (1915). AMP. Columbia MS 7192, and CRI 150 SD.

———. *Songs*. New Music Edition. Recorded on Nonesuch 71209. CD: Etc. KTC-1020 (See Schwann Catalog for complete listing of recorded works.)

———. *Chorale for Quarter-tone Piano.* Recorded on Avant 1008.

———. *Three Pieces for Two Pianos Tuned a Quarter-tone Apart* (1924). C. F. Peters.

Johnston, Ben. *String Quartet No. 2.* Recorded on Nonesuch 71224.

Kagel, Mauricio. *Improvisation ajoutée* (1962). C. F. Peters. Recorded on Odyssey 32-160158.

———. *Sonant.* C. F. Peters.

Liebermann, Rolf. *Concerto for Jazz Band and Symphony Orchestra* (1954). Universal Edition. See p. 1.

Ligeti, György. *Atmosphères* (1961). Universal Edition. Recorded on Columbia MS-6733.

———. *Aventures* (1962). C. F. Peters. Recorded on Candide 31009.

———. *Lontano* (1967). Schott. Recorded on Wergo 322.

———. *Lux Aeterna* (1966). C. F. Peters. Recorded on DG-137004.

———. *Nouvelles Aventures* (1965). Neues. Recorded on Candide 31009.

———. *Requiem* (1965). C. F. Peters. Recorded on Wergo 60045.

———. *Volumina* (1962). Recorded on Musical Heritage Society MHS 3482.

Lucas, Theodore. *Aberrations No. VII.*

Lutoslawski. Witold. *Trois Poèmes d'Henri Michaux* PWM. Recorded on Wergo 60019.

———. *Concerto for Orchestra.* PWM. Recorded on Angel S-36045. Utilizes overlapping improvisation for sound-mass constructs.

———. *Livre Pour Orchestra.* J. & W. Chester Ltd. Polskie Nagrania SX 1370.

———. *Les Espaces du Sommeil.* Published by Chester Music.

Lybbert, Donald. *Lines for the Fallen* (1968). C. F. Peters. Recorded on Odyssey 32–160162. An excellent example of quarter-tone writing.

Macero, Teo. *One-Three Quarters.* Recorded on Odyssey 32–160162.

Messiaen, Oliver. *L' Ascension* (1934). Leduc. Recorded on Argo 5339.

———. *La Nativité du Seigneur.* Leduc. Recorded on Everest 3330. An excellent example of his rhythmic procedures. CD: TELA; CD 80097.

———. *Quatre études de rythme* for piano (1949). Durand. Recorded on Nonesuch H 71334.

Milhaud, Darius. *Piano Sonata* (1916). Salabert. See p. 10.

Moryl, Richard. *Chroma for Chamber Ensemble* (1972). Recorded on Desto 7143.

Nono, Luigi. *Il canto sospeso.* Schott.

———. *Cori di Didone.* Schott.

———. *La terra e la campagna.* Schott.

Oliveros, Pauline. *Sound Patterns.* Recorded on Odyssey 32–160156.

———. *Outline for flute, percussion and string bass: an improvisation chart* (1963). Recording on Nonesuch 71237.

Penderecki, Krzysztof. *Capriccio for Violin and Orchestra* (1967). Moeck. Recorded on Nonesuch 71201.

———. *Passion According to St. Luke.* Moeck. Recorded on Phillips 802771/2.

———. *Threnody for the Victims of Hiroshima.* Eulenberg. Recorded on RCA VICS-1239.

Persichetti, Vincent. *Symphony for Band* (1956). Elkan-Vogel. Recorded on Coronet S-1247.

Riegger, Wallingford. *Music for Brass Choir.* Mercury Music. Recorded on CRI S-229.

Rudhyar, Dane. *Stars* for piano. Recorded on CRI-247.

———. *Tetragram #4* for piano. Recorded on CRI-372.

Ruggles, Carl. *Angels* (1921). Curwen. Recorded on Turnabout 34398. A good example of sound-mass.

———. *Lilacs and Portals* (1926). AME. Recorded on Columbia ML 4986.

———. *Sun Treader* (1932). Recorded on DG 2530048.

Schafer, R. Murray. *Requiem for a Party Girl* (1966). BMI Canada. Recorded on CRI S-245.

———. *Ra.* Recorded on CMC 1283. Based on the mythology and symbolism of ancient Egypt.

———. *East* (1972). Recorded on RCI 434. Work inspired by a Hindu Upanishad.

Schuller, Gunther. *Concertino for Jazz Quartet and Orchestra* (1959). Recorded on Atlantic S-1359.

———. *Conversations.* Recorded by the Modern Jazz Quartet, Atlantic S-1345. These two works explicitly locate the influence of jazz on improvisation within traditional techniques.

———. *Seven Studies on Themes of Paul Klee* (1959). Universal Edition. Recorded on RCA LSC-2879. Fully defined Third Stream.

———. *Transformation.* Recorded on Columbia WL-127.

Schuman, William. *Credendum* (1955). Merion Music. Recorded on CRIS-308. Uses sound-mass effectively.

———. *Symphony No. 8* (1962). Merion Music. Recorded on Columbia ML 5912.

Schwartz, Elliott. *Texture* (1966). A. Broude. Recorded on Ars Nova AN-1002.

Stockhausen, Karlheinz. *Mixtur* (1967). Universal Edition. Recorded on DG 137012.

Strandberg, Newton. *Xerxes.* Recorded on Opus One Records 16. Excellent for use of massive evolutionary sound mass as is his *Sea of Tranquility* (1969), Opus One 21.

Stravinsky, Igor. *Le Sacre du Printemps* (1913). Boosey & Hawkes. Recorded on Columbia M-31520. CD: Decca; 400 084–2DM.

Trythall, Gilbert. *Entropy* for Stereo Brass Improvisation Group and Stereo Tape (1967). Recorded on Golden Crest S-4085.

Varèse, Edgard. *Equatorial.* G. Schirmer. Recorded on Nonesuch 71269.

———. *Hyperprism* (1933), and *Octandre.* G Schirmer. Recorded on Columbia MG 31078.

———. *Octandre.* Ricordi. Recorded on Finnadar 9018 under the supervision of the composer with many other of his works.

Winsor, Phil. *Orgel.* Carl Fischer.

Woodbury, Arthur. *Remembrances.* CPE-*Source.*

Zeitlin, Denny. *Expansions* (recorded in 1973). On 1750 Arch Records 1758.

Mainstream's 5002 includes the live electronic improvisations of the *Musica Elettronica Viva* (Rome) and the AMM (London). Music of the New Music Ensemble is available on two discs from Source Records, Sacramento, Calif. (NME 101 and 102).

4. INSTRUMENT EXPLORATION

Origins and the Futurists

Suprisingly, the desire for new and different sounds is probably the least significant of the driving forces behind the experimental or *avant-garde* composers in the past fifty years. Yet it is within this area that the contemporary composer has had the most serious division with audiences. John Cage referred to this in his 1937 lecture, "The Future of Music: Credo": "Whereas, in the past, the point of disagreement has been between dissonance and consonance, it will be, in the immediate future, between noise and so-called musical sounds."[1] Philosophically, it is not "new" sounds that have disturbed the music world (since no significant new sounds have been developed that had not coexisted with music since the beginning), but the concept that these sounds are potentially valuable as a musical resource.

A group of Italian composers, called Futurists, wrote music for machine guns, steam whistles, sirens, and other "noisemakers" as early as 1912. Deriving their name from Marinetti's 1909 term *futurismo* (referring to extreme radicalism in all the arts), the Futurists were among the first composers to include noise as an inherent part of their music, not merely as a side effect. Francesco Pratella's theoretical "Musica Futurista" (reprinted in Nicolas Slonimsky's *Music Since 1900*) describes the "music" of steamboats, automobiles, battleships, railways, shipyards, and airplanes. Luigi Russolo (1885–1947), the most noted Futurist composer, constructed many of his own "noise instruments." Though his and most of the music of this movement was completely without popular success and approval, its significance lies in the fact that it proposed a concept and laid a foundation for other composers (though no *direct* relationship is implied). Varèse, for example, employed sirens and anvils in *Ionisation*. Mossolov, in his more imitative *Symphony of Machines—Steel Foundry* (1928), included the constant rattling of a metal sheet throughout the work. Equally unsuccessful, the Futurist movement in France (*bruitisme*) enlarged the concept of noise as a viable musical source. George Antheil's *Ballet mécanique* (1924), probably the most "infamous" of noise pieces, was largely influenced by the French movement. Its first Carnegie Hall performance (April 10, 1927) brought

---

1. John Cage, *Silence* (Cambridge, Mass.: The M.I.T. Press, paperback edition, 1961), p. 4.

Figure 4.1 George Antheil arriving in New York for the U.S. premiere performance of his *Ballet mécanique* (1927).

about a violent audience reaction reminiscent of the first performance of Stravinsky's *Le Sacre du Printemps*. Antheil established the paradigm for the *avant-garde* to come, the "predictable" unpredictability of which is expressed in "An Introduction to George Antheil" by Charles Amirkhanian:

> Here is a man who once drew a pistol during a piano recital to silence a restive audience; a man who, in 1923, composed a piece of music calling for the sound of an airplane motor; a man who was mistakenly reported by the news media to have been eaten alive by lions in the Sahara Desert; and a man who collaborated with Hedy Lamarr in the invention and patenting of a World War II torpedo.[2]

Ezra Pound remarks that Antheil was possibly the first American-born musician to be taken seriously in Europe. This might explain John Cage's later successes there. The *Treatise on Harmony* by Antheil (a 25-page book) repetitively dwells on the need for a reappraisal of rhythmic ideas equal to those of melody and harmony: "A sound of any pitch, or combination of such sounds, may be followed by a sound of any other pitch or any combination of such sounds, providing the time interval between them is properly gauged; and this is true for any series of sounds, chords or arpeggios."[3]

In no other period of music history has the performer played such an important role in the development of new sound resources and instrumental techniques. Many instrumentalists have, during the past twenty years, created a significant impact in determining and exploring the sound capabilities of their respective instruments and have more than justified the claim that this immense potential can be applied as easily and as constructively as the use of electronic tape.

2. Charles Amirkhanian, "An Introduction to George Antheil," *Soundings* 7–8:176. Originally printed in a KPFA Folio of November 1970.
3. Ezra Pound, *Antheil* (New York: Da Capo Press, 1968), p. 10.

Figure 4.2. Bertram
Turetzky, bassist.

Bruno Bartolozzi, in his now famous book, *New Sounds for Woodwind,* states
the concept of the contemporary performer's role in new music as well as the role
of instruments:

> Their continued existence in the world of creative composition therefore depends to a
> very large extent on just what they have to offer the composer, just how much they
> can rouse his interest and provoke his fantasy. Some composers already show an
> obvious lack of interest in conventional instruments and have no hesitation in using
> the most unusual means in an effort to find new sonorities. . . .[4]

No traditional instrument has escaped the imagination of the composer's creative mind. Some performers have steadfastly maintained that any other than traditional "acts" upon their instrument violate inherent intention and should not be
attempted. One must wonder if *plucking* and *muting* do not plunder the instrument's virginity. Certainly, short of physical damage to the instrument itself, even
the most critical of traditionalists must admit the impossibility of being "just a little
bit pregnant." Donald Erb sums it up well:

> Music is made by a performer. It comes from him rather than from his instrument,
> the instrument being merely a vehicle. Therefore it seems logical that any sound a
> performer can make may be used in a musical composition.[5]

4. Bruno Bartolozzi, *New Sounds for Woodwind* (New York: Oxford University Press, 1967), p. 1.
5. Bertram Turetzky, "Vocal and Speech Sounds—A Technique of Contemporary writing for the
   Contrabass," *Composer* 1, no. 3 (December 1969): 169.

Four major additions to string techniques have evolved:

1. percussive effects such as knocking, rapping, tapping, or slapping the strings or body of the instrument (especially in the works of Meyer Kupferman, Eugene Kurtz, and Sydney Hodkinson);

2. singing, speaking, or humming while playing (particularly apparent in the works of Russell Peck, Jacob Druckman, Charles Whittenberg, and Richard Felciano);

3. unusual bowings inclusive of circular bowing, bowing on or across the bridge, bowing between the bridge and tailpiece, bowing directly on the tailpiece, and *undertones* (subharmonics) created by bowing with great pressure on a harmonic node (actually creating notes well below the lowest open string of the instrument): these devices are used extensively in the works of Krzysztof Penderecki, Karlheinz Stockhausen, Mauricio Kagel, and George Crumb, among others.

4. combinations and extensions of traditional techniques (e.g., harmonics, glissandi, fingering without bowing, pizzicati, etc.) especially notable in the works of Krzysztof Penderecki, György Ligeti, Donald Erb, and Mauricio Kagel.

Figure 4.3 shows Krzysztof Penderecki's use of playing between the bridge and tailpiece (⌐ and ⫲), highest note pizzicato (↑) and irregular tremolo (⫰) among others in his *Threnody for the Victims of Hiroshima* (for explanation of the proportional notation, see Appendix 3).[6]

Notable performers of innovative works for strings are Paul Zukofsky and Max Pollikov (violin), Walter Trampler (viola), Siegfried Palm ('cello), and Bertram Turetzky and Alvin Brehm (contrabass). String groups particularly dedicated to new music and techniques include the Fine Arts Quartet and the Composers' Quartet, among others.[7]

Though there is a difference between the ways in which innovative techniques are applied to sections (brass and woodwind) and to individual instruments (particularly between the various single-reed, double-reed, and non-reed instruments of the woodwind section), they are combined here for purposes of space and basic similarities. The author has grouped similar effects within six major categories:

6. For a more detailed discussion of new string techniques, see Bertram Turetzky's articles "The Bass as a Drum," *Composer* 1, no. 2 (September 1969): 92–107; and "Vocal and Speech Sounds: A Technique of Contemporary Writing for the Contrabass," *Composer*, 1, no. 3 (December 1969): 118–34; and his book: *The Contemporary Contrabass* (Berkely: University of California Press, 1974).
7. It should be noted that throughout the course of this chapter the mentioning of performers' names is necessarily incomplete due to space limitations. Apologies to those many highly dedicated and talented performers of contemporary music, whose names are not included here.

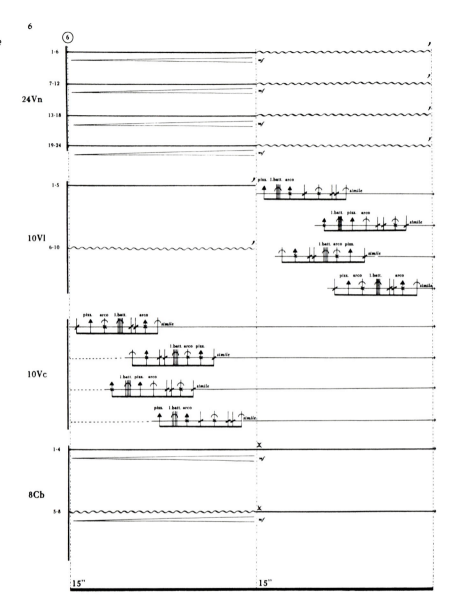

1. multiphonics (or the creation of more than one pitch simultaneously on one instrument) are created by either of two basic methods: singing along with playing and/or forcing the strong overtone content of a given fundamental to become audible (inclusive of altering embouchure, fingerings, overblowing, dynamics, and a combination of these). Figure 4.4 shows Toru Takamitsu's use and notation (in terms of open and closed holes for fingering) in his *Voice* (1971) for solo flute (also found in works of Donald Erb, Roger Reynolds, Russell Peck, and Jacob Druckman, among others);

2. color fingerings involving pitch and timbre fluctuations by changing the available fingerings on the instrument for the same note (particularly notable in the works of George Crumb);

3. jazz effects which include a large variety of hitherto avoided sounds such as *rips, fall offs, bends,* etc. (see particularly the brass works of William Sydeman, Phil Winsor, Donald Erb, and David Cope);

4. percussion effects such as rapping, tapping, fingering without blowing, fingernails on the bell tremolo, and hand-pops (the palm of the hand slapping the open bore of the mouthpiece) as noted in the works of Aurelio de la Vega, Iannis Xenakis, and many others;

5. use of mouthpiece alone or instrument without mouthpiece, both performable with actual or approximate pitch (see works by Donald Erb, Krzysztof Penderecki, and György Ligeti, among others);

6. extension of traditional techniques such as glissandi, harmonics, speed rates of vibrato, pedal tones, flutter tongue, circular breathing, and many others (see works by composers listed under 1–5 as well as works by Luciano Berio, Lukas Foss, and Gunther Schuller).

Donald Scavarda's *Matrix* for solo clarinet (1962), shown in Figure 4.5 contains a wide variety of new wind techniques including multiphonics (one of the very first such usages), smears, breath noise, overtone clusters, inverted mouthpiece, and undertones. Scavarda speaks to this point:

> It was in trying to find sounds that were most natural to the clarinet that I discovered what are now called *multiphonics* in April 1962. Gradually I began to realize the exciting potential of the simultaneity of sounds that could be produced by the

Figure 4.4. Toru Takemitsu: *Voice.* Permission granted by Editions Salabert. All rights reserved. Each small vertical line equals 4.5″. Beamed notes are slurred (n.b. half note beams). Special fingerings above some notes indicate particular timbres or multiphonics (last 2 chords of first system).

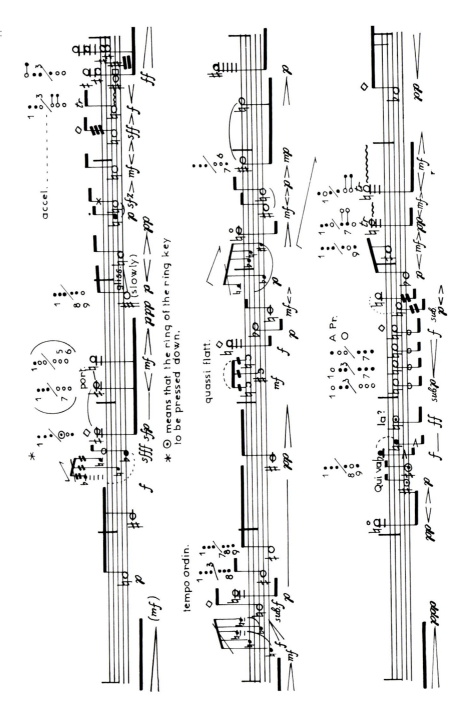

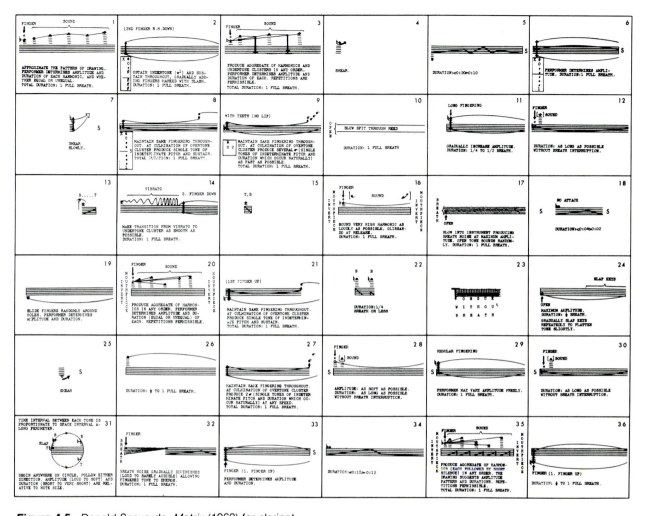

Figure 4.5. Donald Scavarda. *Matrix* (1962) for clarinet.

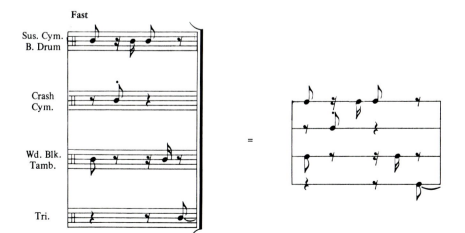

Figure 4.6. An example of traditional (left) *vis à vis* contemporary (right) percussion notation.

instrument. It was necessary first, however, to discard old habits and attitudes about what the clarinet should sound like. It required an open mind and much hard work and patience to explore and 'mine' these rich, natural complex sounds and eventually to bring them to the surface.[8]

Notable performers of woodwind and brass works of the *avant-garde* include: Aurèle Nicolet, Pierluigi Mencarelli, Savarino Gazzeloni, and Harvey Sollberger—flute; Joseph Celli, Lawrence Singer, and Heinz Holliger—oboe; Phillip Rehfeldt, Detalmo Corneti, and William O. Smith—clarinet; William Scribner and Sergio Penazzi—bassoon; Ken Dorn, and James Houlik—saxophone; Gerard Schwarz, Robert Levy, and Marice Stith—trumpet; James Fulkerson, Stuart Dempster, and Vinko Globokar—trombone; and Barton Cummings and Roger Bobo—tuba.

Percussion

It is in the percussion section that the maximum degree of enlargement and experimentation has taken place. Composers using more traditional instruments (timpani, snare drum, xylophone, etc.) developed a wide variety of unusual techniques, and especially experimented with various sizes and types of beaters (metal, wood, cloth, glass), to increase timbral resources. Exotic or foreign folk instruments were added mostly for particular effects, and used sparingly. Surprisingly, in considering the "noises" many percussion instruments (particularly the "whip") emit, many mainstream composers who use them nevertheless refuse to consider the musical potentiality of other less "noisy" instruments, including the oscillator. For a number of years, the most unusual and philosophically significant of these additions to the percussion section was the brake drum. The fact that a part of a car (or truck) had found its way into the standard percussion section of the symphony orchestra seemed to go unnoticed. Its use clearly implied that any object could act as a usable sound source.[9] Early experimenters in percussion music include John Cage, Edgard Varèse, Carlos Chavez, and especially John Becker, whose *Abongo* (1933) marks one of the first serious efforts in true percussion music. Percussion sections, since the late nineteenth century, have also required new notation systems, necessitated by the fact that performers must read as many as six instrumental parts simultaneously, and five-line staves are often impractical (see Figure 4.6).

The increasing need for explicit performance directions indicating type of mallet to be used, the action of the mallet, and its exact placement on the instrument, requires vastly new and different notations. Figure 4.7A shows the exact movement of the mallet across a timpani head within a certain period of time. Figure 4.7B demonstrates the exact direction and striking surface of the crash cymbals. Figure 4.7C notates the sweep action of wire brushes on a brass drum. Since widely variable

8. From notes to the score by the composer. *Matrix.* (1962) published by Lingua Press (1980).
9. The brake drum is described and pictured in a number of contemporary orchestration books (e.g., Reed and Leach, *Scoring for Percussion* [New York: Prentice-Hall, Inc., 1969]).

A

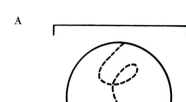

Timpani: mallet motion

B

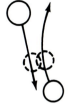

Cymbals: striking procedure

Figure 4.7. *Avant-garde* percussion notations.

C

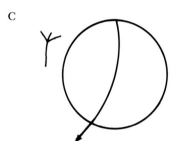

Bass drum: wire brush motion

timbres can result from mallet direction and placement on each of these three per-cussion instruments, as well as from direction and amount of crash for cymbals, new notation becomes inevitable and increasingly more graphic.

An actual listing and numbering of percussion effects would create a book twice the size of this volume for just the unusual uses of the "standard" orchestral per-cussion instruments. The codification of the percussion section defines any instru-ment, no matter whether strings (e.g., piano), air columns (e.g., slide whistle) or others similar in kind to the orchestra "staples," as within "percussion" classifica-tion. This is particularly true when non-Western instruments are used with an or-chestra: no matter what the context, the nature of the instrument, or the method of producing sound.

Notable *avant-garde* composers for percussion include Larry Austin, Karlheinz Stockhausen, Frederic Rzewski, Harry Partch, Edward Miller, Mario Bertoncini, Peter Garland, William Kraft, and many, many others. Performers include Max Neuhaus, Christoph Caskel, Willy Winant and William Kraft. Often, as here in-dicated (and more often than in any other section of the orchestra), percussionists tend to be composers as well. William Kraft is both a percussionist with the Los Angeles Philharmonic Orchestra, and a gifted and well-known composer for all in-struments (which includes his extensive percussion solo and ensemble literature). The well-known Blackearth Percussion Group (see Figure 4.19) performed *avant-garde* music until disbanding several years ago.

Figure 4.8. William Kraft. Photo by A. A. Friedman.

Figure 4.9. Blackearth Percussion Group.

The voice, both in solo and choral situations, has in recent years become a focal point of innovative development realized both in terms of dramatic emphasis of text and as an instrument separate from verbal associations. Its ability to be a "percussively stringed wind instrument" gives it nearly all of the timbre potentials of all the aforementioned instruments. Only the physical limitations of individual performers become obstacles to the composer's available resources (few can equal Roy Hart's eight-octave range and multiphonic abilities).

Vocal

Most vocal experimentation has taken place in three basic areas:

1. effects, such as panting, whistling, sucking, kissing, hissing, clucking, laughing, talking, whispering, etc. (especially in the works of Hans Werner Henze, Krzysztof Penderecki, György Ligeti, Karlheinz Stockhausen, Mauricio Kagel, Pauline Oliveros, Folke Rabe, Richard Felciano, Luciano Berio, and David Cope);

2. multiphonics (especially notable in the *Versuch uber Schweine* by Hans Werner Henze);

3. muting in the forms of humming, hands over mouth and slowly opening and closing the mouth (employed well in works by Donald Erb and Robert Morris).

Figure 4.10, the *Aventures* of György Ligeti, shows the breathing in and out (measures 1–5 shown by symbols ▶ = inhale and ◀ = exhale) as well as muting (closed mouth *m* in second brace). The work is notable for its many other effects, its lack of text (replaced by a 112-letter alphabet for creating sounds), and the exchanging metric and proportional notations (shown clearly here between braces one and two). Hans Werner Henze's *Versuch uber Schweine* (1969) for voice and orchestra is equally impressive in its incredible use of dramatic vocal gymnastics.

Singers who are known for their performance of new music include Roy Hart, Catherine Rowe, Jan DeGaetani, Bethany Beardslee, Elaine Bonazzi, Joan La Barbara, Neva Pilgrim, Paul Sperry, and the late Cathy Berberian. The New Music Choral Ensemble (NMCE), founded by its director (Kenneth Gaburo) in 1966, stood as one of the world's foremost choral ensembles dedicated to the performance of new music.

David Hykes, founder and developer of the Harmonic Choir (1975), practices the art of Harmonic Chant, or the singing of more than one note simultaneously. While Tibetan Buddhist monks and Mongolian "throat" (or *hoomi*) singers have produced music in this manner for centuries, Western singers have only begun using this approach in the past few decades. By performing and recording only in highly resonant spaces (such as large churches and abbeys, including New York City's Cathedral of St. John), the Harmonic Choir is able to take advantage of certain singing techniques to pronounce high harmonics simultaneously with sung fundamentals. With his colleague Timothy Hill, Hykes has developed five types of Harmonic Chant. These move from drones based on subharmonic pitches (higher

Figure 4.10. *Aventures* by György Ligeti (page 1). Copyright © 1964 by Henry Litolff Verlag. Sole selling agents in the Western Hemisphere, C. F. Peters Corporation, 373 Park Avenue South, New York, N.Y. 10016. Reprint permission granted by publisher.

Figure 4.11. From Richard Bunger: *The Well Prepared Piano*. Examples of piano preparations. Used by permission of the author and illustrator, Richard Bunger. Second Edition. Litoral Arts Press, 35 Firefly Lane, Sebastopol, California 95472 (1981).

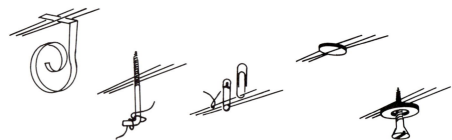

fundamental) through sung fundamentals, as drones over which singers produce melodies based on the overtone series, to contrapuntal harmonic movements of both fundamentals and derived melodies from various related harmonic series.

The early experiments and compositions for piano by Henry Cowell (e.g., 1925, *The Banshee,* which involved plucking and stroking the strings inside the instrument), John Cage (e.g., 1938, *Bacchanale,* and 1946–48, *Sonatas and Interludes* for prepared piano) and Christian Wolff (whose *For Prepared Piano* appeared in *New Music Quarterly* in April, 1951) aroused great interest. At least a few performers became aware of the fantastic array of new sound resources that was available, and that these resources, combined with variable performance techniques, were just as viable as more traditional ones.

The prepared piano (a technique first explored by John Cage in the mid-thirties) involves the placement of objects such as nuts, bolts, and nails on, around, and between the strings, thus converting the piano into an instrument with an almost limitless variety of new timbres. Figure 4.11 shows a number of typical preparations. Resulting timbres can be altered by (a) location of preparation in regard to string length (e.g., placing at harmonic nodes creates a very different sound from that resulting when one places the object between these nodes); (b) striking techniques (i.e., initiating the sound via the keyboard creates a sound distinctly different from that obtained if one strikes the preparation directly with a mallet or similar instrument); and (c) elasticity and density of material utilized. Such preparations should do no damage to the instrument whatsoever if proper precautions are used (see Figure 4.12, which shows the use of a screwdriver covered with masking tape to insert preparations, thus avoiding any harm to the strings).

Aside from preparation, the following new techniques are currently being used and explored:

1. muting (usually done by placing the right hand on the string inside the piano between the pin and the dampers and playing the notes on the keyboard with the left hand) is notated with an + above the note (used particularly in the works of George Crumb and David Cope);

2. harmonics (produced by touching a node of the string inside the piano with one hand and striking the corresponding key with the other) are employed much like those of string instruments (used in works by George Crumb, Larry Barnes, and many others);

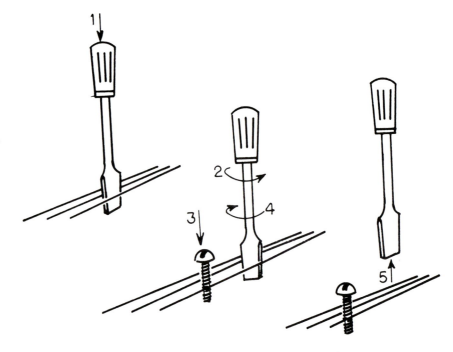

Figure 4.12. From Richard Bunger, *The Well Prepared Piano.* Proper use of screwdriver in inserting preparations. Used by permission of the author and illustrator, Richard Bunger. Second Edition. Litoral Arts Press, 350 Firefly Lane, Sebastopol, California 95472, 1981.

Figure 4.13. Conlon Nancarrow. Photo by Gordon Mumma.

3. bowing the strings (produced by making bows of fishline, threading them around and between the strings, and then drawing back and forth as one would on a string instrument), found particularly in the works of Curtis Curtis-Smith;

4. stroking, rapping, tapping, striking, or plucking the strings directly for a variety of different timbres (used primarily in the works of Henry Cowell, George Crumb, David Cope, Donald Erb, and others);

5. using other parts of the instrument by knocking, tapping, rapping, etc., particularly on the wood of the lid and body, the metal of the internal crossbars and soundboard, etc., with mallets, hands, and various other objects (notable in works like *Knocking Piece* by Ben Johnston, and works by John Cage, George Crumb, Donald Erb, and many others).

Stephen Scott has developed a "bowed piano" influenced by Curtis-Smith's invention. Scott has created sets of miniature "piano bows" similar in design to regular violin bows. Constructed of popsicle sticks with horsehair glued to both sides, he is able to create rich and vibrant continuous sounds on an otherwise struck instrument. Unlike Curtis-Smith's design, however, Scott's invention can play quite fast passages on pre-marked strings.

Pianists who are actively involved in the performance of new *avant-garde* works include David Tudor, David Burge, Richard Bunger, and Aloys Kontarsky. David Tudor, William Albright, and Martha Folts have been active in the performance of new music for the organ, as has Antoinette Vischer with the harpsichord. At present these experiments have been more theatrical (organ) and formal (harpsichord) than real in terms of sonic exploration (note especially works by Mauricio Kagel, Gordon Mumma, Christian Wolff, and William Albright for organ and György Ligeti for harpsichord).

Unique work with the player piano has been accomplished by Conlon Nancarrow in Mexico City. His *Studies for Player Piano* (one of which was published in *New Music Quarterly* in October, 1951 with many now published by *Soundings;* see bibliography) is a series of works (now numbering more than forty) utilizing punched piano rolls inserted in upright player pianos (the composer uses two Marshall and Wendell pianos, both with modified hammers; one set covered with leather and the other with steel straps). His extremely complex and original works vary from jazz-influenced shorter movements (especially the early studies) to mathematically proportioned canons (in the later works). The composer has spoken about his work and its relation to traditional instruments in an interview:

> I'm so tied up now with the player piano. I'd have to start thinking again: "Does the hand reach there?" Can it go here?" The whole thing. No, no. You know, when I do these things for player piano, I just write music; and the notes go here, there, wherever. I don't have to think about anything else. I used to, when I was writing for instruments. It's a real luxury not to have to think about all that.[10]

10. Cole Cagne and Tracy Caras, *Soundpieces: Interviews with American Composers* (London: The Scarecrow Press, Inc., 1982), p. 285.

Harp

Carlos Salzedo (1885–1961) developed an extremely wide range of possible effects on this versatile instrument, as well as highly original notations and names for these techniques ("gushing aeolian chords," etc.). Most have become standard for the harpist and need not be considered *avant-garde,* though they may sound like it to the uninitiated. Composers utilizing these numerous effects include Salzedo himself, Luciano Berio, and George Crumb, in particular.

The harp is indeed unique in that Salzedo, a pioneering and innovative genius, composed during its maturing period. He proved that (more than any other single instrument) it is capable of sounds virtually unexplored by the *avant-garde* composer. It is not much of a gamble to predict that the harp will in future years become a foremost attraction for the contemporary composer.

Ensemble Development

George Crumb's *Songs, Drones, and Refrains of Death* (1969) for baritone, electric guitar, electric contrabass, electric piano, harpischord, and two percussionists, contain a great many of the effects discussed above (see Figure 4.16). The duet here (for electric guitar and electric contrabass) is scored in seven events. Each performer is required to sing or whisper while playing their respective instrument in a variety of unusual ways (e.g., harmonics, glissandi, tremolo, use of metal rod, etc.). Crumb's *Black Angels* (1970) for string quartet employs amplification of the instruments both for balance and for the unique timbre alteration which electronics adds to the ensemble. This procedure, including the use of both contact and acoustic microphones, has become increasingly popular (discussed at greater length under "Electronic Music," see Chapter 7). However, even the instrumentalists often don't recognize sounds from fellow performers, posing a problem contributing to the extreme difficulty of ensemble rhythmic performance. That problem is here solved by a procedure of notating *events,* in which exact timing is not as important as exact performance of the event itself. A broad spectrum of tone colors and "noise" is thus made available to the composer as musical material.

Iannis Xenakis, long interested in preserving live and traditional instruments of the orchestra through creation of new techniques, proves convincingly in *Metastasis* (1953–54) that sixty-one traditional instruments can compete successfully with electronic sound sources.

Roman Haubenstock-Ramati was one of the first, in his *Interpolation* (1958), to utilize an unmanipulated prerecorded tape made by the performer. This enables a single instrumentalist to create a large number of ensemble effects using only a single instrument as source. His 1961 *Liaisons* for vibraphone includes provisions for a previously prepared tape to be started six to ten seconds after the performer begins. In this instance the tape serves not as an electronic device, but as a tool which enables both composer and performer to elicit more combinations of tones and effects, without losing the instrumental timbre.

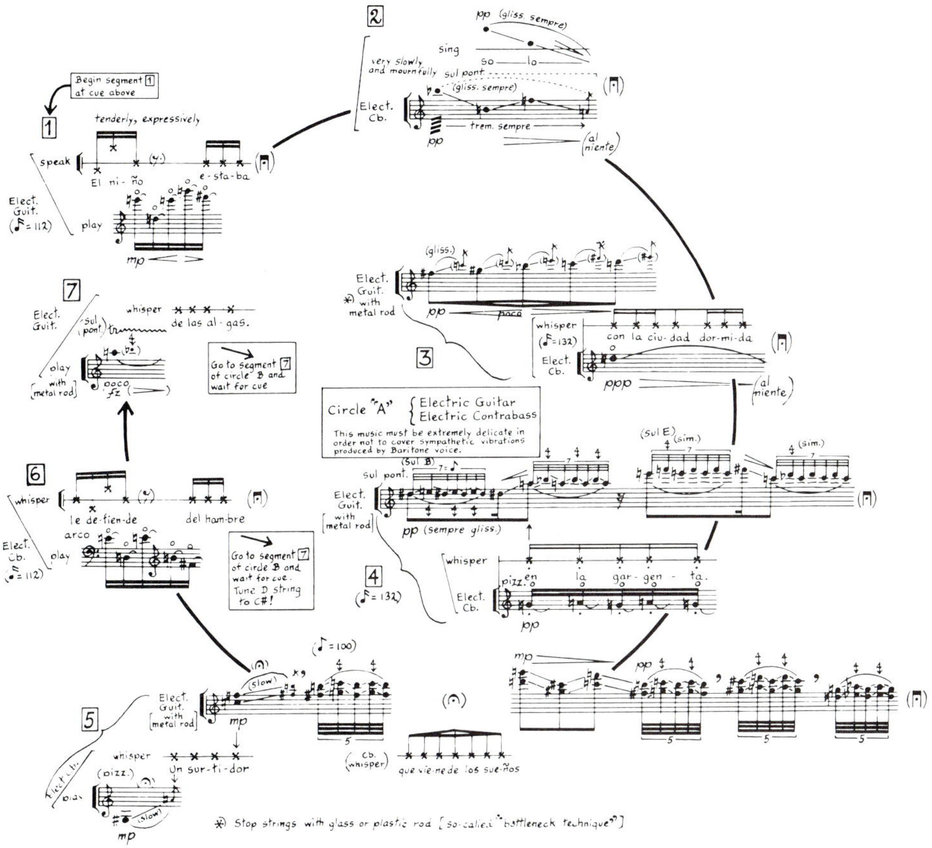

Figure 4.14. George Crumb: *Songs, Drones, and Refrains of Death.*

Figure 4.15. Harry Partch *circa* 1967.

George Green's *Perihelion for Concert Band* (1974) employs an incredible array of new and effective timbres often similar in nature (becoming clusters of like textures), though at times contrasted for purposes of form and direction.

David Cope's *Margins* (1972) ('cello, trumpet, percussion, and two pianos) emphasizes the "marginal" aspects of each insrument in a single movement structure. "The composer equally explores the contrast and developmental possibilities of dynamics and contrapuntal articulations. The tempo remains very slow throughout and the beat divides into multifold groupings of often very quick and pointillistic integrations from instrument to instrument."[11]

The previously discussed effects have also been used in combination or in conjunction with extracurricular performer activity, from finger-snapping and music stand-tapping to such dramatic effects as costumes, theatrical staging, and substitution of the original with other instruments. Often composers use whispers, speaking, and shouting (as in the Crumb example, Figure 4.14) along with the performance of additional instruments such as triangles hung from music stands, maracas, and a variety of other percussion instruments.

Heinz Holliger's *Atembogen* is filled with orchestral effects, most of which involve some machination of subtle nuance or shading of breath or bow technique. Examples for winds include exhaling, inhaling, using voice, embouchure but no tone, whistle-tone; and for strings, bow with too much pressure, bow with too little pressure, bow on tailpiece, and *col legno*. Most of these are used musically and there are no hostile contraptions evident. The piece is shaped in a through-composed series of large dramatic gestures based on quasi-physical motives. For example, *Atembogen*'s opening is four seconds of bowing and blowing without allowing sound to occur, with strings on up-bow and winds inhaling. The work ends similarly with the conductor doing a solo while the orchestra slowly releases bows and breaths from their instruments in exhale fashion. Throughout the work there are like passages lending the "feel" of numerous episodes into deep textures and timbre explorations within the boundaries of the physical motion of bowing/breathing.

Whether in solo or chamber ensembles, the complete realization of all possible sonic events creates an entirely new performance situation with virtually endless combinational possibilities. The audience can no longer attend a string quartet performance, expecting that a traditional string quartet will be heard. New orchestral and multiorchestral combinations create almost endless possibilities equal to that of electronic production. Indeed, recordings of these works, without visual confirmation, distort beyond recognition the imagination's comprehension of the sound source. Ensembles of mixed instrumentation have contributed greatly to the development of instrument exploration. Such active groups commission, perform, and record new music and include the Contemporary Chamber Ensemble, The Aeolian

---

11. From liner notes on recording: ORION ORS 75169.

Chamber Players, Die Reihe Ensemble, the Philadelphia Composers Forum, Cologne New Music Ensemble, The MW 2 Ensemble, da capo Chamber Players, the Melos Ensemble, and the ISKRA ensemble, to name but a few. There also exists a large number of school-affiliated new music ensembles made up of faculty and students possessing both a high degree of professional ability and large repertoires.

New Instruments

Enlargement and transformation of sounds on traditional instruments represents only a part of new, non-electronic sound sources for composers. Harry Partch, unlike Cage and Cowell, created new instruments rather than transforming existing ones (though his first such instrument was an adapted viola). His division of the octave into forty-three tones instead of twelve brought the need to create instruments capable of realizing his theoretical concepts (see his *Genesis of A New Music*). Except for his use of voice, almost all of his works employ original instruments (primarily percussion and struck string). Partch's *U.S. Highball: Account of Hobo Trip* (1943) and *Account of the Normandy Invasion by an American Glider Pilot* (both early works) reflect his fascination with instruments; an attempt at non-imitative music. In *Revelation in the Courthouse Square* (1961), the visual (theatrical) elements—the performers and their instruments—become an integral (in his words: *corporeal*) part of the work. *And on the Seventh Day Petals Fell in Petaluma* (a 1964 work comprising studies in the form of twenty-three duets, for *Delusion of the Fury,* a larger 1967 work) explores the possibilities of harmonic and melodic uses of microtones based on his tonal and polytonal theories of intonation (his word for major is Otonality, for minor, Utonality).

More recent compositions have extended instrumental possibilities to anything which can be beaten, blown, or bowed, with each work demanding a new instrument for realization—cars, brake drums, even a jet engine, for example. Few of these "instruments" enter any standardized orchestra, as their instrinsic theatrical value lies in their being recognized as having a direct relationship to one work or composer.

Yoshimasa Wada has created a number of successful new wind instruments (see Figures 4.17 and 4.18) which, due to size, produce low sounds of soft dynamics often needing amplification for realistic acoustic projection. The KIVA Ensemble of the University of California at San Diego explores new instrumental resources (see Figure 4.20) often coupled with electronic amplification or modification. Arthur Frick has created a wide variety of new instruments (see Figure 4.20), many of which are mobile and often have comic overtones.

George Gonzalez and Peter Richards have built a "Wave Organ" in San Francisco which amplifies the sound of energy created by ocean currents pushing and retreating in large cement pipes. The audience place their ears next to one of several orifices through which both sound and air exit. Different wave and weather conditions affect the type and dynamic of the sounds produced.

Figure 4.16. Various Partch instruments. Photos by Jonathan Glasier.

A. Gourd Tree (1964)
   Cone Gong (1965)

B. Zymo-Xyl (1963)

C. Mazda Marimba (1963)

D. Chromelodeon 1 (1945–1949)

E. Bass Marimba (1951)

F. Diamond Marimba (1946)

Figure 4.16. *(Continued)*

G. Boo (1955–1957)

H. Surrogate Kithara (1953)

Figure 4.17. Instrument by Yoshimasa Wada. Photo by Seiji Kakizaki.

Figure 4.18. Instruments by Yoshimasa Wada. Photo by Seiji Kakizaki.

Figure 4.19. KIVA performance instruments. Photo by Solomon (UCSD).

Figure 4.20. Instrument by
Arthur Frick.

Robert Rutman also creates giant instruments, often out of industrial scrap metals. His "steel 'cello," for example, is a single large piece of this substance twisted into a C-shape with a single large string strung from the top of the instrument to its bottom. His "bow chimes" have a similar shape but are held in place by a bar.

The Pleiades instrument, a proposed 12.5 million dollar structure, represents an interdisciplinary amalgam between astronomy (radio, in this case) and music. Based on the theory that our ears can hear patterns of such sophistication and complexity that visual (graphic displays) and computational models cannot compete, it is a large radio telescope designed so that received information is turned into acoustic sound. This is accomplished through a transducing process that actually excites the plates of the radio "mirror" into sound producers. A radome (a radio translucent geodesic surrounding the instrument) creates a viable acoustic space for the telescope as shown in Figure 4.21.

This cross-section shows both the complementary discs and the resonators. The spherical-shaped mirror allows for the secondary (in the roof of the radome) to collect focused data from only part of the mirror at a time. By moving this (rather than the fixed primary), the telescope can follow objects for periods of up to four hours. Proposed by the Tauceti foundation for a location in the Southern Sierras, the project currently has an electronics site designation from the Sequoia National Forest and a substantial grant for proceeding with investigations. Promoted by both astronomers and musicians, it would be the single largest instrument for music and the second largest in astronomy (to the Arecibo telescope in Puerto Rico).

New instruments require "new" performers, with questioned virtuosity. One could hardly expect as practiced and polished a performance on an instrument created or adapted from one work alone as expected from a (an experienced) violinist after intense study of a Beethoven concerto. One of two alternatives is suggested: (1) a simple but fully notated score, or (2) a more free improvisational structure whereby the performer substitutes freedom and creativity for familiarity. Douglas Leedy chooses the latter in *Usable Music I* (1968), for very small instruments with holes. This work depends almost completely on graphic representation of activities (i.e., the use of symbols to indicate such general directions as "blow" or "draw"), with less emphasis on exact rhythmic and pitch notation. Robert Moran, in *Titus* (1968), has the score projected on the stage upon an automobile, showing pictorially the performers' area and amount of activity (see Figure 4.22). Each of from five to fifteen performers, using contact microphones, files, hammers, and the like, moves around and within the car, visually guided by the score.

In such works, there is an increasing necessity for performer creativity. Once the composer has admitted that the act of composition is a partially shared responsibility it is not difficult to understand the motivation inherent in graphic or less exact notational systems. New instruments and techniques have evolved from concepts of unique sounds, creating implications and philosophies of composer-performer relationships much more significant in their ramifications than the mere searching for different timbres.

Figure 4.21. The *Pleiades* instrument.

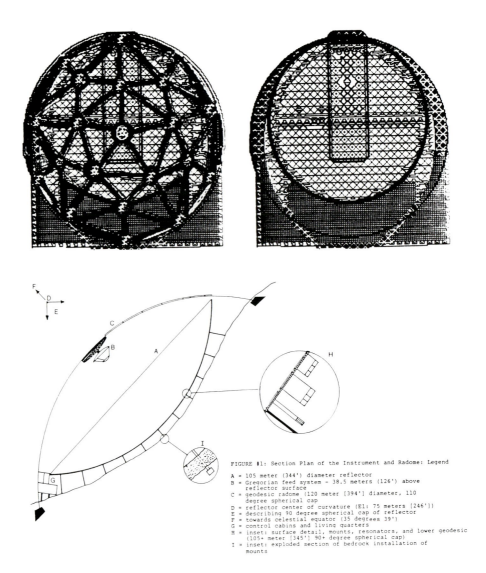

FIGURE #1: Section Plan of the Instrument and Radome: Legend

A = 105 meter (344') diameter reflector
B = Gregorian feed system - 38.5 meters (126') above
    reflector surface
C = geodesic radome (120 meter [394'] diameter, 110
    degree spherical cap
D = reflector center of curvature (E1: 75 meters [246'])
E = describing 90 degree spherical cap of reflector
F = towards celestial equator (35 degrees 39')
G = control cabins and living quarters
H = inset: surface detail, mounts, resonators, and lower geodesic
    (105+ meter [345'] 90+ degree spherical cap)
I = inset: exploded section of bedrock installation of
    mounts

Figure 4.22. Robert Moran: Score of *Titus*. (Permission granted by *Source: Music of the Avant-Garde*, Composer/Performer Edition, Davis, California.)

Other composers and artists deeply involved in the creation of new musical instruments include Laurie Anderson (electronic tape-bow on violins); Christopher Charles Banta (large marimbas); Bob Bates (mechanical instruments and music machines); Harry Bertoia (sound sculptures); Jim Burton (sound installations); Ivor Darreg (large numbers of microtonal string, wind, and electronic instruments similar in scope to those of Harry Partch); Paul De Marinis (electronic modules); Richard Dunlap (nonconventional instruments for improvisation and theater presentation); Stephen Scott (large sound sculptures); Bruce Fier (architectural sound designs); Cris Forster (notably *Chrysalis*); Ron George (original percussion instruments and ensembles); Jonathan Glasier (notably his *Harmonic Canon*); Stephen Goodman (automatic music instruments); Jim Gordon (percussion synthesizers); Jim Hobart (percussion and steel stringed instruments); Alzek Misheff (hot-air balloons containing portable electronic instruments); Max Neuhaus (sound installations); Jim Pomeroy (music boxes); Susan Rawcliffe (wind instruments); Tom Recchion (folk instruments from found objects); Prent Rodgers (electro-acoustical instruments); Stephen von Huene (self-performing sound sculptures); Robert Wilhite (environments); and Richard Waters (notably the metal "waterphone"). More often than not, these composers/instrument builders are also the performers on their instruments, self-taught troubadours of the *avant-garde*.

Timbre and Spatial Modulation

The expansion of possibilities in the area of timbre modulation has proven to be a significant development resulting from instrument exploration. With the composer's increasing awareness of the subtle timbre alterations available in different registers of various instruments—muting, dynamics, attacks, and decays—comes the realization that a wealth of timbre overlap exists between instruments. Figure 4.23 shows three such overlaps with the evolving timbre changes inherent in the combinations. In the first example the piccolo is initially masked by the triangle. Its slow crescendo gradually modulates the sound to solo piccolo through the decay of the triangle sound. In the second example the trumpet (with straight mute) slowly dies away as the like-timbred oboe crescendos, and so takes over. The effect is demonstrated by the intersecting vertical dotted line. At the beginning one hears only the trumpet. At the line one begins to hear a subtle combination of the two. Terms like "obet" or "trumboe" are often employed by composers to emphasize the significance of the truly "new" sound created by the modulation. Finally one hears the oboe alone. The third example demonstrates a direct approach to dynamics (the bass drum masking the piano attack completely) but a unique effect is achieved as the piano "rings" out of the bass drum (the piano chord slowly decaying beyond the hand-stopped percussion attack).

Works effectively employing timbre modulation include *Sinfonia* (1968) by Luciano Berio, *Lontano* (1967) by György Ligeti, *Ancient Voices of Children* (1970) by George Crumb, and *Apotheosis of This Earth* (1971) by Karel Husa.

Spacing and placement play an important role in the struggle for new directional sonorities from traditional instruments. A few historical examples are no-

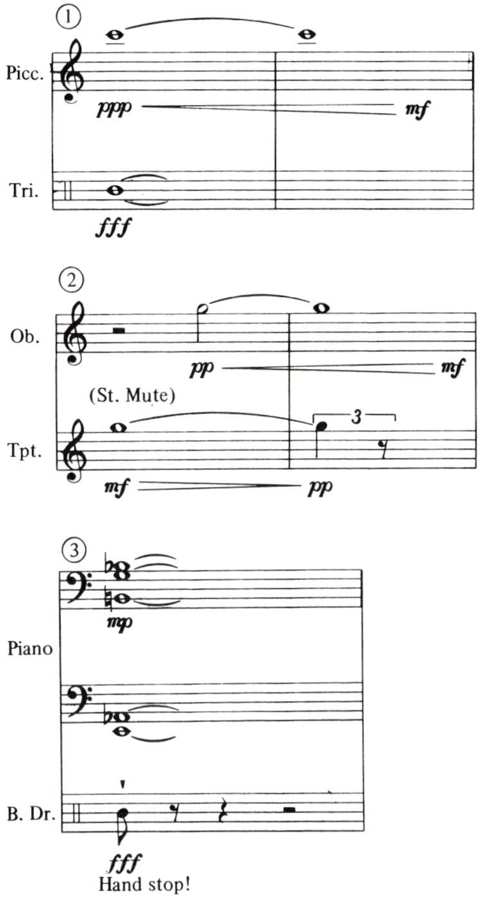

Figure 4.23. Timbre-modulations.

table: Gabrieli's eight- and twelve-part canzonas; Mozart's *Don Giovanni;* Berlioz's *Requiem;* Berg's *Wozzeck;* Mahler's *Das Klagende Lied;* and Ives's *Symphony #4. The Unanswered Question* (1908) for string orchestra, four flutes, and trumpet, isolated. Henry Brant's experiments with the vast potential of vertical, horizontal, and circular arrangements have suggested meaningful solutions to acoustic problems. In his "Space as an Essential Aspect of Musical Composition," Brant describes many of his successful experiments in performer arrangement for optimum directional, acoustical, and balance effectiveness.[12] The spatial composing technique of one of his examples (*Voyage Four,* 1964) involves percussion and brass on stage, violins on one side balcony, violas and 'cellos on the other, basses on floor level at the rear of the auditorium, with various woodwind instruments and a few string instruments on the two rear balconies. Three conductors combine to direct the performers (including tuba, timpani, and chimes in the audience). Brant contends that,

---

12. Elliot Schwartz and Barney Childs, eds., *Contemporary Composers on Contemporary Music* (New York: Holt, Rinehart, and Winston, 1967), pp. 223–42.

if the composer indeed intends to control his performance, each work should contain specific instructions for performer placement. Because every work is different in both structure and instrumentation, rehearsal experimentation is necessary for exact results, with no *right* schematic existing except in individual terms for each work or movement of a work.

Henry Brant discusses his views regarding spatial performance in an interview:

> The competition, from both living and dead composers, is too great for a solo piece; it's also too great for an ensemble that doesn't use spatial separation. What would I write? A string quartet? Besides, I think that particular combination is lopsided. For thirty years I've been trying to devise a rational string quartet; it should be one violin, one viola, one instrument that doesn't exist—a tenor violin, which I'm trying to develop—and 'cello.[13]

Brant's *An American Requiem* utilizes spatial location of six different widely separated instrumental groups and four separated single players including an optional voice. The primary ensemble is a group of sixteen woodwinds sitting on the stage in a semicircle with their backs to the audience (the conductor faces the group and the audience is at centerstage). The horn, trumpet, and trombone sections contrast the individual parts of the woodwinds with unison rhythmic materials and are situated in the hall. The fifth section is made of various bells (including "pipe-chimes," the construction of which is described loosely by the composer as three sets of seven pipes each set, a half inch or so different in diameter, with different pitches obtained by a two- or three-inch length differential). Two tubas join the brass in homorhythmic unison with single parts for pipe organ, voice, church bells (recorded on tape if necessary) and timpani.

An American Requiem is a long (15′) three-section work. The first section opens with the formative material of the work: a nine-note horizontal motive of a half-step cluster bordered on each end by whole steps. Each note of this line is paralleled in the same rhythm by eight other instruments forming a mirror of the horizontal material (i.e., a vertical cluster bordered on each end by whole steps). This kind of consistency of vocabulary between melodic and harmonic content continues throughout the work. Contrasting this dissonant idea in the winds is a static organ part of triadic content (C minor, B♭ minor, etc.) characteristic of both the first and third sections. The quasi-pitched pipe-chimes add a surrealistic touch to the multi-leveled music. The second main section develops the polyphony of the first with contrasting sectional flutters in the brass, trills in the percussion and the carillon in hemiola with the rest of the ensemble. The third main section returns to the organ triads and variations of the initial expository material.

---

13. Cole Cagne and Tracy Caras, *Soundpieces: Interviews with American Composers* (London: The Scarecrow Press, Inc., 1982), p. 61.

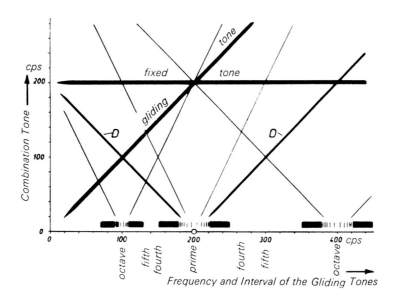

Figure 4.24. Combination tones.

Spatial modulation, aided largely by developments in timbre modulation, involves the active motion of a sound from one point to another. An extreme example of this would be a large number of violins surrounding the audience, the sound beginning with one violin then slowly moving with the same pitch to each violin in turn until the first was encountered again. Works by Henry Brant, Donald Erb (*Fanfare for Brass Ensemble and Percussion,* 1971), Cliff Crego (*Implosions,* 1971), and many others employ this technique.

Music also has elements called "combination tones." Figure 4.24 shows that when two tones, one fixed and the other gliding, occur simultaneously, combination tones result. Differential (difference frequency between two pitches) tones and summational (sum frequency of two pitches) represent the two basic types of combination tones.

Here the D signifies the primary difference tone, and the thickness of line, the acoustical impression of roughness (loudness). Composers such as Ligeti (e.g., *Lontano*) have attempted to create and control these elements in their music. Too often, however, variations in performance or acoustics cause distortion or unsuccessful production. These tones fall generally under discussions of psychoacoustics. The *Center for New Music and Audio Technologies* (CNMAT) founded at the University of California at Berkeley (1988) has been developed to investigate matters relating to this important aspect of the musical experience. Consortiums exist between CNMAT,

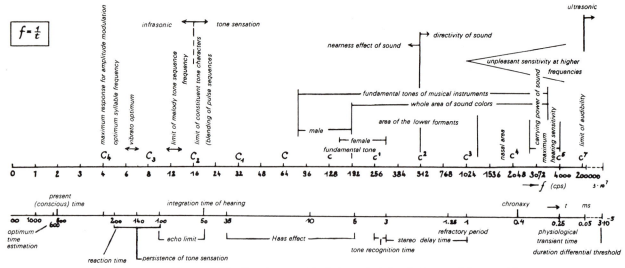

Figure 4.25. Psychoacoustical characteristics in terms of time and frequency. Permission granted by Dover Publications.

IRCAM (Institute for Research and Coordination of Acoustics/Music, a part of the Georges Pompidou Center in Paris) and Stanford's CCRMA (Center for Computer Research in Music and Acoustics). Since performance is indelibly tied to the hearing process, with timbre (especially) and time greatly influencing the manner in which communication takes place, knowledge of these areas seems especially important. Figure 4.25 shows psychoacoustical characteristics in time and frequency scale in rough limits of effectiveness.

Elliott Schwartz's *Elevator Music* (1967) employs the vast acoustical, directional, and movement possibilities which a multi-story building provides. Twelve floors of a building become the performing areas for twenty-four performers (stationary) while the audience rides an elevator up and down through the constantly-changing environment of sound. The small spaces around the elevators make for a leakage of sound between the floors, thus providing an overlay of sound materials. There is no distinct concept of twelve individual entities except when the conductor, who is also the elevator operator, stops at a certain floor and opens the elevator doors, while the performers on *all* floors continue to play regardless of elevator position. Dramatic change is available when the elevator stops at certain empty floors (empty in the sense of visual activity, but completely filled with sound due to the above-mentioned leakage from other floors), as explicitly outlined in the score.[14]

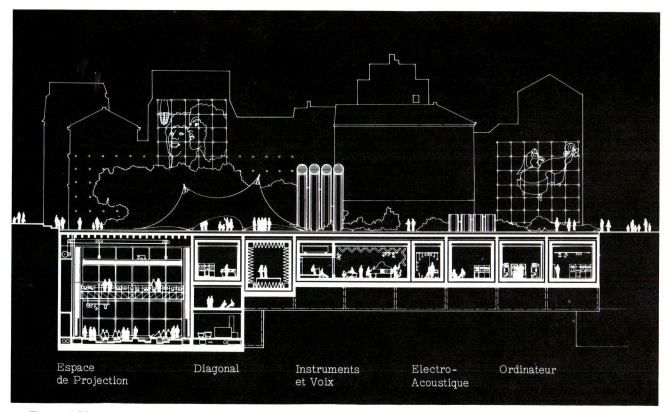

Espace de Projection   Diagonal   Instruments et Voix   Electro-Acoustique   Ordinateur

Figure 4.26. IRCAM installation.

Recording of this, as well as many of Brant's works, become virtually impossible, as the aspects of space, movement, direction, and theater are inherent in the structure of the works.

IRCAM has developed a number of experiments to discover the variety of ways in which sound can be explored in physical spaces. Figure 4.26 is a diagrammatic exposition of the entire IRCAM installation, with figure 4.27 a closer view of the *Espace de Projection,* a performance hall with variable acoustic properties. Figure 4.28 shows Pierre Boulez (director of the Center) and Gerard Buquet (tubist) in the space with the variable shutters and "flats" (controllable by computers). The Center also includes computer and electronic music facilities.

14. For a complete description and score of this work, see *Composer* 2, no. 2 (September 1970).

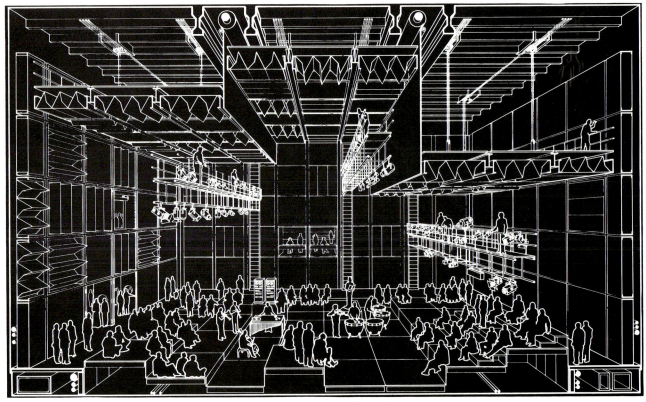

Figure 4.27. IRCAM *Espace de Projection.*

Figure 4.28. Pierre Boulez
with Gerard Buquet in
Espace de Projection.

Chapter 4

For centuries, composers of the mainstream Western-European traditions have borrowed both stylistic flavors and actual folk materials from music of world cultures. The list of works and composers is too long to mention here, but includes Franz Liszt (*Hungarian Rhapsodies*), Georges Bizet (*Carmen*), Edouard Lalo (*Symphonie Espagnole*), Mikhail Glinka (*Spanish Overtures*) and Rimsky-Korsakov (*Capriccio on Spanish Themes*). Notable mainstream composers of this century include Claude Debussy (see Chapter 1), Maurice Ravel (*Bolero*), Igor Stravinsky (use of Russian folk materials), Carlos Chavez (*Sinfonia India* using Indian and Mexican ideas), Heiter Villa-Lobos (*Bachianas Brasileiras*), and Silvestre Revueltas (*Cuauhnahuac* for orchestra, utilizing large numbers of Mexican and Indian musical materials).

Colin McPhee (1901–64) spent a great deal of time in the early 1930s researching and studying the music and instruments of Bali, particularly the Balinese *gamelans*. His style changed considerably as a result, and such works as *Tabuh-Tabuhan* (1936) show considerable influence of the *gamelan gong kebyar* (a 20–25-player ensemble and development of the older *gamelan gong*). McPhee translated the music of Bali into his own style and instrumentation (traditional Western orchestra). Alan Hovhaness (1911–   ) has been strongly influenced by the music of India as well as Armenia (as exemplified by *Avak, The Healer,* 1946, and *Khaldis,* 1951). Again it is the basic style that has influenced Hovhaness's work, rather than direct materials (quotation) or instrument usage. The works of Chou Wen-Chung (Chefoo, China, 1923–   ), particularly *Soliloquy of a Bhiksuni,* and Oliver Messiaen (1908–   ), with the use of Indian *talas* (repeating rhythmic patterns such as ♪ ♩ ♩. ♩. or ♪ ♩. ♩.) in his musical ideas, have been clearly influenced by non-Western world music.

A few contemporary composers employ the use of non-Western instruments in the ensembles for performance of their music. Lou Harrison (1917–   ) has created a wide variety of works utilizing *gamelan*-type (Javanese) instruments suggesting the *kempul, bonang, saron,* and *gender* of the Javanese *gamelan* as well as American folklike homemade ensembles of *gamelan*-like instruments. His *Pacifika Rondo* (1963) is for a chamber orchestra of Western and Asian instruments and *Concerto in Slendro* (1961) for violin, celesta, and percussion orchestra shows strong *gamelan* influence.

Non-Western Influences

Figure 4.29. Lou Harrison teaching at USC during 1978. Photo by Betty Freeman.

Figure 4.30. Lou Harrison and William Colvig. Photo shows a number of instruments built by either or both of these builder/composers. Photo by Betty Freeman.

Harry Partch's instruments (discussed earlier under "New Instruments") show strong influence of Hindu, African, and folk-American crossbreeding. John Cage's prepared piano works of the thirties and forties (particularly the *Sonatas and Interludes* of 1948) show influence of the *gamelan* orchestral style.

Quotation and stylistic embodiment of non-Western traditional music are evident in the works of David Cope (1941–   ). His work includes a great deal of Navajo Indian quotation and influence, particularly *Arena* (1974), *Rituals* (1976), and *The Way* (1981), a part of the score to the former appearing later in this text. Ruth Lomon's *Five Ceremonial Masks* for piano (1980) also show Navajo influence. David Ward-Steinman's (1936) *Rituals for Dancers and Musicians* and *The Tale of Issoumbochi,* Ravi Shankar's (1920–   ) *Concerto for Sitar and Orchestra,* Roy Travis's (1922–   ), *Switched-On Ashanti for Flutes, African Instruments, and Tape* (1933), and *African Sonata for Piano* (1966), are true assimilations of this type. David Fanshawe's (1942–   ) *African Sanctus* is a hybrid of Western and non-Western music.

The styles of some composers fully depend on and develop from non-Western sources. Terry Riley's (1935–   ) *In C* (1964), for example, compares to the *jor* section of an Indian *raga* (term derived from the Sanskrit root *ranja,* "to color, to tinge"). One hears the slow process of variation by textural overlay. Similarly, the works of Steve Reich (1936–   ), especially *Drumming* (1971) and *Four Organs* (1970), show Eastern influence, as does *Einstein on the Beach* by Philip Glass (1937–   ).

The "ritual" elements of some non-Western musics have influenced a number of *avant-garde* composers, including Pauline Oliveros (1932–   ), Jon Gibson (1940–   ), and Alvin Lucier (1931–   ). Each has developed works built on ritual-like elements often taken from Indian, Zen, or Asian concepts. Lucier's *Queen of the South* (1972) takes its title from the mystical personality in alchemy known as *Sapientia Dei* (connected with the south wind, an allegory for the Holy Ghost). The relationship between this work and certain ritual Navajo sand painting techniques is clear in this description of the performance:

> The performers sing into microphones or produce sound with oscillators. By means of electromagnetic transducers, large steel plates which are suspended horizontally near the floor are made to vibrate with these sounds. The vibrational patterns are made visible by sand and other granular materials which the performers sprinkle onto these plates. As they change the pitches of their sounds the granular images on the plates shift from one pattern to another. The performers, each with their own plate, are located throughout the performance space—ideally it is a gallery rather than a traditional proscenium theatre. The spectators move freely around these sonically and visually vibrating islands and choose their own degree of involvement with the ritual.[15]

15. Gordon Mumma, "Witchcraft, Cybersonics and Folkloric Virtuosity," *Darmstädter Beiträge zur Neue Musik,* 1974.

Vectoral Analysis:
Peter Maxwell Davies:
Eight Songs for a
Mad King

(For information on vectoral analysis and procedures see Chapter 1.)

1. Historial Background: Peter Maxwell Davies was born in Manchester, England, in 1934, and studied in England at the Royal College of Music and in America at Princeton University with R   Sessions. He was one of the founders of the Fires of London (*avant-garde* chamber ensemble; formerly the Pierrot Players), who are most noted for performing Davies' works. His music often includes quotations, new instruments, new techniques on traditional instruments, and a kind of stylistic heterophony. His better known works include *Miss Donnithorne's Maggot* (1974), *Vesalii Icones* (1970), and *Dark Angels* (1974), all for chamber ensembles of various makeup.

   In an interview with Paul Griffiths (from *New Sounds, New Personalities*), Davies remarks: "You can be thinking of something entirely different, and then you tune into a process that's going on somewhere. It might be a thematic idea, or a purely structural idea, with its main pivots: a big time span, with departure points and arrival points, but you don't know what's between them. I suspect that before you write down anything on paper, you've probably got, with a big work like a symphony, some small ideas and a big design. Then you start thinking through things in terms of the ideas going into the design, and then you start sketching. I'm not a perfectionist in the way that Boulez and Stockhausen are. Once a piece is done it's part of the past. . . ."

Figure 4.31. Peter Maxwell Davies. Photo by Keith McMillan. Permission by Boosey & Hawkes, Ltd., London.

2. Overview: *Eight Songs for a Mad King* was first peformed on April 22, 1969, in London by Roy Hart (vocals) and the Pierrot Players conducted by the composer. The eight songs are based on texts created by Randolph Stow (suggested by a miniature mechanical organ playing eight tunes, once the property of King George III).

One imagined the King, in his purple flannel dressing-gown and ermine night-cap, struggling to teach birds to make the music which he could so rarely torture out of his flute and harpsichord. Or trying to sing with them, in that ravaged voice, made almost inhuman by day-long soliloquies, which once murdered Handel for Fanny Burney's entertainment. There were echoes of the story of the Emperor's nightingale. But this Emperor was mad; and at times he knew it, and wept.[16]

Each of the songs has a separate indicative title, and the texts resemble old English. Notation is metri-portional (that is, at times the composer writes clear indications of meter and at others the bar-line disappears and a free, time-proportionate-to-space notation takes over).

The forms of each of the movements are similar in that none take the usual part-form (simple AB or ABA), but rather develop intrinsically with the text in organic manner. Humorous colorations of the text and exaggerated gestures in the music of textual ideas are profuse throughout the set of songs (these at times become so obvious and blatant that they tend to create a kind of reverse meaning).

3. Orchestration Techniques: Instrumentation for *Eight Songs* includes flute (doubling piccolo), clarinet, piano (doubling harpsichord and dulcimer), violin, violoncello, and a single percussionist. This latter performer plays twenty-five different instruments, including crow call, steel bars, toy bird calls, foot cymbals, railway whistle, Christmas-type jingle bells, chains, small rachet, etc. The voluminous number of instrumental effects throughout the score includes multiphonics (for voice, clarinet, and flute), tremolo (especially in the voice), use of inside-piano techniques, and vocal effects (breath only, glissandi, screams, harmonics, wide vibrato, etc.). Figure 4.32 shows a number of these effects and the notation used (in autograph score).

Here one can also see the proportional notation in use, notation for multiphonics (free), and the vertical lines that Davies uses to maintain simultaneous attacks.

Aside from unusual techniques and instruments, Davies also incorporates extreme ranges in all instruments, especially in the voice. In figure 4.32, for example, he uses 3½ octaves in the vocal part (eventually the range covers over five octaves).

16. Randolph Stow, Program notes from Introduction to the score.

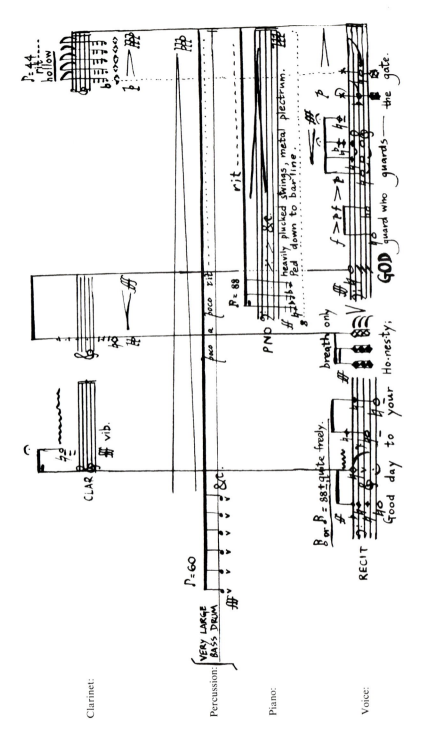

Figure 4.32. Peter Maxwell Davies. *Eight Songs for a Mad King.* Bottom system of page 2. Examples of instrument exploration. Permission granted by Boosey and Hawkes. All rights reserved.

Figure 4.33. David Cope performing *Eight Songs for a Mad King* by Peter Maxwell Davies.

The work also calls for four of the performers (on flute, clarinet, violin, and 'cello) to be placed in large cages on stage, adding an element of media presentation. Figure 4.33 shows a photograph of the author's own performance of this work (note the 'cellist in a large rope cage behind the "king").

Davies comments on the instrumental aspects of the piece:

The flute, clarinet, violin and cello, as well as having their usual accompanimental functions in this work, also represent on one level, the bullfinches the King was trying to teach to sing. . . . In some ways, I regard the work as a collection of musical objects borrowed from many sources, functioning as musical "stage props" around which the reciter's part weaves, lighting them from extraordinary angles, and throwing grotesque and distorted shadows from them, giving the musical objects an unexpected and sometimes sinister significance. . . . The climax of the work is the end of No. 7, where the King snatches the violin through the bars of the player's cage and breaks it. This is not just the killing of a bullfinch—it is a giving-in to insanity, and a ritual murder by the King of a part of himself, after which, at the beginning of 8, he can announce his own death.[17]

4. Basic Techniques: Davies utilizes a hybridization of various techniques embodied in a dramatic and contrasting set of songs. Neotonal (almost impressionistic at times) chromatic techniques contrast a fullbown tonality (created by association with one or more of the many quotes present in the work—particularly from Handel's *Messiah* and jazz inflections). Often the pitches chosen are so clouded by the harsh timbres as to be relatively meaningless. There is little doubt that Davies' consistent inconsistencies (i.e., constantly varying the basic techniques in use) are integral to his style.

17. Ibid.

Figure 4.34. Two vertical models from *8 Songs*.

A   B

5. Vertical Models: Aside from the quoted tonal material and the various "noise" sections where pitch is of litle consequence, the vertical sonorities seem based on a highly chromatic set of interval explorations (the fifth and the third) not unlike triadically based sonorities. Figure 4.34A shows a chord based primarily on different fifths (perfect, augmented, diminished), while Figure 4.34B is triadically centered (G major) with an added minor ninth (G♯).

6. Horizontal Models: As seen in figure 4.32, the vocal melody is characterized by wide leaps and elements of harsh dramatic multiphonics. Most of the nonquoted material irrevocably ties to the text and text meaning.

7. Style: In *Eight Songs for a Mad King,* Davies has created a dynamic and dramatic work fashioned around a mad king whose love/hate relationships with birds abounds. Characateristically, Davies creates a "mad" style replete with quotations, bird imitations, new instrumental techniques, flexible notations, extreme dynamic and timbral contrasts, chromatic yet somewhat triadically based harmonic systems, and word-painting (i.e., the music tends to imitate a word's sound or meaning). The results are a tight fabric of associative songs highly steeped in new instrumental techniques.

This work compares favorably with the Erb Vectoral Analysis presented in Chapter 8 and to some degree with the Glass opera *Einstein on the Beach* presented in Chapter 12. The quotation and free use of pitch in terms of style and chromatic content argue directly with the works in Chapters 2 and 10 where the music depends on rigorously prescribed rules of compositional structure and resource. Dramatic intent agrees favorably with the Penderecki example in the Vectoral Analysis of Chapter 3.

Anhalt, Istvan. *Alternative Voices: Essays on Contemporary Vocal and Choral Composition.* Toronto: The University of Toronto Press, 1984. An excellent (if limited in scope) text which covers recent (last 30 or so years) vocal music. Major drawback is its dependency on European examples with almost no American or other continent examples.

Backus, John. *The Acoustical Foundation of Music.* New York: W. W. Norton & Co., 1969. A must for those seeking expert knowledge in this area for spatial and timbre modulation.

Banek, Reinhold and Jon Scoville. *Sound Designs: A Handbook of Musical Instrument Building.* Berkeley: Ten Speed Press, 1980. An excellent resource for instrument design and specifications.

Bartolozzi, Bruno, *New Sounds for Woodwind.* London: Oxford University Press, 1967. Excellent source for new techniques on woodwind instruments.

Becker, John. "Finding a Personal Orchestral Idiom." *Musical America,* (February 1950). Much insight and subjective information from a man very much an innovator, especially in his use of percussion.

von Bekesy, Georg. "Musical Dynamics by Variation of Apparent Size of Sound Source." *Journal of Music Theory* 14, no. 1 (Winter, 1970):141. A fascinating study of traditional instruments and their acoustic variability in both psychological and spatial terms.

Boulanger, Richard. "Toward a New Age of Performance: Reading the *Book of Dreams* with the Mathews Electronic Violin." *Perspectives of New Music,* 24/2 (Spring-Summer, 1986) 130–152. An excellent description of performance on an electroacoustic (resonator-less) violin created by digital electronic pioneer Max Mathews.

Brant, Henry. "Space as an Essential Aspect of Musical Composition." In *Contemporary Composers on Comtemporary Music.* Edited by Elliott Schwartz and Barney Childs. New York: Holt, Rinehart and Winston, 1967.

Brindle, Reginald Smith. *Contemporary Percussion.* London: Oxford University Press, 1970. A superb book devoted to the growing aspects of this section of instruments. It also includes a rather complete and detailed account of special effects, visual symbology of percussion instruments and mallets, and special performing techniques along with many examples from current literature.

Bunger, Richard. *The Well-Prepared Piano.* Second Edition, Sebastopol, Calif.: Litoral Arts Press, 1981. Superb book dealing with the essentials and potentials of this ever-increasingly-used "instrument."

Chou Wen-Chung. "Asian Music and Western Composers." In *Dictionary of Contemporary Music.* Edited by John Vinton. New York: E. P. Dutton & Co., 1974. An important source for information on ties between Eastern and Western music.

Clough, Rosa Trillo. *Futurism.* New York: Philosophical Library, 1961. A good book which covers futurism in all of the arts. Excellent source of information on the beginnings of the Italian school and how its participants interacted with one another.

Cope, David. "Chronicles of a Cause." *The Composer* 1, no. 1 (June 1969). An interview with I. A. MacKenzie featuring his lucid though incredible accounts of his "sculptures."
———. "Modulations." *The Composer* 8, no. 1 (1977):25–30.

Cowell, Henry. *American Composers on American Music.* New York: Frederick Unger Publishing Co., 1933. Contains a brief but interesting article on Carlos Salzedo (p. 101).

*Addresses for record companies, periodicals, and music publishers mentioned in this Bibliography can be found in Appendix 4.

Bibliography

*Further Readings**

Cummings, Barton. *The Contemporary Tuba.* New London, CT: Whaling Music Publishers, 1984. A resource book for composers and performers. A great deal of new music is discussed in detail with many musical examples.

————. "A Brief Summary of New Techniques for Tuba." *Numus West* 5:62. A very good introduction to new sounds for this instrument in which interest is gaining rapidly among composers of new music.

Dempster, Stuart. *The Modern Trombone: A Definition of its Idiom.* Berkeley: University of California Press, 1980.

Erickson, Robert. *Sound Structure in Music.* Berkeley: University of California Press, 1975. A superb book whose title is a bit misleading in that it deals with timbre and texture primarily in new and *avant-garde* music. Highly recommended reading.

Experimental Music Instruments, P.O. Box 423, Point Reyes Station, CA 94956. (Periodical).

Finkenbeinger, Gerhard and Vera Meyer. "The Glass Harmonica: A Return from Obscurity." *Leonardo* 20, no. 2 (1987): 139–42. A history and prospectus of future use of glass instrument building.

Forsyth, Michael. *Buildings for Music.* Cambridge, MA: MIT Press, 1985.

Garland, Peter. *Americas: Essays on American Music and Culture, 1973–80.* Santa Fe, NM: Soundings Press, 1982. Excellent chapters on Henry Cowell, Harry Partch and Lou Harrison. Conlon Nancarrow also receives significant coverage here.

Goldstein, Malcolm. "Texture." In *Dictionary of Contemporary Music,* edited by John Vinton (New York: E. P. Dutton & Co., 1974.) A fine study of works in depth, often with concentration on both timbre and spatial modulation, though they are not so designated.

Griffiths, Paul. *New Sounds, New Personalities, British Composers of the 1980s in Conversation.* London: Faber Music Ltd., 1985. The Peter Maxwell Davies interview is particularly rewarding.

Heiss, John C. "For the Flute: A List of Double-stops, Triple-stops, Quadruple-stops and Shakes." *Perspectives of New Music* 5, no. 1:189.

————. "Some Multiple Sonorities for Flute, Oboe, Clarinet and Bassoon." *Perspectives of New Music* 7, no. 1 (Fall-Winter, 1968):136.

Howell, Thomas. *The Avant-Garde Flute.* Berkeley: The University of California Press, 1974. An excellent book containing the fingerings for an incredible number of multiphonics. Along with the Turetzky and Rehfeldt books mentioned later, it is the beginning of a most important series of books on new techniques for every orchestral instrument.

The Instrumentalist vol. 28, no. 10 (May 1974). Entire issue dedicated to new directions in instrumental music. Articles feature: strings, by Pat Strange; woodwinds, by Frank McCarty; percussion, by Dennis Kahle; band music, by Larry Livingston; and electronics, by Allen Strange.

Johnston, Ben. "Harry Partch." In *Dictionary of Contemporary Music.* Edited by John Vinton. New York: E. P. Dutton & Co., 1974. Exceptional article; a useful tool in understanding this man and his personal instruments.

Junger, Miguel and David Feit, eds. *Sound, Structures and Their Interaction.* Cambridge, MA: MIT Press, 1986.

Kaufman, Harald. "Ligeti's Zweites Streichquartet." *Melos* 37 (1970):391. A good study of Ligeti's techniques.

Kostelanetz, Richard. *John Cage.* New York: Praeger Publishers, 1968. An excellent source of information of all kinds about this revolutionary figure, especially on his piano preparation techniques and his ideas about new instrumental techniques in general.

Livingston, Larry, and Frank McCarty. "Expanding Woodwind Sound Potential." *The Composer* 3, no. 1 (1971):39. A good broad introduction to the area of using woodwind instruments for new sounds.

Moore, Janet. *Understanding Music through Sound Exploration and Experiments*. New York: University Press of America, 1986.

Musical America vol. 24, no. 4 (April 1974). Contains an interesting article on Jan De Gaetani, one of the most important of avant-garde singers (p. MA-6).

Palm, Siegfried. "Notation for String Instruments." *The Composer* 3, no. 2 (1972):63. A very good cross section of effects in current use for string instruments.

Partch, Harry. "And On the Seventh Day Petals Fell in Petaluma." *Source* 2, no. 1 (January 1968). Includes description of instruments and score.

———. *Genesis of a New Music*. New York: Da Capo Press, 1977. (Reprint of 1949 Edition).

Payton, Rodney J. "The Music of Futurism: Concerts and Polemics." *The Musical Quarterly* 62 no. 1 (January, 1976):25–45. An excellent but all too brief analysis of the futurist movement in Italy and elsewhere (particularly Russolo).

Pooler, Frank and Brent Pierce. *New Choral Notation*. New York: Walton Music, 1973. Fascinating source of various examples of new techniques for writing for the voice.

Read, Gardner. *Thesaurus of Orchestral Devices*. London: Sir Isaac Pitman & Sons, 1953. Huge and extremely useful volume.

———. *Contemporary Instrumental Techniques*. New York: Schirmer Books, 1976.

Reck, David. *Music of the Whole Earth*. New York: Charles Scribner's Sons, 1977. A great source for instruments and instrumental techniques of non-Western tradition music.

Reed, H. Owen, and Joel T. Leach. *Scoring for Percussion*. New York: Prentice-Hall, 1969.

Rehfeldt, Phillip. "Clarinet Resources and Performance." *Procedures* 7, no. 8 (1974). Fine article on multiphonics and other aspects of new clarinet performance.

———. *New Directions for Clarinet*. Berkeley: University of California Press, 1977. Another in the UC series of fine books on new instrumental techniques for the orchestral instruments written by a master performer of new music.

Robson, Ernest. "Research of the Sounds of Literature: Formant Music and a Prosodic Notation for Performance." *Leonardo* 20, no. 2 (1987):131–38. The author creates "whisper music" through novel approaches to literature. "Formant music," discovered by the author in 1940, refers to the frequency band of vowels and diphthongs and their resonant energy levels.

Rossi, Nick, and Robert Choate. *Music of Our Time*. Boston: Crescendo Publishing Co., 1969. Contains two excellent sections on personages involved with instrument exploration: Edgard Varèse (p. 220) and Henry Cowell (p. 339).

Salzedo, Carlos. "Considerations on the Piano and the Harp." *Harp News* vol. 3, no. 4 (Fall 1961). A fascinating article which originally appeared in 1923. The issue of *Harp News* cited here is dedicated to the memory of this innovative genius, and is well worth studying.

———. *Modern Study of the Harp*. New York: G. Schirmer, 1921.

———. *Method for the Harp*. New York: G. Schirmer, 1929. With the above, a classic in new techniques for this instrument which seem far in advance of their time.

Schafer, R. Murray, ed. *Ezra Pound and Music, The Complete Criticism*. New York: New Directions Books, 1977. An excellent compendium of writings by Pound on music. Pound writing on Antheil has a serious ring of truth to it. His choice of words (as a poet's must) mirrors the composer's cluster "slabs."

Schuller, Gunther. "Conversation with Varèse." *Perspectives of New Music,* 3, no. 2:32 and idem, "American Performance and New Music," Ibid. 1, no. 2:1. Two general but very good articles.

Schwartz, Elliott. "Elevator Music." *The Composer* 2, no. 2 (1970):49.

Silber, John. "Writing." *Perspectives of New Music,* Spring–Summer, 1981, pp. 135–183. Excellent examples of new instruments at U.C.S.D. (photos, *et al.*)

Slawson, Wayne. *Sound Color.* Berkeley: University of California Press, 1985. Excellent resource which covers a wide diversity of theories about sonic color perception. The sections on psychoacoustics and speech are particularly notable.

Smith, Jeff. "The Partch Reverberations: Notes on a Musical Rebel." *Soundings* 12 (1982): 46–59. An all too brief biography of this iconoclastic composer. It also speaks to the current (1982) varying conditions of the Partch instruments—for many, a difficult section to endure.

Soundings 2 (April 1972). Half the issue is devoted to Harry Partch and his work, and includes a brief biographical sketch, the score to *Barstow,* and a short article by Partch, "A Somewhat Spoof."

Source: Music of the Avant Garde (Davis, California). Included numerous articles and descriptions of new instruments. See especially Robert Erickson in vol. 3, no. 1 (January 1969), and Harry Partch in vol. 2, no. 1 (January 1968).

Steinberg, Michael. "Some Observations on the Harpsichord in Twentieth Century Music." *Perspectives of New Music* 1, no. 2:189. A good introduction to this instrument's potential.

Turetzky, Bertram. "The Bass as a Drum," *The Composer* 1, no. 2 and "A Technique of Contemporary Writing for the Contrabass," ibid. 1, no. 3.

———. *The Contemporary Contrabass.* Berkeley: University of California Press, 1974. Superb book dealing with this man's original work on his instrument, as well as the many works written for him. Contains chapters covering almost every conceivable aspect of the new techniques for this instrument.

Verkoeyen, Jos. "String Players and New Music," *Sonorum Speculum* 45 (Winter 1970). Short but interesting look into this subject.

Vinton, John, ed. *Dictionary of Contemporary Music.* New York: E. P. Dutton & Co., 1974. Contains numerous articles pertinent to the subject matter of this chapter, including contributions by William Brooks (s.v. "Instrumental and Vocal Resources"), and Henry Brant (s.v. "Orchestration").

Winckel, Fritz. *Music, Sound and Sensation.* New York: Dover Publications, 1967. This is an English translation of a 1960s book called *Phanomene des musikalischen Horens.* An impressive book with a storehouse of charts and diagrams attempting to sound in time and space from an early model of cognitive science.

Yates, Peter. "Lou Harrison." *ACA Bulletin* 9, no. 2:2. Provides a good bibliography of his works, especially those for percussion orchestra.

Recordings and Publishers

Albright, William, *Organbook* (1967). Jobert. Recorded on CRI S-277.

Anderson, Laurie. *Mr. Heartbreak.* Recorded on Warners Records 25077. Anderson uses rock music instruments in her own political and gestural compositional techniques. Her work constantly points out the relation between choice of instrument and musical style.

Antheil, George. *Ballet mécanique* (1924). Templeton.

———. *Sonatas* (3). Weintraub. Recorded on Orion 73119.

———. *Symphony No. 4* (1942). Recorded on Everest 3013.

———. *Transatlantic* (1929). Universal Edition. A most interesting and unusual Antheil opera.

Austin, Larry. *The Maze* (1965). CPE-*Source*. For three percussionists, tape, and projection; performers move from one group of instruments to another.

Bamert, Matthias. *Septuria Lunaris*. Recorded on London S-725. Very effective use of mass orchestral effects.

Becker, John. *Abongo* (1933). Autograph Editions. For percussion orchestra, two solo dancers, dance group.

Berio, Luciano. *Sinfonia*. Universal Edition. Recorded on Columbia MS-7268.

Blank, Allan. *Esther's Monologue*. Recorded on Orion ORS-75169.

Brant, Henry. *An American Requiem* (1973). Henmar Press (Peters).

———. *Angels and Devils* (1932). CD: Centaur; CRC-2014.

———. *Fourth Millennium* (1963). MCA. Recorded on Nonesuch 71222. For brass quintet.

———. *Hieroglyphics* 3 (1957). MCA. Recorded on CRI S-260. For chamber group.

———. *Voyage Four* (1963). MCA. For three orchestral groups.

———. *Music 1970* (1970) MCA. Recorded on Desto 7108.

———. *Verticals Ascending*. MCA. Recorded on New World 211.

Cage, John. *Amores*. C. F. Peters. Recorded on Mainstream 5011.

———. *Bacchanale*. C. F. Peters. Recorded on Columbia M2S-819.

———. *Concerto for Prepared Piano and Chamber Orchestra* (1951). C. F. Peters. Recorded on Nonesuch 71202.

———. *Perilous Night, Suite for Prepared Piano*. C. F. Peters. Recorded on Avant 1008.

———. *Sonatas and Interludes* (1948). C. F. Peters. Recorded on Columbia M2S-819. CD: DENON; CD-7673.

Celli, Joseph. *Organic Oboe*. Recorded on Organic Oboe records O. O. #1. A collection of performances by this master of new oboe techniques, including Stockhausen's *Spiral* and a spectacular performance of Malcolm Goldstein's *A Summoning of Focus*.

Chavez, Carlos. *Toccata for Percussion* (1942). Mills Music. Recorded on Columbia CMS-6447. A standard for the literature.

Chihara, Paul. *Logs* and other works. Recorded on CRI S-269. Use of subtle effects.

Childs, Barney. *Mr. T. His Fancy*. CPE-*Source*.

Chou Wen-Chung. *The Willows Are New* (1957). Published by C. F. Peters. Recorded on CRI 251SD.

Cope, David. *Iceberg Meadow* (1969). Carl Fischer. Recorded on Capra 1210. Use of partially prepared piano.

———. *Margins* (1972). Carl Fischer. Recorded on Orion ORS-75169.

———. *Rituals*. Recorded on Folkways 33869. (For 'cello, percussion, and voice, one performer). Score available from the composer.

———. *The Way* (1981). Recorded on Opus One Records 82. Score available from the composer.

Cowell, Henry. *The Banshee* (1925). AMP. Recorded on Folkways FX6160.

Crumb, George. *Ancient Voices of Children*. C. F. Peters. Recorded on Nonesuch 71255.

———. *Songs, Drones, and Refrains of Death*. C. F. Peters, Recorded on Desto 7155.

———. *Black Angels* (1970). Peters. Recorded on CRI S-283. For amplified string quartet.

Crystal Rainbows: The Sounds of Harmonious Craft. Recorded on Sounds Reasonable SR 7801. Album produced by Jim Harman and William Penn, and includes a number of new and folk instruments (noteworthy: a steel 'cello).

Curtis-Smith, Curtis. *Rhapsodies*. Paris: Editions Salabert. Recorded on CRI S-345. A masterwork for "bowed piano."

Dahl, Ingolf. *Concerto for Saxophone* (1949). MCA. Recorded on Brewster 1203. Brilliant work by a master craftsman.

Davies, Peter Maxwell, *Dark Angels*. Boosey and Hawkes. Recorded on Nonesuch 71342.

———. *Eight Songs for a Mad King.* Boosey and Hawkes. Recorded on Nonesuch 71285.

———. *Vesalii Icones*. Boosey and Hawkes. Recorded on Nonesuch 71295.

Davies, Peter Maxwell. *Voices* (1973). Schott. Recorded on Decca HEAD 5.

Dlugoszewski, Lucia. *Space is a Diamond* (1970). Recorded on Nonesuch 71275. For trumpet and piano.

Druckman, Jacob. *Incenters* (1968). MCA Music. Recorded on Nonesuch 71221.

Erb, Donald. *Fanfare for Brass and Percussion*. Merion Music. Instrumentalists scattered on stage, balcony, etc., for spatial effects.

———. *The Seventh Trumpet* (1969). Merion Music. Recorded on Turnabout 34433. Interesting use of rapping, and tapping, effects from orchestra.

Fanshawe, David. *African Sanctus*. Recorded on Phillips 6558001.

Folkways Records. This company puts out many non-Western musics. Of special interest are:

> 4273 Polynesian Songs
> 4380 Songs of Assam, Uttan, Pradesh and the Andamans—India
> 4401 Music of the Sioux and the Navajo
> 4427 Folk music of the Congo
> 4537AB-CD Music of Indonesia (2 vols.).

Foss, Lukas, *Elytres* (1964). Fischer and Schott. Recorded on Turnabout 34514. For flute, violin, piano, harp, and percussion.

Gaburo, Kenneth. *Lingua II: Maledetto*. Recorded on CRI 316-SD. Composition for 7 virtuoso speakers—important vocal effects.

Gamelan Son of Lion. *Gamelan in the New World*. Recorded on Folkways 31313 with a sister album on Folkways 31312 (Volume 2). Barbara Benary, Daniel Goode and Peter Griggs perform Indonesian-based music on self-constructed instruments. The result is an effective hybrid of East and West influences.

Glass, Philip. *North Star*. Recorded on Virgin PZ-34669.

Globokar, Vinko. *Discours 11* for solo trombone. C. F. Peters. Recorded on DG 137005.

Green, George. *Perihelion for Concert Band* (1974). Recorded by Cornell University Wind Ensemble, Record No. 15.

Harrison, Lou. *Canticle No. 1 for Percussion* (1940). Recorded by Mainstream 5011.

———. *Pacifika Rondo*. Recorded on Desto 6478.

———. *Concert in Slendro*. C. F. Peters. Recorded on Desto 7144.

Haubenstock-Ramati, Roman. *Interpolations: a "Mobile" for Flute* (1, 2, 3), (1958). Universal Edition. Recorded on RCA VICS-1312.

———. *Tableau 1* (1967). Universal Edition. Recorded on Wergo 60049.

Henze, Hans Werner. *Versuch über Schweine*. Schott. Recorded on DG 139456.

Hodkinson, Sydney. *Imagined Quarter* (1967). BMIC.

Holliger, Heinz. *Atembogen* (1975). Mainz: B. Schott's Söhne.

Hovhaness, Alan. *Avak: The Healer*. C. F. Peters. Recorded on Louisville 735.

———. *Khaldis,* op. 91. C. F. Peters. Recorded on Poseidon 1011.

Husa, Karel. *Apotheosis of this Earth* (1971). AMP. Recorded on Golden Crest 4134.

Inuit Throat and Harp Songs. Recorded on Canadian Music Heritage WRC-1-1349. Inuit Eskimo women shout into each other's throats to create music. Located along the shores of the Hudson Bay in Canada, this culture creates most interesting music by using the human body as a resonator.

Johnson, Tom. *Nine Bells.* Recorded on India Navigation 3023. Johnson uses nine alarm bells striking each as he passes through a series of rhythmic excursions. A good example of "found" instruments composition.

Johnston, Ben. *Knocking Piece.* CPE-*Source.* Unconventional use of piano, with knocking on lid, sides, etc., and avoidance of keyboard.

Khan, Ali Akbar. *Pre-Dawn to Sunrise Ragas* (1967). Recorded on Connoisseur Society CS-1967. An extraordinary album consisting of two ragas performed before dawn: the *Bairagi* and *Aheer Bhairow.*

Korte, Karl. *Matrix.* Recorded on CRI S-249. For woodwind quintet.

Kraft, William. *Triangles,* a concerto for percussion, ten instruments (1968). MCA. Recorded on Crystal S104. Very effective use of percussion by a professional percussionist/composer.

Kupferman, Meyer. *Infinities 22* for trumpet and piano. General Music. Recorded on Serenus 12000. Part of a cycle of infinities, all based on the same twelve-tone row.

Leedy, Douglas. *Usable Music I.* CPE-*Source.*

Ligeti, György. *Aventures* (1962). C. F. Peters. Recorded on Candide 31009.

———. *Atmospheres* (1961). Universal Edition. Recorded on Wergo 305.

———. *Lontano* (1967). Schott. Recorded on Wergo 322.

Lomon, Ruth. *Five Ceremonial Masks.* Published by Arsis Press. Recorded on Coronet LPS3121.

Mayuzumi, Toshiro. *Concerto for Percussion.* C.F. Peters. Recorded on Point 101.

McPhee, Colin. *Tabuh-Tabuhan* (1936). AMP. Recorded on Mercury MG 50103.

Messiaen, Oliver. *Oiseaux Exotiques* (1955). Universal Edition. Recorded on Candide 31002.

Meytuss, Julius. *Dnieper Dam.* Recorded on Folkways FX 6160.

Moran, Robert. *Titus.* CPE-*Source.*

Moryl, Richard. *Chroma for Chamber Ensemble* (1972). Recorded on Desto 7143.

Mossolov, Alexander. *Steel Foundry* (1928). Recorded on Folkways FX 6160.

Nancarrow, Conlon. *Studies for Player Piano.* (Published partially in traditional notation by *Soundings.* Book 4. 1977. #1, "Rhythm Study", was published in *New Music Quarterly,* in October, 1951). The complete studies have been released by 1750 Arch Street Records, with 2 volumes out to this date (S-1768 and S-1777).

Nørgård, Per. *Waves* for percussion. Wilhelm Hansen. Recorded on Cambridge 2824.

Other Music. *Prime Numbers.* Recorded on Other Music OMJ14. This group makes its own instruments and performs them masterfully. Their work also shows Indonesian influences.

Partch, Harry. *Daphne of the Dunes* (1958). Recorded on Columbia MQ-31227, which includes other works as well, e.g., *Barstow,* which is published in *Soundings* 2. Features his own unique instruments.

———. *Delusion of the Fury.* Recorded on Columbia M2-30576. Album also contains a color booklet showing a large number of Partch's instruments.

———. *And on the Seventh Day Petals Fell in Petaluma.* CPE-Source. Recorded on CRI S-213.

Pellman, Samuel. *Silent Night.* Published by Alexander Broude Publishers. An amazing virtuoso work for fully prepared piano; a classic of the genre. Similarly the composer's *Dynamic Study* utilizes inner piano techniques in a fully *pianistic* manner.

Penderecki, Krzysztof. *De Natura Sonoris,* for orchestra (1966). Moeck. Recorded on Nonesuch 71201.

———. *Threnody for the Victims of Hiroshima.* PWM. Recorded on RCA VICS-1239. Extraordinary special effects.

Reich, Steve. *Drumming.* Recorded on DG 2740106.

———. *Four Organs.* Recorded on Angel S136059.

Reynolds, Roger. *Ping.* CPE-*Source.* Recorded on CRI S-285.

———. *Quick are the Mouths of the Earth.* C. F. Peters. Recorded on Nonesuch 71219.

Riley, Terry. *In C.* Published and recorded on Columbia MS-7178.

Salzedo, Carlos. *Chanson dans la Nuit.* Recorded on DG 139419. Not so much a composer as a master genius of invention.

Sampson, Peggy. *The Contemporary Viola da Gamba.* Music Gallery Editions. Canada. MGE 7. Fascinating new works for this Renaissance instrument.

Scavarda, Donald. *Matrix.* Published by Lingua Press. Recorded on Advance Records FGR-4.

Schoenberg, Arnold. *Five Pieces for Orchestra* (1909). C. F. Peters. Recorded on Columbia M2S-709 and Mercury. A masterpiece of orchestration.

Schubel, Max. *Insected Surfaces,* a concerto for five instruments (1966). Recorded on Opus One S-1.

Schuller, Gunther. *Seven Studies on Themes of Paul Klee.* Universal Edition. Recorded on RCA LSC-2879.

Scott, Stephen. *New Music for Bowed Piano.* Recorded on New Albion NAL-004. Examples of Scott's unique miniature bows on piano strings.

Shankar, Ravi. *Concerto for Sitar and Orchestra.* Recorded on Angel S-36806.

Smith, William O. *Five Pieces for Clarinet Alone* (1959). Recorded on Crystal Records 332.

Stockhausen, Karlheinz, *Zyklus* (1950). Universal Edition. Recorded on Mainstream 5003. For one percussionist.

———. *Gruppen.* Universal Edition. Recorded on DG-137002. For three orchestras which surround the audience.

Sydeman, William. *Texture Studies for Orchestra.* Okra Music.

Travis, Roy. *African Sonata* (for piano). Recorded on Orion 73121.

———. *Switched-on Ashanti* (1973). Orion 73121.

Varèse, Edgard. *Hyperprism.* G. Schirmer. Recorded on Candide 31028 and Columbia MS-31078.

———. *Ionisation* (1933). G. Schirmer. Recorded on Columbia MS-6146. One of the first full percussion orchestra works.

———. *Intégrales* (1925). G. Schirmer. Recorded on London 6752.

Villa-Lobos, Heitor, *Danses Africaines.* Recorded on Louisville LS-69 5.

Wada, Yoshi. *Lament for the Rise and Fall of the Elephantine Crocodile.* Recorded on India Navigation IN-3025. Uses homemade bagpipes.

———. *Off the Wall.* Recorded on Free Music FMP-SAJ-49. Wade employs reed organ and percussion creating slow moving experiments in overtones, combination tones, and differential tones.

Whittenberg, Charles. *Games of Five for Woodwind Quintet.* Joshua Publishers. Recorded on Advance 11 and Serenus 12028.

Xenakis, Iannis. *Metastasis* (1954). Boosey & Hawkes. Recorded on Vanguard C-10030.

INDETERMINACY

5

William Hayes's *The Art of Composing Music by a Method Entirely New, Suited to the Meanest Capacity* (1751) describes a technique of composition using notes spattered onto staff paper by running a finger over a stiff brush dipped in ink. Mozart used dice-throwing to create music (*Musical Dice Game,* K. 294d). Other such indeterminate techniques have been attempted, even as early as the eleventh and twelfth centuries, but none with the vigor and philosophical implications of endeavors since the late 1940s.

Figure 5.1 is the full score to Paul Ignace's *It Is* (1946). There are no performance instructions for interpretation as a musical composition. Obviously two performances of *It Is* could vary to extreme degrees in instrumentation and harmonic simultaneity. However, without prior knowledge of the composer's procedure or visual access to the score, the audience can make no real decisions concerning determinacy or indeterminacy. Earle Brown's later *December 1952* is similar in nature, but more visually musical in that its short vertical and horizontal bursts of lines of varying thicknesses more easily ignite some form of rhythmic, dynamic, and pitch realization.

Beginning in the early fifties an affinity for chance techniques was developed with the *I Ching*. Christian Wolff had brought the English translation to John Cage's attention at that time (his father Kurt Wolff being founder of the publishing house, Pantheon Press, which published it). The *I Ching,* the first written book of wisdom, philosophy, and oracle (attributed to Fu Hsi, 2953–2838 B.C.), expresses directions of action as a result of six tosses of three coins (originally, the tossing of yarrow sticks). The example in Figure 5.2 shows all combinations of—and—with six tosses (heads = 2, tails = 3: the addition of points, if 2, giving—, if3—). Having asked the question, "Should I use an example of the *I Ching* in this book?" and performing the required tosses, the author received the following answer as a result: "Kun (indicates that in the case which it presupposes) there will be great progress and success, and the advantage will come from being correct and firm. (But) any movement in advance should not be (lightly) undertaken."

A Brief History of Indeterminacy

Figure 5.1. Paul Ignace: *It Is* (full score).

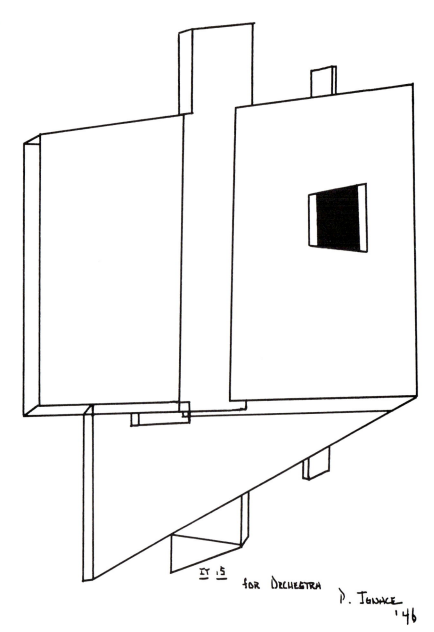

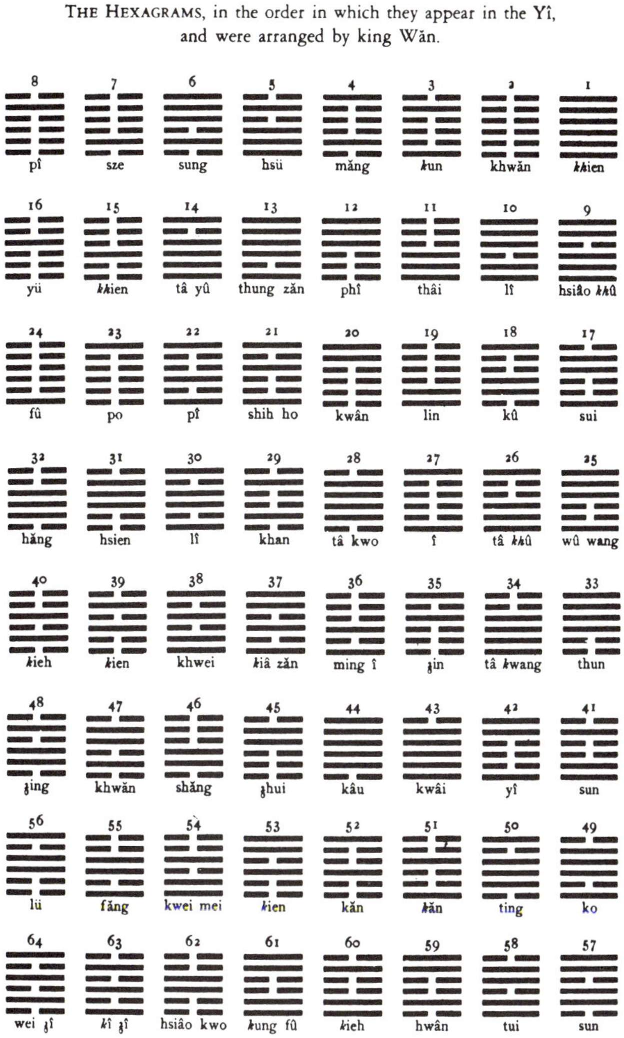

THE HEXAGRAMS, in the order in which they appear in the Yî,
and were arranged by king Wăn.

Figure 5.2. The Hexagrams from *I Ching*. (Permission for reprint granted by University Books, Inc., New Hyde Park, New York 11040. Copyright 1964.)

The Role of Improvisation

One major precursor of musical indeterminacy may be improvisation. The Baroque figured bass and classical concerto cadenzas are two predominant examples of improvisation in traditional music. The figured bass provides only the bass notes and the intervals above them in terms of short-hand numbers below the note, allowing the performer the creative possibility of improvising and developing rhythmic and melodic fragments and motives. The outcome, therefore, was predictable only within certain limits. Cadenzas, up to the late eighteenth century, were very rarely written out in detail, giving each performer a chance to "show off" in the manner best suited to his/her own particular talents (merely suggesting motives and harmonic relevance to the movement or the work as a whole). Donald Erb refers to the latter in remarks about his own *Concerto for Percussion and Orchestra* (1966):

> The work is cast in the traditional concerto format of three movements. The solo part is in the eighteenth and nineteenth century virtuoso tradition. The cadenzas in the second and, especially, the third movements harken back to the eighteenth century tradition of having the performer improvise much or all of the cadenza. A variation on this idea was used in the first movement, where instead of having the soloist improvise a cadenza I had the entire orchestra, other than the soloist, improvise it.[1]

As with the Erb *Concerto* it would seem logical for the composer, rather than refusing to admit the existence of (or making as insignificant as possible) the necessary improvisational aspects of music, to use it to both his/her own and the performer's advantage.

The emphasis in improvisation is more *creative* than *re-creative*. Audiences are often content to quibble over inadequacies in performances of music its hundredth time around. With improvisation they can experience music for the first time, and possibly the last.

Allan Bryant states that improvisation is "Similar to free jazz, oriental and African music, things which are impossible to write out"[2] and "Free, wild music and ideas that wouldn't come about with single composers working alone."[3] Foss adds: "Cardew is right to worry about ethics of improvisation. It needs it. *Improvisation:* one plays what one already knows."[4]

The circumstances under which more recent improvisation developed are less clear. Interest in this century may be rooted in jazz with such artists as Miles Davis (*Bitch's Brew* and beyond), the Modern Jazz Quartet, John Coltrane, Albert Ayler, Denny Zeitlin, Pharoah Sanders, Coleman Hawkins, Django Rheinhardt, and Lenny Tristano, to name just a few.

A major work in *avant-garde* improvisational jazz is "Free Jazz," a 36½-minute uninterrupted "anthem" with Ornette Coleman (plastic alto saxophone) and Don Cherry (pocket trumpet). Eric Dolphy (bass clarinet), Freddie Hubbard (trumpet), Scott LaFaro (bass), Charlie Haden (bass), Billy Higgins and Ed Blackwell (drummers) also contributed to this extraordinary landmark of the jazz avant-garde. Cecil Taylor (first with Steve Lacy and Buell Neidlinger, later with Bill Barron and Ted Curson) was also an important pioneer. His keyboard skills and intense energy created imaginative improvisations. More recently George Lewis, Anthony Braxton, Sun Ra and the Art Ensemble of Chicago all have richly improvised performances and albums.

---

1. Liner notes of the recording: Turnabout TV-S 34433 by the composer. Taken from the program notes of the first performance in 1966.
2. As quoted in "Groups," *Source: Music of the Avant-Garde,* 2, no. 1 (January 1968).
3. Ibid., p. 24.
4. Ibid., p. 17.

A number of contemporary composers associated with improvisation are or were actively involved in jazz (particularly third-stream composers such as Gunther Schuller). It is more plausible, however, that *contemporary* improvisation sprang from the performers' inability to realize accurately the complexities of recent music; the composer, perhaps out of frustration, perhaps because the result was the same (or better), chose to allow a certain freedom in performance. Luciano Berio, for example, in his *Tempi Concertati,* requires the percussionist to hit everything as fast as possible; exact notation would be impractical or even impossible. The effect is generally predictable and effective even without a notated pitch or rhythm.

Some composers disagree that improvisation and indeterminacy share common roots. Speaking to this point William Hellermann clearly defines that distinction:

> It seems to me that there is a fundamental difference between aleatoric and improvisational music. Improvisation is concerned with the realization in real time of defined artistic goals. Aleatory, by its very nature, does not recognize the existence of goals. Both differ from the traditional "classic music" by leaving open to the performer the choice of the specific materials to be used in the piece. They are often lumped together for this reason and, also, because they are both thought to be "free." Actually, freedom is not really the issue. Improvisation, at its highest, seeks meaning through spontaneity. Aleatory declares meaning to be spontaneity. Both of these are very restrictive states. I find that in my own works I am increasingly concerned with improvisation, and never with anything I would call aleatory.[5]

One basic factor in improvisation is that the composer has relinquished some control over musical events to the performer. However, this is done with the full belief that the performer will play with learned skills and an integrity of context and style. In summary, the *reasons* that most composers employ improvisation are:

1. Many composers (as well as performers and listeners) suggest that simply realizing notes from the printed page results in generally strained and somewhat uncreative results. Each performance is predictable and thus not as interesting as a certain amount of flexibility might make it. The "live" and fresh aspect of improvisation can provide a unique performance each time a work is played.

2. In contemporary music, improvisation often results in rhythms and patterns that would paralyze the performer if completely written out. One can note this particularly in certain jazz music, where the subtle and refined improvisatory character of syncopations before and after the beat make full and exact notation a near impossibility. Even if it were possible, would it be performable in that state and, most important, would it have the same kind of fresh musical quality that it does when improvised?

3. Many contemporary composers feel that since improvisation exists in all music to one degree or another, it is only a small step to allowing more freedom with rewards far exceeding risks.

5. Tom Everett, "Questions and Answers," *Composer* 2, no. 4 (March 1971):82.

Figure 5.3. Lukas Foss, Music Director and Conductor, The Brooklyn Philharmonic Orchestra. Photo permission by Carnegie Hall, 154 W. 57th St., New York, N.Y. 10019.

The 1960s brought about a number of groups dedicated to improvisation: the New Music Ensemble (Austin, Lunetta, Mizelle, Woodbury, Alexander, and Johnson); Sonic Arts Group (Mumma, Ashley, Behrman, and Lucier); the *Musica Elettronica Viva* (Allan Bryant, Alvin Curran, Jon Phetteplace, Carol Plantamura, Frederic Rzewski, Richard Teitelbaum, and Ivan Vandor); and the University of Illinois Chamber Players, directed by Jack McKenzie. Whatever the means of producing sound (electronic or instrumental), the immediate and temporary creations were based solely on the interaction of the performers (most of whom were composers). The responsibility was with the ensemble, not a single personality. Lukas Foss remarks: "I thought I had invented a new kind of improvisation. I now know that I was merely the first not to sign my name."[6] The 1957 U.C.L.A.-based Improvisation Chamber Ensemble under the direction of Foss consisted of piano, clarinet, cello, and percussion (among the first of such groups). The ensemble worked primarily from charts indicating only initial ideas (e.g., motive, rhythm, pattern) needed to create a work. Many rehearsals yielded a polished result in performances which varied somewhat, but were more crystalline than live improvisation. The group also performed improvised interludes between the movements of Foss's *Time Cycle* (1960) for soprano and orchestra (first version, 1960).

6. As quoted in "Groups," op. cit.

Cornelius Cardew (of AMM, which also included Lou Gare, Eddie Prevost, and Keith Rowe), in the same article referred to earlier, adds: "The past always seems intentional, but at the time it appears to be accidental."[7]

The MW 2 Ensemble of Poland uses instruments of more traditional origin, while at the same time employing two dancers and an actor, with tapes, projection, and scenery (see Figure 5.4). Performer interaction therefore takes the form of visual as well as musical improvisation.

Figure 5.4. MW 2 Ensemble of Poland.

Group improvisational situations challenge the aesthetic of a "leading personality." The structure and immediate creation resulting from such groups challenges the audience's categorization of individual idols more than they philosophically or aurally alter traditional methods of creative intention.

The concept of *time* provides an essential ingredient in the contemporary composer's approach to improvisation. Morton Feldman expressed his ideas as to how objects exist *as* time, not of, in, or about time:

> . . . This was not how to make an object . . . but how this object exists *as* Time. Time regained, as Proust referred to his work. Time as an Image, as Aristotle suggested. This is the area which the visual arts later began to explore. This is the area which music, deluded that it was counting out the seconds, has neglected.
>
> I once had a conversation with Karlheinz Stockhausen, where he . . . began beating on the table and said: "A sound exists either here—or here—or here." He was convinced that he was demonstrating reality to me. That the beat, and the possible placement of sounds in relation to it, was the only thing the composer could

7. Ibid., p. 18.

realistically hold on to. The fact that he had reduced it to so much a square foot made him think Time was something he could handle and even parcel out, pretty much as he pleased.

Frankly, this approach to Time bores me. I am not a clockmaker. I am interested in getting Time in its unstructured existence. That is, I am interested in how this wild beast lives in the jungle—not in the zoo. I am interested in how Time exists before we put our paws on it—our minds, our imaginations, into it.

One would think that music more than any other art would be exploratory about Time. But is it? Timing—not Time—has been passed off as the real thing in music. . . .[8]

Realization of the inadequacy of traditional notation leads not only to new standards, but to the lack of notation entirely. This destroys the composer/performer relationship, a hierarchy required by most traditional audiences. Lukas Foss, in works like *Echoi* (1963), hints toward this by employing stems without noteheads (though exact indications of rhythm, dynamics, and order are given).

William Duckworth's *Pitch City* (see Figure 5.5) for wind instruments instructs four performers to trace pitches from the corners to the middle. Each note's duration is equivalent to the individual performer's ability to sustain the note(s) as long as possible (breathing between notes). More notes remain unplayed (73) than played (71), while at the same time a twelve-tone row (top line, left to right) is expressed in all versions—original, retrograde (right to left), inversion (top to bottom), and retrograde inversion (bottom to top)—and in every possible transposition. The composer's intention here is unmistakable: to prepare the complete logical and mathematical twelve-tone row structure, and then totally avoid any realization of this organization. This represents a philosophical challenge to twelve-tone rationale that must play a distinct part in any educated performer's realization of the score (none of the outlined portions remotely follow twelve-tone direction). Improvisation occurs in rhythm, instrumentation, and resultant octave (depending on the instrument's range).

Duckworth's *Walden Variations* (see Figure 5.6) demonstrates improvisational graphic notation. The sheet shown (the third and final score page) is a ". . . free improvisation sheet based on the design of the original sheet. The events and movements to and from events are ambiguous and can be freely interpreted. Dancers, readers, slides, movies, and/or lights may be employed as the performers feel it to be in keeping within the general spirit of the piece as they understand it."[9] Completed in 1971, *Walden Variations* is a nonstructured improvisation-based score with open instrumentation.

Etudes for Organ by Lukas Foss requires four different improvisational techniques, one for each movement. In the first, the performer varies an exactly-notated motor-rhythm single-line melody by freely repeating note groups (no more than twelve score notes should be played without returning to some group of notes of the performer's choice). In the second, groups of notes (right hand) are scored for which

8. Morton Feldman, "Between Categories," *Composer* 1, no. 2 (September 1969):75.
9. From notes to the score by the composer.

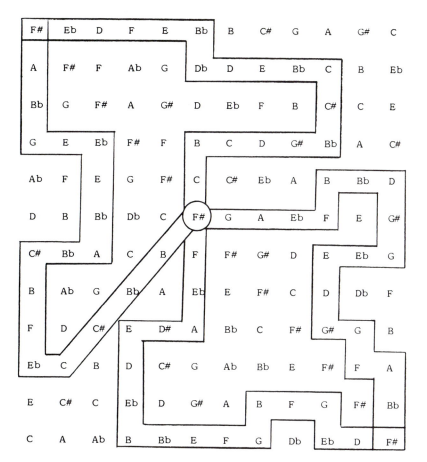

the performer may choose order, rhythm, octave, and/or number of the notes desired. Forearm clusters dominate throughout the third movement, with spontaneous choice of rhythm, white or black key clusters. The form here is more articulate, being verbally presented in four sections: ABA-Coda. The fourth movement includes performer choice of a four-part "religious or patriotic" hymn around which two secondary performers playing four-note clusters at either end of the keyboard are asked (verbally, again) to interfere, *poco a poco,* with the hymn performance. Foss has used notes (in I, II, and IV), rhythms (in I), timbre (in III), dynamics (in II, III, and IV), each in a somewhat traditional manner, at the same time freeing another aspect of composition and performance for improvisation.

In the above discussed works, the composer still claims one or more compositional aspects of his work. Giuseppi Chiari's *Quel Che Volete* is probably more apropos of Morton Feldman's statement: "Down with the Masterpiece; up with art. . . .".[10] The piece consists entirely of verbal instructions ranging from indications suggesting materials not be played in a virtuosic manner, to exchanging instruments among performers. However vague the score may appear, close reading

10. Morton Feldman, "Conversations without Stravinsky," *Source: Music of the Avant-Garde* 1, no. 2 (July 1967):43.

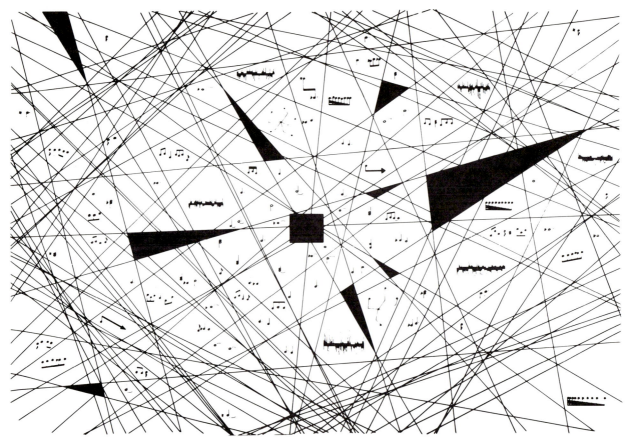

Figure 5.6. William
Duckworth's *Walden
Variations*. Sheet #3. Used
with permission of the
composer.

reveals composer intention, especially in regard to form (from "you must try and
play in a traditional manner" and "play as if playing was a gift" to "We must never
overdo"). Likewise, in *Sonant,* Mauricio Kagel employs verbal descriptions of the
framework within which the performer may improvise. These often intricate instructions may be more accurate in terms of performance ease and understanding
than traditional notation.

Luciano Berio's *Circles* (1960) for female voice, harp, and two percussion players
includes a variety of "improvisation boxes." Figure 5.7 shows the two percussion
parts (top and bottom groups of staves) with the voice in the middle (harp is not
playing at this point). The "improvisation boxes" should not be confused with the
small boxes in which the mallets are graphically shown: i.e., the first small box in
the two top lines from the left. The reasoning behind the "improvisation" is obvious:
the percussion parts would be impossible if written out, or tight and "square." Pitches

Percussion:

Voice:

dis :(appeared cleverly) world   iS Slapped: with;   liGhtninG   !⁰⁰   at

Percussion:

Figure 5.7. Luciano Berio: *Circles* © Copyright 1961 by Universal Edition. Used by permission.

and instrumentation are usually indicated in specific detail. Rhythm is left to the performer. Often Berio stacks the notes vertically in such a way that the performer can proceed in any order he/she "feels." Occasionally the pitches are proportionally distributed within the box to indicate the approximate rhythmic placement or to introduce new "stacks" of notes. Dynamics, on the other hand, are often notated in terms of *limits* (i.e., *mf→pp*) with smooth *crescendi* and *diminuendi* indicated by dovetailing notation. The score contains no performance directions except those of placement of instruments; the composer, it seems, feels that these performance concepts are obvious. With the "boxes" occurring in only one or two parts at a time (there is little flexibility in the vocal line except its proportional non-metered notation), the composer maintains control over the direction and flow of the work, allowing the improvisation to give *life* to each successive performance.

Robert Erickson's *Ricercar à 5* (1966) for five trombones requires a number of improvisational techniques from the performers (the work may be performed with five trombonists or one trombonist and four prerecorded trombones on tape). The work varies from exact notation to control of only one or two elements (e.g., most often dynamics and pitch). The interplay between parts calls for sensitive and interpretative improvisatory techniques. The work was written for trombonist Stuart Dempster who speaks of these points in an interview.

Question (Frank McCarty): So you began to compile a body of new sounds and techniques through research, practice, and mimicry. I assume you incorporated some of these in the improvisational music that was popular among the San Francisco composers of that era.

Answer (Stu Dempster): Yes, those pieces gave me the first opportunity to couple my "funny sounds" with other "funny sounds" made by tapes and by other musical instruments such as Pauline's (Oliveros) accordion and Mort's (Subotnick) clarinet. I also became interested in working with composers, I did a demo for Berio in the early 1960's and asked him for a piece, never thinking he'd really do it. Later (1966), when I was working with Bob Erickson on a commission, I decided to resurrect the Berio idea. I wrote him a letter . . . and learned he was already right in the middle of the piece. The *Sequenza* (also involving improvisation techniques) was written in a way for two of us, myself and (Vinko) Globokar, who had played sketches of what became the B section. But as Berio and I worked together on the final version it became more and more my piece since he saw in me—in my performance—more and more the character of Grock, the famous European clown, about whom the piece is actually written. In the meantime, Erickson and I were spending many a Tuesday morning developing a vocabulary of sounds and sound-mixes which resulted in his composition of the *Ricercar à 5*. . . .[11]

Phil Winsor's *Orgel* includes a sheet of twelve basic improvisatory boxes for organ (and organ recorded on tape). The verbal stylistic indications above each box (see Figure 5.8) plus the timing and overlap directions of the score (not shown) make this "free" improvisation, and not graphic indeterminacy as a quick glance might suggest.

Improvisational techniques in the last few years have created a renaissance of live performance situations. Whether as a result of, or a reaction to, the composer of electronic music, the newfound creative collaboration between composers and performers cannot help but enrich the continuum and significance of all music.

Indeterminacy

Experimental music, that is, actions the outcome of which are not foreseen, is more a philosophical than an audible phenomenon. Form, intended or not, is inherent in all matter and energy, and therefore subject to analysis. It is impossible, without prior knowledge of the composer or work, to distinguish the intention or nonintention of the composer, unless the sounds or actions presented are obviously from another source (intentional or unintentional). For example, John Cage's *4'33"* (1952), wherein the sounds presented are obviously nature or the audience itself, appears realizably unintentional except in concept.

It is with this latter idea, this psychoconceptual aspect, that the greatest single musical antagonism has been born. Audiences can be presented with highly organized and experimental compositions of the same general genre, instrumentation, and techniques, without reacting adversely. However, when prior knowledge exists, or when a work such as *4'33"* is played, and the audience *realizes* the unintention involved, reactions can be much more violent. One struggles with the *concept,* not the sounds. "Therefore my purpose is to remove purpose," spoke John Cage in a 1962 interview with Roger Reynolds (Figure 5.9).[12] The idea is to let sounds

---

11. Frank McCarty, "An Interview with Stuart Dempster," *The Instrumentalist* 28, no. 10 (May 1974). Used by permission of The Instrumentalist Co.
12. *Contemporary Composers on Contemporary Music*, Elliott Schwartz and Barney Childs, eds. (New York: Holt, Rhinehart and Winston, 1967), p. 341.

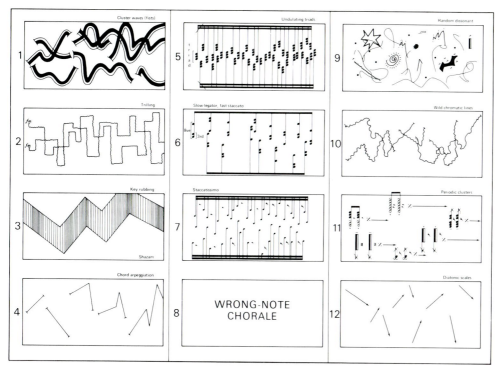

Figure 5.8. Phil Winsor: *ORGEL I.* Copyright © 1975 by Pembroke Music Co., Inc., New York. International Copyright Secured. 62 Cooper Square, New York, N.Y. 10003. Copying or reproducing this publication in whole or in part violates the Federal Copyright Law. All rights reserved including public performance for profit. Used by permission.

Figure 5.9. John Cage. Photo: Dorothy Norman.

"happen," to free them from the composer's control. Can one learn to accept *all* sounds equally? This concept truly rejects the past twelve to fourteen centuries of Western thought; not the music itself, but the *concept of* that music.

Separating oneself so completely from one's acts, artistic or otherwise, through chance or "forced stupidity" frees sound rather than controlling it. If *total* chance, *total* indeterminacy, is not possible, is it pointless to attempt merely to approach it? This question poses possibly the most serious and philosophical antithesis to indeterminacy. Cage has referred to his disappointment and compromise arising from the knowledge that he hasn't really "done it," but merely has been ". . . going along in that general direction."[13]

Indeterminacy is not a game or a passing fancy. It presents *the* philosophical challenge to the aesthetics, art, and ego of history. Its antagonists are numerous (Hindemith refers to chance as "one of the ugliest modern musical diseases."[14]). However, what most antagonists (and some protagonists) fail to realize is that one must deal with the *concept* of indeterminacy, *not* the sounds, *not* the forms, *not* the individuals involved. If it cannot be reckoned with in philosophical terms, then it will destroy (or possibly already has destroyed) the structure, terms, and aesthetics of music and art as contemporary Western civilization has come to know them.

Indeterminacy implies art as process: no beginning, no middle, no end. Each new performance, each new circumstance creates a continually variable process of ideas. As Cage has said, "If one is making an object and then proceeds in an indeterminate fashion, to let happen what will, outside of one's control, then one is simply being careless about the making of that object."[15] If art be process, however, then indeterminacy is the only viable way to proceed.

In "Indeterminacy," Cage describes Bach's *Art of the Fugue* as an example of composition which is indeterminate with respect to its performance, based on lack of directions in regard to timbre, dynamics, sequence of the "determinate" notes, and durations, making available a wide range of possible realizations.[16] This philosophy disavows man's significance as a creator, emphasizing creative performing/listening; understanding being something pedagogical and within the realm of language, not aesthetics.

The terminology surrounding chance operations involves certain basic American/European divisions. The term *aleatoric* (derived by Boulez from *aléa,* French for "risk," and originally from the Latin word meaning *dice*) seems to be primarily a European concept which employs chance techniques within a controlled framework, more related to improvisation than true indeterminacy. Morton Feldman has remarked: "This is true of Boulez. This is true of Stockhausen. You can see this in the way they have approached American 'chance' music. They began by finding

13. Ibid.
14. Ibid., p. 89.
15. Ibid., p. 345.
16. John Cage, *Silence* (Cambridge, Mass.: The M.I.T. Press, paperback edition, 1961), p. 35.

Figure 5.10. Morton Feldman. BMI Archives. Used by permission.

rationalizations for how they could incorporate chance and still keep their precious integrity."[17] After reacting to the personality behind this statement, Boulez expanded on these basic differences between aleatoric and chance techniques:

G. W.:   Feldman refers to "chance" here. Do you feel that you conceive of "chance" in the same way that, say, John Cage conceives of it?

P. B.:   No, not at all. I find that so highly unproductive, because "chance" is not an aesthetic category. "Chance" can bring something interesting only one time in a million. . . . Most of the time you do not get that one time . . . and, if you do get it, you get it in the midst of a hundred thousand possibilities which are not interesting.

G. W.:   Going to a "chance" concert, then, you feel would be like going to a baseball game, gambling for excitement?

P. B.:   Yes, but even a baseball game has rules. Card games, which have much more chance, I suppose, still have rules. Can you imagine a card game with absolutely no rules?

D. C.:   Like Mallarmé saying, "A throw of the dice will not abolish chance," . . . you are saying that, while nothing can be totally chance, nothing can be totally without chance.

17. Schwartz and Childs, op. cit., p. 365.

P. B.: Exactly. With the combination of the two, you must integrate, and it is much more difficult to compose in this way, integrating on a high level than in more traditional ways. Composing by chance is not composing at all. Composing . . . means to put things together. I am interested as to what chance sounds occur on the street, but I will never take them as a musical composition. There is a big difference between unorganized sounds and those placed within complete organization.[18]

The division between American and European concepts of chance has grown deeper in the last several years. Boulez remarks: "Do you see what we are getting back to? Constantly to a refusal of choice. The first conception was purely mechanistic, automatic, fetishistic; the second is still fetishistic but one is freed from choice not by numbers but by the interpreter."[19] England's David Bedford and Brian Tilbury, however, have recently championed the American cause of experimental work in indeterminacy, mirroring in the late sixties much the same discoveries and excitement engendered by Cage and Feldman in the early fifties. Surviving, even thriving upon, the attacks from both here and abroad, the cause for freeing sounds continues.

Indeterminacy, as a step-by-step (even pedagogical) approach to erase control over compositional elements which so many have fought to retain, must first transcend man's loss of individual ego. As such, it is merely the first step to a far-reaching eventuality: rejection of *all* homocentered creativity, and acceptance of *all* of the life around us, with man no longer in control, no longer the creator or destroyer of images or ideals, real or imagined.

Composer Indeterminacy

Indeterminacy involves total lack of knowledge about the outcome of an action in respect to composition, performance, or both. A number of works are *indeterminate in respect to composition but determinate in respect to performance.* This is primarily music which is predictable before performance but was composed with the use of some type of chance operation. Often these works come to the performer in very traditional notation. They always imply *determinate* performance.

In his *Music of Changes* (1951), John Cage used twenty-six large charts indicating aspects of composition (durations, tempos, dynamics), following the *I Ching* to "create" every aspect of the composition. Forty-three minutes (in music) and nine months later, *Music of Changes* (every aspect except conception of which was based on coin tosses; a huge number) was completed. This rigid composition technique (not unlike that of the twelve-tone school), and the dedication and care necessary for the creation of *Music of Changes,* cannot escape philosophical implications, regardless of composer intention. Possibly no other work in the history of music has been so exact in its creation, its composer having purposely attempted to destroy his own control over it. Yet it shows little trace of either the composer or the *I Ching:* it "merely" *sounds*.

18. Galen Wilson and David Cope, "An Interview with Pierre Boulez," *Composer* 1, no. 2 (September 1969):82–83.
19. Pierre Boulez, "Aléa," *Perspectives of New Music* 3, no. 1 (Winter 1964):42.

Some composers utilize more traditional number systems as source material for various parameters of compositions. The Fibonacci series, for example, has been used for pitch, rhythm and timbre control. The series (based on Leonardo Fibonacci's mathematical discoveries of the thirteenth century) creates each new number in its series by adding the previous two (e.g., 1, 1, 2, 3, 5, 8, 13, 21, etc.). As one goes higher in the series a special numerical relationship is created between successive entries. This is known as the "golden mean" (or "section") and, while impossible to express in a pure stable state (each new entry will vary the results), a traditional model averages to .618.[20] Obviously works whose structure and substance derive from Fibonacci series construction have significant "golden mean" import.

György Doczi, for example, using the principle that *proportion* draws things in nature together, creates parallels between architecture and music. Figure 5.11 shows how this translates from different expressions of the *golden section* (another phrase formed from the Fibonacci series).

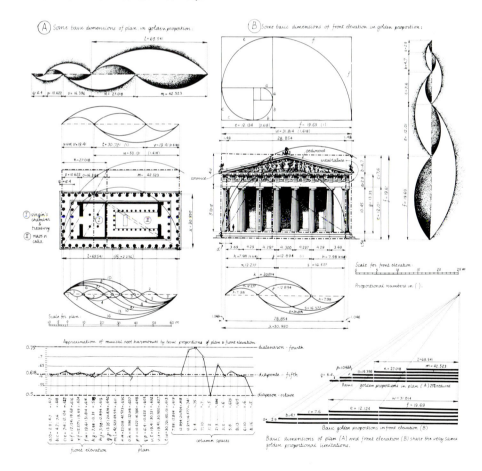

Figure 5.11. From György Doczi's *The Power of Limits,* a view of the Parthenon (Athens) from the perspectives of the golden mean, architecture and music.

20. A number of aestheticians argue the validity of this mean as a conscious or unconscious source of inspiration for many great works of art.

He bases the projections on the proportions of .618, .75 and .5 which he terms diapente, diatessaron and diapason, respectively (translated into the fifth, fourth and octave). In other examples in his visionary book, *The Power of Limits, Proportional Harmonies in Nature, Art and Architecture,* Doczi compares musical root harmonies in galaxies, pine cones, and the human body. Abstracted, as the proportions are in this book, these balances seem appropriate to his schematics. In reality, however, the wandering lines lack any truly musical form or rhythmic direction. He is not the first to make such comparisons, however. Johannes Kepler, a pre-eminent astronomer of the 17th century held that proportions between the planets (*Harmony of the Spheres*) produce musically harmonic motion. Philosopher Robert Fludd (England) suggested a "tuning of the universe" in his two illustrations from *Utrisque Cosmi Historica*. The figure on the left (see Figure 5.12) refers to the dark foreboding and confused world of earthly man, while the one to the right shows the proportionately balanced universe.

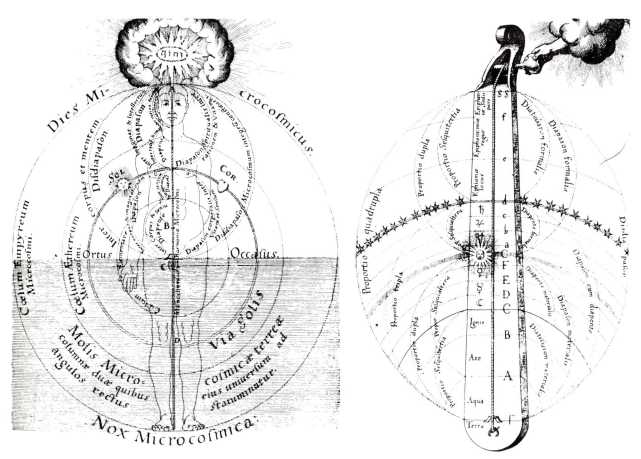

Figure 5.12. Illustrations from Robert Fludd's *Utrisque Cosmi Historica.*

R. Murray Schafer's extraordinary *The Tuning of the World,* while possibly less all-encompassing than these earlier examples, nonetheless continues the tradition of modeling music after the proportions of what he terms the "soundscape." His work covers the field from the post-industrial soundscape to acoustic designs of the soundscape. His process of listening, called "ear cleaning," has significant consequence in his view. His discussions on noise, in particular, seem applicable to the various forms and works of this chapter. (From *Ear Cleaning:* ". . . take a sheet of paper and give it a sound. . . . By giving the paper a voice we have exposed its sound-soul. Every object on the earth has a sound-soul").

Magic squares (and cubes) have also been used as raw material for "formal" compositional techniques. These squares are matrices of numbers which seem to "magically" add, subtract, divide and/or multiply to the same number regardless of the direction taken. Figure 5.13 shows a simple magic square and one possible way it might be interpreted in music values. Note that the addition of every line (including the two diagonal lines) is 15, and no line contains more than one of each of the numbers in use. Interpretation of this data as musical sound is completely at the discretion of the composer and may vary significantly from one work to the next.

1	4	2	3	5
2	3	5	1	4
5	1	4	2	3
4	2	3	5	1
3	5	1	4	2

Figure 5.13. A magic square and possible musical interpretation.

Pitch: (Using 0–11 ordination—beginning on C)
  Line 1—Lines 2 and 1—Lines 2, 1, and 3—etc.
  (Reducing numbers over 11 by 12—e.g.
  C♯ E D D♯ F D♯ G G E A G♯ G♯ B etc.)
Rhythm: 1 = ♪ 2 = ♩ 3 = ♩. 4 = ♩ 5 = 𝅝
Timbre: 1 = horn   2 = flute   3 = piano   4 = violin   5 = cello

Many wonder why such "formalistic" ends could not be achieved in more musical and less mathematical approaches, and so the enigmas around these ideas continue. Writings by and about Xenakis often contribute, for example, to these conflicts. The following is from a discussion between John Cage, Lukas Foss, and Iannis Xenakis:

> Cage: I asked a Spanish lady scientist what she thought about the human mind in a world of computers. She said, "computers are always right but life isn't about being right." What do you say to that?
>
> Xenakis: The opposite—life has reason and computers are often wrong.
>
> Cage: You have been an architect and now you are a musician. Are you going to go to some other activity?
>
> Xenakis: I'd like to but it is difficult.
>
> Foss: Iannis, all the music of yours that I know is built on mathematical premise, mostly probability. Is there any aspect to chance that is not mathematical, that is, not probability theory?
>
> Xenakis: All my music is not based on mathematics—there are parts of it which use mathematics. As to chance, it is not like dice or tossing a coin, this is ignorance, as if there were impossibility of predicting. What does chance mean to you?
>
> Foss: Anything I cannot control. You left architecture for music—why?
>
> Xenakis: Mostly because architecture was a business and music is less business.
>
> Foss: In order to compose you need time, solitude—what else?
>
> Xenakis: To live in a big city.
>
> Foss: If someone imitates you (I know of an instance) does it flatter you or make you angry or both?
>
> Xenakis: I am angry . . . angry and depressed.
>
> Foss: What did you want to be when you were a child?
>
> Xenakis: An elephant.[21]

The creation of Dick Higgin's *Thousand Symphonies* involved the "machine-gunning" of one thousand pages of blank orchestral manuscript. The performance, though necessarily constituting some performer interpretation of the "holes," is basically determinate. "My machine-gunning of scores actually represents the concretization of a fantasy I had of setting the police (or armies) to composing music with their most familiar instruments—guns, machine guns. In fact . . . we actually organized an orchestral performance of the gunshot notations according to a system I worked out, and it sounded quite lovely."[22]

Mauricio Kagel's *1898* (completed in 1973 for Deutsche Grammophon's 75th anniversary) is for eleven to seventeen players with only piano and percussion as obligatory to the orchestration. Twenty to twenty-five children's voices also take part in the form of either taped versions or live performance. The percussion is freely orchestrated so that even "home grown" non-pitched instruments can substitute for the indicated suggestions. Only vague hints regarding orchestration appear in the score.

---

21. John Cage, Lukas Foss, and Iannis Xenakis, "Short Answers to Difficult Questions," *Composer* 2, no. 2 (September 1970):40.

22. From a letter to the author.

Further observation into the instructions of the work provide a great deal of insight:

> The purpose of these tape recordings, among others, is to demonstrate that what is needed is not 'reliable' musical education but the very opposite: an unorthodox system of changeable, ambivalent invitations to express oneself acoustically—rather than 'musically.'[23]

This is later followed by:

> What is the difference between proper and artificial laughter? One can almost be certain that the responses to the ambiguities inherent in this unambiguous question will produce complex aural situations.[24]

Each of these statements, and the others, seems addressed to stochastic solutions (i.e., indeterminacy so complex that determinate results follow). Be this confusing, it is clearly more defined than the composer's own directive: "Variations of a Motive, sung increasingly wrongly."

Performer Indeterminacy

Music which is *determinate in respect to composition but indeterminate in respect to performance* owes much of its development to the idea of "event." These works are "composed" in terms of individual sections or fragments yet mobile in the order of appearance, creating unpredictability before and during performance.

When the timbre, structure, and dynamics of two sounds are so different as to avoid the traditional concept of melody, they become *events* (see chapter 2). Each is equal in importance and does not necessarily build to a climax or cadence. The introduction of silence[25] as an integral part of a composition, and treated equally with sound, helps in identifying these events in time. As sounds move further and further apart, their order becomes less and less important. This reflects much the same concept as a "mobile" in art: that is, the shape, color, and design of each part is fixed, with the order and angle constantly changing.

Karlheinz Stockhausen's *Klavierstück XI, No 7* (1957), printed on a long roll (37 by 21 inches), opens on a special wooden stand (supplied with the score). It contains nineteen "events," which may be played in any order. Performer instructions require glancing at the score and performing whatever event may "catch the eye."

> At the end of the first group, he reads the tempo, dynamic and attack indications that follow, and looks at random to any other group, which he then plays in accordance with the latter indications. "Looking at random to any other group" implies that the

---

23. Mauricio Kagel, *1898*. London: Universal (European American), 1979, p. 89.
24. Ibid.
25. Cage has often pointed out that "real" silence does not exist (see his book *Silence*). The author refers here to lack of intentional sound.

performer will never link up expressly-chosen groups or intentionally leave out others. Each group can be joined to any of the other 18: each can thus be played at any of the six tempi and dynamic levels and with any of the six types of attack.[26]

The composer requires that when a fragment is reached for the third time the piece is concluded. This creates anywhere from three fragments (the first one randomly observed three times in succession) to thirty-eight factorial (that is 38!—or 38 times 37 times 36 times 35 . . . etc.—a truly staggering number indeed: 10! is over 3.5 million).[27] This, along with the tempo, dynamic and attack variances, creates a work whose notes in terms of fragments are controlled by the composer, yet the resultant performance is totally unpredictable.

Figure 5.14 shows the score from measures 27 to 32 of Stockhausen's *Stop* (1965). This "Pariser Version" (the one shown in Figure 5.14—there is another version for full orchestra) is for eighteen performers in six groups (cued with the ◇ sign) of like timbres. This *recipe* work has determinate form (note the duration

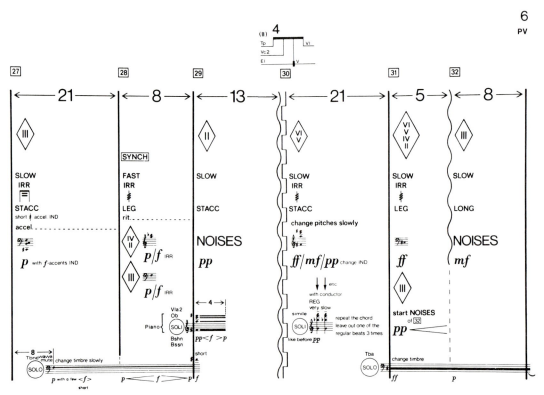

Figure 5.14. Karlheinz Stockhausen: *Stop.* © Copyright Universal Edition. All rights reserved. Used by permission.

26. From the composer's directions on the score. Universal Edition No. 12654 LW.
27. "!" here is not an exclamation point but rather a factorial sign in mathematics (the number preceding the sign multiplied by stepwise diminishing numbers in turn down to 1).

lengths at the top of each "measure") yet lacks "determinate" directions for performance ("noises" is hardly a predictable notation). The composer is obviously very much aware of the outcome in general terms of form, contrast, balance, and direction (note the occasional exact notation overlapping events) but willing to allow performance unpredictability in terms of rhythm, entrance order, and pitch. This type of work, though very different from the *mobile* structures of his *Klavierstück XI, No. 7,* is still primarily composer-determined performer unpredictability.

Henri Pousseur's piano solo *Caractères* (1961) includes cutout windows and randomly placed score pages so that the order of the "events" is not composer-prescribed. Henry Cowell was among the first of composers to provide blocks of sound with which the performer constructed the performance "form" (*Mosaic Quartet,* 1934).

Affected by the mobiles of Alex Calder, Earle Brown has developed concepts of form and order in his music derived primarily from this "event" rationale. Referring to his *Available Forms I* and *II* (1961–62), Brown writes: "The title of the work refers to the availability of many possible forms which these composed elements may assume, spontaneously directed by the conductors in the process of performing the work. The individual musical events are rehearsed, but the performances are not."[28]

In Brown's *Available Forms I* for orchestra, the score is projected on the back of the stage for the performers to read. The conductor then indicates a number which represents one of the large numerals indicated on the score. The performers read and improvise within the context of the information given in the indicated block. The risk parallels that of the Stockhausen example, though it is not so great as to imply complete lack of composer control.

The anti-lyrical aspects of event concepts represent one of the ideas most profoundly antagonistic to Romantic thought. Barney Child's *Nonet* (*Source: Music of the Avant Garde* 3, no. 1 [January 1969]) includes an "event machine" (a numbered acetate overlay and two rotating color-coded discs) which provides the order, timing, and selection of events (provided by the composer). In Feldman's *Intersection 3,* the duration, number, and timbre of sounds are determined by the composer while the dynamics and range (*high, middle,* and *low*) are indeterminate during performance.

John Cage's *Atlas Eclipticalis* (see Figure 5.15), first performed by the New York Philharmonic in 1962, includes the use of contact microphones placed in various locations on the instruments. Though somewhat graphic, this work provides pitch indications and directions of movement. As seen in Figure 5.16 *34'46.776" for a Pianist* (1954) is also a graphic but explicit work.

Musical "games" (or "strategy") take a variety of forms (e.g., Subotnick's *Ritual;* see Chapter 10). Xenakis has characterized music without in-performance "conflict" as *autonomous* (inclusive of most music to the present day) and the music of games (introducing a concept of external conflict between groups or individuals

28. From the program notes of the New York Philharmonic Society, February 1964.

Figure 5.15. John Cage: *Atlas Eclipticalis, French Horn 5, Percussion 4, Cello 7*, pages 245, 309, and 157. Copyright by Henmar Press Inc., 373 Park Avenue South, New York, N.Y. 10016. International Copyright Secured. All rights reserved. Permission granted by the publisher.

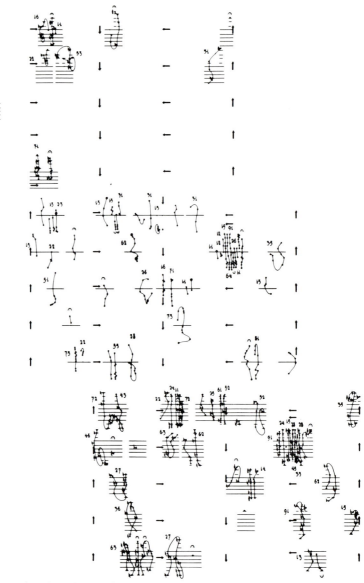

Atlas Eclipticalis, French Horn 5, Percussion 4, Cello 7, pages 245, 309, and 157

Figure 5.16. John Cage: *34'46.776'' for a Pianist,* page 50. Copyright by Henmar Press Inc., 373 Park Avenue South, New York, N.Y. 10016. International Copyright Secured. All rights reserved. Permission granted by the publisher.

in the performance situation) as *heteronomous* music. Xenakis's *Duel* (1958–59) comprises materials like that of the mobile structure: a set of six events, each written in the score in precise manner. Unlike mobiles, however, these strategic games employ definitive *tactics* with the events of length sufficient to permit interruption, and the choice of event a direct result of an "on the spot" performer decision.

Strategie (1962), for two forty-four-member orchestras, employs Xenakis's *strategie musicale* (application to music of the mathematical *theory of games*). Seven basic sound structures have a *stochastic* basis, which was calculated with an IBM 70690 computer with 400 combinations possible between the two orchestras (seated on opposite sides of the stage). An electric scoreboard is set at the end of the stage with points gained and lost by rules set by composer calculations. "At the end of a certain number of exchanges or minutes, as agreed upon by the conductors, one of the two is declared a winner and is awarded a prize."[29]

Roman Haubenstock-Ramati's *Mobile for Shakespeare* (for voice, piano, celeste, vibraphone, and three percussionists) is a prime example of "mobile" type structure indeterminacy (see Figure 5.17). Each box gives a fairly straightforward, mostly traditionally notated fragment (there are a few relatively explicit graphic symbols). The order of each box is not predetermined and therefore while the composer has indeed "composed" each note, the performances are quite different and unpredictable.[30]

29. Xenakis, *Formalized Music,* p. 122.
30. See the score for fuller explanation of complete performance.

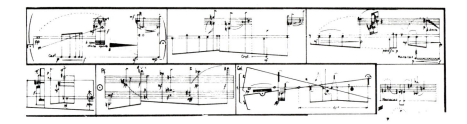

Figure 5.17. Roman Haubenstock-Ramati's *Mobile for Shakespeare.* © Copyright Universal Edition, 1968. All rights reserved. Used by permission.

Composer and Performer Indeterminacy

Music can be *indeterminate in respect to both composition and performance.* "Chance" means produce a "chance" score: at no time is there a predictable outcome. Christian Wolff's *Duo II for Pianists* (1958), for example, involves no score and all materials are indeterminate, the only indication being areas of limitation provided by the composer (the use of pianos with no silences between performer responses). The work has no designated beginning or ending, these being determined only by the situation under which performance takes place. Nam June Paik's *In Homage to John Cage* (1959) is equally indeterminate and in "happening" form. In its first performance Paik leaped offstage to Cage's seat, removed Cage's jacket and, as Tomkins puts it: "slashed his (Cage's) shirt with a wickedly long pair of scissors, cut off his necktie at the knot, poured a bottle of shampoo over his head, and then rushed out of the room."[31] Paik later telephoned the audience to let them know that the work was finished.

Cage has explored "contingency"-type indeterminacy:

I have been writing pieces that I call "music of contingency," in which there is a rupture between cause and effect, so that the causes that are introduced don't necessarily produce effects. That's what contingency is. One piece, *Inlets,* uses conch shells, for example; if instead of blowing a conch shell, you fill it with water and tip it, it will sometimes gurgle and sometimes not. You have no control over it. Even if you try very hard to control it, it gurgles when it wishes to . . . when it's ready to. Sometimes if you rehearse with it and think that you've got it down pat, you'll discover as I do, I'm sure, that it foxes you and gurgles when it chooses.[32]

John Mizelle's *Radial Energy I* (see Figure 5.18) allows the greatest possible freedom in choice of sound sources, number of participants, location of performance, and interpretation (if any). In the sine chart and explanation accompanying the score, the composer describes in detail the silence periods between performances (six, seven, nine, twelve, fifteen, seventeen, eighteen, seventeen, fifteen, twelve, nine, seven, and six *years* for the first phase of the chart, and the first point at which the piece may be concluded: i.e., one hundred fifty years). Other "complete" performances may last over 382 years, depending on initial performance time, with duration of the performances (between the periods of silence) computed by addition,

31. Calvin Tomkins, *The Bride and the Bachelors* (New York: The Viking Press, 1965), p. 134.
32. David Cope, "An Interview with John Cage," *Composer* 10, no. 1 (1980).

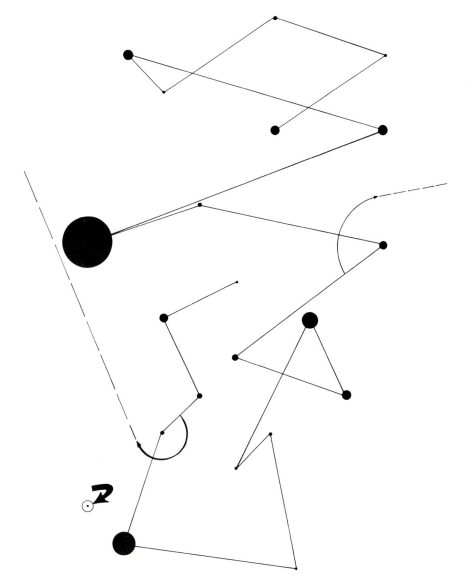

Figure 5.18. John Mizelle: *Radial Energy I.* Permission granted by *Source: Music of the Avant-garde,* Composer/Performer Edition, Davis, California.

squaring, cubing, etc., the initial performance duration (actual sound-producing performances could last over fifteen years). Likewise the area of performance could be expanded, as the composer states, "to other planets, galaxies, etc. When all of time and space are transformed into sound, the piece (and the Universe) ends."

Barney Childs's *The Roachville Project* (a sound sculpture for four to ten performers) verbally describes a situation in which performers *and* audience create an instrument out of available materials, improvising during and after construction. Emphasis is directed *away* from sound and toward situation, theater, and total participation (see Figure 5.19).

"The Roachville Project"

4 to 10 performers, minimum duration 30 minutes.

Provide a great deal of material, most of which should be capable of soundproduction, either immediately (wires, pipes, blocks, tubes, containers, bits and pieces of musical instruments, junk, &c.) or potentially (material which when assembled or altered or worked with can be made, maybe, to produce sound in some fashion).

The piece begins with the arrival of the performers at the material. They begin to assemble the material, as they please, any way they wish, into a "musical instrument" of sorts. The complete construction is to be a unit—that is, separate people may work for a while on separate sub-units, but these must eventually be built into the complete construction. All that is necessary for assembly, finally, is ingenuity: the means of assembly (nails, staples, glue, string, sticky tape, leather straps, baling wire, rivets, &c.) are up to the performers. Performers may converse together concerning problems of assembly and sound potential, but this must be done very quietly, and other conversation is to be avoided; performers may test parts they are working on for sound as they are assembling (i.e. test string tension by plucking, test resonances by tapping, &c.) but this must also be done very quietly. At a stipulated time, or when all agree that the instrument is completed, the performers improvise music on it, for any length of time. The composition is finished with the completion, at a pre-arranged time or by agreement among the performers, of this "piece-within-a-piece." All material provided need not, or perhaps will not, be used. If passing members of the audience with to become performers they may, as long as the total working number of participants never exceeds 10.

Deep Springs
April 1967

°Roachville and White Mountain City were "settlements just over the White Mountain summit from Owens Valley. . . . A writer visiting there in 1864 tells all that we know of those would-be mining centers. The 'city' from which he wrote was on Wyman Creek, on the Deep Spring slope; its rival, Roachville, was on Cottonwood Creek, and was named by its proprietor, William Roach. . . ."

W. A. Chalfant, *The Story of Inyo*

Sylvano Bussotti's *Five Piano Pieces for David Tudor* (1959), on the other hand, reflects a totally graphic concept in which interpretation or non-interpretation is fully within the performer's realm. The artistic drawings of Bussotti are more visual than aural; the composer becomes more an inciter than restrainer. Graphic scores such as this represent a breach with traditional symbols. Inherent in a nonsymbolic abstract representation is a concept of live creation. Bussotti's *Five Pieces* was performed in Los Angeles three times in one concert, by three different performers. More conservative members of the audience, obviously appalled by the lack of recognizable similarities among the performances in structure, length, instrumentation, or motive, reacted antagonistically to both performers and work. The problem seems to be rooted not in the sounds themselves, but in the categorization of who, in fact, is the creator of the sounds.

In reference to these performances Halsey Stevens has pointed out that:

> . . . if Mr. Bussotti had wandered into the hall and didn't know what was going on, he would not have had the remotest idea that those three performances, or any one of them, might have been his own piece. They were so totally different in every respect that the only thing he could lay claim to was having designed the score, not to having composed the piece. Aleatoric music, it seems to me, as it is frequently pursued, is an amusing parlor game. . . .[33]

Had these performances been recorded and subsequently translated into traditional notation for performer "interpretation," they would have avoided the antagonism. Had the piece then been performed three times, repetition would have replaced the creative ideal of the indeterminate composer.

Figures 5.20 to 5.24 show the wide variety of notations John Cage has used, and a cross section of the types of his works. *Concert for Piano and Orchestra* (Figure 5.20, Solo for Piano) was written and first performed for the 1958 Cage Retrospective Concert in New York's Town Hall, with the composer conducting. The staging included a large battery of electronic equipment, with the conductor slowly bringing his hands together over his head, in clocklike fashion. This controlled the duration of the piece more than individual events (which are more or less indeterminate in sequence and number).

26'1.1499" for a String Player, 1955 (see Figure 5.21) is more graphic and has been "realized" by Harold Budd for Bertram Turetzky's Nonesuch recording of the work. Both *Variations I*, 1958 (see Figure 5.22) and *Fontana Mix*, 1958 (see Figure 5.23) graphically plot areas and physical locations for performance. *Variations IV* (1963) involves laying score transparencies over a map of the performance area, determining source and direction, of sounds. The recording (made in a Los Angeles art gallery) includes the various sounds of Cage at work with electronic equipment and the candid conversations of the audience-performers. One microphone was placed outside the building to catch street sounds. Cage created a final realization by splicing and selecting, evaluating and manipulating the resultant tapes.

---

33. David Cope, "An Interview with Halsey Stevens," *Composer* 5, no. 1 (1973):30.

Figure 5.20. John Cage: *Solo for Piano (Concert for Piano and Orchestra)*, page 30. Copyright by Henmar Press Inc., 373 Park Avenue South, New York, N.Y. 10016. International Copyright Secured. All rights reserved. Permission granted by the publisher.

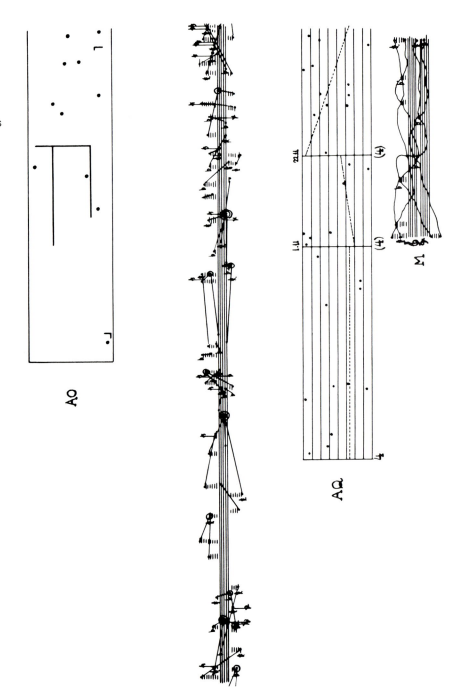

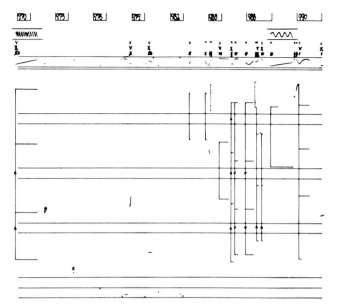

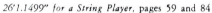

26'1.1499" for a String Player, pages 59 and 84

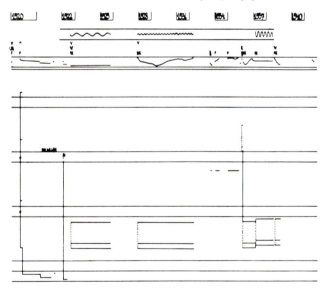

Figure 5.21. John Cage: *26'1.1499'' for a String Player,* pages 59 and 84. Copyright by Henmar Press Inc., 373 Park Avenue South, New York, N.Y. 10016. International Copyright Secured. All rights reserved. Permission granted by the publisher.

Figure 5.22. John Cage: *Variations I.* Copyright by Henmar Press Inc., 373 Park Avenue South, New York, N.Y. 10016. International Copyright Secured. All rights reserved. Permission granted by the publisher.

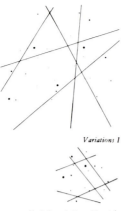

Variations I

Variations I. Extra Materials

Figure 5.23. John Cage: *Fontana Mix.* Copyright by Henmar Press Inc., 373 Park Avenue South, New York, N.Y. 10016. International Copyright Secured. Permission granted by the publisher.

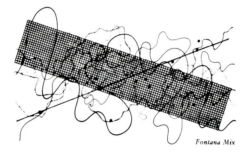

Fontana Mix

The score to *Fontana Mix* represents the physical areas on the instruments used (indeterminate) and intersections (which could be striking areas). Since the composer has not restricted instrumentation, it is not possible to predict any real outcome of the score in performance. Moreover, since the score is randomly made *by* the performer by overlaying various translucent sheets, the score itself looks different in each performance. Once created, however, and the score applied to the instruments used, performers should conform to that score in some very "determined" manner so that improvisation or reliance on past experience will not take place. The piece cannot be predicted or predetermined by either the composer or the performer; this implies full cooperation in indeterminacy by all participants.

Theatre Piece, 1960 (Figure 5.24), in the Cage "happening" tradition, employs number charts significant in their graphic representation of action. *Paintings* (1965) by Louis Andriessen (Figure 5.25), for recorder and piano, exemplifies a totally graphic indeterminate procedure. Even with the instructions, the predictability of the performance is minimal. William Bland's *Speed* (1968) for organ (see Figure 5.26) uses traditional left-to-right reading, up/down pitch level interpretation, and block-cluster chord representation, at the same time graphically encouraging non-predictable performance possibilities (e.g., center triangle with ink blur).

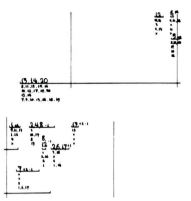

Figure 5.24. John Cage: *Theatre Piece Part VI.* (one of eighteen unnumbered pages). Copyright by Henmar Press Inc., 373 Park Avenue South, New York, N.Y. 10016. International Copyright Secured. All rights reserved. Permission granted by the publisher.

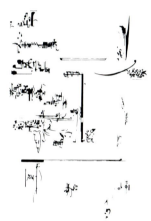

Figure 5.25. Louis Andriessen: *Paintings.* Flötenpart, Blatt 1. Copyright © 1965 by Herman Moeck Verlag. Used with permission. All rights reserved.

Other composers employ varied degrees of *graphic* notations to achieve equally varied ends. Anestis Logothetis's scores seem at first glance to be works of visual art. If one reads the instructions to his works carefully, clues appear that provide partial musical determinacy in terms of performer reaction and interpretation (e.g., *Clusters, Odyssee,* 1963, or *Ichnologia,* 1964). Robert Moran often utilizes *graphic* notations, but unlike Logothetis, gives clear indication of instrumentation and "possible" interpretation of visual symbols (see *Four Visions,* 1963, in Karkoschka's *Notation in New Music,* or *Bombardments No. 2,* 1964, for one to five percussionists). Boguslaw Schäffer has pointed out a number of advantages of *graphic* music (at least for its usefulness to the mainstream of music). In his 1963 *Violin Concerto,* the cadenza (primarily thick black waves and twists of graphic art) is transcribed into one possible traditionally-notated version. The result, based on a rather exact or literal translation, derives time in terms of left to right proportionality, pitch in terms of "up and down" relativity, and flow in terms of visual motion. This revised version is an incredibly complex, nearly unplayable, concrete structure totally foreign to the direction of the work. The plasticity of the *graphic* notation allows for

Figure 5.26. William Bland: *Speed* for organ solo.

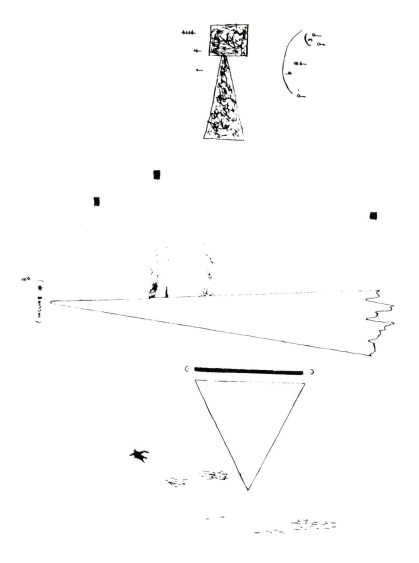

a free sound, every bit as complex as the traditionally notated one, yet without the studied end result (and, of course, without the "performance-to-performance" variability). In Schäffer's *Concerto* one hears the new elements, the surprises each performance offers. One does not judge a performer's mistakes or compare virtuosities in performance: it is indeed "composition in process."

Figure 5.27 is from Roman Haubenstock-Ramati's *Jeux 2,* 1968 (for two percussionists). Though mobile in structure, the graphic nature of the fragments themselves makes determinacy on the part of the composer or performer an impossibility.

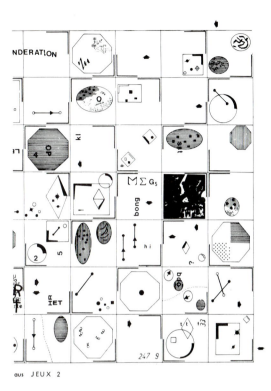

Figure 5.27. Roman Haubenstock Ramati: *Jeux 2* for two percussionists. © Copyright Universal Edition, 1968. All rights reserved. Used by permission.

aus   JEUX 2

Note the difference here between *Jeux 2* and *Mobile for Shakespeare,* 1959 (Figure 5.17), the latter having composer control over the fragments, thus falling distinctly into a different category (that of *performer-indeterminacy*). Possibly Europe's most experimental protagonist of the varieties of indeterminacy, Haubenstock-Ramati continues to explore the areas founded by John Cage, Earle Brown, and Barney Childs (unlike Stockhausen, for example, who now works with *conceptual music, antimusic,* etc., each new area as it comes into view).

Figure 5.28 is Robert Moran's *Sketch for a Tragic One-Act Opera* (score is in colors which cannot be reproduced here). The graphic nature of the score (even though instrumentation is traditional in left margin) contributes to composer-performer indeterminacy. The indications here, since this is only a "sketch," define texture and dynamics more than pitch or exact rhythms.

Other composers involved with indeterminate techniques include Folke Rabe, Bo Nilsson, Cornelius Cardew (though it should be noted that Cardew disowned his former style to compose "political-reformation" music), Roland Kayn, Allan Bryant, Joseph Byrd, Richard Maxfield, Philip Corner, Douglas Leedy, Robert Ashley, and James Fulkerson.

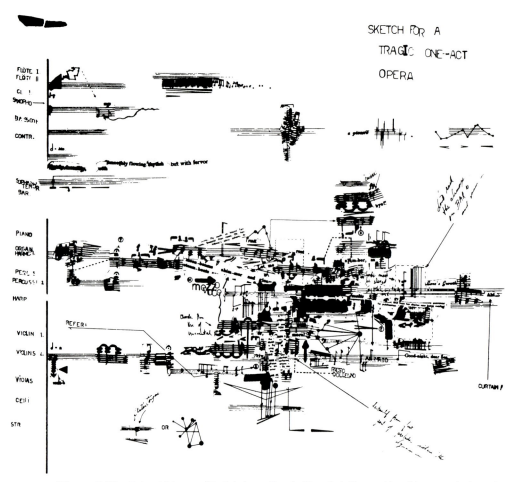

Figure 5.28. Robert Moran. *Sketch for a Tragic One-Act Opera*. Used by permission of the composer.

Vectoral Analysis: John Cage: *Cartridge Music*

(For information on vectoral analysis and procedures, see Chapter 1.)

1. Historical Background: John Cage (b. 1912, Los Angeles, California) began his studies with Henry Cowell and Arnold Schoenberg (with whom he studied counterpoint). Regarding the latter, Cage remarks:

My composition arises out of asking questions. I am reminded of an early story about a class with Schoenberg. He had us go to the blackboard to solve a particular problem in counterpoint (though it was a class in harmony). He said: "When you have a solution, turn around and let me see it." I did that. He then said: "Now another solution, please." I gave another and another until finally, having made seven or eight, I reflected a moment and then said with some certainty: "There aren't any more solutions." He said: "O.K. What is the principle underlying all of the solutions?" I couldn't answer his question; but I had always worshipped the man, and at that point I did even more. He ascended, so to speak. I spent the rest of my life, until recently, hearing him ask that question over and over. And then it occurred to me through the direction that my work has taken, which is renunciation of choices and the substitution of asking questions, that the principle underlying all of the solutions that I had given him was the question that he had asked, because they certainly didn't come from any other point. He would have accepted that answer, I think. The answers have the question in common. Therefore the question underlies the answers. I'm sure that he would have found my answer interesting; though he was very brilliant—he may have been thinking of something else.[34]

Cage's music through the mid-thirties developed chromatic concepts and used tone-row fragments, often with set rhythmic patterns. His *Sonata for Clarinet* (1933) is a good example of his work at this time. The work contains no effects whatsoever, but rather develops a kind of free twelve-tone procedure (definite rows but little working out of systematic serial techniques).

A second period developed in the mid- to late 1930s concentrating on wide diversities of timbral resources and an aesthetic about "noise." The prepared piano (developed in 1938) increased his interest in percussion instruments. The *First Construction in Metal* (1939) and important contributions to electronic music, particularly the *Imaginary Landscape* series begun in 1939, are all characteristic of Cage's imaginative leap into new sonic and timbral realms (Figure 5.29).

Figure 5.29. John Cage (standing at left) conducting a recording session of a percussion work by Lou Harrison (white shirt, far right) about 1940. Accidental overlay of two photos (superimposition) created the music in upper center and bass drum.

34. David Cope, "An Interview with John Cage," *Composer* 10, no. 1 (1980).

Figure 5.30. John Cage and David Cope. Photo by Carol Foote (1980). During preparation of a *Cartridge Music* performance.

A third period developed early in the 1950s when Cage began to infuse indeterminacy into his works. The *Concerto for Prepared Piano and Orchestra* (1951), *4'33"* (blank score in which extraneous sounds to the performance become the work itself; 1952), and *Fontana Mix* (1958; for tape) represent his work at this time.

Throughout his career, Cage has actively referenced his work to the other arts (in collaboration with Merce Cunningham, dance; Robert Rauschenberg, art; and Jasper Johns, sculpture) as well as philosophy (e.g., Buckminster Fuller). His concept of and search for the "possibility of saying nothing" have influenced numerous composers, artists, and writers; few doubt that the present-day evolution of music would not exist without his vast input and contributions (Figure 5.30).

2. Overview: *Cartridge Music* was completed in 1960. The "score" consists of four transparent sheets described as follows: sheet one: nineteen ⅛-inch black dots arranged randomly; sheet two: ten ¼-inch circles arranged randomly; sheet 3: a single two-inch diameter circle numbered as a clock in five-second increments (0 to 60); sheet four: a very long curved dotted line with a circle (¼-inch at one end).

The score also contains twenty numbered nontransparent sheets having various shapes inscribed (the number of shapes corresponding to the number of the sheet). Each performer makes his or her own score from these materials. First, a nontransparent sheet is chosen with its number corresponding to the number of cartridges available to that performer (*cartridge* here referring to a contact mike or record player needle cartridge). The performer then places the transparent sheets randomly over the numbered nontransparent sheet with the last (curved dotted line) arranged so that the circle at the end of the dotted line contains a point outside a shape and so that the dotted line intersects at least one point within one of the shapes. Figure 5.31 shows how the score might look (only one of nearly limitless possibilities). Note that the dotted line (upper left) terminates in a "filled" circle and that it intersects a point *inside* one of the

shapes (i.e., intersects a point inside the large shape, lower right-hand side of the score). One then "reads" the dotted line from one end to the other (either direction is acceptable), making note of intersections with lines, circles, and dots. Each of these intersections correlates with specific actions given in the performance notes (e.g., "intersection of the dotted line with a point within a shape indicates a sound produced in any manner on the object inserted in the cartridge corresponding to that shape.").

Timing of the work is gauged by the circle (stopwatch), here located in the upper center of the Figure (5.31). First, the arrangement shown exists for only one moment of the work (the performer's choice, with total duration being fully at their will of the performers). Second, actions during that minute take place only over periods created by intersections of the dotted line with the time circle (in this case, since the circle has not been intersected, no specific times are given).

The performer should prepare such arrangements for each minute of the scheduled performance prior to the first rehearsal. Exact schedules of actions should be made with clear indications of what procedures are necessary in exact timing sequence. Each part should be prepared separately from any other performer's part. Instruments to be used in performance (i.e., on which the contact microphones are to be used) are at the performer's discretion. "All events, ordinarily thought to be undesirable, such as feed-back, humming, howling, etc. are to be accepted in this situation." Cage refers to a performance of the work in an interview with the author:

D. C.   Did you in the process of recording the piece listen to what you were doing?

J. C.   We did, so to speak, what we had to do. You are usually a bit too busy to listen. And the idea is that the players confound one another. That's one of the ideas of the piece. So that if you do listen to what you're doing, you're apt to get the wrong attitude toward the piece. What you have to develop is an indifference to whether your work is effective or ineffective; let happen what will. In my mind it arises from the experience that is so frequent in American life, of traffic congestion, and how to take it with what I call a sober and quiet mind, how to remain susceptible to divine influences.[35]

35. Ibid.

3. Orchestration: The choice of timbres involved is freely up to the performer (except that the sound will be initiated by the cartridge). In a 1980 performance, the author utilized the insides of a piano, connecting and performing with the contact mikes directly on the strings and the sounding board. Other performers chose percussion instruments (primarily bass drum and tamtam respectively). Springs, wind-up toys, and a variety of other smaller "instruments" were also employed with effective results. Cage remarks further:

> I can't recognize *Cartridge Music* from one performance to the next. Somewhere I tell that story of going into a house . . . and the hostess to be nice had put *Cartridge Music* on in another room. . . . I turned to her and asked, "What is that music?" And she said, "You can't be serious." I said, "It's very interesting; what is it?" And then she told me. I was pleased that I couldn't recognize it. . . . I don't hear it, you see. I performed it . . . with David Tudor, and we made a recording when Earle Brown was in charge of Time Records. Earle asked David and me if . . . we wanted to hear the end result. Neither one of us wanted to hear it.[36]

4. Basic Techniques: Clearly the basic scoring of *Cartridge Music* is experimental in nature (actions for which the final result is not foreseen). Composer indeterminacy is nearly complete, with Cage having no predictable way to foresee the sounds in any given performance situation. The performer's making of the score is indeterminate in the first step (creation of the sequences of actions from the graphs), but rehearsed carefully in the second step (carrying out of those prescribed actions).

> D. C.   In a performance of *Cartridge Music,* does it cross your mind that this is a good performance, a bad performance, or enjoyable. . . ?
>
> J. C.   If I think that way then I won't hear very well. The only time that I think that things are good or bad is when some other intentions than are proper to the piece take over. That happens so frequently with orchestral music, where the players don't do what they're supposed to do. Then I don't think that it's good or bad, but has moved out of the realm of music into the world of society and becomes a theatrical situation that was not intended at all.[37]

5, 6. Vertical and Horizontal Models: Since any and all possible timbres and textures can occur in this piece, no model can exist.

7. Style: *Cartridge Music* is representative of Cage's developed indeterminacy. He has carefully (through obviously involved processes) divorced himself from the process of creative control over the elements of this work. This separation is intricate (some say as intricate as that of trying to put one's personal creative process *into* a composition). *Cartridge Music* demonstrates mature Cage philosophies in full bloom. Relationships with

36. Ibid.
37. Ibid.

Zen (a complex fusion of Western and Eastern ideas deserving far more space than is available here) are significant, with Cage standing as antithetical to the general flow of Western musical traditions.

This Cage analysis demonstrates an indeterminate approach to composition where even the composer will be unaware of the outcome. This closely resembles the stochastic concepts espoused by Iannis Xenakis in Chapter 10. In both cases, rigorous constructs are set in place, the rules of which set composition into motion. The results of both are at least specifically unpredictable, with both composers rigidly adhering to them regardless of any additions or subtractions they (based on hearing) might like to put in place. The Oliveros Vectoral Analysis in the next chapter reveals similar characteristics, but the indeterminacy is left to the particular performance situation. All these examples compare favorably with the serial concepts found in Chapter 2, but not with the "lyricism" expressed by the works found in Chapters 1, 4, 7, 9, 11 and 12.

Attneaw, Fred. "Stochastic Compositional Processes." *Journal of Aesthetics and Art Criticism* 17, no. 4 (1959):503.
Behrman, David. "What Indeterminate Notation Determines." *Perspectives of New Music* 3, no. 2 (Spring 1964).
Boulez, Pierre. "Aléa." *Perspectives of New Music* 3, no. 1 (Winter 1964). A vivid attack on indeterminacy.
Brown, Earle. "Form in New Music." *Source* 1, no. 1 (January 1967). Excellent discussion of the "event" concept, mobile structure, and open form in music.
Cage, John. "History of Experimental Music in the United States." In *Silence: Lectures & Writings* (see details of publication in listing below). Examines the composers and ideas of "events" and musical continuity (especially Cowell, Wolff, Brown, and Cage on p. 71) and "getting rid of glue."
————. *The John Cage Catalog.* New York: C. F. Peters Co., 1962.
————. *Empty Words: Writings '73–'78.* Middletown, Conn.: Wesleyan University Press, 1979.
————. *M: Writings '67–'72.* Middletown, Conn.: Wesleyan University Press, 1973. Continuation of the "collection" form of books that Cage has produced; begins to show a different side of Cage, especially in world and "semi-political" involvement.
————. *Notations.* New York: Something Else Press, 1969. A representation of 270 composers by single-page score reproductions.
————. *Pour les Oiseaux.* Paris: Pierre Belford, 1976.
————. *Silence: Lectures & Writings.* Cambridge, Mass.: The M.I.T. Press, 1966; first edition from Wesleyan University Press, 1961, paperback. See especially the article, "Indeterminacy."
————. *Writings Through Finnegans Wake.* N.Y.: Printed Editions, 1979.
————. *A Year from Monday.* Middletown, Conn.: Wesleyan University Press, 1967.
Cardew, Cornelius. "Notation-Interpretation, etc.," *Tempo* 58:24.

Bibliography

Further Readings*

*Addresses for record companies, periodicals, and music publishers mentioned in this Bibliography can be found in Appendix 4.

————, ed. *Scratch Music.* Cambridge, Massachusetts: The MIT Press; paperback
    edition, 1974. This is a book of scores and ideas by a great many composers involved
    with the *Scratch Orchestra* conducted by Cardew. Many of the works are
    indeterminate.
————. *Stockhausen Serves Imperialism.* London, England: Latimer New Dimensions
    Limited, 1974. Interesting account of this composer's about-face and repudiation of his
    own early works and those of other *avant-garde* composers.
Charles, Daniel. "Entr'acte: 'Formal' or 'Informal' Music." *Musical Quarterly* (1965). A
    good analysis of European/American differences over indeterminacy.
Childs, Barney. "Indeterminacy and Theory: Some Notes," *Composer* 1, no. 1 (June
    1969):15. An excellent "objective" approach to the subject. See also his contribution
    "Indeterminacy" in Vinton's *Dictionary of Contemporary Music.* New York: E. P.
    Dutton & Co., 1974. A superb presentation of the definition, history, and aesthetics of
    the subject (although the dictionary itself does not discriminate clearly between
    improvisation and indeterminacy).
Cone, Edward T. "One Hundred Metronomes." *The American Scholar* 46, no. 4 (Autumn,
    1977). A fascinating article offering alternative viewpoints on new music techniques.
Copland, Aaron. "The Music of Chance," In *Our New Music.* New York: W. W. Norton &
    Co., 1968. Quite fascinating though not as penetrating as the rest of the book is toward
    other areas of new music.
Dallin, Leon. *Techniques of Twentieth Century Composition.* 3rd ed. Dubuque, Iowa:
    Wm. C. Brown Company Publishers, 1974. This third edition has a chapter devoted to
    indeterminate procedures (pp. 237–49) which is a good introduction.
Doczi, György. *The Power of Limits. Proportional Harmonies in Nature, Art and
    Architecture.* Boston: Shambhala Publications, Inc., 1981. Doczi attempts to relate the
    entire universe through a single *dinergy* (a cross between two Greek words: "dia"
    [across] and "energy"). Constant references to the Golden Section provide some
    explanation for the visionary theory which culminates in various comparisons between
    architecture, music, art, life, etc., all in single interpolative graphics.
Feldman, Morton. "Predetermined/Indetermined." *Composer* (England, Fall 1966).
————. "Between Categories." *Composer* 1, no 2 (1969):73. Fine article on *time,*
    indirectly relating to a philosophical construct of indeterminacy.
Fuller, R. Buckminster. *Operating Manual for Spaceship Earth.* Carbondale: Southern
    Illinois University Press, 1969. Though not directly relating to indeterminacy, this book
    indeed relates to Cage and more relevantly to the possible implosion of indeterminate
    procedures in relation to all events, musical and otherwise; truly fascinating reading.
Hansen, Al. *A Primer of Happenings and Time-Space Art.* New York: Something Else
    Press, 1968.
Higgins, Dick. *Postface.* New York: Something Else Press, 1964. Gives some very
    interesting ideas and insights into indeterminate concepts from a neo-Cage point of
    view.
Kayn, Roland. "Random or not Random." *Horyzonty muzyki* (Cracow, 1966). Three
    lectures prepared for the Norddeutscher Rundfunk.
Kirby, Michael. *Happenings.* New York: E. P. Dutton & Co., 1965. Good historical survey
    of this indeterminate form.
Kostelanetz, Richard. *John Cage.* New York: Praeger, 1970. Superb in both text and
    pictures. A real must for any thorough study of Cage and indeterminacy.
————. *Master Minds.* New York: Macmillan, 1969. See especially "The American
    Avant-Garde," with part 2 relating particularly to John Cage and indeterminacy.

Layton, Billy Jim. "The New Liberalism." *Perspectives of New Music* 3, no. 2 (Spring 1964). Presents another attack on indeterminacy.

Logothetis, Anestis. "Gezeichnete Klänge." (*Neues Forum* 183, no. 1:177); "Kurze musikalische Spurenkunde." *Melos* 37:39.

MacKenzie, I. A. "The Critique." *Composer* 2, no. 4 (1971):92. Short but interesting letter to a critic with indeterminate procedures implied.

Metzger, Heinz-Klaus, and Riehn, Rainer, eds. *A Book about John Cage and his Music.* New York: C. F. Peters, 1981. Evaluates Cage's important "Address to an Orchestra."

O'Grady, T. J. "Aesthetic Values in Indeterminate Music." *Musical Quarterly* 67:306–81, N. 3, 1981.

Olson, Harry F., and Herbert Belar. "Aid to Composition Employing a Random Probability System." *Journal of the Acoustical Society of America* 33, no. 9 (1961).

Reynolds, Roger. "It (')s Time." *Electronic Music Review* 7 (July 1968).——— "Indeterminacy: Some Considerations." *Perspectives of New Music* 4, no. 1 (Winter 1965). Exceedingly well-written definitions of terms.

———. *Mind Models.* N.Y.: Praeger Books, 1976. Tough reading, but good discussion of the aesthetics of indeterminacy and other experimentalist techniques.

Schafer, R. Murray. *The Tuning of the World.* New York: Alfred A. Knopf, 1977. An extension of the author's work into environmental acoustic design. Part Four includes some very interesting material, especially "The Acoustic Community," and "The Soniferous Garden." The section on silence in the latter of these two chapters is interesting.

Sumner, Melody, ed. *The Guests Go In To Supper.* New York: Burning Books, 1986. Interviews and texts by John Cage, Robert Ashley, Yoko Ono, Laurie Anderson, Charles Amirkhanian, Michael Peppe and K. Atchley.

Tenney, James. *Meta (÷) Hodos: A Phenomenology of 20th-Century Music and an Approach to the Study of Form.* New Orleans, 1964. Related to a number of sections of this book in addition to indeterminacy.

Tomkins, Calvin. *The Bride and the Bachelors.* New York: Viking Press, 1965. Interesting biographical account of John Cage and related artists (Duchamp, Tinguely, and Rauschenberg).

Wolff, Christian. "On Form." *Die Reihe* 7:26. Relates to indeterminacy as does almost everything that Wolff writes, whether in words or music.

Xenakis, Iannis. *Formalized Music.* Bloomington: Indiana University Press, 1971. Quite interesting though mathematically complex even to those familiar with the subject.

Yates, Peter. *Twentieth Century Music.* New York: Pantheon Books, 1967. A bit outdated but does include some wonderful insights into Cage as well as into indeterminacy (see especially chaps. 30–32, pp. 303ff.).

Young, La Monte, and Jackson Mac Low, eds. *An Anthology of Chance Operations.* New York: La Monte Young & Jackson Mac Low, 1963. Excellent source for readings in chance philosophy and procedures, and includes articles by Young, Mac Low, and Maxfield in particular.

Andriessen, Louis. *Ittrospezione II* (1963). Donemus. For orchestra.

———. *Paintings.* Belwin-Mills.

Ashley, Robert. *in memoriam Crazy Horse* (1963). Recorded on Advance 5.

———. *Wolfman* (1964). CPE-*Source* IV.

Recordings and Publishers

Austin, Larry. *Accidents* (1967). CPE-*Source*.

————. *Piano Set* and *Piano Variations* (1964). Recorded by the Modern Jazz Quartet, Advance S-10.

Bedford, David. *Whitefield Music II*. For six to thirty-six players not trained in music.

Boulez, Pierre. *Structures I for Two Pianos* (1952). Universal Edition.

Brown, Earle. *Available Forms I* and *II*. AMP. The former recorded on RCA Vics1239.

————. *Four Systems*. Recorded on Columbia MS-7139. For amplified cymbals.

————. *Hodograph I*. Recorded on Mainstream 5007.

————. *Music for Violoncello and Pianoforte* (1952). Recorded on Mainstream 5007.

————. *Quartet* (1965). Recorded on Mainstream 5009.

————. *December 1952*. (1952). C. F. Peters. Recorded on CRI S-330.

————. *Du* (1951). Boelke-Bomart. Recorded on Son Nova 1.

Bussotti, Sylvano. *Per tre sul piano* (1959). Universal. Recorded on EMI EMSP 55.

Bussotti, Sylvano. *Coeur pour Batteur—Positively Yes*. Universal Edition. Recorded on Columbia MS-7139.

————. *Frammento*. Ricordi. Recorded on Mainstream 5005.

————. *Five Pieces for David Tudor*. Universal Edition. Recorded on CP2 3–5.

Cage, John. *Amores for Prepared Piano and Percussion*. Peters. Recorded on Mainstream 5011. CD: Bis; CD272.

————. *Aria with Fontana Mix* (1958). C. F. Peters. Recorded on Mainstream 5005 (also includes works of Berio and Bussotti).

————. *Atlas Eclipticalis*. Peters. Recorded on DG-137009.

————. *Concert for Piano and Orchestra*. C. F. Peters.

————. *Cartridge Music* (1960). C. F. Peters. Recorded on Mainstream 5015.

————. *HPSCHD*. C. F. Peters. Recorded on Nonesuch 71224.

————. *Solo for Voice 2*. C. F. Peters. Recorded on Odyssey 32–160156.

————. *Fontana Mix*. C. F. Peters. Recorded on Columbia MS-7139.

————. *Indeterminacy*. (Cage, narrator; Tudor, piano). Recorded on Folkways 3704.

————. *Theatre Piece*. C. F. Peters.

————. *Variations I*. C. F. Peters. Recorded on Wergo 60033.

————. *Variations II*. C. F. Peters. Recorded on Columbia MS-7051.

————. *Variations III*. C. F. Peters. Recorded on DG-139442.

————. *Variations IV*. C. F. Peters. Recorded on Everest 3132.

————. *26'1.1499" for a String Player*. C. F. Peters. Recorded on Nonesuch 71237.

————. *34'46.776" for a Pianist*. C. F. Peters.

————. *4'33"*. C. F. Peters.

Cardew, Cornelius. *Treatise* (1963–67). Buffalo: Gallery Upstairs Press. Graphic music for unspecified ensembles.

Feldman, Morton. *Chorus and Instruments*. C. F. Peters. Recorded on Odyssey 32–160156.

————. *Christian Wolff in Cambridge*. C. F. Peters. Recorded on Odyssey 32–160156.

————. *Durations*. C. F. Peters. Recorded on Mainstream 5007.

————. *False Relationships and the Extended Ending*. C. F. Peters. Recorded on CRI S-276.

————. *In Search of an Orchestration* (1967). C. F. Peters.

————. *Intersection 3*. C. F. Peters. Recorded on DG-139442.

————. *King of Denmark*. C. F. Peters. Recorded on Columbia MS-7139.

————. *Out of "Last Pieces."* C. F. Peters. Recorded on Columbia MS-6733.

————. *Viola in my Life.* C. F. Peters. Recorded on CRI S-276. In addition, Odyssey 32–160302 includes the following Feldman works: *Structures, Three Pieces, Extensions I, Projections 4, Intersection 3, Two Pieces, Extension 4,* and *Piece* (1957). All are published by Peters.

Foss, Lukas. *Geod.* Recorded on Candide 31042.

Haubenstock-Ramati, Roman. *Interpolation: a "Mobile" for Flute* (1,2,3), 1958. Universal Edition. Recorded on RCA Vics-1312.

————. *Jeux 2.* Universal Edition.

————. *Mobile for Shakespeare.* Universal Edition. This composer's works are listed with examples in a brochure published by Universal Edition. Almost all deal in one way or another with indeterminate elements.

Higgins, Dick. *Thousand Symphonies* CPE-*Source.*

————. *Piano Album: Short Pieces* (1962–1982). New York: Printed Editions. Collection of graphic scores.

Hykes, David. *Harmonic Meetings.* Recorded on CHCEL–013/014 (2 record set). Performances by a trio from his Harmonic Choir incorporating words from the Abrahamic religions.

Kagel, Mauricio. *1898* (1973). London: Universal Edition.

Kayn, Roland. *Galaxis* (1962). Moeck. Uses variable instrumentation.

Logothetis, Anestis. *Ichnologia* (1964).

————. *Kulmination.* Edition Modern/Munich. Recorded on Wergo 60057.

————. *Labyrinthos* (1965). Universal Edition. For any soloists or any chamber orchestra.

————. *Odyssee* (1963). Universal Edition.

Maderna, Bruno. *Viola* (open and closed form versions). Recorded on Finnadar 9007.

Mizelle, John. *Radial Energy.* CPE-*Source.*

Moran, Robert. *Bombardments No. 2.* C. F. Peters.

————. *Four Visions.* Universal Edition.

Mumma, Gordon. *Mesa for Cybersonic Bandoneon.* Recorded on Odyssey 32–160158.

Nilsson, Bo. *Reaktionen* (1960). Universal Edition. For four percussionists; uses open form structures.

Pousseur, Henri. *Caractères* (1961). Universal Edition.

————. *Vôtre Faust.* Universal Edition. Variable operatic fantasy.

Rabe, Folke. *Pièce* (1961). W. Hansen. For speaking chorus, done in collaboration with Lasse O'Mansson.

Schäffer, Boguslaw. *S'alto* (1963). PWM. For alto saxophone and orchestra.

————. *Violin Concerto* (1963). PWM.

Stockhausen, Karlheinz. *Klavierstück XI.* Universal Edition. Recorded on Phillips 6500101. CD: Hung; HCD 12569–2.

————. *STOP.* Universal Edition.

Wolff, Christian. *Duo, Duet* and *Summer.* Recorded on Mainstream 5015.

————. *Duo II for Pianists.* C. F. Peters.

————. *Edges* (1968). CPE-*Source.*

————. *For 1, 2 or 3 People.* C. F. Peters. Recorded on Odyssey 32–160158.

————. *Trio 2* (1961). C. F. Peters. Piano, four hands.

Xenakis, Iannis. *Akrata.* Boosey and Hawkes. Recorded on Nonesuch 71201

————. *Duel.* Boosey and Hawkes.

6. EXPERIMENTALISM

6

Chronology and Fundamentals

Experimentalism is, for the purposes of this text, a redefining of the boundaries of a given form. "Art as life" or "art as everything" both qualify. The scope of this book does not permit fully detailed coverage of the cross-disciplinary aspects of the arts in general, and in particular, the added stimulus which the visual arts in particular have given to new music. However, the impetus generated by artists such as Marcel Duchamp, Man Ray, Robert Rauschenberg, Kandinsky, and many others has been profound. In the mainstream of music one finds composers like Schoenberg (who was himself an expressionist painter of repute) and Stravinsky influenced by Expressionism and painters like Picasso (see Chapter 1). In the avant-garde one encounters cross-relationships particularly between composers and artists such as Erik Satie (Man Ray), John Cage (Robert Rauschenberg), and Earle Brown (Alexander Calder).

If one were to trace the roots of experimentalism, the *Musical Sculpture* (undated) by Marcel Duchamp is noteworthy, showing a direct relationship with current concept music. His early work *The Bride Stripped Bare by Her Bachelors, Even* is especially provocative. Duchamp's *Erratum Musical* (1913) is a work of numbers substituting (in realization) a note for each number (Petr Kotik has made two current realizations, one for two pianos, the other for five instruments). The dada artists and later the antiart, concept art, and minimal art movements have all preceded parallel activities in music.

Paul Nougé (active in the surrealistic movement), in his *Music is Dangerous* (written in 1929), points out that its most known "uses" of music (relaxation, forgetting, and pleasure) are but subtle façades for its emotional dangers, drawing proofs from the ancient modal theories wherein each mode provoked distinct emotions (phrygian: excitement; lydian: calming; etc.).[1] His "iatric" music (medicinal music: noting that a great many medical terms end in "iatric" such as pediatric, etc.) further establishes music's profound remedial capabilities (possibly in the sense that a witch doctor has therapeutic powers, predating our current fascination with music therapy). Most important, however, Nougé proposes that the audience is not separate from or even "safe" from musical performance: "Our answer is that the

---

1. Paul Nougé, *Music is Dangerous*, trans. Felix Giovanelli from *View* magazine. Reprinted in book form by *Soundings* (1973).

concept of *spectator,* which seems to play so important a role in certain minds, is one of the grossest imaginable."[2] It is doubtful that Nougé's writings have had a direct influence over the new experimentalism of our present era; however, it is most noteworthy that such expressions as ". . . how we may defend ourselves against music. . . . Evidently, the easiest way is to refuse once and for all to have anything to do with it . . ." are not new or light divertissement as might be supposed.[3]

Questions regarding the most fundamental ideas, often more *about* than *with* sound, inevitably arise from these concepts. The continual expansion of the definition of music to include *all* sound, regardless of origin or "beauty," and all concepts of sound, may eventually annul the new experimental designation used here. The primary motive behind this philosophy, however, remains: to destroy the concept of an "immaculate" art separate from life, with all its dangers and transiency. Indeed, the new experimentalist philosophy returns full circle to the primeval.

Robert Rauschenberg, possibly more than any other artist (aside from Jackson Pollock and Marcel Duchamp), has sustained a creative "antiart" movement which has substantially affected a number of composers. His *Erased de Kooning Drawing* is exactly that: a de Kooning drawing (one he obtained directly from the artist himself) erased as completely as possible using a special selection of erasers collected by Rauschenberg. The act of "decomposing" the work of art becomes in this instance the "act" of creation (of a white sheet of paper only barely showing hints of lines, or even less—slight depressions in the paper where the original drawing once existed). If one can deal with art as *change,* beauty as totally *relative,* any *act* as plausibly artistic, then Rauschenberg's erasure presents a work as significant as the original drawing. Whether one deals with it as such or not is of little consequence: it is antiart.

Robert Rauschenberg's *Black Painting* of 1952 demonstrates both the conceptual nature of his work and the extraordinary complexity of shading provided the right lighting. The lunar landscape quality has been brought forth nicely. The painting itself is entirely black. What the painter has accomplished is to successfully distill a single sculptural feature of painting (reflection). The application of the principle reveals the complex refinement of the concept when applied rigorously.

One composer has come close to this approach in music, but in an entirely different way. He has substituted an entire work of the past *verbatim* for his own. Paul Ignace indicates some of the rationale behind such actions in a letter to the author.

When I was first asked to compose a piece for orchestra I had no idea what they wanted, except an experience of some kind. I wrote and asked for a complete list of the other works included in concerts of the series, and when I discovered that the concert preceding the night of my premiere included Berlioz's *Symphonie Fantastique,* I made up my mind. I insisted that my work be unrehearsed (there wouldn't have been much anyway, as those things go) and that I would bring score and parts the night of the concert. Imagine the shock when the conductor and players opened their music to find the work that they had performed the night before . . . but

2. Ibid., p. 17.
3. Ibid., p. 24.

they performed it, much to the anger and horror of the audience and reviewers. They were angry, of course, not at the sounds but at my plagiarism (legal, according to copyright laws) but few realized they listened to the sounds in an entirely new way—something very good, very creative, in my way of thinking. No, I did not receive $$$ for my endeavor!

(The work, by the way, was titled *Symphonie Fantastique No. 2.*)[4]

Yehuda Yannay's *Houdini's Ninth* (1970) is experimental theater quite apropos of this genre. Bernard Jacobson characterizes one performance in this excerpt in his article in *Stereo Review.*

A man cycled onto the stage, put a record of the (Beethoven) *Choral* Symphony finale on a phonograph, and proceeded to mix some kind of culinary concoction onto the surface of the actual disc, with bizarre effects on the sound. This was interwoven with an episode involving a double-bass player in a sort of straitjacket, and dominating the proceedings was a projection of an incredibly stupid poem published in *Dwight's Journal of Music,* Boston, on December 17, 1870. It was in honor of Beethoven's centenary, and took a very encouraging view of his affliction of deafness: "A price how small," it cheerily informed him, "for privilege how great,/ When thy locked sense groped upward and there/ The shining ladder reaching through the air."[5]

Encouraged by the words of social philosophers Marshall McLuhan and R. Buckminster Fuller, and his own studies with Eastern philosopher Suzuki, John Cage developed a personal philosophy expressed clearly in his sweeping statement: "Everything we do is music." His works encompass every aspect of the new concepts of the last fifty years: electronic, improvisatory, indeterminate, multimedic, exploratory and experimentalistic. From his work in the thirties, when he originated the "prepared piano," to his extension of multimedia "happenings," he has remained the remarkable enigma. His ideas and works amuse, startle, antagonize, and somehow also encourage the worlds of music, dance, and art. If *change,* not idolatry, be the mark of greatness, then John Cage has surely reached this pinnacle. Nothing can or will be the same after him.

Aside from Cage, no other composer has achieved the shock value of, and relevance to, antiart, except perhaps La Monte Young. In particular, his *Composition 1960 #3* (the duration of the piece is announced and the audience told to do whatever they wish for the remainder of the composition) and *Composition 1960 #6,* (the performers stare and react exactly as if they were the audience) are excellent examples of the "anti" aspect at work.[6]

The new experimentalism is a returning to the soil. Works do not cease to exist, but a new awareness of *all* things, their disorder and order, their direction and nondirection in the temporal continuum, takes place. Man is no longer the center of the

---

4. From a letter to the author.
5. Available on film from the composer: 4044 N. Downer Ave., Milwaukee, Wis. 53211 (as of December 1974).
6. Barney Childs discusses these works and others in an excellent article, "Indeterminacy and Theory: Some Notes," *Composer* 1, no. 1 (June 1969):15–34.

universe. As an artist, one no longer attempts gymnastic representations of life, but becomes a part of it. Like the antijoke, one relies on an audience expectancy of traditional forms; funny because it isn't funny, music because it isn't music: inherently temporary as awareness increases, constantly inevitable as all meaning requires opposites for significant identity.

Critics of these and other experimentalists address themselves to the "dead end" and "pointless" philosophies implied. To these, I. A. MacKenzie has replied:

> Art is imitation, repetition, memory, or rejection of life. Nothing is created by man, just recreated: a storeroom to collect the bits and pieces of the whole he feels worthy of saving, to be brought to life again whenever the need occurs, but never as good as the original. Art exists only as a refuge against new experience, un-recreated experience with reality: second-hand living. The terms "musician," "painter," "writer," merely break these limitations down further for easier construction, assimilation and comfort. I am none of these. I am not an artist. I do not imitate, or need of developing [sic] a memory with art for a thousand million possibilities of the present confront me, and I don't want that number diminished by one.
>
> I am a mapmaker, a suggester of possible routes for those interested in experiences with what has already been created—everything. I am similar to the "artist" in that I do not create, dissimilar with him in that I do not pretend to.
>
> Untouched by style, convenience, or tradition, the elements I observe (not manipulate) I discovered, but only for myself and my discovery has style, convenience just as yours.
>
> I do nothing that anyone else could not do easily and do not pretend to. I only give directions when someone wishes them and would be happy to stop anytime. . . .
>
> Everything exists: why should I mechanically alter one thing into another, one thought into another? All exist—it is much more—to find the original.[7]

With these basic concepts and experiments, a transcendental form of expression emerges outside the realm of the arts. Communication rests more directly on the audience than on the creator, often philosophically—more often theatrically—antagonizing the experience of man. New experiments are *necessary, important,* and *contribute* to art without artificial values or misdirected definitions of terms.

Cage speaks of this in *A Year from Monday:* "Art's in process of coming into its own: life."[8] and "We used to have the artist up on a pedestal. Now he's no more extraordinary than we are."[9] Tzara states: "Art is not the most precious manifestation of life. Art has not the celestial and universal value that people like to attribute to it. Life is far more interesting."[10]

These directions extend to include those sounds which destroy the mind (*danger music*), which don't exist (*conceptualism*), and which come about without the hand of man (*biomusic* and *soundscapes*).

7. I. A. MacKenzie, as paraphrased by David Cope in *Notes in Discontinuum* (Los Angeles: Discant Music, 1970), p. 2.
8. John Cage, *A Year from Monday* (Middletown, Conn.: Wesleyan University Press, 1967), p. 6.
9. Ibid., p. 50.
10. Robert Motherwell, *The Dada Painters and Poets: An Anthology* (New York: Wittenborn, Schultz, Inc., 1951), p. 248.

Danger Music

The history of *danger music* is long indeed, and if one follows Paul Nougé's thinking in *Music is Dangerous*,[11] all music has such potential. While, as he points out, we may use it for "relaxation," "forgetting" or "pleasure" it . . . "probably entails serious consequences."[12] This fascinating book describes a number of accounts of man's unfortunate encounters with the dangers of music:

> Sometimes we find peculiar stories in a newspaper. A few weeks ago, a young American went home after coming out of a performance of *Tannhauser,* and killed himself; not without having first written a note in which he explained that where Tannhäuser had weakened, he, yes he, would set a better example of courage and grandeur.[13]

Most current *danger music* involves a more direct attack on the performer or spectator (e.g., Nam June Paik's *Danger Music for Dick Higgins* with the score reading: "Creep into the Vagina of a living Whale.").[14] Figure 6.1 shows Paik during a 1962 *Fluxus* performance.

The visual arts have certainly had direct influence on *danger music*. Ayo, for example, has created a number of finger boxes each containing a substance unknown to the "spectator." One experiences the art by placing fingers into these small creations some of which contain felt, fur, and similar "pleasantries." Some, however, contain razor blades, broken glass, and pocket knives. "Chance" has a new dimension here as one must weigh the odds of pain against pleasure.

Figure 6.1. Nam June Paik during a 1962 *Fluxus* performance.

11. Nougé, op. cit.
12. Ibid., p. 11.
13. Ibid., p. 11.
14. See John Cage's *Notations* (New York: Something Else Press, 1969), unpaged, for a copy of the score in full.

Though blood (and even death) are not unknown to *danger musics,* these seldom occur as a direct result of composer notation. "Accidents" are welcomed, however. Such was the case of two happenings in 1962: the first involved a somewhat "bloodied" Robert Whitman at Bennington College; the second involved a woman spectator/performer at an Al Hansen happening falling from a window down a number of stories and eventually through a glass roof.

The environment around us provides another source of danger: sound pollution. While discussed in more depth later in this chapter under *soundscapes,* the aural dangers of even the average household cannot escape the artist's cognizance. Robert Ashley's *Wolfman* (1964) exemplifies *danger music.* Through use of a prerecorded tape and a voice "screaming" through a microphone involving electronic feedback, all turned to extremely loud levels, the work easily reaches decibel counts above danger level. The recording of this work, with instructions "to be played at the highest possible volume level" indeed constitutes ear annihilation to the uninitiated in a small "live" room.[15]

Figure 6.2. Robert Ashley.

Phil Corner's adaptation of his own *prelude* from *4 Suits* creates interesting danger music:

I threw out a rifle and then slowly picked it up and pointed it at the audience (no one bolted for the doors, by the way) . . . counterpointed by a woman who slowly picked up a bouquet of roses—there was a countdown . . . at the end of which she threw the flowers into the audience, all over, with great love and joy, while I silently let fall the rifle and slunk offstage. Yet this was apparently not the right message for some, as I was accosted afterwards by one of the *Up Against The Wall Motherfucker* crowd, and yelled at: "Next time a real rifle!"[16]

15. *Wolfman* is published in *Source: Music of the Avant-Garde* 2, no. 2 (July 1968). Both the score and the recording are available.
16. From a letter to the author.

Corner's *"One antipersonnel-type CBU bomb will be thrown into the audience"* is another example of danger music used to express antiwar political views. Corner speaks of this work:

> I tried to push the concert situation to a point where those present would *have* to feel the immediacy of the situation—*their* situation, since this had to be something in which those present shared a complicity. Failure! Could I have been that naive? For the audience reaction is *not* predictable. I discovered that right then and there.
> For that reason the thing was not even ever done. The defenses against identifying with the victims, with putting ourselves in their places, is too strong. Guilt is covered up by a selfish fear. A self-serving, even dishonest one, I might add. I felt it then and still do. The idea that that would really be acted on, that a real terrorist act would be announced so and carried out in this way seems to me incredible. Finally though, the "performance" would have been to announce the cancellation of the performance.[17]

Danger music is rarely sound; it is philosophy. Performances merge with reality. Danger music denotes war with music, war with the sanctity of sensual isolation. Daniel Lentz's comments in the Coda of his *Skeletons Don't Say Peek*[18] explicitly attack the hierarchy of traditional concert and instrumental performance routine:

> I too am sad. In fact, I am very sad. Men are still fighting wars and playing music. Some are guerilla wars, and some are guerilla compositions. But they are, nevertheless, war and music. They are fought with weapons and instruments. There is so little difference. One type is used for the defense of an army or nation; the other, for the defense of a vestigial culture. Do we need the protection of generals and composers? Do we need their incredibly scary anti-ballistic-missile systems and synthesizers? Shouldn't we attempt their destruction, before they destroy us? From whom are they protecting us? From the Russians? The Princetonians? What, in the late-middle 20th century does weaponry have to do with music? Can we eliminate one without first eliminating the other? Won't the metaphor be too powerful until it is taken away? Has there ever been an instrument built which wasn't used? Couldn't the players you saw in action tonight just as well have been aggressive soldiers of war? Did you watch closely their gestures? Is there a real difference between them and the Special Forces? Are they not identical mentalities? They are out to kill us and you sit there waiting. Are you all crazy? Can't you see, nor hear? But wait . . . don't blame the players. We are only cogs in the great hierarchy. We follow directions. The artistic generals tell us what to do and when to do it and the manner in which it is to be done. They are not even specific. Aren't they kind, as they destroy us? We are like you: just poor citizens caught up in the immense musical-industrial complex. Sure, if you threaten us or our friends, we will play for you. We have no recourse but to protect our "raison d'être."

17. Ibid.
18. Part of Harold Budd's *California 99* (1969), the movements of which were composed by Turetzky, Oliveros, Austin, Childs, Lunetta, Mizelle, and Sherr.

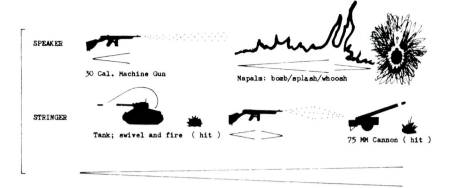

Figure 6.3. Daniel Lentz: *Anti Bass Music*, page 11.

SPEAKER

30 Cal. Machine Gun

Napalm: bomb/splash/whoosh

STRINGER

Tank; swivel and fire (hit)

75 MM Cannon (hit)

Prior to this final "performer" announcement, all the instruments have been taken from the performers, placed in front of the piano, and *saluted*. The act of not playing, the drama of attacking the performance situation, eliminates all vestige of traditional (and, for that matter, nontraditional) equipment, instruments, and concepts.

Daniel Lentz's works are often antiwar as well. *Anti Bass Music,* for example (see Figure 6.3), employs a number of notations relating the concert situation to the battlefield. The work, supplied with four optional endings (which may be performed in multiples; that is, more than one ending may be employed), includes a reading of a list of American composers not killed in Viet Nam, and the use of twenty-five to one hundred laughing machines.

Conceptualism

Minimal and *concept music* are so closely related that separation becomes difficult (though both deserve distinct analysis). Minimal art is the closest "art" relative to *minimal music.* Works such as Robert Rauschenberg's *White Paintings* (canvases covered as evenly as possible with white paint) are parallel to such minimal works as John Cage's classic: *4'33".*

4'33" received its first performance in August, 1952, at Woodstock, New York by pianist David Tudor. Using a stopwatch, he covered the piano keyboard at the beginning of each movement, playing nothing, but timing the silences of each period marked by Cage in the otherwise blank score. Unfortunately, the brilliance of Tudor's dramatic performance had the adverse effect of limiting this work to piano (the score mentions no instrumentation). The title ("for any instrument or combination of instruments") makes realization practical on almost any conceivable plane of sound or nonsound. Virtually anything with a total duration of four minutes and thirty-three seconds (and movements of one minute, forty seconds; two minutes, twenty-three seconds; and thirty seconds respectively) could successfully serve as a realization of the score, from thinking-in-a-bathtub to silence by a symphony orchestra.[19] Cage has clarified the concept behind such works:

> . . . where it is realized that sounds occur whether intended or not, one turns in the direction of those he does not intend. The turning is psychological and seems at first to be a giving up of everything that belongs to humanity—for a musician, the giving up of music. This psychological turning leads to the world of nature, where, gradually or suddenly, one sees that humanity and nature, not separate, are in this world together; that nothing was lost when everything was given away. In fact, everything is gained.[20]

Rauschenberg's *White Paintings* link further with *4'33''* when one realizes that in the former the shadows of spectators, variance of lights, reflections, etc., turn the seemingly blank canvas into a veritable mass of visual activity. In the latter, the coughs, laughter, and other audible movements of the audience as well as the extraneous sounds from without the performance area become, in fact, the work. In both cases the act of the creator is minimal *and* conceptual.

Minimal music (most often minimal in materials and not duration, as will be seen) is also clearly defined in the works of La Monte Young. His *Composition 1960 #7* contains only the notes B and F♯ with the instructions: to be held for a "long time." *Composition 1960 #10* requests the performer to "draw a straight line and follow it."[21] In 1960, at Berkeley, he presented a composition which consisted of turning loose a jar full of butterflies (they made a sound however inaudible). . . .[22]

Others of that same year include his famous (infamous) "line piece":

> My "Composition 1960 No. 9" consists of a straight line drawn on a piece of paper. It is to be performed and comes with no instructions. The night I met Jackson MacLow we went down to my apartment and he read some of his poems for us. Later when he was going home, he said he'd write out directions to get to his place so we could come and visit him sometime. He happened to pick up "Composition No. 9" and said, "Can I write it here?" I said, "No, wait, that's a piece. Don't write on that." He said, "Whadaya mean a piece? That's just a line."[23]

Karlheinz Stockhausen's *Mikrophonie I* (1964) uses only one sound source, a large (about six feet) tam-tam upon which the performers manipulate the various verbal instructions of the score, "scraping, trumpeting," and so on.

Concept music, though often overlapping many of the aforementioned works, is also extremist (more powerful and often more interesting in premise than in the performance situation—if there is one). Eric Andersen's *Opus 48 ("Which turns*

19. This work is published in *Source: Music of the Avant-Garde* 1, no. 2 (July 1967):46 ff.
20. John Cage, *Silence* (Cambridge, Mass.: The M.I.T. Press, paperback edition, 1961), p. 8.
21. A great deal of material on and by LaMonte Young is found in *Selected Writings* by La Monte Young and Marian Zazeela (Munich: Heiner Friedrich, 1969).
22. Richard Kostelanetz, *The Theatre of Mixed Means* (New York: Dial Press, 1968), from the article (first page) on La Monte Young.
23. Young and Zazeela, *Selected Writings,* unpaged (from the Lecture 1960, copyright 1965 by the Tulane Drama Review).

Figure 6.4. Tom Johnson:
Celestial Music for Imaginary
Trumpets. © Copyright 1974
by Tom Johnson. All rights
reserved. Used by
permission. From *Imaginary
Music* by Tom Johnson, Two
Eighteen Press, N.Y.C.

anonymous when the instruction is carried out") is sent through the mail on a piece of cardboard which states in total: "Place the chosen tautology." This is *concept art* (implication of music not being present). Tom Johnson, in his book *Imaginary Music,* includes a number of nonplayable concept pieces.[24] His *Celestial Music for Imaginary Trumpets* (see Figure 6.4) is clearly *concept music,* as performance is impossible; one is able to only "conceptualize" or imagine the work. Robert Moran's *Composition for Piano with Pianist* states: "A pianist comes onto the stage and goes directly to the concert grand piano. He climbs into the piano, and sits on the strings. The piano plays him."[25] This conceptual *message* is more important than any "real" act of sound production.

Concept philosophy is often implied only in the score and is not "real" to the audience. *Accidents* (1967) by Larry Austin, for example, contains instructions in which the pianist performs gestures while avoiding actual sounds. The speed of performance makes accidents unavoidable. As if repenting sins, the performer must return to each gesture in which an accident occurred (i.e., a sound made) and repeat it until error-free (i.e., no sound occurring).

The German-originated but often New York-based movement *Fluxus* (which included Paik, Young, Dick Higgins, Eric Andersen, Thomas Schmidt, Jackson MacLow, and George Brecht) represented the basic directions in concept music for a number of years, finally becoming a publisher of art objects. Blank structures provide objectives in the experiments of these composers, poets, and artists. Often these works do not contain the slightest hint as to what action is intended or what materials are to be used.[26] Figure 6.5 provides a George Maciunas view of what the Fluxus art movement means. The references to "Spikes (sic) Jones" and Duchamp suggest the levity which many members of the various group felt about their projects. Figures 6.6 and 6.7 provide photo documentation of some of the members of Fluxus. Other individuals involved (but not shown here) included Jonas Mekas, Bob Watts, Ben Patterson, and Joe Jones.

24. Tom Johnson, *Imaginary Music.* New York: Two-Eighteen Press (P.O. Box 218, Village Station, New York, N.Y. 10014), 1974.
25. Published in *Soundings* 1:44.
26. *Fluxus* movements have also arisen in other countries, including Japan (Takehisa Kosugi, Chieko Shiomi) and Germany.

Figure 6.5. "Fluxus" by George Maciunas from Happening and Fluxus, materials put together by H. Sohm, Kölnischer Kunstverein 1970.

ART	FLUXUS ART-AMUSEMENT
To justify artist's professional, parasitic and elite status in society, he must demonstrate artist's indispensability and exclusiveness, he must demonstrate the dependability of audience upon him, he must demonstrate that no one but the artist can do art.	To establish artist's nonprofessional status in society, he must demonstrate artist's dispensability and inclusiveness, he must demonstrate the selfsufficiency of the audience, he must demonstrate that anything can be art and anyone can do it.
Therefore, art must appear to be complex, pretentious, profound, serious, intellectual, inspired, skillfull, significant, theatrical, it must appear to be valuable as commodity so as to provide the artist with an income. To raise its value (artist's income and patrons profit), art is made to appear rare, limited in quantity and therefore obtainable and accessible only to the social elite and institutions.	Therefore, art-amusement must be simple, amusing, unpretentious, concerned with insignificances, require no skill or countless rehearsals, have no commodity or institutional value. The value of art-amusement must be lowered by marking it unlimited, massproduced, obtainable by all and eventually produced by all. Fluxus art-amusement is the rear-guard without any pretention or urge to participate in the competition of "one-upmanship" with the avant-garde. It strives for the monostructural and nontheatrical qualities of simple natural event, a game or a gag. It is the fusion of Spikes Jones, Vaudeville, gag, children's games and Duchamp. George Maciunas from: Happening & Fluxus Materials put together by H. Sohm Kölnischer Kunstverein 1970

Figure 6.6. Mieko Shiomi and Alison Knowles during a performance of *"Disappearing Music for Face"* (smile–no smile) at the Washington Square (New York City) gallery on October 30, 1964.

Figure 6.7. Fluxus members (left to right): Emmett Williams, Robert Filliou, George Brecht, Eric Andersen, Thomas Schmit, Robin Page and Ben Vautier at the exhibition of Happening and Fluxus at the Kölnischer Kunstverein in Cologne, Germany. Photo by Ad Petersen.

Text sound music involves minimal procedures and is based on the *textljud kompositioner* of two Swedish composers, Lars-Gunnar Bodin and Bengt-Emil Johnson in 1967. Termed sound poetry, speech music, and even lexical music, its origins extend back to the Futurists (in Italy) just after the turn of the century. Works in this genre expand reading and speaking concepts, utilizing onomatopoeia and other intricate textural mechanics to produce rhythmic and contrapuntal structures. Often these incorporate long repetitions of words in solo or ensemble situations, with changing and developing emphasis, accents, and meaning. Frequently these works are altered through electronic processes.

Composers aware of this form early in this century include Hugo Ball, Tristan Tzara, and Kurt Schwitters in the twenties; Marcel Duchamp in the thirties and forties; and John Cage in the fifties and sixties. Composers currently interested in the genre include John Giorno, Aram Saroyan, Brion Gysin, Beth Anderson, Robert Ashley, Anthony Gnazzo, Tim Bell, Stephen Ruppenthal, and Charles Amirkhanian. Amirkhanian has produced a large number of text sound works, including *Seatbelt Seatbelt* (1973), *Mugic* (1973), *Mahogany Ballpark* (1976), and *Dutiful Ducks* (1977).

Biomusic

Biomusic (music created by natural functions rather than by necessarily conscious attempts at composition) has taken some interesting turns in recent years. A number of composers have become interested in "brain-wave" music. Human (and, for that matter, other advanced animals') brains function with bits of electric currents. Amplifying such energy produces enough current to serve as control voltages on synthesizer functions (utilizing normal electronic music gear such as oscillators, filters, etc.). The brain directly controls sonic output.

"Brain-wave" experiments have created conflicting reports. Stockhausen notes:

> . . . I attended a concert in which David Tudor, together with a composer at Davis, California, where I taught for six months, were performing a piece with "brain waves." The performance, in the beginning, seemed to be very magic-like, a table lifting society, and it seemed to promise quite a lot because of the way they were watching and looking at each other. The speakers' cardboard membranes were pushing the air, and these pulsations—a kind of colored low noise—were produced by the performer's brain waves. It's the same effect as if air were being pumped into a tire. So what? There's a certain periodicity which becomes more or less irregular, maybe interesting for doctors.[27]

Composer David Rosenboom has developed procedures far more sophisticated than those described by Stockhausen.[28] Success, of course, remains in the "heads" of the *performers* and their necessarily practiced art of controlling *alpha* waves.

27. Jonathan Cott, *Stockhausen* (New York: Simon and Schuster, 1973), p. 43.
28. Prevalent in performances on such as the David Frost television show and others on NET (early 1970s).

Possibly one of the most fascinating areas of *biomusic* is the sound of the humpback whale. Initial hearing proves this to be more than a preposterous joke. Indeed these advanced mammals are highly creative:

> Quite apart from any esthetic judgment one might make about them, the sounds produced by Humpback whales can properly be called songs because they occur in complete sequences that are repeated. . . . Humpback whale songs are far longer than bird songs. The shortest Humpback song recorded lasts six minutes and the longest is more than thirty minutes.[29]

Not only have recordings and tapes of the "songs" of the humpback whale become popular in and of themselves, but they have equally impressed composers. George Crumb's *Voice of the Whale* (*Vox Balaenae*, 1971), ". . . was inspired by the singing of the humpback whale, a tape recording of which I had heard two or three years previously."[30] Likewise composers like Allen Strange and Priscilla McLean have completed works influenced by this most highly developed of water mammals.

Works involving a "rediscovery" of bioenvironmental sounds include Pauline Oliveros's *Sonic Meditation XIII.*

Yehuda Yannay's *Bugpiece* involves yet another life form in a slightly different manner, but is definitely *biomusic*. The work uses "live notation" in the form of:

> . . . one beetle, one centipede, and five or six ants. These insects were in a real sense the "composers" and conductors, even if Yannay did set up the parameters as to how the chance operations would work. All the lights in the auditorium were turned off, the overhead projector was turned on so the audience and performers (with their backs to the audience) could see the bugs running around in a plastic box set on the projector. Different areas of the "playing field" represented varieties of loud and soft. Green, yellow, and blue gels represented high and low pitches. The ants did most of the running, even one was maimed. The beetle stayed around the sides, but did make one mad dash across the field. To spark things up, the centipede was a late entry, and he chased the beetle.[31]

An even later entry into the "bio" scene, *plant-created music,* is described vividly in an article from the *Rolling Stone:*

> It could be said they were singing, but that is too anthropomorphic a way to describe the sounds the plants were emitting: strange electronic garglings, ethereal chirpings and shriekings to a mysterious nonlinear rhythm that reveals the secret life-pulse of the vegetable kingdom. Then something very strange happened. A spectator gently held a knife to one of the stalks and addressed the plant. "Hey you! Perk up or you get it." The words plunged the room into sudden silence. The plants stopped singing. Coleuses may be pretty but they certainly aren't dumb. Somehow the threatened

29. Liner notes on Columbia ST-620, ''Songs of the Humpback Whale.''
30. Liner notes on Columbia M-32739.
31. Clifford Barnes, ''Music: Melody sent into exile,'' *Cincinnati Post,* November 15, 1972.

plant conveyed a warning of danger to its pot-mates, and they responded by entering a sort of suspended animation . . . discovery of an early-warning system among plants is just one of the revelations that have come to three electronic music specialists at Sounds Reasonable, Inc., a recording studio in Washington, D.C. There Ed Barnett, Norman Lederman and Gary Burge have been experimenting with ways to create music from the silent vibes of plants. So far their efforts have yielded a single, called *"Stereofernic Orchidstra"* . . . the record is a studio mix of four plants, an Indian azalea, a philodendron, a Boston fern and an amaryllis, recorded at the National Botanical Gardens. The first side features the raw plant "voices" tuned to different pitches on an oscillator. It sounds like a demonic, atonal violin section in electro-frenzy. On the second side the plants control the changes on an ARP music synthesizer. The result is more musical, but no less bizarre.[32]

John Cage speaks of his work in related areas:

I've had for a long time the desire to hear the mushroom itself, and that could be done with very fine technology, because they are dropping spores and those spores are hitting surfaces. There certainly is sound taking place. . . . It leads, of course, to the thought about hearing anything in the world since we know that everything is in a state of vibration, so that not only mushrooms, but also chairs and tables, for instance, could be heard . . . I have a project . . . to amplify a city park for children. It was to be done at Ivrea near Turino. . . . There is a marvelous hill in the center of the city that is high and has a beautiful view of the Alps and is isolated enough from the traffic sounds so that you hear the sounds of the plants. . . . I was spoiled by that marvelous situation in Ivrea where the silence—when you weren't playing the plants—was very audible and beautiful; you could hear it as if you were in a concert hall. In other words, I wanted the silence of the mountain to be heard by the children after they had heard the sounds that they themselves had made by playing the plants. . . . Every now and then the plants were going to become unplayable, and the children would be obliged to hear the silence.[33]

Biomusic, while in and of itself representing some of the oldest forms of organized sound on earth, is still, remarkably, engendering a wide variety of emotions from its spectators. Obviously this, as with most of the music described within this chapter, is primarily natural *artifact* becoming *art-in-fact.*

Many composers articulate aural expression in terms of natural sound quite apart from *biomusic.* Among these are many of Pauline Oliveros's *Sonic Meditations.*[34]

Soundscapes

V:
Take a walk at night. Walk so silently that the bottoms of your feet become ears.

32. Jim Wiggins, "Lily Sings the Blues," *Rolling Stone,* September 12, 1975, p. 12. © 1975 by Straight Arrow Publishers Inc. All Rights Reserved. Reprinted by Permission.
33. David Cope, "An Interview with John Cage," *Composer* 10, no. 1 (1980).
34. Copyright 1974 by Smith Publications. ALL RIGHTS RESERVED.

and

XVII:
Ear Ly
(For Kenneth Gaburo's NMCE)

1. Enhance or paraphrase the auditory environment so perfectly that a listener cannot distinguish between the real sounds of the environment and the performed sounds.
2. Become performers by not performing.

The latter work combines all possible available sounds of the organic and inorganic environments.

Other composers, such as I. A. MacKenzie, verbally express actions, or concepts which often contain written directions toward action, but without any reference to sound other than that inherent in the environment of the situation (Figures 6.8, 6.9). His "wind sound sculptures" (1930s) involve the principle of instruments played by wind (later, he also produced water and fire sculptures) and need neither performer nor audience (see Figure 6.10). The wish, before he died, of having these placed in places where man would not be able to hear them, has been carried out, bearing close resemblance to the self-destructing sculptures of Jean Tinguely.

The following excerpts from an interview between the author and MacKenzie in 1968, just three months before his death, represent his direction towards anti-ego in art. He considered the concert stage the archvillain of true equality of sounds.

I. A.: Basically, I was curious about the fundamental concept of whether I, or mankind for that matter, was really important in the functioning of music. . . . I still followed traditional notation . . . but demanded less and less skill for the performer since it was not to be had anyway . . . my preoccupation seemed to be with creating instruments which played themselves. . . . Musicians and composers . . . seem to delight in creating codes and systems that will separate them more from the common man and, I'm afraid, their audiences. . . .

D. C.: Was publication possible?

I. A.: Out of the question. By 1927 my music had become so involved in new instruments of my own invention, the publisher would have had to publish the instrument with the music. By 1930, I abandoned the written music completely anyway, believing that I should be more interested in sound than codes. . . .

D. C.: . . . What was your . . . reaction (to universities)?

I. A.: My reaction was harsh. . . . The teachers were very dull; more interested in talking *about* sound than *in* sound; mostly more interested in themselves. Many times I would hear visiting composers lecture on their works . . . only to find that the lecturer was just flesh and blood, not a god. . . . I found quickly that for me, at least, the university and its intellect and pomposity was creatively bankrupt: it offered nothing but security . . . and the same old traditional claptrap. . . . As long as people continue to raise gods, not people, the situation won't change. As long as so-called "great" performers are regarded as towering musical figures, instead of rather grotesque finger gymnasts, the situation won't change. The university has contributed to this as well, creating a caste system. . . .

D. C.: . . . you say that around 1930 you began just creating instruments.

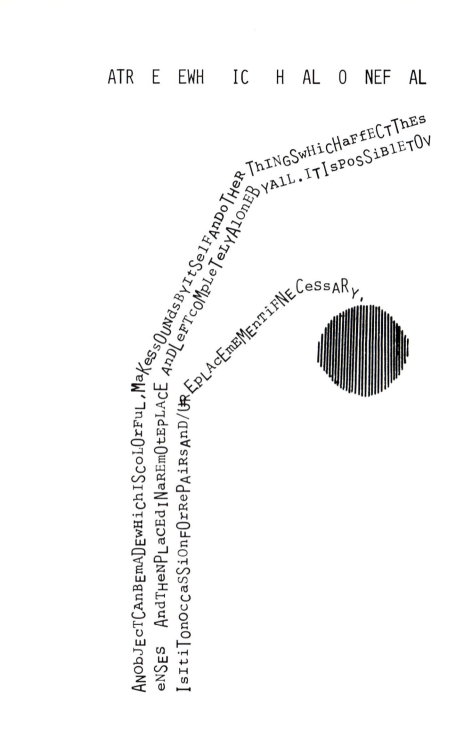

Figure 6.8. Copyright by Discant Music, Los Angeles, California.

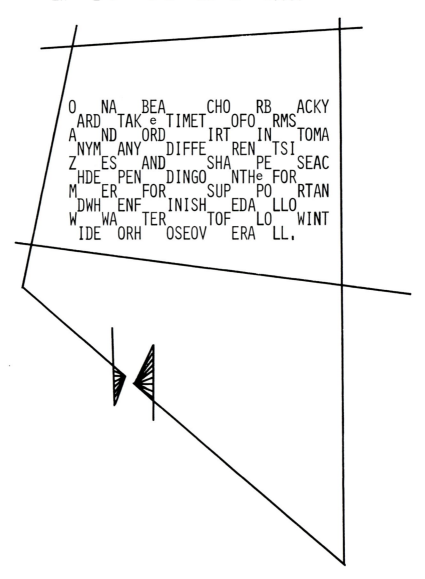

FEWeR LoVEs THaN tIME ALLoWS....

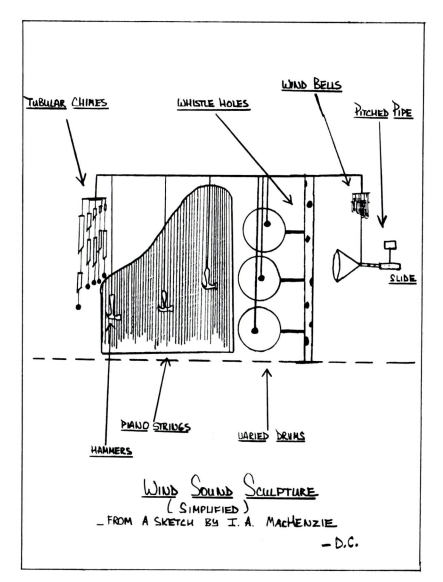

Figure 6.10. From *The Composer,* Vol. I, no. 1 (June 1969). Copyright by *Composer Magazine,* 1969.

TUBULAR CHIMES

WHISTLE HOLES

WIND BELLS

PITCHED PIPE

SLIDE

PIANO STRINGS

VARIED DRUMS

HAMMERS

WIND SOUND SCULPTURE
(SIMPLIFIED)
_ FROM A SKETCH BY I. A. MacHENZIE
— D.C.

I. A.: Yes. But, more important, instruments without human performers. By 1934, early spring, I had created my first wind-sound sculpture . . . an elaboration of the old Chinese wind chimes . . . in fact, that's where I got the idea. . . . I used to listen to storms approach through their sound and somehow felt I was "tuning in" on nature (nature being something I have always felt to be more impressive and profound than man or myself, to be exact). . . .

D. C.: What do you consider yourself?

I. A.: I don't. Categorizing, defining and such limit creativity. . . . Whether one thing is a work of art, and another not, is unimportant. This is cataloguing, not problem-solving. Problems are: God, beauty, nature; creating with or without them, or to them or from them. Creating is solving; cataloguing is avoiding. . . . I don't dislike systems or codes any more than money; but, as before, if these are used by someone to catalogue their own or someone else's work, they have become destructive rather than helpful. . . . I create what I like, in hopes that God, nature, and people (in that order) may like some or all of them. . . .

. . . My sketches are, I suppose, my musical notation. However . . . when I create the work, I let it go its own way, and I sort of follow along. Problems of balance and so forth are worked out as I go along; intonation is achieved through experimentation until I have what I want. . . . I am in complete control of pitch, timbre, and . . . length. . . . I hope the sculpture will last forever, though forever is a long time (I think).

D. C.: How do you regard the partially controlled aspects?

I. A.: With joy. Certainly rhythm is partially controlled . . . and the same with harmony and melody, which are the least controlled.

D. C.: Does it disturb you when, leaving the instrument alone, it is performing without human audience?

I. A.: Human audience? That's up to humans. It's never without an audience. . . . . . . I have been moving toward something, not away from something. I have never maintained that I am right or even important; I am just doing what I think I can do best. . . . I have learned two very important things about sound: (1) it exists, period. No more, no less. There is no good or bad except in individual terms . . . and (2) music (sound) communicates nothing. If I were to define (not categorize) Art, I would have to say it is that which communicates nothing. Rather, it incites or creates something new in each of us (I can say "Hello" and you can reply "Hello." This is communication, bad as it is, but it is not Art. Art's beauty and importance is that it does not communicate!) . . . *Sounds* hold an interest for me; I don't give a damn how one produces them. . . .

. . . One last thing: if one should consider the nightingale and its music and inspect closely the battery of technique in use, he might reconsider his own bloated self-view: certainly music is sound (the existence of the former term owes to social implications only) and man, or even his life, has contributed little enough to expand its vocabulary.[35]

Other sculptors and artists have begun work in similar areas. The German sculptor Hans Haacke, a member of *Atelier 17* in Paris and a founder (along with Pene, Mack, and Vecker) of *Group Zero* (a group dedicated to breaking ties with

35. David Cope, "Chronicles of a Cause: I. A. MacKenzie," *Composer* 1, no. 1 (June 1969):35–42.

the past of nonobjective art), creates wind and water sculptures, as did Harry Bertoia. Japanese environmental artist Shinoda creates elaborate metal sculptures with sound as a by-product. Composer Jon Hassell has recently explored acoustical environments and objects, and large-scale outdoor sound-sculpture events (especially *Nadam,* a "sound-space" work). His *Landmusic Series* (1969–72) is a combination of minimal music and *soundscapes.* Some are like the Oliveros *Sonic Meditations,* being but brief suggestions: "Underground thunder spreading across an open field." Another in the series calls for compact battery-powered speaker, microphone, amplifier combinations to be planted in trees to produce subtle sound amplifications of "wind, leaves, birds, and squirrels who come near. . . ."[36] Terry Allen's three lead-covered eucalyptus trees (1986) installed in San Diego are equipped with specially designed loudspeakers which gently call to passersby with Navajo chants, Aztec poems, and Thai bands. The trees are inconspicuously hidden in a forest of eucalyptus on the campus of the University of California, San Diego.

The struggle, gaining intensity in the late sixties, for the safety and revitalization of the environment holds close ties with the antiart movement. Besides the creation of works which incorporate the environment as is (without artistic distortion), the direction implies an immaculate concept of nature, with distrust of man's creations (and re-creations) in what appears to be their inherent destructiveness. Sound pollution, the technique of discounting the aural by-product of twentieth-century convenience living (e.g., the noise of freeways, airways, refrigeration), has exponentially compounded the situation. The need for *intensity* of sound to compensate for the increased level of accepted background noise, subsequently leads to a battle over dominance between organized and unorganized sound.

The *World Soundscape Project* was designed to explore and note trends in man's relation to his sonic environment. Based in Canada near Vancouver, and directed by R. Murray Schafer, the project attempted to bring together research on the scientific, sociological and aesthetic aspects of the environment and has five significant documents to date:

1. *The Book of Noise;*
2. *Okeanos* (a ninety-minute quadraphonic tape composition by Bruce Davis, Brian Fawcett, and R. Murray Schafer, dealing with the symbolism of the ocean);
3. *The Music of the Environment* (an article on the concept of the World Soundscape; the first treatment of the acoustic environment as a macro-cultural composition);
4. *A Survey of Community Noise By-Laws in Canada;*
5. *The Vancouver Soundscape* (a combination two-record set and booklet detailing a sonic study of the city of Vancouver and its environs, and concluding with two most significant chapters dealing in turn with "Noise Pollution Problems" and "Toward Acoustic Design").[37]

36. Tom Johnson, "New Music," *Musical America* 24, no. 11 (November 1974): MA-14.
37. Available from Sonic Research Studio, Communication Studies, Simon Fraser University, Burnaby 2, British Columbia, Canada.

The records of this latter document include a variety of sounds, from surf to suburban baseball games. Most remarkable are the extremes of everyday sounds pinpointed in this collection; sounds which ". . . too often people ignore (or think they ignore). . . ."[38] The thrust of these concepts is focused in these comments taken from an open letter called "a brief introduction. . . .":

> Acoustics as a design study has been limited to closed environments: concert halls, sound-proof rooms and the like. It is time that acoustic design be applied to the environment as a great macro-cultural composition, of which man and nature are the composers/performers. To disguise an acoustic ambience with background music or masking noise, to block it out with ear muffs, cocoon-like sound-proof rooms or automobiles is not, in our view, a satisfactory solution to the problem of noise nor is it a creative approach to acoustic design.[39]

Within the framework of "Moozak at the Oakridge Shopping Mall," and "A Ventilator at Eaton's Department Store," one can hardly escape the immediate intimacy and beauty of "Full Surf . . . on a Gusty March Afternoon," or "Children's Voices, Recorded on the Playground of Seymour School. . . ."

Though quite a few years must pass before the trials of many of the experimental concepts and works included here expose their real contribution, their vitality and originality cannot be overlooked, regardless of their inherent threats to tradition.

Vectoral Analysis: Pauline Oliveros: *Sonic Meditation XIII*

1. Historical Background: Pauline Oliveros was born in Houston, Texas, on May 30, 1932, and studied composition at the University of Houston (1949–52) with Paul Koepe. She received her B.A. degree from San Francisco State College. She studied with Robert Erickson from 1954–60 and was co-director with Ramon Sender and Morton Subotnick of the San Francisco Tape Center from 1961 to 1965 and first year director of the Mills Tape Music Center in 1966. In 1967 she became Professor of Music at the University of California at San Diego where she taught until 1981 when she retired to become a Consulting Director of the Creative Music Foundation at West Hurley in New York State. She currently resides in New York City and operates a foundation bearing her name. This organization dedicates its efforts to encouraging the creative efforts of other artists and especially collaborative and educational projects in the arts.

   Oliveros is a professional accordianist who has added significant literature to that medium including *The Wanderer* (with the 22 piece Springfield Accordian Orchestra) and *Horse Sings from Cloud* (accordian and voice). Her work ranges from musique concrète (early) to conceptual pieces. She consistently explores the furthest edge of experimentalism

---

38. From "A Brief Introduction to the World Soundscape Project": open letter by R. Murray Schafer, Peter Huse, Bruce Davis, Howard Broomfield, Hildegarde Westerkamp, Barry Truax, and Adam Woog, Vancouver, 1973.
39. Ibid.

Figure 6.11. "Training of musical consciousness is a large order." Composer Pauline Oliveros. Photo credit: Becky Cohen, Del Mar, Calif.

Listen to the environment as a drone. Establish contact mentally with all of the continuous external sounds and include all of your own continuous internal sounds, such as blood pressure, heart beat and nervous system. When you feel prepared, or when you are triggered by a random or intermittent sound from the external or internal environment, make any sound you like in one breath, or a cycle of sounds. When a sound or a cycle of sounds, is completed re-establish mental connection with the drone, which you first established before making another sound or cycle of like sounds.

Figure 6.12. Pauline Oliveros: *Sonic Meditation XIII.*

without ever imitating others in the field. She has been an outspoken proponent for women's rights in a world of new music dominated by male composers.

2. Overview: The work of Pauline Oliveros, especially that of her conceptual period, requires serious analysis and direct involvement for a true understanding of intent and impact. Having been a performer under the composer's direction of this particular work in April, 1978, the author has realized in a very special way the focus and implications of the series of works titled *Sonic Meditations.* Figure 6.12 provides the entire score to *Meditation XIII.*

Gone is the entire traditional assemblage of musical notations and directions. Here the composer merely assists the performers (read "audience") as a "horse to water." In performance, the group in which the author participated focused on a series of breathing exercises for relaxation while incense burned in the four corners of the concert hall. Then, lying on their backs in a feet first circle, all explicitly followed the directions provided in the score. The "cycle" referred to in Figure 6.12 originated from the ensemble as a whole rather than any individual (such egocentric utterances or "solos" being implicitly destructive in the mind of the composer). Since loud sounds would disrupt the otherwise introspective posture of the experience, sounds from the performers invariably were as soft as those from the environment of the performance space creating a cushion of sounds having little direction and impact. Lasting 20 or more minutes, one could find no real beginning and the ending seemed fashioned more by the exhaustion of the quiet and disarming fear of interruption rather than by a planned or composed sequence of events during the work.

3. Orchestration Techniques: With the environmental references in *Meditation XIII* one assumes that natural sounds, ones made by the voice or body, best serve the composer's wishes. These then follow the prescription of "listening" to the droning aspects of the performance area. Oliveros's use of the term "continuous" here voids most of the sounds one ordinarily finds in a daily environment. Natural drones are, in fact, difficult to find at all. Birds, dogs, etc. all take staccato and quasi-random forms, obviously not what she wishes us to contemplate. In the 1978 performance, a steady hum of the hall's heating system combined with a 60 cycle hum from the electric lighting system provided the necessary drone elements. Internal sounds, such as heartbeats or blood flow, were difficult to perceive. In fact, careful listening produced the hallucinatory effect that the aforementioned drones were, in fact, growing to a deafening roar. All participants used humming variants (their choice, not preplanned) in "breath" length phrases on pitches matching (as closely as possible) those of the perceived drones. The resultant work was subtle and effete, not only minimal but fragile. Its consistency and dynamics created a suspension of the ordinary performance situation and, when the work seemed completed, the audience, mesmerized by the exhaustion of listening, did not applaud for minutes, providing a special magic to the concert.

4. Basic Techniques: This kind of prose format has been used successfully by a number of minimal composers. Critics suggest that these brief and poetic models contain no technique. Once in rehearsal, however, the predictability of the final outcome becomes obvious. Clearly, no two performances will be exactly alike. However, if the instructions are followed to the letter (critically important here), broad and lengthy vocalized pitches reinforcing the existing sounds in the performance space will be the rule. Since such are relatively predictable, at least in proscenium situations, one can reasonably expect similar results from one performance to the next.

5. Vertical Models: In five different run-throughs during rehearsals for the 1978 performance, and with three different sets of personnel, these consisted of one to four voice soft textures with hairpin articulations at the beginning and ending of each voice. The tuning is naturally based on the extant pitches of the drones encountered in the performance arena.

6. Horizontal Models: In the 1978 performance, a melody resulted in the entrance patterns of the four different voices. This varied depending on the various breath lengths of the individuals in the ensemble. Since so little happens during the performance, this becomes a very important feature of the work.

7. Style: Pauline Oliveros' *Sonic Meditation XIII* is a minimal work notated in prose English. If the instructions are followed exactly, a subtle work emerges through very soft and slow modulations of environment reinforcing drones. This (and the other works in this series) are aptly named.

The Oliveros Vectoral Analysis points out similarities with Cage's *Cartridge Music* presented in the last chapter. Only general constraints are placed on performers who are (within the guidelines laid out by the score) free to explore a variety of possibilities. Surprisingly favorable comparisons can be made with the strictness of the Webern work, the subject of a Vectoral Analysis in Chapter 2, if one realizes the rigor of performance here compared to the rigor of compositional process in the *Concerto*. The lack of perceivable lyric qualities (in the traditional sense) argues with the works presented in the Vectoral Analysis in Chapters 1, 3, 11 and 12 (in particular).

Bibliography

Further Readings*

Ahlstrom, David. "Footnotes for Mr. T." *Composer* 2, no. 1 (1970):24. Annotated bibliography of writings about the *avant-garde*.

Austin, Larry. "Music is Dead, Long Live Music." *New York Times* (July 6, 1969).

Brindle, Reginald Smith. *The New Music: The Avant Garde since 1945*. New York: Oxford Press, (2nd edition; 1988). This is an excellent overview of experimental tradition though very slanted toward European composers.

Brown, Anthony. "An Introduction to the Music of Morton Feldman,"* *asterisk* 1 (December 1974).

———. "An Interview with John Cage." * *asterisk* 1 (December 1974).

Byron, Michael, ed. *Pieces: An Anthology*. Vancouver. A.R.C., 1975.

Cage, John. *Notations*. New York: Something Else Press, 1969. Many of the selections contained herein fall into the categories covered in this chapter.

———. "To Describe the Process of Composition 'Music for Piano 21–52.' " *Die Reihe* 3:41. A most important example of the new experimentalism in process. Though "indeterminate" in initial look, this article leads one immediately to new concepts and analogies.

———. "Lecture on Nothing." In *Silence: Lectures & Writings*. Cambridge, Mass.: The M.I.T. Press, 1966, p. 109.

———. *Themes and Variations*. New York: Station Hill Press, 1982. A collection of mesostics on names of persons who have most influenced his work.

——— and Geoffrey Bornard. *Conversations without Feldman*. New York: Printed Editions, 1982. First published by Black Ram Books in 1980. A long 1978 interview with Cage.

*Addresses for record companies, periodicals, and music publishers mentioned in this Bibliography can be found in Appendix 4.

————. *Empty Words*. Middletown: Wesleyan University Press, 1973. This is a collection of Cage's writings between 1973 and 1978.

Cardew, Cornelius. ed. *Scratch Music*. Cambridge, Mass.: The M.I.T. Press; paperback edition, 1974. This is a book of scores and ideas by a great many composers involved with the *Scratch Orchestra* once conducted by Cardew. Many of the works are indeterminate and quite a few belong to the new "experimentalist" category. Fascinating study for this area.

Cardew, Cornelius. *Stockhausen Serves Imperialism*. London, England: Latimer New Dimensions Limited, 1974. Interesting account of the author's about-face and repudiation of his own early works and those of other *avant-garde* composers.

Comte, Pierre. "Leonardo in Orbit: Satellite Art." *Leonardo* 20, no. 1 (1987):17–21. A description of ARSAT ("art-satellite") whose only purpose is to orbit the earth and present visibility of "such brilliance that nothing could eclipse it."

Cope, David. *Notes in Discontinuum*. Originally published by Discant Music in 1970. Reprinted with biographical notes added in *Allos*. San Diego: Lingua Press, 1980.

————. "An Interview with John Cage." *The Composer* 10, no. 1 (1980).

Corner, Philip. *I can walk through the World as Music*. New York: Printed Editions, 1982. Verbal tales of a three-week private performance in 1966.

Davis, Bob, and Rich Gold. *Break Glass in Case of Fire*. Oakland: Mills College (Center for Contemporary Music). An Anthology of experimental music from this West Coast source of new music.

Everett, Tom. "Five Questions: 35 Answers." *Composer* 2, no. 4 (1971):79. Quite contrasting views on a number of different subjects related to the new experimentalism by Earle Brown, Harold Budd, Philip Corner, Jim Fulkerson, William Hellermann, Karel Husa, and Elliott Schwartz.

The Experimental Music Catalogue. Published at 208 Ladbroke Crove, London, England.

Fontana, Bill. "The Relocation of Ambient Sound: Urban Sound Sculpture." *Leonardo* 20, no. 2 (1987):143–47. An excellent survey of recent developments paralleled most notably by the performing of the "Golden Gate Bridge" during its 50th anniversary (1987). This article chronicles such works as *Oscillating Steel Grids along the Brooklyn Bridge* (1983) and *Metropolis Köln*.

Gaburo, Kenneth. *Collection of Works*. San Diego: Lingua Press, 1975. A very important collection of 32 compositions by this experimental composer.

Garland, Peter. *The Music of James Tenney*. Santa Fe, NM: SOUNDINGS Press, 1984. An excellent reference source for the music of this important (and generally unrecognized) innovator of the avant-garde. Tenney's "long term specific short term random" compositions cover a wide expanse of divergent forms. This volume contains a great deal of Tenney's music as well as some serious analytical articles by various composers including Tenney himself (e.g. Larry Polansky, Philip Corner, Malcolm Goldstein, Carolee Schneemann, etc.).

Grayson, John. *Sound Sculpture*. Vancouver: A.R.C., 1977. A collection of essays by artists surveying the techniques, applications, and future directions of sound sculpture.

————. *Environments of Musical Sculpture You Can Build*. Vancouver: A.R.C. 1977.

Griffiths, Paul. *Modern Music: "The avant garde since 1945"* N.Y.: George Brazillen, 1981.

Henahan, Donal. "Music Draws Strains Direct from Brains." *New York Times* (November 25, 1970). Interesting account of David Rosenboom's work with brain-wave music.

Higgins, Dick. "Boredom and Danger." *Source* 3, no. 1 (January 1966). An excellent explanation of new experiments.

————. *A Dialectic of Centuries: Notes Towards a Theory of the New Arts.* 2d ed. West Glover, Vt.: Printed Editions, 1979. Many of the essays printed here are reprints from *foew & ombwhnw* brought out by Something Else Press in the 1960's. Important aesthetic inquiry into the *avant-garde.*

————. "Henry Cowell: Some Personal Recollections." *Soundings* 14–15 (1986). Written in 1978, this piece fondly recalls Columbia University lessons with the major American composer.

Huff, Jay. "An Interview with David Behrman." *Composer* 4, no. 1 (1972):29. Fascinating view of this man well-versed both as composer and "man of letters" in the *avant-garde.*

Johnson, Roger. *Scores: An Anthology of New Music.* New York: Schirmer Books, 1980. A good collection of experimental scores that can be performed with a modicum of resources.

Johnson, Tom. *Imaginary Music.* New York: Two-Eighteen Press, 1974. An exceptional contribution to the various aspects discussed in this chapter. See also his extremely informative columns on expressions of antimusic in *The Village Voice.*

Knowles, Alison. *More by Alison Knowles.* New York: Printed Editions, 1976. Performance pieces and environments.

Kostelanetz, Richard. *John Cage.* New York: Praeger, 1970.

————. *Conversing with Cage.* New York: Praeger, 1988.

————. *The Theatre of Mixed Means.* New York: Dial Press, 1968.

————. *Music of Today.* New York: Time-Life Books, 1967.

Kupbovic, L. "The Role of Tonality in Contemporary and 'Up-to-date' Composition." *Tempo* N. 135:16–19 (December 1980).

Lentz, Daniel. "Music Lib." *Composer* 4, no. 1 (1972):6. Interesting article on experimentalism as well as the activities of the California Time Machine's European Tour of 1970.

MacLow, Jackson. *An Anthology.* New York: Heiner Friedrich, 1970.

Maconie, Robin. "Stockhausen's *Mikrophonie 1.*" *Perspectives of New Music* 10, no. 2:92. Interesting and sympathetic view of this piece.

Moore, Carmen. "The Sound of Mind." *Village Voice* (December 24, 1970). Another article about David Rosenboom's works with brain-wave music.

Motherwell, Robert. *The Dada Painters and Poets: An Anthology.* New York: Wittenborn, Schultz, 1951. Interesting as *art* background and insight into experimental concepts.

Nougé, Paul. "Music is Dangerous." *Soundings* 1 (1973). See this same issue for Andre Breton's *Silence is Golden.* Both are truly unique and well worth reading.

Nyman, Michael. *Experimental Music.* New York: Schirmer Books, 1974. An excellent and well-balanced chronicle of 'the new experimentalism'.

Oliveros, Pauline. "Many Strands." *Numus West* 3 (1973):6. By an active contributor and innovator in new music.

————. *Software for People.* New York: Printed Editions, 1982. A collection of theoretical and historical writings and texts from 1962–1980.

Osterreich, Norbert. "Music with Roots in the Aether." *Perspectives of New Music* (Fall/Winter, 1977), pp. 215–28. Review of the video (by the same name) which is a series of interviews with avant-garde composers: Ashley, Behrman, Glass, Lucier, Mumma, Oliveros, Riley. These in-depth interviews reveal a great deal about these composers.

Paik, Nam June. See this author's articles in each of the first five numbers of *Decollage* (Cologne).

Palmer, Robert. "A Father Figure for the Avant Garde." *Atlantic Monthly,* May 1981, pp. 48–56. Excellent article on La Monte Young and his recent works.

Partch, Harry. "Show Horses in the Concert Ring." *Soundings:* 1:66. Good source for philosophical contributions to the subject area covered in this chapter.

Reich, Steve. "Music as a Gradual Process." In *Anti-Illusion Catalog of the Whitney Museum* (New York, 1969).

———. *Writings About Music.* New York: NYU Press, 1974.

Rosenboom, David, ed. *Biofeedback and the Arts: Results of Early Experimentation.* Vancouver: A.R.C., 1976. An important landmark in experimental works of biomusic; excellent resource.

Rzewski, Frederick. "Prose Music." In *Dictionary of Contemporary Music,* edited by John Vinton. (New York: E. P. Dutton & Co., 1974), p. 593.

Schafer, R. Murray. "Ezra Pound and Music." *Canadian Music Journal* 4:15. Interesting view of this poet's relation to music and the effects those relationships might have on experimental concepts.

———. *Ear Cleaning.* Vancouver: BMI Canada Ltd., 1974. This book, along with *The Composer in the Classroom,* is most helpful in acquainting the young (and young in experience) with experimental concepts through simple but effective performances.

Schwarz, K. Robert. "Steve Reich: Music as a Gradual Process." *Perspectives of New Music,* Spring-Summer 1981, pp. 373–94.

Soundings 7/8. Contains several works valuable to this chapter, including Harold Budd's *Madrigals of the Rose Angel* and Daniel Lentz's *You Can't See the Forest . . . Music (for three drinkers and eight echoes),* as well as a large number of other highly interesting works.

Stockhausen, Karlheinz. *"Mikrophonie I and II." Melos* 33:144.

Tenney, James. *James Tenney.* Toronto: Musicworks. Edited by Tina Pearson and Gordon Monahan with a cassette edited by John Oswald, this book presents a number of Tenney's compositions and writings on new music.

Young, La Monte, and Jackson Mac Low, eds. *An Anthology of Chance Operations.* New York: La Monte Young and Jackson Mac Low, 1963.

Young, La Monte, and Marian Zazeela. *Selected Writings.* Munich: Heiner Friedrich, 1969. Excellent source for materials by this composer inclusive of interviews and the like. It also contains the concepts and drawings of *Dream House.*

———. "Sound is God: The Singing of Pran Nath." *Village Voice* (April 30, 1970). More a study of the author than of the singer.

Zimmerman, Walter. *Desert Plants.* Vancouver. A.R.C., 1976. Conversations with 23 *avant-garde* composers.

Recordings and Publishers

10 + 2: *12 American Text Sound Pieces.* Recorded on 1750 Arch Record, 1752 and contains works by Cage, Giorno, Saroyan, Bysin, Dodge, Coolidge, Anderson, Amirkhanian, O'Gallagher, Gnazzo, and Ashley in text-sound composition.

Amirkhanian, Charles. *Lexical Music.* Recorded on 1750 Arch Street Records, S-1779. Album contains a number of Amirkhanian's text sound compositions including *Mahogany Ballpark, She She and She,* and *Muchrooms.*

Anderson, Laurie. *Mister Heartbreak* (1984). Recorded on Warner Brothers 25077-2. These classic text-sound compositions represent important contributions to the experimentalism of the 1980s.

Ashley, Robert. *Wolfman.* CPE-*Source* 2, no. 2 (July 1968); special record issue. Recorded on Source Records 4.

———. *Private Parts.* Recorded on Lovely Music LML-1001 and VR 4904.

Austin, Larry. *Accidents*. CPE-*Source* 2, no. 2 (July 1968). See Ashley, above.

Budd, Harold. *Coeur D'Orr* (1969). For tape, soprano saxophone, and/or voices. Recorded on Advance 16.

―――. *Oak of Golden Dreams* (1970). Recorded on Advance 16.

Cage, John. *Variations IV*. Recorded on Everest 3132.

Corner, Philip. *Rounds. Soundings* 3, no. 4:92.

―――. *Ear Journeys: Water* (1977). Printed Editions. Score includes a seaweed insert.

Crumb, George. *Voice of the Whale*. C. F. Peters. Recorded on Columbia M-32739.

Duchamp, Marcel. *The Bride Stripped Bare by Her Bachelors, Even, Erratum Musical* (1913). Recorded on Finnidar 9017.

Fulkerson, James. *Folio of Scores for the Composers Forum. Soundings* 3, no. 4:2.

Gibson, Jon. *Visitations*. Recorded on Chatham Square CS-LP-12. A 16-track multi-textured environmental soundscape.

Glass, Philip. *Music in Fifths*. Recorded on Chatham Square CS-LP-1003.

―――. *Music in Similar Motion*. Recorded on Chatham Square CS-LP-1003.

―――. *Music with Changing Parts*. Recorded on Chatham Square CS-LP-1001/2.

―――. *Einstein on the Beach* (1976). Recorded on Tomato 4–2901. CD: CBS; M4K-38875.

Hassell, Jon. *Vernal Equinox*. Recorded on Lovely Music LML 1021.

Leedy, Douglas. *Entropical Paradise*. Recorded on Seraphim S-6060.

Monk, Meredith. *Key*. Lovely Music LML 1051. Expressive experimental music.

Moran, Robert. *Four Visions*. Universal Edition. Graphic score for flute, harp, string quartet.

Mother Mallard's Portable Masterpiece Company. Steve Drews, Linda Fisher, and David Borden. Recorded on Earthquack EQ-0001. Drones and steady pulses.

Oliveros, Pauline. *Accordian and Voice*. Recorded on Lovely Music 1901.

―――. *Sonic Meditations* (1974). Smith Publications.

Pearson, Tina and Hildegard Westerkamp, eds. *Women Voicing*. This cassette, which is accompanied by a book of scores and annotations, includes works by Pauline Oliveros (*Talking Bottles and Bones*), Wendy Bartley (*Rising Tides of Generations Lost*) and Susan Frykberg (*Saxerbra*). Musicworks 31.

Reich, Steve. *Four Organs* (1970). Recorded on Angel S-36059. *The Desert Music*. CD: Nonesuch; 79101-2.

―――. *It's gonna Rain; Violin Phase*. Recorded on Columbia MS-7265.

―――. *Music for 18 Musicians* (1976). Recorded on ECM/Warners 1129.

Riley, Terry. *In C*. Recorded on Columbia MS-7178, and published with the recording.

―――. *Poppy Nogood and the Phantom Band*. Recorded on Columbia MS-7315.

―――. *A Rainbow in Curved Air*. Recorded on Columbia MS-7315.

Rosenboom, David. *Ecology of the Skin* (1970). Available from the composer, c/o Mills College, Oakland, California. Bio-feedback for performer and audience brain-wave encounters.

―――. *Portable Gold and Philosopher's Stones* (for brains in fours). Recorded on A.R.C. ST-1002 (Canada). Brainwave bio-music album also containing *Chilean Drought* and *Piano Etude #1*.

Rzewski, Frederick. *Coming Together. Soundings* 3, no. 4, with composer commentary. Recorded on Opus One No. 20.

Satie, Erik. *Vexations* (1893). Salabert.

Songs of the Humpback Whale. Recorded on Columbia ST-620.

The Sounds of Sound Sculpture. A.R.C. ST-1001. Sounds from sound sculptures by Harry Bertoia, von Huene, Marxhausen, and David Jacobs. Excellent book is provided with the album.

Stockhausen, Karlheinz. *Aus den Sieben Tagen.* Universal Edition.

———. *Mikrophonie I.* Universal Edition. Recorded on Columbia MS-7355.

The Vancouver Soundscape (Sonic Research Studio, Simon Fraser University, Burnaby 2, B.C., Canada). Recorded on EPM 186.

Young, La Monte. *Dream House.* Recorded on Shandar 83.510. Long drone-filled music which also includes his *Drift Study.*

Winsor, Phil. *Melted Ears* (1967). Carl Fischer. Recorded on Advance S-14.

ANALOG ELECTRONIC MUSIC

7

Electronic music,[1] or that music composed with or altered by electronic apparatus, has a long and involved history. Early experimental instruments include the "Clavecin Electrique" or "Electric Harpsichord" of Delaborde in Paris, 1761 and Elisha Gray's "Electroharmonic Piano" in Chicago, 1876.[2] Some composers typically utilized these instruments to imitate styles and materials of their times. Many composers, however, attempted to develop a unique aesthetic wherein *all* sounds could act as material for compositions. E. T. A. Hoffman's *The Automaton* in the early nineteenth century, and *The Art of Noises,* 1913, by the Italian futurist Luigi Russolo evidence these attempts. From 1920 to 1940, experiments with electronic instruments began to take place with composers such as Otto Luening, Norman McLaren, Pierre Schaeffer, Leon Theremin (who in 1923 invented the Theremin), Friederich Trautwein, Paul Hindemith, Ernst Toch, and many others contributing significantly to the new sound resources.

The following series of photographs represents a brief synopsis of the evolution of electronic music in the 20th century. The telharmonium, devised by Thaddeus Cahill around the turn of the century (his first patent for an "electric music" machine was filed on February 4, 1896), began auspiciously in 1906 with its installation in "Telharmonic Hall" in New York City. The largest of these instruments is shown in Figure 7.1. Figures 7.2 and 7.3 show (respectively) the telharmonium in performance and some detail of its construction.

Around 1920, Leo Theremin invented the Theremin which was originally called the "etherophone" and "thereminovox." The instrument was performed by moving one's hands in its vicinity creating pitches and (importantly) glissandi between pitches

Origins and Evolutions

1. It must be made abundantly clear that the author does not seek to imply, by the use of the term *electronic music,* any stylistic or material similarity among composers who employ this medium. The term as used here does not connote an inherent style, something which is in fact nonexistent. In a lecture given in Los Angeles, Milton Babbitt argued that a recording of a Tschaikovsky symphony is actually electronic music, in that all the sound actually heard is electronically produced. The term as used by the author here refers *only* to that music composed from or altered by electronic apparatus, and as such is as limitless stylistically as music for string quartet or symphony orchestra.
2. For more detailed history, see Otto Luening, "Some Random Remarks on Electronic Music," *Journal of Music Theory* 8, no. 1 (Spring 1964):89–98.

Figure 7.1. Thaddeus Cahill's *Telharmonium* in 1906. Located in the basement of ''Telharmonic Hall,'' it utilized twelve cogged metal wheels which, when contacting a metal brush, created an electric current. (Smithsonian Institution photo number #77494)

Figure 7.2. Performing the telharmonium.

Figure 7.3. The patent diagram of the telharmonium (note that Cahill used the word ''synthesizing'' to describe the process by which his machine worked).

Figure 7.4. Leon Theremin (left) in a performance with his namesake instrument. (Smithsonian Institution photo number #77461)

Figure 7.5. Joerg Mager performing on the *Klaviatur-Spaerophon* around 1925.

caused by "heterodyning." Figure 7.4 shows Theremin in a performance for two Theremins and traditional instruments.

Joerg Mager created his *Klaviatur-Spaerophon* in 1925. This instrument, using inductance capacitance principles and audio-frequency generators, voided the glissando effects of the *Theremin*. Performing classical masterworks, Mager was supported by both the Heinrich Hertz Institute and the German Telegraph-Technical Office. Figure 7.5 shows both the instrument builder performing and the triple-keyboard performance technique.

Concurrently with Mager's creations in Germany, John Hays Hammond (father of the Hammond organ) began experimenting with electrical sound production in the United States. His first major effort (called the "breathing piano") involved the

Figure 7.6. Hammond's "Breathing Piano."

Figure 7.7. Edouard Coupleus and Joseph Givelet with their "automatic synthesizer."

use of reflective slats within a soundproof case which opened by the use of an extra pedal. While not explicitly electronic, the concept paralleled that of regenerative procedures in radio. Figure 7.6 shows a working model of the instrument.

By 1929, Edouard Coulpeus and Joseph Givelet had created the automatic synthesizer which they exhibited at the Paris Exposition. Their "Automatically Operating Musical Instrument of the Electric Oscillation Type" (AOMIEOT) utilized oscillators performed much the way player pianos operate (paper tape). However, both timbre (using filters) and pitch bending (tremolo) could be affected with the potentials far exceeding its counterpart in the non-electronic world. Figure 7.7 is a photo of the AOMIEOT.

One year later, Emerick Spielmann created the *Superpiano,* an instrument which utilized "light-choppers," interrupting light on photoelectric cells which in turn generated alternating currents for pitch. Figure 7.8 and Figure 7.9 provide examples of performance and of the tone wheels built into the machine.

Figure 7.8. The *Superpiano* in performance.

Figure 7.9. The *Superpiano* in construction.

One of the most successful pioneering electronic musical instruments prior to the present day analog and digital synthesizers was the *ondes martenot*. The instrument was created by Maurice Martenot around 1928 (but not fully discovered until the mid-thirties) when it received a solo performance at the premiere of Dimitri Levidis' *Symphonic Poem*. Looking like a clavichord, it followed the same basic principles of the Theremin but with a much more traditional look and touch. Monophonic in nature, the pitch was controlled by a lateral movement of a finger ring attached to a metal ribbon. Using an intriguing silencing device, the performer could cover up the glissandi so obvious when using the *Theremin*. Figure 7.10 shows a performance model of the *ondes martenot*.

Many composers (including Oliver Messiaen, Darius Milhaud, Arthur Honegger and Edgard Varèse) have effectively used the *ondes martenot* in their works. In 1936, Edgard Varèse said: "I am sure that the time will come when the composer, after he has graphically realized his score, will see this score automatically put on

Figure 7.10. The *ondes martenot* (1977 construction).

a machine that will faithfully transmit the musical content to the listener. . . ."[3] A year later, John Cage remarked: "To make music . . . will continue to increase until we reach a music produced through the aid of electrical instruments."[4]

French composers Pierre Schaeffer and Pierre Henry developed *musique concrète* by re-recording "natural" sounds at various speeds and splicing in composer-controlled rhythms, the first truly serious analog electronic music. In Germany (until 1956) composers tended to shun *concrète,* using only electronic sources, often only sine waves. In America, the pioneering work of composers like Percy Grainger (whose *Free Music* of 1935 used four Theremins) explored electronic resources. Along with Burnett Cross, Grainger later created a "free music" machine using various oscillators. The works of John Cage, Vladimir Ussachevsky, and Otto Luening brought attention to these new sound sources (all during the five-year period 1948–52—the years of real discovery and experimentation). The "Tapesichordists" (as Luening and Ussachevsky were termed in a *Time* magazine review of their renowned Museum of Modern Art concert of October 28, 1952), while not taken seriously until the early sixties, steadfastly and consistently improved their working conditions, equipment, and technical knowledge.

One of the major philosophical concepts that became suspect at the dawn of the electronic-music age was that of "instrument." Heretofore composers had been constrained to traditional or nontraditional instruments which have limitations. No matter how much experimentation one might encounter, a string quartet has but four players and all the exclusion that suggests. With electronic means, however, composers faced an expansion of those sonic possibilities. In fact, each work began with the potential of *any* timbre. Audiences were not prepared conceptually for the demands placed on their expectations. Composers could no longer avoid making decisions that previously were made automatically by the mere selection of a traditional instrument or group of instruments (which of course produces many new questions—and definite new problems). More interestingly, each sound could become

3. From a lecture given at Mary Austin House, Santa Fe, New Mexico, 1936.
4. John Cage, *Silence* (Cambridge, Mass.: The M.I.T. Press, 1961), p. 3.

Figure 7.11. Pierre Henry.

an instrument played only "once" during composition creating virtually thousands of "performers" (hence the extreme focus on the vertical "moment" in composition during the 1960s and 1970s).

New sounds, however, become old quickly. New control (the composer becoming the performer capable of literally any microcosm of controllable elements in time) was equally available to those preferring lack of control. This latter point is strikingly evidenced by such contrasting works as Milton Babbitt's *Vison and Prayer* (1961) and Karlheinz Stockhausen's *Mikrophonie I* (1965). The former is composed of pure electronic sounds (with "live" voice) carefully notated by the composer, while the latter involves two performers acting on one six-foot gong with a score composed primarily of verbal descriptions of how the sounds should affect the listener ("grating," "scraping," etc.). Two other performers control directional microphones, filters, and potentiometers (electronic timbre and volume control respectively).

Certainly the creation of new, nonequal-tempered scales combined with nearly limitless rhythmic possibilities (no longer restricted to the ten fingers of the pianist or the thousand of an orchestra), present opportunities that many composers cannot resist. Few, however, would agree with "New Music for an Old World Dr. Thaddeus Cahill's Dynamophone An Extraordinary Electrical Invention for Producing Scientifically Perfect Music" titling a *McClures' Magazine* article of July 1906[5] or Casio's 1981 claim that one can ". . . become an instant musician . . . easily, without the long years of training necessary for mastering a regular instrument."

---

5. Elliott Schwartz, *Electronic Music: A Listener's Guide* (New York: Praeger Publishers, 1973), p. 241 (from Otto Luening's remarks).

Nourished by the 1948 invention of the long-playing record, electronic music became accessible to every listener's living room despite the singular neglect shown it by "serious music" radio stations. Moreover, electronic music's lack of visual interest in the concert hall has helped spawn a whole genre of interesting combinations of "live electronics"—tape with "live" performers—and has contributed greatly to the refinement and growth of media-forms.

Aesthetic Challenges

With the advent of tape and unlimited resources of sound and rhythm, such concepts as "noise," "consonance-dissonance," and "live performance" have become increasingly difficult to define. Synthesizers enable composers to control all the elements of production (dynamics, envelope, duration, etc.) except performance acoustics and audience receptivity. This philosophy, if one is implied, has not gained a universal acceptance. Igor Stravinsky remarked:

> What about the much publicized "infinity of possibilities" in connection with the new art material of electronically produced sound? With few exceptions "infinite possibilities" has meant collages of organ burbling, rubber suction (indecent, this), machine-gunning, and other—this is curious—representational and associative noises more appropriate to Mr. Disney's musical mimicries.[6]

Ernst Krenek seems almost to answer Stravinsky's objection in his article "A Glance over the Shoulders of the Young":

> To the superficial observer, it appears that the phenomena demonstrated so far in electronic music: levels of colour, texture, density, consistency and mass of sound material, are of a considerably lower intellectual level of musical consciousness than the aspirations which were associated with the demanding music of the past. Perhaps this only represents a beginning; history cites us many examples of the way in which creative energy has been expended on the achievement of progress of one dimension while temporarily impoverishing the other dimensions of the subject.[7]

Inexperienced electronic music composers can very often be "hypnotized" by the time required to make the exact sound needed. Other composers have noted that, up until the era of mechanical music, a composer/performer needed a certain physical energy to produce a *forte,* an energy corresponding in some ways, at least, to the energy of the sound itself. It is possible for one to lose that perspective when a small flick of the finger can create huge volumes of sound or the same flick can quiet the flow to nothing. Obviously a very different quality of action/reaction is present

---

6. Igor Stravinsky and Robert Craft, *Dialogues and A Diary* (Garden City, New York: Doubleday & Co., Inc., 1963), p. 25.
7. Ernst Krěnek, "A Glance over the Shoulders of the Young," *Die Reihe I* (Bryn Mawr, Pennsylvania: Theodore Presser Co., in association with Universal Edition, c. 1958), p. 16.

in electronic music, comparable only to pipe organs and certain mechanical instruments of the past. *Psychoacoustics,* the study of listener discrimination and receptivity of these complexities, has become a real and vital tool of the composer attempting to communicate.[8] Luciano Berio has commented:

> When someone hears electronic music it doesn't reverberate to other levels of his experience, as instrumental music has and does. Up to now I feel electronic music has been developing, evolving as a bridge between what we know and what we don't know yet. It is not without reason that the best musical works that have been produced up until now (from the early 50s to the present) are those that try to make this connection.[9]

Two basic sound sources exist: electronic, including the oscillators and generators; and nonelectronic, or *musique concrète* (e.g., instrumental sounds, sounds of nature). There seems to have been, at least in the early fifties, a definite desire by composers to make a choice between one or the other (with France dedicated to the *concrète* and Germany to the electronic). However, by 1960 (especially in Stockhausen's *Gesang der Jünglinge*), both sources were considered of equal potential. Certainly *musique concrète* involves less control and determinability. Experimentation with tape loops (continuous lengths of tape looped so as to pass and repass the playback head, creating rhythmic ostinati or continuous sound flow), and with gluing bits of recorded magnetic tape to white leader tape resulted in either a very controlled and measurable (in fractions of inches) rhythmic base or a random flux of sounds.

Fundamental Concepts

After choosing sound materials as shown in the following extremely simplified schematic (Figure 7.12), manipulation becomes important. At this point, material can be altered by combining sounds (with mixer, ring modulator), eliminating certain sounds (the use of various filters such as low-pass, high-pass, band-pass and band reject and filter banks—see Figure 7.13), or distorting sounds (by reverberation and/or various types of modulations; frequency, amplitude, and ring; along with speed changes of the tape recorder, etc.).

Amplitude modulation (AM), or continuously changing dynamics (also known as *tremolo*), and frequency modulation (FM), or continuously changing pitch (also known as *vibrato*) have brought about an important concept known as *voltage control*. When, for example, a composer wishes to "warm" a sound with vibrato, quick hand manipulation of the frequency control (repeatedly turning it back and forth) creates the desired effect. Assigning such repetitions to another module (i.e., the sine wave output of another oscillator at the proper frequency) however, is more efficient. The capacity of one oscillator (or for that matter any electronic instrument) to manipulate another oscillator is termed *voltage control*.

8. See especially: Fritz Winckel, "The Psycho-Acoustical Analysis of Structure as Applied to Electronic Music," *Journal of Music Theory* 7, no. 2:194; and Milton Babbitt, "An Introduction to the R.C.A. Synthesizer," *Journal of Music Theory* 8, no. 2:251.
9. David Felder, "An Interview with Luciano Berio," *Composer* 7, no. 1 (1976):11.

Figure 7.12. Electronic music diagram: from source to playback.

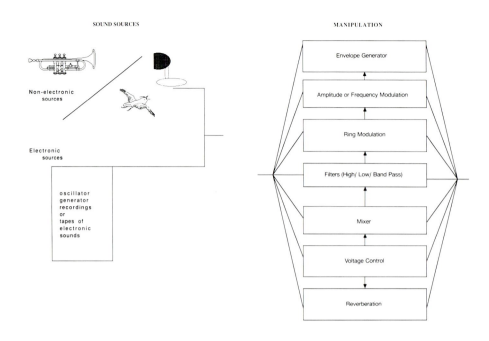

SOUND SOURCES

Non-electronic sources

Electronic sources

oscillator
generator
recordings
or
tapes of
electronic
sounds

MANIPULATION

Envelope Generator

Amplitude or Frequency Modulation

Ring Modulation

Filters (High/ Low/ Band Pass)

Mixer

Voltage Control

Reverberation

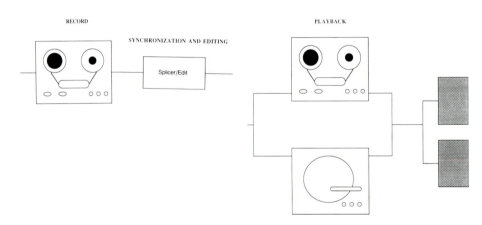

RECORD

SYNCHRONIZATION AND EDITING

Splicer/Edit

PLAYBACK

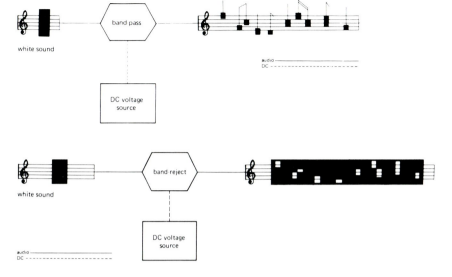

Figure 7.13. Band-pass and band-reject filtering. From *Electronic Music*, by Allen Strange. © Copyright 1972. Wm. C. Brown Company Publishers, Dubuque, Iowa. Permission granted.

Synchronization, or the placing of all events into a composed order (by means of such devices as splicing, rerecording, mixing, speed alteration), readies the tape for playback. *Classic* studios utilize previously recorded sounds (or short groups of sounds), and splicing techniques. While most electronic music involves a certain amount of splicing, *classic* electronic music evolves *all* timing, order, etc., by splicing. This *classic* approach (used for example in the *Poème électronique,* 1958 by Edgard Varèse out of necessity, since synthesizers were not yet in use) is still employed by a number of composers, including Mario Davidovsky and Vladimir Ussachevsky. Prolongation of this tedious and time-consuming approach means one constantly confronts the splicing block for each new sound. The introduction of keyboards, sequencers, etc., and multitrack recorders, making "live" production on tape of as many consecutive sounds as the composer wishes without splicing, has eliminated many such *classical* approaches. While keyboards, sequencers, etc., make near "real-time" performance possible, some feel this leads to sonic masturbation rather than to great music. No doubt, *classic* and "live" electronic means can both serve the talented composer well, each having its share of advantages and drawbacks.

The playback stage cannot be underestimated in importance. The viability of a majority of compositions on tape require specific placement of loudspeakers. Some composers have even "composed" proper placement of the tape machine itself for theatrical or dramatic effect. In *Musik für ein Haus* (1968) by Karlheinz Stockhausen, exact locations of all electronic materials in a two-story house are inherent to the "real" performance of the tape work. Acoustical considerations likewise become extremely important for the composer and/or performer in the placement of loudspeakers. Stockhausen discusses this:

> . . . I should like to explain . . . just how loudspeakers are properly placed in an auditorium (a procedure which is becoming better and better known to me and which demands the greatest care in the particular place in question, as well as often up to four hours of time from me and several other collaborators sitting in various parts of the hall; in Madrid, for example, Kontarsky, Fritsch, Gehlhaar, Alings, Boje, and I took several hours to set the loudspeakers up; some of them were even lying on their backs up in the balcony, and others were on stands on the stage, and we had put pieces of wood under the front edge of each speaker so that they were pointed up at the ceiling and the sound was only reflected into the house at an angle at a greater distance; we set up two loudspeakers contrary to the usual way with their diaphragm sides at an acute angle directly toward the wooden walls in order to prevent hiss and to enable the people sitting right in front of these loudspeakers—at a distance of about 5–7 meters (16½ to 23 feet)—to hear the loudspeakers standing on the opposite side, as well as those which were diagonally opposite; in principle we try to send the sound of the loudspeakers, particularly when instrumentalists are playing at the same time, as *high* as possible into the house and to achieve a smooth acoustic match, especially in four-track reproduction).[10]

Analog Synthesizers

"Electronic studios" vary from a single tape recorder and splicing machine to the R.C.A. Synthesizer valued at $250,000.[11] Unlike instrumental music, in which the performance may vary with both the instrument and performer, tape music generally has *one* performing version, that made by the composer under studio conditions.

Analog synthesizers (synthesized sound producers) are a collection of devices as shown in Figure 7.12, usually in module form (i.e., independent and removable instruments). More important, analog synthesizers contain many voltage control devices so that parameters of one module may be automatically controllable by other modules (see Figure 7.14).

10. Karlheinz Stockhausen, "Not A Special Day," *Composer* 1, no. 2 (September 1969):65–66.
11. *Music Educators Journal* 55, no. 3 (November 1968). A number of kits and guides to electronic music are currently available, including *Electronic Music* (with pictures and leaflets, from Keyboard Jr. Publications); *Exploring Music: Grade Six* (New York: Holt, Rinehart, and Winston); and *Nonesuch Guide to Electronic Music* (Nonesuch HC-73018, a two-record set).

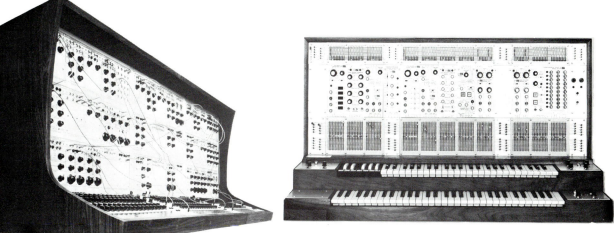

Figure 7.14. (a) The Moog Synthesizer (produced by R. A. Moog Co., Williamsville, N.Y. 14222); (b) The Buchla Electronic Music System (Buchla and Associates, Box 5051, Berkeley, Calif. 94705); (c) The ARP Synthesizer (Tonus Inc., 45 Kenneth St., Newton Highlands, Mass. 02161): (d) SYNTHI 100 (London).

Analog synthesizers come in either portable or console models. Larger models which include sample-hold units, sequencers, ring modulators, digital controllers, and built-in linear mixers may cost upwards of $6,000, again depending on make and model.[12]

Early Studios

Pierre Boulez, in an interview with the author, offered the following observations:

> I think that you cannot do good work in this area until you have teams working together. You must have composer and technician alike. Four things, really: composer, technician, good equipment, and a company or factory with money to back the operation, as well as performers in some cases, and as long as these elements cannot work together you will have small laboratories without any outstanding results.[13]

Highly sophisticated studios do exist, among them the Institute of Sonology at Utrecht State University in Holland (which contains four studios, six scientific staff members, four technical staff members, and two secretaries, with computer, *classic,* "live" and DC/AC patch panels and combination availabilities);[14] the EMS studio in Putney, England (see Figure 7.15) and a host of advanced studios based at American universities, including the aforementioned Columbia-Princeton Laboratory, studios at the University of Illinois, North Texas State University, University of California at San Diego, the Cleveland Institute of Music, and many others. The RCA Mark II Synthesizer, located at the Columbia-Princeton Center since 1959, has served as the source of a large number of important compositions by Babbitt, Ussachevsky, and Luening—especially the first totally synthesized extended work, *Composition for Synthesizer* (1961) by Milton Babbitt.[15].

Experiments in 1940 by Norman McLaren with film sound tracks have created a unique and less expensive approach to electronic "notation." By cutting notches in the film, and by scratching and painting on the sound track portion of the film, McLaren produced a wide variety of "electronic" sounds from the projector (the performer). Lejaren Hiller who with Leonard Isaacson wrote *Experimental Music* (McGraw-Hill, 1959), describes situations in which the composer, with a pen filled with magnetic dyes, could sit at his desk and compose on unmagnetized tape without the aid of any electronic equipment, excepting a tape recorder for experimentation and synchronization.

12. As of April, 1980. Prices subject to change; this sample from the Moog catalog gives the reader an idea of price ranges. Up-to-date catalogs can be obtained by writing to the individual companies (see Figure 7.14 for addresses).

13. Galen Wilson and David Cope, "An Interview with Pierre Boulez," *Composer* 1, no. 2 (September 1969):84–85.

14. For a more detailed and complete description of the Insitute of Sonology with photos and block diagrams see *Sonorum Speculum #52* (Donemus, 51 Jacob Obrechstraat, Amsterdam, Netherlands).

15. Unlike the *analog* synthesizers previously mentioned, the RCA Mark II uses punched paper tape relatively the size of a player-piano roll instead of a keyboard. Though computer-like in appearance (with the *digital* input), the Mark II is not a computer: for computer information see the next chapter.

Figure 7.15. The SYNTHI 100 of Electronic Music Studios (London) Limited, 277 Putney Bridge Road, London SW 15 2 pt, England. By permission.

One of the most popular of early tape pieces, Stockhausen's *Gesang der Jünglinge* (1955–56), combines singing with electronically produced sounds. *Musique concrète* manipulation produces variable comprehensibility of the text (Daniel 3, "Song of the Men in the Fiery Furnace"). The score calls for five groups of loudspeakers to surround the audience. Stockhausen uses the spatial direction and movement of the sounds to create form, avoiding the traditional melodic or timbre repetitions.

Stockhausen's numerous other electronic works, especially *Kontakte* (1960), *Telemusik* (1966), and *Hymnen* (1969)—the latter a collage of electronically altered hymns and *concrète* sounds—has made him one of the most widely known of Europe's electronic composers.

Examples of Concrète and Synthesized Music

Figure 7.16. Karlheinz Stockhausen. (Copyright: Werner Scholz.)

Luciano Berio's *Thema: Omaggio à Joyce* (1958) uses the human voice (completely *concrète*) first recognizably and then slowly transformed into a fantastic array of sounds (by means of splicing and tape speed variation) exploring an absolute minimum of materials. His *Visage* is a "classic" of electronic music (1961); an imaginative vocal-electronic treatment in a strikingly dramatic form (originally composed as a radio program). A voice (Cathy Berberian) speaks only one word (*parole:* Italian for "words"), but through intense crying, whispering, laughing, etc., evokes an emotional gamut virtually without peer in the history of music.

John Cage was among the first of the Americans to employ tape techniques. His *Imaginary Landscape No. 5* (1951–52) uses a prepared score for making a recording on tape. All of Cage's works must, however, be studied in the light of his *indeterminate concepts* of musical technique (see Chapter 5) and as such must be considered for the most part a cooperative effort between himself and the performer. Therefore, the bulk of his electronic music is found scattered throughout this book, especially under the subject headings of Chapters 5 and 6.

A large percentage of Vladimir Ussachevsky's early works (from 1951 to 1954), including *Sonic Contours, Transposition, Reverberation,* and *Composition* (all on Folkways FX 6160), were experiments only, principally based on sounds of piano and flute. His *A Piece for Tape Recorder* (1955) is less of an experiment, yet obvious enough in construction to serve well as a good educational or introductory tool in electronic music. His long-time associates Otto Luening and Milton Babbitt have produced, especially at the Columbia-Princeton Electronic Music Center, a large number of works, particularly tape in combination with live instruments. Ussachevsky's *Of Wood and Brass* (1965) is a unique work employing tape loops of varying lengths (on which are recorded *concrète* sounds "of wood and brass") fed through

Figure 7.17. Vladimir Ussachevsky. BMI Archives. Used by permission.

a ring modulator (which collects the sidebands and nullifies the original inputs, creating neo-electronic effects). This and others of Ussachevsky's later works are highly sophisticated examples of electronic music—quite individualistic and advanced in comparison with the early embryonic years.

Mario Davidovsky's *Study No. II* (1966) for tape is a truly incredible creation in that each of the extremely quick-moving electronic sounds were placed in order by splicing (*classic* electronic music). The straightforward ABA form and the use of more or less "pure" electronic material (sine and square waves) marks another unusual feature of this work. The "limitless possibilities" are almost completely unexplored and, except for the obvious performance limitations, one could easily imagine the work as a string quartet.

Figure 7.18. Mario Davidovsky.

More recently, Morton Subotnick (one of the founders of the San Francisco Tape Center) achieved much success with *Silver Apples of the Moon* (1967), commissioned to fit the two sides of an LP recording, and *The Wild Bull* (1968). Both works employ contrasts in texture and timbre as organizational principles, and the composer has distinctly abandoned the "pure" electronic sounds (e.g., sine waves, traditionally the most "hostile" of the new materials) for more instrumental- and natural-like sounds. More recent works (in the 1970s) in this genre by Subotnick include *Touch, Sidewinder,* and *4 Butterflies.*

Milton Babbitt's *Ensembles for Synthesizer* (1961–63) concentrates on compact rhythmic textures and formal aspects of the tape medium avoiding timbral displays. Charles Wuorinen's *Time's Encomium* (1968–69), also realized on the RCA Mark II Synthesizer at the Columbia-Princeton Center, evidences instrumental style in both its clear composer control (often twelve-tone) and its extremely

Figure 7.19. Milton Babbitt. By permission.

Figure 7.20. Charles Wuorinen.

complicated rhythmic passages. The work contrasts what the composer calls "synthesized sound" (clarity of pitch) with "processed synthesized sound" (i.e., utilizing reverberation).

A number of rock groups have employed electronic sound materials in their music. The Beatles (especially in *Sgt. Pepper's Lonely Hearts Club Band,* Capitol MAS-2653), Jimi Hendrix Experience (Reprise 6261), and The United States of America (Columbia CS-9614) used electronically produced or altered sound but, for the most part, these were only experiments, exploiting such sounds for shock or text emphasis rather than actual musical development. More recently, however, rock and pop groups have used portable synthesizers and various effects modules as standard instruments of their ensembles. Notable among these groups are The Grateful Dead ("Dark Star"), Soft Machine ("Joy of a Toy"), Mothers of Invention ("Penguin in Bondage"), Todd Rundgren ("Born to Synthesize"), King Crimson ("Pictures of a City"), Yes ("Close to the Edge"), Weather Report ("Nubian Sundance"), Tangerine Dream ("Rubycon"), and Frank Zappa ("Roxy and Elsewhere," "Lumpy Gravy," and "Uncle Meat"). The Who's Pete Townshend employs feedback effectively in "My Generation," a work which was quite influential in the creation of "punk" rock. Devo (described by *Rolling Stone* as "a group of Captain Beefheart-influenced dadaists") includes massive electronic instrumentation. Even the singers' voices are continually modified by electronic devices. As rock enters the 1990s it is difficult to find a group not "plugged-in" in some way. Most groups have an entourage of "roadies" who control mixer consoles that feed giant sets of speakers with electronically synthesized samples, modified, or amplified sound.

Walter Carlos (now Wendy Carlos), on the other hand, developed electronic "orchestrations" of works by Bach (e.g., *Switched-on Bach* and *"The Well-Tempered Synthesizer"*) which represent an interesting application of the Moog instrument. These works demonstrate levels of speed and accuracy far beyond human capability. Isao Tomita's realizations of Stravinsky's *Firebird,* Holst's *Planets* and Mussorgsky's *Pictures at an Exhibition* demonstrate the synthesizer's ability both to imitate acoustic timbres as well as to orchestrate quasi-real sounds in novel and striking ways. These records have provided the stimulus for some of the ever-increasing manifestations of the popularity of electronic sounds among the general public.[16]

Electronic music has also flourished in Latin America with composers working in a variety of private and institutional studios. Important composers represented on recording include Joaquin Orellana (b. Guatemala, 1939; particularly *Human-ofonía I,* 1971); Oscar Bazán (b. Argentina, 1936; particularly *Parca,* 1974); Jacqueline Nova, (b. Belgium, 1936, d. Columbia, 1975; especially *Creación de la Tierra,* 1972); and Graciela Paraskevaidís (b. Buenos Aires, 1940; especially *Huauqui,* 1975); and Coriún Aharonián (b. Montevideo, 1940; particularly *Homenaje a la Flecha Clavada en el Pecho de Don Juan Diáz de Solís,* 1975).

Performance Considerations

One of the major performance considerations facing electronic music composers is the quality of speaker systems. Even an extraordinary work can be reduced to drivel by poor reproduction. One of the newest advances in speaker design is the *magneplanar* design which offers literal translation of the musical wave form it transmits. Called "maggies" in the trade, these are constructed with a flat and thin plastic sheet bonded to a very thin layer of vapor-deposited metal. This allows the sheet to

16. For a listing of these, see under "Electronic Music" in the Schwann Catalog.

respond to magnetic impulses originating with narrowly spaced rows of small magnets covering the whole area of the speaker. When these magnets are connected to an amplifier, the entire metalized plastic sheet vibrates in accordance with the musical signal. This process avoids the problem with cone speakers which derives from the central placement of a single electromagnet. This "colors" musical sound with the resonance of the cone and of the speaker enclosure. Neither is present in the "maggie."

The obvious loss (to the audience) of more or less theatrical or visual activity during performance of works on tape has inspired three alternatives: (1) combination of live performer with tape; (2) live electronic music: from the Synket (a complex, compact live electronic instrument invented and developed by Paul Ketoff in 1963) to extremely complex situations involving recording and playback in numerous arrangements in concert, and performers or audience intercepting light beams to set off oscillators; (3) tape used in conjunction with projections and/or theatrical events. In fact, as will be discussed in a later chapter, the need for auxiliary action in electronic music performance played a large part in the need for developing mixed-media presentations.

Figure 7.21. John Eaton playing the Synket. Photo used by permission.

Works for live performer(s) and tape have been popular over the past few decades. Henri Pousseur (b. 1929), for example, in *Rimes pour Différentes Sources Sonores* (1959), treats orchestra and tape as antiphonal bodies, contrasting the available materials of each. The speakers are placed on stage, in "live" performance, in such a way as to visually accentuate the contrast. Otto Luening (b. 1900) and Vladimir Ussachevsky, who worked together on *Rhapsodic Variations for Tape Recorder and Orchestra* (1954), were among the first in America to realize and ex-

Figure 7.22. Otto Luening. By permission of the composer.

periment with live and prerecorded sound sources. Bruno Maderna (in *Musica su due Dimensioni*) began studies in this area in 1952 at the NW German Radio in Cologne. These early examples extended the contrast possibilities of live and recorded sources.

One of the most dynamic works written for tape and orchestra is *Collages* (Symphony No. 3) by Roberto Gerhard (1960). This large seven-section work employs a *concrète*/electronic tape (not unlike that used by Varèse in *Déserts*) contrasting a dramatically pointillistic orchestral score.

Mario Davidovsky has composed a number of *Synchronisms* for a variety of traditional instruments and tape. The first, third, and sixth of these are for solo instruments and tape (flute, 'cello, and piano respectively, the latter winning a Pulitzer Prize). These intense compositions require a great deal of "synchronized" rhythmic interchange from "live" to recorded source (all the *Synchronisms* are recorded; see chapter Bibliography for record numbers).

Kenneth Gaburo's 1962 work *Antiphony III (Pearl-white Moments)* combines sixteen soloists in four groups performing live with tape (through two speaker systems), incorporating antiphonal interplay between live and tape sounds (both acoustically and visually). *Antiphony III's* tape materials include both purely electronic sound sources and those more imitative of the live performers, expanding the echo and reiterative effects inherently restricted in totally live performances.

Donald Erb (b. 1927), in *In No Strange Land* (1968) for trombone, double bass, and tape, reflects more complementary possibilities of electronic and instrumental sounds. Imitative techniques involve instruments in neoelectronic sound effects, thus minimizing the musical and sonic disparities between electronic and instrumental materials. Composers like Robert Erickson have used prerecorded instrumental sounds with live performance. In *Ricercar à 3* (1967), Erickson (b. 1917) employs two prerecorded contrabasses with one live contrabass, allowing the performer to play with and against the tape (a source of unusual combinative effects).

David Cope's *Arena,* 1974 ('cello and tape), is a *classical* studio composition which reflects both a dialogue between live instrument and tape, and contrasting cohesion. Figure 7.23 shows a passage in which the tape "takes over" each pitch begun by the 'cello, in turn creating vertical sonorities from the horizontal line. The rhythm and pitch of the 'cello must be precisely in "sync" for the passage to work (including the quarter-tone inflection indicated by the arrows attached to the accidentals). The bottom staff reflects more interplay—the harmonics on the tape are only symbolically represented—answered by the artificial harmonics on the 'cello. This score reflects the often necessary, exact, and graphic notations used by composers for tape with "live" instruments.

Figure 7.23. David Cope: *Arena* ('cello and tape), page 7. © Copyright 1974 by David Cope. All rights reserved.

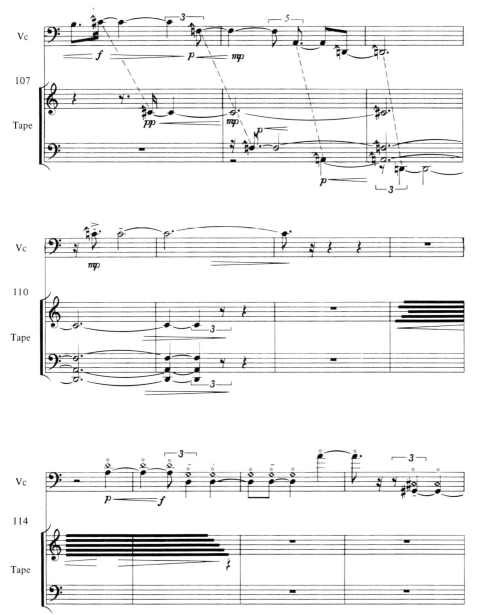

Figure 7.23. (Continued)

Figure 7.24. Richard Felciano. Photo © Michelle Vignes. By permission.

Richard Felciano has written many works for a wide variety of combinations of traditional instruments and tape. *God of the Expanding Universe* and *Litany* are excellent examples of works for organ and tape. His *Crasis* and *Lamentations for Jani Christou* represent examples of chamber music with tape.

John Watts' *WARP* (1972) includes ARP-created electronic sounds on tape with brass quintet. The four-channel quadraphonic speaker setup heightens both the balance and the effective humor and drama of this work. Combinations of large ensembles with tape occupy an increasing bulk of current tape music composition. Works for tape and band include Donald Erb's *Reticulation* (1965), and Herbert Bielawa's *Spectrum*. Vladimir Ussachevsky's *Creation-Prologue* (1961) is for tape and choir.[17]

John Eaton combines the compact "live performance" *Syn-Ket* and full orchestra in his *Concert Piece for Synket and Symphony Orchestra* (effectively utilizing visual "concerto" performance techniques with specially designed electronic

17. For a more complete listing, see *Music Educators Journal* 55, no. 3 (November 1968):73. Also consult publishers' listings.

equipment). Merrill Ellis included soprano, live synthesizer, and orchestra in his *Kaleidoscope*. These last two works concentrate on the "live" performability of synthesizers or *live electronic music*.

John Cage (b. 1912) was the first to employ entirely live electronic techniques in his *Imaginary Landscape No. 4* (c. 1949, first performed in 1951) in which twelve radios are performed by two performers each (twenty-four performers in all). His *Imaginary Landscape No. 1* (1939) uses recordings of constant and variable pitch frequencies in combination with more conventional percussion instruments.

Live Electronic Music

In *Reconnaissance* (1967) Donald Erb employs a Moog synthesizer performed live with a group of other live instrumentalists (viola, piano, bass, percussion), achieving both the visual complement of "live" performance and the available sonic resources of electronic equipment. The work also utilizes a Moog polyphonic instrument (live, also): a keyboard instrument of four octaves (each divided into forty-three tones) capable of producing polyphony in a live performance situation (the synthesizer in use here can only produce chords of the same ratio in live performance).

The "Chapman Stick" is a live-performed electronic instrument resembling an enlarged guitar without an associated resonator. Because the instrument can amplify very small touches on the string surface, the performer need not strum the strings. Hence, it is possible, even promoted, for one to use both hands to "finger" the instrument. This allows for vastly increased potential for chords and counterpoint. With the appropriate straps for support, one can even use thumbs to produce ten pitches simultaneously. Max Mathews has also created an electronic "resonator-less" violin. Similar percussion and wind instruments have been created but usually employ contact microphone enhancement rather than a completely new form of construction.

A number of groups dedicated to the live performance of electronic music (most now disbanded) were formed in the 60s: The Sonic Arts Union (formed in 1966), with Gordon Mumma, Robert Ashley, Alvin Lucier, and David Behrman; *Musica Elettronica Viva* (1967, in Italy), with Frederic Rzewski, Allan Bryant, and Alvin Curran; the Once Group (Michigan), with Robert Ashley, Gordon Mumma, and others. Festivals of live electronic music at Davis, California (1967), Buffalo (1968), and Los Angeles (1968 and 1969), among others, have proved this concept of lasting signficance. A live electronics group "It takes a year one earth to go around the sun," formed in 1970 by David Rosenboom (originator and director of New York's Electric Circus until 1969), with Jon Hassell, Gerald Shapiro, and Terry Riley, spent the summer of that year performing on electronic instruments designed by the members themselves, on "mesas in Wyoming, ghost towns in Death Valley, and lava caves in New Mexico." The works performed (by the composer/performers) are extremely loose in construction, serving as "launching pads" for the performers' rehearsed interplay.

Figure 7.25. Alvin Lucier.
Photo by Mary Lucier.

Alvin Lucier's *North American Time Capsule 1967* involves a vocoder (Sylvania design), an instrument designed to encode speech sounds into digital information. The speech of the performers (coded material) acts as the electronic source material in "live" performance. Gordon Mumma's *Mesa* (1966) uses electronic sound modification as well. He uses a Bandoneon (an accordion-like instrument) instead of voices. Work with tape-delay techniques (in effect, echoes and canon) have been used in live performance by Pauline Oliveros (*I of IV,* 1966, and *Lightpiece for David Tudor,* 1965).[18] By separation of record and playback heads and cross-coupling, a large number of reiterative compositional techniques can be employed.

Several composers in the sixties explored the possibilities of interactive electro-acoustical, process-oriented composition. Representative works of this time include David Behrman's *Wavetrain* (1964), John Cage's *Variations V* (1965), Gordon Mumma's *Hornpipe* (1967), and Alvin Lucier's *Queen of the South* (1972). Behrman's *Wavetrain* involves the acoustical resonances of chordophones (typically grand pianos or zithers). Cage's *Variations V* uses the movements of dancers on the stage translated by photoelectric cells and capacitance sensors into electronic articulations for the accompanying sound. Lucier's *Queen of the South* (which is discussed in Chapter 4), employs large plate surfaces, which are resonated with special loud-speakerlike transducers.

Mumma's *Hornpipe* is described in detail by the composer himself:

> *Hornpipe* is an interactive live-electronic work for solo hornist, cybersonic[19] console, and a performance space. The hornist performs with various techniques on a valveless waldhorn and a standard "French horn." These techniques include a traditional embouchure, and the production of multiphonics with special double-reeds.
>
> The cybersonic console, attached to the hornist's belt, has microphones with which it "hears" the sounds made by the hornist and the acoustical resonances of the space.

18. See Pauline Oliveros, "Tape Delay Techniques for Electronic Music Composition," *Composer* 1, no. 3 (December 1969): 135–42.
19. A term coined by Mumma; refers to sound-control procedures in which the controls are automatically derived from the sounds being controlled.

Figure 7.26. Gordon Mumma performing *Hornpipe* (1967). Photo by Narrye Caldwell, 1974.

The electronic circuitry of the console analyzes the acoustical resonances of the space, and responds interactively with the hornist. The console is connected by an umbilical cable to a stereophonic sound system, so that its responses are heard from loudspeakers. (See Figure 7.26.)

The cybersonic console has several functions. First, it makes an electronic map of the acoustical resonances of the space. This is achieved during the first few minutes of the performance by eight electronically resonant circuits that become automatically tuned to the acoustical resonances of the space. Second, each circuit has a memory that accumulates information about its resonant condition.

Technically, this condition is determined from the frequency (f) and the resonant efficiency (Q) of the circuit. (See Figure 7.27.) Third, when sufficient information is obtained, a VCA (voltage controlled amplifier) for each circuit is gated on, sending its electronically resonant response through the umbilical to the loudspeakers. Because each of the eight resonant circuits is somewhat independent, and has different memory and gating characteristics, these responses can occur in many different combinations.

A performance of *Hornpipe* begins as a solo, without electronic sound. When the responses of the cybersonic console are heard from the loudspeakers, the hornist can then interact with the electronic map of the cybersonic console. By playing sounds

Figure 7.27. Functional diagram, Gordon Mumma's *Hornpipe* (1967).

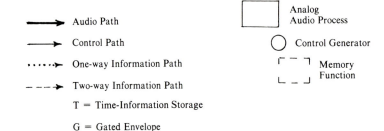

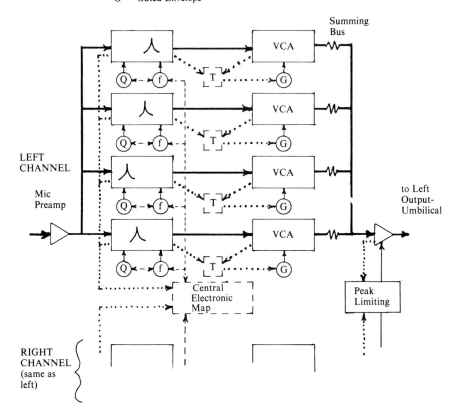

which reinforce the electronic map, the hornist can increase the responses of the cybersonic console. By playing sounds which are anti-resonant (opposed) to the resonances of the electronic map, the hornist can decrease the responses of the cybersonic console.

The performer's choice of anti-resonant sounds strongly influences the continuity of a performance. Without the reinforcement of its original electronic map, the cybersonic console gradually makes a new map representing the hornist's anti-resonant sounds. In other words, having interacted with the responses of the

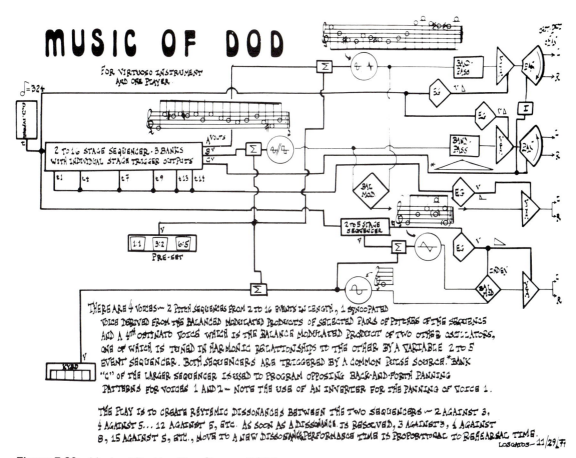

Figure 7.28. *Music of Dod* by Allen Strange (1977).

cybersonic console, and learned the electronic map of the acoustical resonances of the space, the hornist can choose sounds which deceive the console into thinking it is in a different performance space. After the cybersonic console has developed a new map (of the hornist's anti-resonant sounds), it no longer responds to the natural acoustical resonances of the space. The performance of Hornpipe has evolved from an introductory solo, through an ensemble between hornist, cybersonic console and performance space, to a concluding solo section for horn.[20]

The score to Allen Strange's *Music of DOD* (1977), for virtuoso instrument and one player, lays out the design for an electronic instrument with a short performance note regarding dissonance and resolution (see Figure 7.28).

20. Gordon Mumma, performance notes for *Hornpipe*.

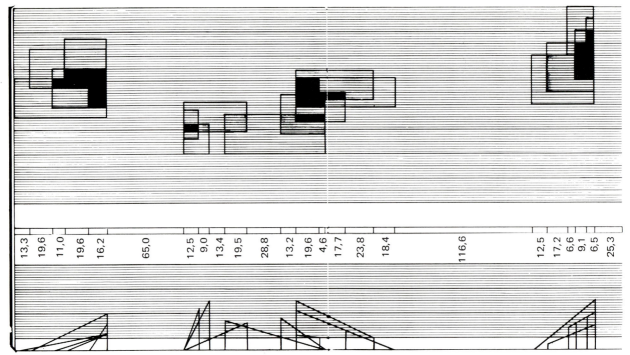

Figure 7.29. Karlheinz Stockhausen: *Studie II.* (Reprinted by permission of Universal Edition; as it appeared in the English edition of *Die Reihe* No. 1, copyright 1958 by Theodore Presser Company, Bryn Mawr, Pa.)

Notation Techniques

The notation of electronic music is complicated by U.S. Public Law 92–140 which makes it possible to copyright certain sound recordings if published with the notice after February 15, 1972 (note that tapes, as of the late 70s, can now be copyrighted). At the same time this does not really solve the problem of unpublished tape compositions. Composers have reacted to these problems in a variety of ways.

Figure 7.29 is from Stockhausen's *Studie II* (1956, Universal Edition). The lower portion indicates dynamics (envelope). The upper portion denotes pitch (100 to 17,200 Hertz, or cycles per second) based on a scale of 81 steps "equal-tempered" at a constant interval ratio of $\sqrt[25]{5}$ (piano at $\sqrt[5]{2}$) and timbre. The middle portion indicates centimeters of tape at 76.2 centimeters per second. This score represents less than seven seconds of performing time.

Another reason for electronic notation is that of synchronization in tape and traditional instrument performances (see Figure 7.23, David Cope's *Arena,* for example).

Notation differs in exactness and form to the same degree composers and works differ. Standardization may come when exact methods for analog to digital processes are perfected with resultant computer printouts serving as notation (see Chapter 6 for more details). Paul Beaver's *Nonesuch Guide to Electronic Music* booklet indicates only the bare essentials of necessities for re-creation of sound on tape. Unusual instruments such as the *Mellotron* (a keyboard instrument with pre-recorded tape loops of traditional sounds activated by depressing the keys and producing neotraditional sounds of violins, etc.) create just that much more confusion in the dilemma of notation.

The close association of live electronic music performance and aleatoric procedures has caused most composers to rely on graphs and diagrams as "before the fact" scores (if indeed any score or directions are used at all). The extremely complex notation necessary for exact re-creation on electronic instruments complicates possibilities of live performance.

(For information on vectoral analysis and procedures, see Chapter 1.)

For Background information on Varèse, see Chapter 1.

Vectoral Analysis: Edgard Varèse: *Poème électronique*

1. Historical Background: *Poème électronique* (1956–58) was composed at the Philips Studio at Eindhaven, having been commissioned for performance in the Philips Pavilion at the 1958 Brussels Worlds Fair. The pavilion was designed by the French architect Le Corbusier (who was assisted, interestingly enough, by then architect Iannis Xenakis. The design of the

Figure 7.30. The Philips Pavilion at the Brussels Exposition (World's Fair) built by Le Corbusier where *Poème électronique* was first performed in 1958.

pavilion included 400 or more loudspeakers, most of which were hidden in the walls or above the ceilings. David Ernst speaks of the elaborate setup:

The taped sounds were distributed by telephone relays among various combinations of loudspeakers. These "sound paths" were determined by a fifteen channel control tape, each track of which contained twelve separate signals. Therefore 180 (15×12) control signals were available to regulate the sound routes, lighting effects and a variety of light sources which consisted of film projectors and projection lanterns, spotlights, ultraviolet lamps, bulbs, and fluorescent lamps of various colors.[21]

Nearly 16,000 people per day for six months provided an audience for the performance of this work of purely taped sounds (both *musique concrète* and electronic sources). The projected images (various photographs of paintings, script, or other montages) were not synchronized with the sound in any particular manner (the projections were chosen by Le Corbusier to fit the elaborate and complex internal design of the pavilion).

2. Overview: Varèse often referred to his work as "organized sound" rather than traditional composition. Clearly *Poème électronique* is very highly organized sound. One method of analyzing electronic music visually "keys" certain sounds so that "paper" analysis becomes possible. Figure 7.31 shows one possible such "keying."

While there are obviously more than seven different sound sources and variants present in this piece, one can clearly identify the ones shown here as basic to its structure. The visual identities are drawn to resemble in some way the aural image presented or in some cases the instruments suggested by the sounds.

Figure 7.32 shows how these symbols can be organized to represent a timeline of the piece (left-to-right, top-to-bottom). Occasional numbers within a diagram represent repetitions of a sound. Assorted "doodlings" between connections represent important but nonformal materials. When one symbol becomes an offshoot of another symbol, it represents a counterpoint, with the first stated material being more significant. Occasional reference to subjects represented by words (e.g., "low voice solo") clearly identify important characteristics that are varied in the context of the work.

The form of the piece takes two distinct shapes. First one perceives a characteristic rondo (return) quality even on first hearing. One such interpretation is shown above the symbols: the "inverted rondo" (here meaning that the main repeating sequence appears second rather than first). Note that the "A" portion repeats twice (occurs three times) in the body of the work between sections of other materials (some of which, like "B," also

21. David Ernst, *The Evolution of Electronic Music* (New York: Schirmer Books, 1977), p. 42.

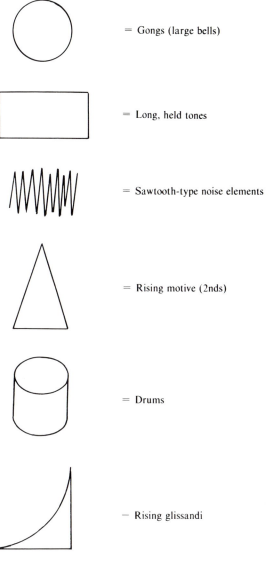

Figure 7.31. Key to diagrams used in figure 7.32.

= Gongs (large bells)

= Long, held tones

= Sawtooth-type noise elements

= Rising motive (2nds)

= Drums

— Rising glissandi

= Voice(s)

Figure 7.32. Diagrammatic formal analysis of Varèse's *Poème électronique.*

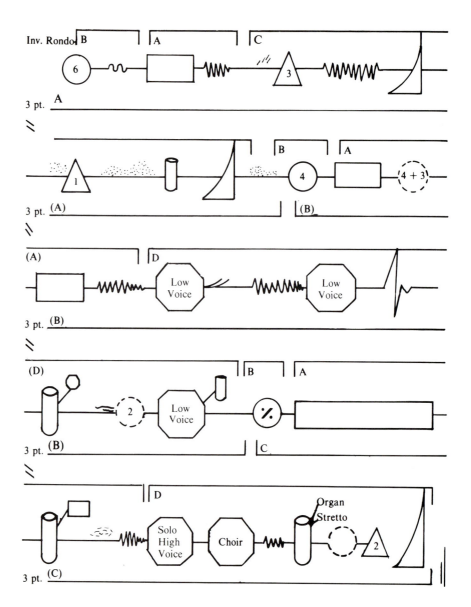

repeat). At least two other rondo possibilities exist here: one, with the opening gongs being "A" and occurring three main times with two "shadow" occurrences; and two, with the rising motive (the triangle) as the main idea (A) occurring on three different occasions.

A second possibility is shown (under the symbols) as "three-part." Here the form is defined as sectional (in three large parts), with each part beginning in nearly the same manner (i.e., gongs followed by long held notes). This separate and distinct formal possibility (from the rondo interpretation discussed above) should not be discarded even though it is less audible on first hearing.

3. Orchestration Techniques: Varèse uses two basic sound materials: *concrète* and electronic. Within each of those categories there are two main divisions: *concrète,* instrumental and vocal; electronic, sine-type tones (simple resonances) and complex (nearly noise) elements. His techniques of variation within these timbres are extremely subtle. A good example of this is the way in which he varies the initial six attacks of the gong-type motive at the beginning of the work. The sixth sound is filtered so that it sounds nearly an octave lower in pitch. The reverberation characteristic, as well as timbre of each of the bells is clearly different in the succeeding appearances of the motivic structure.

4. Basic Techniques: Most techniques presented here are a by-product of *classical* tape composition discussed earlier in this chapter. Most notable in *Poème électronique* are the tape speed changes (N. B.: the solo female entrance where her range is extended beyond human potential), envelope control (cutoffs on the opening long note section, for example, show strong hints of editing executions), synchronization (e.g., the fast switching between drums and organ in the final stretto), and other techniques typical of this period of electronic composition.

5, 6. Vertical and Horizontal Models: Neither of these categories is particularly important in a work whose sonorities are determinates of chosen percussive materials. However, the final "long note" section before the entrance of the low-voice solo clearly defines the harmonic context of the piece (near overtone information and of complex [upper partials] definition). The horizontal materials that most noticeably represent clear identities suggest either secondal (in seconds, minor or major) or widely leaping pointillistic diversity.

7. Style: *Poème électronique* represents an important work (along with Stockhausen's *Gesang der Jünglinge,* 1954) in the hybridization of electronic principles which are highly organized and defined. The recognizable sounds (jet airplane, drums, temple bells, human voices, for example) represent an interesting layer of separate identities, which, along with the often humorous "squeaks and squawks," present a dynamic and linear design not unlike the composer's instrumental works of earlier vintage.

This classic of the electronic music genre compares favorably in concept and stylistic approach to both the works presented in the Vectoral Analyses of Chapter 9 (Risset) and Chapter 3 (Penderecki). In the former case, the centricity of interest in timbre and the electronic medium resemble one another. In the latter case, even though Penderecki's work does not employ electronics of any kind, there are abstract sonorities that create new resonances and hence a vertical sense of depth. While the technology of Varèse's use of electronics suggests a very different kind of music than appeared in his earlier *Density 21.5* (see Vectoral Analysis of Chapter 1), one finds much of the same lyrical and phrase structure present.

Bibliography

*Further Readings**

Appleton, Jon, and Ronald Perera, eds. *The Development and Practice of Electronic Music.* Englewood Cliffs, N.J.: Prentice-Hall, 1974. Another in the growing list of excellent textbooks on electronic music.

Babbitt, Milton, "An Introduction to the RCA Synthesizer." *Journal of Music Theory* 8 (Winter-Spring 1964):251. Excellent survey and introduction to this instrument.

Beckwith, John, and Udo Kasmets, eds. *The Modern Composer and His World.* Toronto: University of Toronto Press, 1961. Has a group of articles and discussion (p. 109) by a number of active composers and physicists dealing with electronic music: Hugh LeCaine, Josef Tal, Vladimir Ussachevsky, among others.

Berio, Luciano. "The Studio di Fonologia Musicale of the Milan Radio." *Score* 15 (March 1956). Fascinating view of this, one of the early studios of electronic music in Europe.

Cage, John. *Silence.* Cambridge, Mass.: The M.I.T. Press, paperback edition, 1961. Provides many insights into the early experiments in electronics by this innovator in the field.

Ceely, Robert. "Thoughts about Electronic Music." *Composer* 5, no. 1 (1973): 11. A fascinating and direct view of this Boston composer.

Chavez, Carlos. *Toward a New Music: Music and Electricity.* New York: W. W. Norton, Inc., 1937. Outdated but visionary for its date (compare to Varèse and Cage predictions).

Christiansen, Louis. "A Visit to the Electronic Music Studios in Moscow." *Numus West* 5:34. Interesting look at Russia's progress in the art form.

Coker, Cecil, Peter Denes, and Elliot Pinson. *Speech/Synthesis.* Farmingdale, N.Y.: Comspace Corp., 1963 (reprinted in 1970). Fascinating book on the physics of speech production and the mechanics of "reproductive" electronic instruments.

Cole, Hugo. *Sounds and Signs.* London: Oxford University Press, 1974. Has some interesting information on the notation of electronic music (p. 112).

Cope, David. "A View on Electronic Music." *db: The Sound Engineering Magazine* (August 1975). This is a broad article covering the problems encountered in the electronic music studio as relevant to the sound engineer.

————. "An Approach to Electronic Music Composition." *Composer* 6, no. 1 (1975): 14. One composer's view of the creation of electronic music.

Cott, Jonathan. *Stockhausen.* New York: Simon & Schuster, 1973. A fascinating view of the composer if one's tastes run to studies of the egocentric.

Cross, Lowell M., ed. *A Bibliography of Electronic Music.* Toronto: University of Toronto Press, 1967. A thorough source from one of the capitals of experimental music.

Dallin, Leon. *Techniques of Twentieth Century Composition.* 3rd ed. Dubuque, Iowa: Wm. C. Brown Company Publishers, 1974. Has a very good section covering electronic music.

Davies, Hugh. "A Discography of Electronic Music and *Musique Concrète.*" *Recorded Sound* 14 (April 1964):205. An excellent source, though in need of updating.

Davies, Hugh, ed. *International Electronic Music Catalog.* Cambridge, Mass.: M.I.T. Press, 1968. Presents a wealth of material including an international list of electronic music studios, both public and private.

Dockstader, Tod. "Inside-Out: Electronic Rock." *Electronic Music Review* 5 (January 1968):15.

*Addresses for record companies, periodicals, and music publishers mentioned in this Bibliography can be found in Appendix 4.

Douglas, Alan. *Electronic Music Production.* London: Pitman Publishing, 1973. An interesting book, though very much slanted towards British equipment and its usage.

———. *Electronic Music Instrument Manual.* 4th ed. London: Pitman, 1972.

Eimert, Herbert, and Karlheinz Stockhausen, eds. *Die Reihe* 1 (Theodore Presser Co., 1965; original German edition, 1955). Presents articles by the editors and Krěnek, Klebe, Stuckenschmidt, Pousseur, Boulez, and Meyer-Eppler; a fascinating general text in the European mid-fifties concept of the development and structuring of electronic music.

Eimert, Herbert, F. Enkel, and Karlheinz Stockhausen. *Problems of Electronic Music Notation.* Translated by D. A. Sinclair. Ottawa, Canada: 1956.

Electronotes (see Appendix 4). A veritable "tome" of information for the serious and knowledgeable electronic music buff.

Ellis, Merrill. "*Musique Concrète* at Home." *Music Educators Journal* 55, no. 3 (November 1968):94. Offers suggestions concerning small "tape manipulation centers."

Emmerson, Simon. *The Language of Electromagnetic Music.* London: Macmillan Press, 1986. A fascinating collection of articles dealing with various approaches to electronic and computer music. The works by McNabb, Truax, and Harvey are particularly interesting.

Ernst, David. *The Evolution of Electronic Music.* New York: Schirmer Books, 1977.

Everett, Tom. "Five Questions: Forty Answers." *Composer* 3, no. 1 (1971):30. Questions dealing with electronic music with varied answers from N. K. Brown, Barney Childs, Sydney Hodkinson, Donald Martino, Richard Moryl, Pauline Oliveros, Elie Siegmeister, and John Watts.

"Four Views of the Music Department of the University of San Diego." *Synthesis* 1, no. 2 (July 1971). Diverse study of this school dedicated to new music, and of its electronic studios.

Fulkerson, James. "What Defines a Piece of Music." *Composer* 5, no. 1:15. An interview with Joel Chadabe, and good insight into new constructs and ideas for electronic music.

Griffiths, Paul. *A Concise History of Avant-Garde Music.* New York: Oxford University Press, 1978.

———. *A Guide to Electronic Music.* London: Thane & Hudson, 1979.

Henry, Thomas. *Build a Better Music Synthesizer.* Blue Ridge Summit, PA: Tab Books, 1987. An excellent book of rudiments for those who wish to construct interesting analog modules. Some fascinating and futuristic possibilities as well as standard components.

Holmes, Thomas B. *Electronic and Experimental Music.* New York: Charles Scribner's Sons, 1985. A popularized and superficial book with some extraordinary photos of early electronic music instruments (particularly the telharmonium, theremin and martenot). There are interesting sections on "intuitive music" and "Interactive Computer Systems."

Horn, Delton. *Music Synthesizers, A Manual of Design and Construction.* Blue Ridge Summit, PA: Tab Books, 1984. A good primer in the electronic basics of synthesizer construction.

Judd, F. C. *Electronic Music and Musique Concrète.* London: Neville Spearman, 1961. Interesting but outdated.

———. *Electronics in Music.* London: Neville Spearman. 1972.

Kondracki, M. *et al. International Electronic Music Discography.* Mainz: B. Schott, 1979. The most current bibliography of recordings of electronic music.

Leitner, Gerhard. *Sound: Space*. New York: New York University Press, 1978. An unusual book of photos, diagrams, and text describing a variety of works by the author involving speakers and electronics in various spaces. The author refers to "expanding-contracting spaces, spiraling space, oscillating boundaries," all of which attest to the acoustic centricity of the book and the author's works.

Luening, Otto. "Some Random Remarks about Electronic Music." *Journal of Music Theory* 8 (Winter-Spring 1964).

———. "An Unfinished History of Electronic Music." *Music Educators Journal* 55 (November 1968):35. Superb study of the long history of electronic music.

———. *The Odyssey of An American Composer: The Autobiography of Otto Luening.* New York: C. F. Peters, 1981.

Manning, Peter. *Electronic and Computer Music*. Oxford, England: Clarendon Press, 1985. A strangely laid out book with the first few chapters chronicling electronic music by country. The section on the voltage-controlled synthesizer is well written with some excellent graphic descriptions.

"The Many Worlds of Music." *BMI* (Summer 1970). Entire issue devoted to electronic music, with an excellent discography by Peter Frank and articles by Carter Harman and Louis Chapin.

Mellotron: information available from Dallas Music Industries, 301 Island Rd., Mahwah, N.J. 07430.

Meyer, Robert G. "Technical Basis of Electronic Music." *Journal of Music: Theory* 8. An interesting, mathematical and electronically oriented introduction (in four parts) to the basic mechanics of electronic sound production for those interested in their scientific foundation.

Naumann, J. and James Wagner. *Analog Electronic Music Technologies and Voltage-Controlled Synthesizer Studios*. New York: Schirmer Books, 1986. An extensive survey of the major studios (university and otherwise) extant at press time.

Nyman, Michael. *Experimental Music*. London: Studio Vista, 1974. Fascinating accounts of some provocative experiments with electronics as well as other avante-garde gadgetry.

Oliveros, Pauline. "Tape Delay Techniques for Electronic Music." *Composer* 1, no. 3 (1969), 135. Excellent source of information on "live" performance possibilities of electronic music.

Olsen, Harry F. *Music, Physics and Engineering*. New York: Dover, 1967. Short on electronic music but quite long on extremely important facts pertaining to acoustics, operation of instruments, etc.

Oram, Daphne. *An Individual Note*. London: Galliard Ltd. 1972. Most provocative, even bizarre book on "Oramics equipment" for electronic synthesis which, despite the "Cagean" writing, is far more significant than it at first appears.

Pousseur, Henri, "Calculation and Imagination in Electronic Music." *Electronic Music Review* 5 (January 1968):21.

Prieberg, F. K. *Musica ex Machina*. Berlin: Verlag Ullstein, 1960. Written in German; a truly classic history of electronic music.

Rossi, Nick, and Robert Choate, eds. *Music of Our Time*. Boston: Crescendo Publishing Co., 1969. Has a number of excellent studies of composers involved in the electronic medium (biographical as well as informative for study of works): Stockhausen, p. 181; Ussachevsky, p. 326; Babbitt, p. 348; Subotnick and Wuorinen, p. 380.

Russcol, Herbert. *The Liberation of Sound*. Englewood Cliffs, N.J.: Prentice-Hall, 1972. Good book on electronic music but suffers from erratic organization.

Schaeffer, Pierre. *A la Recherche d'une Musique Concrète.* Paris: Editions du Seuil, 1952. Valuable and incredibly fascinating study of Schaeffer's early work in *musique concrète.*

Schrader, Barry. *Introduction to Electro-Acoustic Music.* Englewood Cliffs, NJ: Prentice-Hall, Inc., 1982. A well-organized but somewhat superifical book important for its interview with a number of prominent composers including Pauline Oliveros, Luciano Berio, Gordon Mumma, and Jean-Claude Risset. The computer music section is already out-of-date even though the book is recent.

Schwartz, Elliott. *Electronic Music: A Listener's Guide.* New York: Praeger Publishers, 1972. Fine book on the subject with accurate materials on all aspects of the art from live electronic to computer sources.

Stockhausen, Karlheinz. "The Concept of Unity in Electronic Music." In *Perspectives on Contemporary Music Theory.* Edited by Benjamin Boretz and Edward T. Cone. New York: W. W. Norton & Co., 1972. Excellent article on this subject but a bit egocentric in relating to the author-composer's own works.

———. "Mikrophonie I and II." *Melos* 33:144. Fascinating and revealing study of these works by the composer himself.

Strange, Allen. *Electronic Music,* 2nd edition. Dubuque, Iowa: Wm. C. Brown Company Publishers, 1982. Fine textbook for use in electronic music classes. Introduction by Gordon Mumma.

———. "Tape Piece." *Composer* 2, no. 1 (1970):12. Explanation of the correct care and use of the most important element of electronic music: the tape itself.

Stroh, W. M. *Zur Sociologie der elektronischen Musik.* Zurich: Amadeus, 1980.

Trythall, Gilbet, *Electronic Music.* New York: Grosset & Dunlap, 1973. Brief but very good textbook on the subject.

Ussachevsky, Vladimir. "Note on a Piece for Tape Recorder." In *Problems of Modern Music.* Edited by Paul Henry Lang. New York: W. W. Norton & Co., 1960. Excellent personal analysis of this historic work by its composer.

———. "Sound Materials in the Experimental Media of *Musique Concrète,* Tape Music and Electronic Music." *Journal of the Acoustical Society of America* 29:768. Quite interesting and informative.

de la Vega, Aurelio. "Electronic Music, Tool of Creativity." *Music Journal* 2 (September, October, November 1965). A defensive and more philosophical reflection on electronic music in general.

Vercoe, Barry. "Electronic Sounds and the Sensitive Performer." *Music Educators Journal* 55, no. 3 (Novermber 1968).

Vinton, John, ed. *Dictionary of Contemporary Music.* New York: E. P. Dutton & Co., 1974. See in particular the following, dealing with electronic music: "Apparatus and Technology," p. 205; "History and Development," p. 212; "Notation," p. 216. Volume also contains biographies of a great many of the composers discussed in this chapter.

Weilland, Fritz. "The Institute of Sonology at Utrecht State University." *Sonorum Speculum.* A fascinating article on what is possibly one of the world's finest electronic laboratories.

Weinland, John David. "An Electronic Music Primer," *Journal of Music Theory* 13, no. 1 (1969).

Wells, Thomas, and Eric Vogel. *The Technique of Electronic Music.* Austin, Tex.: University Stores, 1974.

Wörner, Karl, *Stockhausen, Life and Work.* Translated by Bill Hopkins. Berkeley: University of California Press, 1973. A good view of this composer's work but like Cott's book, a bit premature in its gamble on this composer's "greatness."

Albright, William. *Organbook II*. Jobert. Recorded on Nonesuch 71260. Uses organ and
   tape.

AMM "live electronic" improvisation group is featured on Mainstream's 5002, which also
   has the Musica Elettronica Viva.

Anderson, Ruth. *Points* (1973–4). Recorded on 1750 Arch Records S-1765. Realized at
   the Hunter College Electronic Studio.

Ashley, Robert. *Purposeful Lady, Slow Afternoon* (1968). Recorded on Mainstream 5010.
   This nearly pornographic "lady" highlights a collection of works performed by the
   Sonic Arts Union, including works by David Behrman, Alvin Lucier, and Gordon
   Mumma.

Babbitt, Milton. *Composition for Synthesizer* (1963). Columbia MS-6566.

———. *Ensemble for Synthesizer* (1967). Recorded on Columbia MS-7051.

Beerman, Burton. *Sensations for Clarinet and Tape*. ACA. Recorded on Advance
   Recordings FGR 15S.

Electronic Music: The Pioneers. Recorded on CRI ACS 6010. An eclectic but important
   collection of 1950–1970 electronic music including the work of Luening, Ussachevsky
   and Babbitt (among others).

Ellis, Merrill. *Kaleidoscope*. Recorded on Louisville S-711.

Erb, Donald. *In No Strange Land*. Merion Music. Recorded on Nonesuch 71223.

———. *Reconnaissance*. Recorded on Nonesuch 71223.

———. *Reticulation*. Merion Music.

Felciano, Richard. *God of the Expanding Universe*. E. C. Schirmer.

———. *Litany*. E. C. Schirmer.

———. *Crasis*. E. C. Schirmer.

———. *Lamentations for Jani Christou*. E. C. Schirmer.

Gaburo, Kenneth. *Antiphony III (Pearl White Moments)*. Recorded on Nonesuch 71199.

Gerhard, Roberto. *Collages (Symphony #3)*. Recorded on Angel S-36558.

Henry, Pierre. *Apocalypse de Jean*. Recorded on Philips 6521 002. By a master of
   musique concrète.

Henry, Pierre, and Pierre Schaeffer. *Symphonie pour un Homme. Seul*. Recorded on
   Philips 6510 012. Two giants of early electronic music presented at their best.

Hiller, Lejaren. *Machine Music* (1964). Presser. Recorded on Turnabout 34536. For piano,
   percussion, and tape.

———. *Malta* (for tuba and tape, 1975). Recorded on CAPRA Records 1206.

Ichiyanagi, Toshi. *Life Music* (for tape and orchestra, 1966). Varèse/Sarabande 81060.

Kagel, Mauricio. *Acoustica* (1970). Recorded on DG-2707059. For experimental sound
   generators and loudspeakers.

Korte, Karl. *Remembrances*. Recorded on Nonesuch 71289. For flute and tape.

Kupferman, Meyer. *Superflute*. Recorded on Nonesuch 71289.

Ligeti, György. *Articulation* (1958). Recorded on Wergo 60059.

Lockwood, Annea. *World Rhythms* (1975). Recorded on 1750 Arch Records S-1765.
   Realized at the Hunter College Electronic Music Studios.

Lucier, Alvin. *North American Time Capsule* (1967). Recorded on Odyssey 32-160156.

———. *Vespers* (1968). Recorded on Mainstream Records 5010.

Lucier, Alvin. *Music on a Long Thin Wire*. Recorded on Lovely Music 1011/2.

Luening, Otto. *Synthesis* (1960). Peters. Recorded on CRI S-219. For orchestra and tape.

MacInnis. Donald. *Collide-a-Scope* (1968). Recorded on Golden Crest S-4085. For twelve
   brass instruments and tape.

Marshall, Ingram. *Fragility Cycle*. Recorded on IBU Records. Live electronic music with voice and other instruments.

McLean, Barton. *Genesis*. Recorded on Orion ORS 75192. This album also contains two other electronic works by this composer: *The Sorcerer Revisited and Dimensions II* (the latter for piano and tape).

————. *Song of the Nahuatl*. Recorded on Folkways FTS 33450. A graphic score was also made of this piece (part of which appears on the cover of *Composer Magazine* 10, no. 1, 1980).

McLean, Priscilla. *Dance of Dawn*. Recorded on CRI SD 335. This album also contains an electronic work by her composer husband Barton McLean: *Spirals*.

————. *Invisible Chariots,* Recorded on Folkways Records FTS 33450.

Messiaen, Oliver. *Trois petites liturgies de la présence divine*. Recorded on Music Guild S-142. This piece uses the ondes martenot very effectively.

Miller, Edward. *Piece for Clarinet and Tape* (1967). Recorded on advance FGR 17S.

Mimaroglu, Ilhan. *Wings of the Delirious Demon,* and other works. Recorded on Finnadar 9001.

Mother Mallard's Portable Masterpiece Company. Music for 5 synthesizers with music by David Borden and Steve Drews. Recorded on Earthquack EQ 001 and 002.

Mumma, Gordon. *Mesa* (1966). Recorded on Odyssey 32-160158.

————. *Hornpipe*. Recorded on Mainstream 5010.

————. *Megaton for Wm. Burroughs*. Recorded on Lovely Music LML/VR-1091.

Nonesuch Guide to Electronic Music. Recorded on Nonesuch HC-73018.

Oliveros, Pauline. *I of IV* (1966). Recorded on Odyssey 32-160160.

————. *Bye Bye Butterfly*. Recorded on 1750 Arch Records S-1765. A classic tape composition made in 1965 at the San Francisco Tape Center.

Ross, Eric. *Electronic Études* (opus 18). Recorded on Doria Records ER-103. This album utilizes the solid-state "theremin."

Souster, Tim. *Spectral* (viola/tape dealy/live electronics). (1972). Recorded on Transatlantic Records TRAG 343.

Stockhausen, Karlheinz. *Gesang der Jünglinge*. Recorded on DG-138811.

————. *Stimmung*. Universal Edition. CD: Hype; CDA66115.

————. *Hymnen*. Universal Edition. Recorded on DG-2707039.

————. *Kontakte*. Universal Edition. Recorded on DG-138811.

————. *Telemusik*. Universal Edition. Recorded on DG-17012.

Strange, Allen. *Two x Two* (1968). Recorded on Capra 1210.

Subotnick, Morton. *After the Butterfly* (1980). Recorded on Nonesuch N-78001.

————. *4 Butterflies*. Recorded on Columbia M-32741. One of his major "music box" works written for a record.

————. *Sidewinder*. Recorded on Columbia M-30683.

————. *Silver Apples of the Moon*. Recorded on Nonesuch 71174.

————. *The Wild Bull*. Recorded on Nonesuch 71208.

Taylor, Dub. *Lumière*. Recorded on Varèse 81001. For synthesized and *concrète* sounds.

Thome, Diane. *Anäis* (for piano, 'cello and tape, 1967). CRI S-437.

Truax, Barry. *Solar Eclipse* (1985). Recorded on Cambridge Street Records CSR 8501.

Ussachevsky, Vladimir. *Creation-Prologue*. Recorded on Columbia MS-6566.

————. *A Piece for Tape Recorder,* Recorded on CRI-122.

————. *Of Wood and Brass*. Recorded on CRI S-227.

———— and Otto Luening. *Concerted Piece for Tape Recorder and Orchestra*. Recorded on CRI 227-SD. A masterwork for tape and orchestra.

————. *A Poem in Cycles and Bells for Tape Recorder and Orchestra* (1954). One of the first (and most well-known) works for this combination.

Varèse, Edgard. *Poème électronique.* Recorded on Columbia MS-6146.

————. *Déserts.* Published by G. Schirmer and recorded on Angel S-36786.

Wilson, Galen. *Applications.* Recorded on Capra 1201.

Wilson, George Blach. *Exigencies* Recorded on CRI S-271.

Wuorinen, Charles. *Times Encomium* (1969). Recorded on Nonesuch 71225.

Xenakis, Iannis. His electronic music is featured on Nonesuch 71246.

Folkways 6301 and 33436 include collections of a variety of electronic music. Folkways FX 6160 contains some early electronic experiments including Ussachevsky's *Sonic Contours, Transposition, Reverberation,* and *Composition,* and Otto Luening's *Fantasy in Space.* Luening's and Ussachevsky's *Concerted Piece for Tape Recorder and Orchestra,* made at the Columbia-Princeton Music Center, is available on CRI S-227-SD, along with works by Mel Powell and Ussachevsky.

Milton Babbitt's *Vision and Prayer* (1961) for soprano and tape (AMP) is part of CRI-268, a large two-disc collection, which includes also Varèse's *Déserts,* 1961 (AMP); Luening's *In the Beginning* (1956); Ussachevsky's *Computer Piece No. 1* (1968), and *Two Sketches* (1971); together with works by Smiley, Shields, and Davidovsky.

Orion 7021 features electronic works by Swickard and Heller. DG 137011 includes four works composed at the Utrecht Institute of Sonology. Desto 6466 has works by Luening and Ussachevsky as well as *Incantation,* on which they collaborated.

The Schwann Record Catalog has a separate listing of electronic music records which is of value even though a number of European labels are not included (especially Wergo). A short list of works and records is listed in the *Music Educators Journal,* November 1968. The *Repertoire International des Musiques Electro-acoustiques* (Electronic Music Catalog) which appeared as *Electronic Music Review* No. 2/3 (April/July 1967), compiled by Hugh Davies is, though out-of-date, still the best source for information on early non-recorded electronic music.

8

EXTENDED MEDIA RESOURCES

Media forms involving music are both the rational extension of composite forms such as ballet and opera, and the result of the need for visual activity in connection with tape music. Many multimedia forms grew from experiments with "chance" relationships between simultaneously produced art forms (e.g., *happenings*).

Alexander Scriabin's *Prometheus—The Poem of Fire* (1910) is one of the first examples of mixed-media compositions with origins not directly related to opera or ballet. The scoring calls for large orchestra, chorus, piano, organ, and *clavier à lumières*, an instrument with a keyboard-controlled lighting console. The part for the *clavier à lumières* employs traditional musical notation, and each key is associated with a color. Scriabin directly ascribed tonal regions with colors (e.g., *f* is blue, *the color of reason;* F, *the blood red of hell;* D, *the sunny key;* etc.). With *Prometheus* he envisioned far more than a superfluous "light-show." His concepts embodied a deeply philosophical and religious symbolism with beams and "clouds" of light moving throughout the hall. The chorus was to be draped in white robes and vocalize on ritualistic closed lips or vowel sounds. Unfortunately, *Prometheus* (which was completed in early 1910) was premiered in 1911 without the *clavier à lumières*—without any lighting, in fact. It waited until March 20, 1915 (just five weeks before the composer's death) to receive any mixed-media complement at all. Even then only weak color projections moved on a small screen, falling considerably short of the composer's intentions.

Schoenberg's *Die glückliche Hand* (opus 18, 1910–13) also required lighting effects, which proved technologically unfeasible. The resulting presentation was a poor realization of the composer's intent. *Prometheus,* at least, has had a media "revival" in the past few years, with numerous attempts made at fulfilling the composer's wishes. Unfortunately, most of the results seem diluted by the architecture of the concert hall's interior, or by the lack of real musical translation of sound into light.

The Dadaists and those who worked in the Bauhaus were among the first to openly confront media concepts (that is, try to *integrate* all the art forms available). While certainly one can trace other attempts through Wagner's *gesamtkunstwerk* back to Greek concepts, to do so would go beyond the scope of this book and thereby

Background and Aesthetics

neglect unique attributes of the "audience participation" aspects of today's media forms.[1] Aside from early commercial "shows" which employed perfumes (*The Song of Solomon* was performed in Paris in 1891 with sound, light, and perfumes, for example) and Scriabin's aforementioned *Poem of Fire* which was not truly realized, Erik Satie's *Relâche* (1924) was one of the first landmarks in media forms. René Clair's film (also a landmark in cinematography for 1924), the understated Satie music, the ballet, the surrealistic scenery—all combined to create a vessel of often interplaying, often contradicting images.

Theatrical elements in new music seem to have closer historical ties with the ballet than with opera or oratorio. Though many mainstream composers (notably William Schuman and Aaron Copland) have created ballets for dance groups (especially for Martha Graham), it was John Cage and the Merce Cunningham dance group that injected theater into the combination of art forms, with each surviving by its dependence upon the other.

These directions, combined with the television-cinema age, and the need in electronic music for auxiliary visual material, have contributed largely to the contemporary revival of the *gesamtkunstwerk* concept in the form of "happenings." Richard Maxfield writes: "I view as irrelevant the repetitious sawing on strings and baton-wielding spectacle we focus our eyes upon during a conventional concert. Much more sensible either no visual counterpart or one more imaginatively selected such as lighting, cinema, choreography, fireworks, trees. . . ."[2] The sophistication of equipment and techniques of lighting, still and moving projections have made many new multimedia possibilities available to the twentieth-century artist-composer. Like all other facets of midcentury life, the new forms of art must inevitably share responsibility with the electromechanical environment in which they develop.

The aesthetics of media forms remain targets at which many an active as well as passive participant or bystander seem to take special aim. Coming to grips with the definitions and categorization of varieties of intentions involved may help in the conciliation of some antagonists. Two composers, Robert Ceely and Paul Goldstaub, tend to sum up the points of view quite succinctly:

Ceely: . . . it [multimedia] is most interesting in that it usually fails.
Goldstaub: The first time I conducted [Toshiro] Mayazumi's *Metamusic* (certainly a multimedia work of classic stature) it brought home the simple truth that people have overlooked for centuries: concert going is partially a visual and social experience, as well as musical. If composers can *use* this to enrich the quality of the experience of their music, everyone gains.[3]

1. The Bauhaus, founded by Walter Gropius in 1919, included very basic interdisciplinary media such as art, architecture, and design. Though short-lived (until 1933) it served as an example in the arts that has founded very solid ground for media studies in the American university.
2. As quoted in *An Anthology of Chance Operations*, La Monte Young and Jackson Mac Low, eds. (New York: 1963). No page numbers.
3. Tom Everett, "Questions and Answers," *Composer Magazine* 4, no. 1 (Fall-Winter 1972): 20–21.

Multimedia is often used synonymously with a number of terms, most often *inter-media* and *mixed-media*. Adding to the confusion are the terms *theatre pieces, merged-medium, environmental works, happenings,* etc. To avoid continuing this terminology explosion, the author defines three major categories of *media forms:*

1. Multimedia: this form is a loose structure in which the various media do not depend on each other for meaning (*happenings* are excellent examples of multimedia events, in that each element is significant and structured in such a way that it could stand on its own merits);
2. Mixed-media: this form tends "toward equalization of elements," though "any hierarchial order is possible" (*environments* more often than not fit this media form in that, though the elements are dependent on each other, "they are mixed, but not truly integrated"[4]);
3. Inter-media: this form has all of its elements in equal balance and integrated to the fullest degree (*merged-medium* fits this category well in that ". . . all elements are equal and integrated"[5]).

A number of terms fall within these three main categories (some in more than one category as they may or may not attain balance or integration):

Multimedia	*Mixed-media*	*Inter-media*
(loosely knit composite forms)	(more integrated, with varying degrees of importance of elements)	(very integrated, each element depending on the others for the work to hold together)
happenings	environments	merged-medium
collage	opera	environments
theatre pieces	film and TV	films
opera	kinetic theatre	meditations
ballet		
light-show		
film and TV		

Two important factors must be considered carefully in observing the above listings:

1. Composers have been very flexible in their usage of the above terms. Indeed, their use of certain terminologies may not fit the above chart (the author's own *Deadliest Angel Revision*, 1971, is a good example: it is billed as

---

4. Stanley Gibb, "Understanding Terminology and Concepts Related to Media Art Forms," *The American Music Teacher* (April-May 1973), pp. 23–25. This is possibly the most well thought out and formulated writing on this subject and is highly recommended to those seeking real insight into media art forms.
5. Ibid.

multimedia or a *theatre piece* when in fact it is *inter-media*). Therefore one cannot always accurately judge the composition by its "nomer."

2. None of the above classifications implies a quality judgment. Each is merely a starting point from which one can discuss the forms with some degree of consistency. Important works exist in each of the categories.

With this in mind it is necessary to note that the author has attempted to choose works which emphasize in particular each of the above categories.

Multimedia

April 17, 1958 saw the introduction of *Poème électronique* by Edgard Varèse at the Brussels World's Fair (see Chapter 7). This multimedia presentation by Varèse, in collaboration with architect Le Corbusier, took place within a pavilion which was shaped externally like a three-peaked circus tent and internally like a cow's stomach. The composition, 480 seconds in length, was accompanied by projected images of paintings, written script, and montages. Neither of the artists made attempts at correlation between visual and aural images. The result produced occasional simultaneity of rhythm or spatial relationships, but more often separation of concepts. The intense organization of each artist's approach to his own material, however, was so apparent that correlation seemed almost inappropriate. The performance, attended by nearly three million people, remains as the most culturally significant representation of multimedia in history.

The summer of 1952 marked some of the first multimedia "happenings" when John Cage, David Tudor, Robert Rauschenberg, and Merce Cunningham teamed to play records, read lectures from stepladders, dance, use projections, and display "white paintings" at Black Mountain College. The concept was a random sequence of nonrandom materials. That is, the order and combinations were chance, but the lectures, projections, and paintings in themselves were not. The resultant "theater" of events allowed each art form to remain isolated, contributing to the whole only as each performer reacted to another's event or personality.

An important experimental media contribution developed during the late fifties and early sixties with the ONCE group in Ann Arbor, Michigan. Composers, artists, filmmakers, and architects focused their activities into the ONCE festival of contemporary music, the Space Theatre of Milton Cohen, the Cooperative Studio for Electronic Music of Robert Ashley and Gordon Mumma, and the Ann Arbor Film Festival of George Manupeli. Mumma's *Music from the Venezia Space Theatre* (1964), composed for Cohen's Space Theatre, was ". . . an hour long program of light projection, film, sculpture, modern dance and electronic music, and (first) performed by an ensemble of the ONCE group. The projected images of the Space Theatre, which evolved continuously between the realistic and the abstract, were as diverse as the sound sources, and moved through the entire space surrounding the audience."[6]

6. Gordon Mumma, Program notes on Lovely Music, VR 1091.

Multimedia, as an offshoot of the American experimental school, has also developed along lines more indeterminate than structured. The thread of separation lies in the area of "theater": the necessity of partial indeterminacy for a play to "happen." Roger Reynolds's *Ping* (1968), based on a text by Samuel Beckett, is an excellent example of a somewhat improvisatory work which explores "theatrical" possibilities. Three performers (flute, piano, harmonium, bowed cymbal, and bowed tam-tam) create the "live" situation, augmented by a 25-minute tape. Their instruments are amplified using contact microphones. A 22-minute film and 160 slides (projected alternately to the left and right) of Beckett's story add visual material. Effects in and around the performance area are created by matrixed mirrors projecting secondary images, blurs, and colors: a cohesive factor enjoining sight and sound experience. The score[7], explicit as to materials, duration, pitches (for the most part), and dynamics, allows improvisation from *all* performers, including the projectionists. For example, the projectionists may, within certain limitations, alter images through the use of such devices as filters and prisms. Reynolds's *The Emperor of Ice Cream* (1962) includes the projection of the score (both graphic and traditional in notation) for the performers (eight singers, piano, percussion, and bass). Each projection, or score page, represents twenty seconds of time, and the position, movement, and "choreography" of each performer is indicated by dotted lines and the positioning of sound-symbols. Theatrical effects are written on the score in words, some as performance cues, others spoken, with performers becoming actors and dancers as well as sound producers.

Morton Subotnick's *Ritual Electronic Chamber Music* involves four performers at "game boards" (lighted buttons for channel or amplitude of the electronic tape or one of four projections). Each performer's choice of which button to

Figure 8.1. Morton Subotnick.

7. Roger Reynolds, *Ping,* as published in *Source: Music of the Avant-Garde* (Composer/Performer Edition) 3, no. 2 (July 1969):70–86.

press sets up choices for other "players." In the center, a "High Priestess" moves about, playing lights on her body and moving the sound throughout the room. The work may be performed without an audience or in a very small chamber group of interested persons.

"Relevant action is theatrical (music [imaginary separation of hearing from the other senses] does not exist) . . ."[8] speaks John Cage of, among other things, the audience's ability to see and hear other sounds outside the performance area. Feelings, smells, and even tastes seem somehow neglected by most composers in the superficially imposed restriction of their creativity to sound alone. More often than not, Cage's approach to multimedia is philosophical: accept *all* sounds, sights, and other sensory experiences which occur in and around a performance situation, *equally,* regardless of their origin (this would include such things as car noises and coughs). Some of his works involve "stage" multimedia. *Water Walk,* for example (first performed over Milan television in 1958 by Cage, who was a quiz show contestant), includes banging a rubber fish inside a piano on the strings, Cage watering a vase of roses, and a pressure cooker spurting steam, among other "props."

Whether initiated by determinate or indeterminate procedures, multimedia is the result of a natural concern by the composer and artist alike to allow and/or control *all* the apsects of the human sensory system within the framework of the performance situation. Peter Maxwell Davies's *Eight Songs for a Mad King* (see analysis, Chapter 4) requires that the flute, clarinet, violin, and 'cello players sit in cages "representing, on one level, the bullfinches the King (George III) was trying to teach to sing . . . the percussion player . . . the King's brutal keeper, who plays him off stage at the end, beating a bass drum with a cat-o'-nine-tails."[9] While the visual forms of drama and setting contribute to live performance intensity, the significance of this highly acclaimed work is caught aurally on the recording (the media form is born in the listener's mind via program notes, while listening to the record).

Boguslaw Schäffer is an active composer of theatre music and happenings. His *Audiences No. 1–5* (1964; see Figure 8.2) is "music for actors" with the texts by the composer, and involves projections, drama, and musical events. His happenings include *Non-stop* (1960) for piano (with a duration varying from six to four hundred and eighty hours), and *Incident* (1966) for an "ensemble" of *audience* (lasting four hours).

George Crumb's *Voice of the Whale* (*Vox Balaenae*) (1971), like the Davies work, has multimedia aspects which are related to live performance only, and which in no real way detract from the music by their absence (i.e., when the music is on a record). The composer requests that the performers wear black half masks (or visor masks) and the stage be bathed in deep blue light. Clearly, the music can easily stand alone and the visual aspects, though interesting in performance, are by no means absolutely essential to the work (i.e., the music retains its artistic identity without the visual complement).

8. John Cage, *Silence* (Cambridge, Mass.: The M.I.T. Press, paperback edition, 1961), p. 15.
9. Liner notes on the recording (Nonesuch H-71285) by Peter Maxwell Davies.

Figure 8.2. Boguslaw Schäffer: *Audiences No. 4.*

Multimedia techniques have invaded *rock* idioms, with extraordinary results. The Velvet Underground, for example, toured America as a part of Andy Warhol's mixed media show *The Exploding Plastic Inevitable* in the mid-sixties. Pink Floyd's 1980 performance of *The Wall,* an extensive light show, proved influential in commercial circles. The group played in front of and behind a huge wall (70 feet high) which was both constructed and destroyed during performance. Multidirectional speaker setups, along with complicated lighting and projections, contributed to an ambitious multimedia event. Led Zeppelin's laser shows and Funkadelic have since developed extensive media programs. Visual theatrics seem almost a requisite for rock performances in the 1980s, with Devo and other *new wave* groups equally preoccupied with visuals and sound effects. Kiss, Ted Nugent, Black Sabbath, Alice Cooper and Ozzy Ozborne (who eats chickens' heads!) all contribute to a diverse popular multimedia (and theatrical) culture.

Work by Nam June Paik and James Searight in the area of video feedback (camera focused directly into the screen to which it feeds; i.e., looping) create interesting potential for the multimedia composer.

Allan Kaprow catalogs some of his basic concepts for multimedia categories in the following ways:

    a. The line between art and life should be kept as fluid, and perhaps indistinct, as possible. . . .

    b. Therefore, the source of themes, materials, actions, and the relationships between them are to be derived from any place or period *except* from the arts, their derivatives and their milieu. . . .

    c. The performance of a Happening should take place over several widely spaced, sometimes moving and changing locales. . . .

    d. Time, which follows closely on space consideration, should be variable and discontinuous. . . .

    e. Happenings should be performed once only. . . .

    f. It follows that audiences should be eliminated entirely.[10]

Clearly these techniques revoke the basic tenets of Western World artistic heritage and begin important contributions to the New Experimentalism (see Chapter 6). Composers and artists involved in these techniques include Jean-Jacques Lebel, Wolf Vostell, George Brecht, Kenneth Dewey, and Allan Kaprow.

Mixed and Intermedia

When superficially (man-made) imposed definitions of art (e.g., music, painting, sculpture) exist psychologically within audiences, domination of one art form over another can exist. Projected scores or performer-interpreted projections share equally the difficulty of misinterpretation; "music seen" or "paintings as sound" represent displacement of traditional dogmatic categorization of the arts. Daniel Lentz's *Sermon* (1970) for string quartet modified by electronic filters, reverberation, ring modulation, and gate device, involves score projection. Once a score is visible to the audience it becomes obvious that it must be made visually interesting and artistic. Lentz has solved this problem by creating an artistic score in color: red = played, blue = sung, green = hummed, yellow = whistled, violet = spoken, brown = whispered, with an orange line surrounding the score page referring to time (a ten-by-twelve-inch projection, each half-inch representing one second). The result is greater visual excitement *and* more meaningful notation for the performers.

Allen Strange's *No Dead Horses on the Moon* requires seven 16mm projectors to surround the audience with visual images (see Figure 8.3). The recorded sound, projected from the four corners of the room, creates an environment. Correlation between visual and aural materials is obtained by written instructions to the performers (in this case the projectionists). In No. 6, for example, the projectionist is instructed to move his projector. The films are created by scraping the emulsion from 16mm black leader film and then constructing loops, creating a seven-fold visual ostinato (see example). The resulting flashing dots, lines, and "strobe" effects, along with the sound, engulf the audience in an imaginative "light-show."

At the same time, these concepts alter a basic concert ritual of audience-performer separation. Robert Ashley's *Public Opinion Descends Upon the Demonstrators* (1961) embraces the ideal of "total theater." Specific prerecorded sounds are produced by a single performer on electronic playback equipment only when a member of the audience acts or reacts in a certain manner (e.g., by speaking, glancing, looking about, gesturing, looking toward a loudspeaker, or leaving). Whether or not performance precludes knowledge on the part of the audience of the compositional concept, it soon becomes obvious that all participants (composer, performer, audience) share equal responsibility in creating the work.

10. Allan Kaprow, *Assemblage, Environments & Happenings* (New York: Abrams, 1966), unpaged.

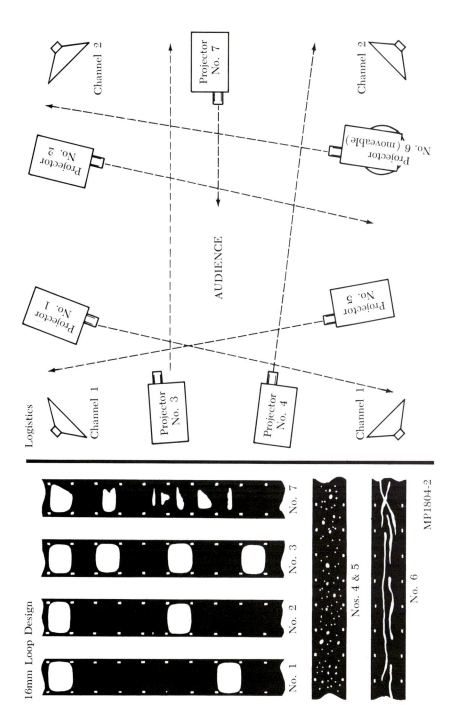

Barton McLean's *Identity* series of compositions deal directly with man's relationship with his surroundings, perception of a work in a complete environmental setting, and audience control over sounds. More complete and detailed than Stockhausen's *Musik für ein Haus* or Sigmund Krauze's experiments with environmental music in Poland and Germany, McLean's *Identity* series includes works for specific buildings and situations. One of these (for the Cultural Center in South Bend, Indiana) is, in the composer's words:

> . . . a true environmental experience in that the hearer who walks through it reacts to the sounds both passively and actively. This latter aspect, perhaps the most unique in its conception, although allowing for the overall direction and control of the work to remain in the hands of the composer, nevertheless provides to the listener the opportunity to participate in smaller, but highly meaningful choices. Thus, the hearer, in exercising creative choices of his own which shape the smaller details of the work, enters into the actual creative experience. Furthermore, no musical training is necessary for this interaction, since it is set up so that all choices made by the hearer on this smaller structural level are equally valid. On the other hand, for those who have more time and intuitive ability, it is possible to grow with the work and, upon repeated hearings, to exercise intelligent choices on gradually higher and higher planes.[11]

The work (building) is controlled in terms of lighting, speaker activity, etc., by the audience motion which triggers a wide variety of sounds. By movement and by the audience's discovery of the planned placement of photoelectric cells, microphones, and various visual control devices, the building becomes a self-contained environment.

Figures 8.4 and 8.5 show the extent to which media techniques have become sophisticated during the past few years. These diagrams represent two of the media aspects of the Learning Resources Center at Middle Tennessee State University in Murfreesboro. The figures demonstrate the incredible future and potential of media in education, the sciences, and communications, as well as in the arts.[12]

Ron Pellegrino has developed laser scanning and projection systems which extend electronic music instrumentation into the realm of light. Figure 8.6 shows a simple laser scanning system. Sound (here from a synthesizer, computer or collection of function generators) controls a power amplifier which in turn uses the galvanometers (and "chopper") for the projection of a single laser beam into three components. Figure 8.7 presents three possible laser setups using (in turn) frequency modulation (first example), frequency, amplitude and ring modulation (second example) and frequency and amplitude modulation.

---

11. The quote from the composer is from materials about the work made available to the author.
12. More information on this most interesting media center is available from the Director of the Learning Resources Center at Middle Tennessee State University.

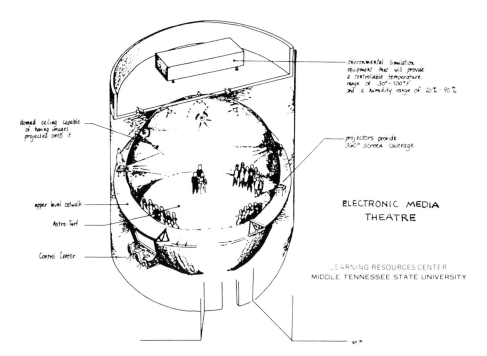

Figure 8.4. Electronic media theatre. Permission granted by the Learning Resources Center, Dr. Marshall Gunselman, Director; Middle Tennessee State University.

environmental simulation equipment that will provide a controllable temperature range of 30°-100°F and a humidity range of 20%-90%

domed ceiling capable of having images projected onto it

projectors provide 360° screen coverage.

upper level catwalk

Astro-Turf

Control Center

ELECTRONIC MEDIA THEATRE

LEARNING RESOURCES CENTER
MIDDLE TENNESSEE STATE UNIVERSITY

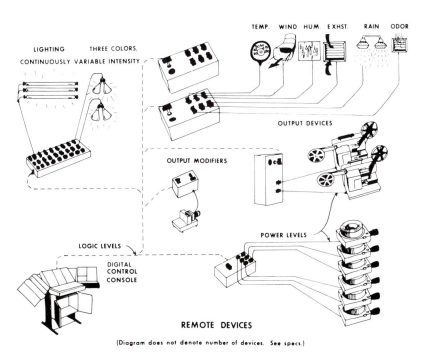

Figure 8.5. Remote devices. Permission granted by the Learning Resources Center, Dr. Marshall Gunselman, Director; Middle Tennessee State University.

LIGHTING   THREE COLORS,
CONTINUOUSLY VARIABLE INTENSITY

TEMP. WIND HUM. EXHST.   RAIN   ODOR

OUTPUT DEVICES

OUTPUT MODIFIERS

LOGIC LEVELS

POWER LEVELS

DIGITAL CONTROL CONSOLE

REMOTE DEVICES

(Diagram does not denote number of devices. See specs.)

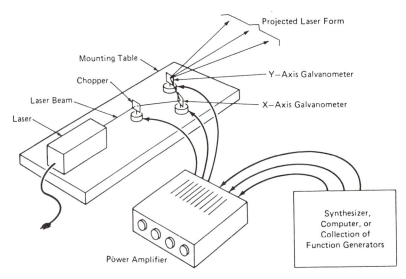

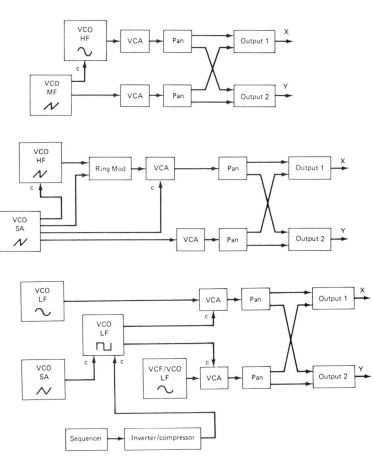

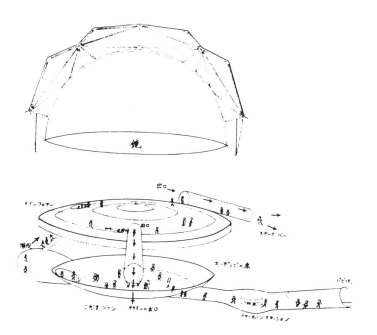

Figure 8.8. Schematic drawings of the main building of *Pavilion* in Japan, 1969.

Composers, often lacking legitimate theater backgrounds, have consequently improvised techniques beyond the "time-honored" Grecian concepts of dramatic ritual. The physical aspect of any sensual act no longer distinctly separates one artistic ideal from another. Paul Ignace's *Feast* (1964) culminates all possible environmental encounters within the framework of a mixed-media work. The performers (even the composer) no longer exist except in concept. The audience is fed all aspects of sensual experience, the menu requiring only individual choice within reason. Preferably for two people, *Feast* enacts the "last request" prerogative of an imaginary death victim, making choices available on most levels of immediate desire, including choices of sounds, smells, tastes, touches, and sights. The composer here does not evoke *certain* responses, but makes available as many responses as possible. In *Feast*, mixed-media achieves the ideal philosophically implied and inherent within its thesis: no action (relevant or not) can be considered unimportant to the totality of a composition. Total theater environments cannot avoid the direction toward complete involvement in what traditionally has been called *life*. All the categories between "theater" and "reality" eventually fall away as even the simplest of media concepts projects to it ultimate end.

Figure 8.8 shows two views (the first exploded) of *Pavilion,* completed in 1969. This extraordinary building was the site for many multi-media compositions, some of which included theater and dynamic effects such as enshrouding the building in fog, mirroring the internal ceiling, etc. A wide range of stylistically different composers have used the facility for exploration and performance.

Mauricio Kagel's *Match* (for two violoncelli and percussion) is a dramatic game which unfolded in full-blown detail to the composer in a dream. Characterized by visual humor (which met with immediate applause at its premiere in Berlin in October of 1965), it is strikingly serious music (leading to what the composer has called a "shaking concert of derision" at the end of the first live performance).[13] The intense and dramatic music, when fused with the visual wittiness, results in a complicated *collage* of constantly varying grades of emotional polarities. Regarding a portion of *Match* the composer has noted:

> During the first rehearsal of these uncertain measures I was told by the interpreters that the passage in question reminded them of the most memorable of the *circene* scenes: the death leap. Such an appreciation was already known to me; the similarity between this situation with what was dreamed a few weeks previously left no room for doubt: both musicians were suspended in mid-air with their cellos on top of their heads and by means of slow pirouettes they produced very sharp, brilliant sounds. The roll of the drum, that from some point in space resounded over the entire environment, maintained the spectators in pure tension until leading to an aggressive attack on the cymbal. Thus was overcome the first of the mortal leap with good fortune.[14]

13. Mauricio Kagel, "On Match for Three Performers," *Composer* 3, no. 2 (Spring 1972); translated from *Sonda #3* (Juventudes Musicales, Madrid) June 1968, pp. 70–78.
14. Ibid., p. 73.

Figure 8.9. Mauricio Kagel.

Possibly one of the most prolific and well-known mixed-media composers is Robert Moran. His *Hallelujah* (for twenty marching bands, forty church choirs and organs, carrillons, rock groups, a gospel group, and the entire city of Bethlehem, Pennsylvania) was first performed in 1971 and is truly a landmark in mixed-media performance. His earlier *39 Minutes for 39 Autos* (for thirty-nine amplified auto horns, auto lights, Moog Synthesizer, thirty skyscrapers, radio stations, a television station, dancers, etc.—first performed on August 29, 1969 in San Francisco) provides further example of equally staggering proportions. Of these the composer has remarked:

> In my work, *39 Minutes for 39 Autos,* I attempted to make everyone a musician. One hundred thousand persons participated in the premiere. My *Hallelujah,* commissioned by Lehigh University, used hundreds of musicians . . . in this composition I tried to make every musician a human being.[15]

Moran's works embrace an incredible variety of mixed-media explorations. *Divertissement No. 1,* 1967 (for popcorn, electric frying pan, and any instrumental soloist), for example, requires the performer to read popping corn as noteheads on five-lined white-staved dark sunglasses. *Bombardments No. 4,* 1968 (for trombone and tape, commissioned by Stu Dempster) requests that the trombonist, wrapped in a sack, become a visual analog gargoyle (legs, slide, arms, and body movements all sharing in the vision of struggling shape, lit dimly from both sides), and its aural counterpart.

15. Robert Moran in a letter to the author.

In general, film music does not qualify as a particularly significant exploration of media forms. There are, however, a number of exceptions which should be noted. Aside from the *Relâche* film of 1924 by René Clair mentioned previously, work by composer John Whitney and his painter brother James is particularly significant. Beginning in 1940 they began their experiments with abstract film and infrasonics (in this case, a series of pendulums mechanically connected to a wedge-shaped aperture and influencing an optical sound track producing sine wave oscillations with a frequency range of a little more than four octaves). Like the sound track notations of Norman McLaren (discussed under *Electronic Music*), the Whitney experiments have provided a vast new source of media materials. However, these have not as yet produced a significant body of artistic achievement.[16] John Whitney speaks to this point:

> It is hoped that the partnership of sound and picture will attract the attention it deserves in artistic circles. The problem that confronts the individual consists of a number of difficulties whose acquaintance he may already have made in the course of his experiences in modern music or painting. Whether the necessary technical apparatus will always be placed at the disposal of the artist is a question that touches on an elementary problem, whose solution lies hidden in the darkness of the future.[17]

Salvatore Martirano's *L'sGA* (1968) is a massive and intense mixed-media work overloading the senses with dramatic, visual, and aural messages. *L'sGA,* in the composer's words, is:

> Lincoln's *Gettysburg Address* for actor, tape, and film, using a helium "bomb" which the actor breathes from at the end of the piece so that his voice goes up a couple of octaves . . . all you need to do is catch a few words now and then to understand what the meaning is. You hear "government" and you hear "people." And thus I would hope that the person watching would create the framework of specific and exact meaning according to how he sees things. Because I'm not forcing him to catch on to a sequence of events in which each one has to be understood for the next one to make sense. It's almost kind of throwing it in all different places and gradually, I would hope, the conception is built up in the audience.[18]

Groups devoted to mixed-media performance include ZAJ (pronounced *thack;* a Mexican Theater of the Absurd); THE; Harkins and Larson (formed in 1975 at CME in San Diego); and individual performers such as Stuart Dempster (performance of Robert Erickson's *General Speech for Trombone,* 1969, being most notable).

---

16. Recent "popular" *visual music* devices wherein strobes or 3-D "color-organs" translate bass, treble, and midrange sounds into visual abstractions, while interesting, prove to be little more than *light-shows* of the most simplistic order.
17. John Whitney, "Moving Pictures and Electronic Music," *Die Reihe* 7 (1960):71.
18. Panel Discussion: *ASUC Proceedings* 3 (1968):43.

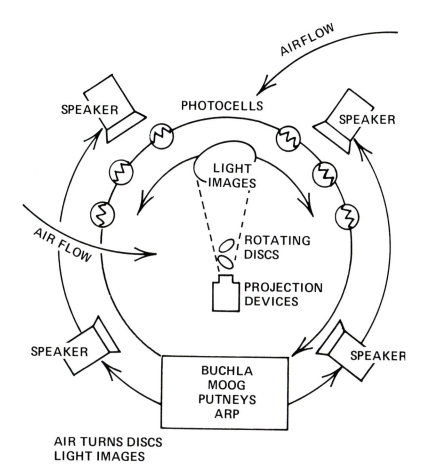

AIRFLOW

SPEAKER

PHOTOCELLS

SPEAKER

LIGHT IMAGES

AIR FLOW

ROTATING DISCS

PROJECTION DEVICES

SPEAKER

SPEAKER

BUCHLA
MOOG
PUTNEYS
ARP

AIR TURNS DISCS
LIGHT IMAGES

Figure 8.10. *Metabiosis V: A Light, Sound, and Audience Environment* by Ron Pellegrino. Used by permission of *Proceedings* of the American Society of University Composers 7/8 (72–73) © ASUC, Inc., c/o American Music Center, 210 Broadway, Suite 15–79, New York, N.Y. 10023.

Figure 8.10 is *Metabiosis V: 'A Light, Sound and Audience Environment'* (1972) by Ronald Pellegrino. The total environmental system is explored in this world[19] with the incorporation of the given space and natural variables an intrinsic part of the design.

Merrill Ellis's *Mutations* for brass choir, electronic tape, and light projections is a dramatic and integrated approach to intermedia. The work begins with a standard concert setting. Suddenly the hall is plunged into darkness, the players leave the stage (making vocal and other unusual sounds) and, with the electronic tape becoming the main aural source, projections (in the form of films, lights, etc.) flash on the ceiling and walls, engulfing the audience in a "sea" of visual activity. *Mutating* the ABA form (not as simplistic as it may appear here), the players return to the hall (rear this time) and perform again under a dim flashing light. The work concludes in total darkness and silence.

19. To be published as part of a book, *Thinking for the Electronic Music Synthesizer* (chapter 6) as outlined in *ASUC Proceedings*, 7/8.

Figure 8.11. Merrill Ellis (photo by Ron Bray: North Texas State University, Electronic Music Center, Denton, Texas).

Landscape Journey (1963) by Donald Scavarda, for clarinet, piano and film projection, reflects the contrasting elements of aural and visual materials. Sections of sound alone interplay with soundless projections to create an obvious alternating formal structure. The abstract fast-moving shapes and colors on *two* screens balance the contrast and dependence of the two instruments in use.

Scavarda speaks of the inter-media implications in his work:

> . . . these sounds (are synthesized) with abstract color film to create a filmic extension of the instrumental timbres. The plasticity of the slowly shifting instrumental timbre is further "pushed" by the use of dramatic silences and contrasts with the rapidly moving film which is gradually introduced as the work evolves. . . . Here the film does not have a notational function but rather is an intrinsic part of the structure of the piece. Thus, timbre is perceived visually as well as aurally. The two projectors, placed immediately in back of the piano bench, are "performed" by the pianist, who also operates a rheostat controlling a single lamp (which lights the scores) in an otherwise darkened hall.[20]

Videos

"The TV extension of our nerves in hirsute pattern possesses the power to evoke a flood of related imagery in clothing, hairdo, walk and gesture. All this adds up to the compressional implosion—the return to nonspecialized forms of clothes and spaces, the seeking of multi-uses for rooms and things and objects in a single word—the iconic. In music, poetry and painting, the tactile implosion means the insistence on qualities that are close to casual speech. Thus Schoenberg and Stravinsky and Carl Orff and Bartók, far from being advanced seekers of esoteric effects, seem now to

20. From a letter to the author.

have brought music very close to the condition of ordinary human speech . . . the great explosion of the Renaissance that split musical instruments off from song and speech and gave them specialist functions is now being played backward in our age of electronic implosion."—Marshall McLuhan from *Understanding Media.*

In music videos, composers have the opportunity to correlate their rhythmic and timbral techniques with the visual arts, roaming freely (because of the advent of sophisticated digital editing machines) between reality and the abstract. Monitor screen size and the home video cassette machine boom allow for intimate viewing and possibilities of a non-linear experience (the ability to freeze frame, fast-forward and otherwise create your own version of the video). In certain styles of music (predominantly rock) the music video has become a staple of the medium, more secure in some ways than the more traditional aural-only performance of records, compact discs and tapes. While slower to develop in the avant-garde, certain composers and idioms have found themselves immediately successsful in this format.

In the 1960s, Nam June Paik began to study the television (video) medium seriously. Experiments with video feedback and loops as well as other abstract techniques proved seminal in the history of the medium as an art form. More recently, Robert Ashley has used videos as a part of the theater he creates. As these pioneers have developed significant alternatives to its naive and often commercial use, other composers have turned to the medium which may have the single biggest technological impact in the music world (note the incredible success of music video programs: *MTV, VH-1* and *Friday Night Videos*).

To date, experimentation in music videos relevant to this book has been somewhat limited to five areas or styles: (1) avant-garde jazz, (2) new age music, (3) performance art, (4) minimalism and (5) experimental rock. Each of these seems especially well suited to the medium with each able to have real-world equivalents to their form. For example, the night-club performance tradition of jazz fits the visual experience of the video format. In performance art, seeing has equal impact (often) to hearing. New age music (discussed more thoroughly in Chapter 12) has ambient overtones which metaphorically suggest real-world equivalents (waves, meadows, waterfalls, etc.) and minimalism, with its lack of material, seems only heightened by the added hallucinatory abilities of the music video. It is clear that all work with video will not be limited to these four styles; however, for the reasons presented, it is most useful to direct our attention to them in particular.

Aside from the standard video camera recording of jazz group performances, the following stand out as examples of good work in both the visual and aural fields. The video by *The Art Ensemble of Chicago* (1982 University of Illinois performance—52 minutes), called "Live from the Jazz Showcase," creates a surreal blend of dance, costume, and music. The performers wear masks and body paint and dance while the music fuses American jazz with African traditional music. Directed by William Mahin, the video is a collection of long-shots and close-ups which artfully capture the extraordinary nature of the performance. Likewise, "The New Music" (1985, directed by Peter Bull and Alex Gibney), by Bobby Bradford and John Carter, represents an Ornette Coleman-derived free-jazz experimentation. This is a brief portrait of the performers during an avant-garde performance using a variety of instrumental exploration techniques. Elvion Jones' "Different Drummer" (directed by Edward Gray—1984) is an explosive documentary of the drummer's life and unbridled performance techniques. In contrast, the *Weather Report* video titled "The Evolutionary Spiral" (1984, directed by Larry Lachman) is an abstract work which strives to "travel·from the birth of the universe, through ancient cultures and the high tech world of today, then on to a vision of art in the future . . ." (from the cover of the cassette).

New age videos represent the work of composers on the Windham Hill label (particularly Mark Isham, William Ackerman, George Winston and Alex De Grassi). Most notable of their recent issues is "Autumn Portrait" (directed by Stanley Dorfman, 1985). The soft ambient music mirrors the autumnal New England which washes across the screen with no comment necessary. No apparent correlation is made from image to sound; however, the tempo seems linked to the speed of camera motion. The various works (by different performers and composers) each blend into the next with no distinction save their different instrumentation. Brian Eno's "Thursday Afternoon" (directed by himself [1986] and *not* a Windham Hill artist) creates an extremely slow moving abstract portrait of Christine Alicino with a backdrop of very soft ambient music by the composer.

With the advent of composer/performers (such as Laurie Anderson and many others), video provides the perfect medium for melding their visual-physical actions and their music. Yoko Ono's "Then and Now" (directed by Barbara Braustark, 1984) attests remarkably to these possibilities in the *then* part of the video, for example, many "happenings" and "bag art performances" of the 1960s are relived (with John Lennon). The *now* portion reveals Ono through a series of intimate interviews and reflections on those performances.

In the minimalistic school of film (video), Philip Glass's *Koyaanisqatsi* stands out. Directed by Godfrey Reggio, this work (originally a film made in 1984) uses only image and music in a tapestry of natural and unnatural scenes with slow and fast camera speeds mirrored in the tempi of the music. There is no narrative here or need of one; it is beautifully photographed (by Ron Fricke) and mesmerizing in effect. The wordless choral vocals add immeasurably to this effective work.

Most rock video follows the formulaic traditions of television and media in general and warrants little but social commentary. A few performers, works and visuals, however, have significant merit and when viewed separately from the onslaught of other types (in the stream that rails from various cable TV stations), merit viewing and analysis. "The Mothership Connection Live from Houston," for example, by George Clinton and the Parliament-Funkadelic (1986, directed by Archie Ivey, Peter Conn and Wayne Isham) represents what some have called the "post-hippie funk-rock traveling circus." This video has an assortment of live performances and shorter video clips, one of which, "Atomic Dog," is a classic music video with computer animation and appropriate musical accompaniment. "Danspak" (directed by Merrill Aldighieri and Joe Tripician, 1983) represents rock music from a number of avant-garde underground artists of New York City. The group Devo, visually interesting in live performance, makes the natural transition to music videos in their

"The Men Who Make Music" (1979, directed by Charles Statler and Gerald Casale) and "We're All Devo" (1983, directed by Gerald Casale). The former was, by some accounts, the first rock video ever made. The latter is technically professional and conceptually masterful. It also includes "Worried Man" by Neil Young, a work from his never released "Human Highway." Pink Floyd's "The Wall," while it does not do justice to the live performance, has nonetheless classic footage of this amorphous rock quasi-opera. "Gimme Shelter" (1981, directed by David Maysles, Albert Maysles and Charlotte Zwerin) is a video-verité of the 1969 Altamont Speedway concert of the Rolling Stones. The video includes the murder of Meredith Hunter in what must be the most horrifying and terrible moments on tape. Except for this, however, the classic action of the veteran and venerable group is classic. The chaotic camera work only heightens the effect of being in this nightmarish scene.

The art of video making has had immense impact on motion photography. The opportunity of immediate playback (some cameras have built-in replay monitors), for example, as well as the inexpensive nature of video tape (over film) have added to the extraordinary popularity of the medium. Large-scale video projectors have likewise expanded the potential for theater presentation. Thus video is *the* future of film and hence the future for those composers and performers interested in the extended media applications of their work. When digital editing equipment prices fall into the general market range, the tendency for most performance-oriented musicians, even traditional concert hall performers, will be to tape their performance, if only for personal uses. These will be archived becoming the next in a series of technological tools begun with the work of Edison on the cylinder tape recorder in the 19th century.

As with laser beams, videos may also have direct audio control of imaging through MIDI interface mechanisms. Very Vivid of Toronto has created such an instrument called *Mandala*. Video animation effects may be generated directly from a composition in virtually hundreds of combinations or approaches. Since digitized music and digitized visual images represent the same kind of data, they may be mixed, controlled, generated and edited in a wide variety of ways allowing composers to interrelate directly with visual imagery and vice versa.

(For information on vectoral analysis and procedures, see Chapter 1).

Vectoral Analysis: Donald Erb: *Souvenir* (1970)

1. Historical Background: Donald Erb was born in Youngstown, Ohio, in 1927. After early years as a jazz trumpeter, he studied composition formally with, among others, Bernard Heiden (at Indiana University) and Nadia Boulanger. He is currently Composer-in-Residence at Indiana University in Bloomington, Indiana. His major works include *Symphony of Overtures* (1964) and *The Seventh Trumpet* (1969) for orchestra, *Harold's Trip to the Sky* (1972) for chamber ensemble, and *Concerto for Percussion and Orchestra* (1966).

Figure 8.12. Donald Erb.

Souvenir, for dancers, instrumental ensemble, electronic tape, projections, and props, was completed early in 1970 and first performed in February of that year at Oberlin College. Laurence Berger (dance) and Royce Dendler (sculpture) premiered the work and created subsequent performances in northern Ohio.

2. Overview: *Souvenir* is a brief (8½ minutes in duration) work of driving intensity. The sonic form of the work derives from the skeletal scoring for the 12–20 wind and percussion players (who surround the audience in the dark) and the electronic tape (created from electronic sources in the Cleveland Institute of Music electronic laboratory). The tape portion exists throughout the work and consists of a slightly out-of-tune "perfect" fifth interval (B— F♯), which acts as a continual drone. The live performers begin during the second minute (signaled by the conductor, whose primary job is to flash a light cue at the end of each minute during the performance). All play *pianissimo* using either long tones within a minor second of either of the tape pitches or short pointillistic effects on their respective instruments. These slowly and consistently grow throughout the piece until the *crescendo* reaches *fortissimo* (at around 7½ minutes). The parts are written in English and are easy to memorize (almost a necessity, since the piece is performed in the dark).

Elements are added according to the following schematic:

minutes: 0—1   action: nothing; just tape
1—2   players quietly begin to play
2—3   slide projections begin
3—4   dancers enter
4—5   weather balloons are added
5—6   silly string is sprayed
6—7½   continue
7—8½   (or end) conductor strikes gong, signaling
ping-pong balls to be "dumped"

The hall is filled with "black light" (nonvisible light that excites certain luminescent paints). The dancers, covered with luminescent tape, bring small props (i.e., sponge rubber balls of various sizes) also covered with luminescent paints of various colors (all of these glow in the dark). The projections (optional) are of the performers' choice, but in fitting with the joyous, positive nature of the work, and not so bright as to nullify the effect of the black lights. The weather balloons (8- to 12-feet war surplus balloons) are also covered with luminescent paints and bounced into the hall (whereupon the audience usually begins to participate). Luminescent "silly string" is sprayed into the whole auditorium, inundating the performers and audience. The ping-pong balls (about 5,000) have been painted with luminescent paint and fall into the audience (becoming "souvenirs" of the performance). The activity clearly accelerates in correspondence with the sounds: a singular and direct *crescendo* from beginning to end.

3. Orchestration: The taped "perfect" fifth drone is created by sawtooth waves drawn through low pass filters. These in turn are slowly adjusted so that the timbre is continually altering during performance. The slight "beating" of the inharmonic fifth also contributes to the perception of change.

   The live performance ensemble is free enough so that exact sounds are unpredictable. It is interesting to note, however, that the long tones, in the interval of seconds with the tape, create subtle shifts in motion and dissonant threads against which the pointillistic events are superimposed. All these occur spatially within the concert space.

4. Basic Techniques: Erb has employed a quasi-improvisatory verbal score that clearly defines limits in performance. The sensual overload that slowly occurs with aural, visual, and tactile elements gradually develops a counterpoint inherent in the "play-by-play" scoring.

5,6. Vertical and Horizontal Models: Pitch content is limited (in the noneffect material) to seconds surrounding the taped fifth (i.e., B♭—C and F—G). These contribute to a dissonant yet static quality lacking the tension suggested by their "cluster" content. The stretto of effects (both aural and visual) add to the momentum of intensity that ensues during the performance.

7. Style: The style of *Souvenir* is possibly best summed up in the composer's own words: "One reason that it works (is that) it is an outgoing and happy work; non-neurotic."[21] The style is inter-media. Audiences (at least those observed by this author) become first mesmerized by the visual material and then, with growing anticipation, actively involved with pushing balloons in the air, dodging silly string and throwing ping pong balls during the near cataclysm of sound and energy surrounding them.

This work, while outwardly expressing a disdain for the seriousness with which most of the composers in this book take their work, also shows a distinct relationship with a number of other examples presented in Vectoral Analysis: particularly those of Chapter 4 (sets, costume, dramatics, etc.) and Chapter 12 (staging, costumes, special lighting, etc.). Its extreme "direction" toward climax and explosion contradict the formal structures of many works lacking such as a compositional device (such as the works found in the Vectoral Analysis of Chapters 2, 5, 6 and 10).

Bibliography

Further Readings*

Ashley, Robert, "Notes for *Public Opinion Descends Upon the Demonstrators." Asterisk* 1, no. 1 (1961):49. Presents score and performance information about this work.

Austin, Larry. "SYCOM—Systems Complex for the Studio and Performing Arts." *Numus West* 5:57. A most interesting article pertaining to the potentials of media research and study of new combinational art forms.

Baschet, Bernard and F. Baschet. "Sound Sculpture: Sounds, Shapes, Public Participation, Education. *Leonardo,* 20, No. 2 (1987): 107–14. The authors describe their work with sound sculptures (accompanied by an extraordinary collection of photographs). These pieces resemble the waterphone (or vice versa) and usually possess various metal horns as amplifiers.

Becker, Jurgen, and Wolf Vostell, eds. *Happenings.* Hamburg: Rowohlt, 1965. A good source of information on this topic from a European viewpoint.

Beckwith, John, and Udo Kasemets, eds. *The Modern Composer and His World.* Toronto: University of Toronto Press, 1961.

Cage, John, *M. Writings '67–'72.* Middletown, Conn.: Wesleyan University Press, 1973.

———. *Silence.* Middletown, Conn.: Wesleyan University Press, 1961.

———. *A Year from Monday.* Middletown, Conn.: Wesleyan University Press, 1967. All very useful books and collections of articles, many of which are related to this man's efforts at media connections, be they relevant or not. A bibliography of Cage articles and interviews exists in Kostelanetz's book on Cage and need not be reprinted here.

Chase, Gilbert. "Toward a Total Musical Theatre." *Arts in Society* (Spring 1969): p. 25. Good primer on this concept.

Cross, Lowell. "David Tudor," In *Dictionary of Contemporary Music,* edited by John Vinton. New York: E. P. Dutton & Co., 1974. Article ends with a group of works by Tudor who is probably the most prolific, in media forms, of any living composer aside from Cage himself.

21. In a telephone interview with the author.

*Addresses for record companies, periodicals, and music publishers mentioned in this Bibliography can be found in Appendix 4.

Cunningham, Merce. *Changes: Notes on Choreography.* Edited by Frances Starr. New York: Something Else Press, 1969. Fascinating source book not only for the dance contribution to media forms but also for the variety of ways in which it has been included in the past.

Dallin, Leon. *Techniques of Twentieth Century Composition.* 3rd ed. Dubuque: Wm. C. Brown Company Publishers, 1974. Contains a brief but interesting commentary on multimedia.

Doubravova, J. "Music and Visual Art: Their Relation as a Topical Problem of Contemporary Music in Czechoslovakia." *International Review of the Aesthetics and Sociology of Music,* 11:19–28, No. 2 (1980).

Evans, Brian. "Integration of Music and Graphics through Algorithmic Congruence." *Proceedings of the 1987 International Computer Music Conference.* San Francisco: Computer Music Association, pp. 17–24. This account of the creation of the *Marie Duet* begins to demonstrate the optical and aural mix and quality inherent in mixed-media.

Gibb, Stanley. "Understanding Terminology and Concepts Related to Media Art Forms." *The American Music Teacher,* 22, no. 5:23. Superb article which brought many insights to this author's consideration of the various forms.

Goddard, Don. *Sound/Art-Exhibition Catalog.* New York: SoundArt Foundation, 1983.

Hansen, Al. *A Primer of Happenings and Time-Space Art.* New York: Something Else Press, 1968. Fascinating contribution to the media-forms literature.

Higgins, Dick. *Postface.* New York: Something Else Press, 1964.

———. *FOEW & OMBWHNW* New York: Something Else Press, 1969. Reprinted by Printed Editions. Both are interesting contributions to the literature.

———. *A Dialectic of Centuries: Notes Towards a Theory of the New Arts,* 2nd ed. New York: Printed Editions, 1979. An important collection of essays on Higgins' work in inter-media.

Hiller, Lejaren. "HPSCHD." *Source* 2, no. 2 (1968). Discusses the work of the same name by Hiller and Cage, with photographs of both composers at the computers.

Hoffman, Paul. "An Interview with Robert Moran." *Composer* 4, no. 2 (1973):46.

Kagel, Mauricio. "On *Match* for Three Performers," *Composer* 3, no. 2 (1972):70. Fascinating account of one very involved in "media" works from the most bizarre to the most conventional.

———. "Uber das instrumentale Theater." *Neue Musik* (Munich, 1961). Interesting study of this man's views on the subject.

Kaprow, Allan. *Assemblage, Environments and Happenings.* New York: Abrams, 1966. Good source with interesting photographs.

Khatchadourian, Haig. *Music, Film and Art.* New York: Gordon and Breach, 1985. Brilliant survey of current techniques in each of these areas as they relate to one another.

Kirby, E. T. *Total Theatre.* New York: E. P. Dutton & Co., 1969. Most fascinating and a very good contribution to the literature though it is slanted in the indeterminate direction: multimedia.

Kirby, Michael. *The Art of Time.* New York: E. P. Dutton & Co., 1969. Relevant and interesting "conceptual" study of media-related forms and structures.

———. *Happenings.* New York: E. P. Dutton & Co., 1965. Good insight into the structure and beginnings of this multimedia form.

Klüver, Billy, Julie Martin, and Barbara Rose. *Pavilion.* New York: Dutton, 1972. A close look into arts and technology; a wide variety of media techniques are explored.

Kostelanetz, Richard. *The Theatre of Mixed Means.* New York: Dial, 1968. Though out of print, one of the best sources on the subject yet available.

———, ed. *John Cage.* New York: Praeger Publishers, 1970. Fine book containing photographs and documents of the tradition of experimentalism started by Cage. Also contains excellent bibliographies relating to media presentations.

MacLow, Jackson. *The Pronouns: A Collection of Forty Dances for the Dancer's Station.* Barrytown, N.Y.: Station Hill Press, 1980.

"Conversation with Robert Moran." *Numus West* 3:30. Fascinating account of this man's work in multimedia.

Mumma, Gordon. "Four Sound Environments for Modern Dance." *Impulse, the Annual of Contemporary Dance,* 1967. Writing particularly on Cage's work.

Muscutt, Keith. "Projected Kinetic Displays and Photomicrographs based on the use of Polarized Light." *Leonardo* 11: 97–102. An excellent article demonstrating the result of experiments with polarized light. The resulting photomicrographs are elegant and sophisticated works of art often used in multimedia performances.

McLuhan, Marshall. *Understanding Media. The Extensions of Man.* New York: New American Library, 1964. The classic McLuhan work on how media has affected contemporary mankind. The sections on television ("The Timid Giant") and automation are particularly insightful.

Nyman, Michael. *Experimental Music.* London: Macmillan Ltd., 1974. Interesting look into a number of experimental media works of the 1960s.

Pellegrino, Ronald. "Some Thoughts on Thinking for the Electronic Music Synthesizer." *Proceedings* (American Society of University Composers) 7, no. 8 (1972–73):52. Interesting approach to many problems facing the media composer today.

———. *The Electronic Arts of Sound and Light.* New York: Van Nostrand Reinhold Company, 1983. The "Brief History," while incomplete, presents good information about multimedia in the 1960s and 1970s. The rest of the book devotes far too much space to Pellegrino's work at the expense of that of other composers in the field (John Whitney, for example, only gets a brief mention).

Penn, William. "The Celluloid Image and Mixed Media." *Composer* 1, no. 4 (1970): 179. Discusses philosophical aspects of the form.

Proceedings 3. (American Society of University Composers [August 1968].) Includes two very interesting discussions: "Theatre Music" with Richard Browne as chairman and a panel of Barney Childs, Ben Johnston, Salvatore Martirano and Roy Travis; and "Mixed-Media Composition" with Ross Lee Finney as moderator and panelists George Cacioppo, Edwin London, and Salvatore Martirano. Both are of value and interest, and show a multiplicity of views toward both media composition and the personalities involved.

Reynolds, Roger. "Happenings in Japan and Elsewhere." *Arts in Society* 5, no. 1 (Spring-Summer, 1968). Short but quite good reference on some significant activities in the sixties in Japan by a number of visiting American composers as well as by composers from Japan.

Rossi, Nick, and Robert Choate. *Music of Our Time.* Boston: Crescendo, 1969. A number of references to multimedia with coverage of Cage (*HPSCHD,* p. 337ff.) and Subotnick (*Play! No. 1,* p. 377).

Salzman, Eric. "Mixed Media." In *Dictionary of Contemporary Music,* edited by John Vinton. New York: E. P. Dutton & Co., 1974. Good introduction to the subject. The *Dictionary* also includes many biographies of composers mentioned in this chapter.

Shore, Michael. *Music Video: A Consumers Guide.* New York: Ballantine, 1987. An excellent compendium of reviews on music videos. Although it limits its content particularly to rock and pop idioms, some of the hybrid experimentation in those fields crosses new music boundaries. All of the information is provided (e.g., duration, production company, director, producer, etc.).

Sondheim, Alan, ed. *Individuals.* (*Post-movement Art in America*). New York: Dutton, 1977. Interesting work on Acconci and Lucier.

Subotnick, Morton. "Extending the Stuff Music is Made of." *Music Educators Journal* 55, no. 3 (November 1968): 109. Short but good study in the problems and origins of multimedia.

Tomkins, Calvin. *The Bride and the Bachelors.* New York: Viking Press, 1965. A brilliant book examining the lives of four extremely important contributors to the media concept: Marcel Duchamp, Jean Tinguely, Robert Rauschenberg, and John Cage.

Weidnenaar, Reynold. "Live Music and Moving Images: Composing and Producing the Concert Video." *Perspectives of New Music,* 24/2 (Spring-summer, 1986):271–79. A good primer on the basic principles of contemporary music videos.

Whitney, John. "Moving Pictures and Electronic Music." In *Die Reihe* 7. Bryn Mawr, Pa.: Theodore Presser, 1965. Superb study in inter-media and a most important contribution to the literature.

———. *Digital Harmony.* Peterborough, N.H.: Byte Books, 1980. An extraordinarily encyclopedic text by a pioneer of multimedia techniques.

Yates, Peter. *Twentieth Century Music.* New York: Pantheon Books, 1967. Follows the history of the experimental "ideal" in America, including happenings and multimedia developments.

Young, La Monte, and Marian Zazeela. *Selected Writings.* Munich: Heiner Friedrich, 1969. Interesting but centered around the activities of the two authors.

Youngblood, Gene. *Expanded Cinema.* New York: Dutton, 1970. Important information regarding computer films and inter-media concepts.

Zahler, Noel. "Isomorphism, Computers and the Multi-media Work." *Proceedings of the International Computer Music Conference.* San Francisco: Computer Music Association, 1987, pp. 228–29. A brief but useful document for relating current technology to media expressions (especially note: *TIS*).

13th Annual Conference on Computer Graphics and Interactive Techniques. The proceedings of this convention provide important information on the use of computers with graphics and light in media presentations. The theme "integrating music and graphics" has produced a sizeable amount of imaginative material for future research.

Ashley, Robert. *Public Opinion Descends Upon the Demonstrators* (1961). *Asterisk* (magazine) 1, no. 1.

Austin, Larry. *Bass* (1967). CPE-*Source.* For bass, tape, and film. Performed over N.E.T. by Bertram Turetzky. Involves exaggerated gestures and mime.

———. *The Maze* (1965). Audience involvement with lights and dramatic actions by the performers. Both these works show the theatrical possibilities of standard performing situations.

Beerman, Burton. *Mixtures.* Media Press. Ensemble, tape, and candlelight procession.

Berio, Luciano. *Laborintus II* (1965). Universal Edition. Recorded on RCA LSC-3267. For voices, instruments, reciter, and tape.

———. *Sinfonia* (1968). Universal Edition. Recorded on Columbia MS-7268.

Recordings and Publishers

Cage, John. Media works include:

————. *Theatre Piece* (1960). Peters.

————. *Variations III*. Peters. Recorded on DG-139442.

————. *Water Music* (1952).

Cage, John and Lejaren Hiller. *HPSCHD*. Peters. Recorded on Nonesuch H-71224. A "happening."

Colgrass, Michael. *As Quiet As* (1966). MCA. Recorded on RCA LSC-3001.

Cope, David. *BTRB* (1970). Brass Press. For any brass player; theatre piece.

————. *Cradle Falling* (1985). For chamber ensemble performing in costume with airplane runway lights and black light effects.

————. *Deadliest Angel Revision* (1971). Seesaw Music Corp.

Crumb, George. *Ancient Voices of Children*. Peters. Recorded on Nonesuch 71255.

————. *Voice of the Whale (Vox Balaenae)*. Peters. Recorded on Columbia M-32739.

Davies, Peter Maxwell. *8 Songs for a Mad King*. Boosey & Hawkes. Recorded on Nonesuch H-71285.

Ellis, Merrill. *Mutations*. Shawnee Press (New York).

Erb, Donald. *Souvenir*. Merion Music.

Erickson, Robert. *General Speech, for Trombone* (1969). Recorded on New World 254. An amazing theatre piece composed for (and played here by) Stu Dempster.

Foss, Lukas. *Baroque Variations* (1967). Carl Fischer. Recorded on Nonesuch 71202.

Ives, Charles. *Central Park in the Dark* (1906). AMP. Recorded on Columbia MS-6843.

Kagel, Mauricio. *Die Himmelsmechanik* (1965). Composition using vivid images of suns, moons, clouds, etc.

————. *Kommentar und Extempore* (1967). For three actors, singer, and seven brass instruments.

————. *Ludwig Van*. Recorded on DG-2530014.

————. *Match* (1966). Universal Edition. Recorded on DG-137006.

————. *Variaktionen* (1967). Universal Edition. For four actors, three singers, and tapes.

Kasemets, Udo. *"It: Tribute to Buckminster Fuller, Marshall McLuhan and John Cage*. A computer-controlled audio-visual audience participation work.

Knowles, Alison. *Natural Assemblages and the True Crow*. New York: Printed Editions, 1980. A sound-tape collage with visuals.

Kraft, William. *Contextures: Riots—Decade '60*. Recorded on London 6613. For orchestra and projections.

Lunetta, Stanley. Four excellent theater pieces complete with flashing lights, projections, and sets: *The Wringer, Mr. Machine, A Piece for Bandoneon and Strings, Spider Song*.

Martirano, Salvatore. *L'sGA* (1968). MCA. Recorded on Polidor 245001.

————. *Underworld*. MCA. For four actors, two basses, tenor saxophone, and tape.

Moran, Robert. The following are available only from the composer: *Bombardments No. 4; Divertissement No. 1; Hallelujah; 39 Minutes for 39 Autos*.

de Oliveira, Jocy. *Probabilistic Theatre 1*. Uses a map projection as score for musicians, actors, dancers, and lights.

Reck, David. *Blues and Screamer.* CPE-*Source.* An excellent aural-visual composite including an antiwar film and dramatic performer remarks (near the end of the score).

Reynolds, Roger. *Emperor of Ice Cream.* Peters.

———. *Ping.* CPE-*Source.* Recorded on CRI-285.

Rochberg, George. *Music for the Magic Theatre.* Theodore Presser. For orchestra. Desto DC-6444.

Satie, Erik. *Relâche* (1924). Salabert. Recorded on Vanguard C-10037/8.

Schäffer, Boguslaw. *Audiences No. 1–5* (1964). PWM.

———. *Non-Stop* (1960). PWM.

———. *Incident* (1966). PWM.

Scriabin, Alexander. *Poem of Fire.* Balawe Publishers. Recorded on London 6732.

Somers, Harry. *Improvisation.* A theater piece for voices and instruments.

Stockhausen, Karlheinz. *Momente* (1963). Recorded on Nonesuch 71157. Begins with players applauding the audience, with rhythmic notations.

———. *Opus 1970.* Recorded on DG-139461.

Strange, Allan. *No Dead Horses on the Moon.* Media Press.

———. *Palace.* CAP. For violin, tape, projections, and staging.

———. *Vanity Fair.* Another dramatic multimedia work.

Subotnick, Morton. *Mandolin* (1960). MCA. For viola, tape, and film.

———. *Play* (1962). MCA. Woodwind quintet, piano, tape, film.

———. *A Ritual Game Room* (1970). MCA. Without audience.

Tudor, David. See p. 769 of John Vinton's *Dictionary of Contemporary Music* for a compilation by Lowell Cross of Tudor's work in media forms.

9 · DIGITAL ELECTRONIC MUSIC

Early Developments

Computer music differentiates between the terms *analog* and *digital*. The electronic music discussed in Chapter 7 is *analog:* continuous, noninterrupted magnetic information. Sound (singing, breathing, etc., most of the activities of life) is analog. *Digital,* on the other hand, refers to information stated in *digits* (commonly numbers); i.e., discrete, noncontinuous bits of information. Unlike analog synthesizers, computers are digital in nature, working only with numbers.

The *digits* that *digital* refers to in computers are binary (or containing two states). The binary system incorporates only the symbols "0" and "1." These occur in columns referencing the more traditional decimal (or base 10) system, and are listed right to left in exponential order:

$$\begin{array}{ccccccc}
\text{etc.} & 32 & 16 & 8 & 4 & 2 & 1 & \text{decimal columns} \\
& 0 & 0 & 0 & 1 & 0 & 0 & \text{binary digits}
\end{array}$$

A "1" in any column "trips" that amount into existence, while a "0" signals that the column is not in operation. In the above example, the number presented is 4. Typically, the exponential listing is not shown, but rather taken for granted. These binary numbers can exist in traditional mathematical operations with one example shown below:

$$\begin{array}{cccc}
0 & 0 & 0 & 1 \\
1 & 0 & 0 & 0 \\
\hline
1 & 0 & 0 & 1
\end{array}$$

Note here that addition exists in much the same way it does in decimal mathematics (i.e., $0 + 0 = 0$; $1 + 0 = 1$, etc.). Here the number 1 was added to the number 8, with the result (adding all "tripped" digits) equalling 9.

Understanding binary mathematics is important to one's understanding of computers (and consequently of computer music). The fact that numbers of any amount can be represented by two digits (0 and 1) makes computers possible. Doors (opened/closed), mousetraps (set/unset), or even directions (up/down) all present real world binary equivalents. More importantly magnetic fields (positive/negative) or electric current (on/off) represent ways in which computers can operate using binary concepts. Since objects require only two states of existence, the operations can be quick (often less than a trillionth of a second) and take little space (some designers are now talking in terms of "molecular" operations). It is this concept (that computers can operate with extreme speed and take little space) that makes the "digital" nature of computers important. In contrast, computers can lose a bit of their mystique; the complicated innards are often merely rows upon rows of millions of devices housing smaller devices whose only job is to be on/off, open/closed, or the equivalent.

Since sound is *analog* and computers *digital,* composers interested in the use of computers found inherent contradictions in the compositional possibilities of the instrument. The speed at which computers operate, however, and the mass of material and control they offer are important attractions for composers exploring new compositional techniques. Composers (primarily in the early and mid sixties) such as Lejaren Hiller, Max Matthews, James Tenney, J. K. Randall, and Hubert Howe were among the first to become dedicated to the problems and advantages of computer music. Work at the Bell Laboratories (beginning in 1959) proved enlightening and led to the first MUSIC series of programs (discussed later in the chapter). Figure 9.1 provides a demonstration of the process. Sound is first produced as numerical amplitude values. These are then smoothed, allowing each of the differences between samples in memory to be transformed into analog sound. The process may also be reversed (as will be discussed in detail later in this chapter).

Significant to these early experiments was the exploration of an instrument called the *digital to analog converter* (often called the DAC). It is conceptually similar to that of motion pictures. If one looks at film it is quickly apparent that material

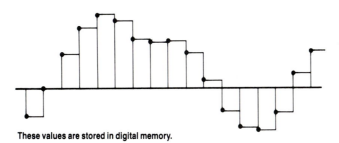

These values are stored in digital memory.

Figure 9.1. How analog sounds are computed and used to create waveforms.

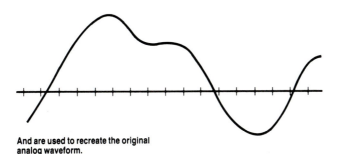

And are used to recreate the original analog waveform.

Figure 9.2. Stages of *computer generated sound.* J. Tenney. (Permission granted by the *Journal of Music Theory,* New Haven, Conn.)

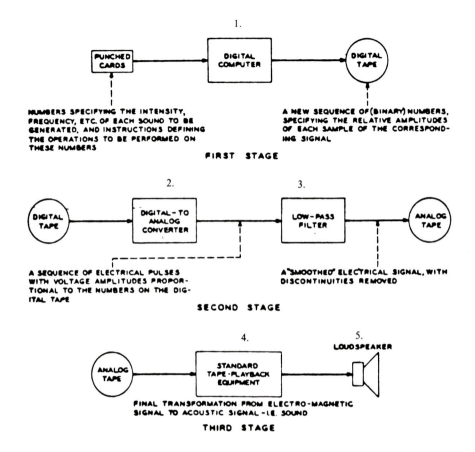

1.

PUNCHED CARDS → DIGITAL COMPUTER → DIGITAL TAPE

NUMBERS SPECIFYING THE INTENSITY, FREQUENCY, ETC. OF EACH SOUND TO BE GENERATED, AND INSTRUCTIONS DEFINING THE OPERATIONS TO BE PERFORMED ON THESE NUMBERS

A NEW SEQUENCE OF (BINARY) NUMBERS, SPECIFYING THE RELATIVE AMPLITUDES OF EACH SAMPLE OF THE CORRESPONDING SIGNAL

FIRST STAGE

2. 3.

DIGITAL TAPE → DIGITAL-TO ANALOG CONVERTER → LOW-PASS FILTER → ANALOG TAPE

A SEQUENCE OF ELECTRICAL PULSES WITH VOLTAGE AMPLITUDES PROPORTIONAL TO THE NUMBERS ON THE DIGITAL TAPE

A "SMOOTHED" ELECTRICAL SIGNAL, WITH DISCONTINUITIES REMOVED

SECOND STAGE

4. 5. LOUDSPEAKER

ANALOG TAPE → STANDARD TAPE-PLAYBACK EQUIPMENT →

FINAL TRANSFORMATION FROM ELECTRO-MAGNETIC SIGNAL TO ACOUSTIC SIGNAL -I.E. SOUND

THIRD STAGE

present is "digital" (i.e., "fixed" images of discrete material); there is no analog motion. However, when these digital elements are shown through a projector at the typical speed of 24 per second, a "feel" of analog motion occurs. The same is possible with computers and sound. If one takes enough numbers representing waveforms and "projects" them through alternations in voltage, the analog impression of sound results. Though this concept is a simplified one, it does give the basic essence of the converter concept. Figure 9.2 demonstrates the ways in which computers are able to produce sound.

In "stage one," the vast amount of numbers (termed *samples*) is produced typically between 20,000 and 55,000 per second of sound. The second stage converts these numbers into voltages that are smoothed and filtered in order to cancel the "rate" of numbers, which can sometimes be read as an extra frequency: called *aliasing*. The third stage produces the "electronic" sound through a standard "hi-fi" system. It should be noted that this early diagram contains a number of elements that today's computer composer finds unnecessary. The computer can now feed directly to the DAC and filter, and subsequently to playback facilities (note the five numbers over the appropriate equipment). This voids the need for so many stages and particularly for punched cards (replaced by video terminals) and digital/analog

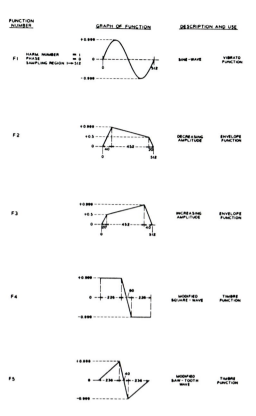

Figure 9.3. Outline of a series of functions. J. Tenney. (Permission granted by the *Journal of Music Theory*, New Haven, Conn.)

tapes. Figure 9.3 shows a series of functions and how they might be presented in terms of vibrato, envelope, and timbre.

With the parameters of sound existing (in the initial state) in numbers, composers can control extremely small and often very precise data. Editing, for example, can be accomplished quickly by extracting "numbers," avoiding the complicated physical necessity of splicing common to "classical" electronic music studios. Careful control of tuning (previously relegated to hand manipulation of knobs) and dynamics is possible and practical. In these ways, the computer offers the composer *more* control and precision in the compositional process.

Analog to digital (A/D) aspects of computer operation often prove as valuable as DAC. Here the composer or experimenter replaces speakers with microphones, and the computer acts as an analytical midwife. Instead of sound being initiated in terms of numbers, it is first analog and then translated into numbers for storage (digital recording), editing (manipulation), or composition (*musique concrète*). Live acoustical events can be recorded via digital mechanics and carefully categorized according to a wide variety of different available techniques for timbral data, spatial content, and reference to compositional potential.

The author has divided composer use of computers into two basic categories: (1) computer-generated sound, wherein the composer has precise control possibilities over musical materials and parameters; and (2) hybrid operations, wherein the computer controls synthesizer functions. In addition to the discussion of these which follows, computer applications in notation and teaching will also be examined.

Computer-Generated Sound

Computer-generated sound (sometimes referred to as "computer sound synthesis") began at the Bell Telephone Laboratories in 1959 with Max Matthews and James Tenney. J. K. Randall and Hubert Howe, among others at Princeton, collaborated with the Bell Laboratories to produce the first effective computer program for sound generation: MUSIC IVB. This program, as well as the host of programs designed since, allows the composer extensive control over all the elements of composition (MUSIC IVB was a culmination of MUSIC IV designed by Matthews using the IBM 7090 computer; it eventually became MUSIC V for the GE 645 computer).

Other programs include the Music Simulator-Interpreter for Compositional Procedure (Musicomp) developed for the IBM 7090 by Hiller and Robert Baker, MUSIGOL developed by Donald MacInnis for the Burroughs 5500, and the Transformational Electronic Music Process Organizer (TEMPO) developed by John Clough at Oberlin College. All of these programs deal explicitly with composer control of all the available parameters of sound and use the computer (with digital input) as a high-speed "performer" to achieve a magnetic tape recording of their works as output (analog voltage on tape).

Research into computer-generated sound continues at many locations, most notably at the Center for Computer Research in Music and Acoustics (CCRMA) at Stanford University. There John Chowning and Leland Smith study digital recording techniques, digital signal processing, psychoacoustical information, advanced synthesis techniques, and the automatic production of musical manuscripts.

The Center for New Music and Audio Technologies (CNMAT) founded at the University of California at Berkeley (1988) has been developed to investigate matters relating to this important aspect of the musical experience. Consortiums exist between it, IRCAM in Paris and Stanford.

John Chowning's research and composition have received considerable acclaim. His early work centered on sound production and basic modulation procedures. Early MUSIC V techniques called for instrument definition in terms of building complex tones (called Fourier or additive synthesis, with each overtone added separately—a tedious and time-consuming process, though the results are often highly controllable). Chowning has worked primarily with concepts of frequency modulation, developing techniques using program and carrier waves. These produce highly complex tones including "inharmonic" materials and frequently sound like "bell tones." This procedure became so important to the development of certain computer programs for music that *Chowning FM* is the term often used to designate the technique. As well, his research of musical *space* using computer techniques and discoveries correlating reverberation (as well as dynamics, direction, and doppler) to spatial modulation have contributed greatly to the development of new programs and works.

Figure 9.4. John Chowning. Photo courtesy of the Stanford University News and Publications Service.

Both space and FM principles are apparent in his *Turenas* (1972) and *Stria* (1977), both computer-generated quadraphonic tape compositions.

He speaks of the former work in an interview:

> In *Turenas,* I used only the FM technique for generating the tones, I used it in both a harmonic series mode and a noisy inharmonic series mode, with transformations between the two. One of the compositional uses of FM was in timbral transformation. This was often coupled with spatial manipulation. As the sounds crossed the space they underwent a timbral transformation.[1]

1. Curtis Roads, *Composers and the Computer* (Los Altos, CA: William Kaufmann, Inc., 1985), p. 21.

Figure 9.5. From David Cope's *Glassworks* (1979); output from PDP 10 computer at Stanford showing controlled parameters (p numbers) in a basic spatial motion of computer-generated sound.

```
21 JUL 1978     4:53        WHIP[222,DHC]
RR MCVX/8 .01,.1/7 .1,.3;
END;

TION 53,68;
P2 MOVE/8 .01,.03 .2,.4/7 .2,.4 1.5,2.9;
P3 SUBR MOVX/3 1260,1260 1239,1272/5 1239,1272 1074,1111/
7 1074,1111 1067,1080;
P4 .167;
P5 F1;
P6 .5 "F8" .5 "F6";
P7 0;
P8 0;
P9 0;
P10 0;
P11 MOVE/4 45,-345/11 -345,-340;
P12 1;
P13 .05;
P14 DF MOVE/8 1,1/7 1,3;
P15 "1";
RR MCVX/8 .01,.1/7 .1,.2;
END;

PROG 0,99;
P2 -66;
P14 F2; P15 F5; P16 F4;
P17 "1";
END;

PROG 66;
P2 NUM/2/4//3/5/6/9;
P3 SUBR NUM/27,3/1,4/10,4/13,5/24,6/27,8/26,8/25,9/24,8;
P4 .14;
P5 MOVP/10 14,14,99 15,15,99/23 15,15,99  16,16,99;
P14 F2; P15 F5; P16 F4;
P6 F8;
P7 0;
P8 0;
P9 0;
P10 0;
P11 MOVE/33 150,200;
P12 1;
P13 .05;
P14 DF 1.5;
P17 "1";
END;

NOS 0,100;
P2 -66;
P14 F2; P15 F5; P16 F4;
P17 "1";
END;
```

Chowning's *Phonè,* completed in 1981, forms elegant vocal effects derived from the use of vibrato (in quasi-random formant structure). Figure 9.5 shows part of program input to the tape portion of David Cope's *Glassworks* for computer-generated tape and two pianos (1979) completed at CCRMA. P's stand for "parameter input data" with the format in SAIL (Stanford Artificial Intelligence Language).

Excellent examples of current computer uses with computer-generated sound are described in *Proceedings 7/8, American Society of University Composers*. A complete recording of the works referred to by their respective composers or programmers is included (Hubert S. Howe, Jr.: *Freeze;* David Cohen: seven examples including a Bach fugue, original studies, and computer-generated fragments; John Melby; *Forandrer;* and Donald MacInnis: *Quadrilith*). These, with their verbal annotations, prove invaluable to the uninitiated as well as to the experienced. Computer-generated sound has proven to be a most prolific and fertile resource for composers.

Dreamsong, a highly regarded computer composition (1977/1978 at Stanford CCRMA) by Michael McNabb, integrates sets of synthesized sounds and digitally recorded natural sounds. The title derives from the fact that many of the sounds presented are vaguely recognizable (as in a dream) while others shift in and out of recognition. This work, unlike most in the genre, is relatively simple in harmonic and melodic structure in order to enable the composer (and hence the audience) to focus on the more important elements of texture and timbre (usually in transition or modulating). Figure 9.6 shows the two modes from which most of the pitch material in *Dreamsong* was derived. This work, considered by many a classic of the field, has revitalized a sense of the lyric even in the world of electronic abstractions.

Figure 9.6. Modes used in Michael McNabb's *Dreamsong* with synthesized and digitally recorded sounds.

Visual artists have explored digital technology parallel to those in music. Computer graphics have become a staple of the industry. Surprisingly, one of the most elegant artists of the past twenty years is a composer: Herbert Brün. His plotted graphics (at the University of Illinois) have achieved fame in both music and art. Figure 9.7 (untitled) presents vintage Brün with lines at subtle angles criss-crossing in a nebula of complex counterpoint.

Hybrid Composition

Research and composition in the area of direct computer control over synthesizer modules (oscillators, filters, etc.) has become very impressive in the past few years. In a sense, the sequencer referred to in Chapter 7 is a mini-analog computer. With various potentiometer settings (usually three to five per note) on a sequence of notes (variable number depending on the make and model of the sequencer) one can "program" a *series* of notes rather than one or two at a time.

New developments include the Synthi 100's Digital Sequencer 256 (E.M.S.), with solid-state storage capacity of 10,240 bits of information. It is capable of precisely controlling six different simultaneous parameters over a sequence of 256 successive events. Through several modes of operation, any or all of the 256 stored items and their time relationships can be retrieved and even varied without difficulty. The Sequencer 256 is indeed a small special-purpose digital computer, complete with analog-to-digital and digital-to-analog converters. Surprisingly compact (about the length of a five-octave piano keyboard, but one-third its depth and width), the 256 provides high-speed operation and full information retrieval. Buchla's (see Chapter 7 for addresses of this and the E.M.S. studios) late '70's *Music Easel* has full analog retrieval and is especially designed for storage of traditional instrument sounds. More recently, Buchla's *300 Series Music Box* combines microprocessing units with an analog synthesizer. The two instruments function in a truly symbiotic relationship with "hands-on" capabilities in both analog and digital spheres.

Salvatore Martirano's *Sal-Mar Construction* (1973) is a semiportable "live-performance" computer with retrieval and storage capabilities. His performances and tours with this instrument have brought much attention to the "live" potential of the computer-synthesizer combination. MUSYS, developed by Peter Zinovieff, Peter Grogono, and David Cockerell, uses PDP8/L and PDP8/S computers to control special-purpose electronic equipment.

Many composers have begun to research and utilize the potential for microprocessors (small microcomputers) to be used in live performance situations. David Behrman has worked extensively in this area. His *On the Other Ocean* (1977), for example, involves flute, bassoon, and the Kim-1 micro-computer-controlled polyphonic analog synthesizer (hybrid microprocessor utilization). The live performers choose their pitches according to the synthesizer's accompaniment and the synthesizer chooses its accompaniment according to the live performers' pitches, producing a kind of 'live-looping' compositional process.

Figure 9.7. A computer graphic by composer Herbert Brün which serves as an example of computer graphics, many of which pre-date sophisticated technologies for digitally synthesizing sound. *Untitled Computer Graphic.* Permission granted by the composer.

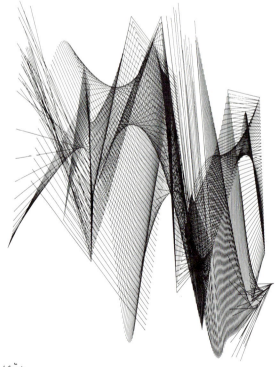

Figure 9.8. David Behrman. Photo by Mary Lucier.

Notation Techniques

Composers continue to explore new concepts and applications of the computer. Visual input is an increasingly viable source for future experimentation. One method is to *draw* (using a special light pen) graph representations of wave forms directly on a cathode-ray tube (CRT-television-like computer input). The computer then translates these to digital information, processes and, through a D/A converter, produces an electromagnetic force on tape (and/or "live" through studio speakers as the composer may wish). Printed graphs can also be assimilated by computer functions through *Graphos I*. Computer recognition of traditionally notated scores creates the potential for actual performances of extremely difficult music without the composer having any knowledge of computer languages. It presents composers with an incredible experimental laboratory: immediate performance of works (with any degree of complexity included) for experimentation, revision, and/or re-orchestration.

Leland Smith at Stanford's Artificial Intelligence Laboratory uses a large PDP 10 computer to create exacting traditional music notation. The computer (using light-sensitive paper similar to Xerox) is actually taught to "print" music according to data fed into the terminal. Figure 9.9 is an example of this notation. Advantages of this kind of notation/copying are:

1. Speed: the computer can produce copies rapidly once the information is stored internally;

Figure 9.9. Example of computer notation. System designed by Leland Smith at Stanford's CCRMA. Work is *Intermezzo and Capriccio for Piano* by Leland Smith. Computer Music Graphics, San Andreas Press, 3732 Laguna Ave., Palo Alto, CA 94306.

2. Editing: since the storage is digital, simple computations can create quick transpositions (for transposing instruments) and corrections;
3. Flexibility: with data in numbers, it is easy to rearrange measure distribution for part-page turns as well as score layout;
4. Extractions: once a score is in the computer, parts can be extracted in seconds (in transposition if necessary);
5. Versatility: pages can be rearranged quickly in a variety of ways for determination of best readability.

Smith's program, *Score,* is now available for the IBM PC computer (thus competing with the *Professional Composer* for the Apple Macintosh discussed later in this section). The elegance of his notation techniques translates beautifully from mainframe to mini. With such programs, digital processes have brought engraving quality music printing to everyone with such a need. And, with the advent of laser printers, the output quality rivals the very best of traditional copyists. Symbols are added to staves in one of three ways: from the standard typing keyboard, by use of the mouse, or using a synthesizer keyboard. In the first two modes, the user indicates which of the symbols shown in Figure 9.10 should be added to the staff where a blinking cursor has been set to the correct pitch. This screendump is from the program *Professional Composer,* the first such program readily available. Clicking on the appropriate box causes the object to be added to the current location of the cursor. Other menu items (such as tempo signs, meter, etc.) exist in this powerful program. Figure 9.11 shows one of these (tuplet) which allows any number of pitches to exist within a beat or division of the beat and adds the appropriate number above or below the set (whichever makes the most sense).

Figure 9.10. Choices of notes, rests, clefs, effects, and special symbols in *Professional Composer.* Permission granted by Mark of the Unicorn. All rights reserved.

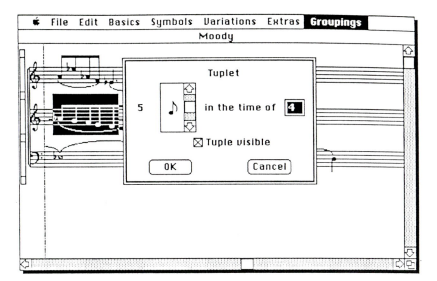

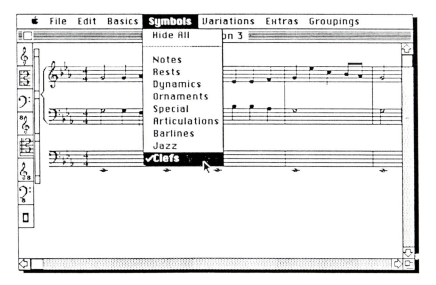

Here five eighth notes will be set into the place reserved for four. Appropriate vertical alignment is automatic in this program. Figure 9.12 shows the "symbols" menu pulled down and how items such as clefs are added and/or subtracted from the screen area.

Figure 9.13. Adding a grace note in *Professional Composer*. Permission granted by Mark of the Unicorn. All rights reserved.

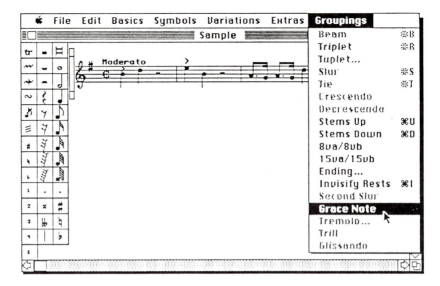

Here, clefs are being removed from the open window. In Figure 9.13 (again from *Professional Composer*), a grace note is being added by selecting it from the "groupings" menu. The music may be varied at any time and performed through the computer's speaker or a stereo system.

The third manner of using *Professional Composer* requires a separate software package called *Professional Performer*. The user simply plays the material to be notated on a synthesizer connected through a MIDI interface (see next section) to the computer. Once the file is stored it can be translated into notation by having *Professional Performer* communicate to *Professional Composer*.

One immediate and typical result from this process is that, if no rounding-off sub-program is used, the resulting manuscript is fraught with 128th notes, syncopations and rests since human performers are not very accurate in even the best of circumstances and with the best of training. Hence programs use "resolving" programs to diminish the number of mistakes in interpretation. In *Professional Composer* one uses a *quantizing* approach. This involves a rounding off of all pitches to a certain level (typically 8th notes) to get a more accurate representation of the performance in *Performer* and then adding legitimate 16th and 128th notes as needed.

Other programs, especially the one by Leland Smith called *Score* and another produced by Oxford in England, effectively employ the same general techniques as *Composer/Performer* except that they are written for the IBM PC or compatible (*Composer* uses the Macintosh as does *Finale,* a most recent edition to the music printing market place). In all of these instances, users are able (at sometimes 5 times the speed of ordinary pen and paper copying) to create engraved quality music printing using microcomputers (laser writer printing services exist in some cities for those who can't afford the $5,000 purchase price of current models). All can handle part-extraction, transposition of parts, etc. Clearly these procedures are significant tools for composers, even those who are not interested in computers for sonic applications and composition.

Figure 9.14. Mountain Hardware's *MusicSystem;* a digital synthesizer audio output (left) and light pen for notation on video (lower right).

With the advent of inexpensive "home" minicomputers, classroom applications have increased (see Figure 9.14). Digital synthesizers of computers such as the APPLE II and *Syntauri* create inroads and potential in a wide variety of situations. ALF products and Mountain Hardware have developed both software (programs) and hardware (instruments) for less than $1,000. Theorists and teachers, such as Arthur Hunkins (University of North Carolina), Dorothy Gross (University of Minnesota), Fred Hofstetter (University of Delaware), Rosemary Killam (North Texas State University), Gary Wittlich (Indiana University), Wolfgang Kuhn (Stanford), Paul Lorton (University of San Francisco) and Herb Bielawa (San Francisco State), have all developed teaching programs (primarily sight-singing and ear-training) involving computers. The advantages that the computer offers include: (1) immediate feedback (visual); (2) storage and retrieval of scoring; (3) timbre versatility; (4) notation speed; and (5) long-term correlation of instructional viability of materials used. Recent programs such as *Listen, Perceive* and *Practica Musica* have made computer music theory affordable and dynamic.

Digital instruments such as the SYNCLAVIER II (see Figure 9.15) have made computers as viable a resource for composers as the synthesizer became in the early sixties.

Figure 9.15. *Synclavier II.* New England Digital Corp.

The table shown in Figure 9.16 provides a list of 51 different pieces of digital music equipment (a fraction of the actual number available). Rough retail costs are provided in column 3. The comments refer to whether the equipment is a synthesizer (creates sound from oscillators), sampler (to be discussed in some detail later) both of these ("DIGI/SYN"), drum machine or MIDI-PIANO. In some cases, special synthesis (additive or *Fourier*) has been added to further identify the type in use. Lists of MIDI data for performance may be stored in associated computer memory or in MIDI sequencers (in resident RAM and/or associated tape decks or disc drives).

Figure 9.16. Table of synthesizers/samplers with manufacturers and approximate costs listed.

producer	product	cost	comments
AKAI	S900	$2995	SAMPLER
AKAI	AX-60 OR AX-73	$895 - 1199	DIGI/SYN
CASIO	CZ-101, CZ1-6000	$499 - $999	DIGI/SYN
CASIO	RZ-1	$599	MIDI DRUMS
DIGITAL-KBS	SYNERGY	$5,295	DIGI/SYN
DYNACORD	PERCUTER-S	??	MIDI DRUMS
E-MU	EMAX	$2400	SAMPLER
E-MU	EMULATOR III	??	SAMPLER
E-MU	DRUMULATOR	$745	DRUM MACHINE
ENSONIQ	ESQ-1	$1395	DIGI/SYN
ENSONIQ	MIRAGE	$1695	MIDI SAMPLER
ENSONIQ	SDP-1	$1395	MIDI-PIANO
EUROPA	PPG	??	DIGI/SYN
FAIRLIGHT	SERIES III	??	DIGI/SYN
FENDER	CHROMA POLARIS	$1195	DIGI/SYN
HOHNER	PK-150,PK-250	$995 - 1250	DIGI/SYN
KAWAI	SX-240,K3	$1295	DIGI/SYN
KAWAI	MODEL 150	$1395	MIDI PIANO
KORG	POLY800, DWSERIES	$799-1459	SIGI/SYN
KORG	DDD-1	$999	DRUM MACHINE
KORG	SGI-D	$2399	MIDI PIANO
KURZWEIL	250	$10715	MIDI SAMPLER
KURZWEIL	MIDIBOARD	??	FOURIER SYNTHESIS
LYRE INC.	FDSS	??	ADDITIVE SYNTHESIS
MOOG	MEMORY MOOG	??	DIDI/SYN
NEW ENGLAND DIGITA	SYNCLAVIER	$72000	MIDI SAMPLER
OBERHEIM	MATRIX 6 - 12	$1595 - 4995	SIGI/SYN
OBERHEIM	OB-8	$4545	DIDI/SYN
OBERHEIM	DX	$1395	MIDI DRUMS
PPG WAVE	2.3, PRK	$8995 - 2995	DIGI/SYN
ROLAND	JUNO 1, 2	$795 - 1295	DIGI/SYN
ROLAND	S-10, S-50	$2995	DIGI/SYN
ROLAND	JX-8P, 10	$2995	MIDI SAMPLER
ROLAND	TR909	$925	DRUM MACHINE
SEIKO	DS - 250	$700	DIGI/SYN
SEQUENTIAL CIRCUITS	SIXTRACK, MAX	$895 - 599	DIGI/SYN

producer	product	cost	comments
SEIKO	DS - 250	$700	DIGI/SYN
SEQUENTIAL CIRCUITS	SIXTRACK, MAX	$895 - 599	DIGI/SYN
SEQUENTIAL CIRCUITS	PROPHET 2000	$2495	MIDI SAMPLER
SEQUENTIAL CIRCUITS	PROPHET T8, VS	$5895 - 2599	DIGISYN
SEQUENTIAL CIRCUITS	DRUMTRACKS	$1295	DRUM MACHINE
SEIL	MK-490,DK-600	$299 - 999	DIGI/SYN
SIMMONS	ELEC. PERC.	??	DRUM MACHINE
TECHNICS	SX-K350,450	??	DIGI/SYN
TECHNICS	SX-PXIM	??	MIDI PIANO
UNIQUE	DBK, DBM	$1299 - 1199	DIGI/SYN
VOYETRA	VOYETRA EIGHT	$4595	DIGI/SYN
WERSI	MKI/SII	??	DIGI/SYN
WERSI	ALPHADX350S	$7900	MIDI PIANO
YAMAHA	DX1, 5, 7	$10900 - 2095	FM
YAMAHA	DX21, 27	$895 - 695	FM
YAMAHA	RX-11	$925	DRUM MACHINE
YAMAHA	CP70M	$5295	MIDI PIANO

Figure 9.16. *(Continued)*

With the exception of New England Digital Corporation's entry, the elegant *Synclavier,* synthesizers have obviously entered the arena of anyone interested in music produced digitally. Since these machines in no way influence the *style* of music performed on them, the business of creating and selling them has become widespead in the popular music industry. Hence, competition has become vigorous and new developments are reviewed by a stream of new monthly magazines devoted to electronic music (see Appendix IV).

A new digital guitar contains metal touch-plates and plucking bars instead of frets and strings. Built by Oncor Sound of Salt Lake City, it was adapted (by Cal Gold of New England Digital Corporation) for use with the Synclavier computerized synthesizer. Jazz artist Pat Methany was one of the first professionals to use the instrument.

Constant emphasis on miniaturization have increased accessibility. Casio, for example, has created a number of fairly inexpensive digital instruments capable of a wide range of functions. Figure 9.17 shows one of their larger models. Note the multitude of options, memory, and especially the encoding reading device storage function (coiled wire and nozzle attached to the rear of the Casiotone 701). This equipment can "read" music from a coded sheet (see Figure 9.18) which can then be played back at various speeds and with different timbres. This $5'' \times 13'' \times 37''$ computer has more options than many electronic organs of a decade past, yet is but a fraction of their size. Yamaha's PS-20 exemplifies the competitive nature of the industry (see Figure 9.19).

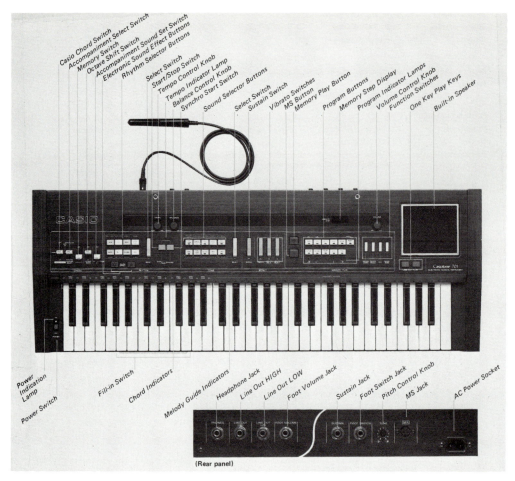

Figure 9.17. The Casiotone 701 (Casio Inc., 15 Gardner Road, Fairfield, NJ 07006).

Figure 9.18. The Casiotone's MS memory function "reading" an encoded score.

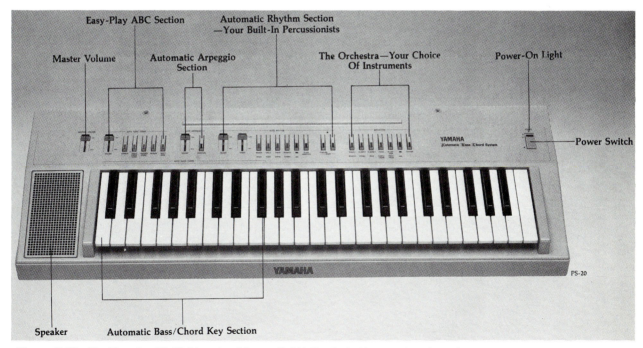

Figure 9.19. The Yamaha PS-20 (Yamaha; Nippon Gakki Co., Ltd., Hamamatsu, Japan).

MIDI: The Default Standard

MIDI (acronym for Musical Instrument Digital Interface) is the industry standard for communication links between synthesizers, drum machines, and other digital equipment. It was intended to create a cooperative standard for what had become, by the middle 1980s, a nightmare of different pieces of equipment with almost no opportunity to develop compatible "systems." Figure 9.20 shows a typical MIDI-chained network of synthesizers. Allowing the synthesizers (different brands) to "talk" to one another enables composers to mix the sound qualities and various advantages of one unit over another during composition without having to create completely separate (and highly redundant) setups. Figure 9.21 provides a summary of MIDI commands.

Figure 9.20. A "MIDI-chained" network of synthesizers and drum unit.

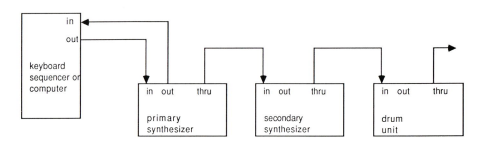

Figure 9.21. A summary of MIDI commands.

MIDI Command Summary

Code: c = channel; k = key number (middle C is 60); v = velocity (0 is slow and 127 is fast); p = pressure or p = patch (depending on circumstance); d = device number; h = pitch wheel change.

```
1001cccc      = note "on" event
0kkkkkkk
0vvvvvvv

1000cccc      = note "off" event
0kkkkkkk
0vvvvvvv

1010cccc      = note "pressure" update
0kkkkkkk
0ppppppp

1101cccc      = "channel pressure"update
0ppppppp

1011cccc      = control change
0ddddddd
0vvvvvvv

1110cccc      = pitch wheel change
0hhhhhhh
01111111

1100cccc      = patch change
0ppppppp
```

Note how the first four digits (binary code) determine how the remaining code will be translated in each case.

The command bytes follow the description that begins this chapter and allow for 128 different states of descriptive elements about note-on and note-off states. The approach is very simple. It avoids, however, any control of timbre (turning this over to the synthesizer being addressed with the code). This has alienated many composers who wish to analyze and digitally dictate timbre between machines. However, as the title of this section suggests, the MIDI standard is just that. As of this writing, virtually all major manufacturers of synthesizers and related equipment have adopted this procedure for transmission of keystroke information. As well, many mini-computer companies have added MIDI ports to their line of personal computers so that available software can be used to create music by hooking up computers to synthesizers. As well, MIDI equipment may be added to device outputs if none has been provided with the original instrument. In each case, the actual transmission of MIDI code takes place through a special MIDI cord with two XLR type connectors.

The implications of MIDI include (1) a central (digital) control of many "instruments" simultaneously; (2) a virtually limitless ability to add to one's equipment assemblage; (3) creation of a "tapeless" recording facility since works can be saved on "floppy discs"; (4) greater cost-efficiency since add-on synthesizers do not require keyboards and other redundant modules; (5) less obsolescence in that new developments may simply be included in the system since whole new "installations" are not required. Curiously, MIDI allows software companies to create systems which employ conventional notes, meters, etc. Driven no doubt by the popular music industry, several current implementations of music programs utilize this process voided in the early days of electronic music by the use of knobs. This return to traditional notation heralds the synthesizer into the world of the traditional instrument and the composer's return, in many respects, to the traditional world of composition. Musically user-friendly programs should greatly enhance even the computer illiterate's abilities to have easy access to the world of digitized sounds and electronic synthesis.

Two important organizations, the International MIDI Association and the MIDI Manufacturers Association (see Appendix 4), are charged with updating and extending the MIDI code. The former includes users as well as manufacturers. However, the manufacturers of digital musical equipment exert tremendous influence over the available directions of new music. As well, the wide acceptability of MIDI as the industry standard suggests that composers in the last decade of this century will not be required to be electronics experts as has often been the case during the past two decades. The consequences of this may be extraordinary. In the past, the presentation of less than perfect equipment or synthesizers without user demanded features was not well received by the generally electronically wise community capable of building their own equipment if not satisfied. The "new" digital electroacoustic composer, on the other hand, may be so unversed in the electrical and digital aspects of his/her system as to exist at the mercy of the economics of the largely untrained business moguls.

Mentioned in the last chapter, SMPTE (Society of Motion Picture and Television Engineers) time code is the industry standard for linking multi-track digital recording and video together. Several MIDI/SMPTE synchronizers now exist. These operate by translating SMPTE time code into the number of MIDI elapsed beats.

Since video production has made inexpensive what was, with film, an extremely costly process, the impact of these synchronizers should be profound for both popular and non-popular forms of contemporary music.

Despite MIDI universality, however, the non-conformity of language access to the MIDI driver has caused much confusion. MIDI BASIC and MIDILISP represent two of the approaches adaptable for programmers. Both, however, have the drawbacks created by their own biases: BASIC, while simple to use, is cumbersome and awkward; LISP, on the other hand, is elegant but very difficult to learn. Doubtless there will soon be versions in SMALLTALK, C and other major languages. The requirements, however, of having to learn a full programming language will be heavy and most individuals attracted to MIDI use will be bound by specific program limitations. As well, full control may be obscured in order to avoid theft or copying of code.

Digital software (not languages) has proliferated abundantly in the past few years as evidenced in the table in Figure 9.22. The prices are average consumer costs based on retail encouraged by the producing company. The abbreviations in

Figure 9.22. Table showing 90 software programs for developing synthesizer/ sequencing music.

PRODUCER	PRODUCT	PRICE	COMMENTS	
ACTIVISION	MUSIC STUDIO	$49	IBM (S/E)	
ALTECH SYSTEMS	MIDIBASIC	$30	MAC (M)	
ASSIMILATION	MIDI-COMPOSER	$29	MAC (S)	
BACCHUS	VOICE MANAGER	$169	IBM (L - DX7)	
BEAM TEAM	MIRAGE EDITOR	$119	COMM64 (E)	
BEAM TEAM	MM1 COMPOSER	$149	COMM64 (S)	
BEAM TEAM	TRANSFORM JX-8P	$99	MAC (R/E)	
BLACKHAWK DATA	TUNESMITH/PC	$29	IBM (P)	
BLANK	SOUND FILE	$99	MAC (L)	
C-LAB	SUPERTRACK	$150	COMM64 (S)	
CAGED ARTISTS	CZ RIDER	$99	COMM64 (E)	
CREATIVE SOLUTION	STUDIO MAC	$125	MAC (N)	
DECILLIONIX	SYTHESTRA	$120	APPLE II (S)	
DECILLIONIS	INTERPOLATOR	$99	APPLE II (E)	
DELTA MUSIC	DELTA-PCM	?	COMM64 (L)	
DIGIDESIGN	SOUND DESIGNER	$495	MAC (E/P)	
DIGIDESIGN	SOFTSYNTH	$295	MAC (S)	
DIGITAL MUSIC	DX PRO	$149	APPLE II (E/L)	
DR. T'S SOFTWARE	ALGORITHMIC COMP	$99	COMM64 (S)	
DR. T'S	THE COPYIST	$195	IBM (N)	
ELECTRONIC ARTS	DELUXE MUSIC CONS.	$49	MAC (S/N)	
ELECTRONIC ARTS	MUSIC CONSTRUCTION	$49	IBM (S/N)	
ELECTRONIC ARTS	INSTANT MUSIC	$49	AMIGA (S)	
ELECTRONIC MUSIC	MIDI PLAY	$20	ATARI (R)	
EMR	MIDI TRACK	$125	COMM64 (S)	
ENSONIQ	MIRAGE	$299	APPLE II (E)	
EVERYWARE	MIDI CONTROL	?	AMIGA (C)	
FAIRLIGHT	SERIES III	?	FAIR (S)	
FIREBIRD	ADV. MUSIC SYS.	$79	COMM64 (S)	
GREATWAVE	CONCERTWARE +	$49	MAC (S/N)	
GW INSTRUMENTS	MACADIOS	$2500	MAC (E)	
HAMEL	MUSPRINT	$89	MAC (N)	
HAYDEN	MUSIC WORKS	?	MAC (N)	
HESWARE	SYNTHESOUND 64	$19	COMM64 (S)	
HYBRID ARTS	EZ-TRACK ST	$65	ATARI ST (S)	
HYBRID ARTS	DX-DROID	$244	ATARI ST (E)	

Figure 9.22. *(Continued)*

PRODUCER	PRODUCT	PRICE	COMMENTS	
IMPULSE	SOUNDWAVE	$25	MAC (E)	
IMPULSE	STUDIO SESSION	$89	MAC (P)	
JORETH	TONE EDITOR	$119	COMM64 (E)	
KEY CLIQUE	FILM MUSIC TOOL	$100	APPLE II (E)	
KORG	800 VE	$100	APPLE II (S/L)	
KURZWEIL	MACATTACK	?	MAC (E/L)	
MAGNETIC MUSIC	TEXTURE	$495	IBM (S)	
MARK OF UNICORN	PERFORMER	$295	MAC (S)	
MARK OF UNICORN	PRO COMPOSER	$495	MAC (N)	
MELODIAN SYSTEMS	CONCERTMASTER	$59	IBM (L)	
MIDI SOFT	METATRACK	$99	ATARI ST (S)	
MILLER	PERSONAL COMPOSER	$495	IBM (S/N/L)	
MIMETICS	DATA 6	$75	IBM (L)	
MIMETICS	SOUNDSCAPE DIGI.	$19	AMIGA (D)	
MINDSCAPE	MUSIC WRITER	$22	MAC (S)	
MOOG ELEC.	SONG PRODUCER	$395	COMM64 (S)	
NEXUS	FM DRAWING	$200	APPLE II (L)	
OCTAVE PLATEAU	SEQUENCER PLUS	$495	IBM (R)	
OPCODE	MIDIMAC ED/LIB	$200	MAC (E/L)	
OPCODE	MUSIC MOUSE	$59	MAC (S)	
OPCODE	CUE	$499	MAC (F)	
OPCODE SYSTEMS	MIDI MAC SEQ	$200	MAC (S)	
PASSPORT DESIGN	MASTER TRKS PRO	?	MAC (E)	
PASSPORT DESIGNS	MIDI VOICE LIBR	$79	IBM (L)	
PASSPORT DESIGNS	MASTER TRACKS	$249	APPLE II (S)	
PASSPORT DESIGNS	POLYWRITER	$199	APPLE II (N)	
PASSPORT DESIGNS	MIDI/8 PLUS	$169	COMM64 (S)	
PASSPORT DESIGNS	MUSIC SHOP	$149	COMM64 (N)	
PASSPORT DESIGNS	SCORE	$495	IBM (N)	
PASSPORT DESIGNS	POLYWRITER	$299	APPLE II (S)	
ROLAND	MPS	$495	IBM (S/N)	
ROLAND	MUSE	$150	APPLE II (S)	
SFX COMPUTER	SOUND SAMPLER	?	COMM64 (S)	
SHAHERAZAM	MUSICTYPE	$59	MAC (N)	
SIGNT & SOUND	MIDI ENSEMBLE	$499	IBM (S)	
SONG WRIGHT	SONGWRIGHT +	$49	(S/E)	

PRODUCER	PRODUCT	PRICE	COMMENTS	
SONIC ACCESS	MIRAGE	$149	MIRAGE (E)	
SONUS	SUPER SEQUENCER	$275	COMM64 (S)	
SOUTHWORTH MUSIC	TOTAL MUSIC	$495	MAC (S/N)	
STEINBERG	PRO 24	$295	ATARI ST (S)	
STEINBERG	TRACKSTAR	$169	COMM64 (R)	
STEINBERG	PRO-CREATOR	$240	IBM (E/L)	
SYNTECH	48-TRK PC	$449	IBM (S)	
SYNTECH	STUDIO TWO	$225	APPLE II (S)	
SYNTECH	CZ MASTER	$149	APPLE II (E/L)	
SYNTECH	STUDIO ONE	$225	COMM64 (S)	
SYNTECH	SONG PLAYER	$99	COMM64 (S)	
SYNTECH	CZ/MASTER	$149	COMM64 (E/L)	
SYSTEMS DESIGN	PROMIDI	$595	IBM (S)	
TURTLE BEACH	VISION	$349	IBM (E)	
TRIANGLE AUDIO	DX7/TX7 LIBR.	$29	COMM64 (L)	
VOYETRA TECH	SEQUENCER PLUS	$495	IBM (S)	
VOYETRA	PATCH MASTER	$149	IBM (P)	
YAMAHA	COMPOSE	?	IBM (S)	

the comments section reference thus: S = synthesizer/sampler; E = editor; P = performer; L = library (of sounds); R = recorder; N = notation; C = controller; M = Mac language. This chart represents but a fraction of the available software now on the market. Addresses for the companies listed here are provided in Appendix 4.

Sampling and Digital Recording

Digital electronic information flow is inherently cleaner than its analog counterpart. The latter suffers generation noise (added machine hum during copying), line impedence and circuit static which multiplies significantly as modules are added to the system. Digital information, however, proceeds through editing as discrete bits of information (the on/off states described at the beginning of the chapter). Hence, even when an analog system is "noisy," the digital information flows without distortion or added gains of unwanted and distracting frequencies or glitches.

CDs (compact discs) provide a good example of this. The immediate popularity of this digital approach to recording playback rests with the fact that the laser which reads the data from the disc reads only the digitized bumps that grace the grooves of the recording. Dust and other potentially distorting material are ignored. There is no system interference. The results are excellent playback with an almost infinite lifetime. These records show virtually no sign of wear since there is no contact involved. These attributes have served the CD well. Indeed, many experts suggest that by the turn of the century, CDs will be the main form of recording.

Figure 9.23 presents a straightforward comparison of compact discs and long playing records. The advantages of the CD appear distinctly obvious in the areas of signal-to-noise ratio and life expectancy. At the present writing, a number of WORM (Write-Once-Read-Manytimes) type CDs for recording have been introduced. The Dyaxis 16-bit DA conversion to 280 megabyte hard discs represents an example of this new technology. Typically it stores up to 30 minutes of digitally recorded music at 48 kHz sampling rates. The CD-ROM (600 megabytes of storage) from Optical Media International, while it does not allow recording, presents up to 1400 pre-recorded sounds for use in composition.

Digital recording, the other end of the process, has also experienced important changes due to the current technology. DAT (or "digital audio tape") has added one more digital component to the recording process. While DAT technology suffers the same lack of random access (i.e., requires fast-forward and reverse for finding material whereas discs, traditional or laser, allow immediate accessibility) that analog cassettes do, they nonetheless provide inexpensive routes to high quality low-noise recording. The discovery that Sony Beta type VCRs make extremely good music tape recorders has brought the process economically within the average recording studio's budget. The PCM.F1 Sony encoder allows users to record sound on the large video tracks of the machine with playback through headphones or traditional amplifiers and speaker combinations. Until now the availability of editing systems for digital music has been a problem.

	Compact Disc	LP Record
Disc diameter (mm)	120	300
Disc thickness (mm)	1·2	1·5 2·3
Disc playing time (min)	60	50- 60
Rotation speed (rpm)	200-500	33⅓ or 45
Scanning velocity (m/s)	1·2 - 1·4	0·4 approx.
Width of grooves or tracks (μm)	1·6	100 approx.
Diameter of center hole (mm)	15	7·24
Number of channels	2	2
Frequency range (Hz)	20-20,000 (±0·5dB)	30-20,000 (±2dB)
Typical dynamic range (dB)	90	55
Signal-to-noise ratio (dB)	90	60
Channel separation (dB)	90	25-35
Total harmonic distortion	0·005%	0·2%
Wow-and-flutter	Quartz accuracy	0·03%
Disc material	Transparent PVC with aluminum reflective coating and lacquer protective layer	Black vinyl
Life expectancy (disc)	Indefinite (no physical contact)	100 playings approx.
Life expectancy (laser/ stylus)	5,000 hours	400 - 800 hours
Effect of dust, scratches and static charges	Largely ignored by the laser beam	Causes increasing background noise and mistracking

Figure 9.23. A comparison of CDs versus LPs.

The optimum system envisaged by most computer music composers and recording engineers would be one that has the sound represented digitally as long as possible with only two processes involving a change in the form of the data: analog to digital (A/D) and digital to analog (D/A). This, combined with access to the information (editing and splicing), creates the perfect environment for composition and processing. Recent advances now make this package possible. Some of these systems are listed in the hardware chart provided in the previous section (listed as "samplers").

Synthesis techniques have long been digitized from their inception (with the advent of CDs which can hold up to 74 minutes and 33 seconds worth of music) to final amplification. Recording has only recently had this advantage. Called by many the "sampling" approach (to mark the contrast to "synthesize"), this process makes the potentials of *musique concrète* real. Most new synthesizers have sampling as a built-in option or feature. Figure 9.24 demonstrates the sampling process.

Here an instant of a percussive voice is represented first by a waveform and then by a series of vertical lines each representing a sample. Note how the last example accurately reflects the middle snapshot. Figure 9.25 shows the makeup of a complete "sampling" system.

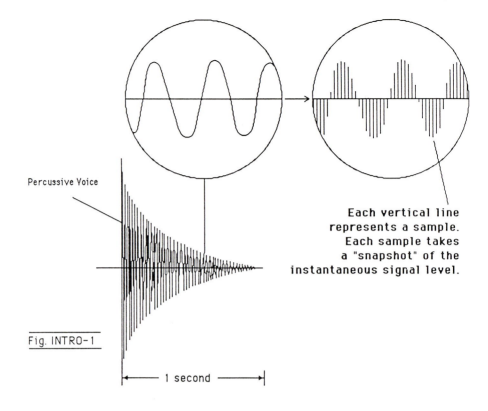

Percussive Voice

Each vertical line represents a sample. Each sample takes a "snapshot" of the instantaneous signal level.

Fig. INTRO-1

|← 1 second →|

Figure 9.25. Example of a simple "sampling" system.

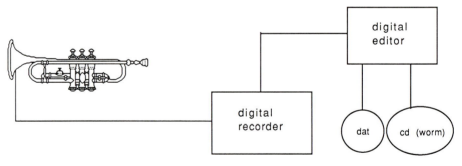

digital editor

digital recorder

dat

cd (worm)

In this example (only one of many possibilities), the live analog sound is converted to a digital imprint as quickly as possible. It is then committed to RAM (Random Access Memory). Editing (discussed at a later point in this section) is then possible. At some point, after the user has what he/she wishes, the music is converted to disc or tape (this may be necessary immediately if the sound sampling requires more RAM than available). When completed, the digital information is then stored on a CD for ultimate performance over a traditional system. Two major problems exist with this model:

1. As indicated earlier in the chapter, sampling requires an immense amount of memory, typically 1 megabyte per every 21 seconds depending on sampling rate (rates vary with 48k/sec standard). Storing this data and retaining random access potential (ability to get to any point quickly and directly and not have to rewind/fast-forward as with tape), requires immense hard disc capacity.

2. Editing processes must be clean (free of adding noise inadvertently to the music) and friendly. The user must be able to access each harmonic in the sound being processed and must be able to add or subtract energy anywhere in the spectrum.

As the end of the 1980s approaches, both problems appear to be solved by a wealth of new products, principally for the mini- and micro-computer markets. In the first instance, hard discs have become more available in significantly large sizes. A number of manufacturers have created (in some instances particularly *for* the music industry) 800 megabyte discs which hold between 30 and 50 minutes of digitally sampled music. As well, WORM (discussed earlier) laser discs allow massive storage of sampled sounds and even complete works of great complexity. While their use is limited (the laser initially "burns" in the information onto a blank disc and once done the process cannot be repeated on that disc), current technology has also created open architecture instruments which have expandable RAM (up to 8 megabytes in some computers at this writing). Thus, the storage and access problems are beginning to be solved. Figure 9.26 shows a more elaborate sampling system which includes CD-ROM interface to an Emulator II with SMPTE Time Code synchronization for video combinations and editing.

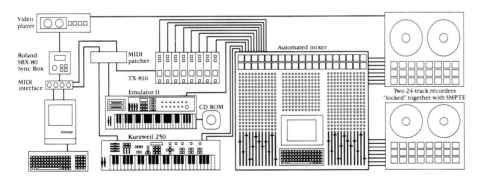

Figure 9.26. An elaborate sampling system with video "sync" capabilities.

Figure 9.27. Visual diagram of the amplitude characteristics of various harmonics of a sampled sound on the EMAX using *Sound Designer*. Permission granted by Digidesign, Inc. All rights reserved.

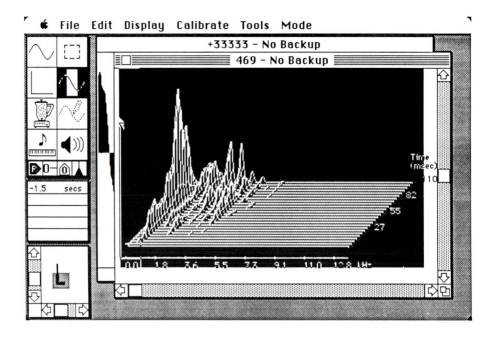

Problems of editing have been addressed by the advent of a series of software programs which provide user control of the various harmonics of a given instant of time. Figure 9.27 shows a typical screen in *Sound Designer's* program with the EMAX sampling device (discussed later in the chapter). Here the figure represents 110 milliseconds of time and shows a sound heavy in harmonics between 0 and 55 kHz in frequency. It also shows their envelopes. The display on the left shows various applications including playback (the speaker icon), select (inverted sine wave with white box), etc. The menus on the top (e.g., "File, Edit," etc.) may all be pulled down by the mouse for a host of other possible choices. The sound may also be viewed as a waveform. Figure 9.28 shows how sine waves may be stretched over both amplitude and time using various built-in features of this particular system.

Figure 9.29 shows *Sound Designer's* mechanics for editing a section of a sound by capturing a repeating loop. Here the recording of a D on the piano has been selected as source material. Note the single millisecond clicks at the bottom of the window. Movement within the sound takes place by scrolling through it (bottom of last three figures). By using the mouse and controlling the pointer, one can alter and invent envelopes for many different time elements. Figure 9.30 shows filter and amplitude envelopes. By grabbing any black segment or line with the pointer arrow, holding down the mouse's button and pulling, a new node is created.

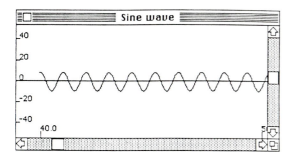

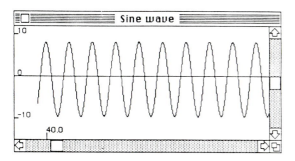

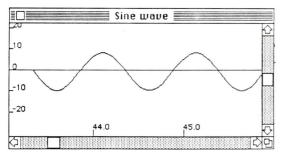

Figure 9.28. Various scaling box adjustments including (here) normal scaling, amplitude axis stretched, and time axis stretched.

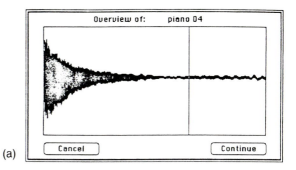

(a)

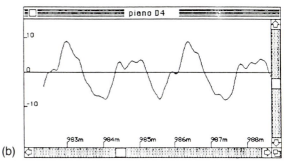

(b)

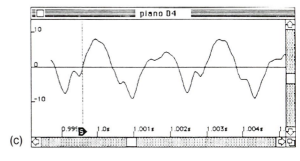

(c)

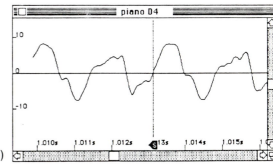

(d)

Figure 9.29. Finding a good loop (a) overview provides location of stable sustain area; (b) scaling waveform displays one or two periods; (c) placing of loop marker; (d) placing loop end marker at zero crossing (using *Sound Designer* software). Permission granted by Digidesign, Inc. All rights reserved.

Digital Electronic Music 309

Figure 9.30. Filter and amplifier envelope-adjusting process using the EMAX and *Sound Designer* software. Permission granted by Digidesign, Inc. All rights reserved.

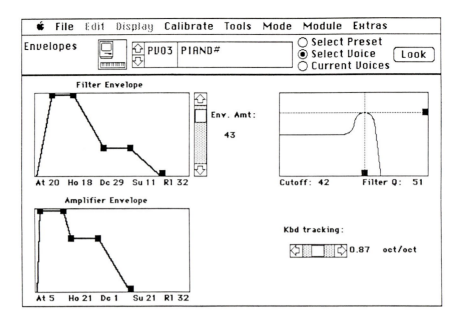

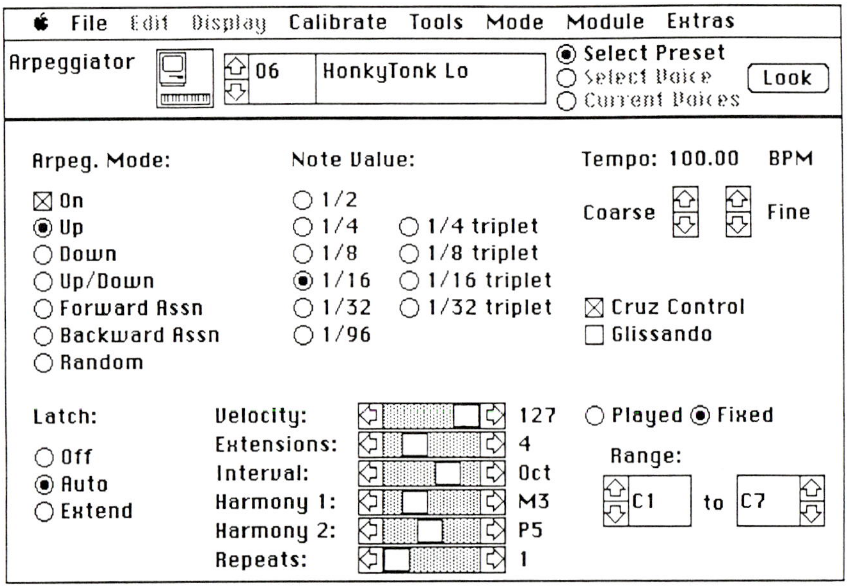

Figure 9.31. The arpeggiator module of *Sound Designer's* software. Permission granted by Digidesign, Inc. All rights reserved.

Larger (and more musical) editing potential exists at higher levels. Figure 9.31, for example, shows how the tempo for a segment of music can be altered, rhythm varied, etc. With a single acoustic sound sampled and edited, digital samples like the EMAX can take the digital information and manipulate it in many ways. For example, a single sung human voice can be duplicated and set at different pitch levels so that it can be turned into a complete choir. This can then be assigned to a keyboard (for example) and the composer may create an entire choral composition that is, in reality, a "real" choir constructed from one voice.

Music thus created may then be re-edited and varied. One option provided by *Professional Performer* allows the composer to view the operation from the perspective of a traditional tape recorder. Figure 9.32 shows a screen dump of a typical set up. Here, screen buttons (accessed via the button on the mouse) allow standard applications of rewind, stop, play, etc. while measures, beats, and counter ticks are counted. The object to the lower left (partially hidden by the "counter") allows mouse control over tempo. Tracks may be added, deleted, or independently edited. The system allows for step-recording and editing as seen in the two examples of Figures 9.33 and 9.34.

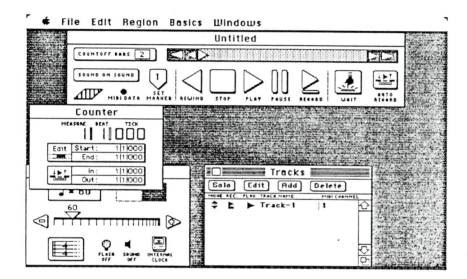

Figure 9.32. The traditional tape recorder look of the *Professional Performer* software. Permission granted by Mark of the Unicorn. All rights reserved.

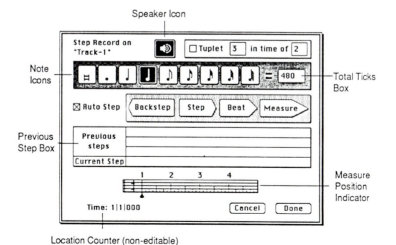

Figure 9.33. An example of step-recording using *Professional Performer* software. Permission granted by Mark of the Unicorn. All rights reserved.

Figure 9.34. The Macintosh keypad for use with *Professional Performer* software. Permission granted by Mark of the Unicorn. All rights reserved.

This provides more traditionally musical editing as one proceeds, not by instants of time, but by notes. The second example also demonstrates a non-mouse option: use of the main keyboard's keypad. Digidesign (manufacturer of *Sound Designer* and *Softsynth*) also shows waveforms in real time (optional) emulating an oscilloscope. Remembering that such instruments have scientific as well as artistic uses suggests that many new editors (applicable to the world of digital recording) will be made available from the technological community. Many of these will have applications outside music (such as speech synthesis, voice analysis [voiceprint checkers for security are now a reality] and speech pathology, to name just a few) but still be of use to recording engineers. *MacADIOS* (made by GW Instruments of Cambridge, MA) performs mathematical spectral analysis based on the Fast Fourier Transform (FFT) in characterizing any given signal by way of measuring the component harmonics.

Real time requires that the computer (in these cases in Apple Macintosh) have direct and quick communication links with the editor through a MIDI-like interface at 500k+ baud rates. Using this kind of feature and looping live sounds allows for experimentation on the effects and/or differences in acoustical situations. For example, capturing the acoustics of a room at different temperatures or with different placements of furniture or speakers would allow for careful "tuning" of concert halls for different ensembles. It would also allow almost immediate replication of any given environment. Such programs should have significant effect in the world of acoustic engineering in the next few years.

Certainly the hardware and software of sampling represents the future of digital editing and recording. It also marks the first occasion in history when composers may have opportunity to master their electronic medium technologically. Many composers, dissatisfied with the electronic purity of synthesized imitations of real world sounds while concomitantly unable to retain traditional performances of their music, will no doubt turn to this substitute. Since the composer will probably do the performance, it will retain, in turn, an importance beyond simple rendition and likewise the real performance, if it ever then occurs, will be a secondary vehicle.

(For information on vectoral analysis and procedures, see Chapter 1).

1. Historical Background: Jean-Claude Risset (b. 1936, France) is the head of computer research at IRCAM (Institute de Recherche et Coordination Acoustique/Musique) in Paris. He studied piano with Robert Trimaille and composition with Suzanne Demarquez and André Jolivet. He earned the *Doctorates-Sciences Physiques* in 1967 at the *Ecole Normale Superieure*. He spent three years working with Max Matthews at the Bell Laboratories in the early sixties researching sound synthesis, imitation of real timbres, and pitch paradoxes. He published a catalog of computer-synthesized sounds in 1969 and set up a computer music installation in Orsay, France, in 1971.

    Inharmonic Soundscapes is a reduction for tape of a larger work titled *Inharmonique* for soprano and tape (first performed in April, 1977, at IRCAM). All of the computer-synthesis for the work was done at IRCAM with a basic MUSIC V type program. Some sections were digitally mixed with the Stanford program titled MIXSND (mix-sounds).

2. Overview: *Inharmonic Soundscapes* falls cleanly into a cyclic arrangement of three main sections preceded by an introduction and followed by a brief coda (both of similar material). If one assigns basic block symbols to the sounds as in Figure 9.35, then a formal layout would look like that shown in Figure 9.36.

    The quote (three-fourths of the way through line one) indicates a timbral and pitch reference to the work analyzed in a previous chapter— *Poème électronique* by Edgard Varèse. Though possibly not intentional, it is certainly and immediately observable when one is familiar with both works. The two transitions (overlapped symbols at the end of the first A and the end of the second A) integrate the basic sound materials.

3. Orchestration: The bell-like sonorities of both basic materials (the bowed glass of "A" and the rung bells of "B") are the direct result of the "inharmonicity" described by the work's title. The spectrum of these types of sounds characteristically includes partials that do not conform exactly to the tuning specifications of the overtone series. This, combined with bell-like envelopes (dynamic characteristics), provides the basic consistency for the entire work. There is very little material present here, as well as only slight alterations and variants to that material. Yet the resulting diversity in terms of color is extraordinary.

    Risset speaks of his timbral studies in an interview:

Instrument-like tones can be transformed in subtle ways. For example, it is possible to construct an inharmonic bell-like tone with a more or less distinct pitch in a fashion similar to building up a chord. That is, the amplitudes of selected frequency components all follow the same amplitude envelope (for example, an abrupt attack and a long decay). However, in contrast to a standard chord, the amplitude envelope of each component is given a different duration. Then one can take the same

Figure 9.35. Symbology for analysis of Risset's *Inharmonic Soundscapes*.

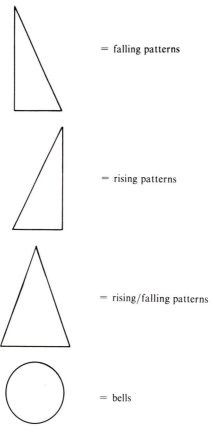

= falling patterns

= rising patterns

= rising/falling patterns

= bells

Figure 9.36. Symbolic analysis of Risset's *Inharmonic Soundscapes*.

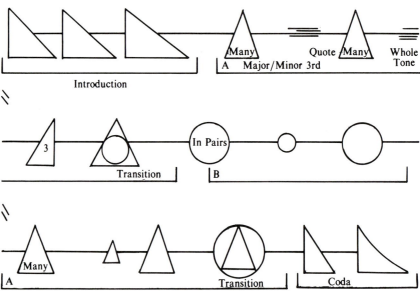

Figure 9.37. Jean-Claude Risset. Photo by Rozenn Risset. Permission granted.

frequency components and apply a different amplitude envelope—one that builds slowly. As a result, the character of the tones changes. Because of the different lengths of the components, they do not swell in synchrony. Hence, instead of fusing into a bell-like sound, the components are diffracted, although the underlying harmony remains the same. Thus, by changing a single function in the score, one can change the internal structure of a sound.[2]

4. Basic Techniques: The most notable technique, aside from the timbral resources, is rhythmic diversity. A random quality, edged with a directional (climax) touch, suggests computer control within parameters guided subtly by the composer.

5, 6. Vertical and Horizontal Models: For the most part, the harmonic sonorities of this piece result from the extended durations of the melodic attacks. Note that there are suggestions of pitch content, at two points in the top line in Figure 9.36. In the first instance, a major/minor third is heard in varying guises (e.g., E♭, E♮, C) while in the second appearance, a whole-tone scale is implied (i.e., E, D, C, B♭, with a G below). Both of these are typical materials and suggest a relatively consonant vocabulary with tuning logically derived from the inharmonic materials.

7. Style: Risset has created a consistent vocabulary of inharmonic timbral material in *Inharmonic Soundscapes*. The form, while simple, supplies balance and direction to a work constructed from subtle variations of glass and bell-like timbres. The composer speaks of his use of the computer:

The computer, a powerful tool, makes new sound sources available. However, it is necessary to learn how to use these new possibilities to produce the desired results . . . in order to take full advantage of the vast potential of direct digital synthesis of sound, one needs a deep understanding of the nature of sounds and of the correlations between the physical parameters and the aural effects of sound: this psychoacoustic science is still in its infancy, but its present growth is promising.[3]

2. Ibid.
3. From IRCAM (31 Rue Saint-Merri F-75004, Paris); "document paru" or introductory booklet.

This work exemplifies some of the major technological developments of the past thirty years and yet, strangely, very few of the new paradigms for compositional approaches; in short, it is exploratory by instrumentation but traditional by design. It therefore resembles the works presented in Vectoral Analysis in Chapters 4 and 11 very closely with ties to those analyzed in Chapters 3 and 8 (as previously mentioned in that chapter). It contrasts the Webern of Chapter 2 (though influenced by it in some very real ways [pointillism]) and the Xenakis of Chapter 10. It bears little relation to Glass' *Einstein on the Beach* (Chapter 12).

Bibliography

*Further Readings**

Abbott, Curtis. "Machine Tongues II." *Computer Music Journal* 2, no. 2 (1978):4. Good article on programming techniques.

Alles, H. G. "A Portable Digital Sound Synthesis System." *Computer Music Journal* 1, no. 4 (1977):5.

Baker, Robert A. "Music Composition—Music-Simulator for Compositional Procedures for the IBM 70/90 Electronic Digital Computer." *Technical Report No. 9,* University of Illinois Experimental Music Studio, 1962. Fascinating early account of techniques for computer-aided composition.

Anderton, Craig. *MIDI for Musicians.* New York: Amsco, 1986. This eminently practical book on MIDI operations, equipment and coding devices provides readable and well organized information. Of the rush of books on this important corporate standard, *MIDI for Musicians* is one of the best.

———. *Digital Delay Handbook.* New York: Amsco, 1985. An excellent source of information on this important subject (includes echo, feedback, resonance, etc.). Though presented in a fairly simple manner, the author obviously knows the material fluently and communicates this well.

Baird, Jock. *Understanding MIDI.* New York: Amsco, 1986. Provides many different views on the subject and along with *The MIDI Resource Book* and *The MIDI Book* indicates the explosion of available texts on the subject of MIDI instrumentation and code.

Bateman, Wayne. *Introduction to Computer Music.* N.Y.: John Wiley and Sons, 1980. A most practical (layman's) guide.

Bayer, Douglas. "Real-Time Software for a Digital Music Synthesizer." *Computer Music Journal* 1, no. 4 (1977):22. Good article on the creation of a language for interconnecting the synthesizer hardware and organizing software.

Chadabe, Joel, and Roger Meyers. "An Introduction to the Play Program." *Computer Music Journal* 2, no. 1 (1978):12.

Chamberlin, Hal. *Musical Applications of Microprocessors* (second edition). Berkley, CA: Hayden Book Company, 1986. This greatly expanded version of an important book by one of the pioneers in the field includes critical information on MIDI, digital synthesizers and D/A interfaces. If it has a weakness it is in the area of samplers.

Chowning, John. "The Simulation of Moving Sound Sources." *Journal of the Audio Engineering Society* 2–6 (1971). One of the first articles discussing computer control of spatial modulation.

———. "The Synthesis of Complex Audio Spectra by Means of Frequency Modulation." *Journal of the Audio Engineering Society* no. 21 (1973):526. The *classic* article on this important technique of computer sound synthesis.

*Addresses for record companies, periodicals, and music publishers mentioned in this Bibliography can be found in Appendix 4.

Cohen, David. "Computer Generated Music." *Southeastern Composers League Newsletter* 66. Fascinating early account of the origins and study of this area of music.

Colbeck, Julian. *KEYFAX Complete Guide to Electronic Keyboards.* New York: Amsco, 1985. A generally interesting and well laid out text on the subject of electronic keyboards.

Crombie, David. *The Complete Synthesizer.* London: Omnibus Press, 1982. A competent book on the subject, however far removed from the adjective in its title.

Crombie, David and Paul Wiffen. *The Casio CZ Book.* New York: Amsco, 1986. An excellent resource for this digital synthesizer (adds significantly to the information available in the manual).

Darter, Tom, editor. *The Whole Synthesizer Catalog.* Milwaukee: Hal Leonard Publishing, 1985. Directed particularly at the rock scene of the mid-1980s, this book still holds some interesting information for the less popularly inclined composer, performer, or interested bystander.

Darter, Tom. *The Art of Electronic Music.* New York: Quill, 1984. A rich resource for photos and historical documentation of the early years of electronic music. Most of the remainder of the book centers on personalities rather than actual procedures or instrumentation and hence the book has little value for instruction.

DeFurio, Steve. *The Secrets of Analog and Digital Synthesis.* New York: Ferro, 1985. A generic book on the current state of technology with few "secrets" revealed.

DeFurio, Steve and Joe Scacciaferro. *The MIDI Implementation Book.* Pompton Lakes, NJ: Ferro Technologies, 1986. Lists all models to date with their MIDI configurations.

De Poli, Giovanni. "A Tutorial on Digital Sound Synthesis Techniques." *Computer Music Journal* 7, no. 4 (Winter, 1983):8–26. An excellent article on the fundamentals of digital synthesis. The material on "granular" and "subtractive" synthesis is particularly good. The mathematics can easily be skipped for those who find them opaque (notably Italy and France [IRCAM]).

DeWitt, Tom. "Visual Music: Searching for an Aesthetic." *Leonardo* 20, no. 2 (1987):115–22. A general introduction to the current (1987) visual "harmonies" and available software for digitization of images.

Divilbiss, J. L. "Real-time Generation of Music with a Digital Computer." *Journal of Music Theory* 8:99. Good treatment of its subject matter.

Dodge, C. and T. A. Jerse. *Computer Music Synthesis, Composition and Performance.* New York: Schirmer Books, 1985.

von Foerster, Heinz, and James W. Beauchamp, eds. *Music by Computers.* New York: John Wiley & Sons, 1969.

Francois, Jean-Charles, Xavier Chabot and John Silber. "MIDI Synthesizers in Performance: Realtime Dynamic Timbre Production." *Proceedings of the International Computer Music Conference.* San Francisco: Computer Music Association, 1987, pp. 238–40. A brief but important article on the experiments of the authors in MIDI performance.

Friedman, Dean. *The Complete Guide to Synthesizers, Sequencers and Drum Machines.* New York: Amsco, 1985. A generally good book on the subject (little competition in the field with the exception of production company literature), though certainly not "complete."

Fukuda, Yasuhiko. *DX7.* New York: Amsco, 1984. A very good introduction to this important digital synthesizer.

Garnett, Guy. "Modeling Piano Sound using Waveguide Digital Filtering Techniques." *Proceedings of the International Computer Music Conference.* San Francisco: Computer Music Association, 1987, pp. 89–95. A prototype of its kind, this article explores the aspect of recreating digital images of string lengths, types and key velocities in order to create a straightforward series of parallels between the analog and digital worlds of sonic design.

Garten, Brad. "Elthar—A Signal Processing Expert that Learns." *Proceedings of the International Computer Music Conference.* San Francisco: Computer Music Association, 1987, pp. 96–103. This natural language interface translates user requests into a command format for the activation of various signal processing algorithms.

Gill, S. A. "A Technic for the Composition of Music in a Computer." *Computer Journal* 6, no. 2 (1963):129. Good account of early computer music techniques.

Gordon, John, and John Grey. "Perception of Spectral Modifications on Orchestral Instrument Tones." *Computer Music Journal* 2, no. 1 (1978):24. Interesting psychoacoustical phenomena.

Grey, John. "An Exploration of Musical Timbre." *CCRMA Report No. STAN-M-2* (February 1975). Stanford University report; important for synthesis information on traditional timbres.

———. "Multidimensional Perceptual Scaling of Musical Timbres." *Journal of the Acoustical Society of America* (May 1977). Good source for the computer composer interested in synthesis of unique timbres.

Hiller, Lejaren, and Leonard Isaacson. *Experimental Music.* New York: McGraw-Hill, 1959.

Holtzman, S. R. "Using Generative Grammars for Music Composition." *Computer Music Journal* 5:51–64, No. 1, 1981.

Howe, Hubert S., Jr. "Electronic Music and Microcomputers." *Perspectives of New Music* (Spring-Summer 1979):70. Good source of information concerning background, use, and futures of microcomputers in new music synthesis.

———. *Electronic Music Synthesis.* New York: W. W. Norton & Co., 1975. Most informative.

Interface 2, no. 2 (December 1973). Contains a number of articles relating to computer music, including Steven Smoliar's "Basic Research in Computer-Music Studies"; "A Data Structure for an Interactive Music System"; and Barry Truax's "Some Programs for Real-Time Computer Synthesis and Composition."

Koenig, Gottfried Michael. "Aesthetic Integration of Computer-Composed Scores." *Computer Music Journal* 7, no. 4 (Winter 1983):27–32. An algorithmic description of the production (composing) process.

Laske, Otto. "Toward a Theory of Interfaces for Computer Music Systems." *Computer Music Journal* 1, no. 4 (1977):53.

Lawson, James, and Max Mathews. "Computer Program to Control a Digital Real-Time Sound Synthesizer." *Computer Music Journal* 1, no. 4 (1977):16. Work at IRCAM in software involving minicomputers.

Le Brun, Marc. "Digital Waveshaping Synthesis." *Journal of the Audio Engineering Society* 27, no. 4 (1979).

Lincoln, Harry. *The Computer and Music.* Ithaca, N.Y.: Cornell University Press, 1970. Directed more towards analysis and bibliographical techniques, but still an important source and tool for the composer.

Longton, M. "SAM: Priorities in the Design of a Microprocessor-based Music Program." *Interface* 10:83–95, no. 1, 1981.

Loy, Gareth. "The Composer Seduced into Programming." *Perspectives of New Music,* Spring-Summer, 1981.

———. "On the Scheduling of Multiple Parallel Processors Executing Synchronously." *Proceedings of the International Computer Music Conference.* San Francisco: Computer Music Association, 1987, pp. 117–24. An excellent article dealing with multi-tasking in realtime environments.

———. "Musicians Make a Standard: The MIDI Phenomenon." *Computer Music Journal* 9, no. 4 (Winter 1985):8–26. This is a useful look at the reasoning behind the MIDI default standard.

Machover, Tod. *Musical Thought at IRCAM.* New York: Harwood Academic Publishers, 1984. A limited but useful survey of the current computer and electronic work in Paris.

Massey, Howard. *The Complete Guide to MIDI Software.* New York: Amsco, 1987. This is a compendium of various software programs for IBM PC, Macintosh, Apple II, Atari ST, Commodore 64 (and 128) and TI 99/4a computers. It covers the features of each program in both a window (brief) format and an in-depth narrative. Screen dumps help explain the text.

———. *The Complete DX7.* New York: Amsco, 1986. A very good post-manual description of some of the power of this digital synthesizer (includes three records with excellent examples on each).

Mathews, M. V., and Joan E. Miller. *Music IV Programmer's Manual.* Murray Hill, N.J.: Bell Telephone Laboratories. An important source for those interested in pursuing detailed information on computer programming.

Mathews, Max. *The Technology of Computer Music.* Cambridge, Mass.: M.I.T. Press, 1969. A superb book and the first major edition in its field; now suffers from outdatedness, but still a landmark on the subject.

McNabb, Michael. "Dreamsong: The Composition." *Computer Music Journal* 5, no. 4, (Winter 1981):36–53. A good article by the composer of a classic of the computer music genre.

Moore, F. Richard. "The Dysfunctions of MIDI." *Proceedings of the International Computer Music Conference.* San Francisco: Computer Music Association, 1987, pp. 256–63. An important discussion of the shortcomings of MIDI.

Moore, F. R. "An Introduction to the Mathematics of Digital Signal Processing." *Computer Music Journal* 2, no. 1 (1978):38. First in a series of articles dealing with an important subject for the serious minded computer music composer.

———. "The Futures of Music." *Perspectives of New Music,* Spring-Summer, 1981, pp. 212–226. Moore's law: our computer knowledge and capability doubles each year.

Moorer, James. "Music and Computer Composition." *Communications of the ACM* 15, no. 2 (1972).

———. "Signal Processing Aspects of Computer Music—A Survey." *Proceedings of the IEEE* 65, no. 8 (1977):1108. An extremely good survey of basic computer techniques and developments through 1977.

Morgan, Christopher. *The BYTE Book of Computer Music.* New York: BYTE, 1980. Brief but interesting developments and experiments mostly for microcomputer technology.

Numus West 4. Entire issue devoted to computer music, with articles by Bruce Rogers, Otto Laske, Barry Truax, Leland Smith, Louis Christiansen, Herbert Brün, and Pauline Oliveros. A very good study in the variety of uses of the computer.

Otsuka, Akira and Akihiko Nakajima. *MIDI Basics.* New York: Amsco, 1987. A generally good book on the subject. Provides a free MIDI signal tracer with purchase indicating the high level competition in the business and the corporate nature of the subject.

Pohlmann, Ken C. *Principles of Digital Audio.* Indianapolis: Howard W. Sams Company, 1985. A very good book that more than adequately fulfills its title's promise.

Polanski, Larry, David Rosenboom and Phil Burk. "HMSL: Overview (Version 3.1) and Notes on Intelligent Instrument Design." *Proceedings of the 1987 International Computer Music Conference.* San Francisco: Computer Music Association, 1987. The Hierarchical Music Programming Language is an "open architecture" language for describing musical environments (real and non-real time).

Proceedings of the Audio Engineering Society 5th International Conference, 1987. Some excellent papers presented at this conference on music and digital technology. Dave Rossum's piece, "Digital Musical Instrument Design: The Art of Compromise" and Kimball Stickney's "Computer Tools for Engraving-Quality Music Notation" are particularly interesting and useful articles.

Proceedings (American Society of University Composers). Vol.1 has a series of articles by J. K. Randall, Herbert Brün, Ercolino Ferretti, Godfrey Winham, Lejaren Hiller, David Lewin, and Harold Shapero, relating to computer music; also excellent reference material and diverse comments.

Risset, Jean-Claude. "Computer Music Experiments 1964–" *Computer Music Journal* 9, no. 1 (Spring 1985):11–18. An interesting and useful account of experiments the author (principally) carried out over the indicated years. This is particularly useful information about the development of computer music in Europe in general and France in particular.

Roads, Curtis. "Artificial Intelligence and Music." *Computer Music Journal* 4, no. 2 (1980):60–65.

Robinson, Charlie Q. "Real Time Synthesis of Bowed String Timbres." *Proceedings of the International Computer Music Conference.* San Francisco: Computer Music Association, 1987, pp. 125–29. A description of bowed string models through MIDI.

Shortess, George K. "Interactive Sound Installations Using Microcomputers." *Leonardo* 20, no. 2 (1987):149–53. A brief but informative piece on more recent sound installations, especially those of the author.

Slawson, Wayne. "A Speech-Oriented Synthesizer of Computer Music." *Journal of Music Theory* 13, no. 1 (1969):94. A most important article and, though a bit technical for the layman, highly original.

Smith, L. C. "Score, A Musician's Approach to Computer Music." *Journal of the Audio Engineering Society* (January 1972).

———. "Editing and Printing Music by Computers." *Journal of Music Theory* (Fall 1973).

Smith, Stuart. "Communications." *Perspectives of New Music* (Spring-Summer, 1973). Fascinating but highly mathematical study of some of Xenakis's remarks in *Formalized Music.*

"Sound Generation by Means of a Digital Computer." *Journal of Music Theory* 7, no. 1 (Spring 1963):24. An excellent general source for coverage of printout cards, programming, digital tape, etc.

Tenney, James. "Computer Music Experiences 1961–64." *Electronic Music Reports* 1:23. Account of this composer's work in the studio at Utrecht State University.

———. "Musical Composition with the Computer." *Journal of the Acoustical Society of America* 34, no. 6 (1964):1245.

Truax, Barry. "Organizational Techniques for C:M Ratios in Frequency Modulation." *Computer Music Journal* 1, no. 4 (1977):39.

Traux, Barry. "Real-time Granulation of Sampled Sound with the DMX-1000." *Proceedings of the International Computer Music Conference.* San Francisco: Computer Music Association, 1987, pp. 138–45. This paper describes the generation of high density sounds via small "grains" on the order of magnitude of 10–20 ms duration.

Vercoe, Barry. "The Music 360 Languages for Sound Synthesis." *Computer Music Newsletter* 2 (June 1971).

Vilordi, Frank and Steve Tarshis. *Electronic Drums.* New York: Amsco, 1985. This somewhat superficial production-oriented text (which includes a record) provides an interesting review of the "drumulating" (fake drums mostly for rock music) equipment.

Wessel, David, David Bristow and Zack Settel. "Control of Phrasing and Articulation in Synthesis." *Proceedings of the International Computer Music Conference.* San Francisco: Computer Music Association, 1987, pp. 108–16. An impressive experiment with rubato, time maps, timbral differences and articulation effects.

Yavelow, Christopher. "MIDI and the Apple Macintosh." *Computer Music Journal,* pp. 11–47. An excellent (as of 1986) review of various software for the Macintosh.

Zinovieff, Peter. "A Computerized Electronic Music Studio." *Electronic Music Reports* 1:5.

Appleton, Jon. *In Deserto* (1977). Recorded on Folkways 33445. This record also contains *Synthrophia* (1977), *Zoetrope* (1974), and other works incorporating the Synclavier and other digital systems. As well, Folkways 3746 contains *Four Fantasies for Synclavier* (1979–81).

———. *Georganne's Farewell.* Recorded on Folkways 33442 along with works by Bodin, Pinkston and Brunson.

———. *Four Fantasies for Synclavier* (1982). Recorded on Folkways FTS 37461. An excellent example of the kind of elegant work this incredible instrument can produce (*both* synthesizing and sampling).

Behrman, David. *On the Other Ocean.* Lovely Music Records LWL-1041.

Computer Music from CCRMA (in three volumes). A fine collection of works from CCRMA recorded on the Stanford Center for Computer Research in Music and Acoustics Digital Recordings. CD: Number #3.

Cope, David. *Glassworks* (1979) for two pianos and computer-generated tape. Recorded on Folkways FTS-33452.

Dartmouth Digital Synthesizer. Folkways FTS-33442. Record containing computer-synthesized works by Appleton (*Georganna's Farewell*), Pinkston (*Emergence*), Brunson (*Tapestry*), and Bodin (*Bilder*).

Dashow, James. *Effetti Collaterali* (1976). Published by Dawsonville. Recorded on Tulstar Productions, New Directions in Music, 1978.

Dodge, Charles. *Earth's Magnetic Field* (1970). Recorded on Nonesuch 71250. A computer-generated work.

———. *In Celebration: Speech Songs. The Story of Our Lives.* Recorded on CRI S-348. Examples of extraordinary speech synthesis techniques.

Ghent, Emmanuel. *Brazen.* Recorded on Tulstar Productions, New Directions in Music, 1978. Computer-synthesized sound using GROOVE at Bell Laboratories.

Greesel, Joel. *Crossings* (1976). Recorded on CRI 393-SD. Record also contains works by Hoffmann, Vercoe, Winham, and others for computer tape.

Hiller, Lejaren, and Robert Baker. *Computer Cantata.* Recorded on CRI 310-SD.

Hiller, L. and John Cage. *HPSCHD* (1968). Peters. Recorded on Nonesuch H-71224.

Recordings and Publishers

Hoffmann, Richard. *In Memoriam Patris* (1976). Recorded on CRI 393-SD.

Jaffe, Stephen. *Silicon Valley Breakdown.* Recorded on the Stanford Center for Computer Research in Music and Acoustics Digital Recordings Number 1. This album also includes Schottstaedt's *Water Music I* and *II* and *Dinosaur Music.*

Lansky, Paul. *Idle Chatter.* Recorded on Wergo Schallplatten. A CD which explores the newest wave of computer music composers including Lansky, Curtis Roads (*nscor*), James Dashow (*Sequence Symbols*), Michel Waisvisz (*The Hands [Movement 1]*), Clarence Barlow (*Relationships for Melody Instruments*) and Stephan Kaske (*Transition Nr. 2*).

McKee, William. *Episodes I and II.* Available on Tulstar Productions, New Directions in Music, 1978.

McNabb, Michael. *Dreamsong* (1978). Recorded on the Stanford Center for Computer Research in Music and Acoustics Digital Recordings CD: Number 2. This album also contains his *Love in the Asylum* and *Orbital View.*

Melby, John. *91 Plus 5 for Brass Quintet and Computer.* Recorded on CRI SD-310.

———. *Concerto for Violin and Computer-Synthesized Tape.* Recorded on New World NW-333.

Morrill, Dexter. *Studies for Trumpet and Computer.* Recorded on Golden Crest Records RE-7068. Interesting use of "Chowning FM" in combination with a live instrument.

———. *Six Dark Questions for Soprano and Computer* (1979). Available on Redwood ES-10 and includes works by Pennycook, Sullivan and Boyer, all completed at the Colgate Computer Music Studio.

Olive, Joseph. *Mar-ri-ia-a* (1973—an opera for soprano, chamber ensemble, and computer tape). Recorded on Tulstar Productions, New Directions in Music.

Peterson, Tracy. *Voices.* Tulstar Productions, New Directions in Music. Fascinating computer voice synthesis.

Randall, J. K. *Lyric Variations for Violin and Computer* (1967). Recorded on Vanguard C-10057.

———. *Quartets in Pairs* (1964). Recorded on Nonesuch 71245, which also includes works by Charles Dodge and Barry Vercoe. *Quartets in Pairs* is computer-generated.

Risset, Jean-Claude. *Inharmonic Soundscapes.* Published by Dawsonville. Recorded on Tulstar, New Directions in Music.

Thome, Diane. *Los Nombres.* Published by Paul Price. Recorded on Tulstar, New Directions in Music.

Truax, Barry. *Sonic Landscapes.* Melbourne SMLP 4033 (Vancouver Canada).

Wallraff, Dean. *Dance.* Published by Dawsonville. Recorded on Tulstar, New Directions in Music. Also contains the work of David Wessel (*Antony*).

Winham, Godfrey. *NP (Two Pieces for Computer-Synthesized Sound).* Recorded on CRI 39 3-SD.

Vercoe, Barry. *Synapse* for viola and computer. Recorded on CRI S-393.

AUTOMATED AND CYBERNETIC[1] MUSIC

10

In a generic sense, music played automatically by machines has a rich and varied tradition. Aeolian harps (stringed instruments played by the wind), for example, date back to ancient China. Musical clocks and boxes enjoyed popularity in the fourteenth century as did barrel-organs, musical chimes and carillons.

Background

More recently, player pianos (pianolas—see Chapter 4 on Instrument Exploration and the work of Conlon Nancarrow) and other mechanical instruments have been employed by composers. In most of these cases, however, the intention, no matter how automatic the process, was an exact as possible repetition of a provided musical statement or work. This chapter will be devoted to studying automated music and programs designed to extend the composer's technique by sharing in the *process* of composition or by composing independently.

Since most of the work in cybernetics during the past thirty years has been accomplished with the use of computers, it is important to differentiate between this type of use and computer-generated synthesis. The work covered in this chapter does not relate to the manner in which sound is actually produced, edited, or broadcast. It is rather dedicated to the choice of which sound will go where in a composition. Some have distinguished these by using the terms *computer-realized music* and *computer-composed music* (or *computer-assisted composition* [CAC]).

Understanding parallels in the visual arts proves valuable. Russell and Joan Kirsch, specialists in natural language processing and art history (respectively) have used formal grammars in automatic language translation to develop computational pattern recognition. Their efforts, investigating whether a visual arts grammar might exist, have produced recognizable art. Using an Ocean Park Series of paintings by the abstract expressionist Richard Diebenkorn and an elaborate geometric compositional program, they created "pseudo-Diebenkorns," randomly generated images based on rules using what they perceived as his artistic *language*. When they sent a "pseudo-Diebenkorn" to the real Diebenkorn they received a simple reply: "Yes, that's me!" Shortly afterwards they discovered that their artificial work was a twin of the *Ocean Park #126* by Diebenkorn himself. Color is equated with semantics, as opposed to the context-free grammar of pen and ink, and shading represents

---

1. Defined as a collaboration between man and machine.

nuance. Further interpretation raises problems especially in non-representational art. At the same time, the work of the Kirsches has produced significant controversy in the visual art community.

AARON, the Hebrew name of its inventor, Harold Cohen, at the University of California at San Diego, is an art robot who draws pictures (without the visual feedback of the results of its efforts) using rules-based procedures. Deriving a set of primitive concepts from paleolithic artists, Cohen created a programming language which enabled AARON to form sets of drawings. This program uses generalized properties of freehand drawing called "standing-for-ness." Attempts at re-creating figurative drawing based on conceptual frames of the human figure have proven very successful. Frolicking male and female bodies (gender seems an easy concept for AARON to grasp) have appeared regularly during 1986–87.

Nelson Goodman's distinctions between painting as a one-stage or autographic art, beginning and ending with the artist and music (as a two-stage or allographic art with a composer and many performers) has proven meaningless. As Cohen has said: "In my own case the program is responsible for all the performances, as if a score could play itself." Certainly the analogies between aural and visual arts extend far beyond this simple "performance" metaphor. John Anderson, a leading cognitive psychologist has stated: "I am betting that at the higher cognitive level, yet to be fully understood, a set of universals are embedded in all human expression, the visual arts only one aspect of that expression."[2]

Stravinsky noted: "I merely report—I cannot verify—that composers already claim to have discovered musical applications of decision theory, mathematical group theory, and the idea of 'shape' in algebraic topology. Mathematicians will undoubtedly think this all very naive, and rightly so, but I consider that any inquiry, naive or not, is of value if only because it must lead to larger questions—in fact, to the eventual mathematical formulation of musical theory, and to, at long last, an empirical study of musical facts—and I mean the facts of the art of combination which is composition."[3]

The first serious work to take place in this area was by Lejaren Hiller and Leonard Isaacson in the creation of the *Illiac Suite for String Quartet* (1956; discussed more fully under automated music in this chapter). Largely based on traditional techniques, their work employed style rules and controls over lists of random numbers with results printed in standard notation. About this same time, Iannis Xenakis began works based on stochastic techniques and developed computer programs based on mathematical processes (see Vectoral Analysis of this chapter). Works such as *Metastasis* (1954), *Pithoprakta* (1956), and *Achoripsis* (1957) all were based on calculations of this sort.

Around the same time, a popular tune called *Push Button Bertha* (1956) by Martin Klein and Douglas Bolito of Burroughs, Inc. used a DATATRON computer.

2. McCorduck. "Science and Meanings in Art," *Whole Earth Review* 55 (Summer 1987): 45–51. An excellent article on AARON and its art as well as the extraordinary work of Russell and Joan Kirsch.
3. Igor Stravinsky and Robert Craft. *Expositions and Developments*. Berkeley: The University of California Press, 1959, p. 99.

An anonymous Burroughs publication describes the compositional process as follows: "The operator inspires DATATRON by first keying in a 10-digit random number. This causes the machine to generate and store 1000 single digits, each representing one of the eight diatonic notes in the scale with two allowable accidentals. The program then motivates DATATRON to pick notes at random, testing each for melodic acceptability as it goes along." (From "Syncopation by Automation," *Data from ElectroData,* August 1956, Pasadena, CA: Electro-data Division of Burroughs, Inc.)

In 1960, Pierre Barbaud began studying the potential of algorithmic composition. He worked principally with permutational methods applied to traditional harmonies and 12-tone processes of random selection. In the late 1960s he developed an aesthetic that included automated music with music composed by humans. "It is 'human' inasmuch as it is the product of rational beings." (See his "Algorithmic Music" listing in the Bibliography.)

Gottfried Michael Koenig's work at the Institute of Sonology in Utrecht has, since 1964, been very involved with automated composition. His work *PROJECT 2* (1969) demonstrates an effective use of statistical procedures which fit together in various combinations. His *Übung für Klavier* (Study for Piano), written in 1970, uses this program.

Other experiments during this time included computer generation of hymn tunes based on the statistical analysis of 37 hymns up to the eighth-order approximation. These were carried out by F. Brooks, A. Hopkins, P. Neumann and W. Wright. Robert Baker's *CSX-1 Study* employed the MUSICOMP (MUsic Simulator Interpreter for COMPositional Procedures) at the University of Illinois. Baker and Hiller then collaborated in the creation of *Computer Cantata,* completed in 1963 and one of the most powerful of the early pioneering works in computer composition. This highly serialized work employs various tempered tuning systems (from 9 to 15 notes per octave) and has been performed extensively and internationally.

Beginning in this same year, Herbert Brün completed *Sonoriferous Loops* for instrumental ensemble and tape using MUSICOMP. This work and his *Nonsequitur VI* (1966, tape and ensemble) are based on various probability distributions entered as data into the computer. Cage and Hiller's dynamic *HPSCHD* (discussed later in this chapter) utilizes a subroutine of MUSICOMP called *ICHING* (justifiably involving 1 to 64 integers). James Tenney's work at Bell Laboratories produced a number of important works involving computer composition including *Four Stochastic Studies* (1962), *Stochastic String Quartet* (1963), and *Dialogue* (1963). Hiller (in his seminal article in Lincoln's *The Computer and Music;* see Bibliography) has expounded Harriet Padberg's work in 1964 of assigning notes to letters of the alphabet, then creating meaningful phrases in English and using computer programs to transform the results into music employing transformations of group theory. The *Canon and Free Fugue* which resulted from her labors has proven "integrally bound to its 'title' in melody and rhythm." Pierre Barbaud and Roger Blanchard worked as well during this period, completing a number of important papers on the subject.

More recently, Hiller has completed a set of three *Algorithms* (I, 1968; II, 1972; and III, 1981) which employ various stochastic and random elements. Figure 10.1

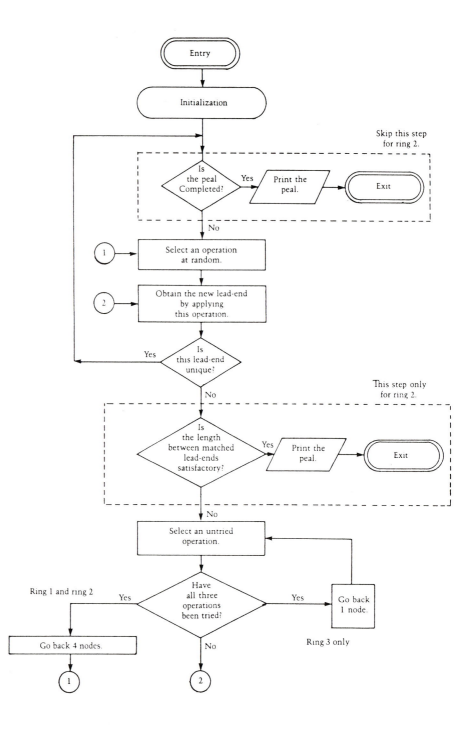

Figure 10.1. The flow chart for change ringing used in Lejaren Hiller's *Algorithms II*. From Lejaren Hiller's "Composing with Computers" from *Computer Music Journal*, Volume 5, Number 4, p. 17 (Figure 5).

gives the flow chart for change ringing used in *Algorithms II*. Each of the steps of composition are clearly laid out and described in English. The circled numbers (bottom and at the left) are connect points. Each of the exits shows a successful operation. Hiller's program called PHRASE produced the orchestral work *A Preview of Coming Attractions* (1975).

The League of Automated Composers (principally Jim Horton, Tim Perkis, John Bishoff, and Rich Gold) have involved mathematics and random sources. Their work includes ensemble pieces and usually employs electronic output. In *Network Piece,* (1980), each of the group works out his materials independently communicating the results from one minicomputer to another through digital-to-analog converters. Since one composer's work could influence another, the outcome is a dialogue. Figure 10.2 shows the ensemble before a 1980 performance of *Network Piece.*

Figure 10.2. The League of Automated Music Composers in performance in San Francisco on November 15, 1980. From the left: Jim Horton, Tim Perkis and John Bishoff. Photograph by John Grau (from Curtis Roads' 1985 book, p. 596, figure 335 [see bibliography for further information]).

More recently, Bishoff and Perkis, along with Chris Brown, Scot Gresham-Lancaster, Phil Stone, and Mark Trayle have created *The Hub*. This is a computer music "band" whose members are all designers and builders of their own hardware and software instruments. The group electronically coordinates the activities of their individual systems through a central microcomputer, *The Hub* itself, as well as through ears, hands, and eyes. Their performances (June 6 and 7, 1987) at the Clocktower and the Experimental Intermedia Foundation received wide acclaim. Tim Perkis noted: "I see the asethetic informing this work perhaps counter to other trends in computer music: instead of attempting to gain more individual control over every aspect of the music, we see more surprise through the lively and unpredictable response of these systems and hope to encourage an active response to surprise in hearing (from program notes to their recital)." The word *we* here is important. The groups hooks their machines, their software, and themselves into *The Hub* and what happens, happens (though real-time control is possible).

Figure 10.3. *Percussion Machine* by Joe Jones, performed first at the Pocket Theatre in New York City on August 8, 1963.

Joe Jones has created many automatic composing instruments. These range from mechanical orchestras of percussion batteries to his percussion machine (shown in figure 10.3) which looks more like an intrepid 'cellist with trappings.

Recent advances in artificial intelligence techniques have produced a number of interesting developments related to music. Translating algorithmic data into AI languages and utilizing traditional chaining techniques and inference engines allows composers to develop intelligent (and, it is hoped, musical) programs for composition.

Automated Music

Studies (primarily by Lejaren Hiller and Leonard Isaacson in 1955–56) began at the University of Illinois with the Illiac high-speed digital computer and involved the programming of basic material and stylistic parameters. The computer was limited to choices it could make within number systems coded by composer input to basic musical note tables. In other words, the computer was "taught" certain conditional limits and fed the results (in terms of numbers) to researchers, who then translated such into traditional notes. The *Illiac Suite for String Quartet* (1957) resulted and was published in the April 1957 edition of *New Music Quarterly*. It was composed by the computer, but transposed to traditional musical notation by researchers for "live" nonelectronic performance.

The score of this work and research leading to its composition are described in *Experimental Music*.[4] Though these directions in "computer control" have not proven to be great artistic successes, the experiments were extraordinarily important, for they indeed opened the door to new vistas in the expansion of the computer's development as a unique instrument with significant potential. Research and composition involving the computer in this manner continue since (1) no special equipment (e.g., the DAC) is required (the computer does exactly what it was designed to do), and (2) extensive data concerning composition and music analysis, especially as it relates to "random" materials, can be important to a number of concepts.

4. Lejaren Hiller and Leonard Isaacson, *Experimental Music* (New York: McGraw-Hill, 1959).

Figure 10.4. Lejaren Hiller. By permission.

In 1969, Lejaren Hiller and John Cage teamed to produce *HPSCHD*. Through the use of computer printout sheets of "highly sophisticated random numbers," they created the first recording with indeterminate performance possibilities. The listener performs on the record player knobs. Each printout sheet contains a different set of numbers for loudness and treble/bass control on each speaker. With both Xenakis and Cage, the computer serves (though to different ends) to achieve otherwise impossible results. In neither case has the computer actually produced the resultant sound; it has only aided the composer by virtue of its high-speed computations.

Hiller speaks of his work with automated music in an interview:

> Nowadays I think that my computer pieces possess more expressive content than I would have first guessed. In other words, I hear in the pieces more of a reflection of my general approach to music than I would have supposed at the beginning. I don't find even the Illiac Suite that far disjunct from the other things I do. I suppose that my programming contains biases that are subjective.

The Tsukuba *Musical Robot* (presented for the first time at the 1985 International Exposition in Tsukuba, Japan) is a fully implemented pianist capable of performing many works either from sight or from a limited repertoire. Figure 10.5 shows this technical marvel during performance. Seated at a Yamaha digital organ, it scans scores with a video camera and speaks with bystanders about its performance. Its control system consists of 17 Z8001 and Z8002 16-bit computers and 50 Z8094 8-bit computers interconnected by fiberoptic data links. The robot's eye utilizes a charge-coupled device (CCD) camera and frame buffer with a resolution of 2000 by 3000 pixels. The limb design follows anthropomorphic models and consist of two-joint thumbs and four three-joint fingers moving at the speed of 1.5 m/sec.

Figure 10.5. The Tsukuba *Musical Robot* at the keyboard.

Figure 10.6. Tsukuba *Musical Robot* fingering the keyboard.

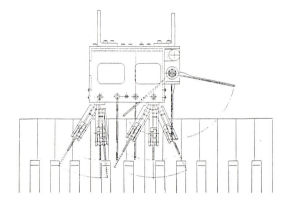

The robot is designed to accompany a human who sings into a microphone attached to the system. If the live performer is out of tune, the robot has been designed to adjust the synthesizer/organ accordingly to match the pitch level. Figure 10.6 shows the posture of the individual fingers at the keyboard.

Charles Ames spent six months developing a *Cybernetic Composer.* His system uses a Kurzweil 250 digital sampling keyboard and sound system with the user choosing the style of music desired: rock, standard jazz (à la Art Blakely), or Latin jazz. Ames-developed software creates original compositions within that style (usually taking many hours). *Cybernetic Composer* was exhibited along with many other original music products for computers on tour with Digital Equipment Corporation's "Robots and Beyond: The Age of Intelligent Machines."

Charles Ames also leads the Kurzweil Foundation's Automated Composition Project in Eggertsville, New York (68 Stevenson Boulevard—14226–3211). Here he has developed a number of significant "constraint-based" programs for the development of automated musics. Ames uses heuristic guidelines and form-generating procedures with the aesthetic goals of individual works in mind. He also employs mechanisms that maintain pitches in statistical balance by favoring the least-used pitch in any decision. Ames's *Crystals,* in particular, exemplifies his use of both AI processes and contextual sensitivity to produce successful compositions.

Figure 10.7 shows a basic program for computer creation of twelve-tone rows and subsequent matrices. It is written in the BASIC computer language and can provide quick (usually less than a second, depending on computer use) generation of data. Extending this program could provide full compositions using the rows created and experimentation for the composer interested in the varieties of ways that random materials can interact.

```
10 PRINT "THIS PROGRAM GENERATES RANDOM 12 TONE ROWS AS WELL AS  "
11 PRINT "THEIR INVERSIONS, RETROGRADES AND INVERSION RETRO-"
12 PRINT "GRADES."
13 RANDOMIZE
20 DIM N(12),M(12),N$(12)
21 DIM A(12,12)
30 N$(1)="C ":N$(2)="C#":N$(3)="D ":N$(4)="D#"
40 N$(5)="E ":N$(6)="F ":N$(7)="F#":N$(8)="G "
50 N$(9)="G#":N$(10)="A ":N$(11)="A#"
60 N$(12)="B "
80 FOR I= 1 TO 12
90 N(I)=INT(1+(12*RND))
100 IF I=1 THEN 140
110 I1=I-1
120 FOR J=1 TO I1
130 IF N(I)=N(J) THEN 90
140 NEXT J
145 NEXT I
150 REM INVERSION
160 FOR K=1 TO 12
164 IF   K=1 THEN M(1)=N(1)
165 IF   K=1 THEN 230
170 Q=K-1
180 P=N(K)-N(Q)
190 R=M(Q)-P
200 IF R<1 THEN R=R+12
210 IF R>12 THEN R=R-12
220 M(K)=R
230 NEXT K
240 &"ORIGINAL"
250 FOR A=1 TO 12
260 G=N(A)
270 &N$(G)"   ";
280 NEXT A
290 &""
300 & "INVERSION"
310 FOR B=1 TO 12
320 G=M(B)
330 &N$(G)"   ";
340 NEXT B
350 &"  "
360 &"RETROGRADE"
370 FOR C=1 TO 12
380 H=13-C
390 G=N(H)
400 &N$(G)"   ";
410 NEXT C
420 &"  "
430 &"RETROGRADE INVERSION"
440 FOR D=1 TO 12
450 H=13-D
460 G=M(H)
470 &N$(G)"   ";
```

Figure 10.7. An example of how LISP (first function) and BASIC programs compare. Here, both functions produce random 12-tone rows.

Figure 10.7. *(Continued)*

```
480 NEXT D
482 &" ":&" ":&" ";
485 &"DO YOU WISH TO SEE TRANSPOSITION MATRIX";:INPUT A$
490 IF A$="NO" THEN 999
500 REM THE TRANSPOSITION MATRIX MADE HERE
510 FOR E=1 TO 12
520   IF E=1 THEN R=0
530   IF E=1 THEN 570
540   R=M(E)-N(1)
550   IF R<1 THEN R=R+12
560   IF R>12 THEN R=R+12
570    FOR F=1 TO 12
580     G=N(F)+R
590     IF G<1 THEN G=G+12
600     IF G>12 THEN G=G-12
610     A(E,F)=G
620    NEXT F
630 NEXT E
632 FOR Q=1 TO 30
635 &" "
636 NEXT Q
640 &"MATRIX GENERATED BY ROW AND ITS INVERSION"
645 FOR G=1 TO 12
650   FOR H=1 TO 12
660   I=A(G,H)
670   &N$(I)" ";
680 NEXT H
690 &" "
700 NEXT G
999 END
```

```
(defun create-row (&optional (number-list (create-mixed-list)))
   (if (null (rest-of number-list)) ()
         (cons (- (first number-list)(second number-list))
                (create-row (rest-of number-list)))))
```

Artificial Intelligence and Symbolic Logic

Eugene Charniak and Drew McDermott define artificial intelligence as "the study of mental faculties through the use of computational models" (see Bibliography for reference). Such studies can take many forms: linguistic, search, logic, deduction, expert, and management to name but a few. In general, however, most approaches take a hierarchical view. The principle is to take large actions and break them into smaller and smaller sub-actions until no further subdivision need take place. These smallest common denominators are then usually formed into functions which can then be built into larger and larger functions so that the computational model will be able to match the large action required.

Since the computer language LISP (LISt Processing) operates in just this manner, it is usually the language of choice for AI researchers. It differs significantly from languages like BASIC which develop long linear (and numbered) progressions of detailed instructions. LISP proceeds by the accumulation of many small "expert" functions ultimately building them into networks capable of powerful top level routines. At present, there is no LISP standard, however. Instead, many different dialects exist (MacLISP, interLISP, even Franz LISP), all reasonably similar yet different enough to cause significant problems when transferring files between programs. In this text, the author has chosen to use "common LISP" (the proposed new standard dialect). Figure 10.7 shows the power of LISP when compared to a BASIC program.

Obviously the LISP version is simpler, more readable, and faster, even though both produce exactly the same results: a random 12-tone row ("create-row" returns numbers for intervals, the BASIC version produces note-names). It isn't that the BASIC version is badly written. It is just as elegant as BASIC will allow. The LISP version points out a number of other key points about the language. First, it is *recursive*. This means that it calls itself while operating using less and less of its argument until it runs out of material and creates a new list (e.g., reason for ()) of the correct response to its being called. Secondly, LISP is extremely flexible and users can change the format at any time (here the use of "first," for example, precludes, for the sake of readability, the more standard "car" operation). Last, and possibly most significant, LISP exemplifies *symbolic logic*. This means that it can associate data with symbols, making it a natural for real world modeling. "Ocean," for example can easily be associated with "blue," etc. thus making pattern matching, one of the traditional AI database techniques, easy and efficient.

These features make LISP exceptionally well suited to music analysis and models of composition. The language is so adaptable as to make any form or approach possible whether it be based on serialism, set theory, tonal roots or motives. Schenkerian processes fit since they parallel the hierarchical structure of LISP itself. As well, any of the traditional AI concepts expressed at the beginning of this section can be applied to music through LISP (i.e., linguistic principles or inference properties). Hence, many researchers in both fields have attempted studies of the properties of music based on "use computational models."

As an example, the function shown in figure 10.8 (in LISP) lists prioritized motives according to how many repetitions or slight variations occur within its second argument (the reference to "window" here simply indicates how close the found variant must be to the original with 0 being exact and 5 representing remote). For example, (analyze 3 '(1 3 2 2 1)) returns ((1 (1 5))(1 (1 3))(1 (3 4))(1 (3 2))(1 (2 3))(1 (2 2))(1 (2 1))) and (analyze 4 '(1 2 1 2 3)) returns ((2 (1 5))(2 (1 2))(2 (2 3))(1 (1 3))(1 (2 6))(1 (2 1))(1 (1 5))(1 (1 2))(1 (2 3))).

```
(defun analyze (window number-list)
  (cond ((null number-list) ())
        ((listp (car number-list))
         (cons (analyze window (car number-list))
               (analyze window (cdr number-list))))
        (t (sort-by-first 'max
             (count-all-occurances (add-numbers
               (collect-motive-lists window number-list))))))))
```

Figure 10.8. An analysis function written in LISP.

Note that in LISP all parenthetical statements must eventually be completed (reason for all the final right parentheses) and that functions always occur after a left parenthesis. Hence, "(sort-by-first 'max (. . . . . .))" means "sort first elements by their maximums (exactly the process shown in the sample runs given before the figure).

Composition programs can be created in a variety of ways using LISP. Approaching the concept using the processes given earlier allow for a variety of techniques to be employed. Traditionally, the model derives from a top-down structure. That is, one begins with the largest issue (probably a work or style) and breaks it into smaller and smaller elements until no further subdivision is possible. However, since music is most often composed in exactly the opposite way (i.e., placing notes one after another on a microscopic scale), a bottom-up approach may be employed (LISP lends itself comfortably to either method). As example, work-section-period-phrase-subphrase-pitch-dynamic may be one way to model a traditional top-down composing process with dynamic-pitch-subphrase-phrase-period-section-work representing the bottom-up approach. Figure 10.9 shows functions demonstrating the two extremes in terms of LISP.

Figure 10.9. Two examples of functions written in LISP. The first explores compositional tools and produces music. The second is a sub-function of the first.

a)

```
(defun proto-compose (&rest work-parameters-and-bindings);flexible # of args
    (let ((principal-motive (create-initial-motive)))          ;creates main motive
        (let ((motive-value (get-motive-value principal-motive)))  ;creates # of phrases
        (let ((number-of-voices                                ;creates the # of
                (create-texture (convert-definitions-to-numbers principal-motive);voices
                motive-value))                                 ;in each phrase
            (init-values (separation))                         ;sets separation of voices
            (window (define-window))                           ;sets window size
                (limit-number (motive-limit)))                 ;sets general size of parsing
        (and (apply 'primal-compose                            ;applies "primal"
                (find-and-order work-parameters-and-bindings   ;to its argument-list
                    (list 'new-work motive-value number-of-voices ;list of default values
                        init-values window limit-number principal-motive)));required
            (if (equal input 'y)(proto-compose input)  t))))))     ;continue?
```

b)

```
(defun count-the (object list-of-objects)
    (cond ((equal object list-of-objects) 1)  ;add 1 for each success
            ((atom list-of-objects) 0)           ;if it didn't pass above, then 0
            (t (+ count-the object (car list-of-objects));double recurse
                (count-the object (cdr list-of-objects))))))
```

Note that the statements following the semicolon are remarks only, to help the reader understand the programming techniques involved. Figure 10.9a is a high-level function which will require the writing of many subfunctions to operate. However, it does indicate an approach to determining major work-related issues such as texture, motive, etc. The function defined in Figure 10.9b is built only of LISP primitives. It is found (in this particular program) in "count-the-occurrences-of" which in turn is found in "analysis," "primal-compose," and, finally, "proto-compose," the function above it.

Modeling analytical and compositional processes in this way allows for better understanding of the musical intelligence required by the computer in order to create reasonable facsimiles of given styles or to create wholly new styles based on mathematical formulas, statistics, and/or random processes. Artificial intelligence techniques may then be applied in a wide variety of different implementations.

One of the simplest ways to describe the process of defining musical intelligence is to follow an orchestration model. Since a great deal of cybernetic music has been composed for traditional ensembles, it seems plausible to study the area most foreign to such application: idiomatic scoring for standard orchestral instruments. The tactile nature of performance, the physical limitations of human performers, the layout of the instruments, etc., combine to create a cumulation of limitations often difficult to describe in machine terms. Fingering, for example, is possible in one circumstance and not another. The C♯ shown at the top of Figure 10.10 is easily accomplished given its immediate environment while impossible in the following case. In fact, as one begins to sift through the various elements of possibilities in performance, one quickly begins to understand a very simple axiom: the question in music is never *whether* something can be done, but *when* it can be done. This mirrors the temporal aspects of the art form, and requires the use of *if/then/else* concepts inherent in most computer languages. In LISP the functions *when* and *while* serve exceptionally well for this purpose. Put simply, these functions do not operate unless what follows their appearance corresponds to every stated condition in the musical situation. (when (equal (xp1v1i1 'interval) 7)(and (<> (xp1v2i1 'interval) 1 − 7)(eq (position 2) (> (pitch 440))))) would be a useful rule for the 'cello example. It states that when a fifth occurs, the next interval may not be more than a minor second up or a fifth in the other direction if the performer is in more than second position on the a string. This could be further qualified for tempo, etc. Combining this approach with the inferential structures discussed in the previous section allows the computer to relate to real world terms.

Figure 10.10. Two high 'cello examples, one possible and the other not.

Music intelligence may be further defined by a second axiom: the number of possible musical situations that exist is infinite. This is not only true for performance in general but for the example cited above; i.e., the number of possible durations, tempo, etc., just for the C♯, is infinite. A third axiom provides the ultimate realization: "computers cannot create or manipulate infinite data or rules." There is thus far no manner in which the computer can deal with the complex phenomenon of "thinking" musically.

One approach to dealing with this problem rests with the concept of *musical sense*. This parallels the model of the AI "blocks world" where one does not describe the infinite number of sizes and weights of blocks which, when stacked off center, may or may not fall down. Rather, the concepts of gravity, balance, and leverage are taught to the machine with the remaining *situational* conditions removed from the problem. For the musical examples already given, this means that the computer will be taught to think like a 'cellist with no situation rules given initially.

This approach to compositional problems suggests that computers could be instructed to think in musical terms rather than just plodding through a list of endless rules and regulations about when and where they might allow a certain action to take place. Since the computer, using its own digital instrumentation, can create any sonic image, the concept is to teach it that in the human world, some things are more musical than others and that this musicality can originate in physical as well as intellectual terms.

If one ignores the rules concept and situational descriptions of events and takes a *gestural* approach based on musical positive feedback, then music cybernetics becomes possible on a macro level. For example, implementing a model of the human voice box in a computer, with all the concepts of complex (and often unconscious) actions and reactions in performance, would force composition toward more potentially musical processes. Even a description of the human ear would be useful for this real-world parallel to become fully possible. Hence this translation could allow the computer to facilitate the concepts of range limits and detail limits so important (and so taken for granted) in our human world. There are, for example, gradations of vibrato, intonation, etc., which the human ear simply cannot detect. Knowing that reduces the infinite numbers of variations the computer must deal with.

This discussion of modeling is predicated on the assumption that musicality follows a combination of tactile as well as reasoning processes. It places the human composer and performer at the center of the cybernetic relationship (not the case with a good deal of music composed in this manner thus far). It is also based, however, on the concept that continuing to build computer systems on definitions of something which is impossible to define using situational rules seems itself irrational.

Figure 10.11 shows the results of a computer program which includes a *musical sensing* process. Descriptions of the ear, two hands (fingering and bowing), and the fingerboard of a 'cello were included in the composing programs for EMI (*Experiments in Musical Intelligence,* an author-created computer project). Note that the phrase follows traditionally idiomatic principles. The fingering and bowing have been included to show how the computer verifies the practicality of its choices (which were linguistically influenced according to the linguistic processes described in the next section). Musical gestures are based on concepts of smooth transitions of hand position (positions 1 and 4 take dominance over 2, 3, 5, etc., since they physically represent easy locations for actual 'cellists). The range of the passage falls in the register most traditional to the instrument.

Obviously, the intricate balance between intellectual potential and physical limitation is difficult to define. Also, knowing how to write for real-world instruments

Figure 10.11. Computer-composed musical example. The program incorporates a musical "sensing" process.

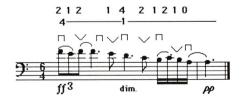

is no guarantee that the results of composition will be good music (history abounds with good orchestrators being poor composers). However, the added intelligence for the computer could, at least, cover more musically viable examples while speeding up the composing process by limiting the otherwise highly flexible computational world to real-world limits of human perception and performance.

Studies of cybernetic processes with computers have created a renewed interest in a linguistic approach to music composition. This is principally due to the need for programmers to base their programs on some kind of natural process. Since language uses sound, and order proceeds by analogous organizations (i.e., sentence to phrase), it has received attention in recent years. This requires a substantial leap of faith not corroborated by a significant body of empirical evidence. However, studying linguistic models has proven useful to a number of composers.

Music grammar has, at present, only been defined crudely in terms of syntax and semantics. These definitions generally take the form of personal rather than universal representations of rules and values applicable during composition. Syntax is often applied both horizontally and vertically since these may have significantly different meanings. Parsing helps understand written languages and thus offers potential for parallels in music. Work in this area has proven fruitful especially in GGDL (Generative Grammar Definition Language compiler) and EMI (Experiments in Music Intelligence discussed later in this chapter). Augmented Transition Network (ATN) Parsing provides transformational rules to the context-free syntax of grammar. Of the nine grammar types, only ATN allows the recursive possibilities inherent in LISP and is thus usually the approach of choice. Figure 10.12 shows a simple sentence parsed according to the rudimentary rules of ATN. In a, *s* refers to sentence part, *np* to noun-phrase and *vp* to verb-phrase. In b, the upper symbols show an alternative notation to the statements below.

Linguistics, Graph Grammars, and Fractals

Figure 10.12. An example of sentence parsing.

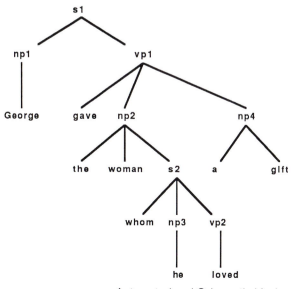

Figure 10.13. Crude examples of musical parsing.

Many theorists have postulated musical parsing mechanisms appropriate for tonal grammars. Among these are Curtis Roads, Fred Lerdahl, and the author of this text. Typically they metaphorically reference such concepts as noun-phrase and verb-phrase (the basic syntax of the English language). Figures 10.13a–c present crude but useful examples of the possibilities of parsing. Part 10.13a shows a combination of a leap and its tonal resolution, followed by a stepwise progression to a traditional cadence. A simple progression in 10.13b demonstrates potential harmonic analysis. In 10.13c, a 12-tone row shows aspects of interval dependence. Note that all similar intervals have the same analysis. The letter/number combinations show repetition and variation of intervals in the relevant series.

Parsing music requires that the language equivalents have meanings and that rules will restrict usage. Figure 10.14a lists one possible set. In this case, the initial symbol may only be followed by the symbol in the corresponding list. In 10.14b, a motive followed by three parsed phrases demonstrates how these rules produce examples of style syntax.

This gives an example of simple parsing and the varieties of syntactically correct replications of simple phrases. Note that each of the last three is an extended version of the first. Musical parsing may be straightforward variations or complex projections.

Simple dictionaries require only that one or more numbers (representing defined parameters of the composition) be assigned to the current definition. The fewer the possibilities, the more restrictive the composing process. For example (a1 'entry (4 3 2 1 –2 – 1 –3)) (a2 'entry '(– 3 2 – 1 – 2 – 2 3)) (a3 'entry '(1 – 2 2 3 – 3)) rudimentarily demonstrates entries for one set of musical "words." This dictionary example is elastic and useful for testing. It restricts motion to small intervals.

```
(a)     (a1 = (c1 c2 o1 o2 o3 s1 s2))
            (a2 = (c1 c2 c3 o3 s2 s3))
            (a3 = (c2 c3 s3))
        (c1 = (a1 a2 a3 02 03))
            (c2 = (a1 a2 a3 o3))
            (c3 = (o2 o3 a2 a3))
        (o1 = (a1 a2 a3 c1 c2 c3 s1))
            (o2 = (a2 a3 c1 c2 c3 s1 s2 s3))
            (o3 = (a3 c2 c3 s2 s3))
        (s1 = (a1 a2 a3 o1 o2 o3))
            (s2 = (a2 a3 o1 o2 o3))
            (s3 = (a3 o2 o3))
```

Figure 10.14. Examples of symbolic musical parsing through a linguistic rules-base.

```
(b)     (o1 c2 a3 s3)=(o1 a1 c2 a1 s2 a3 c3 a2 s3 o3)
            (a1 o1 c1 o2  c2 a3 s3)
            (a1 o1 c2 o3 a3 s3 a3 s3)
```

Since there may be many correct next intervals, the order of possibilities in the dictionary will have significant influence. Reordering, unless the process occurs by keyboard input, requires biasing. This can obviously be random or based on some mathematical formula. The Fibonacci series or golden section (the series adds each of the two preceding numbers: 1, 1, 2, 3, 5, 8, 13 . . . ∞) has proven very successful.

Figure 10.15 gives an overview of one possible syntax relevant to sentence parsing in English. The legend of figure 10.16 shows only one of the several possibilities for representing hierarchical structure. Hierarchy ascends through section and movement to the work's surface with structural relationships at each level. The system's self-similar (discussed further in fractals at the end of this section) concepts in linear and vertical structuring provide logical skeletal frames on which to fabricate musical phrases. The musical example shows one possible translation of the phrase above it.

In the author's implementation of a LISP-based linguistic composing program (EMI), the system may have any type of style dictionary. Figure 10.17 shows a fragment of music created from a J. S. Bach dictionary. Figure 10.18 provides an example of an author-initiated composition (*Cradle Falling* for mixed ensemble) using the EMI system in various composer configurations.

Figure 10.19 shows how one composition system operates. This algorithmic layout of the various components move from the composer's input to the final result. Usually these are associated with building and discovering patterns in data and forming definitions from these recognitions. The program then proceeds to create further data.

Figure 10.15. Parse tree in English.

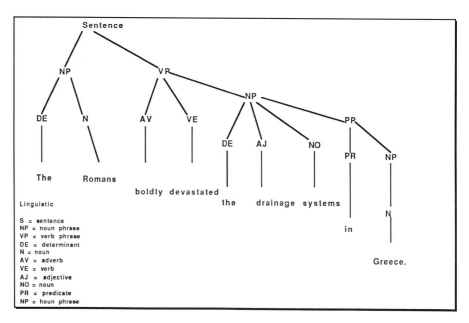

Linguistic

S = sentence
NP = noun phrase
VP = verb phrase
DE = determinant
N = noun
AV = adverb
VE = verb
AJ = adjective
NO = noun
PR = predicate
NP = noun phrase

Figure 10.16. A parse tree using identifiers and musical example of computation.

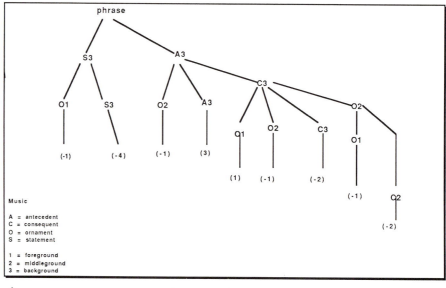

Music

A = antecedent
C = consequent
O = ornament
S = statement

1 = foreground
2 = middleground
3 = background

Figure 10.17. Example of the use of linguistics in music: a machine-composed Bach example.

Figure 10.18. A cybernetically composed work (with the author): *Cradle Falling.*

Fred Lerdahl and Ray Jackendoff (see Bibliography) have created what they term a "generative grammar for tonal music" which incorporates a number of linguistically associated approaches to certain musical styles. Figure 10.20 presents their "well-formedness" rules based on musical "surface," and possible underlying analyses (based on linguistic principles). Figure 10.21 demonstrates their "layer" approach to Beethoven's "Tempest" Sonata, Opus 31, No. 2. Here only the most important and critical material survives to the last (bottom) layer of the analysis. Primary material is shown (in the toplevel parsing) as initial splinters from main lines while secondary and tertiary material is represented by angular departures.

Figure 10.22 shows a parser developed by K. S. Fu for syntax analysis of programmed languages. It is a top-down parsing algorithm consisting of generation and backtracking sub-algorithms which can systematically trace out the programmed grammar of strings (lists of letters surrounded by double quotes ["]). This is used here to show parallel activity for linguistic application in fields other than music or language.

Graph grammars, especially context-driven grammars (inclusive of semantics), encourage pattern recognition and have been applied extensively in many diverse areas such as biology, chemistry and economics. These grammars, to a degree, expand reductive mathematical processes by providing semantics to otherwise context-free environments.

Grammars such as these provide basic grist from which computers may draw material for the creation of musically useful results, and ensure that the results of composition will not be random. Connecting with nature in this way also suggests that all things are connected in some very special ways attractive to some composers

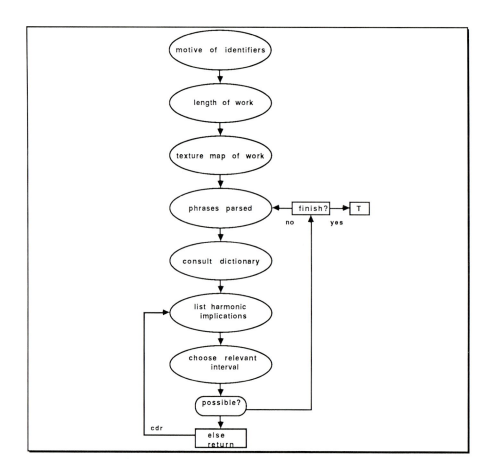

Figure 10.19. A block diagram of one approach to linguistic composition.

who decry the continued specialization of the sciences and arts. They appear reasonable directions since the composers involved in linguistics, artificial intelligence, and cybernetics have already crossed over into other fields and are not hesitant to add yet another to their interdisciplinary research.

Fractals (so named by their creator Benoit Mendelbrot) offer further variations for modeling musical composition. These are roughly defined as reticular structures which imitate themselves at succeedingly larger and smaller levels. Self-similar by nature, they are found in many real-world (life and lifeless) objects. Many trees, for example, have their branch and root structures implanted in the vein structures of their leaves. Shore lines can best be defined in terms of fractal relations.

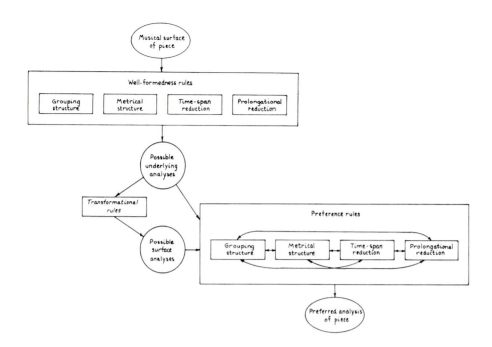

When analyzing the form and shape of each sonic *event* following these "quasi-phonetic" procedures, composers may utilize similar models. Each level of the work, beginning with any sonic *event,* resembles the next layer so as to create a musical fractal. The exactness of each level may be as perfect or as "fuzzy" as the composer requires. Hence, the first sound of a given work may genetically contain the germ of the entire work though it may not be fully perceived by the listener at that point. Motives mold around the amplitude characteristics of sonic *events,* with phrases paralleling motives, periods, sections, and full works. Composers may connect the larger differentials between musical strata: timbre, structure, time, etc.

Inference Engines

Inferences imply deduction of new facts about something based on knowledge which does not specifically contain the information. As an example, consider that "Nipper" is a cat and that cats are mammals. We can make a simple deduction based on this information: "Bob" is also a cat: therefore, "Bob" is a mammal. This example also demonstrates "chaining techniques" which are utilized in some form in almost all artificial intelligence programs. In the following "chain," information about a radio can be stored: object << electric << tunable << radio. We can now be assured, if the chain is correct, that a radio belongs to a group of objects that are tunable and electric. Now, assigning computer to object (i.e., object << computer) allows us to infer nothing. However, stating that computer is electric allows for a further deduction: object << electric << computer. We have gained a piece of new information.

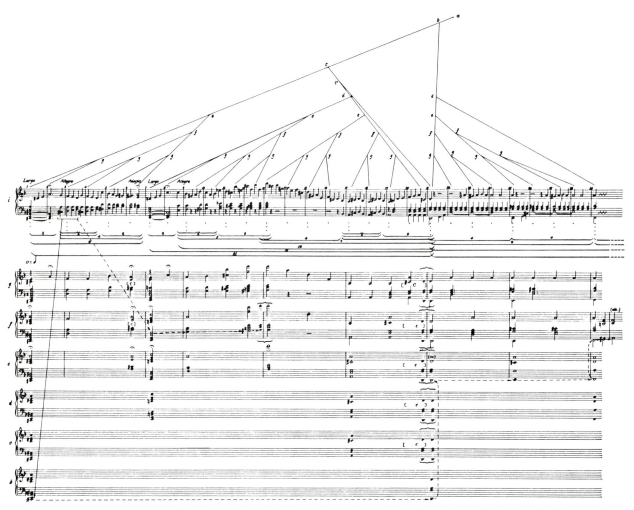

Figure 10.21. Fred Lerdahl and Ray Jackendoff's analysis of Beethoven's "Tempest" Sonata, Opus 31, No. 2. From "A Generative Theory of Tonal Music." By Fred Lerdahl and Ray Jackendoff. Printed by the MIT Press (1983). Permission granted. All rights reserved.

Inferential structures abound in the world of music. When a 'cello is played, for example, the timbre excites chaining procedures which inform the audience that it: is a stringed instrument, performer sits with it between his legs, sits to the right of the stage in orchestras, Casals' instrument, Bach wrote 'cello suites for it, etc. Some of the deductions are the results of memories of learned information and don't really count as new information. As well, most are reasonably uninteresting and uninformative. However, timbre has some very useful corollaries when, for example, a computer-synthesized sound *resembles* a 'cello. Here, the human ear and mind must access stored chains of data about the attacks of harmonics, the delay characteristics of reverberant 'cello fundamentals, etc., even though the sound may continue for a minute without a hint of necessary elements such as bow changes or extraneous imperfections found regularly in real performances of instruments.

One of the many ways LISP works with inferential structure is by using *objects*. Objects which have certain qualities belong to classes of objects, all of which share the same description but not necessarily the same values. For example, a 'cello C♯ belongs to a class (pitch) of notes that has certain frequency characteristics with all of those in its class. However, a C♯ on the clarinet differs in many profound ways. The 'cello *sound* while it plays the C♯ shares elements with all other 'cello sounds. Hence that 'cello C♯ belongs to many classes of objects (here pitch and timbre), all of which overlap to some degree. This is called object oriented programming.

A frequently used example should clarify further how objects can be used for memory and deduction while belonging to many classes simultaneously. Imagine that a mechanic wishes first to fix his car and then to fix his refrigerator. One trick to remember the steps involved in doing both similar but different tasks would be to put wet green paint on his hands while he repaired the car. When finished he would have a coded record of (1) which tools he used for the job, and (2) the order based on the amount of paint left on each one. If he repeated the process using red paint for the refrigerator, he would have a similar record. But he would also have something else: a list of tools that were required for both jobs. He might infer from this that some tools have more universal uses than others and create a new class of general purpose objects. After several such operations he could create a purchase-class of objects (absolute necessities to have for any repair job) and a borrow-object class (ones he would like to have but which are only needed for specialized uses and hence may be borrowed from another person when the repair is made).

Some languages, principally *prolog,* are designed as chaining processes. LISP, however, simply has it as one of many options available. In either case, the process usually involves parentheses that define characteristics of objects and rules about them. Question marks almost universally represent unknown parts of equations. For example, (animal horse) (horse name) (name Bill) links three characteristics together. Querying the process by direct means, e.g., (? horse) = animal, achieves non-chained data. Asking more difficult questions, however, such as (? animal Bill) provides a structural inference that since Bill is the name of a horse who is an animal means that Bill is therefore an animal even though the explicit fact is not in the database. Called unification, such techniques may be forward or backward driven. When a complete program is built on these techniques, it is said to have an "inference engine."

In music, inference and chaining techniques can be useful when used in relation to "message passing." In LISP, or for that matter, any object-oriented language, messages may be sent between any object and another regardless of where they exist in the system or work. Usually these follow the concept that *if* some value is exceeded, *then* it implies effects elsewhere *or* it remains only a local phenomenon. If, for example, a musical object's pitch exceeds a certain dynamic the implication for the remainder of the passage may suggest that other performers will also be slightly

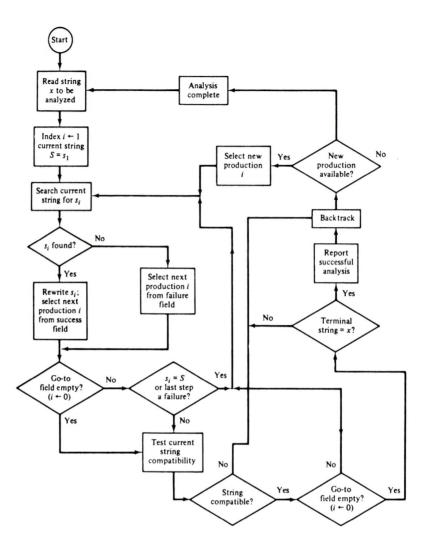

Figure 10.22. A programmed grammar with a syntax of programming languages. King Sun Fu, *Syntactic Pattern Recognition and Applications*, Copyright 1982, p. 192. Reprinted by permission of Prentice-Hall, Inc., Englewood Cliffs, New Jersey.

Figure 10.23. Two phrases with different performance implications.

louder than previous. Musicians make such complicated inferences continually while playing. Contextually juggling dynamics is but one of the numerous ways in which music requires inference engines.

In actual computer code, however, the business of mirroring such complex issues in terms of mechanically understandable logic is very difficult. Retaining the 'cello and dynamics as examples, Figure 10.23 should serve as a good reference to this complexity. This example contains two solo 'cello passages imagined in the context of a full orchestral work. Remembering that the C♯ already belongs to a number of classes (see first part of section), note that it now fits into the classes of loud, phrase, legato, orchestral, and many other classes as well. Constraints from each of these are remarkable. What if the orchestra plays louder than it should? How does this compare with the solo flute playing the same melody in the second phrase? What does the conductor want the performer to do? These are all relevant questions that performers face regularly. A machine, on the other hand, unless it is instructed to do otherwise, will simply iterate the passage exactly each time this program is addressed. Inference engines can, however, by allowing complex messages to be sent from the flutist, the conductor, the other members of the imagined orchestra, combine to inform the 'cello object C♯ that it should be louder to compensate (or softer should the flute performance takes precedence over balance, etc.).

Current Programs and Research

At the present time, many computer-assisted composition programs are emerging, particularly in the microcomputer market. These often border on legitimate AI potential. Most are based on straightforward random and improvisatory functions rather than truly intelligent programs. Of these, *M,* written by David Zicarelli, Joel Chadabe, John Offenhartz and Antony Widoff, has proven successful. Dubbed "the intelligent composing and performing system," *M* stores composer defined musical material as patterns and varies these according to such characteristics as order, orchestration, and density. As with most of the programs mentioned herein, *M* has been written for the Macintosh line of Apple computers. Figure 10.24 shows a sample screen from the *M* program.

Jam Factory, another program from Intelligent Music, follows more of an improvisatory structure based on an interactive sequencer-type system. Billed as a "real-time improvisation enhancement and performance system," users may work with the program while it is performing (real-time capabilities). Neither *M* nor *Jam Factory* have any real AI applications. However, they both have powerful algorithms which could serve as a template upon which an intelligence could reside.

Music Mouse, created by Laurie Spiegel, turns the Macintosh into what the publishers call "an intelligent instrument." The program utilizes the computer's "mouse" and allows the user to control a wide variety of sequencing note formations by physically moving the cursor while it is performing. The keyboard can then be used to control volume, tempo, tone control, pitch collection, transposition, and various MIDI parameters. The principal variables on the instrument are tempo and articulation and not pitch or loudness. *Music Mouse* is an example of computer-assisted improvisation, automating parts of the process and leaving users free to shape and direct the flow of the music. Like *Music Mouse, Instant Music* (for the Apple IIGS computer) requires holding down the button on the mouse while performing a work. Moving the cursor across the screen adds improvisational (called the "mousejam") changes to the music.

Cybernetic Composer, on the other hand, comes very close to legitimate "intelligence." Charles Ames developed this program for stylistic imitation of various popular music (jazz, Latin jazz, and rock) and, using a MIDI interface, it performs unique compositions faithful to the conventions of these styles. The program, not available commercially at this point, takes a great deal of time to compose a work. The results, however, have been encouraging and successful.

Figure 10.24. Screen from *M,* from Intelligent Music. Permission granted by Intelligent Music, Albany, New York.

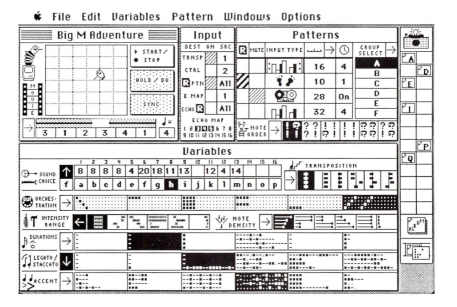

Linda Sorisio has developed a program called *THE MUSES* (acronym for THEory of MUSic Expert Systems). Primarily devised for music theorists, *THE MUSES* has AI potential for composition as well. Written on an IBM mainframe, the program utilizes nonlinguistic pattern recognition for the analysis of music in many styles. Sounds are typically entered into *THE MUSES* through a MIDI port by electronic instruments. Then, the program can apply many different timbral and pitch modifications before playback and analysis begins. It was designed to use AI processes in creating intelligent courseware for graduate students in music. It is written in IBM's own expert system tool for mainframes: the Expert System Environment utilizing Turbo Pascal. The intention was to devise a kind of computerized music theory professor.

Choice of language has created a difficulty in this field since so many varieties exist, even within the LISP language itself. Like so many of the early attempts at consolidation, the development of commonLISP has simply created more (rather than less) versions (dialects) of itself. As a result, even when programs are written in LISP, they are not necessarily compatible on other machines or other implementations of LISP. Hence, many new programs, both commercial and academic, have been written in C, Pascal or even BASIC, which to date have commonality. Different versions of these languages tend to have various computational speeds but have essentially the same top-level protocol. This has caused some composers, developers, and institutions to create new languages specifically designed to meet the general needs of composers and AI researchers in new music.

HMSL (Hierarchical Music Programming Language), designed by Larry Polansky, David Rosenboom and Phil Burke at the Center for Contemporary Music at Mills College in Oakland, California, creates a flexible and highly general environment, whose data structures and high-level programming tools provide users with the resources to realize works and experiments in a wide variety of styles (i.e., a "non-stylistic" based language). The language has real and non-real-time environments and has been dubbed a WYSIWYH (what-you-see-is-what-you hear) language. Morphologies ("morphs") are hierarchical approaches where a series of points may represent single data or collections of data (such as pitches, motives, phrases, etc.). *HMSL* is itself written in Forth-83. The *MASC* (Meta Adaptive Synthesis and Computational) language also has artificial intelligence applications, although at the time of writing had not been fully developed, tested or made available to the public.

Experiments in Music Intelligence (EMI) employs a linguistic approach to music intelligence. It solves the dialect riddle in LISP by implementations in many different versions at the same time. Hence, users need not rewrite code to fit their own particular dialect of LISP. The program employs the workstation shown in Figure 10.25. The project that operates this workstation is described in the following outline:

Experiments in Music Intelligence (EMI) is an object-oriented system written in LISP. It was designed to assist composers in their creative work. Based on natural language processing augmented transition network parsing (NLP-ATN), it assigns

Figure 10.25. One possible workstation involving AI, sampling, MIDI and natural language processing.

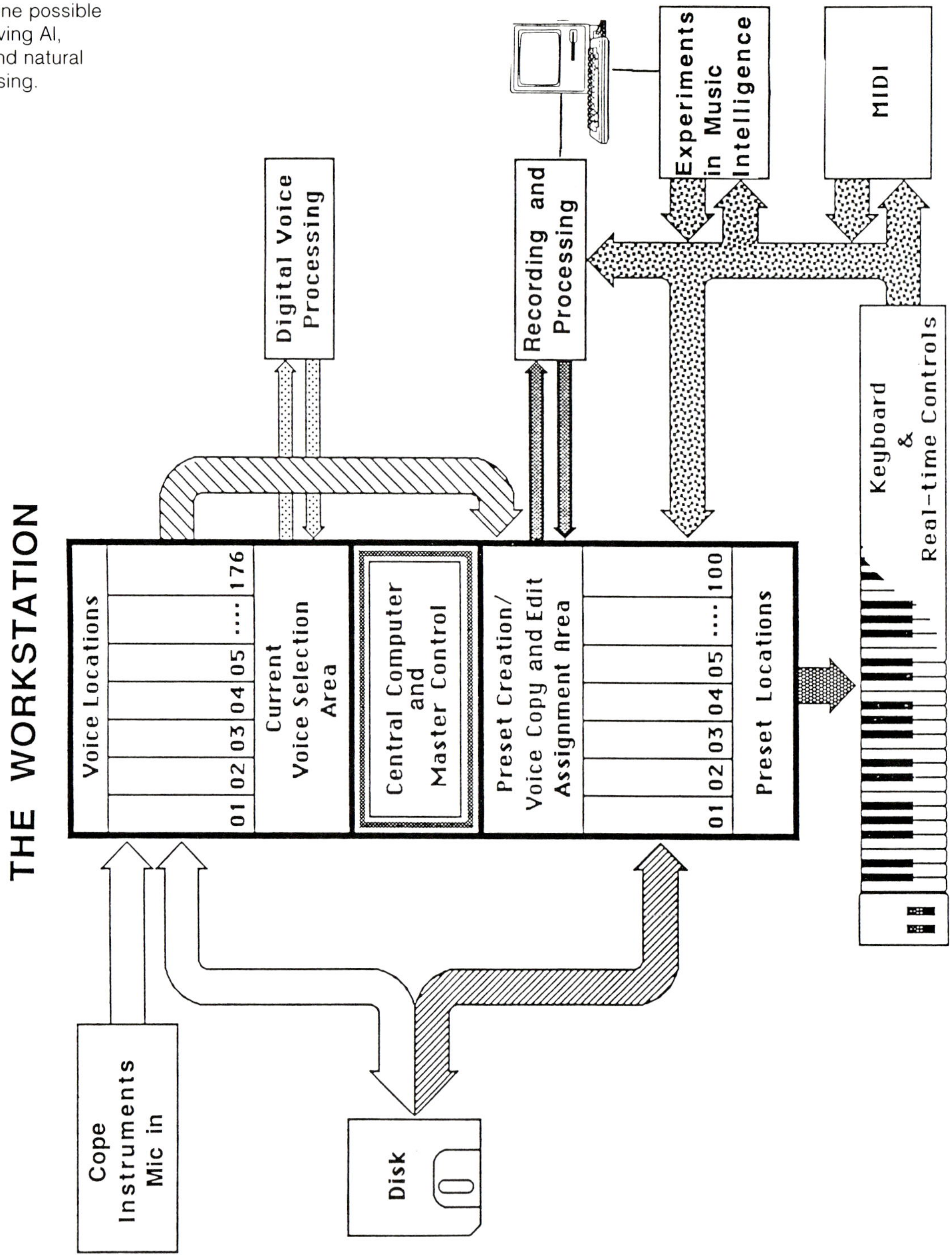

syntax definitions to dictionaries containing rules about when and where intervals may exist. A motive engine guarantees that composition will produce logical structures. Composers may explore many gradations of machine versus human control. Message passing and inheritance add depth by allowing the implications of a choice in one part of the composition to affect the nature of another (*non-linear composition*). The use of *k-lines* (knowledge-lines) for timbral development significantly reduces sampling and synthesizing rates by accurately tuning harmonic coordinates to conform to "remembered" object *events*. Musical examples range from imitations of styles to unique man/machine collaborations.

Since the principal investigator in the project (the author) has a predilection for acoustic sounds, the particular program involves an *EMAX* (see Chapter 9 on digital music) sampler which is then controlled by the system using LISP. Keyboards and real-time control (à la synthesizer) are still available during the composing process. These (and many other) approaches are generally noncommercial and have been utilized purely for research and as aids to composition.

Otto Laske, one of the major proponents of musical intelligence as related to computers and cybernetics over the past few years, sums up many current views when he states:

> The question is: How can we transfer human musical expertise to a computer and represent it within the machine? How can we construct musical knowledge bases incrementally? How can we get the machine to explain its musical reasoning to a human being? There is nothing peculiar about musical expertise that would force us to use different methods from those used in artificial intelligence applications today to solve these very legitimate problems.[5]

Many are further convinced that by studying the problem of style through applications of AI and cybernetic approaches (as well as defining what music and style really are) may have significant impact on the development of a new universal style.

(For information on vectoral analysis and procedures see Chapter 1.)

(For information on vectoral analysis and procedures see Chapter 1.)

Vectoral Analysis: Iannis Xenakis: *Atrées*

1. Historical Background: Iannis Xenakis was born in Braïla, Roumania on May 29, 1922. Both of his parents were Greeks and he currently holds French citizenship. He lived for ten years near the Danube before he moved with his family to Greece and obtained an education at a private college in Spetsai. He entered the Athens Polytechnic school majoring in engineering but soon became heavily involved with the Resistance. On January 1, 1945,

---

5. C. Roads, *Composers and the Computer* (Los Altos, CA: William Kaufmann, Inc., 1985).

Figure 10.26. Iannis Xenakis. Photo courtesy of Indiana University.

he was badly wounded and blinded in his left eye. In 1947, Xenakis met Honegger, Milhaud, and Messiaen in Paris with the latter providing him much encouragement to go into music. He also met LeCorbusier, the architect, who accepted him as a collaborator (using Xenakis's engineering talents). The two worked closely together on many projects including the Baghdad stadium and the convent of La Tourette. In 1958, he helped with the design of the Philips pavilion at the Brussels Exposition (discussed in Chapter 7 on electroacoustic music) which developed further his ideas about architecture, acoustics, and music, ideas he finds inexorably linked. In 1966, he founded EMAMu (Equipe de Mathématique et d'Automatique Musicales) in Paris. He taught at Indiana University (Bloomington) during 1967–72, during which time he founded the Center for Musical Mathematics and Automation (similar to EMAMu). Most recently, he toured in America and Europe giving classes in composition and attending peformances of his music.

His works center around mathematical models and are often composed, per se, by machines (automated music). His writings (particularly *Formalized Music*) represent a standard reference for work relating to the early developments of computer composition (termed cybernetic music in this book). He has used probability laws, stochastics, Markovian chains, game theory, group theory, set theory, Boolean algebra, and Gaussian distributions as formalized projections and "galaxies." His music typically contains thick textures with many diverse elements sounding at once. Sometimes, as in *Metastasis* where the textures are sliding glissandi, techniques are limited to one or two effects. More often, however, his computer programs will produce variations with astounding contrasts. As well, some works contain extended silences punctuated by seemingly random points or fragments of sound.

2. Overview: The *stochastic* and mathematical approach to music as represented in the music of Iannis Xenakis is often deeply rooted in a chance framework. Arbitrary materials feed into an extremely determinate composition system. The resultant structure is composer indeterminacy written out in traditional notation for predictable results. Xenakis describes his concepts and procedures in his book *Formalized Music:*

As a result of the impasse in serial music, as well as other causes, I originated in 1954 a music constructed from the principle of indeterminism; two years later I named it "Stochastic Music." The laws of the calculus of probabilities entered composition through musical necessity. But other paths also led to the same stochastic crossroads—first of all, natural events such as the collision of hail or rain with hard surfaces, or the song of cicadas in a summer field. These sonic events are made out of thousands of isolated sounds; this multitude of sounds, seen as a totality, is a new sonic event. This mass event is articulated and forms a plastic mold of time, which itself follows aleatory and stochastic laws. If one then wishes to form a large mass of point-notes, such as string pizzicati, one must know these mathematical laws, which, in any case, are no more than a tight and concise expression of chains of logical reasoning. Everyone has observed the sonic phenomena of a political crowd of dozens of hundreds of thousands of people. The human river shouts a slogan in a uniform rhythm. Then another slogan springs from the head of the demonstration; it spreads toward the tail, replacing the first. A wave of transition thus passes from the head to the tail. . . . The statistical laws of these events, separated from their political or moral context, are the same as those of the cicadas or the rain. They are the laws of the passage from complete order to total disorder in a continuous or explosive manner. They are stochastic laws.[6]

Some have argued that Xenakis's music is not indeterminate at all. Bernard Jacobson has written:

He uses chance, but his music leaves nothing to chance. This is not the paradox it might seem. To Xenakis—as indeed, to most philosophers—chance itself is a scientific concept. Central among the scientific laws he has applied to music is Bernoulli's Law of large numbers, which provides that as the number of repetitions of a given "chance" trial (such as flipping a coin) increases, so the probability that the results will tend to a determinate end approaches certainty.[7]

---

6. Iannis Xenakis, *Formalized Music* (Bloomington: Indiana University Press, 1971), p. 9.
7. From the liner notes to Nonesuch Records H-71201 (*Akrat·· Pithoprakta*).

Figure 10.27. Some of the mathematical theory behind Xenakis' work (p. 142, *Formalized Music,* see bibliography).

$$(0 \le x \le x_0) = \int_0^{x_0} f(x)\, dx = 1 - e^{-cx_0} = F(x_0),$$

$$F(x_0) = \text{prob.}\, (0 \le y \le y_0) = y_0$$

$$1 - e^{-cx_0} = y_0$$

$$x_0 = -\frac{\ln\,(1 - y_0)}{c}$$

$$f(x)\, dx = ce^{-cx}\, dx.$$

Iannis Xenakis, using FORTRAN IV programming with the IBM-7090, has produced data for his free *stochastic music* (detailed in his *Formalized Music*). A number of his works (for traditional instruments) were composed with the aid of high-speed computations of probability theory made accessible by computer application. These works include *ST/10-1, 080262* (1962, with first performance on May 24 of that year at the headquarters of IBM in France), *ST/48–1, 240162* (for large orchestra), *Atrées* (for ten soloists, 1962), and *Morsima-Amorsima* (for violin, 'cello, bass, and piano, 1962; the processes are described in the performance notes for this work). Pitches were calculated by the electronic brain 7090 IBM in Paris in obedience to a special stochastic (probabilist) "programme" devised by Xenakis. This was derived from the thesis of "Minimum Rules of Composition," which he had already formulated in 1958 in *Achorripsis*. The "programme" is a complex of stochastic laws which the composer had been introducing into musical composition for a number of years. The computer defines all the sounds of a sequence, previously calculated, including the time of occurrence, kind of timbre (*arco, pizzicato, glissando,* etc.), instrument, pitch, the gradient of *glissando* (where it occurs), and the duration and dynamic of the emission of sound.[8]

Atrées (ST/10-3,060962) was completed in 1962 (the last 6 digits represent that date: 6, September, 1962) and composed with the same computer program known as ST (for stochastic) used for ST/10 (1962 10

8. See Iannis Xenakis, *Morsima-Amorsima* (Boosey & Hawkes, 1967). From notes to the score.

the number of performers), Morsima-Amorsima, Achorripsis and ST/48–1, 240162. The work is 15 minutes long, following a free form, at times dramatic, often halting and formidable. Pitches are fixed by determining the mean density of notes occurring during preconceived sequence lengths. Dynamic intensities derive from a chart of 44 values based on the dynamics ppp, p, f, and ff with all other values existing only briefly within crescendi and diminuendi, giving the work a constant feel of movement (since 40 of the 44 values have such changing dynamics) towards or away from these guideposts. Figure 10.27 gives an example of some of the mathematical theory behind this work.

The first formula represents an elementary law of probability (a density function) with the others showing the logic of producing a distribution function which can be translated into machine language. These programs were run on an IBM 7090 computer using punch cards, a process which could take (in the early 1960s) up to 6 months. The composer further ran many tests for errors in logic and orthography before actually translating his work into music notation. Figures 10.28 and 10.29 show examples of the Fortran IV language employment and the provisional results from one phase of the analysis program.

This work, like *Metastasis,* aptly demonstrates Xenakis's penchant for glissandi in his music. It also clearly emphasizes the fact that he uses the numbers (statistics) separate from musical meaning (i.e., the computer simply processes numbers). The composer relates to this with his comment: "There exists in all the arts what we may call rationalism in the etymological sense: the search for proportion" and "Now everything that is rule or repeated constraint is part of the mental machine."[9] He further refers to his use of science and art: "Computers resolve logical problems by heuristic methods. But computers are not really responsible for the introduction of mathematics into music; rather it is mathematics that makes use of the computer in composition.[10]

3. Orchestration Techniques: *Atrées* is scored for clarinet, bass clarinet, 2 French horns, percussion, 2 violins, viola and 'cello (though there are various versions). The percussionist employs maracas, suspended cymbals, a gong, 5 temple-blocks, 4 tom-toms and a vibraphone. Determination of which instruments play together at any given time is achieved by breaking them into timbre classes. For example, there exist classes for flute/clarinet, brass, struck-strings (*col legno*), bowed-strings, and glissando. Effects are treated similarly to instruments. As an example, the texture densities provided by the chart in Figure 10.30 show 8 classes, four of which are instruments (played normally), with the other four being effects.

The vertical numbers refer to percentages (summing to 100) of each of the eight categories of timbres which contribute to the overall textural shape. The harp and clarinet have the least and most (respectively) deviation (2 and 26 percents). By and large, the patterns tend to imitate one another

9. Xenakis, Iannis,"Free Stochastic Music from the Computer," in *Cybernetics, Art and Ideas,* ed. by Jasia Reichardt, p. 124.
10. Ibid.

```
C     PROGRAM FREE STOCHASTIC MUSIC   (FORTRAN IV)                      XEN    6
C                                                                       XEN    7
C     GLOSSARY OF THE PRINCIPAL ABBREVIATIONS                           XEN    8
C                                                                       XEN    9
C     A - DURATION OF EACH SEQUENCE IN SECONDS                          XEN    9
C     A10,A20,A17,A35,A30 - NUMBERS FOR GLISSANDO CALCULATION           XEN   10
C     ALEA - PARAMETER USED TO ALTER THE RESULT OF A SECOND RUN WITH THEXEN   11
C     SAME INPUT DATA                                                   XEN   12
C     ALFA(3) - THREE EXPRESSIONS ENTERING INTO THE THREE SPEED VALUES  XEN   13
C     OF THE SLIDING TONES ( GLISSANDI )                                XEN   14
C     ALIM - MAXIMUM LIMIT OF SEQUENCE DURATION A                       XEN   15
C     (AMAX(I),I=1,KTR) TABLE OF AN EXPRESSION ENTERING INTO THE        XEN   16
C     CALCULATION OF THE NOTE LENGTH IN PART 8                          XEN   17
C     BF - DYNAMIC FORM NUMBER. THE LIST IS ESTABLISHED INDEPENDENTLY   XEN   18
C     OF THIS PROGRAM AND IS SUBJECT TO MODIFICATION                    XEN   19
C     DELTA - THE RECIPROCAL OF THE MEAN DENSITY OF SOUND EVENTS DURING XEN   20
C     A SEQUENCE OF DURATION A                                          XEN   21
C     (E(I,J),I=1,KTR,J=1,KTE) - PROBABILITIES OF THE KTR TIMBRE CLASSESXEN   22
C     INTRODUCED AS INPUT DATA, DEPENDING ON THE CLASS NUMBER I=KR AND  XEN   23
C     ON THE POWER J=U OBTAINED FROM V3*EXPF(U)=DA                       XEN   24
C     EPSI - EPSILON FOR ACCURACY IN CALCULATING PN AND E(I,J),WHICH    XEN   25
C     IT IS ADVISABLE TO RETAIN.                                        XEN   26
C     (GN(I,J),I=1,KTR,J=1,KTS) - TABLE OF THE GIVEN LENGTH OF BREATH   XEN   27
C     FOR EACH INSTRUMENT, DEPENDING ON CLASS I AND INSTRUMENT J        XEN   28
C     GTNA - GREATEST NUMBER OF NOTES IN THE SEQUENCE OF DURATION A     XEN   29
C     GTNS - GREATEST NUMBER OF NOTES IN KW LOOPS                       XEN   30
C     (HAMIN(I,J),HAMAX(I,J),HBMIN(I,J),HBMAX(I,J),I=1,KTR,J=1,KTS)     XEN   31
C     TABLE OF INSTRUMENT COMPASS LIMITS, DEPENDING ON TIMBRE CLASS I   XEN   32
C     AND INSTRUMENT J.   TEST INSTRUCTION 480 IN PART 6 DETERMINES     XEN   33
C     WHETHER THE HA OR THE HB TABLE IS FOLLOWED. THE NUMBER 7 IS       XEN   34
C     ARBITRARY.                                                        XEN   35
C     JW - ORDINAL NUMBER OF THE SEQUENCE COMPUTED.                     XEN   36
C     KNL - NUMBER OF LINES PER PAGE OF THE PRINTED RESULT.KNL=50       XEN   37
C     KR1 - NUMBER IN THE CLASS KR=1 USED FOR PERCUSSION OR INSTRUMENTS XEN   38
C     WITHOUT A DEFINITE PITCH.                                         XEN   39
C     KTE - POWER OF THE EXPONENTIAL COEFFICIENT E SUCH THAT            XEN   40
C     DA(MAX)=V3*(E**(KTE-1))                                           XEN   41
C     KTR - NUMBER OF TIMBRE CLASSES                                    XEN   42
C     KW - MAXIMUM NUMBER OF JW                                         XEN   43
C     KTEST1,TAV1,ETC - EXPRESSIONS USEFUL IN CALCULATING HOW LONG THE  XEN   44
C     VARIOUS PARTS OF THE PROGRAM WILL RUN.                            XEN   45
C     KT1 - ZERO IF THE PROGRAM IS BEING RUN, NONZERO DURING DEBUGGING  XEN   46
C     KT2 - NUMBER OF LOOPS, EQUAL TO 15 BY ARBITRARY DEFINITION.       XEN   47
C     (MODI(IX8),IX8=7,1)  AUXILIARY FUNCTION TO INTERPOLATE VALUES IN  XEN   48
C     THE TETA(256) TABLE (SEE PART 7)                                  XEN   49
C     NA - NUMBER OF SOUNDS CALCULATED FOR THE SEQUENCE A(NA=DA*A)      XEN   50
C     (NT(I),I=1,KTR) NUMBER OF INSTRUMENTS ALLOCATED TO EACH OF THE    XEN   51
C     KTR TIMBRE CLASSES.                                               XEN   52
C     (PN(I,J),I=1,KTR,J=1,KTS),(KTS=NT(I),I=1,KTR) TABLE OF PROBABILITYXEN   53
C     OF EACH INSTRUMENT OF THE CLASS I.                                XEN   54
C     (Q(I),I=1,KTR) PROBABILITIES OF THE KTR TIMBRE CLASSES, CONSIDEREDXEN   55
C     AS LINEAR FUNCTIONS OF THE DENSITY DA.                            XEN   56
C     (S(I),I=1,KTR) SUM OF THE SUCCESSIVE G(I) PROBABILITIES, USED TO  XEN   57
C     CHOOSE THE CLASS KR BY COMPARING IT TO A RANDOM NUMBER X1 (SEE    XEN   58
C     PART 3, LOOP 380 AND PART 5, LOOP 430).                           XEN   59
C     SINA - SUM OF THE COMPUTED NOTES IN THE JW CLOUDS NA, ALWAYS LESS XEN   60
C     THAN GTNS ( SEE TEST IN PART 10 ).                                XEN   61
C     SQPI - SQUARE ROOT OF PI ( 3.14159...)                            XEN   62
C     TA - SOUND ATTACK TIME ABCISSA.                                   XEN   63
C     TETA(256) - TABLE OF THE 256 VALUES OF THE INTEGRAL OF THE NORMAL XEN   64
C     DISTRIBUTION CURVE WHICH IS USEFUL IN CALCULATING GLISSANDO SPEED XEN   65
```

Figure 10.28. The principal glossary of Xenakis' stochastic music writing in FORTRAN IV (p. 145, *Formalized Music,* see bibliography).

N	START	CLASS	INSTRM	PITCH	GLISS1	GLISS2	GLISS3	DURATION	DYNAM
1	0.00	7	1	34.0	0.0	0.0	0.0	0.00	3
2	0.10	10	1	43.2	0.0	0.0	0.0	0.41	50
3	0.11	6	8	81.3	0.0	0.0	0.0	0.63	21
4	0.13	6	3	47.0	0.0	0.0	0.0	0.18	10
5	0.18	1	4	0.0	0.0	0.0	0.0	1.90	29
6	0.25	9	1	48.7	0.0	0.0	0.0	0.51	35
7	0.33	6	7	11.4	0.0	0.0	0.0	0.37	42
8	0.34	9	1	38.1	0.0	0.0	0.0	0.00	59
9	0.40	1	1	0.0	0.0	0.0	0.0	2.20	45
10	0.41	6	9	55.0	0.0	0.0	0.0	1.07	0
11	0.76	6	7	11.5	0.0	0.0	0.0	0.40	7
12	0.90	8	2	23.2	0.0	0.0	0.0	0.00	19
13	1.00	7	2	26.9	0.0	0.0	0.0	0.00	6
14	1.09	10	1	46.2	0.0	0.0	0.0	0.32	57
15	1.09	6	2	68.5	0.0	0.0	0.0	0.71	25
16	1.23	6	3	46.9	0.0	0.0	0.0	0.64	32
17	1.42	6	1	44.0	0.0	0.0	0.0	0.44	1
18	1.57	10	1	36.2	0.0	0.0	0.0	0.22	21
19	1.65	4	2	32.5	0.0	0.0	0.0	1.09	13
20	1.78	6	8	72.6	0.0	0.0	0.0	0.06	60
21	1.92	6	3	38.9	0.0	0.0	0.0	0.55	60
22	1.94	5	1	74.6	71.0	-25.0	-71.0	0.80	62
23	2.18	4	1	32.6	0.0	0.0	0.0	1.50	50
24	2.18	6	6	50.9	0.0	0.0	0.0	0.60	26
25	2.19	1	12	0.0	0.0	0.0	0.0	4.58	24
26	2.20	9	1	49.3	0.0	0.0	0.0	0.02	58
27	2.23	9	1	51.0	0.0	0.0	0.0	0.22	13
28	2.32	7	1	36.9	0.0	0.0	0.0	0.00	43
29	2.33	4	1	31.8	0.0	0.0	0.0	1.38	56
30	2.54	1	6	0.0	0.0	0.0	0.0	0.28	14
31	2.57	11	2	12.2	0.0	0.0	0.0	1.65	40
32	2.71	9	1	48.5	0.0	0.0	0.0	0.37	55
33	2.80	1	5	0.0	0.0	0.0	0.0	1.50	58
34	3.28	5	2	15.4	49.0	5.0	-31.0	0.52	21
35	3.33	1	7	0.0	0.0	0.0	0.0	1.38	8
36	3.38	5	2	47.3	-71.0	-17.0	46.0	1.05	4
37	3.55	10	1	37.6	0.0	0.0	0.0	0.14	24
38	3.56	1	9	0.0	0.0	0.0	0.0	1.30	0
39	3.60	9	1	64.3	0.0	0.0	0.0	0.19	13
40	3.64	12	2	52.2	0.0	0.0	0.0	3.72	9
41	3.65	6	5	59.0	0.0	0.0	0.0	0.83	28
42	3.71	5	3	38.8	25.0	2.0	-15.0	0.00	11
43	3.80	6	8	75.6	0.0	0.0	0.0	0.43	17
44	3.87	6	2	51.5	0.0	0.0	0.0	0.77	57
45	3.89	6	7	12.1	0.0	0.0	0.0	0.39	2
46	4.15	5	2	43.0	-71.0	24.0	71.0	1.16	2
47	4.15	5	1	80.3	36.0	4.0	22.0	0.85	50
48	4.25	9	1	59.9	0.0	0.0	0.0	0.10	10
49	4.31	12	2	40.1	0.0	0.0	0.0	2.49	33
50	4.33	1	10	0.0	0.0	0.0	0.0	0.46	34

Figure 10.29. Provisional results of one phase of the analysis (p. 153, *Formalized Music*, see bibliography).

Figure 10.30. Percents of use utilized in *Atrées* (from *Cybernetics, Art and Ideas,* ed. by Jadis Reichardt, p. 128, see bibliography).

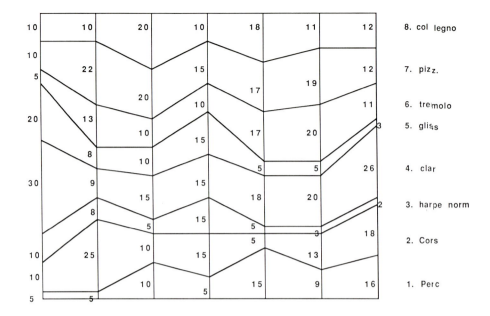

(partially out of necessity) with only the percussion moving somewhat independently at times.

4. Basic Techniques: Much of Xenakis's work with probability derives from a given voice's "memory" of a preceding pitch and choosing then from a given compass within a prescribed set of semitones (typically 86). This is given by the formula in Figure 10.31 where P_z is the probability of the interval z chosen from the compass s. Lengths of notes and even sliding speeds of glissandi are similarly determined. Part of an early flow chart of work in the ST series provides an example of the composer's processes (shown in figure 10.32). The random number is used as a selection number from a table of correct possibilities. The formula creates values as a result of system-defined determinants.

Figure 10.31. One probability formula used by Xenakis.

$$P_z = 2/S\ (1 - Z/S)DZ$$

5. Vertical Models: Figure 10.33 shows the first bar of *Atrées ST/10–1, 080262*.
   All 12 pitches exist here but clearly no rows or established protocol for their use. Centers (e.g., G♯ and E near the beginning) occur and pass so quickly that the word has little meaning. In fact, pitch itself seems elusive and often unimportant, bowing to the rapidity of the changing harmonic rhythm. The texture varies on a microscale; that is, from instant to instant one is constantly provided with *change*. Polyrhythms abound (i.e., 6 against 5 against 4, etc., in the first half measure). Effects (harmonics, pizzicato,

358   Chapter 10

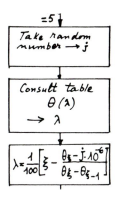

Figure 10.32. Example of aspects of Xenakis' algorithm for random processes.

tremolo, glissando) occur simultaneously or in near proximity. Dynamics are volatile (subject to changes every note) and mixed in a nontraditional manner. Often this causes some instruments not to be heard during a performance. This level of complexity abounds in this and other of Xenakis's works, no doubt a reflection of the processes which contributed to its composition.

6. Horizontal Models: Figure 10.33 also provides an example of melodic order in *Atrées*. Only two melodic intervals are seconds (A–G♯ in the clarinet and C–C♯ in the viola) with most larger than an octave. Even when factoring in a pitch-class component, one finds few seconds or thirds. The pointillism thus achieved, however, is often clouded by the complex counterpoint taking place. It is difficult to follow any line independently from the others. Since each voice often changes timbres as well as pitches, this further confuses the issue.

7. Style: *Atrées ST/10–1, 080262* is a stochastically determined work based on probability calculations using an IBM 7090 computer. The complex process of developing programs for the work is as important as the piece itself. Writing the formulae, the resultant programs, and the charts of data from which the computer may choose possible notes requires intense scrutiny. Debugging the large functions properly is crucial if the process is to succeed. Translating the resultant data to music also claims great time and care to avoid mistakes. The result is a complex work demanding of its performers and audience alike. Some critics, confused by the pluralistic societies of new music, have dubbed Xenakis the founder of *maximalism*. Certainly this work, if not in size of orchestration in terms of event numbers per performer, ranks high in size.

This work, while similar to Webern's *Symphonie* in terms of pointillism, varies with respect to texture and lack of premeditated pitch control. It is most different, however, when compared to Oliveros's *Sonic Meditations XIII* which, by virtue of its outspoken simplicity and lack of tangible movement, represents the opposite extreme from Xenakis. Interestingly, however, *Atrées* holds more conceptual ties with

Figure 10.33. First few bars from *ST/10-1, 080262.*

Oliveros's work: for example, both were conceived with a high degree of indeterminacy yet they have very predictable results in performance. Comparisons to the Vectoral Analyses found in Chapters 2 and 5 prove very revealing, especially in the former case where apparently opposite approaches to control reveal comparatively similar results.

Bibliography

Further Readings*

Allen, John. *Anatomy of LISP*. New York: McGraw-Hill, 1978. A good general account of the LISP language and its applications to artificial intelligence.

Ames, Charles. "Automated Composition in Retrospect: 1956–1986." *Leonardo: Journal of the International Society for Science, Technology and the Arts*. Oxford: Pergamon Press, 1987. This is an extraordinarily well written account of various aspects of automation in music. It actually creates a better update of Hiller's article "Music Composed with Computers: A Historical Survey" than Hiller's own article avowing such. The initialization of computer (and other) generation of music includes the famed *Push Button Bertha* written by "Datatron."

———. "Crystals: Recursive Structures in Automated Composition." *Computer Music Journal,* Volume 6, Number 3, 1982 p. 46.

———. "Notes on *Undulant*," *Interface*, 12, No. 3 (1983):505.

———. "AI in Music." *Encyclopedia of Artificial Intelligence*. New York: John Wiley and Sons, 1987, pp. 638–42. A good introduction to the subject of artificial intelligence and music composition.

Austin, Larry and Eugene DeLisa. "Modeling Processes of Musical Invention." *Proceedings of the International Computer Music Conference.* San Francisco: Computer Music Association, 1987, pp. 206–11. While based on Austin's "love of randomness" this piece does present some interesting experiments with definitions of ordering and inversion.

Balzano, Gerald J. "The Group-theoretic Description of 12-Fold and Microtonal Pitch Systems." *Computer Music Journal* 4, No. 4 (Winter 1980):66–84. The author proposes a "cyclic group structure" approach to systematic pitch description. This important piece of research provides useful theoretical backbone for tonal versus non-tonal distinctions.

―――. "What are Musical Pitch and Timbre?" *Music Perception.* 3, No. 3 (Spring 1986):297–314. A review and perspective on Fourier spectral analysis as a determinant for pitch and timbre analysis.

Barbaud, P. "Algorithmic Music." From a trade publication. Paris: Systems Bulletin, 1969.

Baroni, Mario and Callegari, L. editors. *Musical Grammars and Computer Analysis.* Bolognia: Società Italiana di Musicologia, 1984. The printed papers of an Italian conference regarding the linguistic applications of music. The Curtis Roads and Michel Imberty articles (the latter published in Italian) are very important. The overview of the former represents a serious attempt at outlining possible interrelationships between language and music.

Barr, A. and E. Feigenbaum. *Handbook of Artificial Intelligence.* Stanford: Stanford Computer Science Department, 1979. Somewhat outdated at this point, but still a fundamentally sound handbook on generic programs and algorithms for AI research.

Bolognesi, Tommaso. "Automated Composition: Experiments with Self-Similar Music." *Computer Music Journal* 7/1 (Spring 1983):25–36. Excellent though idiosyncratic account of fractal-like experiments in automated music composition.

Caianiello, E. R. *Cybernetic Systems.* London: Research Studies Press, 1984. A classic textbook on this subject. A somewhat removed from the arts but nonetheless useful outline of cybernetics from definition to realization in the form of actual projects.

Carne, E. B. *Artificial Intelligence Techniques.* London: Macmillan, 1965. A basic treatise on the general principles of AI.

Charniak, D. and C. Riesbeck and D. McDermott. *Artificial Intelligence Programming Techniques.* Hillsdale, N.J.: Lawrence Erlbaum Associates, 1979. An excellent beginning text in this field.

Charniak, Eugene, and Drew McDermott. *Introduction to Artificial Intelligence.* Reading, MA: Addison-Wesley Publishing Company, 1984. A revision and simplification of the aforementioned text, this book deals quite effectively with the principles of AI.

Chomsky, Noam. *Aspects of the Theory of Syntax.* Cambridge, MA: MIT Press, 1965. One of the classics of linguistic theory. While it does not broach the subject of music or the arts in general, it does articulate the "augmented transition network" so important in translating parse concepts to digital technology.

―――. *Syntactic Structures.* The Hague: Mouton, 1957. This text (earlier than the one above) set the standard for seminal research in linguistics over the past 30 years.

Clynes, Manfred, ed. *Music, Mind, and Brain.* New York: Penguin Press, 1982. A good collection of articles on musical perception, especially those by Minsky, Lerdahl, and Balzano. The latter piece is particularly important in that it references not only pitch structures but *dynamics.* Minsky's contribution demonstrates his "inclusive" concepts of AI and music.

Cogan, Robert and Pozzi Escot. *Sonic Design, Practice and Problems.* Englewood Cliffs: Prentice-Hall, 1981. While this text is for beginning music students, it represents one of the first attempts to popularize the concept that music is a language and hence has parsing rules following linguistic models.

Cope, David. "Experiments in Music Intelligence." *Proceedings of the International Computer Music Conference.* San Francisco: Computer Music Association, 1987. A brief synopsis of the author's linguistic approach to cybernetic music.

————. "An Expert System for Computer-Assisted Music Composition." *Computer Music Journal* 11/2 (Fall 1987). Briefly described in this chapter. This is a linguistically based program dedicated to ascribing dictionaries and rules-based functions to a motive engine capable of creating imitative music for solving compositional blocks.

Dodge, Charles and Curtis Bahn. "Musical Fractals." *BYTE Magazine,* June 1986, pp. 185–66. An excellent proposal for a fractal approach to composition and analysis.

Dodge, Charles. "Profile of A Musical Fractal." *Proceedings of the 1986 Symposium on the Arts and Technology at Connecticut College.* Shoestring Press, 1987.

Dowling, W. Jay and Dane L. Harwood. *Music Cognition.* New York: Academic Press, Inc., 1986. An excellent book if only for its "cross-cultural" materials and its extensive reference list.

Duisberg, Robert. "On the Role of Affect in Artificial Intelligence and Music." *Perspectives of New Music* 23/1 (Fall-Winter 1984):6–35. One of the best overviews of the field. The author covers all of the literature and experiments in an unbiased and comprehensive manner.

Dewdney, A. K. "Computer Recreations." *Scientific American,* April 1987. This article describes its author's creation: a program called *SOLFEGGIO.* It creates (among other things) examples of correct two-part first species counterpoint.

Ennals, R. *Artificial Intelligence.* West Sussex, England: John Wiley and Sons Ltd., 1985. A good primer on the subject.

Evans, Brian. "Integration of Music and Graphics through Algorithmic Congruence." *Proceedings of the International Computer Music Conference.* San Francisco: Computer Music Association, 1987, pp. 17–24. This description of the creation of the *Maria Duet* as a work with fractal graphics and related music is a fine example of research and aesthetic realization.

Foderaro, John. *The Franz LISP Manual.* Berkeley: University of California Press, 1979. One of the best manuals dealing with the concepts of LISP and this particular dialect. Another text, called the *Franz LISP Common LISP Manual* has now been published.

von Foerster, Heinz and James Beauchamp, editors. *Music by Computers.* New York: John Wiley and Sons, 1969. For its time, one of the best books in the field. The Hiller retrospective and the Lefkoff articles (among others) are especially important.

Forte, A. "Computer-implemented Analysis of Musical Structure." *Computer Applications in Music,* 1967. An excellent resource for "intelligent" analysis of music.

Fry, C. "Flavors Band: A Language for Specifying Musical Style." *Computer Music Journal.* Cambridge: MIT 8/4(1984). This object-oriented approach has been especially useful for composers.

Fu, K. S. *Syntactic Pattern Recognition and Applications.* Englewood Cliffs: Prentice-Hall, 1982. This is a classic in the field of linguistic applications and grammars in non-linguistic areas.

Gil, S. "A Technique for the Composition of Music in a Computer." *The Computer Journal* 6, No. 2 (1963). An early implementation of techniques for computational composition. Useful reading if only for historical reasons.

Goldberg, Adele and David Robson. *SMALLTALK-80: The Language and its Implementation.* Reading, MA: Addison-Wesley, 1983. Smalltalk is an object-oriented environment. This text is one of the best in its field in explaining how this concept pervades this particular language and currently dominates the field.

Goos, G. and J. Hartmanis, eds. *Lecture Notes in Computer Science.* New York: Springer-Verlag, 1979. Sub-titled "Graph-Grammars and Their Application to Computer Science and Biology," this book presents a variety of diverse ways of viewing linguistics and grammars applied to the biological sciences.

Greenberg, Gary. "Procedural Composition." *Proceedings of the International Computer Music Conference.* San Francisco: Computer Music Association, 1987, pp. 25–32. Uses *Object Logo* in order to create a list of procedures for direct communication between composing programs and the composer.

Grossman, Gary. "Instruments, Cybernetics and Computer Music." *Proceedings of the International Computer Music Conference.* San Francisco: Computer Music Association (1987):212–19. An interesting paper dealing with music objects as "tools." "Music N" and "Sawdust" present interesting resolutions of the theories.

Hamel, Keith, Bruce Pennycook, Bill Ripley and Eli Blevis. "Composition Design System: A functional Approach to Composition." *Proceedings of the International Computer Music Conference.* San Francisco: Computer Music Association, 1987, pp. 33–39. Describes the notions of gestures and devices for computational models of composition.

Hasty, Christopher. "Phrase Formation in Post-Tonal Music." *Journal of Music Theory* 28/2(Fall 1984):67–190. A prime source of concepts regarding atonal phrasing, cadencing and shaping processes.

Hiller, Lejaren. "Music Composed with Computers: A Historical Survey." *The Computer and Music.* ed. H. Lincoln. Ithaca: Cornell University Press, 1970, pp. 42–96. The classic retrospective. Out of date, but nonetheless important.

———. "Composing with Computers: A Progress Report." *Computer Music Journal* 5/4 (Winter 1981):7–21. A good history of this composer's recent work (albeit not informative about others in the field as his earlier article was).

———. "Programming a Computer for Musical Composition." In *Computer Applications in Music,* Gerald Lefkoff, ed. Morgantown, West Virginia: West Virginia University Library, 1967, pp. 65–88. An excellent account of Hiller's attempt to program compositional algorithms.

Hiller, Lejaren and Leonard Isaacson. *Experimental Music.* New York: McGraw-Hill, 1959. This book describes the first true experiments with automated music and descriptions of musical style.

Hofstadter, Douglas. *Godel, Escher, Bach.* New York: Random House, 1980. Arguably one of the better recent books attempting to integrate a variety of different fields of expertise (here music, visual art and mathematics—computers being central).

Holland, Simon. "New Cognitive Theories of Harmony Applied to Direct Manipulation Tools for Novices." *Proceedings of the International Computer Music Conference.* San Francisco: Computer Music Association, 1987, pp. 182–89. Excellent practical use (for educational purposes) of both Balzano and Longuet-Higgins' theories of harmonic and rhythmic perception.

Holtzman, S. R. "Using Generative Grammars for Music Composition." *Computer Music Journal* 5/1 (Spring 1981):51–64. A general but important piece on the use of grammars in computer software techniques.

———. "A Generative Grammar Definitional Language for Music," *Interface* 9, No. 1 (1982):46. A good preparatory article to the one mentioned above.

Kivy, Peter, *Sound and Semblance: Reflections on Musical Representation*. Princeton: Princeton University Press, 1984.

Koenig, G. M. "Project 1," *Electronic Music Reports* 1, No. 2 (1970):32. An excellent account of this researcher/composer's early experiments.

———. "PROJECT 2: A Programme for Musical Composition," *Electronic Music Reports* 1, No. 3 (1970).

Laske, Otto. "In Search of a Generative Grammar for Music." *Perspectives of New Music* 12/1 (Fall-Winter):351–78. A seminal article on the force of grammar in the understanding of music.

———. "Musical Semantics: A Procedural Point of View." *Proceedings of the International Conference on the Semiotics of Music*. Belgrade, 1973. A bit obscure, but nonetheless interesting in content.

Lerdahl, Fred, and Ray Jackendoff. "Toward a Formal Theory of Music." *Journal of Music Theory* 21/1 (Spring 1977): 111–72. A forerunner of the book whose entry follows.

———. *A Generative Theory of Tonal Music*. Cambridge, MA: The MIT Press, 1983. A masterpiece of original applications of linguistics to tonal music. Applications of the principles to other types of music should have significant results.

Lerdahl, Fred. "Cognitive Constraints on Compositional Systems." *Generative Processes in Music,* J. Sloboda, ed. London: Oxford University Press, 1987, p. 229. An excellent set of applications of the Jackendoff/Lerdahl language ideas on contemporary (nontonal) works.

Levitt, David. "Machine Tongues X: Constraint Languages." *Computer Music Journal* 8, No. 1 (Spring 1984). A good general article on the subject using popular software of the time. Especially good evolution of "iterative solution algorithms."

Lewin, David. "On Formal Intervals between Time-Spans." *Music Perception* 1, No. 1 (Summer 1984): 414–23. A complicated but important reference in describing temporal events.

Lidov, D., and J. Gabura. "A Melody Writing Algorithm Using a Formal Language Model." *Computer Studies in the Humanities* 4(3/4) (1973):138–48.

Lincoln, Harry, editor. *The Computer and Music*. Ithaca, NY: Cornell University Press, 1970. This now out-dated classic includes some very important information on music composed by computers (especially Lejaren Hiller's article documenting a number of serious early attempts at music automatons).

Lischka, Christoph. "Connectionist Models of Musical Thinking." *Proceedings of the International Computer Music Conference*. San Francisco: Computer Music Association, 1987, pp. 190–96. Describes the "connectionist paradigm" in somewhat vague mathematical terms. Presents, however, a good beginning to a representation of musical knowledge.

Longuet-Higgins, H. Christopher. *Mental Processes*. Cambridge, MA: The MIT Press, 1987. An extraordinary book wherein the author (who collaborates in many chapters) covers the subjects of artificial intelligence, linguistics, music, vision and memory. The interdisciplinary approach survives the scientific model well and the author provides the reader with many compelling insights.

Longuet-Higgins, H. C. and C. S. Lee. "The Rhythmic Interpretation of Monophonic Music." *Music Perception* 1, No. 1 (Summer 1984):424–41. An excellent introduction to parsing rhythm Longuet-Higgins style.

Meehan, James R. "An Artificial Intelligence Approach to Tonal Music Theory." *Computer Music Journal* 4/2 (Summer 1980):60–65. A very solid piece of research dedicated to theoretical applications of AI in music analysis.

Minsky, Marvin. *K-lines: A Theory of Memory*. Cambridge: MIT AI Memo 516, 1979, pp. 1–35. A critical study of *knowledge-lines,* the Minsky theory that complex interconnections between certain nodal intersections create complex memory potentials.

———. *The Society of Mind*. New York: Simon and Schuster, 1986. Minsky's LISP-like theory of intelligence propagation. This somewhat controversial work has been well accepted by the general AI community but has doubters in other scientific academia.

Narmour, Eugene. *Beyond Schenkerism*. Chicago: University of Chicago Press, 1977. A major step towards expanding and creating alternates to Schenker hierarchical analytical procedures.

———. "Some Major Theoretical Problems Concerning the Concept of Hierarchy in the Analysis of Tonal Music." *Music Perception* 1, No. 2 (Winter 1983–4):129–99. Arguments against the Schenker theories of foreground, middleground and background levels of analysis.

Newcomb, Steven R. "LASSO: An Intelligent Computer-based Tutorial in Sixteenth-Century Counterpoint." *Computer Music Journal* 9, No. 4 (Winter 1985). Presents one model of the processes necessary for creating stylistic imitators.

Olschki, Leo, ed. *Musical Grammars and Computer Analysis*. Quaderni Della Rivista Italiana Di Musicologia A. Cura Della Società Italiana Di Musicologia, 1986. An important document on computer music and especially the use of linguistics in music analysis (especially the articles by Roads and Pelinski).

Oppenheim, Daniel Vincent. "The P-G-G Environment for Music Composition." *Proceedings of the International Computer Music Conference*. San Francisco: Computer Music Association, 1987, pp. 40–48. This article describes visual interfaces (real-time) between composers and computers.

Polansky, Larry, David Rosenboom and Phil Burk. "HMSL: Overview (Version 3.1) and Notes on Intelligent Instrument Design." *Proceedings of the International Computer Music Conference*. San Francisco: Computer Music Association, 1987, pp. 220–27. An elegant if generic language for possibly representing what its name suggests: *Hierarchical Music Specification Language*.

Pierce, J. R. *Symbols, Signals and Noise*. New York: Harper, pp. 238–49. A good philosophical summary of the attempts to distinguish between these phenomena.

Prieberg, Fred. *Musica ex Machina*. Berlin: Verlag Ullstein, 1960. While this book has still not been translated into English, it remains a very special addition to the German literature concerning the history of man's infatuation with the machine as a source for music inspiration.

Reichardt, Jasia, editor. *Cybernetics, Art and Ideas*. Greenwich, Connecticut: New York Graphic Society Ltd., 1971. An excellent compendium of various attempts at artistic cybernetics in the early 1970s. The articles by Donald Michie, Iannis Xenakis and Ali Irtem are particularly important.

Roads, C. "Grammars as Representations for Music." in *Foundations of Computer Music*. (Curtis Roads and John Strawn, eds.) Cambridge: MIT Press, 1985. An expanded version of the article found in Computer Music Journal 3/1 (1979):48–55.

———. "Artificial Intelligence and Music." *Computer Music Journal*. Cambridge: MIT 4/2:1980. An important survey of the various potentials of AI and music. Now out of date, it nonetheless was ahead of its time.

———. *Composers and the Computer*. Los Altos, CA: William Kaufmann, Inc., 1985. This is a series of interviews with composers (Brün and Xenakis of particular interest for this chapter) with accompanying scores and photographs.

———. "Composing Grammars." *Proceedings of the 1977 International Computer Music Conference*. San Francisco: Computer Music Association. 1978.

———. "Symposium on Computer Music Composition." *Computer Music Journal,* pp. 40–63. A collection of composers speaking about their particular brand of computer music. The section on automation is quite good (especially the responses by Otto Laske and Giuseppe Englert).

———. "The Tsukuba Musical Robot." *Computer Music Journal* 10, No. 2 (Summer 1986):39–43. An interesting account of this expensive robot designed to perform music on command.

———. "An Overview of Music Representations." Musical Grammars and Computer Analysis. Leo S. Olschki, ed. Quaderni Della Rivista Italiana De Musicologia A Cura Della Società Italiana Di Musicologia, 1986. This is an extraordinary contribution to the literature on music and linguistics.

———. "Research in Music and Artificial Intelligence," *Computing Surveys* 17, No. 2 (June 1985). A good overview of the subject of AI and music with special attention paid to constraints and algorithmic composition.

Rodet, Xavier and Pierre Cointe. "FORMES: Composition and Scheduling of Processes." *Computer Music Journal.* Cambridge: MIT 8/3: 1984. Excellent survey of the object-oriented LeLISP-based music programming environment of IRCAM.

Ruwet, N. "Théorie et Méthodes dans les Études Musicales." *Musique en Jeu* 17 (1975):11–36. A classic for those interested in music linguistics.

Slawson, A. W. "Review of Computer Applications in Music." *Journal of Music Theory.* 12, 1 (1968):105–11.

———. *Sound Color.* Berkeley: University of California Press, 1985. This book presents a theory of timbre relevant to language on a "literal" level. It includes a section on "speech" and on speech-like sounds with instruments in electronic music.

Smoliar, Stephen W. "A Computer Aid for Schenkerian Analysis." *Computer Music Journal* 4/2 (Summer 1980): 41–59. A standard for those interested in layer approaches to music through computer analysis.

Snell, James L. "Musical Grammars and Computer Analysis: A Review." *Perspectives of New Music* 23/2 (Spring-Summer 1985):220–34. Excellent, if brief, study of music and grammar.

Steedman, Mark J. "A Generative Grammar for Jazz Chord Sequences." *Music Perception* 2, No. 1 (Fall 1984):52–77. An excellent article for developing an intellectual (previously intuitive) approach to parsing jazz harmonic sequences.

"Syncopation by Automation," *Data from ElectroData,* August 1956, Pasadena: Electro-Data Division of Burroughs, Inc.

Thomas, M. T. "VIVACE: A Rule-Based AI System for Composition." *Proceedings of the 1985 ICMC,* p. 267–75. Good (even if the title is misleading) article on the subject.

Truax, Barry. "The PODX System: Interactive Compositional Software for the DMX-1000." *Computer Music Journal* 9/1 (Spring 1985):29–38.

Winograd, T. "Linguistics and the Computer Analysis of Tonal Harmony." *Journal of Music Theory* 12(Spring 1968):2–49. A classic study of musical linguistics and their application to tonality in particular.

Winsor, Phil. *Computer-Assisted Music Composition.* Princeton, New Jersey: Petrocelli Books, Inc., 1987. A book addressed to those wishing to develop programming skills in BASIC for the purposes of CAC (Computer-Assisted Composition).

Winston, P. H. *Artificial Intelligence,* 2nd ed. Reading, MA: Addison-Wesley, 1984. One of the finest basic introductions to the subject. With little question, this remains the seminal primer on the subject for the uninitiated.

Winston, P. H. and B. K P. Horn. *LISP,* 2nd ed. Reading, Mass: Addison-Wesley, 1984. A good standard reading for those wanting the best in common LISP reference tools.

Xenakis, Iannis. "Free Stochastic Music from the Computer." *Cybernetics, Art and Ideas,* edited by Jasia Reichardt. Greenwich: New York Graphic Society Ltd., 1971, pp. 124–42.

———. *Formalized Music.* Bloomington: Indiana University Press, 1971. This is the standard text in the field. It defines *stochastics* and musical interactions. It also includes Xenakis's approach to composing with games and various mathematical formulae.

———. *Arts/Sciences: Alloys.* New York: Pendragon Press, 1985. An excellent translation of the composer's thesis defense (with Messiaen, d'Allonnes, Ragon, Serres, and Teyssèdre).

———. *Musique. Architecture.* Paris: Casterman, 1976. In French, this book has many extraordinary illustrations and a bibliography of Xenakis's works (including a discography).

Yavelow, Christopher. "Composition or Improvisation? Only the Computer Knows." *AES 5th Annual Conference Proceedings.* Los Angeles: Audio Engineering Society, 1987. An interesting account of "interactive composition."

This section is necessarily brief due to the newness of the field in terms of actual production of music.

Recordings and Publishers

Bischoff, John. *Lovely Little Records.* Recorded on Lovely Records 101/06. This is a box of six 7-inch records including a booklet of notes and biographies. Performers include Bischoff, DeMarinis, Phil Harmonic, Maggie Payne, Blue Gene Tyranny, and others.

Brün, Herbert. *Gestures for Eleven* (1964). Recorded on CRIs-321. Not the work of choice for this composer but the only one available on recording. Excellent introduction to his compositional techniques using cybernetics.

Cage, John and Lejaren Hiller. *HPSCHD* (1968). C. F. Peters. Recorded on Nonesuch 71224. This classic of cybernetic music involves the use of many composing algorithms.

Chadabe, Joel. *Daisy.* Recorded on Opus One #16. An interactive cybernetic work for English Horn and tape.

———. *Settings for Spirituals.* Recorded on Lovely Music 1302. This album also contains *Solo* and includes computer-controlled electronics and voice.

Cope, David. *Out From This Breathing Earth.* Opus One Records, 1988. This linguistic (EMI) work (from programs created by the author) is monophonic and based on dictionaries similar to the composer's own style.

Hiller, Lejaren. *An Avalanche for Pitchman, Prima-Donna, Player Piano, Percussionist and Pre-Recorded Playback* (1968). Capra 1206. This work utilizes the CALCOMP program at the University of Illinois.

Hiller, Lejaren and Robert Baker. *Computer Cantata.* (1968). Theodore Presser. Recorded on CRI SD-310. This is the classic automated work for soprano, chamber ensemble, and tape.

Jaffe, David. *Silicon Valley Breakdown.* Involves tempo, rubato, and phrasing automation. CD: Stanford; S#1.

Lerdahl, Fred. *String Quartet No. #2* (1982). Laurel 128. This work shows some influence of the composer's linguistic studies of tonal music.

Xenakis, Iannis. *Akrata* (1965). Salabert. Nonesuch 71201. A stochastic work for 16 wind instruments.

———. *Atrées* (1960). Salabert. Recorded on EMI CVC 2086.

———. *Mikka* and *Mikka "S"* (1971 and 1976 respectively). Salabert. Recorded by Paul Zukofsky on CP2 #6. Work for solo violin employing mathematical procedures.

———. *Morsima-Amorsima.* Salabert. Barclay 920217.

11 · THE POST AVANT-GARDE

Evaluation

In music, the term *avant-garde* has become a designation for those composers or works displaying the newest technique (often anti-technique; i.e., chance music) or sound (often lack of sound; i.e., silence). The apparent dead-end features of this, as projected by its critics and enthusiasts alike, become obvious when, as one composer stated, "anything goes." It is difficult to create something *new* within the framework of that philosophy.

The decay of any movement or social direction begins when the thrust of its reason for existence is silenced. This *raison d'être* of the *avant-garde* movement centers around supposed shock value and "newness" of purpose and effect. Certainly the movement begins its death throes when an event in any of its art forms becomes so new, so shocking, as to virtually negate anything surpassing it.

Saying "anything goes" is still quite a far cry from *doing* "anything goes." Rudolf Schwarzkogler, a Viennese artist born in 1940, began his masterpiece in the late 1960s. It seems, as we pick up the story by Robert Hughes of *Time,* that Schwarzkogler, a prime mover of the *avant-garde* of his time, had decided that *his* art, at least, depended not on the application of paint, but on the removal of his own flesh:

> So he proceeded, inch by inch to amputate his own penis, while a photographer recorded the act as an art event. In 1972, the resulting prints were reverently exhibited in that biennial motor show of Western art, Documenta 5 at Kassel. Successive acts of self-amputation finally did Schwarzkogler in. . . . No doubt it could be argued by the proponents of body art . . . that Schwarzkogler's self-editing was not indulgent but brave, taking the audience's castration fears and reducing them to their most threatening quiddity. That the man was clearly as mad as a hatter, sick beyond rebuke, is not thought important; wasn't Van Gogh crazy too? But Schwarzkogler's gesture has a certain emblematic value. Having nothing to say, and nowhere to go but further out, he lopped himself and called it art.[1]

As the article states, Schwarzkogler is indeed dead, a victim of his own art. One is often reminded of Philip Corner's work entitled "*One anti-personnel type CBU bomb will be thrown into the audience*" (what kind of strange masochist would

---

1. Robert Hughes, "The Decline and Fall of the Avant-Garde," *Time,* December 18, 1972, pp. 111–12.

attend a program which had announced this work's performance?). While one finds the composer's suggestions asking the performers not to fulfill the probably small audience's desires, one wonders why some composer doesn't consider a world war as a next piece. The shock factor here is death, the "newness" that either of these be considered as art in the first place. Whether the act be real (as with Schwarz-kogler) or imagined (as with Corner), it seems topped only by multi-deaths, war, and finally complete annihilation. Since none of these seems real (at least in the form of artistic development), one is led to believe that at least for those of us who are aware of what has been happening in the arts, "newness" and "shock" are over, and with them, the prime movers, the superstructure of the *avant-garde* movement.

Philosophically the *avant-garde* remains one of the most conservative areas of musical thought: a concept in which, indeed, anything does *not* go. The very nature of the *avant-garde* concept binds the composer to reject the past and work within a multitude of limitations often surpassing those of the strictest of traditional con-trapuntalists.

Sensing the oblivion inherent in such rejection of the past, a number of composers have begun to accept the philosophy projected, but not carried out, by the *avant-garde;* that is, truly "anything goes." Not a statement of rejection, this, but of affirmation: the *post avant-garde.* While the phrase "anything goes" may immediately alienate those of us intent on saving the arts for (and in some cases from) people and significance, the words *with purpose* may be added. It is no longer the new sound, the new device, the new trick, that is important, but the new *work*.

Antagonists of this philosophy generally neglect the true depth of such a direction: once the composer has become unprejudiced toward sound, Bach is no longer an enemy; the major triad, tonality, need no longer be avoided; dissonance need not be a requirement to be contemporary. Redefined, the *post avant-garde* composer is *just* the composer, using anything that is necessary to fulfill the need to create music; accepting *all* sound and silence without being limited by current styles.

Likewise consistency, previously designated as the type of materials used (triads, noise, etc.) is implied and governed by the composer, not by period, audience, or fellow composers. The *post avant-garde* composer has also challenged the listener's prejudices: can one truly accept all sound, all styles, all meaning in music? In effect, can one listen to Bach, to Webern, to Cage, to rock; not rejecting any?

The struggle, however taut it may have once seemed, grows less and less tangible with each passing year. The post-*avant-garde* works of this chapter, as different in sound and structure as they may seem, hold a fragile but distinctly recognizable common thread among them. Possibly Ben Johnston says it best in his article *On Context:* "Awareness makes free choice possible. Freedom requires responsiveness: responsibility."[2] Later in the same article his optimism is clearly focused:

> It is as though we have to cross a chasm. If we are to build a bridge over it we will have to anchor its ends far in the past and far in the future. Tradition thoroughly

2. Ben Johnston, "On Context," *ASUC Proceedings # 3* (1968), p. 35.

assimilated will help us anchor in the past; only a sharp eye for where we are going can help us anchor in the future. Technology will help us build the bridge, which will not impose upon nature but will be possible because we understand how things happen and cooperate rather than interfering.[3]

There is no progress in music (or art). That is, while certainly an individual composer may get better and better with time, "newer" music (with its complex new instruments for creating much more diverse sounds) is no better than older music (or any worse for that matter). No invention, or creation, can "outdate" Machaut's *Mass* (c. 1360) as a newer car can, for instance, outdate the horse and buggy.

Notation, deeply rooted in battle during the prolific years of the *avant-garde,* seems best when it communicates the most of its designer's intention. The new techniques of notation engendered by many of the more profitable experiments of the *avant-garde,* are just now becoming standardized (see Appendix 3). These developments, however, cannot be construed to supersede or replace previous notational techniques as "better," but as different means of expression. The battles of improvisation and indeterminacy seem won, to the extent that we now agree—if a composer has no real intention, then unintentional notation certainly is the best vehicle. The return to faith in honest technique and musicality, whatever form it may take (as long as the ultimate purpose is to communicate composer intention), is the focus. Fortunately, even the very patient have tired of the endless scribbles of masturbative visual art (as music notation) possessed of its own purposelessness.

Techniques of Synthesis

There has existed, alongside the *avant-garde,* for the past thirty to forty years, a vast and somewhat sheltered mainstream of composers, often maddened, more often disgusted by what they saw and heard from the *avant-garde.* They have steadfastly held onto their historically justified techniques, and their ears. The *avant-garde* constantly shivered, however, above a pit of self-destruction. That difference, that canyon between the two divergent schools, is now the target of synthesis. The intelligent and talented composers on each side have realized that the radical claims of the initial proponents of both sides were not necessarily true.

One is reminded of the assertions set forth by two of the world's most renowned men of music: Igor Stravinsky, of *Le Sacre de Printemps* ("Very little tradition lies behind *Le Sacre* and no theory. I had only my ear to help me. . . . I am the vessel through which *Le Sacre* passed."[4]); and Pierre Boulez, the director of IRCAM in Paris ("Since the discovery by the Viennese, all composition other than twelve-tone is useless."[5]). Both men are, of course, incorrect; yet each viewpoint retains that grain of truth for which armies of artists and composers will clash for years. The last few years have witnessed the collapse of these camps surrounding the revisionist and the experimental.

---

3. Ibid.
4. Igor Stavinsky, "Apropos Le Sacre du Printemps," as printed on the cover of Columbia Records ML-5719.
5. David Cope and Galen Wilson, "An Interview with Pierre Boulez," *Composer* 1, no. 2 (September 1969):83.

We stand on the verge of one of the most creative and significant eras in the history of music. The prejudiced and insecure may still need shelter behind a mainstream door, yet those who now venture forth freely to take quiet advantage of the evident skills of both recent schools of thought (tradition and innovation, technique and intuition) are, will, and have been braving an exciting new credible sensitivity into new music.

György Ligeti's *Requiem* is a four-movement work (around 26 minutes) for soprano and mezzo-soprano soloists, two choruses, and large orchestra. Composed during the years 1963–65, the *Requiem* fuses two basic concepts. *Klangflachenkomposition* creates sound-mass which ebbs and flows through constant overlapping of timbre and spatial modulations (evident in the extreme in his later *Lontano*). *Mikropolyphonie* creates highly complex densities of polyphonic motion in which no single voice dominates—only the overall fabric of resultant sound (notable in his *Aventures*). There is also a strong synthesis of traditional and *avant-garde* techniques. Conservative procedures are evidenced in the standard musical notation, text, extremely "determinate" articulations, and rhythmic complexities. Special effects include muting bassoons with handkerchiefs and the "Langlois Effect" of squeezing the string with thumb and forefinger rather than pressing it normally against the fingerboard. The score is accompanied by a 23-page booklet of incredibly exacting performance directions. Like his earlier *Aventures*, the *Requiem* occasionally moves from metered notation to "senza tempo" sections (especially in the third movement). Note that in Figure 4.10 (see Chapter 4) his use of this effect is for *contrast*. In the *Requiem* the effect is quite the opposite with even the bar lines

Figure 11.1. György Ligeti. With permission of Universal Edition.

being, in the composer's words, ". . . purely a means of synchronizing the individual parts."[6] Aside from its obvious synthesis of new and old, *Requiem* creates a composer-controlled "spatial movement." The composer has remarked about the work: "You have a drawing in two dimensions and you give it perspective. . . . I was constantly thinking of achieving this illusion of a musical space, which has only an acoustical existence in time."[7]

Figure 11.2. George Crumb. With permission.

George Crumb's *Ancient Voices of Children* (1970) is a 27-minute work for soprano, boy soprano, oboe, mandolin, harp, electric piano, and three percussionists. The work consists of five basic vocal movements separated twice by purely instrumental dances. The texts are by Federico Garcìa Lorca and sung in Spanish. The synthesis present in this work is evidenced by the composer's own words about the piece:

> In composing *Ancient Voices of Children* I was conscious of an urge to fuse various unrelated stylistic elements. I was intrigued by the idea of juxtaposing the seemingly incongruous: a suggestion of Flamenco with a Baroque quotation ("Bist du bei mir," from the Notebook of Anna Magdelena Bach), or a reminiscence of Mahler with a breath of the Orient. It later occurred to me that both Bach and Mahler drew upon many disparate sources in their own music without sacrificing "stylistic purity."[8]

Crumb's "stylistic purity" remains intact in this as well as his earlier works (beginning with his *Five Pieces for Piano,* 1962). It is characterized by three particularly distinct features: (1) extremely defined and thinly exposed textures often

6. From the "Introductory Remarks" of the score: C. F. Peters: 30285.
7. "Conversations with Ligeti at Stanford," *Numus West* 2 (1972):19.
8. From the score: No. 66303. C. F. Peters.

consisting of solo lines (almost one-third of this work is for solo instruments), dramatic silences frequently expressed by square fermatas with duration in seconds (see Figure 11.3) and subtle motivic repetition and development; (2) the use of instruments and voice equally for their pitch and "special" timbral qualities. Crumb remarks:

> Certain special instrumental effects are used to heighten the "expressive intensity" e.g. "bending" the pitch of the piano by application of a chisel to the strings; . . . the mandolin has one set of strings tuned a quarter-tone low in order to give a special pungency to its tone.[9]

IV. Todas las tardes en Granada, todas las tardes se muere un niño
[Each afternoon in Granada, a child dies each afternoon]

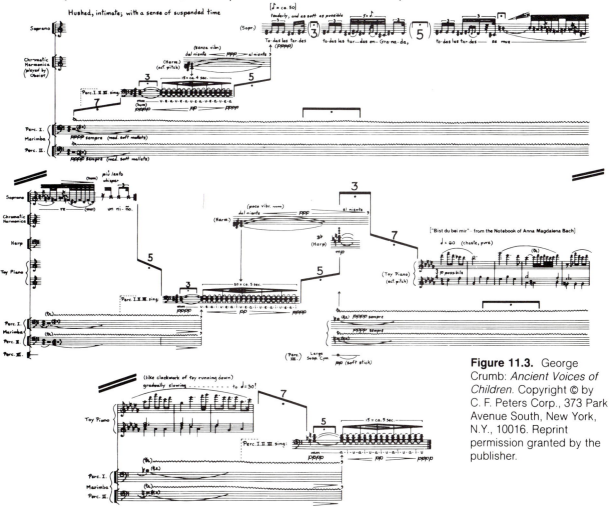

Figure 11.3. George Crumb: *Ancient Voices of Children*. Copyright © by C. F. Peters Corp., 373 Park Avenue South, New York, N.Y., 10016. Reprint permission granted by the publisher.

9. Ibid.

(3) the musical imagery: a reflection of the texts without programmatic connotations.

> I feel that the essential meaning of this poetry is concerned with the most primary things: life, death, love, the smell of the earth, the sounds of the wind and sea. These *"ur*-concepts" are embodied in language which is primitive and stark but which is capable of infinitely subtle nuance.[10]

Figure 11.3 shows the entire fourth movement of *Ancient Voices* and exemplifies the synthesis referred to earlier. The simple use of the whole-tone scale (in the opening vocal part beginning on C#), the triadic harmonies and the simple formal structure are all traditional. The marimba drones, the percussionists singing, and the Bach quote on the toy piano are all *avant-garde* in nature. The movement, and indeed the work, holds together with a high degree of continuity despite the contrasting material and styles.

Ellen Tsaffe Zwilich's *Double Quartet,* a seminal 21-minute work, convincingly demonstrates the composer's predilection for tight formal/modal structures and post *avant-garde* synthesis. This four-movement work begins and ends in D. The opening, a dynamic and fast unison, defines the mode. The second movement begins in D minor with a transition to the third movement via a unison (leading tone) C#. This latter movement concludes on a D *dominant seventh* in 4/2 position. The fourth movement poses an F = F# contradiction with D again playing a very important role. The score centers on a kind of ambiguity between modes and key centers. The lexical implications in this (i.e., a chromatic tapestry without the rigors of a full-blown 12-tone system) create a syntax which balances well with the quasi-tonal harmonic vocabulary. The orchestration employs an effective use of spatial modulations. In the performance notes, Zwilich suggests a seating arrangement which separates two string quartets by an apparent stage width. She then carefully creates a dialogue between the groups, at times complementary, more typically antiphonal.

Toshi Ichiyanagi's *Violin Concerto* is a three-movement 26-minute *tour de force*. The soloist alternately converses with the orchestra and lapses into meditative soliloquies. The chromatic logic, not 12-tone, does occasionally have actual rows (e.g., bar 46, solo violin: C-Eb-F#-G-A-Bb-C#-D-E-F-G#-B transposed in bar 114 to: G-Bb-C#-D-E-F-G#-A-B-C-D♯-F# and thereafter occurring at a variety of pitch levels). Melodies typically ascend using only seconds and thirds. Ichiyanagi's lines tend towards continuous upward or downward motion or lapse into repeating figures which have no direction at all. Harmonic motion remains for the most part opaque. Either roots change so quickly that they blur distinction or they remain steady and without momentum (paralleling the contrast in his melodic writing). Voices tend to follow 5, 8, or 10 mutually exclusive pitch subsets. The composition, with the exception of a few freelance solos (interchanges between orchestral soloists and the violin virtuoso), develops from the opening solo and effectively combines the melodic elements from each successive movement.

---

10. Ibid.

Henri Lazarof's *Second Concerto for Orchestra* (subtitled "Icarus") is a demanding 22-minute three-movement work. Twelve-tone rows and near-rows abound. However, this is clearly not a dodecaphonic piece. The composer freely expresses intense chromaticism with an intuitive source. The harmonic vocabulary builds from the same foundation and panchromatic chords can be found on almost every page of the score. The opening reveals an all-exclusive 12-note pitch set which the composer varies freely throughout the work. His most frequently used technique involves presenting 11 notes of a row and then delaying the 12th until (usually) it appears dramatically (e.g., 11 notes stated and repeated in the strings and percussion in bars 10–12 with a quadrupled twelfth pitch entry in the woodwinds). The beginning of the work also reveals a sentence-like phrase structure which develops throughout the work. Often completely silent bars conclude parsings of the main thematic material. The principal motive of the work (C#-F-G-A-B-C-Eb-Gb-Ab-Bb-D on the piano) announces each of the major sections. Vertical arrows and unevenly drawn stems without note-heads demonstrate notational synthesis techniques. The work gradually builds (by slowly adding instruments) to thundering climaxes which, after stopping abruptly, resolve.

Further Examples

György Kurtág's *Messages of the Late R. V. Troussova,* Opus 17, represents a significant post-*avant-garde* approach. Elements of instrument exploration, time suspension, and use of a variety of notations create an "atmospheric" style similar to that of Crumb yet distinctly his own. The composer uses a gestural approach to timbre and cadence and generates a sense of breath through the use of extensive silence or soft sections.

Apotheosis of This Earth (1970) by Karel Husa, for concert band, is a work "physically" impelled by dynamics and textural momentum. Its synthesis is not easily heard (it is truly a work fused in every sense). Its three-movement structure (Apotheosis, Tragedy of Destruction, Postscript) employs sound-mass resultant of repetitive composite motives (see Figure 3.12 in Chapter 3) and cumulatively sustained

Figure 11.4. Karel Husa.

clusters (often panchromatic, e.g., measure 149, where the horns and trumpets attack and slowly "unvelope" a twelve-note cluster). The final movement employs whispering with both repetitive consonance attacks and text ("this beautiful earth"). In *Apotheosis* one finds the fusion of *avant-garde* and traditional techniques so complete that neither is audible: a work of a unique and personal style.

Other works of varying degrees of synthesis include Donald Erb's *Symphony of Overtures* (1964) and Richard Toensing's *Doxologies I*. Both composers have evolved personal styles fused of elements equally *avant-garde* and traditional. The synthesis is complete: these works no longer "espouse" a single thought or gimmick nor express the fear of the use of any sonic material.

David Cope's *Threshold and Visions* (1979—a concerto for chamber orchestra) evolves a post-*avant-garde* idiom through synthesis of a diverse number of *avant-garde* techniques (including sound-mass, instrument exploration, and a free serial technique). The thirty-five minute work is cast in five movements centered around a basic arch-type format.

Walter Mays's *Icarus* for large orchestra (1976) incorporates sound-mass, new instrumental techniques, electronic tape, improvisatory techniques, proportional notation, and indeterminate methods (stochastic). The effective large orchestration (calling for well over one hundred players) employs musical saw, bowed crotales, and electric organ to develop large volumes of complex sonic environments. David Felder's *Rondàge,* on the other hand, involves only five performers, fusing live electronics, sound-mass, structured improvisations and new instrumental techniques into a comprehensively consistent vocabulary.

Barbara Kolb's *Soundings* is a complex work performable in two versions (chamber orchestra and tape prepared by the ensemble, or full orchestra divided into three groups directed by two conductors). The extensive program notes discuss the central conception of the work: "*Soundings* is a technique which makes it possible to ascertain the depth of water by measuring the interval of time between the sending of a signal and the return echo" with the resultant sounds developing ". . . a sea-change into something rich and strange."[11] A montage of triply overlaid contrapuntal textures results (each mini-orchestra or tape channel, depending on version, being a separate but often simultaneous "sounding").

The piece clearly divides into three major sections. The first section is characterized by a straightforward ostinato in the strings (repeating beat by beat throughout the entire passage) with slowly evolving patterns in first the original "sounding" and then the reflections. Tension is created by thickening texture and increased chromaticism towards a fast rush of sound slowly relaxing in a high tremolo in harp and solo violin. The second section is soloistic, conversational, and full of tightly woven musical gestures interplaying in often very thin textures. The final section reverts to the thick textures of the first, contrasts it in content (often long held notes in rising chromatic lines) but parallels it in direction (again driving to a loud climax sliced by an immediate *pianissimo* passage marked "in the distance").

11. Barbara Kolb, *Soundings* (New York: Boosey & Hawkes, 1981).

Quoting a fragment from another composer or style within the framework of one's own work became a prime focus for many composers in the *avant-garde*. It survives in the post-*avant-garde*. While hardly new (almost every composer has at one time or another quoted other music, from Bach's borrowed chants to Mahler's quotations of his own music), the use of strikingly different styles in the twentieth-century *avant-garde* has taken a decisively novel direction. The hymn quotes of Charles Ives as well as his free borrowings of any material to suit his message (evident in such works as *Central Park in the Dark* and *Symphony No. 4*) are often starkly presented against dissonant textures highlighting the cognizant drama present. Quite unlike the "theme and variations" quoting of previous centuries, this new actively polarized presentation of borrowed material results in "psycho-drama."

Reasons for such quoting vary from composer to composer and often from work to work by the same composer. George Rochberg speaks of his usage:

> The centerpiece of my *Music for the Magic Theatre* is a transcription, that is, a completely new version, of a Mozart adagio. I decided to repeat it in my own way because I loved it. People who understand, love it because they know it began with Mozart and ended with me. People who don't understand think it's by Mozart.[12]

Peter Maxwell Davies's use of Handel quotes in *Eight Songs for a Mad King* (1969) results in a strange periodization (of George III) as well as superimposed *collage* effect (especially in "Comfort Ye, Comfort Ye My People," of Song #7). Michael Colgrass achieves an Ivesian *montage* in *As Quiet As* (1966) for orchestra by using a multitude of effectively varied quotes framed by a background of subtle clouds of modulating chords.

Mauricio Kagel superimposes quote upon quote from Beethoven in his *Ludwig Van* (1970) creating, like Lukas Foss in his *Baroque Variations* (1967) and Stockhausen in his *Opus 1970*, a surrealistic intertwining of raw material stylistically consistent but rhythmically and texturally deranged. Each is contextually dramatic as additive overlays contribute to the increasing cognizant tension of "composer" intention.

The third movement of Luciano Berio's *Sinfonia* (1968) for eight soloists and orchestra, quoting extensively from Mahler and Debussy among others, possesses dramatic power through its use of striking text (likewise quoting from a number of sources including Samuel Beckett) and driving musical force (see analysis at end of chapter). Certainly more innocent, at least in its length and continuity, is George Crumb's use of a short Bach fragment in his *Ancient Voices of Children,* 1970 (shown earlier in this chapter). The performance (on a toy piano) complete with Baroque ornaments is possibly one of the most powerful quotes in recent music, though the dynamics of the movement barely rise above *mezzoforte*.

Phil Winsor's *Orgel I* (for pipe organ and prerecorded tape) includes some performer choice (e.g., *which* Bach fugue, prelude, etc.) yet the incredible diversity creates a constant rationale of forged opposites. Figure 11.6 shows page X, a page

---

12. George Rochberg, "No Center," *Composer* 2, no. 1 (September 1969):89.

Figure 11.5. Phil Winsor.
Photo by Julia Winsor.

Figure 11.6. Phil Winsor's *ORGEL I* (page X). Copyright © 1975 by Pembroke Music Co., Inc. New York. International Copyright Secured. 62 Cooper Square, New York, N.Y. 10003. Copying or reproducing this publication in whole or in part violates the Federal Copyright Law. All rights reserved including public performance for profit. Used by permission.

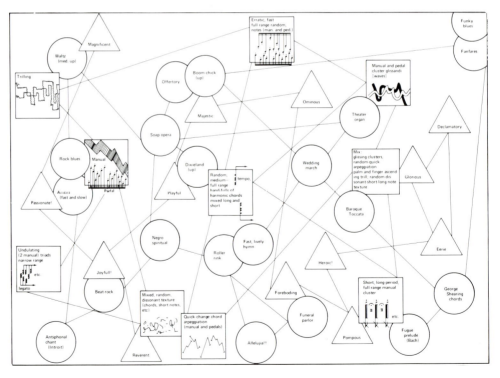

of directed choices from which at points in the score (not shown) the performer may choose items within a prescribed time limit. The tape, made by the performer, contributes further overlays of the given material resulting in massive densities of crowded triadic clashes. Each listener will, of course, recognize from experience only a percentage of the quotes. However, their often simultaneously polarized styles, and indeed the listener's inherent quest for message, create intense drama.

It is no longer possible to avoid the implications of the *post avant-garde*. Whether they be, in the final analysis, friend or enemy (or both), one must know and acknowledge them. Nothing is gained by ignorance. Varèse's comments are most apropos:

> My fight for the liberation of sound and for my right to make music with any sound and all sounds has sometimes been construed as a desire to disparage and even to discard the great music of the past. But that is where my roots are. No matter how original, how different a composer may seem, he has only grafted a little bit of himself on the old plant. But this he should be allowed to do without being accused of wanting to kill the plant. He only wants to produce a new flower. . .[13]

(For information on vectoral analysis and procedures, see Chapter 1.)

Vectoral Analysis: Luciano Berio: *Sinfonia*

1. Historical Background: Luciano Berio (b. 1925, Oneglia, Italy) was a cofounder (with Bruno Maderna) of the electronic music studio in Milan (1955). He later taught at the Juilliard School of Music (until 1973), Mills College in Oakland, California, and has been director of the electronic music studio at IRCAM in Paris.

Figure 11.7. Luciano Berio. BMI Archives. Used by permission.

13. As quoted in *Contemporary Composers on Contemporary Music*. Elliott Schwartz and Barney Childs, eds. (New York: Holt, Rinehart, and Winston, 1967), p. 201.

Berio's music separates into two major periods, though there is a defined continuity throughout his compositional career: (1) through the mid-fifties, a post-Western serialism prevails with *Chamber Music* (1952) as a good example; and (2) through the late seventies, an eclectic theater approach is expressed through electronic means (e.g., *Visage,* 1961) and more recently through large instrumental works (e.g., *Sinfonia,* 1968 and *Coro,* 1976 for voices and instruments). Other important works include *Circles* (for soprano, harp, and two percussion ensembles, 1962; see example in Chapter 5), *Omaggio a Joyce* (1958), *Differences* (for five instruments and tape, 1959), and *Opera* (large "opera," 1972, with a revised version completed in 1977).

Berio is most known for his extraordinary music-theater works, many of which were greatly influenced by the abilities of Cathy Berberian (who for a number of years was married to Berio). Her gymnastic vocal talents fused with Berio's dramatic and lyric style to create *Visage* and particularly *Recital* (1971), a singular study of a singer's mental breakdown. Other works dedicated to Cathy Berberian include *Circles* and *Epifanie* (1960).

2. Overview: *Sinfonia* was originally composed in four movements and later (in 1968) altered to include a fifth (some maintain that the latter was added at a conductor's request for a "flashy" final movement). The work was commissioned by the New York Philharmonic Orchestra and dedicated to Leonard Bernstein (the conductor). It is scored for large orchestra (see orchestration) and eight voices (performed most notably since the premiere by the Swingle Singers).

The first movement is cast in two large sections melded together through a plastic transition. The opening of the work (ominously provoked by three tam-tams) sets repeated notes in motion. These vacillate through a variety of homorhythmic and heterophonic rhythmic variants utilizing timbral development (e.g., slow vowel changes in the voices; use of mutes in brass). This opening material is followed by similar groupings (i.e., initialization/ pitch repetition development) of successively shorter and shorter duration. A second section emerges innocuously from this stretto by a short burst in the background from the piano. These outbursts increase in importance until finally (at J in the score) they take over completely, forming the nucleus of the second main section (characterized by loud quick blasts of sound followed by silences). These develop into an orchestral tutti. Occasionally one or more of the notes rings after being set in motion by the fast bursts. This allows Berio (in the final few measures) to recollect the opening or first section briefly in an illusion of a three-part form. Berio has cleverly allowed the second section to "grow" from the second part of the first section. The end of the movement resembles the first part of the first section (initialization of the repeated note structures).

The second movement (subtitled "O King") is continuous organic form centered on the simple text: "Martin Luther King" (except for the vowel exchange carried over from the first movement, the only text for the

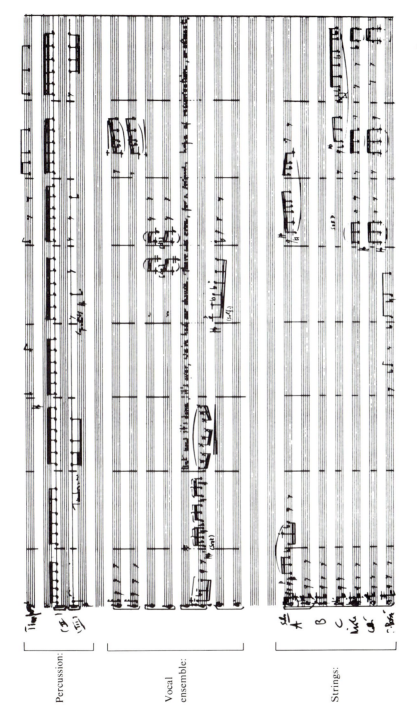

Figure 11.8. Luciano Berio: *Sinfonia* Movement 3. © Copyright 1969 Universal Edition. All rights reserved.

movement). The idea from the first movement (excitation) continues in the piano, whose sudden single attacks on certain notes initiate the held soft pitches by the singers. The material centers on F, and a variety of chromatic scales emerge around this pivotal point (hybrid chromatic gestures, whole-tone scales, etc.). The end of the movement suggests a brief return to the blasts at the end of the first movement, implying (as the first does to itself) a cyclical use of materials. At the outset of the movement, all materials move upward from F, and at the end of the movement, all materials work down from the same F.

The third movement is an Ivesian barrage of quotations. Figure 11.8 shows a portion of the movement. The text here reads: "But now it's done, it's over, we've had our chance. There was even, for a second, hope of resurrection, or almost." It seems to encapsulate the almost narrative "stream-of-consciousness" flow of the work. Eclecticism abounds in both text and music. Text examples are drawn from such sources as Claude Levi-Strauss's book *Du Cru et du Cuit* (on Brazilian origin myths of water), Samuel Beckett, and Berio's own words (all set with performance directions in English, such as "impatient," "indignant," and "bewildered"—these taken, for example, from just four bars on page 12). Music quotes are prevalent throughout the third movement and include fragments from Debussy's *La Mer,* references to Berio's own music (primarily *Epifanie* and *Sequenza 4*), as well as quotations from "Bach, Schoenberg, Ravel, Strauss, Berlioz, Brahms, Berg, Hindemith, Beethoven, Wagner, Stravinsky, Boulez, Stockhausen, Globokar, Pousseur, Ives. . . ."[14] The major quote, however, is from Mahler's Second Symphony (Scherzo), which runs throughout the movement in one form or another. "As a structural point of reference, Mahler is to the totality of the music of this section what Beckett is to the text."[15] (The Beckett referred to is *The Unnameable*). Aside from the diverse juxtapositions of contrasting elements, the movement tends to shift around three centerpins: a short upbeat motion followed by a crashing cluster chord (at L, M, and Y in the score). Between these flow the overkill of musical information for which the work has become so noted.

The fourth movement returns to the reverie of the second and is a reaggregation of materials used in all three previous movements. The material grows higher (as in the second movement), particularly enveloping the major second/minor third intervallic set. Sudden bursts of sound suggest recapitulation of the second part of the first movement.

The treatments of the vocal part in the first, second and fourth sections of *Sinfonia* resemble each other in that the text is not immediately perceivable as such. The words and their components undergo a musical analysis that is integral to the total musical structure of voice and instrument together. It is precisely because the varying

---

14. From liner notes by the composer, Columbia MS 7268.
15. Ibid.

degree of perceptibility of the text at different moments is a part of the musical structure that the words and phrases are not printed here. The experience of 'not quite hearing' them is to be conceived as essential to the nature of the work itself.[16]

The fifth movement is set in a single variations type structure introduced by a piano/voice/flute soli trio section. The music, characterized by materials similar to those in the first movement, is more integrated and involves less contrast. The text continues to expose heterophonic multiple language collage, with clusters waxing and waning in an interlocking repeated pitch, or vacillating tremolo style.

In its five-movement form, *Sinfonia* resembles a Bartókian arch form:

I   II   III   IV   V

with the centerpiece (movement III) a striking compilation of diverse materials surrounded by two quiet, almost passive, sections and bounded externally by two agitated and dramatic movements.

3. Orchestration: *Sinfonia* employs an orchestra of eighty-one players and eight vocalists. The stage layout is given in the performance notes and includes a diagram of spatial locations for each of the orchestral groups. The violins divide into three (not the usual two) sections and are spaced diagonally from left to rear right, across the stage. The three percussionists are situated as far apart as possible, with percussion I in the center. The vocalists usually stand directly in front of the conductor and need amplification to be heard.

Berio gives the percussion (and particularly the piano) a very large role in the orchestra. Orchestration involves some doubling and incorporates a sectional approach (i.e., rare solos). Few effects are used (muting and harmonics are the exceptions) and balance is obtained by careful handling of dynamics.

4. Basic Techniques: While quotation and texts play an important role in *Sinfonia,* the underlying core of consistent materials and vocabulary ties the work together. These center rhythmically around expanding and contracting rhythmic units, metrically evolved through an interplay of duple and triple elements. Figure 11.9 is an example from the first few bars.

These escalate to involved rhythmic schemes around repeated couplets (i.e., two-note groupings recurring in an environment of constantly shifting rhythmic design). Pitch seems lessened in importance by the large structures of sound (discussed more fully under vertical and horizontal models) that are primarily based in seconds and thirds (with leaps developed out of their octave transpositions: sevenths, ninths, etc.).

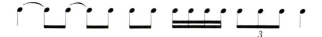

Figure 11.9. Luciano Berio: *Sinfonia*, examples of rhythmic development.

16. Ibid.

Figure 11.10. Luciano Berio: *Sinfonia*, examples of vertical sonorities.

5. Vertical Models: As mentioned earlier, harmonic structures in *Sinfonia* seem to be built primarily out of seconds and thirds. Figure 11.10 shows six of these in ascending order of complexity and dissonance.

    The first is a frequently repeated harmony found at the end of the first and fifth movements in the voices (again suggesting arch form) and in a number of other locations throughout the piece. It consists of a minor triad with a major seventh. The second example, like the first, is generally consonant with suggestions of a whole-tone scale (extracted from the opening of the second movement). Example 3 (from the fourth movement) begins to show deepening complexity and illustrates the growth of dependency on the intervals of seconds and thirds (note the beginning of contradictory chromatism: D♭ and D♮). Example 4 (from the second movement) creates similar tension with slight variations, while example 5 (from the beginning of the first movement) deepens the dissonance. The final example (from one of the large constructs of the third movement) is a near panchromatic (ten different notes) structure, again of stacked seconds and thirds. There is clearly no systematic application of specific rules, but rather an imaginative and intuitive approach to intervallic development.

6. Horizontal Models: Most of the vertical structures mentioned above arise out of slowly adding ntoes horizontally. All chord structures seen in Figure 11.10, except 1 and 6, were created by adding notes from the bottom in orders that incorporate no leap larger than a third. These are typical of the melodic style that Berio incorporates throughout *Sinfonia*.

7. Style: *Sinfonia* is a prime example of the *post avant-garde* musical style. It is a contrapuntal work developing elements of quotation (media), clusters (sound-mass), improvisation (brief but important vocal ornamentations), and serial techniques (inherent in the post-Webern tradition). The culmination of these diverse elements in a *gestalt* represents the essence of the *post avant-garde*.

    It would seem that such diverse elements as the work "talking about itself" ("Keep going, going on, call that going, call that on. But wait. He is barely moving, now almost still. Should I make my introductions?"—at which point the singers are introduced by name while the music continues), the extensive quotation, exploring nearly every conceivable sonority (from major thirds, triads and lush ninth chords to panchromatic clusters) and the use of massive dramatic bursts of sound within delicate frames of textures (the first movement primarily) could not possibly make sense. However, reflecting a society gone mad with self-preoccupation, *Sinfonia* forcefully drives its musical/dramatic point home, leaving few listeners with less than a profound disturbance borne of having indeed heard the through-composed expression of *self* without restraint. The work does indeed have continuity and a kind of frightening "madness," a macrocosm of dramatic fusion. While traditional in notation, material for quotes, form, and rhythmic flow, it is as well a highly *avant-garde* work in text, "act" of quoting, and eclectic, harmonic, and melodic idioms, and is a striking example of the *post avant-garde*.

This work, with its dramatic and often "stream-of-consciousness" feel, resembles the Peter Maxwell Davies work analyzed in Chapter 4. Both rely on quotation of various composers as well as a free use of available resources. It also compares favorably with Penderecki's *Capriccio* of Chapter 3's Vectoral Analysis, though not so explicitly (drama and unordered pitch components primarily). This work relies significantly on many of the experiments in the realms of electronic music (Chapter 7), utilizing them, however, in its imaginative use of timbre with traditional instruments.

Bibliography

*Further Readings**

Burrows, David. "Music and the Biology of Time." *Perspectives of New Music.* (Fall-Winter 1972):241. A stimulating *post avant-garde* reference.

Cage, John. "The Future of Music." *Numus West* 5:6. An interesting article and, though garbed in the usual Cage linguistics, presents a different Cage than usual, and *his* future (". . . if there is one . . .") is one bred not so far from that described herein.

Cope, David. Biography of George Crumb. *George Crumb: Profile of a Composer.* New York: C. F. Peters Corporation, 1986. Photos accompany a straightforward narrative of this composer's life (thus far).

————. "Footnotes." *Composer* 4, no. 2 (1973):52. Relates directly to the *post avant-garde*.

————. *"A Post Avant-Garde." Composer* 3, no. 2 (1972):61.

Gilbert, Steven. "Carl Ruggles (1876–1971): An Appreciation." *Perspectives of New Music* (Fall-Winter 1972):224. A man of early synthesis.

Gillespie, Don, ed. *George Crumb: Profile of a Composer.* New York: C. F. Peters Corporation, 1986. This includes articles by Gilbert Chase, David Burge, David Cope, Suzanne MacLean, Richard Wernick, Eugene Narmour, Jan DeGaetani, Teresa Sterne, and Robert Shuffett.

Harbison, John. "Peter Maxwell Davies' *Taverner." Perspectives of New Music.* (Fall-Winter 1972):233. About a man active in the area of the *post avant-garde*.

Henze, Hans Werner. *Music and Politics.* London: Faber and Faber, 1982. This is a collection of the writings by Henze in this area. It is fascinating reading albeit extraordinarily opinionated.

"Musician of the Month: Karel Husa." *Musical America* (August 1969):5. A good but short biographical sketch.

Ives, Charles. "Music and Its Future." In *American Composers on American Music.* edited by Henry Cowell. New York: Unger Publishing Co., 1962. Most prophetic.

*Addresses for record companies, periodicals, and music publishers mentioned in this Bibliography can be found in Appendix 4.

Johnston, Ben. "On Context." *ASUC Proceedings* 3 (1968):32. Superbly optimistic article on this subject. See p. 35: "That's why I think it's spring." A most sincere and credible quote from this man of diverse musics.

Ligeti, György. "Metamorphosis of Musical Form." *Die Reihe* 7 (1960):5. An excellent article on this man's evolutionary and revolutionary process of thinking.

————. Witold Lutoslawski, and Ingvar Lidholm. *Three Aspects of New Music* (from a composition seminar in Stockholm). Stockholm: Nordiska Musikförlaget, 1968.

Petcock, Stuart. "Multiple Values in New Music." *ASUC Proceedings* 7/8;75. A most interesting and relevant article on the relativity in criticism of new music.

Poissenot, Jacques M. "Luciano Berio." In *Dictionary of Contemporary Music,* edited by John Vinton (New York: E. P. Dutton & Co., 1974), p. 78. Excellent in its breakup of the composer's styles into four major periods to date: "serial, electronic, aleatory, and eclectic."

Rochberg, George. "The New Image of Music." *Perspectives of New Music* 2, no. 1:1. An interesting early approach to the concepts of unity in new music.

Salzman, Eric. *Twentieth-Century Music: An Introduction.* Englewood Cliffs: N.J.: Prentice-Hall, 1967. Has a fascinating *post avant-garde* ending (p. 186).

Santi, Piero. "Luciano Berio." *Die Reihe* 4:98. An interesting view of Luciano Berio at the time (1958).

Varèse, Edgard. "The Liberation of Sound." Edited by Chou Wen-chung. In *Contemporary Composers on Contemporary Music,* edited by Barney Childs and Elliott Schwartz (New York: Holt, Rinehart and Winston, 1967). An incredibly well-edited and "composed" article on the futures of music as diverse as they may be. It prophesies the *post avant-garde* with great clarity (the article is based on lectures given by Varèse during the years 1936 to 1962).

Recordings and
Publishers

Berio, Luciano. *Sinfonia.* Universal Edition. Recorded on Columbia MS-7268. CD. Erato; ECD 88151.

————. *Epifanie.* Universal Edition. Recorded on RCA LSC-3189.

————. *Sequenza IV.* Universal Edition. Recorded on Candide 31015.

————. *Coro.* Universal Edition. Recorded on DG 2531 270.

Cope, David. *Concert for Piano and Orchestra* (1981). Recorded on Opus One No. 82.

————. *Re-birth.* Seesaw Music Corp. Recorded on Cornell CUWE-16A. For Concert Band.

————. *Threshold and Visions.* New York: Alexander Broude. Recorded on Folkways FTS 33452.

Crumb, George. *Ancient Voices of Children.* Peters. Recorded on Nonesuch 71255.

———. *Makrokosmos III.* 1974 Peters. Recorded on AMU 038. A work for two amplified pianos and percussion. BIS-CD 261.

Davies, Peter Maxwell. *Eight Songs for a Mad King.* Boosey and Hawkes. Recorded on Nonesuch H-71285.

del Tredici, David. *Final Alice* (1976). Recorded on London LDR-71018 (D).

Druckman, Jacob. *Windows* (1972). MCA Music. Recorded on CRI S-457. An extraordinary collage of different types of music.

Erb, Donald, *Symphony of Overtures.* Galaxy Music. Recorded on Turnabout 34433.

Felder, David. *Rondâge.* Published by Alexander Broude.

Husa, Karel. *Apotheosis of This Earth.* Associated Music Publishers. Recorded on Golden Crest 4134.

———. *Sonata for Violin and Piano.* Recorded on Grenadilla 1032. A superb example of the *post avant-garde.*

Ives, Charles. *Central Park in the Dark* (1906). AMP. Recorded on Columbia MS-6843. Interesting "pre-logue" of the *post avant-garde.*

Kolb, Barbara. *Soundings* (1981). Boosey & Hawkes.

Ligeti, György. *Requiem.* Peters. Recorded on Wergo 60045.

———. *Lontano.* Schott. Recorded on Wergo 322.

———. *Aventures.* Peters. Recorded on Wergo 60022.

———. *Melodien for Orchestra* (1971). Recorded on Decca Head 12 (England). Also contains versions of his *Double Concerto* (1972) and the *Chamber Concerto* (1970).

———. *Le Grand Macabre.* Recorded on Wergo 60085. This unpublished opera is a masterwork by this extraordinary composer.

Nono, Luigi. *Canti di Vita e d'amore* (1962). Ars Viva. Recorded on Wergo 60067. An interesting *post avant-garde* work for soprano, tenor and orchestra.

Rochberg, George. *Violin Concerto* (1974). Recorded on M-35149. Resurgence of post-Romantic tonality *vis â vis* "new tonality."

Schwantner, Joseph. *Aftertones of Infinity* (1978). Mercury 75141. An extraordinary work, shameless in its tonal references.

Stravinsky, Igor. *Variations (Aldos Huxley in Memoriam, 1964).* Boosey and Hawkes. Masterwork of a man of synthesis. Recorded on Columbia MS-7386.

Takemitsu, Toru. *November Steps* (1967). Peters. Recorded on RCA LSC-7051. Interesting work of culminative opposites.

Toensing, Richard. *Doxologies I.* Recorded on Cornell University #9.

12 · THE NEW CONSERVATISM

Nowhere does influence of Eastern music upon occidental concepts appear so obviously and vigorously as it does in the new conservatism. Both Terry Riley and Philip Glass visited India where they became fascinated by the ragas (melody-type), talas (repeated rhythmic patterns), gamaka (ornamentation), and tamburas (drone) they found there. Indian master sitarist Ravi Shankar had direct and indirect influences on these and other minimalist composers which has had a lasting effect on new music. The result has been a blend in the precision of performance (to wit, the Glass Ensemble) with heavily repeated materials using principally Western instruments and tunings.

As with most new developments in the *avant-garde* (if indeed the new conservatism could be so defined), the influence of John Cage must be acknowledged. While Debussy and others earlier on had crudely investigated the possible resources in the Orient, it was he who first (in 1947) began attending lectures of D. T. Suzuki. His studies of Zen and related Eastern philosophies greatly influenced him and hence the rest of the new music world. Those who worked directly with Cage, particularly Morton Feldman whose soft and effete works show significant Eastern influence, also created much stir. Lou Harrison (influenced by Henry Cowell) has developed extensive Southeast Asian gamelans for the performance of his work (Pacific Rim influence).

Today, while universality is the mainstay of the new conservatism, diversity abounds. In some cases (Steve Reich in particular), repeating materials shift in and out of phase, creating densely populated clouds of sound at times and monophonic lines in juxtaposition. In other cases (namely Philip Glass), the bar line sets the stage for changing meters for different lengths of repeating material. Still others (especially Terry Riley) use slow expansions or reductions which take place over long and mesmerizing spans of time. Some composers (La Monte Young and Harold Budd) distilled the essence of the minimalism and created terse works more conceptual than sonic. Others adapted a perceived aimlessness in Indian and Eastern musics and adapted them to the instruments and triadic emphasis in much of today's new music (*new age,* in particular). In all cases, however, the influence is decidedly conspicuous.

A second source of influence apparent in the new conservatism is the search for a common style roughly analogous to that previous to the 20th century, a style which can speak to a general audience. Philip Glass comments: "[My music] is essentially concert music, which means inventing a new language as opposed to pop, which tends to be imitative. But the idea that concert music is only for a handful of people has only existed since the First World War. The language I've invented is not a purposely difficult one—it's a language of our time. I think people are beginning to hear that" (from an interview in the *Village Voice*). Whether or not this new language has, in fact, been invented by him, that we are speaking of it as a language at all suggests the search for a common voice, a single mode through which composers can express their ideas without reinventing the wheel for each new work.

It should also be noted that the Beatles, and especially the work of George Harrison, invited Eastern (especially Indian music) to enter the world of popular music. An overlap or cross over between these two very different international cultures brought about an invitation for a similar crossing over within the world of concert music (*avant-garde* versus popular). This is most evident in the general popularity of, for example, the music of Glass and the success of new age music.

Whether all of the music presented in this chapter could be considered cross-cultural remains to be seen. Whether future music will be defined by multi-cultural processes, techniques, instruments, or concepts is likewise impossible to infer. However, it is certain that much of the widespread adoption of basic minimalist and conservative tendencies has been influenced directly or indirectly by non-Western sources.

Minimalism

Frederic Rzewski's (founder of the *Musica Elettronica Viva*) *Coming Together* (1972) exemplifies minimalist techniques. The score contains 394 measures of continuous running sixteenth notes (no other rhythm occurs in the piece) over which a vocal line speaks the words of an inmate from the Attica Correction facility. Figure 12.1 provides an example of the repetitious yet varied pulse and the G pitch centricity. Figure 12.2 shows the second and third measures of the work. Here, the first two sixteenths frame the motive and pulse in synchronization. The third, fourth,

Figure 12.1. Measures 1 and 297 of Frederic Rzewski's *Coming Together* demonstrating the lack of significant variation in this minimalist work.

Figure 12.2. Measure 2 and 3 of Frederic Rzewski's *Coming Together.*

Figure 12.3. Copyright © La Monte Young & Marian Zazeela 1971. Courtesy: Heiner Friedrich. (Photo credit: Robert Adler.)

and fifth notes, however, extend the motive to three notes and cross the pulse at beat 2. The sixth and seventh notes are repetitions of the initial note with dual roles. For example, the G can be considered the end of the extended motive or the beginning of the new version. While seemingly unimportant, these dual and even triple role inferences give the work its diversity. Notes 6 and 7 are linked to note 8 in such a way that the opening motive is repeated, but shifted with respect to beat. Notes 9, 10, and 11 repeat the first variant of the motive, metrically altered. Careful evaluation of the two bars (less than 1/100 th of the piece) shows a microcosm of actions and reactions, of cross accents and cross rhythms, all of which contrast the lack of development in new pitch and rhythm material. *Coming Together* is a striking work from the minimalist school which shows its power and potential.

Minimal music is also apparent in the music of Harold Budd. His *Lovely Thing (Piano),* in which one chord is softly attempted many times over a period of fifteen to twenty minutes; *One Sound* for string quartet; and *The Candy Apple Revision* (1970), which states simply, "D-flat Major," all classify as minimal compositions. About his approach, Budd remarks:

> Ever since (a long time ago) I've pushed and pushed towards zero: Running it all down, a kind of on-going process of removal. There's an enormous difference, by the way, between Monotony and Boredom. Boredom, it seems to me, is trying to make something interesting. Monotony is making nothing interesting. And insofar as I feel all art to be utterly worthless (no redeeming social values), I'm interested in that what I do is pretty—("Terrifying," "Gripping," "Sensitive," "Relaxing," "Hypnotic," "Spiritual"—all to the side for a moment) an existential *prettiness;* a king of High-Art Uselessness. . . .[1]

1. From a letter to the author.

Much of minimal music actually is *maximal* [2] in duration. La Monte Young's New York City-based (6 Harrison St.) *Dream Houses* (1968, funded by the Dia Art Foundation) are media works of great duration (Alex Dea singing, Jon Hassell on horn, David Rosenboom, viola, and De Fracia Evans working slide projections). Like most minimal works these contain drones and slowly overlapping (focusing in and out) projections: a minimum of material. These works derive from earlier experiments such as *The Tortoise, His Dream and Journeys* (1964–), performed over extended periods of time by *The Theatre of Eternal Music* (John Cale, a member of the *Velvet Underground* rock group, on viola and Tony Conrad on violin).

Many of these works find precedent in Erik Satie's *Vexations*. This 32-bar piece is to be played softly 840 times. His *musique d'ameublement* (1920) is also minimal music. This "furnishing music" co-composed by Satie and Darius Milhaud was played during intermissions and programs announced: "We urge you to take no notice of it and to behave during the intervals *as if it did not exist.*"[3]

Composers such as Charlemagne Palestine, Yoshima Wada (whose large horns are created from "plumbing pipes") build on drones and/or slowly overlapping motives creating a slowly evolving *somnambulistic* state. Max Neuhaus's underwater work, *Water Whistle,* utilizes 8–10 water driven whistles and can be heard only if you are submerged in the same water as the whistles (as well an overlap with *danger music*). Karlheinz Stockhausen's (*aus den Sieben Tagen,* 1968) is a verbal score containing only very brief performance directions such as "play single sounds with such dedication until you feel the warmth that radiates from you—play on and sustain it as long as you can."

Philip Corner is especially noted for his work with minimal concepts often lasting evenings, at other times lasting brief seconds (for example, his *One Note Once* which is just that; the instrumentation being flexible). His *Metal Meditations* are often collaborations with others involved in the *Sounds out of Silent Spaces* series in New York City: Carole Weber, Julie Winter, Elaine Summers, Annea Lockwood, Alison Knowles,[4] Daniel Goode, and Charles Morrow, among others. These are evening-long events featuring composer-constructed and traditional instruments struck softly but with intense aural expression. These meditations also involve "total experience" with "ritual food events," slide projections, and lights. *Corner's One Note Once, Cage's 4'33"* and Young's *Compositions of 1960* all approach the ultimate minimal structure: 0 duration, 0 instruments, 0 performers, 0 audience.

Many composers feel that the *avant-garde* as such is dead, and that the works in the 1960s point to a return to simplicity, a return to the foundations of sound itself: pitch, duration, and silence. These composers and their works no longer achieve

---

2. The term *process* is also used to describe music which unfolds slowly, one that carries the thrust of invention by slowly processing one idea to another. Music in this genre, while appearing minimal, achieves "mileage" through constantly generating variations of a single idea.

3. Pierre-Daniel Templier, *Erik Satie,* trans. Elena French and David French, 1932 (originally published by Presses Universitaires de France). Cambridge, Mass.: The MIT Press, 1969, p. 45.

4. Knowles (along with Jaran Downey and Gunther Maier) has recently been involved with *Other Media's* production of *Music in the Key of J* in New York City. This was broadcast on Teleprompter's Channel J (produced by Charles Morrow).

the "shock" immediacy and notoriety that *avant-garde* works of the 1950s–60s characteristically received, nor the pretentious complexities of systems and scientific paraphernalia so in evidence with more mainstream academic-based composers. Steve Reich's *It's Gonna Rain* (1965), *Violin Phase,* and *Piano Phase* (both 1967), and *Pulse Music* for phase-shifting gate, an instrument invented by the composer (1968–69), are notable.

The New Tonality

During the late 1960s, many composers began intense experimentation with tonal resources. This reacquaintance seems rooted in two traditions: minimalism and the basic pendulum that swings through music (and all other) history. In the first instance, composers discovered that utilizing basic tonal materials in a repeating minimal fabric allowed their music to have continuity without the phrase/cadence structure of Classical tradition. In the second instance, the timing seemed right for the inevitable return to simplicity at a time when music was fragmented and without common threads.

LaMonte Young's work in the very early sixties (see section on Minimal Music) influenced a diversity of individuals on both coasts of the U.S. (notably New York City and Los Angeles). The simplicity of design and materials in Young's work, often based on justly tuned fifths, provided many composers with intriguing ideas suggesting further development: consonance and minimalism. James Fulkerson's *Triad,* for example, consists of a C major triad performed over a 12- to 20-hour period without variation. Robert Moran's *Illuminatio Nocturna* presents a C-rooted major thirteenth chord repeated slowly and softly for an extended period of time. This work and his subsequent "trance music" represent other manifestations of this drone-like approach to triadic materials.

Terry Riley's *In C* (1964) gave a needed impetus and visibility to this new school of composition. The work is constructed from repeated and overlapped motives in the "key" of C moving, over a period of 45 to 90 minutes, to E, back to C and then to G. This is not the tonality one finds in late Romanticism; rather, it is a minimal work (the complete score can be placed on a single sheet) structured around continuously repeating octave Cs. Two major works follow *In C: Poppy Nogood and the Phantom Band* (1968) and *A Rainbow in Curved Air* (1969). Both of these works continue the explorations begun with *In C.* Each develops richer and more complex interrelationships of tonal materials less associated with drones and rhythmic repetition.

Philip Glass began developing a similar kind of style in the late sixties with pieces like *Music in Fifths* (1969). This work evolves through expanding scalular cells in a kind of F-Dorian mode (three flats in the signature). He creates an "additive" structure common in his later works. For example, a three-note motive becomes four, then five, etc. with the initial motive repeated on each reoccurrence. His opera *Einstein on the Beach* (1976) is a massive tonal work which continues to receive wide acclaim. His audience is as eclectic as his music, with rock and pop followers as well as traditional and experimental "serious" admirers. His work with the Philip Glass Ensemble has contributed enormously to this success. Minimal tonal music is very difficult to perform due to both its maximal length and intonation requirements. Glass's ensemble epitomizes the precision necessary for proper performance.

John Adams's *Shaker Loops* for seven solo strings (1978) and *Phrygian Gates* for piano (1978) utilize triadic source materials. Both works create the atmosphere of self-regenerative energy and at the same time, lyric melodic curves traditionally associated with tonal music. Other composers committed to similar types of minimal/tonal composition include Beth Anderson, Gavin Bryers, Stuart Smith, William Duckworth and Phil Winsor (notably *Kyrie Eleison* for choir and tape drone, 1977).

In England, Cornelius Cardew's work with the *Scratch Orchestra* provided opportunity for both large scale improvisation (performers were largely unskilled) and performances of simple tonal works. His enormous work *The Great Learning* (1971, particularly *Paragraph 2)* provided precedence for renewed tonal activity. Cardew was motivated by political beliefs and moved towards a more traditional tonal style with works such as *Soon,* based on Maoist-like texts and ideals. The music consists of single lines with "chording" similar to popular music (C, F, etc. relating to triads) while at the same time containing an unmistakeable hint of Cardew's inimitable rhythmic subtleties and twists of phrase.

Lou Harrison has long persevered in this tonal realm. His *Mass to St. Anthony* (1962) is modal-tonal in key and sixteenth century in counterpoint. Even traditional cadences balance and direct the lines. Yet there is a subtle twentieth century inflection throughout. His work with the *American gamelan* is the basis for a number of new works using rich tonal materials, though less traditionally Western in cadence and phrasing.

Robert Ashley's cryptic *Perfect Lives (Private Parts)*—"an opera in seven episodes"—is tonal (at least in basic pitch materials). Its composer-created text is "surrealistically" rooted in "sixties" nihilism as it comments on "Rodney's" life. Ashley's voice and the keyboard performance of Blue Gene Tyranny are so authentic in its recorded version (see Bibliography) as to negate reproduction by any other performers. The cultural and anthropomorphic aspects of both the music and the poetry of this piece contextualize the tonal materials. The use of tonality provides a commentary on the soap opera nature of society.

George Rochberg's career spans three periods: rigorous dodecaphony, Ivesian-like quotation, and his own brand of new conservatism. His 23-minute *Trio* (piano, violin, 'cello) falls principally in the latter of these periods. The work begins and ends in E major. The non-tonal syntax exploits the principle that successive chords contradict one another (chromatically) at least once with common tones providing continuity (e.g., G major, g minor, F# major, Eb major, etc.). Polytonality results from the direction of diatonic lines. The first movement spans the key-signatures of E, Bb, E, C, Db, C, Db, G, and E major respectively, though clearly all of the music presented is not within these centers. In fact, Rochberg relentlessly avoids the C triad when in the signature of C major. He provides "ghosts" with C as the common tone (i.e., F and Ab major; f and c minor triads). Ostinato pedal tones on D and G in octaves provide the kind of tonal anticipation that serves as one of the most tasteful and successful aspects of this work. Ultimately, the composer does provide the tonic pitch (without, however, the full triad). Much of the work belies the signature-implied key (a midmovement section ends on a Db major triad in the signature of 4 sharps). The final movement propels the listener through the same key centers as the first movement, but with more bravura and direction. The skeletal attacks which succeed in driving the movement to a close create the *Trio's* most effective moments.

Each of the tonal idioms mentioned above bodes a virulent future for tonality in the latter years of the twentieth century. The static and somnambulistic qualities of single resonant chords, though possibly less immediately conceivable as a style, could begin an entirely new language for tertian harmonies. Minimal tonal music, based on repetitions of ever varying melodic fragments, is reaching wider audiences than most recent *avant-garde* styles. More and more composers seem infatuated with its potential. Even works which imitate traditional models of tonality, either in admiration or parody, have gained significant following in recent years. If any aspect of twentieth century music seems providential, it is most surely this recent trend toward consonance.

New Age Music

The widespread use of minimal techniques has led to the rise of what has been generally called *new age* music. This then breaks into further sub-divisions: "Inner-harmony" (meditative, usually instrumental, supposedly healing) and "progressive" (nondistracting, usually electronic, inspired by the work of Vangelis Papathanas-sious). While many feel that this area has more ties with *muzak* than with serious musical intent, one cannot ignore the fact that various forms of new age music can be found in motion picture soundtracks, new music concert halls, radio stations (some devoted exclusively to it), and to opera and stage soundtracks. Since many of the performers and composers involved in the new age area have roots and traditions in jazz, it is not surprising to find that influence present in much of the work done to date. Its more radical protagonists claim effects from listener tranquility to serious changes in the mentally ill. Others insist that it mirrors the inner harmonies of man. Some believe that the name derives from a proclamation of the sacred writings of India (Vedas) which tell of the incarnation of gifted musicians at the beginning of each new age in order to herald man's increasing ability to understand the mysteries of life. Others contend that it comes from ancient Egypt and even Atlantis where the cultures believed that certain musical notes could stimulate and awaken the *chakra* energy centers that lead to expanded awareness. Most agree that there is a kind of ancient/future aspect to whatever definition is assigned.

Connections between new age music and recent interest in "harmonic convergence" in 1987 (the beginning of a five year world-wide destabilization followed by a 1992 to 2012 period of relaxation in preparation for the new age which begins on December 21, 2012) seem loose but of interest. Special locations such as the 2,000 year-old Tule Tree in Oaxaca, Mexico, Machu Picchu in Peru, Stonehenge in England, Mount Shasta in California, the Great Pyramid in Egypt, Mt. Olympus in Greece and Serpent Mound in Ohio are considered vortices where the harmonies of the universe focus (long believed to be significant in the Sundance tradition).

Unlike pure minimalism, new age music does not necessarily involve constant repetitions. Rather, a constant dynamic state, consistent slow to medium tempi and bluntly tonal environments persist. In "progressive" types of new age, there are more attempts at unusual timbres but the sense of suspended time pervades the music. "Inner-harmony" new age music, on the other hand, often has distinct meters and traditional chord progressions. One critic summed up his views by saying that in new age music "anything goes nowhere."

The simplest forms of new age music employ natural sounds or their synthetic imitations. Don Campbell's *Lightning on the Moon,* for example, is based on a heartbeat and the overtone series. The composer claims that, in general, his music heals, educates, and creates well-being in its listeners. Many such composers refer to the pioneering work done by the French M.D. and hearing psychologist Alfred A. Tomatis who attempted to prove that physical health can be altered by the transmission of certain frequencies of sound to the brain. Known as the Tomatis method, his views suggest that serious health changes can occur by the use of auditory stimulation.

Such beliefs in the power of music have led some composers into cult traditions and studies of drugs which make the same claims on healing and raising of consciousness. Workshops, formed around the general topic of shaman exploration, occur regularly in certain new age circles. Visits to *huichol* (a group of Native Americans who use certain drugs to produce meditative and spiritually exalting hallucinations) sites in Mexico have provoked some to feel strongly that new age music shares a ritual quality with other arts (notably dance) as expressed in these nontraditional cultures.

Brian Eno composes ambient music (self-proclaimed) for airports, businesses, and the home (notably *Ambience I*). Lists of ambient nature recordings now occur regularly in the Schwann record catalog and include the nonedited sounds of meadows, sailing, the sea, thunderstorms, heartbeats, the wind, Okefenokee Swamps, summer cornfields, etc. *Relax Video* (begun by Jacob Podber) produces videotapes of aquariums and fireplaces which stand as uncut, two-hour documentaries of one camera, one-shot life exposures to the subject of their titles with a soundtrack of new age compositions. His new age production called *Ocean TV* is a minimalist production of waves crashing off the Long Island coast with no sound whatsoever. "God did a lot better job than I could have," the composer argues. Other groups such as Windham Hill records and Natural States (views of mountains and waterfalls specifically) continue to develop new age scenes of no plot, no direction video panoramas. Some have termed the style *new impressionism* to indicate the level "time suspension" in many of the works presented on this label. ECM (Germany) is a more jazz-centered new age music record company which produces such composers as Keith Jarrett, Chick Correa, Pat Metheny, and Ralph Towner.

Of the other "inner-harmony" new age composers, Stephen Halpern (piano, usually with some combination of electronics and strings) and George Winston (mostly solo improvisatory piano) stand out. Halpern's *Comfort Zone,* for keyboards and strings, moves with typically meditative and inoffensive diatonicism through a variety of aimless scenes. Long themes roam above moderately moving passages formed of modal pedal points. Winston's *Winter into Spring* demonstrates the composer's freely improvisatory style. Here, the harmonic scheme often uses the circle of fifths with subtle shifts to chromatic (but triadic) sonorities. Mark Isham's film music (most notably *Never Cry Wolf*) exemplifies pure "inner-harmony" techniques. Rarified long melodies are placed over simple triadic ostinati that usually center around a single key center with little variation or development.

The works of Vangelis (noted for film scores of *Blade Runner* and *Chariots of Fire*), on the other hand, exemplify the progressive side of new age music. He uses long themes under which are effects produced from a variety of found (cultural *musique concrète*) and created (usually synthesized) sounds. While this music varies distinctly from its "inner-harmony" sister, it retains the same conformity to nonmetric and time suspended weightlessness. The timbres, though widely varying in source and type, all seem chosen by their associative but relaxed natures. His *Earth* and *To the Unknown Man* particularly emphasize these characteristics.

Vangelis has noted (in an interview reported in *The Art of Electronic Music* by Tom Darter—see the bibliography): "You feel just like you have to start creating." It's like you feel when you have to go to the toilet. Then I just push the tape, and it happens when it happens. I don't know how it happens. I don't *want* to know. I don't *try* to know. It's like riding a bicycle. If you think, "How am I going to do it?", you fall down. If you think about how to breathe, you choke. But when you do things dramatically they happen like that."

Figure 12.4. *New age* composer Vangelis Papathanassious.

Composer Kitaro, like Vangelis, circumscribes large arcs of sound, usually a blend of electronic and live sounds. His *Toward the West* and *India* exemplify new age progressiveness.

Another progressive new age composer, Upper Astral, overlays extremely long tonal melodies on punctuated triadic ostinati reminiscent in some ways of the *alberti bass* of previous centuries. This composer also employs sonic scenes of the surf, wind, and fountains. *Journey to the Edge of the Universe* epitomizes the use of these sources. Frequent synthesizer drones and filter band sweeps (through the overtone series) also occur.

Whether new age music, as both a concept and a reality, will truly develop into a form for future *development* or become a relative of background music for hospitals and bus stations, will be seen during the next decade. Many serious composers and highly qualified musicians are, at present, actively engaged in its creation. Its hallucinogenic qualities combined with a rising popularity among crossover artists has convinced many that it will remain an active force in new music. Some even suggest that a kind of new universal language may someday prevail and develop from this source. Composers claim that since any sound can be used, the form has arisen out of contemporary music over the past few decades. With the generally inoffensive tonal vocabulary and simple and long directed melodic lines, it also has a very solid root in the world of popular music.

Postlude

In Chapter 1, the author attempted to explore the various relationships between the arts and cultural trends of the late nineteenth century in terms of the origins of the *avant garde*. "It is no accident that art parallels the tempo of world events." The comparisons hold true today. In obvious cases such as technology, the relevance appears so striking as to be impossible to refute. Forty-six percent of all musical instruments sold in 1986 were electronic in construction. The digital revolution is exploding onto new fronts daily. The accessibility of personal computers has provided a technology to all musicians that ten years ago was available only in university research centers. This is true in the other arts as well. Computer lighting boards and digitally processed graphic arts programs have given rise to a whole new generation of technically-minded creators and producers.

In less obvious areas, one finds the concepts of specialization and economy as important points of comparison. Styles have not only fragmented into various schools of thought and aesthetic, these schools further have separated into single views of individuals. Many composers, seeking to find a true language, write consecutive works in widely different modes without concern. Gone are the simplicities of a pen and paper mode of composing; now typesetting software and laser printers have brought desktop publishing possibilities to every home. The economics of keeping up technologically have become a major factor even for the "notes on paper" composers. The use of sampled sounds, digital editing, and storage as well as production, will be the greatest single evolution of the late 20th century. These will have a profound effect on performance groups of all kinds. Ensembles and orchestras, which hitherto have depended (at least in part) for their income on the commercial world, whether radio, TV, or live performance, will find the competition stiff. Sampling systems will, as their synthesizer cousins have already proven, drop significantly in price over the next few years. An increase in quality will allow any composer anywhere to perform large scale works without the large scale performance resources.

On subtler levels, one finds the conservatism exemplified in this chapter in every arena: politics, religion (fundamentalist), visual arts, architecture, motion pictures, etc. There is a sense of rondoic return to an earlier period where simplicity abounded and music and all of the arts were a part of cultural heritage and distinctly not in the rarified air of academia or a concert hall setting.

Musical style, as well as instrumentation, shows a distinct return to former aesthetics. One finds, for example, long tapering lines reminiscent of Mahler in new age music. Quasi-tonal progressions abound freely in a variety of new music forms which only ten years ago would have seemed very out of place. Effects, from the "noises" of Russolo to the early efforts in electronic music, have come full circle with sampling devices which imitate traditional instruments. Rhythm, once fragmented by pointillism, has returned in many styles to a steady and predictable metric pulse (sometimes even employing motor-rhythms as in the works of Philip Glass). The free use of pitch class has diminished significantly with lines returning to more traditional and predominantly stepwise motion so prevalent even in turn-of-the-century music. Interests in diverse tuning systems, combinations of various media, indeterminacy and cluster chords have waned significantly since their inceptions in the 1940s and earlier. Even the challenge to tonal harmony seems exhausted, with few who resist the simple graces of triadic consonances on a systematic basis.

While exact counterparts may stretch the point, some are irresistible. Glass and Satie, for example, or Crumb and Ives, new age and impressionism, while not obviously presenting clear parallels, do not beg the point. Even techniques of artificial intelligence and music suggest the introspection so inherent in Schoenberg's self-studies towards serialism and the work of Busoni and others in scientific applications turn to style. Most important, however, is the *ethos* of a period where, with technological advances expanding horizons in a multitude of directions, composers retrench into a reexamination of ages past where subtle hierarchies and nuances of musical structure predominated and individuality emanated from personal statement within a style, not from the shock and newness without it.

Visionary Roberto Pavo has predicted the many changes he feels will take place during the next few decades: "Mice attached to TV sets with Mac-like menus where visual and sonic images can be frozen, digitized, edited and printed in just a few seconds. The body will become cybernetic with all manner of contraptions attached to it including alpha-state Walkmen-like radio-tape-players and automatic massage units as well as the already extant electronic organs; talking machines everywhere, even toaster ovens; intelligent machines will run our houses, our businesses, even our lives—they will even tell our fortunes and our horoscopes (and we'll believe them). They will compose our music, write novels, create videos, fight our wars, run our space program and, generally speaking, our future. It's all fantastic." (from *Future Now!* see Bibliography).

George Crumb sums it up succinctly in his article titled, "Music: Does it have a future?": "I am optimistic about the future of music. I frequently hear our present period described as uncertain, confused, chaotic. The two decades from 1950 to 1970 have been described as 'the rise and fall of the musical *avant-garde*,' the implication being that nothing at all worthwhile was accomplished during those years. My own feeling is that music can never cease evolving; it will continually re-invent the world in its own terms."

As the author looks back over 20 years and five editions of *New Directions in Music,* what is clear is that good music takes the same drive and skills it always did and the same patience on the part of its audience to understand it. New technologies, electronic performance potentials, conservative or *avant garde* styles do not guarantee quality—only composers can do that.

(For information on vectoral analysis and procedures see Chapter 1.)

Vectoral Analysis: Philip Glass: *Einstein on the Beach*

1. Historical background: Philip Glass was born in Baltimore on January 31, 1937. He received his Bachelor's degree from the University of Chicago in 1956 and then studied at Juilliard where he earned another BA (1959) followed by an MA (1961). There he worked with William Bergsma and Vincent Persichetti. He had further studies with Darius Milhaud (at the Aspen Music Festival during the summer of 1960) and with Nadia Boulanger (on a Fulbright scholarship during 1963–65). From 1961–63 he served as composer-in-residence for the Pittsburgh public schools under a Ford Foundation grant. Glass worked with Ravi Shankar in Paris in 1965, teaching him solfège and taking lessons in tabla from Shankar's associate, Allah Rakha. Inspired by the rhythmic and metric centricity of this music, he traveled to India for six months during 1965–66.

    On his return he collaborated in performances with Steve Reich and Arthur Murphy, finally developing his own group, the Philip Glass Ensemble, in 1968. He and his ensemble toured extensively during 1970 both in America and abroad. *Einstein on the Beach* was completed in 1975 as a collaboration between Glass and noted mixed-media conceptualist Robert Wilson. Its first performances in Europe proved quite successful. On November 21, 1976, the American premiere brought immediate attention and acclaim. In 1978 he was awarded a Rockefeller grant for a three-year-period.

    He has completed two other operas: *Satyagraha* (1980) and *Akhnaten* (1984). These and *Einstein* roughly form a trilogy which Glass states is based on "historical figures who changed the course of world events through the wisdom and strength of their inner vision" (Gandhi and an Egyptian pharaoh in the latter cases respectively). His work (especially since 1965) is minimal in nature with repetitions of pitch layered over a finely varied rhythmic base.

Figure 12.5. Philip Glass.

Glass comments about his musical style in an interview with *Keyboard Magazine* (April, 1987): "I'm not interested in exotic and funny weird sounds. To me, that seems like an endless avenue; once you start on it, there's no telling where in the world it might lead. Maybe it's partly a generation thing too. I'm a pencil-and-paper composer. That's how I was taught to write music, and it's easier for me to conceptualize with a paper and pencil than it is with a machine."

2. Overview: *Einstein on the Beach* is an opera in four acts, nine scenes, and five "kneeplays" which occur at the beginning and end of each act. The work involves vocal and instrumental music, dance, and sets resembling traditional opera. However, there is no traditional plot here, no story to follow. Instead the work employs a sequence of events which develop the musical score more than a tangible direction. Indeed, even language, while expressive, is based on mathematical choices.

For example, "I feel the earth move . . . I feel the tumbling down tumbling down. . . . There was a judge who like puts (sic) in a court. And the judge have like in what able jail what it could be a spanking." Stage action follows similar discontinuity. Freud, Queen Victoria, Stalin, and Einstein (among others in the opera) are defined by a rhythmic parceling of the five-hour performance time.

Figure 12.6. From a performance of *Einstein on the Beach*.

The numbers 1, 2, and 3 figure heavily in the structural layout of the work. The first three acts have two scenes each, repeating twice the three elements of train, trial, and field. These elements appear in the final scenes of the last act as building (for train), bed (in the trial scene earlier) and the interior of a time/space/machine seen above the field of Act 2 and 3. The stage is divided into three layers: foreground, middleground, and background (or downstage, centerstage, and upstage). These translate into sections called portrait, still-life, and landscape and intensities termed skin, flesh, and bones.

3. Orchestration techniques: The ensemble for *Einstein* requires 5 to 8 performers on electric organs, viola, 'cello, and soprano saxophones. Much of the work is in unison and at very fast and consistent tempi demanding a high level of technical proficiency from the performers. Effects are nonexistent and timbre exploration minimal. In fact, the music is so sparse vertically at times that when straightforward harmonies do occur they produce extraordinary results even though they seldom extend beyond triads. Sparsity therefore conditions the listener and Glass is able to get expansive results from only minor changes in the music.

4. Basic Techniques: Glass employs repetition, addition/subtraction, and modes
   to create an often hypnotizing effect. The number of repeats follows either
   the score or, in the case of his ensemble performing, directions during the
   course of performance. Figure 12.7 shows measures 3 and 4 of Act 4, Scene
   2, organ solo. Repeats may be extensive. The second measure shows the
   additive procedure (7 to 8 notes), the filling in of structural detail (the E
   between D and G at the end of the second measure) and the harmonic
   variation (A-C-E instead of C-E-A). The drone of the octave C is typical of
   Glass's work. Pedal tones, struck at the beginning of bars of constantly
   changing meters (though not explicitly shown), provide the underpinnings of
   the music's motion. The beat here (eighth notes) remains fixed as exactly as
   possible providing the kind of locomotive charge that persists throughout.

5. Vertical Models: Figure 12.8 demonstrates a typical harmonic progression
   from *Einstein on the Beach.* Common tones proliferate. While triadic, the
   music does not follow other traditional (Western world) voice-leading
   practices though it does move stepwise (a Glass trademark). There is
   virtually no contrary direction in the "voices" and the 6/4 chord at the end
   of this passage suspends every cadential tradition. The chromaticism follows
   that of Hovhaness and others by creating subtle key shifts between chords
   (i.e., difficult to explain the A major triad of measure 3 in the key of F minor
   (measures 1 and 2). The non-triadic structure of measure 4 (A–D♯-B)
   outlines a dominant seventh of E Major (the final chord).

   Glass has commented on this in an interview (Cole Cagne and Tracy
   Caras, *Soundpieces: Interviews with American Composers*—see
   Bibliography):

In *Einstein,* the kind of cadential formula that runs through it, the I-VI-IVb-V-I progression that you hear in the Spaceship and the Knee Plays, the voicing and working out of that was done by somebody who knew very well how traditional harmony operated. I don't think that anyone who didn't have the training that I did could have written that. So even though my music seems so far away from her (Nadia Boulanger), it was only four or five years after studying with her that I began to find uses for the things that I had learned.

Figure 12.9. From the second page of the score *Einstein on the Beach.*

6. Horizontal Models: Measures 16 through 20 of the quoted section of *Einstein* provide an apt model (shown in figure 12.9). Here the measures show metric divisions of 4/3/4/5/6 (no two measures of the same length). Nothing else changes here. The repeating pulse of the pedal point and the left hand (organ) C remain the same in each case. Given that each of these measures will be repeated many times during the actual performance, the constantly changing appearance of these measures is somewhat deceiving. Once a pattern has begun, one may be more than reasonably confident that it will immediately repeat many times; first exactly and then with slight variation, with these in turn repeating.

7. Style: Glass's *Einstein on the Beach* is a major example of music minimalism in the freedom of nonliterary theater. The discontinuity between the various music, choreographic, set, and action elements creates a rich counterpoint at once mesmerizing and confusing. Repetitious and slightly varied fragments of music of different lengths, often performed in unison or within consonant triadic harmonies, suggest a more traditional vocabulary with the exceptional lack of diversity providing a definite contemporary idiom. The success of this work and others in its genre with both concert hall and popular music enthusiasts has given rise to speculation that it may become the universal music language of the latter decades of the 20th century. Glass continues to compose music for the theater, movies, and his ensemble.

This work demonstrates favorable comparisons to the works analyzed in Chapter 1 and Chapter 6 (especially "conceptualism"). It ignores the ongoing technological developments and innovation. The repetitive nature of Glass's style, and that of most of the music reviewed in this chapter, contrasts most sharply with the ideals expressed in Chapters 5 and 10. "Indeterminacy," for example, suggests the exact opposite: a lack of repetition from event to event and even over the largest frame of sonic expression.

Bibliography

Further Readings

Doczi, György. *The Power of Limits*. Boston: Shambhala Publications, Inc., 1981. This author and philosopher strives to explain the world through a vision of the Fibonacci Series Golden Rule. Notable are his theories of expression in art, architecture, and music as the simplest rationalizations of this vision.

The Experimental Music Catalog. Published at 208 Ladbroke Crove, London, England.

Garland, D. "Creating *Einstein on the Beach:* Philip Glass and Robert Wilson speak to Maxime de la Falaise." *The Audience Magazine of BAM's Next Wave Festival* ii/4 (1984): 5.

Glass, Philip and Robert Wilson. *Einstein on the Beach*. New York: EOS Enterprises Inc. This book provides samples of all the various elements of the work including music, story, and choreography (by Andrew de Groat). As these are notated in the hands of the creators, it gives insight into the procedures and elements of the collaboration.

Hamel, Peter Michael. *Through Music to the Self*. Dorset, England: Element Books, 1978. Mantra, psychedelic, intuitive, and esoteric.

Jones, Robert T. "Musician of the Month: Philip Glass." *High Fidelity/Musical America* 29 (April 1979). An interview with the composer on his opera *Einstein on the Beach* (discussed in this chapter).

Kupbovic, L. "The Role of Tonality in Contemporary and 'Up-to-date' Composition." *Tempo* 135 (December 1980) 16–19.

Palmer, R. and Philip Glass. *Einstein on the Beach*. Liner notes to the Tomato 4-2901, 1979 recording. Excellent insights into the music and production.

Pavo, Roberto. *Future Now!* New York: Futurista Publications, 1987.

Rzewski, Frederick. "Prose Music." In *Dictionary of Contemporary Music*. Edited by John Vinton. New York: E. P. Dutton & Co., 1974, p. 593. An excellent and definitive resource for this topic.

Schaeffer, John. *New Sounds, A Listener's Guide to New Music*. New York: Harper and Row, Publishers, 1987. Devotes a page to new age music and covers a number of composers such as Brian Eno and George Winston.

Schwartz, K. Robert. "Steve Reich: Music as a Gradual Process." *Perspectives of New Music* (Spring–Summer 1981): pp. 373–94.

Simms, Bryan R. *Music of the Twentieth Century, Style and Structure*. New York: Schirmer Books, 1986. Covers many aspects of this chapter, especially the work of Philip Glass.

Tame, David. *The Secret Power of Music*. Rochester, Vermont: Destiny Books, 1984. The author attempts to meld the ideals of "new music," world music and jazz using OM (or divine vibration). This esoteric and visionary approach leaps from one proposed gestalt to another often providing insight, more often confusing issues without resolution.

Vandenbroeck, André. *Philosophical Geometry*. Rochester, Vermont: Inner Traditions International, Ltd., 1987. This is an attempt to integrate philosophical, geometrical, and musical concepts through the Pythagorean theorem. The symmetrical concepts parallel those of Doczi but lack the grace and elegance of line and curve (notably the Fibonacci-based Golden Section relevance).

Winckel, Fritz. *Music, Sound and Sensation, A Modern Exposition*. New York: Dover Publications, 1967. An innovative and speculative text on perception and sonic delineation.

Young, La Monte and Marian Zazeela. *Selected Writings*. Munich: Heiner Friedrich, 1969. This is an excellent source for materials by this composer inclusive of interviews. It also contains the concepts and drawings of *Dream Houses*.

———. "Sound is God: The Singing of Pran Nath." *Village Voice*, April 30, 1970. More a study of the author than the singer.

Adams, John. *Shaker Loops.* Phillips 412214-4 PH. For string quartet, this work exemplifies motivic repetition in a quasi-tonal language. CD: PHIL; 412 214-2PM.

———. *Harmonielehre.* (1985) Nonesuch 79115. A lush orchestral work which, in minimalist style, winds out a tremendous amount of music from very little material. CD: Nonesuch; 79115–2.

———. *Phrygian Gates.* New Albion NA-007. For piano.

Ashley, Robert. *Private Parts.* Lovely Music LML-1001 and VR-4904.

Budd, Harold. *Coeur D/Orr* (1969). For tape, soprano saxophone, and voices. Recorded on Advance 16.

———. *Oak of Golden Dreams* (1970). Recorded on Advance 16.

Campbell, Don. *Crystal Meditation.* C-9517 (cassette tape). New age music for meditation and relaxation (according to the composer himself).

Corner, Philip. *Rounds.* Soundings 3, no. 4:92.

———. *Ear Journeys: Water* (1977). Printed Editions. Score includes a seaweed insert.

Eno, Brian. *Here Come the Warm Jets* (1973). Recorded on Island 9268. A good example of Eno's ambient music.

———. *Ambient #2—The Plateau of Mirrors: Eno and Budd* (1980). Recorded on Editions EG.

Glass, Philip. *Music in Fifths.* Recorded on Chatham Square CS-LP-1003.

———. *Music in Similar Motion.* Recorded on Chatham Square CS-LP-1003.

———. *Music with Changing Parts.* Recorded on Chatham Square CS-LP-1001/2.

———. *Einstein on the Beach.* Recorded on Tomato 4-2901.

Halpern, Steven. *Comfort Zone.* Grammavision 18-6786-4 (cassette). New age music for many instruments.

Harrison, Lou. *Suite for 'Cello and Harp* (1949).

Kitaro. *Toward the West.* Recorded on Geffen, GHS-24094.

———. *India.* Geffen GHS 24085.

Isham, Mark. *Vapor Drawings.* Windham Hill WH-1027. New age music. CD: Windham Hill; WD-1027.

Penguin Cafe Orchestra. *Music from the Penguin Cafe.* Recorded on Editions EG EGED-27. This minimalism group creates simple and repetitive music drawing particularly on classical music, pop styles, East African music, and the folk heritage of Venezuela.

Reich, Steve. *Four Organs* (1970). Recorded on Angel S-36059. Incredible work which slowly fades four organs in and out of phase.

———. *It's Gonna Rain; Violin Phase.* Recorded on Columbia MS-7265. The words are first stated and then, by splicing, slowly altered while repeating.

———. *Music for 18 Musicians* (1976). Recorded on ECM Warners 1129.

Riley, Terry. *In C.* Recorded on Columbia MS-7178. Score published with the recording. A riveting high C repeated throughout on a piano with motives slowly changing (usually by extension and diminution) over long periods of time.

———. *Poppy Nogood and the Phantom Band.* Recorded on Columbia MS-7315.

———. *A Rainbow in Curved Air.* Recorded on Columbia MS-7315.

Rzewski, Frederick. *Coming Together.* Soundings 3, no. 4, with composer commentary. Recorded on Opus One No. 20.

———. *Variations on 'No Place To Go But Around' for Piano* (1973). Watt Works. Recorded on Finnadar 9011.

Satie, Erik. *Complete Piano Music.* Denon CD-7485, -86, -87. Several extraordinary works in this collection and an excellent performance by Takahashi. CD: Denon; C37-7486.

Upper Astral. *Journey to the Edge of the Universe*. Recorded on Valley of the Sun Records. Also includes *Celestial Harmonies*.

Vangelis (Papathanassious). *Earth*. Polydor 6499693 PSI. Excellent example of this "progressive" new age composer.

———. *To the Unknown Man*. RCA AFL1-4397. Another example of new age mastery.

Winston, George. *Winter into Spring*. Windham Hill WH-1019. New age music (solo piano) in first rate recording and processing. CD: Windham Hill; WH-1019.

Young, La Monte. *The Tortoise, his Dreams and Journeys* (1964). Recorded on Shandar 83510. Young, listed also in the New Experimentalism chapter, often works with droning minimalistic sounds.

GLOSSARY OF TERMS

This is an alphabetical listing of those terms used in the text which may need further clarification. An asterisk (*) after a term within a definition signifies that the word so starred is itself defined within this glossary.

additive synthesis   the creation of timbres by plotting the amplitude envelopes of the fundamental and harmonics of a timbre.

algorithmic music   music based on algorithms defined as step-by-step procedures (often shown as block diagrams with interconnecting lines) and usually produced by a computer.

amplifier   an instrument used to increase the power of a sound or signal.

amplitude   equivalent to the "loudness" of a pitch; the dynamics of sound.

amplitude modulation (AM)   a periodic variation of amplitude* creating tremolo.

analog computer   a computer whose information is stored and processed using continuous electromagnetic energy on wires or tapes, as opposed to a digital computer,* which employs only off/on states.

antimusic   a term denoting those works the concept or implication of which is "opposed to" the traditional meaning of music. In current terms, it refers to those compositions which either (1) include no reference to sound in their scores; (2) destroy one or more of the traditional composer/performer/audience relationships; or (3) are impossible to perform and exist only in concept.

atonality   literally, away from tonality, or no tonality. Atonality is truly impossible to obtain, as any group of sounds will by acoustical principles have one or more strongest tones (tone center = tonality), just as they will have form (intended or not). *Pantonality** (inclusive of all tonalities) has for the most part replaced the term *atonality* in reference to twelve-tone music (dodecaphony*).

augmentation   expanding the duration of a rhythmic set without disturbing the relationship of elements (e.g., doubling or tripling the value of each note).

autonomous music Xenakis's term for music which does not employ "strategy" or "games" in its performance. This would include all of traditional music and all *indeterminate music** that does not result from group conflict (*heteronomous music** is the opposite term).

avant-garde a French term literally meaning *advance guard* or *vanguard;* in the arts, applies to those who work in the newest areas of creativity. It may come to mean in music a certain period (such as "modern") roughly covering the years 1935–1975. Thus the term *post avant-garde* means after the earlier period: no longer can anything be really "new."

band-reject filter an electronic filtering device that eliminates a particular band (group) of frequencies while allowing the remainder to pass.

band-pass filter an electronic filtering device which allows a certain band to pass while rejecting all the remaining frequencies; often applied to white sound* in order to create a wide variety of timbres.

Bauhaus an art school in Germany (founded in 1919 by Walter Gropius, and closed in 1933) in which the various art forms and crafts were taught interdisciplinarily. Faculty included Paul Klee, Vasily Kandinsky, and Mies van der Rohe (among others of like prominence), and was instrumental in encouraging the development of many of the media-forms extant today.

binary a term used to denote a numbering system in "base 2." Only two numbers need be used (0,1), and can be represented by

any system capable of two states. To create linear* numbers (1,2,3 . . . etc.), a code is created defined by columns proceeding to the left by increments following an exponential series (1,2,4,8,16 . . . etc.). In this way, any number can be represented and operated upon. (0 0 0 1 = 1; 0 0 1 0 = 2; 0 0 1 1 = 3; 0 1 0 0 = 4; etc.) This concept is important for digital computers.

black sound used to denote silences as opposed to white sound* (inclusive of all frequencies).

brake drum the housing of the braking mechanism of an automobile; also used as a percussion instrument.

chance music often used synonymously with *indeterminate* music*, it means any music in which there is a "chance" result whether it be by composer, performer, or both.

circular bowing on string instruments, a procedure whereby the bow is kept in motion (regardless of bow direction change) by a circular action of the bow across the string.

circular breathing on wind instruments, the ability of the performer to breathe in through the nose while expelling air through the mouth, thereby needing no rests or "breaks" to regain breath. Performers well-versed in this procedure can play continuously for great lengths of time.

classic electronic music electronic music created primarily by "splicing" one sound to the next rather than by using keyboards and sequencers.

cluster a chord or sound which contains two or more intervals of a major second or less.

combinatoriality a twelve-tone technique wherein hexachords* of different versions of the same row can be exchanged to create new rows (still twelve different pitches). Forms of newly created rows can be used simultaneously with the original to avoid unisons, octaves, etc., often characteristic of contrapuntal dodecaphonic* techniques.

computer-generated sound timbres produced by computational means by either additive* or FM synthesis.*

contact microphone a certain type of microphone which requires physical contact for reproduction of sound.

cross-coupling a tape-recorder technique of attaching the playback of one channel to the record of the other channel and vice versa to create a reiteration of attack with built-in decay,* usually employed in live-electronic music.*

DAC Digital-to-analog-converter. An instrument designed to translate digital* information into analog* sound (primarily conversion of numbers into voltages and smoothing the result into continuous voltages for sound production).

dada international movement (beginning around 1916) which some feel originated with the poet Tristan Tzara. It included artists such as Man Ray and Marcel Duchamp among others, and attacked all conventional standards and aesthetics of "art." Exemplified by redefining machine-produced objects as works of art, by collages of newspapers, etc., it was (and some still feel it still is) one generating force behind the *avant-garde*.

decay   that aspect of a tone's envelope* in which the amplitude decreases.

digital computer   a computer whose information is stored and processed in binary* numbers.

dodecaphonic   a term commonly used to refer to twelve-tone music.

drift   in electronic music, any unintentional shift of frequency due to equipment inaccuracy. All analog* oscillators* and generators* necessarily include a small amount of drift.

envelope   the amplitude* characteristics of a signal. Most typically: attack, initial decay,* sustain, and final decay.* Envelope generators control both the amount and duration of each of these characteristics.

equal temperament   dividing the octave into twelve equal parts. Based on the twelfth root of two, this system represents to some composers an artificial solution to the problems encountered by just* intonation.

feedback   a result of cross-coupling.* Literally, any electronic device in which sound is fed back through the system one or more times to produce echoes or, depending on gain* adjustment, an increase of sound to limits of system tolerance.

filter   an electronic instrument designed to allow selection of frequencies from a signal: band-pass,* band-reject,* for example.

Fluxus   a group of *avant-garde** composers beginning in the 1960s with intentional direction toward danger and boredom as viable concepts of art.

FM synthesis   the artificial creation of harmonics via sidebands of complex spectral FM.

fractal   a self-replicating object which regenerates at succeeding smaller and larger levels.

frequency modulation (FM)   a periodic variation of frequency creating vibrato.

Futurists   Italian group of composers (1912–20) employing a wide variety of noise*-making instruments.

gain   amount of amplification. Variable gain would be the "loudness" knob on any sound-producing device (e.g., amplifier).

generator   sound source of all types of electronic signals except sine waves.*

gesamtkunstwerk   German term meaning literally "complete art work." Used to denote the nineteenth-century view of opera (particularly Wagner's), the composer creating and controlling all aspects of the work—staging, music, lyrics, dance, etc.—and all aspects contributing equally to the total effect.

graphic   in music, those scores which are more oriented toward visual incitement than communication of directions through symbols.

hardware   a computer term used to denote actual instrument technology as opposed to programmatic (software*) technology. Colloquially, hardware refers to "hard" physical instruments while software* refers to programs.

heteronomous music   music which utilizes "games" and "strategy" during performance, producing *conflict* and indeterminate* results. Term primarily used by Xenakis.

heterophony   "hetero" = several; phony = sounds. This term identifies music that contains many variations of a melody simultaneously.

hexachord   in its simplest form: a six-note chord. Commonly used in twelve-tone music to construct various further computations of the row.

improvisation   music which involves some performer freedom during performance within a certain set of parameters* created by the composer. As opposed to indeterminate* music, improvisation suggests (often demands) that the performer draw upon techniques and intuition (based on his previous experience) within a set stylistic framework.

indeterminacy   act of composer, performer, and/or both, in which the outcome is unpredictable. In general, unlike improvisation (where the performer is asked to draw upon previous experience and techniques), indeterminacy requires a *real* "letting of sounds be themselves" (as John Cage has put it) with performers and performing situations allowing any sound to exist within the framework set by the composer. The term *aleatoric* is sometimes used to denote indeterminacy.

interface   any instrument which allows two different instruments to function together. In computer music (especially computer-generated sound*) the digital-to-analog (D/A) *interface* allows the digital computer to produce analog sounds on tape. A MIDI *interface* allows many different digital instruments to communicate to one another.

inversion stating something upside down. In twelve-tone music this refers to rearranging an entire row exactly by calculating up intervals down and vice versa.

isorhythm a compositional technique of Gothic music (c. twelfth to fifteenth century, primarily in Machaut) in which a set rhythm is repeatedly applied throughout the composition to iso-melodies (isomelos) of different duration and number of notes.

just tuning tuning systems based on the overtone series.* The intervals of the fifth and the major third are calculated (ratios 3:2 and 5:4, respectively) from the series and projected into pitch series.

klangfarbenmelodien German term denoting color pointillism*: individual notes have distinctly different timbre, and are further separated by range.

klangflächenkomposition sound-mass* which ebbs and flows through constant overlapping of timbre* and spatial* modulation.

laser as used loosely in multimedia,* an intense beam of directed light usually connected to a receiving device which, in turn, usually leads to an oscillator.* When the beam is broken (by performer or object), the oscillator is triggered by the receiving device.

linear literal meaning: pertaining to line. In traditional music "linear" refers to melodic or contrapuntal flow. In electronic terminology "linear" refers to a "straight" line flow as opposed to exponential accelerated flow.

live-electronic sound created by a performer working "live" using electronic instruments in a concert situation. "Live" also refers to an approach opposite to that of composing electronic music on tape by splicing procedures (classical*).

matrix a box of 144 squares that provides all versions of a twelve-tone row. The original is placed across the top with the inversion top to bottom; all notes are then filled in according to transpositions. This is an important device for analysis and composition of twleve-tone music.

microtone an interval which is less than an equal-tempered half-step. Quarter-tones* are one example.

MIDI an acronym for Musical Instrument Digital Interface, the default standard in the music industry for digital instrument communication.

mikropolyphonie highly complex densities of polyphonic motion in which no single voice dominates.

mixer an electronic instrument designed to combine signals by algebraically summing their amplitudes.

modulation a process in which any aspect of a sound or signal is varied (e.g., amplitude modulation* and frequency modulation*).

montage a visual overlapping of images.

multimedia a work which employs two or more traditionally separate art forms. "Happenings" are multimedia events which are more or less aleatorically conceived.

multiphonics the technique (particularly on wind instruments) of obtaining two or more sounds simultaneously. Obtained by control of the overtone* series so that one or more of the partials becomes prominent enough to be heard as a separate tone. Another voice can be added by humming.

musique concrète music which employs nonelectronic sounds on tape. The tape recorder is most commonly the compositional tool, and sounds are manipulated after recording to achieve the desired effect.

noise traditionally defined as undesirable sound. Today, however, as composers continually employ sounds which were in the past "disliked," or considered "nonmusical," it has come roughly to mean those sounds whose complexity is such that individual frequencies are no longer determinable and/or audible.

oscillator an electronic instrument designed to create sine waves.*

oscilloscope a device used to show (via cathode-ray tubes) the characteristics of incoming signals (amplitude,* frequency, etc.).

ostinato a rhythmic grouping which is repeated many times.

overtone all sounds except sinusoidal forms contain small secondary pitches called overtones, the alteration or filtering* of which alters timbre.

panchromatic inclusive of all chromatic tones. Usually used to refer to cluster* chords in which all or most of the twelve (traditional) pitches occur.

pandiatonicism inclusive of all diatonic (or key-scale) notes. Pandiatonic clusters* include all seven scale notes (e.g., a white key forearm cluster on piano = key of C pandiatonic cluster).

pantonality inclusive of all tonalities. Like atonality* it is impossible to achieve, and thus very loosely applied to twelve-tone music.

parameter any characteristic element or concept (of sound) which can be controlled.

pitch class the set of pitches related to a given pitch by octave transposition (e.g., all B's belong to the same pitch class).

pointillism a term derived from the graphic arts; as applied to music, each sound becomes more an entity in itself, separated distinctly from those before and after by space (frequency), distance (silence) and/or timbre.

potentiometer (pot) a variable resistor used to control the energy in a system. Most usually found as a volume control.

prepared piano a piano the timbre of which has been altered by the placing of various objects between, on, or around the strings inside the instrument.

program computer software* designed by the programmer to initialize and control the computer in specific operations. In composition, programs are set up in advance to create the parameters* of the computer's "musical" language as well as act as interface* between the "programmer" and the computer.

process music music created by overlaying short motives of different lengths. The "process" is as important as the resultant variations.

psycho acoustics the study of sound and its complexity, and its realistic communication both physically and psychologically to man.

pulse wave any waveform that instantaneously moves from a negative to positive function. This includes all square and rectangular wave forms.

quarter-tone the distance between two tones which are one-half of a semitone (half step) apart. Those instruments capable of variable intonation (e.g., string instruments) approach quarter-tones in correct performance of traditional tonal music (a D♭, for example, is differentiated from a C♯ according to context).

real-time a term used to denote composition time equivalent to performance time (as opposed to abstract or nonreal time, in which, due to notation requirements, conception and composition requires much more time than performance).

retrograde literally meaning "backwards." In twelve-tone music, a row is permutated in twelve retrogrades (R) or readings of the original versions backwards.

ring modulator a signal multiplier circuit, combining signals to produce the sum and difference of their frequencies, with only the resultant sidebands exiting.

sampling the ability of a computer to calculate as points the characteristics of a waveform. The higher the sampling rate the better the resultant fidelity of sound in analog output through speakers. (45K usually the minimum)

sequencer a device capable of storing programmed control voltages in order to "play" them at any given speed.

serialization the ordered and intellectual logic applied to any or all aspects of compositional technique. This term no longer applies to just twelve-tone mechanics.

sine-wave a tone which contains no overtones.*

software computer programs.* As opposed to hardware,* software refers to programs and data; i.e., "soft" as opposed to "hard" instruments (the computer itself).

sound-mass a block of sound in which individual pitches are no longer important and/or perceptible. Used instead of *noise** to avoid negative connotations.

spatial modulation the compositional technique of moving sound evenly and continuously from one physical location to another.

square wave a pulse wave* with equal positive and negative energy.

splicer an instrument to cut and place together segments of tape for synchronization. It is used extensively in classic* electronic music.

stochastic music mathematician Jacques Bernoulli's term from the Greek meaning, literally, "target." Stochastic laws state that the more numerous indeterminate* activities become, the more determinate their outcome. These are often improvisatory or indeterminate in isolation, but in mass create the same construct of sound-mass*, mikropolyphonie* and/or klangflächenkomposition.*

strategic music heteronomous* music composed of "live-performance" games.

synthesizer an electronic device used to artificially create timbres.

tetrachord a group of four notes. Often used to designate one of the three groups of four notes of a twelve-tone row.

timbre modulation the compositional technique of moving sound continuously and evenly from one timbre to another.

triangle wave waveform that, when viewed on an oscilloscope,* takes the shape of a triangle. It contains every other overtone.*

trichord any group of three notes. Often used to designate one of four groups of three notes of a twelve-tone row.

vibrato frequency modulation.* This is different from the tremolo created by amplitude modulation.*

vocoder an instrument designed to code sounds (speech) into digital information for communication over cables or by radio (subsequently decoded upon reception). It is now used by some composers to create new sounds by modifying traditional ones.

voltage control the ability of one module in a synthesizer to control another. A vital concept for electronic music allowing many techniques (AM,* FM,* etc.) to take place without manual control.

white sound sometimes referred to as white noise; sound which contains all possible frequencies (called white, from white—inclusive of all colors—light). Often used in conjunction with various filters* to create a wide variety of timbres.

wind sound sculptures sculptures designed to allow wind to create sound; similar to Oriental wind chimes.

BIOGRAPHICAL DATA

A listing of many of the composers discussed in this book, with brief biographies and/or current information about each, appear here in alphabetical sequence. Omissions are due either to lack of definite information concerning the composer, and/or necessarily limited space. Only non-USA birthplaces are listed.

ANDRIESSEN, Louis (b. 1939, Utrecht. Holland) is a leading composer of Holland where he currently has served as musical advisor to the Globe theater group of Amsterdam.

ANTHEIL, George (1900–59) was noted as America's *Bad Boy of Music* (book by Antheil published in 1945), and during the twenties and thirties as one of the most confusing figures in the world of music. His *Ballet mécanique* (inclusive of airplane motors, doorbells, and the like) is considered by many to be a milestone of the *avant-garde*. His music is as stylistically diverse as his character.

ASHLEY, Robert (b. 1930) was cofounder of ONCE (at one time an annual festival of new music in Ann Arbor, Michigan) and coordinator of the ONCE Group. He is active as both composer and performer of new music and holds degrees from the University of Michigan and the Manhattan School of Music.

AUSTIN, Larry (b. 1930) was the editor of *Source: Music of the Avant-Garde*, a biannual publication devoted to the music of the *avant-garde*. He is currently teaching in the music department at North Texas State University. His works have appeared as part of a number of important festivals, including the New York Philharmonic 1964 *Avant-Garde* Series and the 1965 Rome *Nuova Consonanza*.

BABBITT, Milton (b. 1916) was professor of music at Princeton University and a director of the Columbia-Princeton Electronic Music Center. Educated in mathematics as well as in music, he was particularly well suited for the complicated intricacies of programming and detailed acoustical knowledge necessary for composition using the Mark II Synthesizer. As one of the major representatives of American music, his work has received numerous performances throughout the world. He retains all possible control over compositional elements whether his materials be electronic or instrumental.

BEHRMAN, David (b. 1937) was cofounder of the Sonic Arts Group (performers of live-electronic music) and a producer of recordings of new music for CBS and Odyssey Records. As composer/performer, he has participated in many festivals of new music, including the Angry Arts Festival in New York, and the Lincoln Center Library New Music Concerts. He continues to organize and support concerts and recordings of *avant-garde* music both here and abroad. He currently works with live computer music (via microprocessors).

BERIO, Luciano (b. 1925, Italy) founded the electronic studio at the Italian Radio in Milan with Bruno Maderna in 1955. A prolific composer and conductor, he lived in the U.S. and taught at Juilliard School of Music until 1973. He now conducts and composes in Europe and his music continues to rely on an intuitive "dramatic" approach.

BOULEZ, Pierre (b. 1925, France) is founder (in 1953) of the new music series *Domaine Musicale,* and continues to be active in his support of new music. In 1970, he took up duties as head conductor of the New York Philharmonic, replacing Leonard Bernstein. A prolific composer and author, his music and approach continues to be a major influence in the European *avant-garde.* He founded IRCAM in Paris.

BRANT, Henry (b. 1913), whose first works appeared in the then *avant-garde* publication *New Music Quarterly* (early 1930s), continues to contribute as both theorist and composer to the spatial composing techniques now finding great popularity in the multimedia, electronic, and theatrical arenas.

BROWN, Earle (b. 1926) has been composer-in-residence at several universities including the University of California, Berkeley, the University of Southern California and the Peabody Conservatory of Music. During the 1950s his association with John Cage led to his use of indeterminate techniques. This, together with influences derived from Alex Calder's mobiles, led him further toward graphic and mobile-type structures, a composite of indeterminate and improvisatory techniques.

BUDD, Harold (b. 1936) whose works have appeared at FFLEM (First Festival of Live Electronic Music) has enjoyed numerous performances by Bertram Turetzky among others. He has also composed for documentary and art films. His music and philosophies are influenced in part by recent art, especially "minimal art."

BUSSOTTI, Sylvano (b. 1931, Italy) is active as composer and promoter of *avant-garde* music, notably at the Cologne series *Music of our Time,* the Munich series *New Music,* and the Florence concerts *Vita Musicale Contemporanea.* His scores are primarily graphic with emphasis on live performing/composing situations.

CAGE, John (b. 1912) is unquestionably the world's leading exponent of the *avant-garde.* His writings (*Silence, A Year from Monday* and *Notations,* among others) and music continue to explore and experiment with the basic concepts, techniques, and philosophy of all the *avant-garde* forms presented here. His percussion concerts in early 1936

(Seattle), experiments about the same time with prepared piano techniques, and his first compositions on tape (1951), along with the inclusion of chance operations involved in compositional process, culminated in a 25-year retrospective concert of his music in Town Hall (New York) in 1958. He continues to make extensive US and European lecture tours. Very few concerts of new music have failed to include the name, music, or at least the influence, of John Cage.

CARTER, Elliott (b. 1908), under the encouragement of Charles Ives, studied at Harvard with Walter Piston and in Paris with Nadia Boulanger. He has taught at Juilliard, Columbia, Cornell, Yale, and other schools and is particularly noted for his rigid and iconoclastic views of rhythm (metric modulation) and harmonic space. His works, like those of Carl Ruggles, are composed very slowly (usually at the rate of one every one or two years), and are regarded by their performers (he does not compose electronic music) as *extremely* difficult. His *Double Concerto,* and the *Concerto for Orchestra,* are considered by many to be the most difficult in orchestral literature.

CHIARI, Giuseppe (b. 1926, Italy) was coorganizer (with Bussotti) of the *Musica e Segno* and a member of *Gruppo 70* in Florence. An active member of the European *avant-garde* movement, his works were performed at the 1963 *Internazionale Nuova Musica* at Palermo, the Festival of the *Avant-Garde* in New York, and several *Fluxus* festivals. His concepts point towards a new theatrical form of music dependent on inclusion of all aural materials.

CHILDS, Barney (b. 1926) is a graduate of Stanford University (Ph. D.) and studied at Oxford University as a Rhodes Scholar. His many awards include the Koussevitsky Memorial Award in 1954, and he was an associate editor of *Genesis West*. His endeavors for Advance Records, has furthered the cause and works of new music. His works involve improvisatory and some indeterminate methods, often including audience participation but avoiding the overly-theatrical. He teaches at the University of Redlands in California.

COWELL, Henry (1897–1965) was editor of *New Music* from 1927 until the mid-forties (the periodical continued until the 1950s with Cowell on the executive board), a publication devoted to the innovative scores of that period. His 1930 book *New Musical Resources* is devoted to the new possibilities of harmony and rhythm which would later form a cornerstone for *avant-garde* experimentation. Until his death, he promoted new music with great vitality and composed prolifically in countless styles and with considerable diversity, freely open to new and creative ideas.

CRUMB, George (b. 1929) studied at the University of Michigan with Ross Lee Finney and currently teaches at the University of Pennsylvania in Philadelphia. His *Echoes of Time and the River* for orchestra won the 1968 Pulitzer Prize. His scores are unique both musically and in notation (all of his published works are autograph scores, as his manuscript is both incredibly neat and his notations unique [see examples in the body of this book]).

CURRAN, Alvin (b. 1938) has been a recipient of both the Bearns Prize and BMI Student Composers award. An active member of *Musica Elettronica Viva* in Italy (live electronic performance group), his recent music is theatrical and concerned with new sounds, both electronic and nonelectronic in origin.

DAVIDOVSKY, Mario (b. 1934, Argentina) currently composes and teaches in New York City. His *Synchronisms No. 6* for piano and tape won the 1971 Pulitzer Prize. Like Carter and Ruggles, he composes very slowly and his electronic works are *classical* in construction. He was active for many years in the Columbia-Princeton Electronic Music Center.

DAVIES, Peter Maxwell (b. 1934, England) resides in England and has been active with *The Fires of London* and the *Pierrot Players*. His music, like that of Berio, is highly eclectic and dramatic.

DRUCKMAN, Jacob (b. 1928) teaches at the Yale School of Music and has been active in the Columbia-Princeton Electronic Music Center. His *Windows* for orchestra received a Pulitzer Prize in 1972. A great deal of his music, especially the *Animus* series, is for traditional instruments and tape. He has also been involved in the creation of new sounds for traditional instruments, and their resultant notations.

DUCKWORTH, William (b. 1943) founded and was president of the Association of Independent Composers and Performers, dedicated to the performance of new music. He currently teaches at Bucknell University. His music often employs process techniques.

ERB, Donald (b. 1927) has received grants from the Ford and Guggenheim Foundations and from the National Council on the Arts. He is currently on the faculty of Indiana University. His music often employs both live and taped electronic sounds in combination with performers on traditional instruments. His works are performed widely both here and abroad and are recorded on Nonesuch and Ars Nova discs.

FELCIANO, Richard (b. 1930) currently teaches at the University of California at Berkeley, and has received grants from the Ford (two), Fulbright, and Guggenheim Foundations. His works are primarily for traditional instruments and tape and are published by E. C. Schirmer in Boston.

FELDMAN, Morton (1926–1986) was one of the major influences on young composers, through both his music and his writings about music. His works generally require very soft dynamics and are published by C. F. Peters and recorded on Columbia, Odyssey, and Time Records. His work, though influenced by painting (especially the works of Pollock and Kline) and dance (Merce Cunningham), constantly underplays the theatrical.

FOSS, Lukas (b. 1922) is conductor of the Brooklyn Philharmonic Orchestra. His music revolves around controlled improvisation based on historical concepts of live performance-creation combined with intentionally used "non-musical" sounds for drama and expression.

GLASS, Philip (b. 1937) studied at the University of Chicago and at Juilliard with Bergsma, Persichetti, and Milhand. Known for his three major operas (especially *Einstein on the Beach*), the film score for *Koyaanisqatis*. He champions a minimal (repeating with slight variation) and triadic style.

HAUBENSTOCK-RAMATI, Roman (b. 1919, Poland) studied at the University of Cracow and is living as a free-lance composer in Vienna. His music is predominantly indeterminate.

HILLER, Lejaren (b. 1924) studied with Milton Babbitt and Roger Sessions at Princeton while achieving his Ph.D. in chemistry. After 1955 he turned toward composition and with Leonard Isaacson began experiments in computer music (first at the University of Illinois and later at *SUNY*, Buffalo). A great deal of his recent composition is intermedia.

HUSA, Karel (b. 1921, Prague) studied at the Prague Conservatory as well as at the Ecole Normale de Musique in Paris (composition with Arthur Honegger). Since 1954 he has taught at Cornell University. His music is a fusion of the traditional and *avant-garde*, and his *Music for Prague* and *Apotheosis of this Earth* have made the concert band a more viable ensemble for contemporary composers.

ICHIYANAGI, Toshi (b. 1933, Japan) formed a new music performing group called *New Direction* in 1963. His works have been performed both here and abroad, notably by David Tudor.

His music often is graphic and live-electronic. In the last few years, his concepts have turned to mixed-media in the form of environmental works.

IVES, Charles (1874–1954) was (and still is) a major influence on almost every facet of *avant-garde* tradition. Almost everything done in the *avant-garde* (whether directly traceable to him or not in terms of lineage) seems predated by Ives many years before their so-called discovery.

JOHNSTON, Ben (b. 1926) taught for many years at the University of Illinois and has received a Guggenheim Fellowship and grants from the University of Illinois and the National Council on the Arts and Humanities. His writings have appeared in *Perspectives of New Music* and *The Composer*. His music is highly structured and often utilizes unique sound sources and microtones.

KAGEL, Mauricio (b. 1931, Argentina) resides in Cologne, where he serves as composer/conductor for the *Ensemble for New Music*. Many of his works involve written directions rather than notes, employ some improvisatory and aleatoric elements, and are based primarily on theatrical concepts.

KNOWLES, Alison (b. 1933) is a visual/performance/graphic artist. Her work has been influential in environmental media (e.g., *The Hour of Dust*, 1968–71). She works in New York City.

KRAFT, William (b. 1923) has been a percussionist with the Los Angeles Philharmonic Orchestra. He has studied with Otto Luening,

Vladimir Ussachevsky and Henry Cowell, among others, and has written extensively not only for percussion, but for full orchestra as well. His *Contextures: Riots-Decade '60* is a classic inter-media orchestral composition.

KRENEK, Ernst (b. 1900, Germany) began his composing career as a twelve-tone composer. He has never ceased to explore all available materials and concepts of his craft. His music is intellectual and complex with an approach directed towards individualizing each work both in concept and sound.

LENTZ, Daniel (b. 1942) has had numerous performances of his works both here and abroad. His music, generally graphic and dramatic (multimedia), often expresses political messages, and his unusual use of colors to represent instruments and/or effects gives both the visual and aural image of his works a marked individuality.

LIGETI, György (b. 1923, Transylvania) worked from 1957 to 1958 in the Studio for Electronic Music of WDR in Cologne. Since 1961 he has been professor of Composition at the Hochschule für Musik in Stockholm. Though largely nonelectronic, his music has explored the vast sonic possibilities of traditional orchestral and choral instruments. Despite the fact that his ideas are extremely complex, he continues to employ traditional notation and exact composer control. He has attained wide acclaim as a leader of the *avant-garde* both through his recordings on DG and exposure in the sound track of the motion picture *2001:A Space Odyssey*.

LUENING, Otto (b. 1900) is a foremost representative of electronic music in America. His ideas of the early 1950s continue to represent effective techniques and procedures for contemporary composers. His historical surveys of electronic music remain a primary source of information on the origins and development of this medium. He is co-director of the Columbia-Princeton Electronic Center. His music freely includes all sound sources available, especially *musique concrète*.

LUNETTA, Stanley (b. 1937) was a member of the *New Music Ensemble* and, aside from his work as percussionist (Sacramento Symphony Orchestra), has composed many *avant-garde* works. His music is theatrical and employs multimedia techniques. Through his association and performances with David Tudor and Larry Austin, he has been instrumental in advancing the cause of new music in America.

LUTOSLAWSKI, Witold (b. 1913, Poland) is both an active conductor and a composer in Poland. Most of his early works were destroyed in World War II, but show a marked traditionalism. His works today are a strong fusion of *avant-garde* and traditional techniques. He works very slowly (a large work every two years or so) and has used indeterminate and improvisatory procedures. He attributes much of his style to a hearing of Cage's *Concert for Piano and Orchestra* (divulged in a conversation with the author).

MacKENZIE, I. A. (1894–1969) was an early exponent of experimental ideas involved with novel instrument exploration and

philosophical concepts of ego and art. His music, though for the most part without notation or significant audience approval, concentrates on fantasy vs. reality.

MADERNA, Bruno (b. 1920, Italy-d. 1974) was an active conductor of new music (testament are the large number of recordings and premieres of new works he conducted in both Europe and America), as well as a composer. In 1961 he founded the Darmstadt International Chamber Ensemble which he conducted until his death.

MORAN, Robert (b. 1937) is a freelance composer in New York City. His works often involve humor as well as drama. Primarily a composer of mixed-media compositions, Moran has also been active in performing a good deal of new music (such as the puppet operas of Satie and many others when he was director of the West Coast Music Ensemble, 1968–73).

MUMMA, Gordon (b. 1935) was a member of the Sonic Arts Union (live-electronic music) and is a composer/performer actively concerned with the preservation of live performance and a controlled theatrical/gesture situation. His music is found on the *Music of Our Time* series (Odyssey Records) and Lovely Music. He is Professor of Music at the University of California, Santa Cruz.

OLIVEROS, Pauline (b. 1932) is a composer of electronic, live-electronic, and multimedia compositions and an articulate experimentalist. Her works appear on the *Music of Our Time* series (Odyssey Records) and Columbia Records, and her articles in *Source, Composer* and Printed Editions.

PARTCH, Harry (1901–1974) received many grants, including those from the Carnegie Corporation, Fromm Foundation, and the University of Illinois. A virtually unknown experimentalist in new tunings and instruments for many years, his works and ideas have recently gained wide notice, consideration, and success. His book *Genesis of a Music* and his works serve as a storehouse of new concepts and performing techniques. He lived in San Diego and taught part-time at the University of California until his death.

PENDERECKI, Krzysztof (b. 1933, Poland) has won awards from the Polish Union of Composers and UNESCO (1960) and is a graduate of the University of Cracow. His music explores the vast possibilities of sonic material available within traditional concert bodies (e.g., orchestra, choir). More recently his music follows neoRomantic techniques.

POUSSEUR, Henri (b. 1929, Belgium) works at the Brussels electronic music studio. He is a graduate of the Liège and Brussels Conservatories. Most of his music is electronic, and much of it explores the numerous sonic and acoustical possibilities of tape with live performers (especially orchestra).

REICH, Steve (b. 1936) founded (along with Terry Riley) the phase-music school of composition (principally with the works *It's Gonna Rain* [1965] and *Piano Phase* [1967]).

REYNOLDS, Roger (b. 1934) was cofounder of ONCE and has received Fulbright, Guggenheim, and Rockefeller Foundation fellowships. He teaches at the University of California in San Diego. His works are available from C. F. Peters and are recorded on Nonesuch Records.

ROCHBERG, George (b. 1918) has, since 1960, been on the staff at the University of Pennsylvania in Philadelphia. He used "quotes" freely and a liberal approach to serial techniques. Most recently his work has followed neo classic stylistic principles.

SATIE, Erik (b. 1866, France-d. 1925) was one of the most influential composers of the *avant-garde*. Composers such as John Cage, Robert Moran, and many others have given Satie the highest plaudits in terms of his influence on new music. These influences take the form of ultra-simplicity, new time concepts (i.e., *Vexations*), and inter-media. A number of biographies are available and have been listed in the appropriate chapter bibliographies.

SCRIABIN, Alexander (b. 1872, Russia-d. 1915) was influential in the use of media forms. Biographical information is available in almost any book on twentieth-century music.

STOCKHAUSEN, Karlheinz (b. 1928, Germany) resides in Cologne. His experiments with electronic music in the mid-fifties, co-editorship of *Die Reihe,* and prolific compositions utilizing electronic sound sources on tape (performed over numerous speakers placed acoustically and compositionally in and around the audience), have placed him at the forefront of the European *avant-garde*. His life and works are discussed at length in

Kontrapunkte #6 (P. J. Tonger-Rodenkirchen/Rhein). His writings about music are prolific and complex.

SUBOTNICK, Morton (b. 1933) teaches at the California Institute of the Arts in Valencia. He was one of the co-founders of the San Francisco Tape Center and has worked in the Columbia (New York) electronic studio. His more recent compositions involve "ghost" electronics.

USSACHEVSKY, Vladimir (b. 1911, Russia), together with Otto Luening, presented one of the first American tape music concerts in 1952, and continues to be one of the foremost exponents of *musique concrète* in this country. He teaches at Columbia University in New York.

VARÈSE, Edgard (b. 1885, France-d. 1965) spent the latter forty years of his life working in New York City. His early predictions and pioneering work with tape and electronic sounds, along with his original approach to concepts of music, mark him as one of the major experimentalists and creators of our time. His music is available from G. Schirmer.

WOLFF, Christian (b. 1934, France) teaches at Dartmouth University. His association in the early fifties with Cage and Feldman led to the development of very personal indeterminate procedures, often notated graphically but sometimes traditionally. His works are published by C. F. Peters and recorded on Time and Odyssey Records.

WUORINEN, Charles (b. 1938) is an active composer and pianist. Most of his works (recorded on CRI, Nonesuch, and Advance Records) require immense performer virtuosity and are explicit in notation. He has explored more nontheatrical and formally complex electronic music than most of his American contemporaries.

XENAKIS, Iannis (b. 1922, Rumania) received his early training in science at the Ausbildung am Polytechnikaus in Athens, Greece. From 1947 until 1959 he worked with the famed architect Le Corbusier. His approach to composition is founded primarily on mathematical principles and explores fields of new sounds using traditional instruments and notation. His music is recorded on Columbia, Angel, Vanguard, and Nonesuch Records.

YOUNG, La Monte (b. 1935) is one of the most highly original composers of the *avant-garde*. He studied briefly with Karlheinz Stockhausen in Germany, and is a free-lance composer in New York City. His *Dream Houses* and other mixed-media works, as well as the innovative compositions of 1960, have made him, along with John Cage, one of the most energetic exponents of new music in both America and abroad.

Further biographical information on these as well as many other contemporary composers listed in this book is available in *Dictionary of Contemporary Music,* edited by John Vinton. New York: E. P. Dutton & Co., 1974 (834 pp.).

NOTATIONS

The objective of this Appendix is to provide a skeleton outline of new music notations developed over the past fifteen to thirty years which have become somewhat standard. It is a minimal sketch, intended to illuminate some of the examples in the book. It gives samples of viable solutions to problems posed by *avant-garde* music, and hopefully will stimulate the reader to research this area in greater depth.

Introduction

Most scores over the past thirty years include "performance instructions" which describe the new symbols evolved by the composer for the work. It is usually separate, sometimes multipaged, and often full of symbols in direct conflict with similar symbols of other composers. Until the late sixties there seemed an almost endless stream of "artistic" endeavors—as numerous as composers and works attempting new directions. Since the publication of the *Darmstädter Beiträge zur Neuen Musik* in 1965 there has been a slow but steady pull toward codification of symbology. The short bibliography that follows this introduction indicates a host of articles and books dedicated to this ever-changing subject.

One of the most important new[1] concepts employed in new music is that of *proportional notation*. In most music

since 1600 bar lines serve a variety of purposes:

1. to keep performers together:
2. to provide (in some music) primary and secondary implied accents for *dance suites* and the like;
3. to make the *reading* of music more feasible (even a Clementi *Sonatina* becomes a "nightmare" upon the removal of bar lines).

Contemporary composers often feel that these bar lines conflict with their ideas of freeing musical line, form, drive, and rhythm from imposed "square-ness" and repetition. While some of these composers have solved their problems within a metered structure (i.e., Elliott Carter: *metric modulation;* György Ligeti: involved and intricate rhythmic entrances, etc.) others have felt that the only solution was to dispense with the bar line entirely. *Proportional notation* is a bar-less structure in which the rhythm of the work is derived from the performer "proportioning" left-to-right visual reading speed with the time allotted for the given section. Toru Takemitsu's *Voice* (Figure 4.4) uses small vertical slashes through the upper portion of the staff to indicate approximately 4½ seconds of playing time. Others, like Penderecki (see Figure 3.9—*Threnody*), use large blocks of

---

1. The word "new" is used here with caution: indeed proportionality existed *before* metered notations in many medieval works. In fact, it is probably the oldest concept of music notation. However, it is the new *way* in which the term is used that is of interest here.

space which equal a certain duration of time. The performer then reads at a speed *proportional* to the time given for performance (i.e., if an entrance begins about one-third through a 30-second section the performer waits 10 seconds before entering, etc.). This system eradicates the limits and implied accents of bar lines. At the same time, however, it introduces a certain degree of flexibility in that each performer reads the score differently (therefore giving more "chance" possibilities to the performance).

Some composers, like George Crumb for example (see Figure 11.2), use tempo marks without bar lines. At the same time most of these composers write in a very *thin* soloistic style so that the need for bar lines is minimal (less than, say, trying to perform *Le Sacre du Printemps* without bar lines). In any event, different composers use notations for different reasons. Many mix proportional and metered notations within the same work (see Figure 4.10—Ligeti's *Aventures*), thereby taking advantage of the benefits of both systems. While to the untrained eye these types of scores

may appear unnecessarily difficult and/ or obscure, they have become standard practice.

Following a short bibliography (completely annotated bibliographies on the subject are available in many other sources) is a list of somewhat standard new music notations. Again, this is a bare outline only, and does not in any way pretend to be comprehensive, or to make any major codifying suggestions (this is the subject of another of this author's books: *New Music Notation,* referred to below).

Brief Bibliography

Bartolozzi, Bruno. *New Sounds for Woodwind.* London: Oxford University Press, 1967 Revised, 1980.

———. "Proposals for Changes in Musical Notation." *Journal of Music Theory 5,* no. 2 (1961).

Behrman, David. "What Indeterminate Notation Determines." *Perspectives of New Music* (Spring-Summer 1965).

Brindle, Reginald Smith. *Contemporary Percussion.* London: Oxford University Press, 1970.

Cage, John. *Notations.* New York: Something Else Press, 1969.

Cope, David. *New Music Notation.* Dubuque, Iowa: Kendall/Hunt Publishing Company, 1976.

Cowell, Henry. *New Musical Resources.* New York: Alfred A. Knopf, 1930.

Darmstädter Beiträge zur Neuen Musik. Mainz: B. Schott's Söhne, 1965.

Eimert, Herbert; Fritz Enkel; and Karlheinz Stockhausen. *Problems of Electronic Music Notation.* Ottawa: National Research Council of Canada, 1956.

Howell, Thomas. *The Avant-Garde Flute: A Handbook for Composers and Flutists.* Berkeley: University of California Press, 1974.

Karkoschka, Erhard. *Notation in New Music.* New York: Praeger Publishers, 1972.

Kontarsky, Aloys. "Notation for Piano." *Perspectives of New Music* 10, no. 2 (1972).

Pooler, Frank and Brent Pierce. *New Choral Notation.* New York: Walton Music Corp., 1973.

Read, Gardner. *Twentieth-Century Music Notation* (unpublished as of this writing).

Rehfeldt, Phillip. "Clarinet Resources and Performance." *Proceedings* 7/8, American Society of University Composers (1974).

Salzedo, Carlos. *Modern Study of the Harp.* New York: G. Schirmer, 1921.

Stone, Kurt. "New Music Notation: Why?" *Musical America* 24, no. 7 (July 1974).

———. *Music Notation in the Twentieth Century: A Practical Guidebook.* New York: W. W. Norton, 1980.

Turetzky, Bertram. *The Contemporary Contrabass.* Berkeley: University of California Press, 1974.

Yates, Peter. "The Proof of the Notation." *Twentieth-Century Music.* New York: Pantheon Books, 1967.

A) Pitch meaning	symbol	one composer among the many who use this type of notation
quarter-tones	↑ ↓ = (¼ up or down)	*Béla Bartók*
	♯ ♭ ♮ = (¼ up)	*Mauricio Kagel*
	(sharpen) (flatten) ⌐ ♯ ♭ ⌐ (¼) (¾) (¼) (¾)	*Krzysztof Penderecki*
highest and lowest pitch	↑ ↓	*Krzysztof Penderecki*
clusters	♮ or ♯	*Henry Cowell*
silent pitches	◇	*Arnold Schoenberg*
(to be held down on the piano for ring-off of overtones when other tones are struck)		

B) Rhythm		
half dot	♩· = (♩ ♪)	*George Crumb*
repetition of whole groups of notes	• — • — • — •	*Krzysztof Penderecki*
slow/even speed-up of pitches		*Karel Husa*
slow/even decrease of speed of pitches		*Karel Husa*

long fermata with duration shown in seconds	 5	*George Crumb*
irregular tremolo		*Krzysztof Penderecki*

C) Dynamics

refined dynamic changes	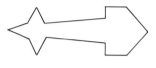	*Henry K. Gorecki*
ad lib dynamics and flux	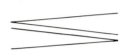	*John Cage*

D) Articulation

articulation of ends of notes	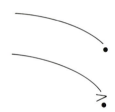	*Richard Bunger*

E) Timbre effects

1. *Winds*

sing while playing	= play = sing	*David Cope*
multiphonics		*Toru Takemitsu*

	+ = in	
mutes (brass)	O = out	*standard*
	Ø = halfway	
slow change	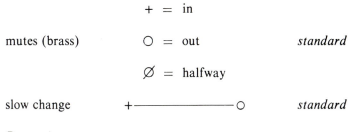	*standard*

2. *Percussion*

visual symbols for instruments (samples)	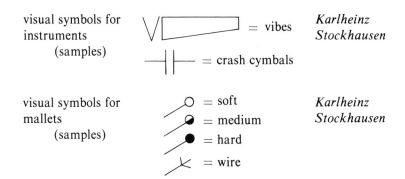	*Karlheinz Stockhausen*
visual symbols for mallets (samples)		*Karlheinz Stockhausen*

(for these last two see Reginald Smith Brindle's book for complete listing)

3. *Harp*

rolling surf effect	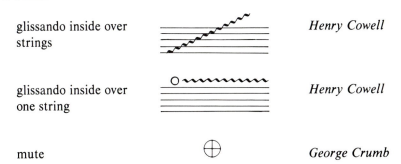	*Carlos Salzedo*

(for a complete listing of such effects and notations, see
Carlos Salzedo's book in the preceding bibliography)

4. *Piano*

glissando inside over strings		*Henry Cowell*
glissando inside over one string		*Henry Cowell*
mute	⊕	*George Crumb*

5. *Strings*

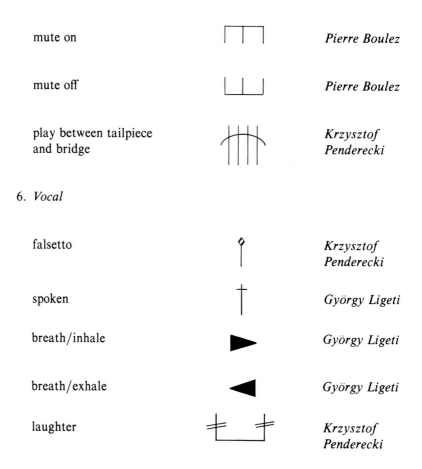

mute on		*Pierre Boulez*
mute off		*Pierre Boulez*
play between tailpiece and bridge		*Krzysztof Penderecki*

6. *Vocal*

falsetto		*Krzysztof Penderecki*
spoken		*György Ligeti*
breath/inhale		*György Ligeti*
breath/exhale		*György Ligeti*
laughter		*Krzysztof Penderecki*

Note that a number of comtemporary scores leave out staves of instruments with empty bars. This contributes to the "new" look of many of the scores of Crumb, Penderecki, and many others shown in this book. Likewise, when non-pitch-related activity is being employed, one-line staves are often used—quite unfamiliar in appearance to those who are used to the standard five-line staff.

SOURCE ADDRESSES

The purpose of this appendix is to furnish addresses of record companies, music periodicals, and music publishers, which dedicate a large part of their services to the promotion of contemporary and *avant-garde* music. The lists are provided to aid the reader in these ways:

1. to obtain works and equipment (hardware and software) for further study and research (since the author has by no means been comprehensive in coverage of *all* works in given areas);
2. to become acquainted with the large number of sources not ordinarily found in music, record and book stores or even in many university libraries;
3. to help support the dissemination of new music by making the names and addresses of its supporters that much more available.

The lists are by no means complete for a variety of reasons:

1. lack of space (with apologies to all those companies who do support new music yet whose names, for one reason or another, were not included in the list);

2. availability to the general public (i.e., Columbia Records does indeed support new music, but their name has not been included in this list as their records are available at any retail record store);
3. new music proportion to output: the emphasis here must of necessity be on companies which devote a *major* portion of their production to new music;
4. emphasis on listing those companies from which the examples in the book were taken, thus giving the reader the opportunity to obtain the score, record, piece of equipment or book discussed with comparative ease.

Record Companies

Advance: Box 17072, Rincon Station, Tucson, Ariz. 85731
Advent: 23366 Commerce Pk. Rd., Cleveland, Ohio 44122
AMG: Box 2866, Sta. A, Champaign, Ill. 61820
Avant: Box 65661, Los Angeles, Calif. 90065
Avant-Garde: 250 W. 57th St., New York, N.Y. 10019
Bowdoin College Music: 6 W. 95th St., New York, N.Y. 10025

Brewster: 1822 Monroe St., Evanston, Ill. 60202

CAPRA: 500 Broadway, New York, N.Y. 10012

Celestial Harmonies: Box 673, Wilton, Conn. 06897

Chatham Square: 500 Broadway, New York, N.Y. 10012

Concept: 500 Broadway, New York, N.Y. 10012

Cornell University: Lincoln Hall, Ithaca, N.Y. 14850

CRI: 170 W. 74th St., New York, N.Y. 10023

Crystal: Box 65661, Los Angeles, Calif. 90065

Desto: 14 Warren St., New York, N.Y. 10007

Deutsche Grammophone: 810 7th Ave., New York, N.Y. 10019

Digital Music Products: Box 2317, Rockefeller Center Station, New York, N.Y. 10185

Earthquack: 500 Broadway, New York, N.Y. 10012

ECM: Box 6868, Burbank, Calif. 91510

Eurock: P.O. Box 13718, Portland, Oregon 97213

Finnadar: 75 Rockefeller Plaza, New York, N.Y. 10019

Flying Fish Records: 1304 West Schubert, Chicago, Ill. 60614

Folkways: 43 W. 61st St., New York, N.Y. 10023

Golden Crest: 220 Broadway, Huntington Station, N.Y. 11746

Harmonia Mundi: P.O. Box 64503, Los Angeles, Calif. 90064

Kama-Sutra: 810 7th Ave., New York, N.Y. 10019

Louisville: 333 W. Broadway, Louisville, Ky. 40202

Mach: 539 W. 25th St., New York, N.Y. 10001

Mainstream: 1700 Broadway, New York, N.Y. 10019

Music of the World: Box 285, Brooklyn, N.Y. 11209

Nonesuch: 15 Columbus Circle, New York, N.Y. 10023

Now: 224 S. Lebanon St., Lebanon, Ind. 46052

Odyssey: 51 W. 52nd St., New York, N.Y. 10019

Opus One: Box 604, Greenville, Maine 04441

Orion: 5840 Busch Dr., Malibu, Calif. 90265

Owl Box: 4536, Boulder, Colo. 80302

Point Park: Wood and Blvd. of the Allies, Pittsburgh, Pa. 15222

Private Music: 220 East 23 St., New York, N.Y. 10010

Redwood: 8 Redwood Lane, Ithaca, N.Y. 14850

Serenus: Box 267, Hastings-on-Hudson, N.Y. 10706

Smithsonian Collection: 955 L'Enfant Plaza, Suite 2100, Washington, D.C., 20560

Trilogy: 723 7th Ave., New York, N.Y. 10017

Turnabout: 211 E. 42nd St., New York, N.Y. 10019

UBRES: P.O. Box 2374, Champaign, Ill. 61020

Wergo: 65 Mainz, Postfach 3640, Weihergarten, Germany

WIM: Box 65661, Los Angeles, Calif. 90065

Windham Hill Records: Box 9388, Stanford, Calif. 94305

Periodicals

American Society of University Composers: Journal of Music Scores: c/o Joseph Boonin, P.O. Box 2124, South Hackensack, N.J. 07606

Canadian Composer: 159 Bay St., Toronto 1, Canada

Computer Music Journal: MIT Press, 28 Carlton Street, Cambridge, Mass. 02142.

Contemporary Music Newsletter: Dept. of Music, New York University, Washington Square, New York, N.Y. 10003

Darmstädter Beiträge zur Neuen Musik: B. Schotts Sohne, Weihergarten 12, Postfach 1403, 6500 Mainz, Germany.

Electronic Musician: 2608 Ninth Street, Berkeley, Calif. 94710

Electronotes: 60 Sheraton Drive, Ithaca, N.Y. 14850

Interface: heerweg 347b Lisse, Netherlands

Interval: Box 8027, San Diego, Calif. 92102

Journal of Music Theory: Yale University, New Haven, Conn. 06520

Keyboard: 20085 Stevens Creek, Cupertino, Calif. 95015

Konzerte Mit Neuer Musik: Rundfunkplatz 1, 8 Munich 2, Germany

Melos: B. Schotts Söhne, Weihergarten 12, Postfach 1403, 6500 Mainz, Germany

Music Technology: 7361 Topanga Canyon Blvd., Canoga Park, Calif. 91303

Musician: P.O. Box 701, 31 Commercial St., Gloucester, Mass. 01930

Music in Poland: ZAIKS 2, Hupoteczna Str., Warsaw, Poland

Musical America: 1 Astor Plaza, New York, N.Y. 10036

Nutida Musik: Sveriges Radio, S-105, 10 Stockholm, Sweden

Perspectives of New Music: Princeton University Press, Princeton University, Princeton, N.J. 08540

Proceedings: American Society of University Composers: c/o American Music Center, 2109 Broadway, Suite 15–79, New York, N.Y. 10023

die Reihe (back issues): c/o Theodore Presser Co., Bryn Mawr, Pa.

Sonda: Juventudes Musicales, Madrid, Spain

Sonorum Speculum: Donemus 51, Jacob Obrechtstraat, Amsterdam, Netherlands

Sonological Reports: Utrecht State University, Utrecht, Netherlands

Soundings: 948 Canyon Rd., Santa Fe, New Mexico 87501

Source: Music of the Avant Garde: 2101 22nd St., Sacramento, Calif. 95818

Studio Sound: Link House, Dingwall Ave., Croydon CR9 2TA, Great Britain

Tempo: c/o Boosey and Hawkes Ltd., 295 Regent St., London, England W1A 1BR

There are a number of other magazines which carry regular columns dealing with new music and/or magazines dealing with more mainstream musical trends. Names and addresses of such magazines can be found in either: *Directory of the Music Industry,* 1418 Lake St., Evanston, Ill. 60204, or *Directory of the World of Music,* Music Information Service, 310 Madison Ave., New York, N.Y. 10017.

Music Publishers

It is very difficult to be complete in this area without filling several hundred pages with addresses. To avoid this, the author has listed only major U.S. music publishers, many of which handle the music of numerous European companies dealing with new music (C. F. Peters, for example, aside from their own nine companies, represents forty publishers of new music from around the world). These "umbrella" publishers are noted with an asterisk. Catalogs and lists of music available from almost all new music publishers are available from these "major" companies.

Music distributors are also included in this list and designated by an asterisk. These companies distribute catalogs of publishers from around the world.

The Internationales Musikinstitut Darmstädt Informationszentrum für zeitgenössische Musik Katalog der Abteilung Noten (Druck und Herstellung: Druckerei und Verlag Jacob Helene KG., Pfungstadt, Ostendstrasse 10, Germany) is a fairly comprehensive listing of new music and publishers (issued annually).

Along with the listing of major publishers and distributors are a number of smaller companies which deal almost exclusively in new and *avant-garde* music. These companies for the most part are not represented through distributors. Other such publisher addresses may be obtained from the *Directory of the World of Music,* Music Information Service, 310 Madison Ave., New York, N.Y. 10017, or *Directory of the Music Industry,* 1418 Lake St., Evanston, Illinois 60204.

ASCAP (1 Lincoln Plaza, New York, N.Y. 10023), BMI (40 W. 57th St., New York, N.Y. 10019), and Sesac (10 Columbus Circle, New York, N.Y. 10019) all have publishers' names and addresses (of their own affiliated "performance rights" publishers).

*Associated Music Publishers: 866 3rd. Ave., New York, N.Y. 10022

Augsburg: 426 S. 5th St., Minneapolis, Minn. 55415

*Baerenreiter-Verlag: Heindrich Schutz Allee 35, 35 Kossel, Germany

*B. H. Blackwell Ltd.: 48–51 Broadstreet, Oxford, England OX1 3BQ

*Belwin Mills: 16 W. 61st. St., New York, N.Y. 10023

Bowdoin College Music Press: Brunswick, Maine 04011

Brass Press: 136 Eighth Avenue North, Nashville, Tenn. 37203

*Alexander Broude, Inc.: 225 West 57th St., New York, N.Y. 10019

Composers' Facsimile Edition: 170 W. 74th St., New York, N.Y. 10023

Composers' Press Inc.: 1211 Ditmas Ave., Brooklyn, N.Y. 10018

*J. W. Chester, Ltd.: Eagle Court, London, E.C.1, England

Dorn Productions: P.O. Box 704, Islington, Mass. 02009

*Carl Fischer, Inc.: 62 Cooper Square, New York, N.Y. 10003

*Galaxy Music: 2121 Broadway, New York, N.Y. 10023

*Otto Harrassowitz: Postfach 349, 6200 Wiesbaben 1, Germany

Lingua Press: 6417 La Jolla Scenic Drive South, La Jolla, Calif. 92037

*Edward Marks: 1790 Broadway, New York, N.Y. 10019

*Mills Music, Inc.: 1619 Broadway, New York, N.Y. 10019

Moeck Verlag: D31 Celle, Postfach 143, Germany

*MCA Music: 225 Park Ave. South, New York, N.Y. 10003

*C. F. Peters: 373 Park Ave. South, New York, N.Y. 10016

*Theodore Presser: Bryn Mawr, Pennsylvania 19010

E. C. Schirmer Music Co.: 112 S. St., Boston, Mass. 02111

G. Schirmer: 866 3rd Ave., New York, N.Y. 10022

Seesaw Music Corp. (also *Okra Music*): 1966 Broadway, New York, N.Y. 10019

Smith Publications: 2617 Gwyndale Ave., Baltimore, Maryland 21207

Source: 2101 22nd St., Sacramento, Calif. 95818

Universal Edition: 195 Allwood Rd., Clifton, N.J. 07012

Walton Music: 17 W. 60th St., New York, N.Y. 10023

*Wilhelm Hansen Group: Gothersgade 9–11, DK 1123 Copenhagen K, Denmark.

Hardware

Akai: P.O. Box 2344, Fort Worth, Texas 76113

Alesis Studio Electronics: P.O. Box 3908, Los Angeles, Calif. 90078

Analytic Systems Group Inc.: P.O. Box 621, Amherst, N.Y. 14226

Axxess: Box 8435, Ft. Collins, Colorado 80525

Art Inc.: 215 Tremont St., Rochester, N.Y. 14608

Casio: 15 Gardner Road, Fairfield, N.J. 07006

Clarity: Nelson Lane, Garrison, N.Y. 10524

J. L. Cooper Electronics: 1931 Pontius Avenue, West Los Angeles, Calif. 90025

Decillionix: P.O. Box 70985, Sunnyvale, Calif. 94086

DigiTech: 5639 South Riley Lane, Salt Lake City, Utah 84107

Drew Engineering: 35 Indiana St., Rochester, N.Y. 14609

D. Drum: 1201 US Highway 1 Suite #280, N. Palm Beach, Florida 33408

Drum Workshop: 2697 Lavery Ct. 16, Dept. MI, Newbury Park, Calif. 91320

E-mu Systems: 1600 Green Hills Rd., Scotts Valley, Calif. 95066

Europa Technology: 1638 W. Washington Blvd., Venice, Calif. 90291

Eventide Inc.: One Alsan Way, Little Ferry, N.J. 07643

Fairlight Instruments: 2945 Westwood Blvd., Los Angeles, Calif. 90064

Fender Musical Instruments: 1130 Columbia Street, Brea, Calif. 92621

Forte Music: Box 6322, San Jose, Calif. 95150

Garfield Electronics: P.O. Box 1941, Burbank, Calif. 91507

Gentle Electric: Dept. P, P.O. Box 132, Delta, Colorado 81416

Harris Sound, Inc.: 6640 Sunset Blvd. Suite #110, Hollywood, Calif. 90028

Hohner Inc.: P.O. Box 15035, Richmond, Virginia 23227

IMS: 1552 Laurel St., San Carlos, Calif. 94070

Industrial Systems: 9811 Owensmouth Suite #10, Chatsworth, Calif. 91311

Kawai: Dept. KM, P.O. Box 438, 24200 S. Vermont, Harbor City, Calif. 90710

K-Muse: 18653 Ventura Blvd., Suite #359, Tarzana, Calif. 91356

Kurzweil Music Systems: 411 Waverly Oaks Rd., Waltham, MA 02154

Lexicon Inc.: 60 Turner Street, Waltham, MA 02154

Mellotron: 36 Main St., Port Washington, N.Y. 11050

Moog Electronics: 2500 Walden Avenue, Buffalo, N.Y. 14225

New England Digital Corporation: Waltham, MA 02154

Oberheim Electronics: 2250 S. Barrington Ave., Los Angeles, Calif. 90064

Roland Corp.: 7200 Dominion Circle, Los Angeles, Calif. 90040

Sequential: 3051 North First Street, San Jose, Calif. 95134

Simmons Group Centre, Inc.: 23917 Craftsman Road, Calabasas, Calif. 91302

Standard Productions: 1314 34th Ave., San Francisco, Calif. 94122

Syncordion: 117 Cedar Lane, Englewood, N.J. 07631

Technics: 1 Panasonic Way, Secaucus, N.J. 07094

TOA Electronics, Inc.: 480 Carlton Court, South San Francisco, Calif. 94080

Voyce Music: P.O. Box 27862, San Diego, Calif. 92128

Voyetra Technologies: 420 Mt. Pleasant Ave., Mamaroneck, N.Y. 10543

WERSI: 1720 Hempstead Road, P.O. Box 5318, Lancaster, PA 17601

Yamaha: Nippon Gakki Co. Ltd., Hamamatsu, Japan

Software

Bacchus Software Systems: 2210 Wilshire Blvd. #330, Santa Monica, Calif. 90403

Blank Software: 2210 Wilshire Blvd. #330, Santa Monica, Calif. 90403

Decillionix: P.O. Box 70985, Sunnyvale, Calif. 95086

DigiDesign Inc.: 920 Commercial Street, Palo Alto, Calif. 94303

Digital Music Services: 23010 Lake Forest, Suite D334, Laguna Hills, Calif. 92653

Dr. T's Music Software: 66 Louise Road, Chestnut Hill, MA 02167

Electronic Arts: 2755 Campus Drive, San Mateo, Calif. 94403

Enharmonik: P.O. Box 22243, Sacramento, Calif. 95822

Great Wave Software: P.O. Box 5847, Stanford, Calif. 94305

Hayden Software: 18 Haviland, Boston, MA 02115

Hippopotamus Software, Inc.: 985 University Ave #12, Los Gatos, Calif. 95030

Hybrid Arts, Inc.: 11920 West Olympic Blvd., Los Angeles, Calif. 90064

Imaja: P.O. Box 638, Middletown, CT 06457

Intelligent Music: P.O. Box 8748, Albany, N.Y. 12208

Joreth Music: Box 20, Evansham, Worcs, WRII5EG, U.K.

Magnetic Music: P.O. Box 328, Rhinebeck, N.Y. 12572

Mark of the Unicorn: 222 Third Street, Cambridge, MA 02142

McNifty Central (Impulse): 6860 Shingle Creek Pkwy #110, Minneapolis, MN 12540

Jim Miller: P.O. Box 648, Honaunau, HI 96726

Mimetics: P.O. Box 60238, Station A, Palo Alto, Calif. 94306

Music Data: Box 28001, Crystal, MN 55428

Music Works: 18 Haviland, Boston, MA 02115

Note Worthy Software: 13119 Pleasant Place, Burnsville, MN 55337

Opcode Systems: 444 Romona, Palo Alto, Calif. 94301

Passport Designs: 625 Miramontes Street, Half Moon Bay, Calif. 94019

Roland Corporation: 7200 Dominion Circle, Los Angeles, Calif. 90840

SFX Computer Software: 1 Hunter Road, North Weldon Industrial Estate, Corby, Northhamptonshire, England

Southworth Music Systems, Inc.: Box 275 RD 1, Harvard, MA 01451

Syntech Corporation: 5699 Kanan Road, Agoura, Calif. 91301

Triangle Audio: P.O. Box 1108, Sterling, VA 22170

Voyetra Technologies: 51 Main Street, Yonkers, N.Y. 10701

World Class Software: 1500 Valley River Drive, Suite 250, Eugene, Oregon 97401

MIDI Organizations and Publications

International MIDI Association: 11857 Hartsook St., North Hollywood, Calif. 91607

MIDI Manufacturers Association: 7200 Dominion Circle, Los Angeles, Calif. 90040

INDEX

AARON, 324
Acoustics, 202, 312
Adams, John, 393
Aleatory, 141, 150–52, 241
Algorithms, 325, 341, 342
Allen, Terry, 201
Ames, Charles, 330, 348
Amirkhanian, Charles, 87, 193
Andersen, Eric
    Opus 48 ("Which turns anonymous
      when the instruction is carried
      out"), 190–91
Anderson, John, 324
Andriessen, Louis, 168
Antheil, George, 86–87
Antiart, 183, 184, 201
Antiwar, 188–89
Architecture, 153, 241–42
Armenia, 120
Art, 1, 3, 182, 185, 186, 189, 290,
    323–24
Artificial intelligence, 347, 348, 351
Ashley, Robert, 271
    Perfect Lives (Private Parts), 393
    Public Opinion Descends Upon the
      Demonstrators, 260
    Wolfman, 187
Astral, Upper, 397
Astronomy, 111, 154
Audience, 21, 140, 148, 150, 165, 260,
    262
Austin, Larry, 191
Avant-garde, 368–70, 391–92

Babbitt, Milton, 42–43, 226
    Ensembles for Synthesizer, 227
    Three Compositions for Piano,
      41–42
    Vision and Prayer, 217
Bach, Johann Sebastian
    Art of the Fugue, 150
    Well-Tempered Clavier, 36
Baker, Robert, 325
Bali, 120
Ballet, 254
Barbaud, Pierre, 325
Bartók, Béla, 16, 71
    Mikrokosmos, 10
    Piano Sonata, 55
Bartolozzi, Bruno, 87
BASIC, 331, 332–33
Bauhaus, 3, 253
Beatles, 228, 389
Beaver, Paul, 240–41
Becker, John
    Abongo, 94
    Symphonia Brevis, 58
Bedford, David, 152
Behrman, David
    On the Other Ocean, 290
    Wavetrain, 236
Bell Telephone Laboratories, 283, 287
Berg, Alban, 39
Berio, Luciano, 219, 379–80
    Circles, 146–47
    Sinfonia, 377, 380–85
    Tempi Concertati, 141
    Thema: Omaggio à Joyce, 226
    Visage, 226